A Brief History of
Christianity

Blackwell Brief Histories of
Religion

This series offers brief, accessible, and lively accounts of key topics within theology and religion. Each volume presents both academic and general readers with a selected history of topics which have had a profound effect on religious and cultural life. The word "history" is, therefore, understood in its broadest cultural and social sense. The volumes are based on serious scholarship but they are written engagingly and in terms readily understood by general readers.

Published

Alister E. McGrath – A Brief History of Heaven
G. R. Evans – A Brief History of Heresy
Tamara Sonn – A Brief History of Islam
Douglas J. Davies – A Brief History of Death
Lawrence S. Cunningham – A Brief History of Saints
Carter Lindberg – A Brief History of Christianity

A Brief History of
Christianity

CARTER LINDBERG

Blackwell
Publishing

© 2006 by Carter Lindberg

BLACKWELL PUBLISHING
350 Main Street, Malden, MA 02148-5020, USA
9600 Garsington Road, Oxford OX4 2DQ, UK
550 Swanston Street, Carlton, Victoria 3053, Australia

The right of Carter Lindberg to be identified as the Author of this Work has been asserted in accordance with the UK Copyright, Designs, and Patents Act 1988.

First published 2006 by Blackwell Publishing Ltd

1 2006

Library of Congress Cataloging-in-Publication Data

Lindberg, Carter, 1937–
    A brief history of Christianity / Carter Lindberg.
        p. cm. — (Blackwell brief histories of religion)
    Includes bibliographical references and index.
    ISBN-13: 978-1-4051-1078-5 (hardcover: alk. paper)
    ISBN-10: 1-4051-1078-3 (hardcover: alk. paper)
    ISBN-13: 978-1-4051-1047-1 (pbk.: alk. paper)
    ISBN-10: 1-4051-1047-3 (pbk.: alk. paper)
    1. Church history. I. Title. II. Series.

    BR145.3.L56 2005
    270—dc22

                                                2005006598

A catalogue record for this title is available from the British Library.

The publisher's policy is to use permanent paper from mills that operate a sustainable forestry policy, and which has been manufactured from pulp processed using acid-free and elementary chlorine-free practices. Furthermore, the publisher ensures that the text paper and cover board used have met acceptable environmental accreditation standards.

For further information on
Blackwell Publishing, visit our website:
www.blackwellpublishing.com

To Teddy and Coco

Contents

Preface

A "brief" history of Christianity falls into the genre of the pro-
verbial final exam question: provide a history of the universe
with a couple of examples. While I hope the following effort will
provide a bit more perspective on the history of Western Christianity than a variation on the theme of curious George goes to
church, I am all too aware of what is missing in the following
narrative. The task has proven to be more daunting than I had
at first thought – though probably not as daunting as the proposed "brief history of eternity" we bandied about in discussing
this proposal. After having taught a survey course on the history
of Christianity for more years than I care to remember, I naively
assumed I could just paste together all my old yellowed notes
and that would be it. But even as cryptic as they were, far more
cutting was required – even with the gracious allowance by
the editors of more space. A very partial remedy for the topics
suffering neglect is the list of suggested reading. The list is not a
bibliography of works consulted, though some of course were,
but resources for addressing the many omissions in the text.
I have also attempted to avoid footnotes. Partially this decision
was to save space, but it also reflects that fact that over the years

I have appropriated the insights of so many scholars that I no longer am aware of specific attributions. Peter of Blois (d. 1212) is justly renowned for his comment: "We are like dwarfs standing on the shoulders of giants; thanks to them, we see farther than they. Busying ourselves with the treatises written by the ancients, we take their choice thoughts." I haven't seen nearly as far as the giant scholars of the history of Christianity, but I am grateful for their broad shoulders for whatever panorama the following text provides, and I beg their forgiveness for not crediting them for their "choice thoughts."

I am also grateful to the editors of Blackwell Publishing, especially Rebecca Harkin, who has supported, but should not be blamed, for this effort; and Andrew Humphries, who not only saw this project into print but also chose excellent reviewers of the manuscript whose insightful criticisms and suggestions have vastly improved the text. In retrospect, I am also grateful now (I wasn't at the time!) to those colleagues of the School of Theology at Boston University who many years ago forced me to accept teaching the survey course. It turned out to be really great fun – mainly because of the generations of lively students who wouldn't allow it to be just a litany of dates. Finally, I am delighted to dedicate this volume to our most recent grandchildren – Theodore (Teddy) and Claudia (aka Coco) – who, like their cousins, provide great reasons to get out of the study and play.

Chapter 1

The Responsibility to Remember: An Introduction to the Historiography of Christianity

In a memorable epigram, the historian Richard Hofstadter stated: "Memory is the thread of personal identity, history of public identity." Memory and historical identity are inseparable. Most of us have experienced the embarrassment of momentarily forgetting a name in the midst of an introduction. Think what life would be like without any memory at all. Life is terribly difficult for an amnesiac, and it is tragic for the person – and his or her family and friends – with Alzheimer's disease. The loss of memory is not just the absence of "facts"; it is the loss of personal identity, family, friends, indeed the whole complex of life's meaning. It is very difficult if not impossible to function in society if we do not know who we are. Our memory is the thread of our personal identity.

What about our religious identities? Are we amnesiacs when someone asks how the Methodist or the Roman Catholic Church came to be? Beyond referring to our parents or a move to a new neighborhood, could we explain why we belong to St. Mary's by the gas station or the Lutheran church by the grocery store?

A French friend once began to explain contemporary French–German relations to me by referring to the significance of the ninth-century division of Charlemagne's empire! Most of us do not go back that far to understand the present, but his perspective illustrates the tenacity of historical memory, all too painfully evident in the eruption of historical ethnic conflicts. On the other hand, if we do not know our personal and communal histories, we are like children easily manipulated by those who would revise the past for their own purposes. Historical perspective is important for counteracting the tyranny of current opinions.

The biblical community has always known that its identity is rooted in history. Isaiah calls Israel to "Look to the rock from which you were hewn, and to the quarry from which your were dug. Look to Abraham your father and to Sarah who bore you" (Isaiah 51:1–2). The genealogies scattered through the Bible remind the people of God of their roots in creation and their destiny in God's plan (Matthew 1:1–25). Christian identity is clearly stated in the historical shorthand of the Christian creeds that confess faith in the historical person of Jesus who was born, suffered, and died. Christians put a unique spin on this history when they confess that this historical Jesus is also the historic Christ who was raised from the dead and who will return to complete history. Thus, from an insider's perspective, the identity of the Christian community is formed by both the historical past and the historical future. In brief, then, Christian identity is rooted in history, not in nature, philosophy, or ethics.

Sociologists suggest that our family identity is passed on to us through our conversations with the mothers and fathers who have gone on before us. We know, of course, from even limited family experience that when we no longer talk to our parents and children we begin to forget who we are. This is not to say that conversations between generations are always pleasant, but to say that they are important for learning "how we got this way." To paraphrase the old saw about watching the making of sausage and political decisions, the study of our personal and communal histories, including the history of Christianity, may be disturbing. But without such conversations we are condemned to presentism, which is a more elegant way of describing a continuous "me generation."

Historical memory provides perspective, a horizon, for judging what is or is not important. Without a horizon it is too easy to overvalue what is before your nose. A horizon enables the valuation of the relative significance of everything within this horizon, as near or far, great or small. The idea of horizon or historical distance bears further reflection.

Historical distance can be a surprising element for understanding the present. Fernand Braudel, the renowned French historian, spoke of this by analogy to living in a foreign city. If you live in a foreign city for a year you may not learn a great deal about that city, but when you return home you will be surprised by your increasing comprehension as well as questions of your homeland. You did not previously understand or perhaps even perceive these characteristics because you were too close to them. Likewise, a visit to the past provides distance and a vantage point for comprehending and questioning the present. In other words, distance – in history as in navigation – is necessary for finding true bearings. Sailors, at least those with some longevity, do not navigate by watching the prow of the boat. Hence the old adage about people who can't see beyond their own noses applies equally to historical myopia.

I have belabored the importance of memory and history for our personal and communal identities because we live in a culture that regards as wisdom Henry Ford's dictum that "history is bunk." I hope the image of the amnesiac will jar loose easy acquiescence to forgetfulness of the past and warn us of the dangers posed by lack of identity. Without a sense of our communal and personal history we are prey for whatever fads and fancies appeal to us. If we do not recognize the role of history in shaping our identities then we unreflectively allow the past to control us. This may not have bad results but it puts us in the position of being misled by those who wish to manipulate us.

Tradition and Confession

Lack of historical consciousness promotes a conversational deficit in the communion of saints, the church. The irony is that this is occurring even as we are acquiring more and more information. We now have a wealth of archeological and textual materials, including texts from the early Christian community not included in the Bible, far beyond the wildest imagination of medieval scribes, but without an interpretive tradition it is difficult to know what to do with this wealth of material.

"Tradition" is not merely a mass of information, but in its root sense means the action of handing on an understanding of that information, not just its rote repetition. The prolific historian of doctrine Jaroslav Pelikan sharpens this point with his clever distinction between tradition and traditionalism: "Tradition is the living faith of the dead; traditionalism is the dead faith of the living." In the Bible and the church fathers, "tradition" means primarily God's self-revelation; God's handing himself over in Jesus. Thus the fundamental structure of the Christian faith and community depends upon tradition, upon passing on significant conversations with prior generations concerning God's activity in history.

In the New Testament, Paul speaks of handing on what he has received. The first place he speaks this way is in connection with the Eucharist (1 Corinthians 11:23–26); the second place is where he cites the confession of the cross and resurrection of Jesus (1 Corinthians 15:3–11). The concept of the tradition as the passing on of the news that God has handed over his Son at a particular moment in world history for the salvation of human-kind is bound up in the New Testament with the concept of remembering (Greek: *anamnesis*, i.e., the exact opposite of forgetting, amnesia). It is no accident that these terms are both present in connection with the Eucharist or Lord's Supper. The tradition that Paul cites presents an exhortation to *anamnesis*. The meal that Jesus held with his disciples the night before his death will continue to be held "in remembrance of me." This is not just a conceptual remembrance, an idea; rather, it is a carrying out of the remembrance that offers, passes on, his presence itself. This "doing in remembrance" has its model in the Hebrew Bible, namely in the Passover as the remembrance of the flight from Egypt. Here too the past event is made present as every co-celebrant becomes a contemporary of the event through remembrance of what is passed on. The essential yet paradoxical point in the biblical understanding of tradition is that it is not fixed upon the past, but that in presenting the past (i.e., making the past present) it has significance for a new future.

Chapter 2

The Law of Praying is the Law of Believing

The title of this chapter is from Prosper of Aquitaine (ca. 390–ca. 463): "The rule of prayer should lay down the rule of faith." By his time, the Christian community had developed from the small group of Jewish followers of Jesus worshipping in the temple in Jerusalem (Acts 2:46), to the established religion of the Roman Empire with scriptures, creeds, and a hierarchical authority all claiming to be "apostolic." This astounding development was marked by tumult and controversy within and without as the various Christian communities with all the pluralism of their theologies and writings created a self-identity that would in turn inform and identify Western culture up to our own time. In the process, the "rule of faith" was not determined by "prayer alone" but with the help of tough, hard-nosed, and bright leaders who vigorously opposed alternative Christian writings, theologies, and ways of life as well as challenges from rival religious perspectives. The Christian protagonists and antagonists in these developments believed salvation depended on to whom one prayed, that is, what one believed and confessed about God and salvation. Normative authorities were needed to answer Jesus' question: "But who do you say that I am?" (Matthew 16:15).

In retrospect, the Christian community believed that its survival was the fulfillment of God's plan. "Now after John was arrested, Jesus came to Galilee, proclaiming the good news of God, and saying, 'The time is fulfilled, and the kingdom of God has come near; repent, and believe in the good news'" (Mark 1:14–15).

"The time is fulfilled." The author of Mark wrote in Greek, and as the saying goes, the Greeks have a word for it. The Greek word used in the above sentence is "kairos," that is, the time for a decision, the time when events are so juxtaposed that a crucial decision or event may occur. Another Greek word for time is "chronos," that is, "chronological" time measured by units of years, days, hours, minutes, etc. "Kairos" has the potential to qualitatively change "chronos." The early Christian community had this sense that the appearance of Jesus in the midst of chronological time marked a crucial (crux, "cross") moment, a time of decision. A "kairotic" event divides time in terms of what precedes and succeeds it. This is what early Christian historians were getting at when they proclaimed Jesus the Christ is the center of history between the creation and the Last Judgment; a conviction eventually enshrined in the dating by years before and after Christ (BC and AD) or in more recent terms before and during the common era of Judaism and Christianity (BCE and CE). The "kairos" occurred at the "chronos" of a number of developments: the dispersion of Judaism, the dominance of the Roman Empire, and the universality of Hellenistic culture.

The early Christian community was convinced the "time is fulfilled" because they believed Jesus was the fulfillment of God's promise to Israel. Persuaded by their experience of Easter that Jesus is the Messiah, the early Christians – themselves Jews – therefore saw the promises in the Hebrew Bible to be transferable to Jesus. Convinced that God gave "all authority in heaven and earth" to Jesus, his followers believed they had the mission to "make disciples of all nations, baptizing them in the name of the Father and of the Son and of the Holy Spirit" (Matthew 28:18–19).

The early community's liturgical confessions and hymns testify to its conviction that Jesus fulfilled the promise God made through his prophets (Romans 1:1–4). In this perspective, history is viewed within the context of God's plan of salvation "that was kept secret for long ages but is now disclosed, and through the prophetic writings is made known" (Romans 16:25–26). Rooted in the life, preaching, and death of Jesus of Nazareth, the early Christian community initially saw itself as a renewal movement within Palestinian Judaism; Easter confirmed God's promises to Israel.

The historical context for Christianity thus first of all is the whole history of Israel and its sacred scriptures, the Bible of early Christianity (there is not an "Old" Testament until the church developed the "New" Testament some 200 years later). As initially a Jewish movement, Christianity was heir to the plurality of influences from the Hebrew Bible, diaspora Judaism, and Hellenistic Judaism. Furthermore, in its formative stages, Christianity benefited from the protective shield Judaism provided as a "licit" religion in the Roman Empire.

At the time of the early Christian community, Jews had long been widely dispersed in Asia Minor and the Roman Empire with sizeable populations in urban centers such as Rome and Alexandria. The Jewish Dispersion (Diaspora), with its origins in the Assyrian and Babylonian deportations beginning in the eighth century BCE, provided a point of contact for Christian missionaries who "proclaimed the word of God in the synagogues of the Jews" (Acts 13:5), addressing both Jews and their Gentile converts (Acts 13:42–43; 14:1; 17:1–4; 17:10–17). The Book of Acts repeatedly states that in his missionary travels Paul would go to the local synagogue "every Sabbath" where he would argue and "try to convince Jews and Greeks" (Acts 18:4).

The ethical monotheism of Judaism appealed to those "Greeks," that is Gentiles, of the Greco-Roman Empire who found philosophical ethics too cerebral and Dionysian religions too emotional and amoral. The drawback however was that Gentile conversion to Judaism included male circumcision and obedience to ritual and dietary laws. The appeal of Christianity was an ethical monotheism without such restrictive and counter-cultural rules. In Christ "neither circumcision nor uncircumcision counts for anything; the only thing that counts is faith working through love" (Galatians 5:6). Furthermore, Christianity appealed to the marginalized, women and the poor, in the proclamation of social equality. "There is no longer Jew or Greek, there is no longer slave or free, there is no longer male and female, for all of you are one in Christ Jesus" (Galatians 3:28).

In a society that blamed the victim, the biblical motif of the great reversal – that the last shall be first and the first last – pointedly expressed in the "Magnificat" (Luke 1:46–55) must have appealed to those on the receiving end of the Roman view that the gods rewarded the good with wealth and punished the evil and lazy with poverty. That God would side with the poor and oppressed was a discordant note to those whose worldview was shaped by the Roman poet Ovid's (43 BCE–CE 17) dictum, "property confers rank," but it was a message of hope to the disenfranchised.

It has been said that the blood of the martyrs is the seed of the church. "Martyr" derives from the Greek word for witness, and in that sense the witness of the early Christians that won Gentiles to the church was not only the witness in the face of persecution, but also the witness of serving the neighbor (cf. Matthew 25:35–40). There are numerous references from the early church fathers concerning the collection of funds during worship that are dedicated to helping the needy. One of the more famous stories is that of Laurence (d. 258), a deacon of Rome who was told by the civil authorities to deliver up the treasure of the church. In response he assembled the poor to whom he had distributed the church's possessions and presented them to the Roman prefect with the words, "These are the treasure of the church." The prefect was not amused, and – the story goes – had Laurence slowly roasted to death on a gridiron. Tertullian (ca. 160–ca. 225) summarized the point when he stated to Roman culture, "our compassion spends more in the street than yours does in the temples."

The Roman Empire and its Political Achievements

The early Christian conviction that Jesus is the Messiah, whom God sent in the fullness of time, meant to them that universal history was prepared for this event. The Roman Empire was thus part of God's providential plan. The *pax romana* had pacified the Mediterranean world and suppressed robbery and piracy along the Roman roads and seaways. The network of roads enabled shipping, commerce and communications – from the British Isles to North Africa, from the Iberian Peninsula to the Near East – and thus facilitated the spread of Christian missions. Roman law also enabled missionary mobility. Paul could travel with relative safety and could appeal to his Roman citizenship when in difficulty (Acts 25:1–12).

Hellenization and its Cultural Achievements

The Greek language of the time, "Koine," was the common language of diplomacy and commerce in the Mediterranean world. Practically everyone understood Koine. Indeed, the culture, especially in the cities and commercial centers, was multilingual. Linguistic universality enabled Christians to spread their message rapidly. Thus early Christian missionaries not only did not have to spend years in language school before setting out to spread their faith, but with their facility with the "lingua franca" of their day they did not appear as an ethnic minority. Furthermore, their scripture (i.e., the Hebrew Bible) was already in a Greek translation known as the "Septuagint" or "LXX" (after the supposed number of translators in the legendary account of its origin). By around 100 BCE the bulk of the Old Testament was circulating in Greek.

Hellenism also created a universal cultural orientation that was not only esteemed and perpetuated by the Romans but was also present in Palestine and influential upon Judaism. Spread by the conquests of Alexander the Great (356–323 BCE), Hellenistic culture provided a common philosophical terminology. Christians borrowed freely from both the terminology of Greek philosophy and its claim to be ancient wisdom. With regard to the latter claim, as we note in the appendix, the early Christians agreed that older is better. Thus, to counter the charge of innovation, defenders of the Christian faith claimed that Christianity goes back to Moses who is even before the ancient philosophers so highly esteemed in the Hellenistic culture of the day. A classic example of the use of philosophical terminology is the Christian use of the term and concept "logos." The term was rich with philosophical meanings as the universal "reason" or "word" that governs and permeates the world. The prologue to the Fourth Gospel gives this a new twist when it proclaims that the logos is not merely an idea but God incarnate: "In the beginning was the Word ["logos"] . . . And the Word became flesh and lived among us" (John 1:1–14). The claim that Christianity is really *the* true philosophy served as a catchy entrée to missionary dialogue, but would in turn be attacked by other Christians as warping the gospel message.

In fact control of the gospel message became an increasing priority as Christian communities developed throughout the empire, often with their own local take on Jesus supported by their own teachers and writings claiming to go back to particular apostles or their disciples. Without an authoritative scripture, how could one know the right teaching (literally, "orthodoxy"), but without the right teaching, how could one know which of the many scriptures extant among the various Christian communities were authoritative? These symbiotic problems stimulated the creation of an authoritative list of New Testament writings even while the early church was dealing with a number of other interrelated concerns at the same time.

Development of the Biblical Canon

Christianity, like Judaism and later Islam, is a religion of the book. It would be difficult to overestimate the significance of the determination of normative biblical writings for the history of the church and its faith. Indeed, the development of the canon of scriptures was the first dogmatic development in the history of Christianity; it has remained fundamental for most Christian communities down to today as *the* source for the Christian faith.

The word "canon" (Greek: *kanon*, "measuring rod") means "rule" or "standard." The Greek and Latin fathers applied the term canon beyond the list of scriptures, for example to lists of church rules, thus canon law; lists of saints or heroes of the faith, thus persons who are canonized. The death of the first Christian generation and the efforts by various Christian communities or individuals to introduce their alternative understandings of Jesus and salvation led to the development of the canon. Since salvation related to confessing Christ, it was crucial to have the right confession and thus the right scripture by which to "measure" that confession. A famous (or infamous as the case may be) example, often cited as a major impetus to the formation of the New Testament, is the canon of Marcion (ca. 100–ca.160). Reputedly the excommunicated son of the bishop of Sinope, a city on the southern shore of the Black Sea, Marcion became very wealthy in the shipping industry. Around 140, he moved to Rome, joined the church there, and made a huge benevolence gift for the mission of the church.

Marcion's theology presented a dualistic opposition between the world of the spirit (deemed good) and the world of matter (deemed evil). In brief, what concerned Marcion was his perceived opposition between the righteousness of the law as he understood it in the Hebrew Bible and the righteousness of faith in the New Testament. To Marcion, the Jewish God of law and wrath and the Christian God of love and mercy were mutually exclusive. Jesus the Christ was not truly a part of the material world created by the God of the Old Testament, but rather only appeared to be human, "in the likeness of sinful flesh" (Romans 8:3), in order to reveal the supreme God of love and fool the Old Testament God. Therefore, Marcion argued, the God of the Old Testament must be rejected in favor of the God of the New Testament, who in the person of Jesus saves people from the God of the Jews. To support his views, Marcion set forth a canon of scripture that completely excluded the Old Testament and included only the epistles of Paul (omitting 1 and 2 Timothy and Titus) expurgated of "Jewish" influences and a form of the Gospel of Luke, perhaps because he accepted the claim that the author was a companion of Paul. Paul, according to Marcion, was the only apostle who rightly understood that Christians are no longer under the law; the Judaistic errors of the other apostles blinded them to the truth.

The Roman church rejected Marcion's views and his canon, excommunicated him, and returned his large donation. Undeterred, Marcion went on to establish numerous Marcionite churches throughout Asia Minor, attestations to the attractiveness of his views. Further testimony to his success in mission were his many significant opponents, including Irenaeus of Lyons (ca. 130–ca. 200), Tertullian (ca. 160–ca. 225), and Justin Martyr (ca. 100–ca. 165), and not least the stimulus to speed up the process of fixing the authoritative list of writings that would become the New Testament. The decision to include the Old Testament was a doctrinal decision of great significance for the church's affirmation of its Jewish roots, and its understanding of creation, redemption, and Christian life in the world. Furthermore, the fixing of the New Testament canon also clearly affirms that valid and binding knowledge of God's revelation in Jesus Christ may be gained only from these writings. Other writings have certainly been and continue to be significant for the faith and life of the church, but they cannot claim the same authority in the church as the canonical scriptures.

As already noted, the process of fixing the New Testament canon was a circular one in which the gospel message was used to determine the writings that were to be the "canonical" source – the measuring rod – of the gospel message. Although the earliest writings of Paul date from about 50 CE, it was not until the latter half of the second century that challenges such as Marcion and prophetic movements such as Montanism that claimed revelations inspired by the Holy Spirit impelled the church to determine its canon. How did the early church decide which Christian writings should be included in the canon? The answer to this question involves a complex and long historical process that we can only generalize about here.

One of the criteria is that indicated by our opening reference to Prosper of Aquitaine: a writing's normative use in worship. Thus, Justin Martyr, who died in Rome about 165, reported about written "memories" of the apostles and their disciples that contained the words of Jesus, called Gospels, that were read during Sunday worship. A second criterion is that a "canonical" writing had to reflect tradition thought to be apostolic in origin. And a third criterion is that the writing be "catholic," that is, universal in the sense of enjoying widespread use in the churches. The process of canonization had a strong community orientation. Here we see the interrelationship of community and canonicity so succinctly expressed by Augustine (354–430): "I would not believe the gospel unless the Catholic Church moved me." In brief, the Bible is the church's book developed in the worshipping community, the community that professes and confesses Jesus is Lord.

It appears that most of the 27 books now constituting the New Testament were in common usage in the church by the end of the second century. The earliest extant list of New Testament books is the Muratorian fragment, named for the Italian scholar Ludovico Muratori who discovered it in a library in Milan and published it in 1740. Held to date from the late second century, the fragment includes the four Gospels, Acts, all 13 Pauline epistles, and rejects the Marcionite epistles of Paul to Laodicea and Alexandria as forgeries. The list also includes Jude, 1 and 2 John, the Wisdom of Solomon, the Apocalypse of John, and the Apocalypse of Peter, with the caveat that the latter is not accepted everywhere. It also mentions the Shepherd of Hermas as an edifying book but that it is too recent to be included in the canon. It does not include 1 and 2 Peter, James, and one Johannine epistle. The oldest witness to the complete New Testament as it now stands is Athanasius (ca. 296–373), the bishop of Alexandria. In 367, in his annual pastoral letter to the churches of Egypt that set that year's date for Easter, he listed the books to be accepted as canonical literature: the four Gospels, Acts, 14 letters of Paul including Hebrews, 7 catholic epistles, and Revelation. The Greek church accepted this list, as did also the Synod of Rome (382) under Pope Damasus I. Athanasius' list was promoted by Augustine and accepted at the North African synods of Hippo (393) and Carthage (397). Thus, by the beginning of the fifth century, there was a common agreement on the canon of the New Testament in most of the churches. Somewhat of an exception was the Syrian church that up to the fifth century had a shorter canon and used the Diatessaron, a synoptic harmony of the four Gospels composed around 170 by Tatian, a Syrian church father.

The Christian community by the fourth and fifth centuries was now handing on the gospel message not only in oral form but also in written form. Already by the end of the second century, Irenaeus, the bishop of Lyons, insisted that the rule of faith is faithfully preserved by the church and finds multiform expression in the canonical books. The gospel preached in the churches continues in scripture. We could speak of an "inscripturization" of the apostolic proclamation that is the foundation of the faith. Thus, for Irenaeus, the Christian community does not "create" the canon, but acknowledges it. The church receives and conserves the rule of faith. From the perspective of the church, this is not something secret or mysterious but a public transmission – handing on (*traditio*) – of the gospel under the guidance of the Holy Spirit who permeates the church.

As Tertullian maintained, only the person who belongs to the true, orthodox church is authorized for the exposition of scripture. And the only true support for an orthodox interpretation of scripture over against the variations of individual interpretations is the rule of faith. The rule of faith, the shorthand for the later Trinitarian creeds, structured the responses of catechumens at their baptism to the questions, "Do you believe in God the Father Almighty?" "Do you believe in Jesus Christ his only Son our Lord?" "Do you believe in the Holy Spirit?" There is here the reciprocal relationship between the New Testament canon and the community's confession of faith. Scripture, therefore, according to 2 Peter 1:20, is not a "matter of one's own interpretation."

The canon determined the identity of holy scripture. While the fixing of the canon was a foundational decision by the church, and thereby the source for future theological reflection, it did not guarantee the unity of the church. It became apparent that even such a small collection of writings could yield alternative answers to Jesus' question, "Who do you say that I am?" In response, the church continued to spell out its faith in the form of creeds.

Chapter 3

Sibling Rivalry: Heresy, Orthodoxy, and Ecumenical Councils

The early Christian community understood itself in continuity with Israel, God's chosen people. Yet Christians prayed to the risen Jesus, their Lord – a blasphemous act to their fellow Jews because it went counter to exclusive devotion to God: "Hear, O Israel: The Lord is our God, the Lord alone" (Deuteronomy 6:4). The first sibling rivalry then was between the Jews who confessed Jesus is the Messiah and those who rejected this claim as blasphemous. Again we see the locus of tension in worship – the law of praying is the law of believing. As the Christian community was forced from the temple and began its mission to the Gentiles, further rivalries arose as the Christian communities first rejected Greco-Roman culture and then began to appropriate it. The developing church thus strove to delineate its faith in Jesus in relation to both its Jewish roots and heritage on the one hand and the Hellenistic context into which it was moving on the other hand. This is the context for the development of formal confessions of faith: creeds. Those who chose and advocated confessions that conflicted with what the church believed, taught, and confessed came to be called heretics (from the Greek, *hairesis*, "a choosing"). The issues about which the confessions developed focused on the relationship of Jesus to God and the relationship of Jesus to humankind; the Christian claim in both issues is that in Jesus one definitively encounters God's own self.

The Structure of Tradition: Confession and Doctrine

The passing on of the tradition concerning Jesus the Christ occurred from the very beginning of the Christian community in many different ways, among others in the form of confessions of faith for catechumens preparing for baptism (1 Corinthians 15:3–6) and the command to proclaim the gospel (Matthew 28:19). Such confessions formulated central statements of the faith and very early became expressions of ecclesial consensus, traditionally termed "orthodoxy." These confessions had to an increasing extent the function of validating ecclesial teaching, and as a "rule of faith" that defined apostolic teaching they governed the proclamation of the gospel and served to detect heterodoxy and heresy. Such validating teaching in the churches, together with the developing canon of apostolic writings and the churches' office of bishop, functioned to preserve the identity of the church in conformity to the gospel. At this point it can only be noted that considerable problems have arisen in the history of Christianity in relation to the relationship between apostolic writings (the Bible), the apostolic creeds, and the apostolic office of bishop.

The form of confessions reflected the language, concepts, and culture of the particular times of their formulations, as well as the questions and issues uppermost in the mind of the community at the time. This was not a tidy process; what one community or generation believed "orthodox" could appear to the next as problematic or even heretical. What the church believes, teaches, and confesses is therefore not a collection of timeless truths but the historical expression of the community's convictions. Thus confessions such as the classic creeds (Apostles',

Nicene, and Athanasian), as well as later confessions such as in the Reformation period and the Barmen Declaration against Nazism, are provisional expressions that both express and form Christian identities in history.

Doctrine as a Key to Christian Memory and Identity

It is a popular modern cliché that religion should be free of doctrine. This reflects both the awareness that doctrine has been a source of intolerance and that doctrine is historically conditioned. The modern development of historical relativism that posits doctrines are historically contingent has also eroded their role in the maintenance of Christian memory. The very phrase "history of doctrine" denotes the modern dilemma of trying to mesh what appear to be antithetical phenomena. "History" denotes relativity and change, whereas "doctrine" connotes unchanging truths.

However, the Christian community has for most of its history held that without a grasp of and commitment to what the church has believed, taught, and confessed over the centuries, the church will be prey to what we may call "chameleonism," that is, it will take on the coloring of its environment. And reflecting the environment means losing or suppressing the church's memory and identity. As the saying goes, salt without savor should be thrown out.

The acknowledgment of doctrines in imperial law contributed to their character as infallible propositions. This is also how doctrine acquired the overtones of compulsion, as those who did not subscribe to the dogmatic decisions of the church were banished or worse by the state. But doctrine need not be conceived this way. To use a homely analogy: doctrine has too often been perceived as an electric fence designed to keep the ecclesiastical cows from straying far from home. If such an ecclesial cow is foolish enough to stray, she will be zapped. In the temporal realm, until recently, the electrical current was supplied by the state. Now, with the separation of church and state, the power is turned off; and with the rise of historical relativism, the fences themselves are largely gone. Therefore it may be more helpful to return to an earlier understanding of doctrine as analogous to a feed box, the purpose of which is to gather the herd by providing nourishment. This image correlates well with our earlier comments that link tradition with the Lord's Supper. Confession and its articulation in doctrine serve to nourish the self-understanding and identity of the Christian community. For the early church the purpose of dogma was both to develop the community's reflection on salvation wrought by God through Jesus and to impart meaning to earlier reflections that was not originally perceived.

There has never been a time when Christians did not face the task of expressing their faith in the form of confessions (a kind of shorthand of the faith). From the outset, the community was called to answer Jesus' question: "But who do you say that I am?" (Matthew 16:15), and to defend the hope Jesus inspired (1 Peter 3:15). The community's self-definition also needed to be maintained in the face of internal and external challenges. At their best, these endeavors were not ecclesiastical power trips or intellectual parlor games, but served as norms for worship and proclamation of the gospel. In other words, doctrine makes no sense outside the worshipping community. Doctrine was not intended to explain the mystery of God, but confess it. Doctrines are the consequence of baptism, Eucharist, preaching, evangelism, mission, and opposition to and dialogue with rival religions; doctrines arose from the liturgy (literally, "the work of the people"), from worship. That is why the Nicene and Apostles' creeds are often embedded in worship services.

Certainly, it has sometimes been the case that confessions and doctrines have been used to externalize and formalize the faith. Nevertheless, without doctrine, without confession, the church was in danger of no longer knowing what it believed. What the church believes, teaches, and confesses is the community's affirmation that "not anything goes."

Heresy

Orthodoxy is the language that preserves the promise character of the gospel, that salvation is received from God, not achieved by humans. In contrast, heresy is the language that in one or another way vitiates the promise of the gospel by making it contingent upon human achievement. It is important to realize at the outset that the historical relationship of heresy and orthodoxy is complex. The early church did not begin with a handy catalogue of orthodox dogmas by which to determine the presence of heresies. Rather, heresy and orthodoxy grew together in mutual interaction. That historical process was so complex that it will be useful to begin with a formal way to conceive of heresy; to get a sense of what the Christian community believed to be at stake as they developed their confessions of faith. Friedrich Schleiermacher (1768–1834), one of the most influential theologians of the nineteenth century, provided just such a useful formal way to conceive of heresy. "Now, if the distinctive essence of Christianity consists in the fact that in it all religious emotions are related to the redemption wrought by Jesus of Nazareth, there will be two ways in which heresy can arise . . . *Either* human nature will be so defined that a redemption in the strict sense cannot be accomplished, *or* the Redeemer will be defined in such a way that He cannot accomplish redemption."

Schleiermacher continues by positing that each option has two basic forms. Anthropological heresies (i.e., those defining human nature in ways that preclude redemption) either conceive of human nature as so intrinsically good that redemption is not necessary or as so intrinsically evil that redemption is impossible. The classical expressions of these positions are associated with Pelagianism (the former) and Manichaeism (the latter). Soteriological (from Greek *soter*, "savior") heresies (i.e., those defining the Redeemer in ways that preclude redemption) either conceive of the nature of Jesus as so like that of humankind that he lacks the power to redeem or as so different from that of humankind that there is no point of contact. The classical expressions of these positions are Ebionitism (the former) and Docetism (the latter). Logically, how one conceives of theological anthropology influences the conception of soteriology and vice versa; that is, these heresies are bound in pairs. Thus a Pelagian view of humankind as basically good will tend to view Jesus in Ebionite terms as a human being whose contribution is little more than moral instruction or guidance in the way of salvation. Historically, this has been the orientation of rationalism. The problem of humankind is perceived as ignorance of the good, and Jesus is the teacher and model of the good life. A Manichaean view that humankind is so evil that no God worth his salt would participate in human life will view Jesus in Docetic terms (i.e., as only an apparent person). Historically, this has been the orientation of supernaturalism or strict dualism.

Schleiermacher's formal definition of heresy is useful but not foolproof in efforts to unravel the historically tangled skein of heresy and orthodoxy. Hence, Schleiermacher cautioned "it is highly important that people should go to work with the greatest caution when it comes to declaring anything heretical." Such caution, however, appeared to be in short supply in the bitter disputes that racked the early church. Since we are engaged in a *brief* history, we shall focus on the central dogmatic developments: the doctrines of the Trinity and Christology.

Jesus' Relationship to God: The Doctrine of the Trinity

The fundamental doctrines of the Trinity and Christology have to do, respectively, with Jesus' relationship with God and with humankind. While the doctrine of the Trinity is associated with the Councils of Nicaea (325) and Constantinople (381), and the doctrine of Christology with the Council of Chalcedon (451), it is important to realize once again that historical developments are not very tidy, and that both doctrines developed simultaneously.

The historical context of the development of the doctrine of the Trinity was framed not only by theological disputes among and within the urban centers of Christianity but also very significantly by the rise of the "imperial church." By the early fourth century the sporadic imperial persecutions of Christians ceased and leading thinkers in the church were carrying on constructive dialogues with Greco-Roman culture. In 312, Constantine, earlier proclaimed ruler of the western provinces by the Roman army in Britain, led his troops south into Italy and victoriously entered Rome after fierce battles against the larger army of the Roman emperor Maxentius. Prior to the final battle at the Milvian Bridge outside Rome, Constantine reportedly had a vision of the cross with the promise that under this sign he would conquer. He then replaced the emblems on the shields and standards of his troops with an intersecting X-P. Whether Constantine had in mind the emblem of the Sun god, Sol invictus, of whom he was then a devotee, or the first two letters of the Greek word for Christ (*chi* – "X," *rho* – "P") as Christian propagandists would later claim, the outcome was a change in policy toward the Christian faith. It was said that Constantine attributed his victory to the God of the Christians. In 324 he defeated his Eastern rival, Licinius, under the same standard and thus became sole master of the Greco-Roman world until his death in 337.

The Christian church now had an imperial patron. In 313 the Edict of Milan not only granted Christians freedom of worship but also restored church property taken during the persecutions, whether held by individuals or the state. Constantine's wife, Fausta, gave her palace on the Lateran to the church, and numerous other properties and monies soon followed. In 321 Constantine legalized bequests to the church, and its income was now also supplemented by the estates of all those who died without an heir; a firm foundation for the growing wealth of the church was established. The clergy were granted immunity from various civil responsibilities; bishops were provided imperial support for travel and administration; and the jurisdiction of church courts began extending to civil matters such as the manumission of slaves.

Constantine also displaced the many "immortal gods," hitherto seen as the protectors of the empire, with the God of Christianity. The French kings would later express this drive for a unified empire in their phrase: "one king, one law, one faith." In this regard sociologists of religion speak of the role religion plays in the construction of society by providing an ontological basis for civil institutions. That is, the society and its institutions are rooted in the mind of God. Almost immediately, however, Constantine discovered that the Christian faith he believed would be the glue to cement in place his vast empire was functioning in some major areas more as a corrosive acid eating away at the desired social unity.

The focal point for the spread of disunity in the church and hence the danger to the newly united empire was Alexandria. The size and cultural significance of Alexandria ranked it second only to Rome, and its renown as a center of Christian learning was already widespread in the second and third centuries in connection with the catechetical school led most famously by Clement (ca. 190–ca. 202) and then Origen (ca. 202–31). The theologian who created the crisis for the church and for Constantine was Arius (ca. 256–336), a priest in the port district of the city, popular among his parishioners for his preaching and ascetic life. The controversy associated with Arius concerned the relationship of Jesus to God. Arius emphasized the one God's absolute transcendence and indivisibility. Therefore, since God's substance cannot be shared with any other being – for then God would be divisible and changeable, a horror to Greek metaphysics – everything that exists outside of God – including Christ – must be created from nothing. Christ, the Word of God, did not exist prior to his creation by God; hence the famous phrase of the Arians: "there was [a time] when he [Christ] was not." Arius was concerned to maintain a Christian monotheism against what appeared to him to be the introduction of ideas of change in the Godhead. Ironically, his opponents thought that Arius ran the danger of presenting Christ as a demigod, and thus the question arose as to how this differed from pagan polytheism. Furthermore, it appeared that Arius was claiming that Christ's perfection was not therefore in his nature, his being one in substance with God, but in his voluntary fulfillment of God's will. In following or imitating Christ, therefore, humankind can also attain favor with God through ethical progress. This was a theology of salvation that appealed to the largest and most influential group of "spiritual athletes" of the day, the monks. Hence it was a brilliant propaganda coup when Arius' later opponent, Athanasius, wrote a *Life of Antony*, the most revered of the Egyptian ascetics, that argued that Antony's holiness was a gift of God's grace, not an ethical achievement.

Arius' views spread widely thanks to his persuasive rhetoric and ability to cast his theology in verse to popular tunes so that even the dockworkers of Alexandria began to propagate his theology. The consequent turmoil led his bishop, Alexander of Alexandria, to call upon him and his "Ariomaniacs" to recant. Arius refused, fled, and enlisted support from a number of bishops in northwestern Asia Minor. The controversy was not easily settled by appealing to scripture, for each side found biblical passages to support their position. Arius cited Colossians that Christ was "the firstborn of all creation" (Colossians 1:15), and his opponents appealed to the affirmation in the Gospel of John (1:1–5) that the "Word was with God . . . in the beginning."

As the controversy raged on, Constantine became increasingly concerned that religious division would erode political unity. After fruitless appeals for harmony, Constantine called a council of all the bishops to meet in Nicaea. This was not an invitation the bishops could refuse! All told, though there are no extant accurate lists of attendees, between 220 and 300 bishops assembled at Nicaea in 325. This was the first ecumenical council (Greek: *oikoumene*, "the inhabited world," i.e., universal, meaning in practical terms, the empire). The significance of this meeting would reverberate theologically and institutionally throughout the history of the church. Theologically, the council formulated a creed that rejected the Arian doctrine that Christ, the Son, was not of the same substance of God, the Father; and also rejected the Arian teaching that Christ is the Son by virtue of his will. The council affirmed that the Son is of the same substance (*homoousios*) of the Father.

Institutionally, Constantine's calling of the council presaged centuries of struggles between church and empire that would continue up to the last crowning of an emperor, that of Napoleon. From Constantine's perspective he had the right to call a council because in the context of Greco-Roman culture the emperor represented God on earth, and was thus legally entitled to intervene in religious affairs. The council itself was procedurally modeled on the Roman Senate. This allowed the bishops relative autonomy in resolving doctrinal issues because the emperor did not have the right to vote in the Senate. But Constantine did confirm the decisions of the bishops and made them binding under Roman law.

From the Council of Nicaea to the Council of Constantinople

In 328 Athanasius became the bishop of Alexandria. His genius was to formulate the rule: "All that is said of the Father is also said of the Son, except that the Son is Son, and not Father." But Athanasius did not become the "father of catholic orthodoxy" without a long and costly struggle. Immediately after Nicaea, Arius was condemned and exiled. Yet not all the council fathers were pleased by the use of the Nicene term *homoousios*, a term central to Athanasius' argument. Constantine allowed an anti-Nicene coalition to take root in his court and by the end of his reign it had become an anti-Athanasian force. As bishop, Athanasius was soon faced by riots and intrigues against the Nicene party. He stood firm, but by the time of Constantine's death and the succession of his sons, the leaders of the Nicene party in the East had been deposed or exiled. A relentless and dirty campaign began against Athanasius. Since his opponents could not attack his orthodoxy, they attacked his person, accusing him, among other things, of murdering another bishop and using his hand in magic rites – a charge refuted by producing the person in question with both hands still attached. In 335 Athanasius was banished to Trier. The attempt to rehabilitate Arius was prevented by his death in a public lavatory in 336 – a sign to the orthodox party of God's judgment.

On the eve of the Council of Constantinople (381), the Cappadocian bishop, Gregory of Nyssa (d. 394), declared that it was the destiny of his time to bring to full clarity the mystery that in the New Testament was only dimly intimated. A daring pronouncement, but it outlined the theological task of the day. The emperor Theodosius (379–95) sealed the peace with the imperial Council of Constantinople that endorsed the Council of Nicaea and also defined the divinity of the Holy Spirit. He also outlawed the Arians.

The Nicene-Constantinopolitan creed quickly became the baptismal creed of the East and also became popular in the West. It was incorporated in the eucharistic liturgy and used in East and West, and continues to be regarded as a truly ecumenical and therefore catholic summation of the Christian faith.

The development of the "Nicene" creed differs from the creation of the New Testament canon and the rule of faith in that its specific concern is the doctrine of God. By means of this doctrine the church erected a barrier against the Hellenism that threatened to inundate the Christian faith. Neither council attempted to plumb the depth of the divine mystery or to define God's essence.

Their intention was to indicate that God himself encounters us in Jesus Christ and that in the Holy Spirit God himself is present with the church. That the councils were not in their own self-understanding eliminating all theological reflection may be seen in the continuing reflection on these dogmas in the history of the church. One of the next persons to take up this task was Augustine (354–430), who in 381 was not yet a Christian.

Augustine – never accused of being an intellectual slouch – spent some fifteen years (400–16) laboring on his treatise *On the Trinity*. His concern was to warn the West of the dangers of tritheism. In the course of his work he commented: "Human speech at once toils with great insufficiency. Yet we say three persons, not in order to express it, but in order not to be silent." Again, the intent of doctrine is not to define the mystery of God but to confess it.

Jesus and Humankind: Christology

The development of the doctrine of the Trinity entailed Christological reflection in that every affirmation about Christ carried an understanding of the Trinity and vice versa. Now that the fourth-century church confessed the unity of God with the assertion of the divinity of the Son and Holy Spirit, questions arose concerning the relationship between divinity and humanity in the person of Jesus Christ. The New Testament authors had no doubt concerning the true humanity of Jesus – they had known him "according to the flesh" (2 Corinthians 5:16) – they had shared their lives with him. Yet, at the same time, the disciples were convinced that Jesus was not just another prophet sent by God, but rather that in Jesus, God met them in a unique and incomparable way. In some sense they were convinced that Jesus himself is divine; that Jesus had broken through the category of the prophetic. But how are the human and the divine related in Jesus? Does the divine Word replace the human mind or soul? A sense of the integrity of human nature criticized such a view on the basis that a person's soul and not merely his or her flesh must be saved through Christ. Furthermore, the locus of sin is not the body but the mind. As Gregory of Nazianzus (d. ca. 390), another Cappadocian bishop, succinctly put it, what is not assumed by God is not redeemed. Orthodox Christian tradition tended to oppose the Neoplatonic view that the spirit seeks the good but is imprisoned in a corrupt body. Gregory saw that it is the person's highest faculties that rebel. Therefore, if Christ has not assumed all of human nature, then not all of human nature is redeemed.

The Christological issue came to a head through Nestorius (d. ca. 451), the bishop of Constantinople, and his opponent Cyril (ca. 370–444), bishop of Alexandria. Here, too, of course, there were numerous non-doctrinal factors in the controversy leading to the councils of Ephesus (431) and Chalcedon (451) – rivalry between the theological schools of Antioch and Alexandria; jealousy of Alexandria toward Constantinople (Alexandria, long esteemed as the seat of learning and the bulwark of orthodoxy, was being overshadowed by the rise of Constantinople as the imperial residence); the power of monasticism; and the role of women.

The heresy associated with Nestorius, who had been a priest and monk in Antioch before becoming bishop of Constantinople – Nestorianism – basically held that there were two persons in Christ. However, it seems he did not actually teach this; and so like many heresies attributed to particular persons there is some inaccuracy here. The Antiochene emphasis upon the reality of Christ's human experiences of temptation and suffering led to the view that in Christ there were two persons in moral rather than in essential union. Since the Logos is eternal and only like can bear like, that which was born of Mary was the human only. The Incarnation was the indwelling of the Logos in a perfect man, as of God in a temple. In contrast, Cyril held the Alexandrian teaching that the divine and human natures were united in Jesus, who was God become man. Cyril's argument was that if Jesus did not suffer on the cross as the Word become flesh, his sacrifice did not truly bring salvation. In short, if only a man died on the cross, what is salvific about another victim of human cruelty?

When Nestorius became bishop of Constantinople he inherited a dispute over a title applied to Mary. Some insisted on calling her "theotokos," God-bearer or Mother of God, while others were calling her Mother of man. Nestorius, hoping for compromise, suggested that she should be called Mother of Christ ("Christotokos"), a term which he argued represented both God and man, as it is used in the gospels.

However, theotokos was a term that had become deeply rooted in liturgy and popular piety. In light of the formulation of Nicaea and Constantinople, the theotokos title expressed, especially for the Alexandrians, the belief that, in the Incarnation, deity and humanity were so closely united that neither birth nor death nor salvation could be attributed to one nature without the other. Alexandrian Christology used the liturgical term theotokos to support its emphasis on the unity of the person of Christ. To Cyril of Alexandria it was of course a natural expression. Indeed, it was used everywhere in the East except where the school of Antioch was influential.

Thus Nestorius' position ran aground on popular piety both in terms of the worship of Christ and the growing veneration for Mary. Furthermore, Nestorius, a powerful preacher, lacked discretion in using provocative phrases such as Mary could not carry God for nine months in her womb and God could hardly be wrapped in diapers. Cyril's counter-claim was to profess the unity of God with the man Jesus – it was God himself who was born, lived, taught, labored, and died in history. From Cyril's point of view, Nestorian Christology denied the affirmation that the divine Word truly became a human person, thus implying there can be no true redemption. Furthermore, for Cyril, the liturgical consequences of Nestorianism would mean that in the Eucharist only the body of a man would be resting on the altar, and this would rob the Eucharist of its life-giving power.

Nestorius also exhibited his inability to win friends and influence people by railing against the city's popular entertainments of circus races and theater; and demanding that monks remain in the monasteries rather than engage in public ministry. And he raised the question of whether the patriarch of Constantinople could overrule the patriarch of Alexandria. The "last straw" was Nestorius' confrontation with the emperor's sister, Pulcheria, who had dedicated her life to holy virginity.

Nestorius was certainly not the first – nor the last! – church leader who believed women should stay in their place. In his view, women who attended evening psalms and prayers as well as night vigils for the dead were inviting problems; so he locked women out of evening services. Nestorius then personally blocked Pulcheria from entering the sanctuary when, as her custom, she was to take communion with her brother and the priests, proclaiming that "only priests may walk here." She responded: "Why? Have I not given birth to God?" Nestorius drove her away with the incensed charge: "You? You have given birth to Satan!" As if this were not enough, Nestorius then cancelled a popular festival dedicated to Mary that had become an occasion during the liturgical year when virgins and religious women were honored. Mary was not the mother of God, claimed Nestorius, but only the mother of Jesus the man, Christ-bearer, not God-bearer.

The emperor called the Council of Ephesus to settle the theological question. Ephesus, however, was both a haven for adherents of Cyril's position and the ancient cult center of the virgin goddess Artemis/Diana that by now had been co-opted to the cult of the theotokos. Whether or not Pulcheria had a hand in choosing this site, the city was packed with pro-Cyril supporters and monks angry at Nestorius. To cap it all off, the council met in a church dedicated to the Virgin Mary. Nestorius was excommunicated, and Jesus was declared fully God and fully human. Jubilant women escorted Cyril from the meeting.

The reaction to Nestorianism led to monophysitism – a Christology that merged Christ's divinity and humanity into one entity (*physis*). The strength of the Monophysite orientation was in the areas of Syria and Egypt where strong Semitic roots of the faith militated against any suggestions that the person of Jesus might be divided. In contrast, the Greco-Latin churches were influenced by their roots in classical antiquity.

In response, the emperor called a council to meet at Chalcedon, on the eastern shore of the Bosphorus, opposite Constantinople. Its dogmatic decision was decisively influenced by a doctrinal letter written by the bishop of Rome, Leo I, known as "Leo's Tome." Leo insisted that in Jesus there are two natures complete in one person, God and man. How this can be, Leo leaves a mystery – which is perhaps Leo's greatest wisdom. Leo summarized briefly and succinctly the Christology of the West that in Christ there are two full and complete natures which "without detracting from the properties of either nature and substance, came together in one person." Leo argued that the unity of the two natures is essential for redemption. The mediator between God and humankind, Jesus Christ, had to be able to die (according to his human nature) and not to die (according to his divine nature). He further emphasized that the two natures of Christ have separate modes of operation but one always acts in unison with the other. This is the doctrine of the *communicatio idomatum* – in the unity of the person there is an exchange or "communication" of properties or attributes. It is therefore proper to say that the Son of God was crucified and buried or that the Son of Man came down from heaven. There is one indivisible God-man. Christ is to be acknowledged in two natures "inconfusedly, unchangeably, indivisibly, inseparably." The first two terms exclude Monophysitism and the last two exclude Nestorianism. The acclamation in response to Leo's proposal – "Peter has spoken through Leo" – enhanced the prestige of the bishop of Rome, and thus the eventual papacy rooted there.

The decision at Chalcedon was not an attempt to force the inexpressible into conceptual clarity. In the face of the endless discussions and controversies concerning the relationship of divinity and humanity in Jesus Christ, Chalcedon simply asserted that Jesus Christ is one person and at the same time he is truly God and truly man. The decision did not eliminate speculative questions, but it gave the questions a direction for speaking about the divinity and humanity of Jesus Christ.

The rivalry of the patriarchs of Constantinople and Alexandria brought grief upon both of them and allowed the eastern emperors to subject the church to their own authority. The Christological controversies enflamed the national passions of Egypt and Syria and fed the struggle for freedom from Byzantine overlordship. Monophysite bishops were placed in the sees of Egypt and Syria, thus eroding the unity of empire and church. Some scholars have suggested that this area of the empire was thus less able later to fend off Islam. Although subject to isolation and oppression, the Coptic Church in Egypt and its daughter church, the Ethiopian Church, have continued to today and are members of the World Council of Churches. Nestorianism also took root in Persia, from whence it sent missionaries to India and China. Another aftermath of these lengthy Christological controversies was the iconoclastic controversy that rocked the Greek Church in the eighth and ninth centuries. Here too there were non-doctrinal factors at play, such as the role and authority of monasticism, but the Christological issue was also present. The opponents of images argued that a representation of Christ's divine nature comes under the prohibition of images of God found in scripture. The proponents of images, on the other hand, appealed to the affirmation that the divine Logos did in fact become human.

Chalcedon's concerns were made known to the West in the so-called Athanasian creed that was cited at least partially for the first time by Caesarius of Arles (470–552). In 40 short statements it summarized the catholic dogma on the union in two natures of the person of Christ and the divine Trinity. But the Athanasian creed also contained a formulation that led to division in the church. It emphasized that "the Holy Spirit is from the Father and the Son, neither made nor created, but proceeding." This reference of filioque ("and from the Son") sought originally to emphasize that Christ is one essence with the Father. But it also stated that the Spirit proceeds in the same manner from the Father and the Son. This formulation distinguishes the creed from the usual emphasis of the Eastern theologians that the Spirit proceeds from the Father through the Son and is distributed over the whole creation.

That this formulation led to division between East and West lay not only in the different theological orientations – Eastern theologians started from the Trinitarian and Christological considerations of the unity of the Trinity, while Western theologians understood in their reflections that the Holy Spirit is the person uniting the Father and the Son. The early medieval Western insertion of the filioque into the Nicene-Constantinopolitan creed raised an essential point of contention between the Eastern and Western churches, that is, whether a part of the church could change by its own unilateral action the common confession of the church formulated by an ecumenical council. According to the Eastern church only an ecumenical council of the Eastern and Western churches could expand a confession that a council had determined. The controversy over the filioque in addition to other political and ecclesial tensions finally led to the Great Schism in 1054 between the East and the West. The East continues to view the addition of the filioque as a matter of schism while it is generally accepted in the West.

Chapter 4

The Heavenly City: The Augustinian Synthesis of Biblical Religion and Hellenism

The person in the West who more than any other put his stamp on the competing interpretations of salvation was St. Augustine (354–430), who also bequeathed to Western culture its penchant for introspection, pilgrimage, and alienation. No other theologian has been as influential upon the West as Augustine. He marked the theological–spiritual course for the church up to the modern period.

Aurelius Augustinus was born in Thagaste (in contemporary Algeria), a provincial bourgeois milieu. His father was a pagan and his mother, Monica, was a very devout Christian. Augustine lived in a time of great political and social crisis. By the time of his death while the bishop of Hippo Regius, a small North African seaport and Roman military post, the city was under siege by the Vandals. Aleric's Visigoths had pillaged Rome and shaken the Roman world to its foundations in 410, the symbolic date for the end of the Roman Empire in the West. The empire had been divided in 395. Whereas Byzantium, the Eastern Roman Empire, was able to defend its population, the defenses of the western half of the empire were too weak to withstand barbarian pressures. Indeed, Rome itself was no longer the capital of the empire. In 330 Constantine had established a new capital in the town of Byzantium strategically located in the isthmus between the Black and Aegean Seas, that he in all humility named Constantinople. By 404 Rome was no longer even the capital of the Western Roman Empire, having been displaced by the exarchate of Ravenna. These events marked a major break with the existing Roman Empire, and left a political vacuum that would be filled by the bishops of Rome. Next to the political and economic upheaval in Augustine's time there were also significant theological controversies threatening the unity of the church, in particular Donatism and Pelagianism.

Augustine lived in an afflicted society that appeared to be rushing pell-mell towards disintegration. "Eternal Rome" was collapsing as it faced perpetual warfare with barbarian war bands in the north and the challenge of Persia in the east. Taxation skyrocketed to finance the military; the poor were victimized by horrendous inflation; and the rich sought refuge in unparalleled accumulations of property. To add insult to injury for the Christians, the charge arose that all these disasters were the consequence of the abandonment of the traditional gods of the empire.

Augustine's family, though not rich, was free and he was bright. His father, Patricius, a minor official, perceived that economic advancement was through a classical education, and thus he scraped together the means for Augustine to gain such an education with its emphasis upon rhetoric. Hot tempered but generous, Patricius was admired by fellow townsfolk for his sacrifices for Augustine's education, yet Augustine himself makes only passing reference to his father's death. His mother, Monica, however, was convinced through a dream that he would be converted to Christianity. She followed Augustine relentlessly in pursuit of her vision of Augustine's conversion. Augustine himself seems to have realized that her devouring love had an element of "unspiritual desire" in it for in his *Confessions* he wrote: "She loved to have me with her, as is the way with mothers, but far more than most mothers."

Insight into Augustine's development is provided by his *Confessions*, written between 397 and 401. This book takes his story to the death of his mother in 387; in his unfinished *Retractions*, begun in 426, he corrects and discusses those aspects of his writings that he came to see were in error or were misunderstood.

Augustine's *Confessions* present his reflections on his family origins and development. Indeed, this writing is the means by which Augustine came to terms with his own history; it was an act of therapy for what we might now call a midlife crisis. Since 391 he had been forced to adjust to a new life-situation as a priest and then as a bishop. He received the latter responsibility against his will. His own plan for his life after his dramatic conversion to Christianity was to live in a monastic community apart from the world; but this desire had to be set aside. The ecstasy and optimism of his conversion was now sobered by increasing introspection into his past, into his sins, into his ability to function in his new ecclesiastical responsibility. Augustine felt he had to assess himself, and he did this by reinterpreting his past life as it led to his conversion. The *Confessions* are Augustine's effort to find himself.

This was an intensely personal period of adjustment for Augustine. In being thrust into the life of episcopal action he was not only losing his treasured life of contemplative withdrawal (John Calvin will have a similar experience) but was also now exposed to the spiritual temptations he thought he had escaped by renouncing in 386 his acclaimed public position as a rhetorician. He had rejected a life as a public figure because of its seductive dangers of ambition, desire for praise, temptation to dominate others, and the sensitivity to insult. Now he found himself faced once again by the hazards of pride in what he called "the puffed-up existence" of a bishop. All that had horrified him at his conversion was reappearing, never mind that it was now in service of the church.

Thus, immediately after his ordination as a priest, Augustine wrote a desperate letter to his bishop begging for time to retire and study scripture. Why? He was already an accomplished theologian. The actual life of a priest, he discovered, revealed his limitations. "I found it," Augustine wrote, "far, far more than I had thought . . . I just had not known my own powers: I still thought they counted for something. But the Lord laughed me to scorn and, by real experience, wished to show me to myself." As he put it later in his *Confessions*, the office of ministry bit into him and he was "made deeply afraid by the weight of his sins."

To face his ministry, Augustine worked through his past. His conversion alone was not enough to sustain him. He had to work through his emotions regarding the death of his mother, for example, and reached the conclusion that the idealized figure who had haunted his youth is finally just an ordinary person, a sinner like himself. Augustine could have cut himself off from his past – not an unusual reaction to a conversion experience. Instead, he called on his memory to understand his present. He dealt specifically with his feelings in relation to his personal growth and the nature of human motivation. Hence his account of stealing a pear is a paradigm for the sinful human condition. One would think that a cosmopolitan person like Augustine could have come up with a more lurid example! But, as he noted, it was not the pear he wanted to enjoy, but rather "the theft for its own sake, and the sin." He "derived pleasure from the deed simply because it was forbidden." He recalled how in his pagan life he had enjoyed crying at the theater, but had no reaction to the news of his father's death. In his reflections Augustine set the tone that will permeate medieval culture and theology up to the Reformation period and in many respects up to today. That tone is introspection.

Introspective self-scrutiny, seen in the *Confessions*, is the soul's longing for God, a longing to return to its maker, a longing experienced as restlessness, a pressing sense that in all things there lies something beyond, something that calls to God. The sense of not being at home in the world, the sense of alienation, is fundamental to Augustine. But of course it is not unique to him or to

Christianity. It is the Hellenistic tension between the transient and the permanent, the temporal and the eternal. It is what Plato expressed in the longing to escape the shadows of the cave and enter the sunshine of the intelligible world. It is even more clearly expressed by Plotinus, whose writings influenced Augustine. But in Augustine the longing for God is transposed from human restlessness to a response to God's love and condescension; it is, in the opening lines of the *Confessions*, the movement of the Holy Spirit in the human heart: "for you have formed us for yourself, and our hearts are restless till they find rest in you."

Augustine's experience is a transitory foretaste of the joys of heaven. Its transitoriness reminds Augustine and his culture – as if it needed reminding as the empire collapsed – of mortality and the destiny of death. The experience is also a way of ascent – both upwards and inwards – that passes beyond material things to the depths of the soul. Here is also Augustine's debt to Plotinus. Here too is reflected the changed context of Augustine's Christianity from that of pre-establishment Christianity – the enemy of the Christian is no longer the external persecutor but the internal tempter. While early Christians faced external pressures that at times led to martyrdom, the worst enemies of the Christians of Augustine's time were sin and doubt; the climax of a person's life would not be martyrdom but conversion from the past. That is why to Augustine's contemporaries the *Confessions* was a startling book. Their ideal was to present conversion as the beginning of a new life that leaves the past behind.

In contrast, Augustine regarded the past as alive in the person's present. Personal differences related to unique past experiences. His mother would have become a drunkard had she not been caught tippling at age six, and his friend Alypius' unsatisfactory experience of sex as a boy contributed to his chastity. Augustine explored the ability of persons to imprison themselves by their past. Thus he reflected on the theft of a pear as a paradigm of the limitations of human freedom and the proclivity to self-destruction. He described the bondage of the will as a chain of iron. Unlike so many ancient and medieval biographies where the heroes are described in terms of their ideal qualities, Augustine revealed his past and its grip on him. He made it clear that a person's past is very much alive in the present, and that no dramatic conversion experience should delude a person into believing he or she could easily discard a past identity.

Augustine's Path to Conversion

One of Augustine's first crucial concerns was the question of truth. Cicero's *Hortensius*, a work that summoned philosophy to the truth, influenced him as a student. He also tried reading the Bible, but thought it was an inferior writing compared to the works of the Latins. The next influence was Manichaeism, an Asian-Hellenistic religion somewhat similar to Gnosticism in its equation of good and evil with spirit and matter. The religion attracted Augustine because it provided a rational explanation of sin in terms of an ultimate principle of evil in the world fighting against the ultimate principle of good. The material world should be avoided by an ascetic discipline designed to free the soul from the matter that enmeshed it in evil. Manichaeism was a system of salvation in which truth is seen as saving truth. However, Augustine's disappointment in the intellects of leading Manichaeans he met, and his encounter with Neoplatonism and the church in the figure of Ambrose, bishop of Milan, led him to forsake this religion. Some, however, have suggested that the profound pessimism concerning created nature inculcated by Manichaeism influenced Augustine's later doctrine of sin.

Augustine's search for philosophical certainty was aided by his discovery of Neoplatonism. Instead of the forces of good and evil, Neoplatonism spoke of being and non-being. In this schema, evil is seen as a defect, a lack of being. Persons are pulled downward or direct their attention downward away from being toward non-being, and therefore are not what they ought to be. But as attractive as this was intellectually for Augustine, he was unable to put it into practice. Neoplatonism showed him the good, but did not enable him to reach it. He wondered how Christian monks, who to him were not very bright, could control themselves, but he with all his publicly acclaimed brilliance could not. Yet Platonic thought helped prepare him for acceptance of the gospel. It was, Augustine says, God's design that he read the Platonists before the scriptures.

The other major influence was the church in the person of Ambrose of Milan, a brilliant rhetorician who had embraced Christianity and then been acclaimed bishop. Ambrose exhibited in his own person to Augustine that he did not have to sacrifice his intellect to become a Christian. A further impetus to conversion was the story recounted by his countryman Ponticianus of the conversion of two of his friends on reading Athanasius' *Life of St. Antony.*

In his *Confessions* Augustine recounts his conversion as a highly emotional event. He withdrew into his garden and flung himself down under a fig tree, weeping for release from the anger and judgment of God, and heard a child chanting: "Take up and read; take up and read." Interpreting this as a divine command, he opened the Bible and read the first passage he saw, Romans 13:13–14: "Let us live honorably as in the day, not in reveling and drunkenness, not in debauchery and licentiousness, not in quarreling and jealousy. Instead, put on the Lord Jesus Christ, and make no provision for the flesh, to gratify its desires." Instantly, his gloom and doubt vanished.

Augustine's Theological Contributions

Augustine's contributions to Western theology and church history are legion. Most noteworthy are his grounding of Christian faith in the concept of love, and his responses to the challenges posed in his time – and ever after – by Donatism and Pelagianism.

Augustine attempted to subsume Christianity as a whole under the aspect of love. Christianity is purely and simply the religion of love. He articulated this motif so powerfully that it became axiomatic for Roman Catholic and much of Protestant theology to affirm Christianity is a religion of love.

Augustine's mother tongue was Latin, thus the word he used for Christian love is *caritas*, the word from which we get "charity." Caritas in Augustine's sense is primarily love to God made possible because God first loved humankind. Love to God is the central virtue; all other virtues are expressions of it. With this theological orientation Augustine is free from all legalistic ethics. Only love is enjoined upon the Christian; where love is, no other requirements are necessary. Hence, Augustine's famous ethical injunction: "Love God and do what you will." Caritas is the root of all that is good; its opposite, the root of all that is evil, is *cupiditas*, the word from which we get "cupidity" and also "Cupid," the Roman god of love. Both caritas and cupiditas are terms for love. The difference between them is that caritas is directed to the sole true and real possibility for happiness, God; whereas cupiditas is (mis)directed love toward things assumed to provide happiness but which are only transient. Both terms refer to "love" but are polar opposites – caritas ascends to God, Being itself; cupiditas descends to inferior beings and then nothingness. Augustine's fundamental assumption – gained from his acquaintance with Neoplatonism – is that all love is acquisitive. That is, persons desire what they believe will fulfill them. In short, Augustine perceives that the eudaemonism – the drive for fulfillment – of ancient philosophy has apologetic value. Everyone wants to be happy. By linking love closely to the desire for happiness, Augustine finds it possible to regard love as the most elementary of all manifestations of human life. There is no one who does not seek his or her happiness. For Augustine this is synonymous with the claim that there is no one who does not love.

Here is the foundation for the theology of ordered love that will develop in medieval scholasticism. Anything may be an object of good *for me* – thus even in evil the person loves nothing other than what he or she thinks is his or her good. Creatures, being incomplete, always desire their completeness.

This leads to consideration of the opposition between loves, between caritas and cupiditas. Cupiditas is sin because it is misdirected love; it is love directed to inferior objects; it is curved down toward the earth rather than toward God. But God is above us, and thus we are to direct our love upward toward the good that is God. Earthly goods confuse us, and drag our love downwards toward them. Cupiditas then is the search for the good, which while good, is nevertheless incapable of providing final satisfaction. Here again we see the influence of Neoplatonism. Being itself is the highest good; to turn away from the highest good, from Being, is to turn toward non-being. Augustine was thus using Hellenistic philosophy to express to his audience the biblical view that sin is not just breaking rules or laws but breaking relationships by turning away from God and the neighbor, breaking the chain of being. Since only God is the highest good, the immutable good, only God can give persons complete fulfillment. When love is directed to lower goods in the search for fulfillment it then becomes idolatrous, it mistakes the creature for the Creator; by loving perishable goods, sin is a turn or perversion toward privation and death.

The distinction between true and false love raises the question of Augustine's understanding of the creation. He rejected Manichaeism with its denigration of the material world, and he affirmed the goodness of creation because it is God's creation. Hence love of the creation is not in itself sin if this love is rightly understood. He clarified this by making a distinction between enjoyment (*frui*) and use (*uti*). Frui is the love that "enjoys" its object, whereas uti is the love that "uses" its object. The analogy Augustine used to illustrate this distinction is that of a voyage to our homeland. The ship is "used" as a means to get us to our home that we "enjoy." But the danger is that the voyage may so appeal to us that we forget home and enjoy the trip to the extent that it becomes an end in itself.

The earthly city is not the true home of the Christian, but rather the vehicle (the ship) for our travel to our true home in the heavenly city. The world, our earthly city, is given as a means and vehicle for our return to God; it is to be used, not enjoyed. The world, if enjoyed, drags us down and away from God. In his theology of history, *The City of God*, Augustine wrote: "Accordingly, two cities have been formed by two loves: the earthly by the love of self, even to the contempt of God; the heavenly by the love of God, even to the contempt of self. The former, in a word, glories in itself, the latter in the Lord." The issue in the succeeding history of Western Christendom became whether this disjuncture is spiritualized toward an ascetic otherworldliness or understood as the critical perspective for life in this world. One major aspect of the Augustinian heritage was an emphasis upon Christians as pilgrims in an alien land. In Augustine we find the themes of pilgrimage and alienation that become so influential in Western Christendom and culture. The motif of ascent to God will be illustrated in art and literature by images of the ladder to heaven. To be sure, Augustine emphasized that human ascent to God depends first of all upon God's descent to humankind; the descent of Christ enables human ascent to God.

Augustine and Donatism

Donatism was a movement concerned for the moral purity of the church, especially its ministry, and as such has been a perennial occurrence in the history of the church, especially in relation to renewal movements such as the Gregorian reform (eleventh century), Reformation radicalism (sixteenth century), and modern charismatic movements.

In the African Christianity of Augustine's time, the purity of the church was a central concern. To the Donatists of North Africa, however, the moral purity and holiness of Christianity had been severely compromised by the failure of nerve of many of its members, including priests and bishops, during the major persecutions. In 303 the emperor Diocletian launched a major attack, the "Great Persecution" (303–5), upon the church. Churches were destroyed, Christians were forced to hand over their sacred writings, bishops and congregational leaders were arrested and forced to make sacrifices to imperial divinities.

During this and prior persecutions numerous Christians had witnessed to their faith to the extent of losing their lives. Moved by these martyrdoms, pagans had joined the church; hence the famous phrase "the blood of the martyrs is the seed of the church." Not all Christians, however, when confronted by the choice of torture and possibly a grisly death or renouncing their faith, chose the former. Bishops who opted for the better part of valor were known as "traditors" because they "handed over" the scriptures to the authorities. After the persecutions subsided, there were "traditors" or "collaborators" who wished to rejoin the community. We can imagine the mixed emotions of those who had remained steadfast at great cost. At any rate, it was believed by the Donatists that those bishops who had handed the scriptures over to the authorities had thereby deprived themselves of all spiritual power.

It was believed that Caecilian, bishop of Carthage, had been ordained by a traditor. Thus, in 311, 80 Numidian bishops declared his ordination invalid and elected another bishop in his place. The new bishop was soon succeeded by another bishop named Donatus. Hence arose the "Donatist party."

Caecilian held on as bishop. The case of the Donatists was perceived as weak because some of them also had been traditors. And the rest of the Latin church was more open to tolerating past collaborators. Furthermore, Constantine wanted a unified and respectable church. Since Caecilian was the existing bishop,

Constantine supported him against what appeared to non-Africans as exaggerated and parochial grievances.

Division was hardened by military persecution of the Donatists. When Julian the Apostate was emperor (361–3), tolerance was renewed for the Donatists and the Catholic party was attacked.

Augustine's response to the Donatists was influenced by the fact that he became a Christian in Milan, not in North Africa. In the former context the major issues were philosophical and cultural rather than the generations of rancor about purity in North Africa. To Augustine, the Donatists threatened the universality and unity of the church by their advocacy of isolation for the sake of purity. Whereas the Donatists regarded their church as an alternative to society, a place of refuge like the biblical ark, Augustine believed the church should become coextensive with human society as a whole and thereby transform and perfect the bonds of human relations.

The questions sharpened by the Donatist controversy were whether the church is defined by the purity of its ministers or the catholicity of its sacraments; whether the church is "in" society or should separate from society in order to live the faith; whether the church is a community of saints and sinners or the company of the pure. What is the source of the true unity of the church?

Already at the Council of Arles (316) under the influence of Constantine, the principle was decreed that ordination and baptism are not dependent upon the worthiness of the administrant. Augustine continued this principle with the argument that the holiness of the church is due to the divine presence in it in the sacraments. In other words, the message is not dependent upon the moral character of the messenger. If the contrary was held, then the gospel would always be in doubt because the hearts of the ministers cannot be read. The Word of God and the sacraments are valid whether or not the minister runs off with the choir director or even contemplates doing so in the future. Hence the Conference of Carthage (411) affirmed that salvation depends upon God, not humankind. The Donatists were not won back to the church, but were condemned. One of the historical consequences was that Augustine turned to the power of the state to repress the Donatists by appealing to the parable of the banquet in Luke 14:16–23 that ends with the mandate: "compel them to come in." Thus the emperor Honorius around 400 applied heresy laws against schismatics. Throughout the history of the church Donatism has been a temptation that can also take the form of a congregational Donatism that claims that the truth of the church depends upon the moral purity of the assembly rather than Word and sacrament. The Donatist party was concerned that the church would forsake its prophetic critique of culture and succumb to moral complacency, whereas the "Catholic" concern was that Donatism would lead to moralism and sectarianism.

The Pelagian Controversy

Augustine had been involved with the Donatist controversy for nearly fifteen years (396–411), but that did not deter him from continuing theological reflection on the problems of evil and salvation. His own conversion experience naturally led him in the direction of emphasizing the absolute priority of divine providence for salvation. He rejected any suggestion that persons could make the smallest step toward righteousness before God without divine assistance. Thus, well before the Irish monk Pelagius (355–420) appeared on the scene advocating human freedom to choose righteousness, Augustine through his personal experience and intense study of the Bible held that humankind was a *massa peccati*, a "lump of sin," since the fall of Adam, with no merit of its own. Indeed, he held that sin was passed on seminally from Adam. The sense of original sin as the original sexually transmitted disease was derived from his (mis)reading of Romans 5:12 as "In whom, that is, in Adam, all sinned." Augustine did not read Greek and depended on a Latin translation of the second century that rendered the Greek as *in quo omnes peccaverunt* ("in whom all have sinned"). The *in quo* was read in the masculine by Augustine to mean "in Adam." Sin therefore is universal and inevitable since all humankind descended from Adam. What was at stake for Augustine in this reasoning was the affirmation that redemption depends solely upon God, since all are sinners. Humankind cannot depend upon any natural capacity for salvation; salvation is received, not achieved. The downside of Augustine's interpretation of the universality of sin as hereditary has been a suspicion about sexuality.

Pelagius, however, heard Augustine to be advocating fatalism. Augustine's dictum in his *Confessions*, "Give what you [God] command, and command what you will," clearly appeared to Pelagius to jeopardize human morality. He and his followers were already concerned that now that Christianity had become the established religion, people were entering the church for convenience or political and economic advantage rather than as disciples. As Søren Kierkegaard, nineteenth-century critic of the Danish state church, would later charge, when everyone is a Christian no one is a Christian.

Like the Donatist party, the Pelagians were also interested in perfection. Pelagius called upon Christians to live out their faith in perfection. Certainly, grace was necessary for humankind because the power to be good had been weakened by Adam's fall into sin. But baptism gives forgiveness, and Christ has provided a new law and example to guide humankind toward perfection and the consequent eternal reward. Pelagius believed that Christians through divinely provided free will and through God's law could carry out Christ's commands as laid down in the New Testament, and thereby live a virtuous life. Pelagius neither admitted original sin nor original fall. A person's sin is his or her own. Adam was certainly a bad example, but he did not infect the whole human race.

Pelagius preached repentance with great zeal. To an insecure age with a "pull-yourself-up-by-your-bootstraps mentality" comparable to American ideology, such moral exhortation was well received. By 418 Pelagius was joined by impressive champions of his views, including the bishop of Eclanum, Julian. Their theology emphasized the freedom of the human will. The rationalist strain here is apparent with the argument that since God has given us the law, it must follow that we have the ability to do it. Centuries later during the Enlightenment, Immanuel Kant would phrase this: "You ought, therefore you can." Since we have free will, it is possible for us to decide for or against the good. Christ would not have commanded divine perfection had he known this was beyond achievement (Matthew 5:48: "Be perfect, therefore, as your heavenly Father is perfect"). The Old Testament law and the Sermon on the Mount emphasize our responsibility to God's command. Human difficulties in fulfilling the law are removed by grace. The law is further supplemented by the teachings and example of Christ; thus God's assistance may be seen as instruction through moral example.

To Augustine the tendency to identify grace with the exemplary life and moral teaching of Christ displaced Christ's atoning death and perverted the good news into bad news, a new legalism that placed the burden of proof for salvation upon human effort. Furthermore, the assumption that humans have the capability to fulfill the law of God would lead to naive optimism.

In 417 pope Innocent I (reign 401–17) took the side of Augustine against Pelagius in a way that contributed to the growing power of the Roman bishop, later expressed in the phrase: *Roma locuta, causa finita* – "Rome has spoken, the case is closed." In 418 the Synod of Carthage confirmed the condemnation of Pelagianism, and variations on its theme of human free will in relation to salvation were condemned at the Synod of Orange in 529. Like Donatism, however, Pelagianism has a perennial appeal and continually crops up in the history of Christianity.

In the last decades of his life Augustine wrote two of his greatest works, *On the Trinity* and *The City of God*. The former is a brilliant exposition of the doctrine that seeks to free it from the metaphysical puzzles that had beset the East since the Council of Nicaea. Augustine presented the divine quality of love binding the three persons of the Trinity descending to humankind as the creative force of forgiveness by which God recreates his own image in each sinner. The *City of God*, begun in 411 and completed in 426, responded to the questions of whether the fall of Rome and other disasters were the consequences of the imperial establishment of Christianity. Were the neglected gods of old Rome taking vengeance? In this theology of history, Augustine rejected such views and also set forth a schema of church–state relations. The earthly images of the two cities are the church and the state. But the earthly church is still not the city of God; and the state is necessary to preserve peace and human righteousness. Augustine presented the two cities as ideal types, even though these were reflected in earthly governments according to the purpose of their existence. Thus the state too could reflect divine purpose.

Augustine presented a whole theory of society that drew upon classical culture yet also consciously criticized it. Here too he was a great influence upon the medieval church and culture that, under his influence, would continue to aspire to the city of God. In the Augustinian theology of history the problems of human society relate to sin, and thus even the virtues of humankind are but "splendid vices." Therefore no political and social system can make people good. The best that government can do is to provide enough peace to enable the pilgrimage to the heavenly city to continue. Augustine also attacked in his theology of history the classic cyclical view of history, the endless wheel of the pagans. The church's mission is to convert and transform society. In this, the goal is not withdrawal into purity but engagement with the world. The medieval church clearly took this to heart.

Chapter 5

The Development of Medieval Christendom

The church may indeed in Augustine's eyes be a reflection of the heavenly city, but he also recognized it existed in the earthly city. Vital to the church's existence in the world was its developing institutional structure as it expanded outward from the collapsing Roman Empire into the lands it would shape to become what we call Europe. The institutionalization of the Augustinian aspiration to the city of God that formed the foundation and then shaped the contours of medieval Europe included a number of often simultaneously interweaving factors, through which ran the red thread of imperial–papal relations. The warp and woof of this tapestry of medieval development included the authority of the bishop of Rome; the Roman cultural heritage of jurisprudence and language; the barbarian invasions that eroded imperial power and left the church as the major integrating force in the West; the rise of monasticism as a missionary movement; and the two-pronged evangelization of the Continent from the south by Roman missions under Gregory the Great and from the north by Celtic missions from the British Isles. The temporal parameters of this complex development are the papal reigns of Gregory the Great (590–604) and Gregory VII (1073–85).

Monasticism to Mission

Monastic life exerted such influence that its significance is almost impossible to overestimate. The monastery provided a glimpse of order in the midst of the prevalent disorder of early medieval life so marked by dearth, disease, and death. It was a place for penitence, for refuge, for protection, and above all for the worship and collective prayer to obtain God's favor in the combat against sin, death, and the devil.

Monasticism was rooted in one of the most cited passages of the Middle Ages: "What must I do to inherit eternal life? . . . sell what you own, and give the money to the poor . . . then come, follow me" (Luke 10:21ff.; Matthew 19:16ff.; Mark 10:17ff.). Monasticism was the liturgical and spiritual "exercise"(Greek: *askesis*, "exercise," "training," also asceticism; see Mark 8:34) in the battle against sin. A characteristic mark of monasticism was separation from the world. Its early form in the East (Palestine, Syria, Asia Minor, and Egypt) was hermitic marked by self-denial and seclusion. Ironically, the extreme asceticism of hermits often attracted visitors and then disciples. Thus there arose a form of religious communal life first advanced by Antony (d. 356) and Pachomius (d. 346) in Egypt that became the dominant form of Western monasticism. Life in a community, strictly controlled by the abbot ("father"), was gradually formalized by rules. An early rule for Byzantine monasticism was that of Basil of Caesarea (ca. 330–79); in the West the Rule of St. Benedict of Nursia (ca. 480–ca. 560) dominated the development of "Benedictine" monasticism.

In addition to the crucial recitation of psalms and prayers in eight daily services, the monasteries provided pastoral care, homes for "surplus" noble children, education, preservation of classical culture, promotion of civilization, and evangelization.

Monasticism initially entered Europe via southern Gaul. Many bishops and even popes such as Gregory the Great came from the ranks of monks, and close ties between monastery and diocese promoted monastic expansion. Most important however for the thriving of monastic culture was the patronage provided by kings and nobles. In return for their support, founding families and donors were remembered in the prayers of the monks. Medieval religion thus has been described as "the living in service to the dead." The nobles who built churches and monasteries assumed they could install the clergy in them. Noble support was of course crucial for these foundations, but at the same time their view of the church and its activities as their own property created tension down the line with the papacy, and set the stage for the struggles between pope and emperor that culminated in the Investiture Controversy.

Roman monasticism was rivaled by Irish–Scottish monasticism with its rigorous penitential discipline and missionary drive, derived from its orientation to ascetic wandering for the sake of Christ represented by Colomba (ca. 521–97), founder of the Iona monastic center of missions. The major wave of missionaries to the Continent consisted of Anglo-Saxons affiliated with Rome after the mission to Britain impelled by Gregory the Great in the seventh century. The rigorous piety of the Irish monastic church and the organizational strength of the Roman church were epitomized in the missions of Winfried (Boniface, 672–754). He worked on the Continent organizing churches, closely tying his work to Rome and the papacy; and also relating classical culture and Christian piety, thereby creating the groundwork for the so-called "Carolingian Renaissance." After a fruitless mission to the Frisians in 716, Pope Gregory II sent Boniface to the German peoples. After a second journey to Rome where he rendered an oath of obedience to the pope, he returned to Germany and was active from 723–32. Upon his third journey to Rome (732), Gregory III made him an archbishop. During a final mission to the Frisians he received the perfect ending for a saint – martyrdom! He is buried in his church in Fulda.

The cultural and educational work of the church and especially the monasteries related initially to the reality that whole peoples were brought into the church by actions of kings or nobles who upon conversion forced mass baptism upon their people. Missionary work thus began mostly after baptism. The use of Latin as the church's language created a cultural–intellectual unity that was a significant aspect of medieval culture. The cloisters were centers for education where ancient wisdom was collected in "florilegia" (anthologies). The pedagogical role of monasteries extended beyond collecting wisdom to promoting it through writing and copying. Such work was deemed meritorious for salvation. Hence the story that a sinful monk saved his soul because God cancelled a sin for every letter he copied; and fortunately, he had just one remaining letter to his credit.

Monastic culture was not limited to copying texts from the past, but also engaged in a variety of intellectual pursuits related to monastic life. These included maintaining a liturgical calendar; mathematics for managing estates; calculations for determining times of prayer, readings, and manual labor; legal work related to monastic estates; histories and biographies of founding monks and their monasteries; rhetoric for preaching; theological and philosophical reflection concerning the Bible and tradition; art for adorning manuscripts with exquisite miniatures, places of worship, vestments, liturgical materials and vessels; music for worship; and architecture. Inspired by the biblical description of the construction of Solomon's Temple (1 Kings 5–7), magnificent churches were built to honor the saints and worship God.

The Emergence of the Papacy

The papacy developed from unassuming beginnings to become the most significant institution of Western Christianity. Beginning with collegial relationships, the office of bishop – guarantor of apostolic truth – gradually developed in the direction of a monarchical office. In Rome the claim to be an apostolic church rested upon the tradition of its founding by the two most significant apostles, Peter and Paul. The Roman church also benefited from its political and cultural significance as a world capital, and its noteworthy charitable activities. By the later fourth century the Petrine basis of the papacy was generally acknowledged in the Roman environs, but lacked a "documentary" basis outside the New Testament promise that Peter will be the rock on which Christ will build his church (Matthew 16:18ff.). Early documentation for a "foundation narrative" came around 500 with the translation and embellishment of a second-century Greek document, the "Epistle of Clement." Purported to be a letter by Clement I to James, the brother of Jesus, it claimed that Peter himself passed his authority to Clement before a gathering of the Roman Christian community. The document thereby affirmed the institution of succession by claiming a historical link between Peter and the Roman line of bishops, and its use of the head and body metaphor contributed to the monarchical claim of the papacy.

Pope Leo I (r. 440–61), himself a superb jurist, used Roman law to clarify the relationship of successive bishops to Peter. Inheritance law stated that the heir legally took the place of the dead person, including estate, assets and liabilities, and rights and duties. The pope thus became Peter's heir in regard to his powers though not his personal merit. Leo expressed this juristic point with the formula of the pope as "the unworthy heir of St. Peter."

Leo further developed papal primacy with the argument that Christ founded a new society for which monarchical government was given to Peter and then inherited by Peter's successors. This is the beginning of the concept of a Christian commonwealth or society (corpus Christianum). The difference, Leo argued, between the papacy and the empire is that the papal monarchy was the result of a unique divine act, whereas the imperial monarchy was a historical development of human organization and administration and therefore divinely willed only in a secondary sense. Leo enhanced his theoretical argument through the prestige he gained by his "Tome" presented at the Council of Chalcedon, and by his convincing Attila and later Geiselich not to pillage Rome in 452 and 455.

Leo's program reached its classical formulation under pope Gelasius I (r. 492–6). The Gelasian theory, sometimes called the "Great Charter of the Medieval Papacy," distinguished sacred power from royal power by use of the Roman distinction between legislative and executive authority. To Gelasius, the authority of the church was legislative, while the authority of the secular ruler was executive. In Roman law legislative authority was above executive authority. Thus Gelasius both distinguished church and state – in order to keep the emperor out of church affairs – and at the same time implied that the church as legislative institution gave power to the emperor as executive. Here is the legal formulation of the position stated earlier by Ambrose of Milan: "The emperor is in the church, not above it."

Needless to say, emperors were not enthusiastic about these developing positions. Indeed the emperor Justinian (527–65) turned Gelasian theory on its head, claiming that the emperor as legislator was "divinity walking on earth." The consequent imperial program to reduce the Roman bishop to the level of an imperial appointee, along with other tensions, led the Roman church to turn to the West. The person who epitomizes this shift is Gregory the Great, often called the father of the medieval papacy.

Gregory was of aristocratic descent, thoroughly trained in Roman law, and had been a papal ambassador to the court in Constantinople. Aware that Rome would be little able to dent imperial ideology, Gregory was already prepared to turn to the West when he became pope in 590. Thus Gregory intensified papal activities in Spain, Gaul, and Britain. His vision was to unite these areas into a Christian commonwealth under the Roman faith. His policy bore fruit in papal dealings with the Franks.

By the mid-eighth century, the Frankish Merovingian house had declined to the point that the government was being run by the mayor of the palace, Pepin the Short, who exercised royal authority on behalf of the crown and was contemplating a coup. Pepin approached the papacy for support through the famous missionary Boniface. Pope Zacharias (r. 741–52) responded that he who ruled should be king. With this sanction, Pepin became king in 750. In 751 he was anointed by archbishop Boniface – the first anointing of a Frankish ruler.

Meanwhile the political situation in Italy was deteriorating. In 751 the Lombards drove the imperial garrison from northern Italy and expelled the imperial representative from Ravenna, the seat of Byzantine rule in the West. Pope Stephen II (r. 752–7) perceived that the Frankish monarchy could be a means for extricating the papacy from Lombard pressure and imperial control from Constantinople. In 754 Stephen met and negotiated with Pepin for the restoration of papal lands taken by the Lombards in exchange for papal prohibition of the choice of a Frankish king outside the family of Pepin. At St. Denis in 754 the pope anointed Pepin as patrician of the Romans, thereby designating him regent and protector of Italy. The charisma of blood, the hereditary Merovingian line, was now replaced by the charisma of divine grace conferred by the pope upon a usurper king.

Pepin fulfilled his promise by crushing the Lombards and donating the lands to St. Peter and thus to the papacy in a solemn document deposited at the tomb of St. Peter – the "Donation of Pepin" (756). Thereby the papal state was created that would last for more than the next 1,000 years. The emperor in Constantinople was not pleased! The papacy, however, found precedent in the "Donation of Constantine." The Donation of Constantine was a novelistic product that portrayed Constantine being healed of leprosy by his baptism by the pope. The grateful Constantine then proclaimed the pope and his successors to be forever over all other bishops, and then gave the pope the imperial crown and all the imperial territory in the West with the right to create consuls and patricians. The pope, not a greedy fellow, retained only Italy as a papal patrimony, returned the imperial regalia to Constantine, and allowed him to establish a new seat of government in Byzantium. The legend served a number of vital papal interests. It explained the establishment of Constantinople in 330 as the new capital of the empire as a direct result of papal permission; it established the papacy's secular prerogatives; and by the return of the imperial insignia to Constantine, it established the papal right to create the emperor by crowning him. In 1440 the Italian Humanist Lorenzo Valla exposed the Donation of Constantine as an eighth-century forgery.

It was Pepin's son, Charlemagne, who from his accession in 768 fully lived up to the crucial role of patrician of the Romans. He added more territory to the papal patrimony, and carried forth a marked Romanization in religious matters. He also came to the rescue of pope Leo III (r. 795–816) when local Roman nobles tried to depose him.

Charlemagne agreed to go to Rome in support of Leo in his quarrel with the Roman nobles, who by now had charged him with lechery and perjury. Leo cleared himself of the charges by taking a solemn oath on the basis that the pope could not be judged by anyone (see 1 Corinthians 2:15). This principle had first been set forth in the early sixth century in the so-called Symmachan forgeries that included the decree: "Nobody can sit in judgment on the first (apostolic) see which distributes rightful justice to all. Neither the emperor nor the whole clergy nor kings nor people can judge the supreme judge."

At this time, Christmas 800, Leo took the initiative to crown Charlemagne Roman emperor in a highly orchestrated event. Prior to the celebration of the Christmas mass – held for a change at St. Peter's rather than the customary Santa Maria Maggiore because of the pope's awareness of Frankish veneration of Peter – Charlemagne had agreed to take the title of emperor. While Charlemagne was kneeling at the altar, Leo came up behind him and placed a crown on his head. The carefully coached crowd responded: "Charles, most pious Augustus, crowned by God, great and peace-loving emperor, life and victory!" The function of universal ruler – as certainly intended by Leo – meant that the East would no longer be considered the legitimate Roman Empire, for it was now "translated" to the West. Leo thereby extricated the papacy from the East, and placed the center of the Christian world in Rome rather than either in Constantinople or Aachen, Charlemagne's capital. This was the birth of the Holy Roman Empire as a religious, geographical, and political phenomenon.

Papacy and Empire

The Carolingian church prospered under Charlemagne. As the authority and power of the bishops and archbishops increased, the lower clergy looked to the papacy as a source of unity and court of final appeal. They desired a strengthening of the papacy not for its own sake but as a means of checking both the growing secular control of the church (the proprietary church system wherein clergy were appointed by secular lords and kings) and as a restraint upon the autonomous behavior of the archbishops. It was this circle of the lower clergy that developed the Pseudo-Isidorian Decretals, a mid-ninth century collection of doctrine and laws attributed to the Spanish archbishop Isidore of Seville (560–636). The papal ideology expressed in this collection was not new, but the laws fabricated to support these concerns were. A recurrent theme throughout the Decretals is papal primacy with the concomitant emphasis upon the Roman church as the mother of all churches; the head from which all jurisdictional and governing authority and power flows.

The first pope to make full use of the Pseudo-Isidorian Decretals was Nicholas I (r. 858–67), the most effective pope between Gregory I and Gregory VII. According to Nicholas, the pope is Christ's vice regent on earth and speaks with the authority of God. Papal decisions have the force of law, and councils are only the means for carrying out papal decrees. No one may sit in judgment on the pope, not even the emperor. This exalted claim led Nicholas to oppose both Frankish and Byzantine rulers. Since spiritual authority is higher than secular authority, the church must at times exercise direct influence over the state, but not the reverse, for the state exists to support the church. Nicholas saw in the Pseudo-Isidorian Decretals the power for creating a homogeneous Europe under Roman papal authority. His skill and genius in pursuing his goal may be seen in three cases: the marriage affair of Lothair II, king of Lorraine; the Hincmar case; and the Photian Schism.

When Lothair became the king of Lorraine in 855 he was married according to German law to Waldrada, who bore him three children. The opinion of the time was that German marriages were dissoluble. After becoming king, Lothair married a noblewoman, Theutberga, in a lawful Christian marriage. When it appeared she would remain childless, Lothair wished to put her aside and take back Waldrada. The archbishops of Cologne and Trier supported the king, as did two papal legates at the Synod of Metz. The papacy, however, came out strongly in favor of the Christian marriage and declared Theutberga his legal wife. The consequences were the displacement of Germanic marriage custom, the unprecedented deposition of two archbishops and the threat of excommunicating the king.

The Hincmar case involved the powerful archbishop of Rheims, who had excommunicated bishop Rothad of Soissons for refusing to accept a ruling by the archbishop. Rothad appealed to the papacy on the basis of the Pseudo-Isidorian Decretals. Nicholas then forced Hincmar to reinstate Rothad as well as other deposed clerics.

The Photian Schism provided the opportunity for Nicholas to assert papal rights in the East. The complicated – indeed, truly Byzantine – context included the deposition of the patriarch Ignatius of Constantinople for his refusal to commune the immoral imperial regent, Bardas. Bardas then appointed a learned layman, Photius (ca. 820–ca. 897), to take the place of Ignatius as patriarch. Ignatius appealed to the papacy, but Nicholas' legates joined in approving Photius. Nicholas then repudiated his legates and declared Photius deposed. Photius replied in kind, and for good measure added the charge of heresy to the Western church for adding the filioque to the creed. The fortunes of Ignatius and Photius continued to go up and down in relation to Byzantine intrigues, but what is important in terms of the development of the papacy is Nicholas' conviction that the papacy had authority over the East, and the consequent separation of the Eastern and Western churches.

The Gregorian Reform

With the death of Charlemagne in 814 rule passed to his son Louis the Pious (r. 814–40), who divided the reign with his three sons, Lothair, Pippin, and Louis. Carolingian power however was now under assault both internally and externally. Sibling rivalry is an understatement for the constant conflicts among the brothers whose striving for power was abetted by the self-interest of semi-royal dukes. Further serious disruption was caused by Viking, Magyar, and Saracen invasions. In 843 the Treaty of Verdun split the kingdom in three, and the death of the last Carolingian, Louis the Child, in 911 facilitated the reassertion of tribal duchies.

Henry, Duke of Saxony (r. 919–36), revived the German monarchy and the Carolingian ideal of empire and its unity with the church. The expansion of the realm under his son Otto the Great (r. 936–73) used the church for political goals, a policy that also preserved the church's holdings. Otto's vigorous assertion of royal authority over the church expressed not only his ambition but also his devotion to advance the church's ideals, culture, and civilizing mission. Otto nominated bishops who for the most part had been trained in the royal chapel; as bishops they received royal support that extended even to jurisdiction over serious criminal cases. From the time of Otto III (r. 983–1002) even whole counties with all their rights were bestowed on episcopal sees and royal abbeys. The financial benefits included not only lands but also profits from tolls and markets. These Ottonian privileges laid the foundation for episcopal territorial power. At the same time, the imposition of clerical celibacy meant that the clergy could not pass on power and wealth, but only receive it from the kings.

The bishops also received the symbols of their office – ring and staff – from the rulers. Otto would hand the crozier to the newly appointed bishop or abbot with the words, "receive the church." Such investiture was possible because the king was not simply a layman. His anointment as ruler, at that time regarded as a sacrament, raised him to the sphere of a vicar of Christ. Thus an anointing formula from Mainz presented the king as a participant in ecclesiastical office and an intermediary between the clergy and the people. Again we are reminded of the importance of liturgy – here utilized in the establishment of political legitimacy. Otto III, Henry II (r. 1002–24), and Henry III (r. 1039–56) all took this theocratic ideal very seriously. The downside was that bishoprics were filled with men who had reason to be loyal to the monarchy, and rulers began to think they were responsible for reform of the church.

Otto the Great's increasing hegemony over other nations pointed to the goal of imperial anointing and coronation. Since this presupposed the possession of Italy, the Saxon dynasty focused its politics on the conquest of the Lombard kingdom. Otto's motives – as mixed as political goals are – were also formed in a political and religious climate that blended aspirations for royal power and a renewed empire with Christian universalism and the awe of the sacred transmitted in an imperial anointing.

In 951 Otto I assumed the crown of Italy, but Pope Agapetus II refused him the imperial crown. In 961 Pope John XII appealed to Otto for protection, and in return Otto was crowned Roman emperor in 962. John XII intended that Otto serve the church as its military protector – an ornamental copy of the Donation of Constantine was presented to Otto – but Otto had his own aspirations. He had the papal enemies he conquered swear allegiance to him instead of the pope. The pope was enraged and instigated a revolt in Rome. Otto put down the revolt, deposed the pope (963), and appointed a layman as successor, Leo VIII (r. 963–5). Otto then inserted into the papal oath of election an oath of obedience to the emperor. Termed the "Ottonianum," this remained the basis for numerous imperial interventions in papal affairs for nearly a century.

Barely had Otto left Rome when John XII returned, expelled Leo VIII, and took vengeance on his adversaries with the help of the Romans. The pope died soon after this, allegedly from a stroke after being caught in bed with a Roman's wife. Benedict V succeeded him but was exiled by Otto, who reinstalled Leo VIII.

The Ottonian line ended with the death of Otto III in 1003. The Ottonians had succeeded in renewing the empire of Charlemagne. In the north, east, and southeast the Poles, Hungarians, and Bohemians formed nations whose churches were oriented toward Rome. Farther east, the Russian church was under the influence of Byzantium. In the eleventh century Denmark, Norway, and Iceland were also Christianized, and in the twelfth century so too was Sweden.

A fundamental turn in the relationship of the papacy and the empire came from the monastic reform movement associated with the Cluny monastery. Cluny struck a spark of hope for the late ninth-century world of Viking-devastated monasteries and an enfeebled papacy seemingly intent on wading deeper and deeper into moral and political swamps. Cluny was founded in 910 in Burgundy on land given by Duke William of Aquitaine, the Pious. The charter affirmed that Cluny was to be self-governing under the protection of the pope. The abbot had the right to choose his own successor and thus insure continuity. Its lands were to be secure from all invasion or secularization. And the Benedictine Rule as interpreted by the Benedictine reformer,

Benedict of Aniane (ca. 750–821), was to be strictly observed. The Cluny movement quickly spread throughout France and Italy. Cluny itself progressed from an example emulated by other monasteries to the exercise of direct control over other monasteries. By the beginning of the twelfth century there were more than 1,500 monastic houses tied to Cluny whose heads were appointed by or responsible to the abbot of Cluny. Cluny also became the most renowned center of liturgy and ecclesiastical splendor of the time.

The Cluniac reform movement caught fire with the nobles as well as the monastics and prompted the laity to expect increasingly higher standards of the clergy. The German king Henry III (r. 1039–56) was deeply religious and impressed by his duties as a Christian king. So, for example, in 1043 he proclaimed a "day of indulgence" forgiving all his foes and urging his subjects to do likewise. His contemporaries sometimes viewed him as a monk in worldly garb because of his piety and delight in participating in processions and dedicating shrines. His support for Cluny was related not only to his piety but also to the fact that his wife was the daughter of William of Aquitaine. Henry was not unique among the rulers of his day; Edward of England was called Edward the Confessor, and throughout Europe nobility and rulers were building churches and endowing monasteries. Monastic intercession was viewed as a key to heaven, and it was not unusual for nobles to spend their last days in a monastery and desire to be buried in monk's garb.

Cluny expanded its concern for monastic reform to the reform of all clerical life. By the 1050s the reform movement was focused on two issues: simony and Nicolaitanism. Simony (Acts 8:18–24) was the giving or receiving of clerical office for money or other considerations. Nicolaitanism (Revelation 2:6, 14–15) was the breach of clerical celibacy. The most explosive issue was simony, viewed by the Cluniacs as any lay investiture in clerical office.

A noted exponent of Cluniac reform was the monk Peter Damian (1007–72), later cardinal bishop of Ostia. An orphan from a poor family in Ravenna, Damian rose to a comfortable life and then suddenly at 29 resolved to become a monk. He entered the Benedictine monastery at Fonte Avellana and soon excelled at study and a rigorous asceticism that might appear to us as self-torture. He wrote a biography of the ascetic St. Romuald (c. 950–1027) and after being chosen abbot introduced Romuald's Rule, which emphasized asceticism. Each psalm recited was to be accompanied by 100 lashes on the bare back. The whole Psalter was equal to 15,000 lashes – those were the days when it paid to be a slow reader! The practice became a craze and led to the Flagellant movement. Damian insisted on separation from the contemporary world, which he denounced as worse than Sodom and Gomorrah, and he never tired of railing against simony, clerical marriage, and clergy bearing arms. He became the spiritual counselor and censor of seven reform popes, and called himself "lord of the pope" and Hildebrand's "holy Satan." He died in 1072, just a year before Hildebrand became pope Gregory VII.

The degeneracy of the papacy at this time stirred Henry III to reform it. Between 955 and 1057 there were 25 popes, 12 by imperial appointment and the rest by the Roman aristocracy, five of whom were deposed by emperors – hardly an affirmation of the claim that the pope could be judged by no one. In 1046 Henry entered Italy and called for a synod that met at Sutri where he had pope Sylvester III deposed and Gregory VI exiled, and then made a German bishop, Suidger of Bamberg, pope Clement II. From Henry's perspective his coronation gave him authority to bestow symbols of ecclesiastical office and order the affairs of the church, including the appointment of three popes, all men of high caliber and all Germans (Clement II, Leo IX, Nicholas II). Henry's choice of Germans was not in order to incorporate the papacy into the German church but to insure reform by independence from the Roman nobility. The preliminary condition for renewal was a free papacy; this Henry accomplished by recourse to the old imperial right of participating in the papal election established by the Ottonianum. Ironically, Henry's papal choices ushered in an age of papal reform that turned against imperial intervention.

Among the popes named by Henry, Leo IX (r. 1048–54) was the most significant. Leo brought the spirit of monastic reform into the papacy, thereby strengthening it and the entire church. Leo regularly held synods at which simony and clerical marriage were condemned, and he laid the groundwork for the College of Cardinals. Two men from this circle were especially important for the further development of the papacy, the monk Humbert (d. 1061), later cardinal bishop of Silvia Candida, and the Cluniac monk Hildebrand (ca. 1033–85), later pope Gregory VII. Humbert was a master of literature and law, especially the Pseudo-Isidorian Decretals. He pushed for the abolition of the proprietary church system and condemned simony and concubinage.

The strengthened papacy under Leo IX conflicted with Byzantium when he asserted papal primacy over southern Italy, an area claimed by Constantinople since the eighth century. The patriarch of Constantinople, Michael Cerularius (r. 1043–58), refused to accede to the papal claim. The ante was upped when the patriarch closed the Latin churches in Constantinople and took over the few Latin monasteries. Humbert attacked the patriarch with fiery and passionate claims, including the Donation of Constantine. Escalating tensions included further points of conflict such as the mission to the Slavs and the filioque. Humbert then led a legation to Constantinople and on July 16, 1054 laid a papal decree of excommunication on the high altar of St. Sophia. The patriarch returned the favor, and the Eastern and Western churches were now in open schism.

The Investiture Conflict

Humbert gave the starting signal for the Investiture Conflict in 1057 with his three books against simony (*Adversus simoniacos*), defined as any participation of a layperson in the conferral of ecclesiastical office, thus condemning lay investiture. The insignia of the office of bishop (staff and ring) could only be given by one who himself held this office. In 1059 a Roman Synod, presided over by pope Nicholas II, issued a papal election decree that precluded the right of the German king to introduce an election proposal.

The monk Hildebrand as pope Gregory VII (r. 1073–85) reiterated laws against simony and Nicolaitanism in synod after synod. He summarized his convictions in his *Dictatus Papae*, a list of 27 chapter headings for a projected collection of canon law. These sentences, largely mined from the Pseudo-Isidorian Decretals, presented the most important primatial rights and were to guide reform. Significant among them are that the pope "alone has the power to depose emperors"; "that no general synod may be called without his order"; "that his decree can be annulled by no one, and that he can annul the decree of anyone"; "that he can be judged by no one"; "that the Roman Church has never erred and will never err to all eternity"; and "that he has the power to absolve subjects from their oath of fidelity to wicked rulers." He based these rights upon Matthew 16:18ff., Augustine's *City of God*, and the claims of Gregory I and Nicholas I. Gregory, never renowned for flexibility, became exceedingly rigid on the matter of secular investiture. Clerics were forbidden under pain of excommunication and annulment of the completed action to accept from a layperson the investiture of bishoprics, abbeys, and churches; the investing layman would also be excommunicated.

When king Henry IV (1056–1106) invested the archbishop of Milan, a man whom the papacy did not even know, Gregory sent Henry a letter of admonition. Henry himself declared on the basis of his authority as Protector of the Romans that Gregory had forfeited his papal authority and must resign. Gregory's response was to suspend Henry from governing, annul oaths of loyalty to him, and excommunicate him. This prompted the German princes to form an alliance against Henry in order to advance their own interests. Gregory, however, wanted Henry's obedience not his head, and provided a compromise that forestalled the election of a new king so long as Henry promised obedience and penance. This is the setting for the famous confrontation at Canossa, the fortress of countess Matilda, a strong supporter of Gregory. For three days in January 1077 Henry stood bareheaded and barefoot in the snow outside the castle. Within the castle, Matilda as well as abbot Hugh of Cluny, Henry's godfather, implored clemency. In the end, Gregory could not refuse his priestly office and received Henry back into the Christian community. In the history of the German kingship, Canossa was such a profound humiliation that the phrase "nach Kanossa gehen" (to go to Canossa) came to mean "to eat humble pie."

The investiture struggle ended with a compromise between king Henry V and pope Callistus II in the Concordat of Worms (1122): the king renounced investiture with ring and staff, but retained investiture with the scepter before the vows. That the Concordat of Worms did not finally settle tensions between church and state is evident in England in the struggle between king Henry II and Thomas Becket, archbishop of Canterbury (d. 1170). However, the Gregorian reform movement reflects the appeal of churchly ideals and the concomitant growth of lay religiosity in the tenth and eleventh centuries. This in turn created increasing demand that the clergy should be superior in piety and morality. The ideological struggle arising in this context pushed the papacy to strive for the sort of distinctiveness and freedom from state control that in turn led to papal efforts to negate the sacramental power of kingship and to dominate secular rulers.

The Crusades

The ascetic and penitential revival stimulated by the Cluniac movement and the increased power of the papacy found an unwholesome outlet in the crusades. Penitential pilgrimages to Jerusalem had occurred for centuries and continued after the Muslim conquest of the city in 638, for Jerusalem was considered a joint shrine for Christian and Muslim. This changed with the rise of the Seljuk sultans (1055–1194), whose armies defeated the Byzantine army in 1071 and captured large areas of Asia Minor that had been a source of wealth and manpower for the Roman Empire of the East. Over the next centuries the Byzantines would periodically appeal for help from the West, only to discover the truth of the adage "with (Christian) friends like these who needs enemies."

The Byzantine emperor, Alexios I Komnenos (r. 1081–1118), petitioned the papacy for help. It was a call that found an enthusiastic echo in the Western church, whose increased self-consciousness in the time of Gregory VII supported the conviction that the holy places should be rescued from the hands of unbelievers. The long held sense of pilgrimage combined with the concept of forcible mission and conversion since Charlemagne and the church's ethos of the "Christian knight" formed the background for the enthusiastic response to pope Urban II's call for a crusade at the Synod of Clermont in 1095.

Urban spoke of the suffering of Christian pilgrims and the desecration and destruction of holy places, and called upon Western Christendom to combat Islam and liberate the Holy Land. Urban sweetened the pot with the promises of spiritual and temporal rewards – a plenary indulgence, earthly treasures, the diversion of feuding into combat against a common enemy, and political and economic expansion. The mixed motives of the crusades and crusaders are reflected in archbishop William of Tyre's (ca. 1130–ca. 1187) *History of the Deeds Done Beyond the Sea*: "Not all of them, indeed, were there on behalf of the Lord . . . All of them went for different reasons."

Whatever the reasons, the series of crusades lasting to the final Turkish victory in 1244 left bloody tracks as so-called crusader states were established and fell, Constantinople was sacked by the Western "Christians" who went to rescue it, and various efforts such as the "children's crusade" of 1212 went horribly wrong (thousands of children died or were sold into slavery). The crusades did not permanently conquer the Holy Land nor did much to impede the advance of Islam. They exacted a great toll in life and treasure, and whatever idealistic spirit impelled them degenerated into savage conduct. Crusader attacks on the Byzantine Empire severely damaged East–West relations and contributed to the ultimate triumph of the Ottoman Turks in 1453. The sense that a military crusade for the Prince of Peace is an oxymoron began to be recognized before the crusades petered out. Also, the church's need for funds in order to finance the crusades led to criticism of the church's turn from apostolic poverty.

The crusades did strengthen the role of the papacy, and gave rise to military orders – the Templars, the Hospitallers or Knights of St. John, and the Teutonic Order – that continued to play important roles in Europe, and brought nobles into service of the church. The crusades also stimulated the trading cities of northern Italy and their influence. Along with the rise of trade, the drain on feudal lands and properties made possible a new political role for towns, and the rise of a "third estate," the bourgeoisie, especially in France. Knowledge in the West was greatly expanded by contact with the East, and led to an intellectual awakening. The soil was prepared for the later Renaissance as Europeans rediscovered the classics, became interested in history and literature, and supported the development of universities. These streams flowed into the marked theological development of the Middle Ages: scholasticism. The crusades also stimulated the demand for relics and indulgences. The encounter with non-Christian culture called into question the universality and uniqueness of the church, and stimulated theological reflection.

Chapter 6

Faith in Search of Understanding: Anselm, Abelard, and the Beginnings of Scholasticism

The early period of scholasticism, so-called for its systematic use of reason utilized in the schools, stretches from the eighth century to the twelfth. The critical investigation of the received tradition and its authority is the essential beginning of scholasticism.

Medieval intellectual life was nourished by the Bible and the Augustinian heritage transmitted to the West by Gregory the Great. Efforts to collect and transmit the classical heritage and the theology of the church fathers were furthered by Charlemagne and the so-called Carolingian Renaissance. In 782 he recruited the most renowned scholars of the day, Alcuin of York (ca. 735–804) and Theodulf of Orleans (ca. 750–821), to improve the Frankish monastic schools and to raise the educational level of the court. Alcuin, former master of the cathedral school at York, established Charlemagne's palace library as well as a library and school in Tours, and promoted instruction in the works of Boethius, Augustine, and Latin grammarians. Theodulf, a leading theologian and poet of the time, wrote treatises on a number of theological subjects, including a defense of the filioque; his hymn "All glory, laud, and honor" continues to be sung today as the Palm Sunday processional. At court, Charlemagne surrounded himself with learned and zealous churchmen whose advice he sought and sometimes followed. Charlemagne himself was said to understand Greek and Latin, although he could not write. When in 794 Charlemagne decided to make Aachen his capital, he conceived of it as a new Rome, a center not only of political and administrative power but also of learning and the passing on of knowledge. He proceeded to establish new schools, to patronize scholars, and to mandate study in all monasteries and bishops' houses under the rubric "let those who can, teach." The preservation and dissemination of classical learning in these schools and monasteries is the source of much of the classical literature in the West.

With few exceptions, organized study in the tenth century depended upon monasteries and cathedral schools. Cathedral schools, so-called because they were connected to cathedrals, did not have the regulated life of the monastic schools and included boys not dedicated to the clerical life. In addition to similar concerns with regulating the liturgy, the cathedral schools were engaged in correspondence and business transactions. By the eleventh century there appeared to be a growing intellectual restlessness, evident in the willingness of students to go most anywhere for the sake of learning. By the mid-twelfth century it was clear that students knew where they wanted to go to study, and that they knew their studies would have market value in relation to the growing bureaucratic and economic needs of royal courts and cities. These students then created a demand for more teachers, and the eventual creation of universities.

The extent of the growing Carolingian political and educational self-consciousness is manifest in the *Libri Carolini* (The Caroline Books, ca. 791), themselves a testament to the revival of learning in the West. The occasion for the *Libri* was the iconoclastic controversy in the East. The Byzantine Empire, under pressure from Islam and the growing power of its own monks, had tried to dampen the fervor of both by limiting the use of icons, especially on the outside of churches. The theological rationale advanced by the imperial party was that since icons represented only the humanity of Christ, they either divided Christ's unity like the Nestorians or confounded it like the Monophysites. The persecutions and social unrest in the wake of emperor Leo III's 726 edict that images must be destroyed led to the Second Council of Nicaea (787) led by the new patriarch of Constantinople, Tarasius, in concert with the empress Irene and attended by papal legates. The council defined and restored the veneration of icons.

The Franks learned of the iconoclastic controversy and then received a faulty translation of the Acts of the Second Nicene Council from pope Hadrian I. The Frankish response in the *Libri* condemned the Second Nicene Council, thinking it had enjoined adoration of images equal to that due to God. The non-doctrinal factors affecting the composition of the *Libri* included general Frankish dislike for the Byzantines, and Charlemagne's own irritation with the empress Irene. In 794 Charlemagne presided over a synod at Frankfurt attended by all the Frankish and English bishops, and two legates of the pope that responded to the "heresy" of Second Nicaea. Hadrian, however, refused to withdraw his recognition of the Nicene assembly or to obey Charlemagne's demand that the Byzantine emperor be excommunicated. Apart from the political and theological conflicts here, we see the increasing self-confidence in learning and appropriating the theological tradition in the West, and an additional impetus toward the separation of the churches of East and West.

Universities and Scholasticism

The Carolingian concern for education lived on in the great schools of Aachen and Tours, hence the term "scholasticism" for the knowledge of this time occurring expressly in the schools. The basis for formal education, directed almost exclusively to the clergy and monks, was the classical Roman focus on the liberal arts (the subjects thought appropriate for a *liber*, a "free" man). The basic three, the *trivium*, were grammar, rhetoric, and dialectic. It should be noted that *the* language of education was Latin; thus all students began their education by learning this foreign language. The *trivium* was supplemented by the *quadrivium*: geometry, arithmetic, astronomy, and music. The "higher" professional studies were theology, law, and medicine. The intellectual capital of the medieval world consisted basically of the Bible and the church fathers, supplemented by the work of Boethius (d. 524), whose ambition was to preserve and present Greek learning to a Latin world rapidly being driven back on its own resources. The medieval excitement and enthusiasm for schools may be elusive to the modern mind. Thanks to the polemics of the sixteenth-century reformers and intellectuals, the medieval era in general and scholasticism in particular has received a bad press. The bias that scholastics were more interested in intellectual parlor games than "real life" continues with the old question that always arises when scholasticism is mentioned – "how many angels can dance on the head of a pin?" Historically, however, there is no doubt about the flesh and blood character of the leading intellectuals as they wrestled with the realities of their day.

Anselm (1033–109), known as the "father of scholasticism," left his home in northern Italy after quarreling with his father and set off in search of knowledge. He ended up in northern France at the monastery of Bec because of the intellectual renown of its prior, Lanfranc (ca. 1005–89), a fellow Italian called in 1070 by William the Conqueror to become archbishop of Canterbury. Anselm stayed on at Bec, became a monk at the age of 26, and gained renown as a teacher. The last 16 years of his life were in public political service as the archbishop of Canterbury, a position forced on him against his will. The English king, William Rufus, not renowned for his piety, had kept the see vacant in order to use its funds, but upon becoming very ill and fearful of eternity he hoped to make amends with the church by appointing an archbishop. Anselm, on a visit to England in 1093, was seen by the local bishops and the king's councilors to be the ideal candidate, but Anselm refused the honor. So the councilors and bishops literally carried Anselm off to the church with the bishop's staff pressed against his closed fist. Anselm wrote to his brothers at Bec: "It would have been difficult to make out whether madmen were dragging along one in his senses, or sane men a madman, save that they were chanting, and I, pale with amazement and pain, looked more like one dead than alive." The king survived his purported mortal illness only to be assassinated a few years later. Before that, however, Anselm went into self-imposed exile because the king continued to exploit the church and resist Gregorian reform measures.

The other great contributor to scholasticism, Peter Abelard (1070–1142), had an even more colorful life. The eldest son of an educated knight, Abelard became a knight errant of the mind, willing to go anywhere in search of his holy grail, knowledge. An exceptionally brilliant youth with an ego to match, Abelard trekked off to Paris to study with reputed scholars whom he soon dismissed as without substance. For example, jealous of the attention paid to theologians, Abelard sought out the illustrious Anselm of Laon (ca. 1050–1117), whom he then described as a barren tree – all leaves and no fruit. After disagreeing with some of the Paris Masters, Abelard began his own lectures in competition, and attracted their best students. Abelard's lack of the better part of valor was also evident in his affair with Heloise, the brilliant and comely niece of his fellow canon at the Cathedral of Notre Dame. Engaged to tutor her in philosophy and Greek, Abelard soon became engaged in extracurricular activities and she became pregnant. The rage of her guardian led to a gang attack on Abelard that in his words "cut off those parts of my body with which I had done that which was the cause of their sorrow." That event also cut short his teaching career at Paris. Having incurred the wrath of his teachers and colleagues, Abelard next incurred the wrath of ecclesiastical authorities with his book on the Trinity that he was himself forced to consign to the flames at the Council of Soissons in 1121. To round things off, angry monks chased Abelard from his monastery because he had argued that the patron saint of the monastery was not Dionysius the Areopagite, companion of St. Paul. Abelard aptly titled his autobiography, *The History of My Calamities*. For Abelard, academics was clearly neither an ivory tower nor a spectator sport.

Abelard certainly disturbed the guardians of the old order – recall that a generation earlier Gregory VII and his colleagues had condemned clerical incontinence. But Abelard's danger was not that he slept with a woman, but that his life and theology were an expression of a new understanding of love arising in twelfth-century southern France and making its way north. Romantic love – celebrated by troubadours and expressed in the poems and songs of courtly love – was a new idea of love destined to take over Western ideas until its banalization in Hollywood movies, "true confessions" journalism, and "bodice-ripping" novels. To Abelard and to Heloise, the relationship of individuals should trump the oppressive institution of marriage. Indeed, it was Heloise who did not want the marriage pushed on her by Abelard. "God knows," she later wrote to him from her nunnery, "I never sought anything in you except yourself; I wanted simply you, nothing of yours. I looked for no marriage-bond, no marriage portion." Heloise shared Abelard's low view of marriage, a view transmitted to their time from the early church fathers such as Jerome and Augustine. They also shared the "ethic of intention" set forth in Abelard's *Scito te ipsum* (Know Thyself). So Heloise wrote to him: "It is not the deed but the intention of the doer which makes the crime, and justice should weigh not what was done but the spirit in which it is done." They both thought marriage could add nothing to their relationship, but would rather detract from it by interfering with Abelard's intellectual work. So Abelard wrote: "What man, intent on his religious or philosophical meditations, can possible endure the whining of children . . . or the noisy confusion of family life?"

It may be suggested that Abelard's experience of the love of Heloise – with both its heady joy from which he composed love songs, as well as its profound pain and loss – was influential upon his understanding of the atonement, sometimes called an anthropocentric theory of the atonement. The significance of the Incarnation now is not in satisfying the claims of either Satan or God, but rather in the example and teaching of love manifest in Jesus, and the renewed love of humankind for God and others that Jesus' example stimulates. The monastic and feudal inspirations of Anselm's theology are displaced by worldly and humanistic inspirations in Abelard. As already noted, the guardians of the old order were not ready for that kind of subjectivity.

The major excitement of the time however was not the lives of the academics, but logic! Logic became the exciting discipline, for it was an instrument by which it was thought order could be imposed on a chaotic world. The world was a realm of natural and supernatural forces, demonic and otherwise, over which persons had little or no control. The realms of politics and economics – even more so than today! – were similarly dis-ordered and intractable to thought. But logic – however weakly at first – began to open a window to an orderly and systematic view of the world. The whole process of simplification and arrange-ment was a revelation of the powers of the mind and provided a sense of order residing behind a bewildering complexity of appar-ently unrelated facts. From the end of the tenth to the end of the twelfth century the digestion of Aristotle's logic was the greatest intellectual task. By the thirteenth century, the curricula at Paris and Oxford made Aristotelian logic the main feature of under-graduate studies.

There were various steps and turning points in the develop-ment of scholasticism, including the development around 1200 of universities as a higher form of the school with the ideal of ordering knowledge into a coherent whole, the *summa*. The expansion of knowledge created a new organization of teaching and scholarly apprenticeship the purpose of which was, above all, to pass on the accumulating body of knowledge. Over time, there arose awareness of contradictory elements in the tradition and the necessity for responsible explanation or reconciliation of such conflicts. From this developed the critical examination of tradition by the use of reason. The critical relating of reason and the authority of tradition is essentially the beginning of scholasticism as a methodological phenomenon. Medieval scholasticism, then, is a methodology that received the classical heritage and theology of the church fathers, above all Augustine, and treated it with the help of dialectics and logic. The distinction of early, high, and late scholasticism is only a construct to aid discussion. The turning points are associated with distinguishable degrees of dealing with the classical heritage, especially of Aristotle. Early scholasticism is the period from 1000 to 1200. A new level of development appears from about 1150 as Aristotle's logical writings become known. High scholasticism begins about 1200 as the West became acquainted with the whole of the Aristotelian corpus, including his ethics and metaphysics, mediated through Arabic and Jewish writings. At the same time there arose the first universities in Europe in Bologna, Paris, Oxford, and Cambridge. The University of Paris, developing from the cathedral schools in the twelfth century, received its foundation charter in 1200, and by 1213 had a curriculum that included theology, canon law, and medicine along with the liberal arts. Pope Innocent III recognized the University of Paris as a corporation under the jurisdiction of the papacy in 1215. In 1257 it received an endowment from Robert de Sorbon, hence the Sorbonne. In Italy the Investiture Controversy stimulated Matilda of Tuscany to endow a school for the study of law that became the University of Bologna. Bologna then became famous for the study of canon law through Gratian's *Decretum* (1140), and added a theology faculty in 1360. The University of Naples was the first to be founded by royal charter (1224) to train state officials.

Contributions of Early Scholastic Theology

It is important to note that the use of reason for the critical analysis of the tradition was not the autonomous use of reason, unbound by authority and free of faith, that is the characteristic ideal of modern reason after the seventeenth and eighteenth-century Enlightenment. Reason, as understood by Anselm and his contemporaries, is theonomous reason, that is, it is rooted in God and is a gift to humankind. Anselm thus saw faith – indeed, prayer – as the foundation for the right use of reason; hence his famous expressions *credo ut intelligam* ("I believe in order to understand") and *fides quaerens intellectum* ("faith seeking understanding"). His emphasis upon meditation liberated theology from his day's slavishness to the arranging and harmonizing of past authorities; the task of science is not merely to repeat the words of others but to inquire and examine the data. He presented his rational proof for God in two writings. In the *Monologion* he set forth the later so-called cosmological argument for the existence of God on the basis of the appropriateness and order of creation. In the *Proslogion* he presented the so-called ontological argument for the existence of God: the idea of God is given in reason which holds that nothing greater than God can be conceived. Even the fool who says there is no God (Psalm 14:1) understands this statement. What is understood must exist in his understanding. But that than which nothing greater can be conceived cannot exist merely in understanding, for then it would not be that than which no greater can be thought. For it is greater to exist in fact as well as in the mind. Thus, God must exist in reality, not just in the mind, because otherwise God lacks being. Although this argument has been criticized on various grounds since Anselm proposed it, it continues to fascinate logicians and philosophers.

In his *Cur Deus homo?* (Why Did God Become Human?) Anselm presented a new theology of redemption through his theory of satisfaction. The Incarnation of God is not only conceptually possible but also conceptually necessary. Anselm's understanding of sin posits that sin is an objective deprivation of the honor that belongs to God. The decisive concept of the honor of God reflects Anselm's feudal social world. To deprive a person of his or her honor was a fundamental crime against the social order. Furthermore, such an offense is proportionately magnified according to the status of the person in the hierarchical order and therefore the satisfaction of the offense is also magnified. An insult to the king is far more serious than the same insult to a fellow peasant. If the maintenance of a king's honor was necessary for the preservation of his kingdom, of a baron's honor for his barony, and so on down the social scale, how much more infinitely important for the preservation of the entire social world, indeed, the cosmos, was the maintenance of God's honor. God's honor is so profoundly violated by sin that punishment must be exacted to satisfy God's honor. For God merely to forgive the offense of humankind would vitiate his justice and honor, thereby undermining the stability of the universe itself. For God to reclaim his honor by just punishment of humankind's offense would annihilate all humankind. The honor of God can only be restored by its satisfaction, which God himself does by becoming a human being and himself satisfying the offense of humankind, thus maintaining both God's honor and mercy.

Anselm's "satisfaction" theory of the atonement has also been described as theocentric because he located the satisfaction of God's honor within God himself. Anselm's theory not only reflects his feudal society, it also moves beyond the religious thought of prior generations that posited Satan's legal claim on humankind. Since the "cosmocentric" theory of the atonement advanced by Gregory the Great and earlier by Gregory of Nyssa (ca. 330– ca. 395), the atonement had been viewed as a cosmic struggle between God and Satan. The imagery, dependent upon the Chalcedonian formula that Jesus is fully God and fully human and stimulated by the verse in Job 41:1 ("Can you draw out Leviathan with a fishhook?"), is that Satan claims Jesus with the mistaken assumption that Jesus is just another mortal. Satan is fooled by Jesus' humanity (the bait) and hooked by Jesus' divinity when he tries to devour Jesus.

It was Peter Abelard who most famously promoted the dialectical method in his work *Sic et Non* (Yes and No). Aware of the contradictions within the received tradition, Abelard pointed out that the truth of the church is not simply given but must always be sought. This was a milestone on the road leading away from unexamined reliance upon past authorities. The way to the truth leads through inquiry and doubt. With the help of philological criticism and logical arguments the tradition is worked over in order to balance its contradictions and to find the abiding truth. *Sic et Non* is the first comprehensive exposition of theology as a science rather than as a meditation or a compilation of past authorities. Abelard proposed a series of 156 doctrinal questions with citations from the church fathers in support of both a "yes" and a "no" to each of them. He then proposed a critical methodology for determining the authenticity, reliability, intention, and historical context of the text in question. When resolution of the contradiction by these means was not possible, then the strongest witness with the greatest support was to be preferred. This method became obligatory for the whole of scholasticism.

The drive to impose order on the tradition was carried forth by Peter Lombard's (ca. 1100–60) *Libri quattuor Sententiarum* (Four Books of Sentences), which gave the opinions of different authorities on the basic theological topics of God, creation, fall, redemption, sacraments, and eschatology. Lombard's *Sentences* became one of the all-time bestsellers and remained the basic textbook for theology into the sixteenth century. The monk Gratian of Bologna achieved a similar ordering of the tradition in the realm of church law with his *Concordantia discordantium canonum* (*Concordance of Disconcordant Canons*, 1140). The so-called *Decretum Gratiani* was a foundational text for generations of law students and judges. The supplements to Gratian's work were published with his *Decretum* in 1582 as the *Corpus Juris Canonici* (Code of Canon Law).

Not all of the leading intellectuals of the time were enamored of the new scholastic method, however. Bernard of Clairvaux (1090–1153), the monastic reformer and mystic, self-appointed judge, jury, and prosecutor of Abelard, turned against rational criticism and the dialectical method. For him the presupposition for theological work is not rational knowledge but rather the humble adaptation of the human will to the divine. It is ironic that Bernard, who hounded Abelard with inquisitorial fervor, himself refined further than Abelard the introspective conscience that Augustine bequeathed to the West. Born into a noble family, Bernard by the age of 22 persuaded 30 other young noblemen, including his brothers, to join the Benedictine renewal movement that had recently developed an order in its own right, the Cistercians (named after its foundation in Citeaux). The rigor of the Cistercians had already brought the order to the edge of extinction when Bernard's impact so transformed it that it came to be known as the Bernardines. Bernard has been called the "uncrowned ruler of Europe" because of his multifaceted influence on the election of popes, politics of kings, preaching of crusades, reforms of the church, and pursuit of heretics. But above all it was his promotion of mystical piety that secured his fame, then and now. Thus Dante (1265–1321) presented Bernard in the *Divine Comedy* as the representative of mystic contemplation who leads him to the Virgin Mary in Paradise.

The meditative literature that flowed from the Cistercians under the dominating influence of Bernard emphasized personal experience, appealed to the individual conscience, and plumbed the spirit of humankind. In a sense, this was scholasticism experienced, for it did not reject the age's love of logic but shifted it to the self-conscious, systematic search of the soul. Ascent to God was posited in the progress of self-knowledge, and presented in terms of logical steps of an intelligible development beginning with self-love and moving through self-knowledge to union with God. Logic was used to investigate the internal movements of the soul and states of mind. This "psychologizing" of theology is already present in Bernard's reworking of Benedict's treatise on the 12 steps of humility.

Bernard's tremendous spiritual influence resided not only in the power of his personality and perception but also in the readiness of his age to look inward, a readiness that also informed and received Anselm's emphasis upon meditation and Abelard's call to know oneself. The humanism and romanticism of this so-called "twelfth century renaissance" was graphically expressed in its changing art. Images of the crucifixion shifted from representations of divine power and majesty to depictions of extreme human suffering. The heroic images of Christ the King, a crowned and royally clothed warrior on the cross with head erect and open eyes expressing power, slowly changed to images of a humiliated, dishonored man, eyes closed, whose head and arms slump under the pain, and whose naked body shows his wounds. Among Bernard's many hymns still sung in Protestant and Catholic churches today, the new sensibility of the twelfth century comes through in his "O sacred head, now wounded, with grief and shame weighed down, now scornfully surrounded with thorns, thine only crown." Likewise, the images of Mary and the child Jesus once depicted as Mary the God-bearer (theotokos) and Jesus as a miniature adult, right hand raised in benediction, left hand clasping a symbol of dominion, were now transformed into the image of a helpless baby at Mary's breast. Maternal tenderness and infant vulnerability began to come to the fore, and Marian piety blossomed in the universities into heated arguments about the Immaculate Conception. The stage was being set for the Christian romance incarnated in St. Francis. Anselm's faith seeking understanding, Abelard's quest for self-knowledge, and Bernard's love seeking spiritual union will in the person of Francis focus on the symbolism of the wandering homelessness of the beggar, "naked following the naked Christ." The virtue of poverty will be transmuted from the Benedictine renunciation of pride to the romantic embrace of material impoverishment.

Chapter 7

The Medieval Church

Between the tenth and fifteenth centuries the medieval church responded to an array of issues ranging from the number and meaning of the sacraments to the challenges of a developing urban culture and economy. The papacy, recovering from its earlier weakness, realized the aspirations of Gregory VII's "Dictates" in the papal reign of Innocent III, only to find its earthly rule curtailed by the conflict between pope Boniface VIII and the French king Philip the Fair and the consequent rise of conciliarism.

The Cultural and Theological Development of the Sacraments

Medieval humankind at the mercy of natural and social forces largely beyond its control and understanding sought security, peace, and order. Thus in liturgy, art, architecture, political and religious thought, and piety, people strove to create an image of an eternal world within a world of change. The image of the city of God on earth was developed in terms of the biblical image of the Christian community as a body (e.g., 1 Corinthians 12; Ephesians 4; Colossians 3), the corpus Christianum. By the tenth century the functional social expression of this "Christian commonwealth" was parsed into three "orders" or "estates": peasants, priests, and warriors.

Theologians, politicians, and moralists emphasized the cooperation and harmony among these three orders sanctioned by the Trinitarian Godhead. Their complementary functions – supply and maintenance of material life, defense against enemies, and the promotion of spiritual welfare – assisted all in the corpus Christianum to conform to the divine plan. On the other hand, the "divine design" impressed upon the collective consciousness could also sanction social inequalities and exploitation.

The three orders expressed the "feudal" foundation of social relations that lasted in varying degrees up to the French Revolution. The quotation marks indicate that the term "feudal" is a construct by modern historians to describe a social pattern more complicated than the three orders would suggest. Nearly all wealth in the agrarian Middle Ages rested on landholdings and their produce. In feudal society the lord was responsible for protecting his vassals and their lands, and his vassals were obligated to serve the lord through both military service when needed and counsel when called upon. The church was fully involved in the feudal system, having its own fief holdings and lordship as well as being obligated to provide men and material to their lords, secular and religious. The word "lord" was also a term of address to God; and the posture of prayer with hands held together reflected the posture of a vassal doing fealty. By the twelfth century these ideas of lordship and vassalage were also used to describe relationships to women. In courtly literature the man as vassal pledged service to his lady (lord). Hymns to God and the Virgin Mary also began to use this language.

The corpus Christianum encompassed not only such feudal relationships here on earth but also transcended space and time with an ecclesiology that embraced the Christian family in the suffering church in purgatory, the militant church on earth, and the triumphant church in heaven. Through its sacraments the church addressed the major rites of passage in human life from birth to death, and related them to the maintenance of the whole society.

The church's intensive interest in sacraments began very early in its history even though the number of sacraments was not limited to the seven of modern Roman Catholicism (baptism, confirmation, penance, Eucharist, marriage, orders, extreme unction) until the Council of Florence in 1439. The word "sacrament," from the Latin *sacramentum*, translates the Greek term for "mystery." The Latin term originally meant an oath, in particular a soldier's oath of allegiance with its accompanying tattoo of identification. Thus, in the early church, the term itself conveyed the sense that the non-repeatable sacraments – baptism, confirmation, and ordination – impressed an indelible mark, a "tattoo," on the soul.

Baptism initiated a person into the community and the Eucharist nourished the pilgrim traveling toward the heavenly city. The early church had expressed its understanding of the Eucharist in both realistic and symbolic terms. During the Carolingian era, popular piety strengthened and intensified the realistic understanding until it became generally accepted that the bread and wine somehow changed into the body and blood of Christ as the result of priestly consecration of the elements.

There were a number of influences upon this development. The contemporary mentality perceived myriads of miracles and mysteries in nature. It may be that the sacred act of the Eucharist was developed into the wonder of wonders so that it would stand out from the everyday miraculous. Also, the emphasis upon the majesty and omnipotence of God and the growing perception of Christ as divine judge focused attention on the point where the mystery of Christ's presence was most palpable: the Eucharist. Thus the clergy gained social as well as religious power as those who alone could make Christ present in the Eucharist.

A series of eucharistic controversies from the ninth to the eleventh centuries led to the Synod of Rome in 1079, which declared "the bread and wine placed on the altar are, after consecration, not only a sacrament, but also the true body and blood of our Lord Jesus Christ . . . handled by the hands of the priests and crushed by the teeth of the faithful." The doctrine of transubstantiation (Fourth Lateran Council, 1215) later "explained" how this occurred. The sacrament so awed the laity that they began to adore the Host (Latin: *hostia*, a sacrificial victim) and brought their petitions to it. Visions and miracle stories surrounding the sacrament proliferated. Christ as he existed in the sacrament became the greatest of all relics. Popular piety influenced liturgical practices such as a perpetual light before the reserved, consecrated bread; and bells to signal the consecration and elevation of the Host. In 1264 pope Urban IV, influenced by the visions of the French nun Juliana (d. 1258), commanded the Feast of Corpus Christi, the commemoration of the institution of the Eucharist.

The sacrament was so revered that the frequency of reception declined drastically; the sight of the Host alone became a devotional substitute for reception. The laity, fearful of spilling Christ's blood, began withdrawing from taking the cup. In response, the doctrine of concomitance (Council of Constance, 1415) legitimated lay communion with only the bread by affirming the whole Christ in the form of the bread. Since Latin was of little use to the uneducated laity, they no longer "heard" the mass but saw the elevation of the Host as the reenactment of the Passion that the priest, by virtue of the sacrament of orders, "offered" to appease God. By the eve of the Reformation such sacerdotal offerings increased in value as they increased in number.

Nevertheless, the danger of shipwreck on earthly delights was omnipresent. In response to this danger, the church offered the "second plank after shipwreck," the sacrament of penance. The term penance derives from the Latin *poena*, a term that encompasses compensation, satisfaction, expiation, and penalty.

Meditation on the necessity of satisfying the punishment for sin – either here or hereafter – led to the doctrine of purgatory and its purifying fire and the indulgence system for commuting penitential impositions too severe for temporal completion. Thus when cardinal Peter Damian (d. 1072) imposed a 100-year penance on the archbishop of Milan for simony, he also indicated how much money would commute each year of penance. Although the intent of the indulgence system was to adjust satisfaction for sins to changing social conditions, by the late Middle Ages it became so corrupted in service of clerical authority and revenue raising that it evoked Luther's "Ninety-five Theses" on penance and indulgences, sparking the Protestant Reformation.

Individual and collective acts of satisfaction for sin found a variety of outlets. In periods of great social stress, such as the mid-fourteenth-century plague, collective rituals developed such as the penitential bands of flagellants who traveled from town to town scourging themselves. The collective ritual of penance *par excellence* was Lent. Its communal ascetic rigor was such that it spawned a wild collective prelude known as "carnival" (from *carnevalis*, "farewell to flesh") that marked the transition to the meatless period of Lent. Carnival consisted of the days or week preceding Shrove Tuesday, the day before Ash Wednesday, termed in French *Mardi gras*, "fat Tuesday." Carnival was to expose the sins of the community. Carnality, represented as a fat figure carried in procession, was tried, condemned, and executed by fire. The overindulgence in food and drink was vividly expressed by the dedication of Shrove Tuesday in Nantes to St. Dégobillard – St. Vomit! Sexuality and obscenity were equally on display with iconographic representations of the penis such as enormous sausages, as well as symbols of lechery carried in processions that included the town prostitutes. The purpose was to expose that which had been concealed throughout the year, and thus anything regarded as shameful was high on the list for parading.

This was also the period when the hierarchical and patriarchal culture could at least momentarily be overturned, and so men rode backward on asses and women beat the men. The Feast of Fools or the Day of the Boy Bishop, a counterpart to the revels of carnival, often held on January 6, the Feast of Holy Innocents, satirized clerical rules by parading a choirboy as bishop. For a fleeting moment carnival and similar "days of misrule" turned the world upside down.

The Rise of the Mendicant Orders

While not a move to turn the world upside down, the mendicant orders arose from the respective challenges of Dominic (1170–1221) and Francis (ca. 1181–1226) to the socioeconomic and ecclesiastical status quo. The social construction of reality to which the early medieval church had contributed so much now showed signs of stress. The values of stability, tradition, and order expressed in the three orders and the sense of the corpus Christianum set forth by liturgy and ritual were increasingly confronted by change, innovation, and disorder.

The social changes that began around the eleventh century involved population growth and the rise of cities abetted by technological development and a money economy. New personal roles as businessman, citizen, and worker were less all-embracing than the groupings of village and kindred, and involved a shift in relationships and values. An increasing number of people, deprived of kin and community, faced the need to prove themselves rather than play assigned roles. New social experiences exposed them to situations for which the church not only offered no meaningful patterns but also actually resisted changes already underway. What relevance had a religion of stability and humility to a life of mobility and competition? The church's response to these issues tended to reaffirm traditional solutions such as pilgrimage, church building, monastic patronage, eucharistic ritual, and indulgences. The Cluniac and Gregorian renewal movements intended to purify, not change, the church and its theology.

A renewed search for community and divine approbation sought to address the disquieting changes. Both Francis and Dominic incorporated contemporary concerns into their commitment to apostolic poverty as a means for reaching communion with God. In contrast to the Benedictine monasteries that spurned towns as iniquitous, the Franciscans and Dominicans rooted themselves in cities. The Benedictines had emphasized humility, obedience, and stability; poverty to them was understood in terms of poverty of spirit. The mendicant orders, as their name indicates, lived by begging and emphasized material poverty. Their desire to imitate the early church and the wandering, preaching, poor Christ, displaced the older monastic ideal of a fixed role of inter-cession within rural monastic walls with an innovative urban itinerancy; they were able to go to where distressed people longed for the message of the life and poverty of Jesus. For the Benedictine monk in his rural cloister, poverty took the form of the denial of self-will and the embrace of humility – achievements correlated with the fact that the Benedictines drew membership from the feudal nobility and warrior class. For the urban mendicant monk, poverty was understood in terms of the destitute on the margins of society and the questions of conscience that plagued the new urban entrepreneurs.

Although the Dominicans and Franciscans shared these modern concerns, they differed in their origins and development. The Dominicans, or Order of Preachers, were founded by the Spanish priest Dominic Guzman. His encounter with an Albigensian innkeeper inspired him to found an order of itinerant preachers. The Albigensians (from Albi, a city in southern France) were a dualistic heretical sect. Also known as Cathars (from the Greek for "pure"), they attracted a wide following due to their ascetic lifestyle and challenge to perceived corruption in the church. After a nightlong effort, Dominic converted the Albigensian back to the Catholic faith. The experience made Dominic aware of both the prevalence of the Albigensian heresy and the need for persuasive preaching to counter it. He also realized that only by equaling the ascetic austerity of the heretics would it be possible to preach true doctrine with credibility. Thus voluntary poverty was embraced as a means of promoting an itinerant preaching mission.

In 1216 pope Honorius III recognized Dominic and his followers as an order according to the Rule of St. Augustine, a more flexible rule than the Benedictine Rule. Dominic's concern to counter the doctrinal errors of heretics convinced him of the necessity of a learned ministry. Within Dominic's own lifetime his order became established in the intellectual centers of Paris and Bologna. The intellectual focus of the Dominicans formed such outstanding scholars as Albertus Magnus (ca. 1200–80) and Thomas Aquinas (ca. 1225–74), and led to the papal appointment of the Dominicans as inquisitors in 1232.

The most radical exponent of the new evangelical poverty of the twelfth and thirteenth centuries was Francis of Assisi. Francis lived the ideal of "naked, following the naked Christ" and "poor, following the poor Christ." These twelfth-century formulas, adapted from ancient tradition, associated the individual with Christ in a common nakedness or poverty of worldly goods and cares. Francis vividly embraced this ideal when, nearly 25 years of age, he stood before his angry merchant father and the bishop's court of Assisi and stripped himself naked, gave his clothes to his father, and declared that henceforth he would speak only of his Father in heaven.

For Francis, poverty expressed the imitation of Christ. Francis rejected the new urban merchant world of profits and the accumulation of wealth, the world of his father, as something so corrupt that he regarded money as excrement. He urged his followers to flee money as if it were the devil. The 1223 Rule of St. Francis strictly commanded all friars "never to receive coin or money, for themselves or for any other person." Supposedly, Francis once commanded a friar who had absent-mindedly touched a coin to pick it up with his mouth and to place it in a pile of dung.

Although this attitude would seem unlikely to enhance the recruitment process, it nevertheless worked wonders. Whether Francis touched some deep emotional springs of piety or the nerves and anxieties of the urban, profit-oriented society, his ideal of poverty stimulated a remarkable response from his contemporaries. The enthusiasm for Francis led to the formation of a female branch known as the Poor Clares, after Clare of Assisi, the first woman converted to Francis' ideal of poverty; and then a third order for those unable to embrace the full rigor of Franciscan poverty that permitted remaining in secular life while practicing certain elements of the ideal. Francis soon became the reluctant head of an organization that perceived the whole world as its parish.

Why were Francis and his mendicant order so appealing? Certainly, the medieval person was deeply concerned for personal salvation, the path to which was presented as pilgrimage out of this world. The Franciscans gave the radical ascetic expression of this pilgrimage an orthodox expression. Francis himself reputedly received the stigmata, the very wounds of Christ, the highest expression of medieval piety. But there may well have been other motivations. Rebellion against fathers and the rejection of social respectability were not limited to Francis – or his age! The fact that well-to-do families supported the friars but were horrified by the prospect of their children joining them may have imbued the poverty of the friars with a certain appeal to youth. And for the aspiring intellectuals of the time, the Dominicans and the Franciscans offered a university education without the debts and obligations even then incurred by studies. The desire of scholars to live and work in a university community dovetailed nicely with the needs of friars to educate their new recruits.

The Dominican and Franciscan scholars addressed the social and ethical problems confronting the new urban life. Ironically, they legitimated private property as necessary and good for the development of an ordered state. They developed business ethics and a theory of just price in relation to supply and demand.

These contributions made it possible for the urban Christian merchant, previously marginalized by feudal social mores and a religion that condemned and prohibited usury, to be reintegrated into Christian society. Furthermore, as mendicant orders, the Dominicans and Franciscans provided merchants with a meritorious subject for philanthropy. They provided a key to the justification of profits – how else could one have the wherewithal for charity? – and thus an honorable and much preferred option to the penance and opprobrium that had earlier accrued to businesspersons. The mendicant friars supplied city dwellers with a new ethic and an outlet for charity.

The Dominican and Franciscan vision of the world as their parish and education in preaching as the tool for its conversion, unleashed an intellectual energy that transformed universities from trade schools for training clerks into centers of intellectual ferment and creativity. Such intellectual giants as Albertus Magnus, Thomas Aquinas, and Meister Eckhard (ca. 1260–1327) among the Dominicans, and Bonaventure (ca. 1217–74), Duns Scotus (ca. 1265–1308), and William of Ockham (ca. 1285–1347) among the Franciscans made theology the "queen of the sciences." It is, of course, Aquinas who has long been regarded as one of the most brilliant theologians among the scholastics. The range of his thought and the phenomenal synthesis he achieved in relating reason and revelation imparted such an architectonic and aesthetic quality to his theology that it has been likened to the gothic cathedrals of the time.

Thomas was born into the great feudal family of count Landulf of Aquino that was related to both the emperor and the king of France. In consonance with his family's position and prestige, he was sent as a child to the famous Benedictine monastery of Monte Cassino to be trained to become its abbot. As a teenager, however, Thomas decided to enter the new Dominican order. His father and brothers were furious that Thomas intended to reject the respectable ecclesiastical career customary for the younger sons of nobility for what they and their peers perceived to be an order of ecclesial riffraff. When unable to dissuade Thomas from his decision, the family imprisoned him in the family castle; when that did not work, they decided to render his decision impossible through scandal by putting a courtesan in his room. The story is that young Thomas snatched a brand from the fire, chased the woman from his room, and burned a huge black cross into the door.

Obviously, Thomas' decision was not to be trifled with, and he went on to join the Dominicans studying with Albertus Magnus, who introduced him to the philosophy of Aristotle newly mediated to the West by the Spanish Muslim and Jewish philosophers, Averroes of Cordoba (Ibn Rushd, 1126–98) and Moses Maimonides (1135–1204).

Thomas was and continues to be so influential in the life and thought of the church, not only because he addressed clearly and forcefully the intellectual crisis of the day created by Aristotelian metaphysics that ran counter to revelation, but also because he did so in a way that opened faith to dialogue with philosophy, revelation with empirical reason, religion with science. Thomas slaked his contemporaries' great thirst for reality without giving in to their influential cries that one could drink at only the bar of reason or only the bar of faith but not both. For Thomas, there is only truth, not two mutually exclusive truths. He expressed this conviction in his watchword that grace does not destroy nature but fulfills it; that is, there is continuity between reason and revelation, the natural and the supernatural.

Following Aristotle, Thomas agreed that virtues are acquired through practice and thus become a "habit" – "practice makes perfect." The supernatural virtues, however, unlike the natural virtues, are not innate to humankind but must be infused into the person through God's grace mediated by the church's sacraments. Once infused, the supernatural virtues are, analogously to the natural virtues, to be "acquired" or "realized" by practice. In this sense, the person who is in a state of grace does good works that please God and thus cooperates in his or her salvation. The later scholastic phrase that expresses this process is *facere quod in se est*, "do what is within one." Salvation, then, occurs within one through the actualization of faith formed by acts of charity. The person who does his or her best with the aid of grace receives the reward of eternal life as a just due. Later scholastic theologians would be more optimistic about human capability to cooperate with God in salvation and would suggest that good works done in the state of nature would also be rewarded by God with an infusion of grace as an appropriate due.

Not all of Thomas' contemporaries responded positively to his contributions. The archbishops of Paris and Canterbury condemned several of his propositions in 1277, but in 1278 the General Chapter of the Dominicans endorsed his teaching. He was canonized in 1323 and declared a Doctor of the Church (i.e., official teacher) by pope Pius V (a Dominican) in 1567. In 1879 Leo XIII's encyclical *Aeterni Patris* made Thomas' works mandatory for all students of theology. In 1923, the sixth centenary of his canonization, pope Pius XI reiterated Thomas' teaching authority.

The Rise and Decline of Papal Authority

The age of Thomas was the watershed of the medieval era. It included the ideal Christian monarch (St.) Louis IX of France, the English king Henry III, and Thomas' friend, the great Franciscan theologian and mystic, Bonaventure. The creative synthesis constructed during this period covered all realms of life, including not only reason and revelation, but also sacerdotal authority and personal religious experience. The papal embodiment of the age was Innocent III (r. 1198–1216).

Building upon the centuries-long development of papal ideology, Innocent believed that the whole world is the province of the pope and that Christ had commissioned Peter to govern not only the universal church but also the secular world. A gifted administrator and leader as well as canon lawyer, Innocent expressed his conviction of the superiority of the church over the empire by the analogy that the monarchy is related to the papacy as the moon is to the sun.

Innocent first secured papal power and authority in Rome and then decided a disputed imperial election in favor of Otto IV. However, once secure, Otto IV reneged on his recognition of the papal states and his promise not to intervene in Italy. In response, Innocent appointed Frederick II to replace Otto, and organized a coalition of the papacy, Frederick, and Philip Augustus of France against Otto and his ally, king John of England. This is one of the first great examples of the clash of international alliances in European history. Otto was crushed at the battle of Bouvines in 1214, and Frederick publicly swore an oath of allegiance to the papacy.

Innocent paralleled his triumph in the "imperial business" with the English and French kings. In a dispute concerning traditional royal authority over the English church, Innocent forced king John to accept the papal appointee to the see of Canterbury and to become his vassal, thus making England a fief of the papacy. A sidelight to this was that John acquiesced to Innocent's conditions because in 1213 he was unsure of the support of his barons. When in 1215 the barons rebelled and compelled John to sign the *Magna carta libertatum*, which restricted the crown's feudal and sovereign rights, Innocent supported the king and declared the *Magna carta* null and void.

Innocent also placed France under interdict (cessation of the administration of the sacraments throughout the land).to compel Philip Augustus to be reconciled with his wife, Ingeborg of Denmark. In general, however, Innocent's reign benefited Philip's monarchy. Philip cloaked his expansionist policies in southern France in the dubious morality of a crusade against heretics – the Albigenses whom Dominic had hoped to convert through preaching. When in 1208 a papal legate was murdered in the area, a crusade was launched. Innocent had already been energetically attacking heresy in his own territory and had equated heresy with crime against the sovereign power. Because Innocent did not trust local French officials to purge the remnants of heresy following the bloodbath and land grab of the crusade, he sent papal legates to establish courts to deal with heretics, the basis for the Inquisition.

Although Innocent reorganized the church, humiliated kings, and took up the sword against heretics, he also realized the importance of law and piety for Christendom. He commissioned a collection of canon law, the first since Gratian's *Decretum* (ca. 1140), which became the authentic text for teaching at the University of Bologna. He also recognized the value of the mendicant movements for the renewal and reform of the church, thereby co-opting the claim of heretical movements such as the Albigenses to be the only pure church. Finally, Innocent's summoning of the Fourth Lateran Council in 1215 established one of the most important conciliar meetings since Nicaea in 325. The council set the number of sacraments at the seven still recognized in the Roman Catholic Church; made transubstantiation the orthodox teaching on the Eucharist; limited confirmation and ordination to bishops; mandated at least annual penance and communion for all Catholics; and prohibited the public presence of Jews during Holy Week.

The Decline of the Papacy

With the death of Innocent III the links between hierarchical church authority and the political realm could not be maintained. In little more than a generation after Thomas and Innocent III, king Philip of France subjugated pope Boniface VIII (r. 1294–1303).

Boniface VIII was of Roman noble lineage. He studied law at Bologna and served in the Curia before becoming a cardinal and papal legate to France. An able canon lawyer and administrator,

Boniface represented the legacy of Gregory VII and Innocent III that political facts are subject to papal ideology. Unfortunately for both Boniface and the papal office, the world context had shifted markedly since Innocent's triumphs.

Boniface's troubles began with his feud with the Colonna family, two of whom were cardinals he deposed. Boniface then alienated the kings of England and France, who had moved to tax their clergy to finance their mutual conflict (the Hundred Years' War). In the bull *Clericis laicos* (1296) Boniface forbade clergy to provide ecclesiastical revenue or property to any ruler without consent of the pope and forbade laity to exact or receive taxes from the clergy. The kings were not intimidated. Philip IV of France (1285–1314) responded by banning the export of precious metals, thus cutting off revenue to the papal court.

Boniface caved in and explained that he certainly did not want to invalidate feudal clerical obligations to the crown. Therefore, clergy could provide "voluntary" gifts at the king's "friendly suggestion." In cases of necessity, the king could tax the clergy without papal permission. Finally, to show his "affection" for the French monarchy, Boniface canonized Philip's grandfather, Louis IX.

Unmollified, Philip imprisoned the bishop of Pamiers on various charges. Boniface responded by reinstituting *Clericis laicos*, charging the king with violating the freedom and immunity of the church, and summoning the French bishops to Rome to take measures against the king. Boniface's bull *Ausculta fili* (1301) summoned Philip himself to Rome to answer charges. Undaunted, Philip substituted a forged bull that distorted papal claims along with a proclamation that began: "Your utter fatuity may know that we [the king] are not subjected to anyone." The royal chancery also drew up a list of charges against Boniface that included blasphemy, simony, heresy, fornication, and the murder of the previous pope. At the same time, popular pamphlets and academic treatises attacked Boniface in particular and the papacy in general.

This is the context for one of the most famous and debated decrees of the medieval papacy, *Unam sanctam* (1302), in which Boniface stated that both the temporal and spiritual swords are in the power of the church, that temporal power is subject to the papacy, and that "submission on the part of every man to the bishop of Rome is altogether necessary for his salvation." One of Philip's royal ministers is said to have remarked, "My master's sword is of steel, the pope's is made of verbiage." That point was illustrated by storming the papal palace the night before Boniface was to excommunicate the king. Although liberated by the local populace, Boniface soon died a broken man.

The centuries-long development of the ideal of a universal Christian commonwealth with one emperor, one language, and one law under the church, the ark of salvation captained by the papacy, ran aground on the rocks thrust up with the development of national vernaculars, states, and laws. Since the Donation of Constantine, papal ideology had focused attention on the empire and the emperor, and had neglected those rulers whom Gregory VII referred to as mere "kinglets." But these kinglets had become aware of a new national sense and outlook for which the papacy had little or no ideological means of control. Philip's triumph over Boniface concluded one phase in the history of the papacy and initiated another.

Conciliarism

Traumatized by the attack upon Boniface, the papacy attempted to appease France and to restore its own prestige. However, matters only deteriorated with the election of the archbishop of Bordeaux as Clement V (r. 1305–14). He ensconced the papacy in Avignon, a city under the influence of France. Thus began what the Italian poet Francesco Petrarch (1304–74) termed the "Babylonian captivity" of the church (1309–77), during which all the popes were French. A French pope with a French Curia lived in a French-speaking city on the French frontier. The papacy, that under Innocent III had subdued kings and emperors, was now widely perceived to be captive to the French monarchy.

Critical voices were increasingly raised against the papacy. The French Dominican John of Paris (ca. 1250–1306) argued in his *On Papal and Royal Power* that secular government was rooted in the natural human community and that popes had no power therefore to depose kings. Marsilius of Padua (ca. 1275–1342), a former rector of the University of Paris, in *The Defender of the Peace* (1324) blamed the papacy for undermining world peace. His solution was to limit the authority of the papacy by the laws governing all human institutions, laws that derived from the whole community based on Aristotle and Roman law. Dante (1265–1321) assailed the papacy and popes not only in his *Divine Comedy* but also in his *On Monarchy*. In the latter he argued the papacy should abandon all temporal authority and possessions, and that temporal peace required a universal monarchy under the emperor. Petrarch, who had lived in and around Avignon for some years, described the luxury and worldliness of the papal court and building program there as "the sewer of the world." Instead of responding to the philosophical, theological, and literary critiques, the papacy concentrated on bureaucratic efficiency for collecting more and more money, shuffling its thousands of pages of documents concerned with benefices, indulgences, politics, and patronage.

With papal prestige at a low point, there were increasing calls for the papacy to return to Rome, including pressure by the influential women mystics Catherine of Siena (d. 1380) and Bridget of Sweden (d. 1373). Finally, the papacy in the person of Gregory XI (r. 1370–8) reentered Rome and took up official residency at the Vatican. Ironically, this move led almost immediately to the Western Schism of the church.

Conflict over Gregory's successor led to the election of a rival pope. There had been antipopes before in the history of the church, but this was the first time that the same College of

Cardinals had legitimately elected two popes. Urban VI, successor to Gregory, refused to accede to the cardinals' request that he abdicate. He and his successors remained in Rome. Clement VII, elected to replace Urban, and his successors returned to Avignon. It is difficult today to appreciate the depth of the religious insecurity and the intensity of institutional criticism caused by this schism. If, as decreed by *Unam sanctam*, salvation itself was contingent on obedience to the pope, it was crucial to know who was the true Vicar of Christ. But how could this be decided?

Europe itself was split. France, Scotland, Aragon, Castille, and Navarre followed the Avignon line; whereas much of Germany, Hungary, England, Poland, and Scandinavia followed the Roman line. Public opinion was hopelessly confused. Even the learned and the holy clashed over who was the true pope. Catherine of Siena promoted universal recognition of Urban. She called the cardinals who elected Clement "fools, liars, and devils in human form." On the other hand, the Spanish Dominican Vincent Ferrar was equally zealous for the Avignon popes, and labeled the adherents of Urban "dupes of the devil and heretics." The maintenance of two papal courts and their related expenses increased the ecclesial tax burdens; and the disputing popes' appointments of partisans to bishoprics and ecclesial benefices furthered division and acrimony.

The first attempt to resolve the crisis by an ecumenical council, proposed by various professors and universities, occurred with the Council of Pisa (1409). Both popes refused to attend, and thus the council deposed both and elected a new pope, Alexander V (r. 1409–10), a cardinal of the Roman line. The deposed popes, however, declined to recognize the validity of the council, and thus there were now three popes!

To make a long and complicated story blessedly short, the emperor Sigismund, in line with the precedent set by Constantine, accepted arguments that a general council is superior to the pope and that as emperor and protector of the church he had the duty to call a council. He convoked the Council of Constance

(1414–18) to deal with three main issues: the great schism, reform of the church in "head and members," and the extirpation of heresy. In the matter of heresy, the council condemned to death the Englishman John Wyclif (ca. 1330–84) and the Czech Jan Hus (ca. 1372–1415) for heresy. Wyclif cheated the verdict by already being dead, but the burning of Hus, who had been given a safe conduct to come to the council, ignited religious fires in Bohemia that were still burning by the time of the Reformation a century later.

The major agenda item, however, had to do with the schism. The council decided to vote by nations rather than by individuals, with each nation having one vote. The decision counterbalanced the preponderance of Italian prelates upon whom the Roman pope was depending. It was also a democratizing decision because it gave voice to non-prelates. Furthermore, the idea of a nation as a unit contributed to the already developing sense of nationalism that was undermining the old idea of a universal Christian commonwealth under the headship of the papacy.

The council successfully resolved the schism with the election of Martin V. In the process the council passed two significant decrees, *Haec sancta* and *Frequens*. The former placed the authority of an ecumenical council over that of a pope in matters of faith and reform of the church. The latter decreed frequent and regular meetings of ecumenical councils "in perpetuity." Martin V did not confirm or approve the council, an omission probably little noted in the midst of the profound relief at having resolved the schism. His successor, Eugene IV (r. 1431–47), approved the Council of Constance insofar as it was not prejudicial to the rights and supremacy of the papacy. And Pius II (r. 1458–64) in his bull *Execrabilis* (1460) prohibited any and all appeals to a council over the pope; such an appeal in itself to be regarded as heresy and schism.

Further councils – Basel (1433), Ferrara-Florence (1439) – did not accomplish much other than to affirm the view of Pius II and other one-time conciliarists that parliamentary government was not to their liking. Rulers sensed that conciliarism implied too large a voice for the governed. With the demotion of the papacy to the status of one monarchical government among others, it dawned on monarchs that conciliarism was a two-edged sword – the means called upon to control the papacy might become a weapon against them. Consequently, the papacy and monarchs became disposed to cooperate and to conclude concordats with each other for the sake of mutual support. The papacy's efforts to overcome the challenge of conciliarism and to consolidate its patrimony in Italy diverted its energy and attention from the widespread cry for reform of the church in head and members.

In less than a century this cry would become the full-throated roar of the Reformation that blew away the last vestiges of the ideal of the corpus Christianum. Although that roar would include a cacophony of voices, its first sighs and murmurs came from those alienated by poverty, the profit economy, and the stress of urban growth augmented by fears of famine, plague, and war, the anger of the frustrated renewal movements of Wyclif and Hus, and the individualism and intellectual discoveries of the Renaissance.

Chapter 8

The Reformations of the Sixteenth Century

The Reformation era is customarily dated from 1517 and the posting of Martin Luther's "Ninety-five Theses," to 1555 and the Religious Peace of Augsburg. In this short period the Roman papal hegemony over Western Christendom was shattered, and Catholicism came to be known as "Roman Catholicism," now one denomination of Christianity among others. Four major churches arose in this period – Roman Catholic, Lutheran, Reformed (the general name for the various national Calvinist churches), and Anglican – with a variety of other Christian communities – Anabaptists and Spiritualists – espousing more radical reforms. The late-Reformation polarization of Christendom into conflicting denominations with specific confessions of faith is known as the "confessional period." The confessional period extended to the Peace of Westphalia (1648) that concluded the Thirty Years' War (1618–48), the last of the major religious wars stemming from the Reformation.

Context

On the eve of the Reformation the question was not whether the church *should* be reformed but *when*. The papacy, earlier buffeted by conciliarism and national renewal movements, now faced the challenges of the intellectual awakening known as the Renaissance. The watchword of the Renaissance that began in fourteenth-century Italy and spread northward was *ad fontes* – "back to the sources" – of Western culture: the Greek and Latin classics, the Bible, and the writings of the church fathers. Scholars such as Desiderius Erasmus (1469–1536) and Jacques Lefèvre d'Etaples (ca. 1460–1536) provided editions of the New Testament and biblical prefaces and commentaries that went behind the Latin Vulgate to the Greek text, and thereby stimulated a critical rereading of the theological tradition. Other texts too came under the sharp eye and literary methods of the humanists; for example, Lorenzo Valla (ca. 1406–57) proved that the famous Donation of Constantine was spurious. New ideas spread rapidly, widely, and reliably due to the recent invention of the printing press, and found homes in new universities such as the University of Wittenberg, founded in 1502. Indeed, Luther wrote to a friend that courses on the Bible and Augustine's writings were displacing the study of Aristotelian metaphysics and ethics and scholastic theology at Wittenberg. In a sense, then, the Reformation began in a faculty-led curriculum change – hard to believe if you've ever had to sit through a faculty meeting!

Stimulated by the recovery of biblical and early church texts and the excitement of fresh translations and interpretations, reformers throughout Europe urged biblical preaching and pastoral theology. Preachers became translators and translators became preachers. Their conviction that academic theology serves the proclamation of the gospel was succinctly expressed in Erasmus' rendering of the opening verses of the Gospel of John: "In the beginning was the *sermon*." But at the very time the reformers were bringing theology out of the scholastic closet with vernacular sermons and devotional writings, the papacy had reached an advanced stage in the hardening of its pastoral and ethical arteries.

A series of worldly popes not only bequeathed glorious art and architecture to posterity but also anger and anxiety to their contemporaries. Stung by the conciliar movement's encroachment upon papal authority, the major figures of the late medieval papacy sought to squelch voices of renewal. Their success in containing conciliarism may be seen in that, apart from the Council of Trent (1545–63), the late and grudging response to the Reformation, there was not another council until Vatican I (1869–70), which in its declaration of papal primacy and infallibility definitively answered the Council of Constance.

Contemporaries experienced cognitive dissonance when they perceived the opulence and power of the papal court in contrast to the biblical image of the shepherd guarding his flock. Critics pointed out that Jesus' command to Peter was "feed my sheep" (John 21:15–17), not "fleece them." A German woodcut portrayed the mercenary spirit of the papacy by picturing the pope and the Curia counting money in one panel and Jesus driving the moneychangers from the temple in the opposite panel. An Italian proverb stated that the person who goes to Rome will lose his or her faith. And a Latin acrostic for Rome summed up the sense of papal venality: *R[adix] O[mnium] M[alorum] A[varitia]* – "the love of money is the root of all evil." The papacy had become a regal court, and the pope was increasingly perceived to be nothing more than an Italian prince. Two particularly notorious popes exemplify this papal image: Alexander VI (r. 1492–1503) and Julius II (r. 1503–13).

Rodrigo Borgia was made a cardinal by his uncle, pope Callistus III, and won the papacy largely through bribery, taking the title Alexander VI. It is no surprise that continuing familial and financial concerns determined Alexander's reign, rooted in nepotism and simony from the beginning. He is one pope to whom the title "father," if not "holy," may be literally applied. Alexander's involvement in sexual promiscuity, alleged poisonings, and murderous intrigues made the name Borgia a synonym for corruption. He was denounced in his own time by the influential and fiery Dominican preacher Girolamo Savonarola (1452–98), who, unmoved by bribes or threats, was executed in Florence. Alexander's efforts to strengthen the papacy abetted French intervention in northern Italy that in turn contributed to a new period of power politics with Italy as the focus of international intrigue.

Julius II, like Alexander a patron of the arts, supported Raphael, Michelangelo, and Bramante. Julius' enthusiasm for rebuilding St. Peter's – the goal of which was to show other princes that the pope had a more magnificent court – was matched by his zeal for war. So much of his reign involved warfare that people began to wonder what this pontiff had to do with the Prince of Peace. Erasmus, who witnessed Julius' triumphal martial entry into Bologna, satirized him in *Julius Excluded* by depicting him in full armor trying unsuccessfully to force his way into heaven.

Julius' successor was a son of the famous Florentine banking family, the Medici. He took the title Leo X (r. 1513–21). He revealed his sensitivity to the widespread desire for reform of the church by reputedly opening his reign with the words: "Now that God has given us the papacy, let us enjoy it." But as Leo was settling into the papal throne, a young monk named Martin Luther (1483–1546) was struggling to understand the Bible in a newly established university in the German backwater town of Wittenberg.

Luther's reform movement was not initiated by the moral indignation of a Savonarola directed against the Renaissance papacy, but by his anxiety about salvation. Luther and fellow reformers were confronted by this in the praxis of the worshipping community. Hence it is important to remember that Luther's formal academic disputation "Disputation on the Power and Efficacy of Indulgences," better known as the "Ninety-five Theses," focused on the sacrament of penance and its associated issues of justification, indulgences, purgatory, and ecclesiastical authority. In brief, the Reformation began with a focus on the central pastoral praxis of the church: the forgiveness of sins.

The Reformation in Germany

The personal and pastoral problem that plagued Luther was whether salvation is achieved or received. The medieval scholastic answer that it is both did not resolve the issue for him because the necessity of even the smallest human contribution to salvation threw the burden of proof back upon the person. The church's pastoral care made people uncertain of their salvation and thus more dependent upon the intercessions of the church by stimulating spiritual anxiety and introspection in stressing that "no one knows whether he is worthy of God's love or hate" (Ecclesiastes 9:1). Furthermore, people did not need to go to confession to feel insecure and uncertain about their salvation. Everywhere in everyday life, images – those "books of the laity" in pope Gregory the Great's phrase – served to remind people of heaven and hell. Medieval churches presented the image of Christ on the throne of judgment with a sword and a lily extending from either side of his head. The lily represents resurrection to heaven, but the sword of judgment to eternal torment was more vivid in the minds of most people. Pictures and poems presented the theme of the "dance of death" complete with a skeletal Grim Reaper, and provided manuals on the "art of dying."

Luther's teaching responsibilities at Wittenberg as well as his own quest for certainty of salvation led him to intensive study of the Bible. Here he discovered that righteousness before God is not what the sinner achieves but what the sinner receives as a free gift from God. The promise that salvation is no longer the goal of life but rather the foundation of life freed him from preoccupation with his own spiritual pulse and for life in the world. Luther reversed the medieval piety of achievement: good works do not make the sinner acceptable to God, but rather God's acceptance of the sinner prompts good works.

Luther's personal discovery became a public event with his criticism of current indulgence practices in the "Ninety-five Theses." The popular mind, abetted by some preachers, had twisted the meaning of indulgence from that of the remission of a church-imposed penance after priestly absolution to that of a ticket to heaven. Hard-sell medieval indulgence sellers such as John Tetzel offered direct access to heaven even for the dead in purgatory. One of Tetzel's sales jingles was: "As soon as the coin into the box rings, a soul from purgatory to heaven springs." Tetzel's extravagant claims for the power of an indulgence included remission of sin even if one had raped the Virgin Mary. Another claim, according to popular lore, ricocheted back upon Tetzel to his own dismay. A knight bought an indulgence on the basis that it extended to future sins and then robbed Tetzel!

Aside from such an occasional glitch, Tetzel was a well-paid, excellent salesman who today would be the envy of the advertising world. He entered towns with fanfares of trumpets and drums and the flags and symbols of the papacy. Quite a show in the pre-television age! After a vivid sermon on hell in the town square, he proceeded to the largest church and gave an equally vivid sermon on purgatory and the sufferings awaiting the audience and presently endured by their dear departed friends and relatives. After the next sermon depicting heaven, his audience was sufficiently prepped and eager to buy indulgences.

Luther's theses directed at Tetzel's abuse of indulgences were written in Latin, and most Wittenbergers could not even read German. Thus the popular image of Luther as the angry young man pounding incendiary theses to a church door is more romantic fiction than reality. The uproar originated from the fact that Luther sent the theses to Tetzel's superior, archbishop Albrecht of Mainz, with the naive thought that Albrecht did not know his hireling was abusing the authority of the church. In actuality, Luther had unknowingly touched the nerve of a far-reaching political and ecclesiastical scam. Pope Leo X needed funds to build St. Peter's, and Albrecht had agreed to provide such funds in return for a papal dispensation to become the archbishop of Mainz.

Events accelerated rapidly as the establishment proceeded to silence Luther. By January 1521 Luther was excommunicated, and the papacy urged the young, newly elected emperor, Charles V, to issue a mandate against Luther. But the German constitution and Charles' coronation oath upheld the right of Germans to a trial by impartial judges. Thus Luther was promised safe conduct to a hearing at the impending Diet of Worms in April. There, before the emperor, princes, lords, and ecclesiastical authorities – a world away from his monastic cell and classroom – Luther did not receive a hearing but was presented with a pile of his writings and asked to recant their errors. His brief answer that he could not go against his conscience unless convinced by scripture or clear reason included the memorable phrase, "Here I stand, may God help me." The result, the Edict of Worms (1521), proclaimed Luther an outlaw to be seized and delivered to the authorities. Fortunately for Luther, he had a number of powerful supporters, including his own prince, Frederick the Wise, who sequestered Luther in one of his castles for safekeeping. During the six months of Luther's "castle arrest" he translated the New Testament into German.

The Reformation motif of faith active in love energized innovative approaches to a broad range of early modern social issues including reform of social welfare, literacy and public education, and political issues of authority and the right to resistance. The Reformers' rejection of mandatory clerical celibacy not only struck at church authority but "civil"-ized the clergy in the sense that they became citizens with homes, families, and a stake in civil responsibilities. The liberation from striving for salvation released human energy and material resources for this-worldly activities.

While Luther referred to the early evangelical movement in Wittenberg as "our theology," fissures among erstwhile colleagues began appearing by the early 1520s. Andreas Bodenstein von Karlstadt (1486–1541), sometimes referred to as the forerunner of Puritanism, insisted that evangelical insights must be instituted without tarrying for anyone. One effect of this, paralleled in other centers of reform such as Zurich, was an outbreak of iconoclasm during efforts to sweep out the old faith. Luther's response was that to coerce people into gospel perspectives by forced reform was only to revert back to a religion of laws, and thus undermines the insight that justification is a free gift.

Tensions and conflicts between the German Reformers escalated in relation to the Peasants' War (1524–5) as Thomas Müntzer (ca. 1490–1525) joined the late phase of the war with the rallying cry that "the godless have no right to live." The extremely volatile mix of late medieval apocalypticism and oppressive social and economic conditions coupled with the Reformation motifs of the "freedom of the Christian" and theological critiques of canon law and papal authority, fueled the peasants' social and religious expectations for political and economic liberation, but horribly misfired at their disastrous defeat at Frankenhausen in 1525.

The emperor Charles V's (1500–58) military preoccupations with France (the Habsburg–Valois Wars, 1521–59) and the Ottoman Empire (Sultan Süleyman I the Magnificent, r. 1520–66) continually frustrated his efforts to eliminate the Reformation movements in his realm apart from his hereditary lands, the Low Countries. Charles also needed the support of the Protestant princes in his military campaigns. The Protestant princes presented a confession of their faith to the emperor at the 1530 Diet of Augsburg. Composed by Luther's colleague, Philip Melanchthon (1497–1560), the Augsburg Confession did not sway the Catholic emperor to rescind the Edict of Worms, but it did become the foundational document for Lutheran churches up to today.

The rejection of the Augsburg Confession led the Protestants to form a military alliance, the Schmalkald League, that protected the Protestant movement until its defeat by imperial forces in 1547. By this time, however, the evangelicals had gained sufficient strength that a series of settlements led finally to their toleration in the 1555 Peace of Augsburg, with the principle that the religion of the ruler would be the religion of the territory (*cuius regio, eius religio*, "whose reign, his religion").

The Reformation in Switzerland

The Reform movement in Switzerland proceeded along roughly parallel lines in Zurich under the leadership of Huldrych Zwingli (1484–1531), and then in Geneva under the leadership of John Calvin (1509–64). Unlike Luther, these Reformers lacked the protection of a benevolent and supportive prince and thus had to develop and implement their movements in cooperation (and tension) with their respective civic governments.

Zwingli's renown for biblical study and preaching led to his 1518 appointment by the city government to the major preaching post in Zurich. His commitment to the Reformation principle *sola scriptura* was evident immediately. His sermons, no longer based upon the church's lectionary, methodically exposited book after biblical book. By 1525 he had established "prophesyings," weekly Bible studies for the Zurich clergy and advanced students. A similar practice was established in Geneva in 1536 under Calvin. All of life, personal and communal, was to be normed by scripture.

Controversy, however, soon erupted on multiple fronts. At home, Zwingli and his colleagues found themselves in a double-fronted conflict with those who wanted to halt reforms and those who wanted to expand and radicalize them. Hugo, the bishop of Constance, whose diocese included Zurich, led the former; Conrad Grebel (1498–1526), the reputed founder of Anabaptism, led the latter. The Anabaptists (i.e., "re-baptists"), in applying biblical norms to faith and life, understood baptism to be contingent upon a mature confession of faith rather than a sacrament administered to infants who neither understood nor evidenced a Christian life. The Anabaptist confession of faith, the Schleitheim Confession (1527), also rejected what most of their contemporaries assumed were normal obligations of citizenship: oaths, tithes, and military service.

Added to these challenges facing Zwingli was the years-long dispute with Luther over the correct interpretation of the Lord's Supper. The German Lutheran prince Philip of Hesse, hoping for a united Protestant front against Catholic military forces, brought Luther and Zwingli to the negotiating table in Marburg in 1529. At the Marburg Colloquy the Lutherans and Zwinglians agreed on 14 of 15 articles. They repudiated transubstantiation and the belief that the mass is a sacrifice for the living and the dead, and they insisted upon communion in both kinds. However, the two evangelical parties remained apart on whether the Lord's Supper is primarily an act of thanksgiving for the gospel (Zwingli's symbolic and memorial view) or a concrete offer of the gospel (Luther's sacramental emphasis on Christ's real presence). The differing Protestant theologies of the Eucharist continued to be church dividing in spite of Calvin's later ecumenical efforts informed by his own emphasis upon the gift character of the sacrament. Calvin did achieve agreement with Zwingli's successor, Heinrich Bullinger (1504–75) with the Consensus Tigurinus (1549), but by this time many second generation Lutherans suspected this was more Zwinglian than Lutheran.

Unable to achieve recognition at the Diet of Augsburg in 1530, Zurich was vulnerable to Swiss Catholic pressures. In 1531 the Zurich forces were routed at the Second Battle of Kappel, during which Zwingli was killed. The consequent political resolution that divided Switzerland by confessional allegiance foreshadowed the fate of Europe.

At the time of Zwingli's death, Geneva had not yet adopted the Reformation and neither had its future Reformer-to-be, John Calvin, who was just completing his legal studies in France. Sometime in 1533–4 Calvin experienced his so-called "unexpected conversion." Trained in law and imbued with humanist learning, Calvin echoed Luther's fundamental understanding of salvation. In his *Institutes of the Christian Religion* Calvin described justification by faith in terms of God's acquittal of the guilty sinner.

In early 1535 Calvin sought refuge in Basel from the intensifying persecution of Protestants in his native France. Here he completed and published the first edition of his *Institutes* prefaced by a masterful appeal to king Francis I for a fair hearing of the evangelical faith. Calvin then concluded his affairs in France and set out for the city of Strasbourg where he hoped to settle down to a life of evangelical scholarship. Forced to detour through Geneva, Calvin was confronted by his compatriot, Guillaume Farel (1489–1565), who had been preaching reform in Geneva since 1532. Only months before Calvin's arrival in July 1536, Geneva had finally achieved independence, with the aid of its neighbor Bern, from the Duchy of Savoy and its imposed episcopal rule. The citizens voted to adopt the Reformation and to expel all clergy who disagreed. Farel, faced by the enormous task of institutionalizing reform in Geneva, made it clear in no uncertain terms to Calvin that God had sent Calvin to Geneva for precisely this task. Furthermore, Calvin was told that to shirk this duty would incur his damnation; Calvin stayed!

The reforming colleagues' emphasis upon church discipline soon alienated the Geneva council and many of its citizens. Exiled in 1538, Calvin now finally made it to Strasbourg where he spent the next years learning about institutional reform and church organization from that city's reformer, Martin Bucer (1491–1551). Here, too, he married. Geneva, now concerned about faltering reform, appealed to Calvin to return. Not without misgivings, but with the promise that he could develop a reformed order for the church, Calvin returned in 1541. Within six weeks of his return Calvin completed and submitted to the magistrates of Geneva his *Ecclesiastical Ordinances*. Soon ratified, the *Ordinances* organized the Genevan church according to four categories of ministry: doctors, pastors, deacons, and elders. The doctors were to maintain doctrinal purity through theological study and instruction. Pastors were responsible for preaching, administering the sacraments, and admonishing the people. Deacons were responsible for the supervision of poor relief and the hospitals. Elders were responsible for maintaining discipline within the community. The institutional organ for church discipline was the Consistory, a kind of ecclesiastical court, including the pastors and elders. The Consistory was a bone of contention through most of Calvin's career in Geneva due to its supervision of public morality and its power to excommunicate.

Challenges to Calvin's authority came not just from those who resented what they considered meddling by the Consistory. Two doctrinal debates threatened to unravel the fabric of "the most perfect school of Christ," as the Scottish reformer John Knox (1513–72) called Geneva. The first was a sharp public attack on Calvin's doctrine of predestination by Jerome Bolsec (ca. 1524–84), who claimed it was unbiblical. The charge that the Genevan reformers were unclear about a point of scripture was not a narrow theological challenge because the reform movement rested upon popular confidence in its biblical basis. Calvin's response was to reiterate that predestination is an expression of unconditional grace – God chooses the sinner, not vice versa. Bolsec himself was banished from Geneva.

The second controversy was the trial and execution of Michael Servetus (ca. 1511–53) for his denial of the doctrine of the Trinity. Already notorious throughout Europe for his written attacks on the Trinity, Servetus escaped execution in France (where the Catholics had to be satisfied with burning him in effigy) and ended up in Geneva where the Protestants did the "honor." From a political perspective, the Genevans were in a bind if they did not try and execute Servetus because the city had gained a reputation as the haven for heretics, but the operative motive was theological. It was this to which the Genevan schoolmaster exiled by Calvin, Sebastian Castellio (1515–63), responded when he wrote: "To burn a heretic is not to defend a doctrine but to kill a person." Castellio's *Concerning Heretics, Whether They are to be Persecuted* is one of the best known early modern pleas for religious toleration.

Calvin's Protestant contemporaries did not view Geneva as a vengeful theocracy. Thousands of religious refugees flocked to Geneva from nearly every province in France, as well as from England, Scotland, Holland, Italy, Spain, Germany, Poland, and Bohemia. When they returned home, they took Calvinism with them.

The Reformation in France

Once Calvin's leadership was established in Geneva, he and the French exiles living there directed an effective evangelization program toward France. Although French Calvinists were called Huguenots, they preferred the term Reformed. By 1567 over a hundred pastors sent from Geneva were organizing Reformed congregations patterned on the Geneva church. In 1559 the first national synod of the Reformed church in France met in Paris. Calvin himself provided the first draft of its confession of faith, the Gallican Confession. It was modified at the Synod of La Rochelle in 1571 and continues to inform French Reformed churches to this day.

The crown played a major role in the course of the Reformation in France. Until the late 1520s, reform-minded humanists and reformers found shelter under Francis I's enthusiasm for Renaissance humanism. But the Gallican tradition of "one king, one law, one faith" plus the crown's considerable power over the church guaranteed by the Concordat of Bologna (1516) precluded state endorsement of Reformation ideas. By 1516 Francis I had everything that the English king Henry VIII broke with the church to get. Thus, as Reformation ideas began to take root not only in the "middle class" but also in the nobles of the Bourbon (next in line for the throne after the ruling Valois) and Montmorency houses, the crown began a policy of persecution to root out Protestantism.

The resulting civil strife prompted the crown's call for a public Protestant–Catholic debate. Any hope that the Colloquy of Poissy (1561) would contribute to peace was dashed when Theodore Beza (1519–1605), Calvin's heir apparent in Geneva and leader of the Huguenot delegation, unequivocally rejected the bodily presence of Christ in the sacrament. To Beza and his colleagues, the Catholic belief that the mass was the community's supreme good work of offering and receiving the corporeal Christ was no more than idolatry and rejection of the gospel. The Catholic rage against such blasphemy was not merely a reaction to theological disputation, but reflected the offenses visited upon their faith by a generation of iconoclasts who had desecrated churches and holy objects, including the consecrated sacramental bread.

The crown's effort to overcome the failure at Poissy by an Edict of Toleration (January 1562) lasted barely two months before armed attacks on Huguenot congregations occurred, and the country sank into decades of conflict fueled by religious hatred. The most infamous event in the French Wars of Religion was the St. Bartholomew's Day Massacre (August 24, 1572), when thousands of Huguenots were massacred in a frenzy of state terrorism. A generation later, weary of bloodshed and assassinations, the Protestant Bourbon, Henry of Navarre, became king as Henry IV, converted to Catholicism ("Paris is worth a mass"), and set forth a policy of limited toleration in the Edict of Nantes (1598) that lasted until its revocation by Louis XIV in 1685.

The Reformation in England

The traditional view of the English Reformation as an act of state reflects Henry VIII's (1491–1547; reigned from 1509) break with Rome over his desire for a divorce. Indeed, the top-down imposition of ecclesiology continued in his heirs: Protestantism with Edward VI (1537–53); Catholicism with Mary Tudor (1516–58); and Protestantism with Elizabeth I (1533–1603). Yet, without gainsaying the significant roles of the various Tudors, the Reformation in England benefited from a residual Lollard anticlericalism, humanist interest in reform, and continental Reformation influences spread by young Cambridge scholars, pamphlets, Bible translations, the return of English students studying in the centers of Switzerland, and then the influx of Protestant refugees from continental Europe. Later, with the accession of Elizabeth I (1558), the Marian exiles returned from such Protestant centers as Frankfurt and Geneva and began to radicalize reforms in England in the direction of Puritanism.

English translations of the Bible were significant means of introducing Reformation ideas. William Tyndale (ca. 1494–1536), one of the most influential translators, carried out most of his work in exile on the Continent. His translation of the New Testament (first printed in 1525) utilized Luther's translation and included many of Luther's biblical prefaces. Miles Coverdale (1488–1568) assisted Tyndale in translating the Old Testament, and was responsible for the first complete English translation of the Bible (1535). Largely through the influence of Thomas Cromwell (ca. 1485–1540), Henry VIII's chief minister in state and church, and archbishop Thomas Cranmer (1489–1556), the king was persuaded to put the Bible in all the churches.

Theological ideas were not however the source for the English break with Rome, but rather the king's "great matter." Henry's marriage to his brother's widow, Catherine of Aragon, arranged for an alliance with Spain, necessitated a papal dispensation because Leviticus 18:6–18 prohibited marriages within close relationships. The only child to survive from the marriage was Mary Tudor. Henry wanted a male heir and hoped Anne Boleyn would do the honors. He appealed to pope Clement VII for an annulment on the biblical basis that one should not marry a brother's widow (Leviticus 20:21). Henry's demand put Clement in an ecclesiastical and political bind. If he granted an annulment he would undermine papal authority by reversing a previous pope's action. The political problem was that Clement was virtually a prisoner of the emperor Charles V (the Sack of Rome, 1527), who as Catherine's nephew was adamantly opposed to Henry's plan to divorce her. Henry's solution, after a long and convoluted process, was to get satisfaction through the English courts. To free himself from papal interference, Henry declared himself and his successors head of the Church of England (Act of Supremacy, 1534). Henry wanted Rome out of his realm, but not Catholicism. Hence the Act of Six Articles (1539) reaffirmed pre-Reformation orthodoxy.

Reformation theology – oriented to the Swiss Reformed – came to the fore during the reign of the child king, Edward VI (1547–53). Cranmer provided the Prayer Book (1549, revised 1552) and a statement of faith, the Forty-two Articles (revised to Thirty-nine Articles under Elizabeth). The tide was reversed with the accession of the ardent Roman Catholic Mary to the throne (1553–8). Ironically, her efforts to restore Catholicism strengthened Protestant resolve. Her marriage to Philip of Spain linked her faith to foreign influence; her efforts to restore church properties alienated their present owners; her persecution of Protestants created the host of martyrs celebrated by John Foxe's (1517–87) martyrology; and through the flight of hundreds of leading Protestants she exposed English Protestants to continental theology that they eagerly brought back upon her death.

The pendulum of reform swung to the middle with Elizabeth, whose long reign (1558–1603) facilitated the establishment of English Protestantism. Elizabeth's *via media* retained traditional vestments and an English liturgy with sermons and prayers normed by the Thirty-nine Articles. The theology of the Eucharist, perennial focal point of dispute, denied transubstantiation on the one hand and Zwinglian symbolism on the other, while remaining open to a range of Lutheran and Calvinist interpretations. As

"Supreme Governor" of the church (1559 Act of Supremacy), Elizabeth proceeded to appoint moderate clergy who conformed to her program. Significant support came from such apologists as John Jewel (1522–71; *Apology for the Anglican Church*) and Richard Hooker (ca. 1554–1600; *Treatise on the Laws of Ecclesiastical Polity*). Elizabeth responded to Catholic challenges by executing her Catholic rival, Mary Stuart, Queen of Scots (1587), and destroying the Spanish Armada (1588). The challenge from Calvinists of varying persuasions was a continual bother, with "Presbyterians" rejecting episcopal polity and "Puritans" striving to purify the church of all vestiges of Catholicism. Elizabeth charted a course between Catholicism and Calvinism because the former denied her legitimacy and the latter rejected the episcopacy she believed supported monarchy. In order to rule the Church of England through her bishops, she had to reject the decentralized polity of European Reformed churches and of Scottish Presbyterianism. Her successor, James I, agreed with his succinct phrase: "No bishop, no king."

Scandinavia and Eastern Europe

Humanism and Catholic reform movements prepared the ground for the introduction of the Reformation in Denmark, that then included Norway, Iceland, a number of provinces in present-day Sweden, and the associated duchies of Schleswig and Holstein where the Danish king was duke. Lutheran influences were evident in Schleswig already in the early 1520s, and king Christian III (r. 1534–59) officially established the Lutheran Reformation in Denmark in 1537. The king's own evangelical commitment may have begun when he saw Luther at the Diet of Worms; he later married a Lutheran, corresponded extensively with Luther, Melanchthon, and Bugenhagen on theological subjects, and provided economic support to the Wittenberg reformers. Christian appointed Luther's colleague, Johannes Bugenhagen

(1485–1558), known as the "Reformer of the North" for his introduction of the Wittenberg reforms throughout northern German cities and his native Pomerania, to lead the reform of the Danish church. Stationed in Copenhagen from 1537 to 1539, Bugenhagen led the reorganization of the church, ordaining seven Lutheran bishops, thus ending apostolic succession, and reforming the University of Copenhagen according to the model of the University of Wittenberg. Influential Danish theologians such as the bishops Peder Palladius, Hans Tausen, and Niels Palladius were trained at Wittenberg. In 1538 the Augsburg Confession was made the foundational document of the Danish church.

Olaus Petri and his brother Laurentius, previously students in Wittenberg, brought Luther's theology to Sweden-Finland. The Swedish king Gustavus Vasa (r. 1523–60) established the Reformation there in 1527. One consequence in Finland was the sending of Finnish students to Wittenberg, the most famous being Michael Agricola (ca. 1510–57). Agricola is known as the father of written Finnish through his prayer book (1544) and New Testament translation (1548). In Eastern Europe the Reformation was established in Prussia and Livonia but remained a minority movement in other areas.

Early Modern Catholicism

Well before Luther came on the scene, Catholic renewal found personal expression in such movements as the Beguines and Beghards (twelfth century), the Brethren of the Common Life or Devotio Moderna (late fourteenth century), and institutional expression in the conciliar movement (fourteenth century on) that called for reform of the church "in head and members." By the eve of the Reformation, Catholic Humanists and theologians were translating the Bible, preachers were endeavoring to instill piety and ethics, and confraternities and oratories provided vehicles for lay spirituality and charity. The continuation of medieval monastic reforming movements may be seen in Ignatius Loyola (1491–1556), founder of the Society of Jesus (Jesuits), whose interest centered on the promotion of pastoral and mission work rather than the reform of doctrine, and Teresa of Ávila (1515–82), whose mystical writings and work in reforming the Carmelite order remain influential.

On the other hand, the late medieval papacy's antipathy toward conciliarism was a major factor in blocking repeated Protestant calls for a council to deal with the issues raised by the Reformation. When the council finally began in 1546 in Trent, a generation of strife had hardened positions. Mediating efforts – for example, the 1541 Colloquy of Regensburg – had been rejected by both sides as compromises of the "truth."

The Council of Trent, in three distinct assemblies (1545–7, 1551–2, 1561–3), focused on the moral, spiritual, and educational renewal of the Catholic Church, and the refutation of Protestantism. The latter goal found expression in the council's repudiation of *sola scriptura* by stating tradition an equal source of revelation; the supplementation of *sola gratia* with human cooperation; and reaffirmation of the seven sacraments and the doctrine of transubstantiation. Papal authority, although not officially established in the modern sense until Vatican I (1870), was reaffirmed at the conclusion of the Council of Trent by the papal bull *Benedictus Deus* that reserved authentic interpretation of conciliar decrees to the pope.

The Reformations' Aftermath

By the close of the Council of Trent in 1563, Western Christendom was fragmented into "denominations" identified by particular confessions of faith. The hot lava of theological debates and religious innovations that had erupted and flowed over the medieval corpus Christianum solidified into three major communities – Roman Catholicism, Lutheranism, and Reformed Protestantism – each of which had formulated confessions of their beliefs. The consequent intramural and extramural theological conflicts stemmed from each church's effort to consolidate and institutionalize its understanding of the gospel. These efforts have been described under the general term "confessionalization." The confessionalization process was also political and social because all the confessional churches allied themselves with temporal rulers and states to preserve their confessional hegemony and, if possible, extend it to other territories. Non-confessional religious movements such as the Anabaptist and Jewish communities were isolated and marginalized. While on the one hand the confessional churches received legitimacy and support from their respective states, they on the other hand served the development of the modern state by promoting a unified, disciplined society of subjects.

In Protestant states the clergy were integrated into civic life not only by virtue of their participation in marriage and family life, but also by their involvement in the bureaucracy of the state as administrators of the church. In this respect the clergy were civil servants bound by their respective church constitutions and confessions of faith. In Roman Catholic states the administrative structure had similar functions, although it often was more complex. The churches played a significant role in advancing social discipline because they had a legitimacy that the early modern state was still in the process of acquiring in relation to moral, political, and legal norms. Sermons, pastoral care and visitations, religious education through instruction and catechisms, religious services, and the inculcation of discipline promoted the Reformations' sense of vocation in domestic and public affairs. The values of good behavior, honesty, learning, self-discipline, work, and obedience were thereby internalized and provided support for the social and economic transition to the modern European bourgeois society of the industrial age. This so-called "Protestant ethic" was not limited to the Calvinists and their Puritan offspring. Social discipline was a universal expression of confessionalism. For example, the Society of Jesus – the Jesuits – was clearly a meritocracy that rewarded precisely those values esteemed by the developing state and economy: learning, talent, hard work, and piety.

Chapter 9

Pietism and the Enlightenment

Pietism and the Enlightenment usher in a new period of Western Christianity. They may be viewed as siblings, with Pietism the older sister. It is difficult to pinpoint a specific turn from the confessional era to the period of Pietism and the Enlightenment. In the face of the devastation wrought by the religious wars of the Reformation era, capped by the Thirty Years' War (1618–48), it was necessary to begin rebuilding society, a process in which the churches played a role. Politically this is the period from the Peace of Westphalia (1648) to the end of the old Empire (1806). Theologically and philosophically this is the period from Spener's *Pious Desires* (1675) to Kant's *Religion within the Limits of Reason Alone* (1793).

Pietism, the most significant renewal movement since the Reformation, pressed for the individualizing and interiorizing of religious life. Pietism was also a transnational and transconfessional movement wherein Spanish Catholic mysticism influenced English Puritanism and English Puritanism and German Pietism cross-fertilized each other; comparable developments in France were Jansenism and Quietism. The considerable geographical and temporal relationships of these movements combined in implicit and explicit critiques of the establishment churches and prepared the soil for the Enlightenment's call for the emancipation of society from church authorities.

Pietism itself is difficult to define. The name gained currency in the late seventeenth century as a term of abuse and derision. The Pietists themselves, however, accepted the description provided in a poem of the time composed for the funeral of a pious theology student: "What is a Pietist? One who studies God's Word, and also lives a holy life according to it." In brief, then, Pietism as a movement was marked by intense study of the Bible and a focus on sanctification. It was also a strong lay movement. Its participants' diaries and autobiographies focused on conversion and inner life, and are the forerunners of modern, psychological introspection and analysis. Pietism was transdenominational not only in terms of the influences spreading from Roman Catholic mysticism through Puritan devotional literature to Lutheran piety, but also in its ecumenism of religious experience over doctrine. Indeed, one may argue that Pietism so focused on religious experience that it not only transcended, but also undermined the churches' confessions. Hence, Philipp Jakob Spener (1635–1705), the "Father of Pietism," has also been referred to as an impetus for theological liberalism. It is perhaps no accident that the major figures of the Enlightenment – Lessing, Kant, Schiller, Goethe, Fichte, and Schleiermacher – came from Pietist backgrounds. In a sense then, Pietism's efforts to protect the Christian faith from modernity by turning to experience reflected that very modernity. Pietism's borders have always been permeable – both theologically and chronologically. Theologically, the Pietist emphasis upon religious experience and holy living eroded confessional demarcations between Lutheran Orthodoxy, Reformed Puritanism, and Roman Catholicism, and stimulated the early Rationalism and Enlightenment of the Baroque period. Chronologically, the roots of Pietism extend back through such Reformation "enthusiasts" as Karlstadt and Müntzer into medieval mystical spiritualism and forward to modern charismatic movements. Furthermore, the influence of Pietism continues through its devotional writings and hymnody; most modern hymnbooks contain numerous hymns from the period of Pietism.

Faced by the complexity of Pietism, we shall take a very simple path leading from Arndt to Spener to Francke. We begin with Johann Arndt (1555–1621) not only because of his incredible influence but also because he exemplifies the positive connection of Pietism and Protestant Orthodoxy. It is not uncommon to find Pietism described as a reaction to Orthodoxy's fight for right belief during the post-Reformation confessional age. The Pietists' penchant for sloganeering no doubt contributes to this perspective. Their emphasis that the Christian life is a walk not a talk, a becoming not being, that heart religion opposes head religion, and that life is over doctrine, was succinctly summed up by the radical Pietist Christian Hoburg (1606–75), who stated: "Justification is fiction, rebirth is fact." In less extreme formulations, the moderate Pietists affirmed the continuation of the Reformation of doctrine by the Reformation of life. Arndt expressed this theme in the foreword to his immensely popular *Four Books on True Christianity*: "It is not enough to know God's word; one must also practice it in a living, active manner." Arndt's writings were so popular that their hundreds of editions overshadowed Luther's influence in the seventeenth and eighteenth centuries, and his *True Christianity* was reprinted in America by Benjamin Franklin.

Arndt addressed a different context than had Luther. Luther's proclamation of justification by grace alone through faith, the good news that salvation is received not achieved, addressed late medieval people who sought salvation by good works, pilgrimages, and indulgences. Thanks to the acceptance of that message, people's religious interest turned to the consequences of justification. What follows from faith? The emphasis shifted from justification to sanctification and rebirth, to the pious life.

Arndt wrote to supplement justifying faith, not to critique it. Nevertheless, he initiated a piety of interiority and introspection.

While Luther in his Small Catechism petitioned that the Kingdom of God may come *to* us, Arndt spoke of the Kingdom that will be established *in* us. Arndt's interiority did not lead to passivity and quietism. His emphasis on active, living faith stimulated a major renewal movement based upon practical Christianity. Johann Amos Comenius (1592–1670), the bishop of the Moravian Brethren and the most significant reform educator of the early modern period, reckoned himself among the students of Arndt. And Johann Valentin Andreä (1586–1654) dedicated his *Christianopolis* (1619), the first utopian social novel in Lutheran Germany, to Johann Arndt. Andreä pictured an ideal Christian social order developed upon platonic-communistic foundations, and took steps to institutionalize it. His Färber-Stift – founded in 1621 as a foundation for the poor, supported by citizens enriched by cloth-dying – is among the oldest social institutions of the early bourgeois period. After the Thirty Years' War, Andreä introduced in the Württemberg church the Calvinist church discipline he had learned in Geneva. However, the attempt failed because the nobility evaded moral supervision. Andreä lamented lazy Lutheran preachers whose ideal was "short sermons and long bratwursts." He increasingly viewed the "new papacy" of the state-controlled church as the strongest obstacle to any moral improvement.

These developments occurred in the context of the general deterioration of living conditions after 1600 culminating in the Thirty Years' War. The war undermined the unity of church and society. Furthermore, princely absolutism and the seeds of the Enlightenment began to emancipate political and intellectual life from the power of the confessional church bodies and their theological traditions.

The profound upheaval of the war cannot be underestimated. There is no doubt that rural populations suffered the most. City walls provided some protection from the fury of the conflicts, whereas rural towns and villages were totally unprotected. After that war, there was renewed war with the Turks. The Tatars invaded East Prussia in 1656–7 with the loss of some 100,000. In 1709 the plague returned and extended as far as Berlin, carrying away some 155,000. Under these drastic conditions the rural population largely withdrew from the spiritual and political life of the country. The bourgeoisie also had difficult lives. Tradesmen were increasingly oppressed by the rising money economy. And the large numbers of unemployed soldiers contributed to widespread begging and unrest.

Social distinctions were emphasized as never before. The nobles expressed their attitude toward the lower classes by creating physical boundaries. They insulated their homes by parks and iron fences, and their churches by separate areas for prayer and worship. At the Lord's Supper people came up according to class. The parish community reflected the social order of the secular society, and for the lower classes the church was a place of humiliation just like their everyday existence. One no longer spoke of the universal priesthood of the baptized, and the distinction between clergy and laity was reemphasized by the increasing separation of the clerical office from the people. The worst conditions in the cities fell on the laborers in the new manufacturing industries, especially the textile workers. The sharpening of class differences within church and society led to increasing criticism of the churches, which appeared ineffectual in ameliorating social conditions. Separation from the church and a homegrown atheism reached its high point between 1690 and 1730, and in turn stimulated a spate of reform proposals.

It was in this context that Spener presented a "theology of hope" that proclaimed a better future based upon the renewal of society through renewal of the church. In contrast to pessimism concerning the future fostered by the crises of the time, Spener spoke of the coming great time of mission possibilities to the whole world, of Judaism's turn to Christianity, and an overcoming of the Counter-Reformation.

Spener's *Pious Desires or heartfelt desire for a God-pleasing improvement of the true evangelical church* appeared in 1675 as the foreword to a new edition of Arndt's sermons. The church's lack of true, living faith was to be countered by bringing God's Word more fully into the church and world through reading and discussing the Bible in devotional assemblies. Thus Pietism became a Bible movement that strove to activate the universal priesthood of all believers (or at least all the reborn), shift the focus from the theory to the praxis of Christianity, limit confessional polemics, reform theological studies in the sense of the practice of piety, and finally redirect preaching to the edification and cultivation of the "inner man." Spener believed the improvement of the church possible for God promised a splendid future for his church.

The *Pious Desires* became the programmatic writing of Pietism. Spener desired to reform the church through the cultivation of the pious. Among other things, he demanded the revival of the universal priesthood and the freedom for lay activity in the church. The laity should have the opportunity to gather together with the clergy for common Bible study. The people are not to be "objects" of sermons and pastoral activity, but "subjects" to be involved in practicing Christianity by means of the meditative appropriation of the whole Bible. Meditation was also promoted as the means for personal application of the sermon, and for contemporizing the events of the Passion in relation to the Lord's Supper. The formation of voluntary circles within the church, known as the *ecclesiola in ecclesia* ("the little church in the church"), would be the avant-garde for the inbreaking Kingdom of God. At the same time, Spener guarded against the inclination to flee the world through his emphasis upon an active Christianity.

Spener's Pietism placed within Protestantism an active social-political will. In 1666, as the senior pastor in Frankfurt, he re-ordered the city's program of poor relief. He soon became widely known, and Frederick III in 1693 sought his opinion on reducing the widespread begging in Berlin. In one generation, Berlin had grown from about 30,000 to 50,000. Among this expanded population there were numerous discharged soldiers, widows, and orphans. The social need was indescribable; women and their daughters entered prostitution in countless numbers. Spener's plan was to use almsgiving to establish work places. Invalids, widows, and orphans should be cared for in humane fashion in public institutions, without regard to their class and denomination. The financing of social programs was by weekly door-to-door collections, and state subsidies for the discharged soldiers. In 1695 Frederick created a central poor relief fund, and in 1702 the Grosse Friedrichshospital arose, from which developed the Berlin Charité, an orphanage, and an insane asylum. Within two years after establishment, it was already supporting some 2,000 people.

Spener became head court preacher in Dresden in 1686, the highest clerical position in Protestant Germany. In 1691 he was called to Berlin where, protected by the Brandenburg-Prussian state, he defended the Pietist movement against the attacks of the Orthodox. He was able to place his Pietist friends and students in key positions of church and academic life. The far-reaching Pietist character of Halle University (established in 1694) was due to his influence as well as that of his young follower, August Hermann Francke (1663–1727). As a true patriarch of Pietism, Spener died in 1705 in Berlin viewed as the second greatest theologian in Lutheranism after Luther.

Francke – preacher and pastor, theologian and educator, incredible organizer – spent more than three decades developing the most historically significant form of Pietism, Halle Pietism. As a student he had experienced a sudden life-determining conversion after days of inner struggle. It made him certain of God's existence and his own rebirth. The importance of a sudden, datable, and one-time conversion – still alien to Spener – entered Pietism through Francke.

Through Spener's influence, Francke received an academic post as professor of Oriental languages in the new Prussian University of Halle and a pastoral charge in the Halle suburb of Glaucha. There he initiated pastoral and social programs that became legendary. The "Franckean Institutions" included an orphanage, training schools for teachers and pastors, various schools for different levels and classes of students, a *collegium orientale* for scripture study and translation, a publishing house, a science laboratory, and an apothecary. Francke titled his own account of these developments *The Footprints of the Still-Living God* (1701–9). This classic defense of Pietism was printed in English with the Latinized title *Pietas Hallensis* (1727) and influenced both the British Isles and the Atlantic coast of colonial North America. Some of Francke's writings were published in America, and the Boston Puritan Cotton Mather (1663–1728) carried on an extensive correspondence with Francke.

Francke's entrepreneurial ability enabled him to initiate the above-mentioned Institutions with only the few dollars he found left in his parish poor box and then raise the funds for an imposing series of Baroque buildings. He contributed a social advance in separating the orphanage from the poorhouse, the workhouse, and the house of correction. The orphanage itself was the most advanced of its time. Among other things it was a pioneer of modern hygiene. At a time when few took offense at bodily uncleanness, Francke and his colleagues insisted that children brush their teeth, bathe, and have clean clothes and bedding. Here, cleanliness was indeed next to godliness.

The reform of theological studies at Halle soon made it the most frequented faculty for theology students in all Germany, and then a center for foreign missions that extended to America in the West and Russia and India in the East. The study of theology was tied directly to praxis. For example, theology students interned in the hospital. They also learned rudimentary medical and pharmacological skills that, as the Halle missionary to America, Henry Melchior Muhlenberg (1711–87) learned, stood them in good stead in their missionary work. Francke introduced studies into his schools with the motto that a Christian "shall be equipped and sent out so that all the world may see that no more useful people may be found than those who belong to Jesus Christ."

Francke viewed holy living as serious business, and warned against unnecessary laughter at jokes and foolish things that distract the mind. His *Rules for Living* condemned laziness and stressed hard work and obedience to authority. His critique of luxury prohibited spending time on one's appearance, looking in the mirror, or being concerned for finery and jewelry. Francke's emphasis upon introspection is evident in his mandate for constant, diligent self-examination. In lines reminiscent of Loyola's *Spiritual Exercises* Francke exhorted his readers not to weary in examining their consciences. Works, words, desires, and ideas are to be scrutinized. Ideas and thoughts are to be controlled because "a child can more easily stamp out a spark than a hundred men can extinguish a raging fire."

Pietism's strongest moral influence was upon the ethics of the bourgeoisie. As Francke emphasized in his tracts on educating youth, the three central virtues of a God-pleasing life are love of the truth, obedience, and diligence. These virtues of industriousness, thrift, and obedience were obviously pleasing to early modern states. Precisely as demanders of bourgeois virtues the Pietists often found themselves at least indirectly to be supporters of state powers. The alliance of Pietism and the Prussian state occurred under the "Soldier-King" Friedrich Wilhelm I (1713–40). After some hesitation, Francke placed himself in the service of the Prussian state. His Institutions served to create industrious state servants, and Pietism gained special access to the army by providing field chaplains. The most important result of this symbiosis of state authority and piety was the obedient, conscientious, diligent, and selfless civil servant as represented especially in the ethos of the Prussian bureaucracy and officer corps.

Halle Pietism also echoed themes of English devotional literature that presented the ideal of individual praxis-oriented piety in a thoroughly rationalized, psychologically reflective manner relevant to the time's new drive toward analysis, order, and goal-directed thinking. English devotional literature was not confessional-specific but sought to concretize the ideal of the Christian life and make it feasible.

In England as in Germany the new conception of piety promoted personal meditation. One of the most influential devotional works was Lewis Bayly's (d. 1631) *Practice of Piety*. By 1636 it had gone through at least 36 editions in English, and by 1628 a German edition with the Latinized title *Praxis Pietatis* also went through many editions. The greater part of English devotional literature focused on sanctification, including denial of the self and contempt of the world in order to master the Christian's everyday life.

The rules of life are impressively concrete. Reflecting the contemporary fascination with natural science, especially the uncovering of hidden pathologies by the science of anatomy, the Christian life was anatomized into a network of individual rules that regulated the course of the day and especially the hallowing of Sunday. *Praxis Pietatis* meant the "systematic practice" of the Christian life. Richard Baxter (1615–91) exhorted his readers to think not only of consoling words but also to practice the rules he gave them. Practice brings advance in sanctification. When the motive of the pilgrim is evoked, then it comprehends not only the Christian's alienation from the earth but above all his goal-directedness: the Pilgrim's Progress.

The seventeenth century began with the ideal of a uniform state church reflective on a small scale of the old ideal of the corpus Christianum. But that ideal was not sustainable. States and cultures increasingly emancipated themselves from ecclesiastical control, and looked to standards derived from the "nature" of human life and society. Baroque music, for example, began shifting from worship settings to concert halls. The reverse also occurred, and thereby raised anxieties about secular incursion into sacred space and time. In brief, the pluralism initiated, although not intended, by the Reformation was becoming more and more apparent. There were now alternative modes of living and understanding life. What did this mean for Christians who now spent a good portion of their lives in the non-churchly aspects of this developing culture? What could that "Christianity" be that was not the standard and the motive for the whole life of the Christian?

Pietism provided a provisional and, it turned out, a less than helpful answer: the individualization and internalization of the faith. Cultural development and fragmentation could be ignored by seeking religious fellowship with the like-minded; by personal appropriation of religious truth that was no longer accepted as universal; by subjective religious experience and personal devotion and discipline. The downside of this orientation was the segregation of a certain sphere of life as religious, with the rest of life being secular by default. Pietists might lament this state of affairs, but adherents of the Enlightenment rejoiced in it and sought to expand it. In the process the Enlightenment was also heir to some of the fundamental emphases of Pietism: an anthropocentric orientation to religion rooted in personal experience, an orientation toward a better future, and a concern for morality that could be inculcated through education.

The Enlightenment

Unlike previous eras that looked back to classical culture or early Christianity, the Enlightenment was optimistically oriented toward the future in terms of continuing improvement. The modern Swiss theologian Karl Barth (1886–1968) described this period in terms of "absolutism" and the "desire for form." This may be seen in the popular use of plaster in Baroque architecture and the mastery of form in music from Bach to Mozart, as well as new theories of nature that dispensed with the God-hypothesis for scientific explanations. Alexander Pope (1688–1744) succinctly expressed the new orientation with this dictum:

"The proper study of mankind is man." Confidence in human capability found novelistic expression in Daniel Defoe's (1660–1731) *Robinson Crusoe*, whose hero masters nature and life when thrown back on his own resources. The conviction that the mastery of nature and human life resided in education led to a number of Enlightenment treatises, such as Gotthold Ephraim Lessing's (1729–81) *The Education of the Human Race*, Jean-Jacques Rousseau's (1712–78) *Émile, or Treatise on Education*, and Johann Heinrich Pestalozzi's (1746–1827) *How Gertrude Teaches Her Children*. These found pragmatic expression in the rise of teacher training schools. Immanuel Kant (1724–1804), the culmination of Enlightenment philosophy, himself defined the Enlightenment as "the emergence from a self-inflicted state of minority," and challenged his contemporaries to think for themselves, to "have the courage to make use of your own understanding."

Kant's summary definition of the Enlightenment capped a European-wide development. René Descartes (1596–1650), educated by the Jesuits, expressed the modern self-consciousness rooted in reason: *cogito ergo sum* – I think therefore I am! The existence of God becomes rational, and philosophy shifts from its role as the "handmaid of theology" (Aquinas) to a fundamental scientific discipline founded on empirical observations and rational principles. In England, Deism sought a firm foundation for religious propositions so that any person of sound mind and common sense could accept them. Edward Lord Herbert of Cherbury (1581–1648) reduced Christianity to five "reasonable" points: God exists; God is to be served; such service is a matter of morality not ritual; mistakes are to be regretted and made good; ethical living merits reward here and hereafter. Christianity was being reduced to God, moral freedom, and immortality. John Locke (1632–1704) understood Christianity in terms of tolerance, virtue, and morality, and wrote *The Reasonableness of Christianity as Delivered in the Scriptures*.

The drive toward the harmony of reason and revelation reflected battle fatigue from religious controversies; if Christianity could be reduced to reasonable essentials then causes of conflict could be removed. Theological reductionism was also a reflection of the growing awareness of the diversity of the world's religions. The Bible as the record of revelation transcending reason and nature was increasingly questioned. This shift is expressed in two important writings: John Toland's (1670–1722) *Christianity not Mysterious* and Matthew Tindal's (1655–1733) *Christianity as Old as the Creation, or the Gospel a Republication of the Religion of Nature*. The latter became the "Bible" of Deism, and was translated into German. Since Christianity contains nothing mysterious in opposition to human reason, then the miracle stories and resurrection reports are open to criticism.

The effort to reduce Christianity to reasonableness was dealt a major blow by the Scottish empiricist David Hume (1711–76), who was equally critical of metaphysics and theology on the basis that knowledge comes from sense experience and can be shown to be correct only when tested against further experience. In response to the appeal to an inherent religious sense, Hume noted that the earliest forms of religion were not archetypes of English civilization but gross anthropomorphic polytheisms. Primitive gods were mysterious, tricky beings who fell notably short of the moral conduct of humans. Hume's final critique of religion was an ethical one. Religion directs human attention away from life, and preoccupation with salvation is apt to make persons narrow and bigoted. Hume suggested the wise person avoid the disputes of the theologians provided he can make himself immune to their rancor and persecution.

In France, François-Marie Voltaire (1694–1778) used the concepts of English Deism to fight against the Catholic Church. His sharp wit made him a controversial figure. He generally rejected philosophical theories for God, but thought God remained an important presupposition for moral order and the prevention of anarchy. It is in this sense that his famous comment should be read: "If God did not exist, it would be necessary to invent him."

Fascination with the natural sciences – also a preoccupation among leading Pietists, who with their age saw "experience" and "experiment" as synonyms – found expression in the *Encyclopedia* (35 volumes) edited by Denis Diderot (1713–84) and Jean d'Alembert (ca. 1717–83). This monumental digest of eighteenth-century rationalism mediated Enlightenment ideas to the French bourgeoisie, including Francis Bacon's (1561–1626) view that human rule over nature would advance history on the path of freedom and human happiness. Rousseau posited that the future of humankind resides not in reason but the powers and feelings of the natural man, hence the alleged motto "back to nature." Persons are born good but society, culture, the state, and religion pervert humankind's naturally good faculties. Rousseau influenced others through his *The Social Contract*, which presented an ideal, natural order of the state as a democracy served by civil religion. Thus Rousseau has been regarded as a spiritual father of the French Revolution.

In Germany the Enlightenment was less critical toward the state and the church, perhaps because it coexisted with as well as derived from Pietism. Gottfried Wilhelm Leibnitz (1646–1716) emphasized that faith and reason may harmoniously coexist. He addressed the problem of theodicy, the justification of God in the face of evil in the world, by his thesis that our world is "the best of all possible worlds." Evil is based in the restrictedness of finite being. But reason may recognize the good and the divine as the essential structure of the world. Leibnitz's optimistic view of the world conceives of sin only as the imperfect good. However, the Lisbon earthquake (1755) that destroyed the city and tens of thousands of people severely shook his confidence that this is the best of all possible worlds. Voltaire's pessimistic *Candide* (1759) ends with the advice to retire to one's garden and withdraw from the horrors of history.

Since revelation had become suspect, Enlightenment theologians generally strove to depict Christianity in social-ethical terms. Hence, Jesus became the great teacher of wisdom and virtue, the forerunner of the Enlightenment who broke the bonds of error (not sin!) and served as a model for humankind. The Enlightenment also raised critical questions for the churches, not least of which concerned biblical authorship and Christian origins. Hermann Samuel Reimarus (1694–1768) claimed these origins were fraudulent. He viewed Jesus as a failed political messiah whose resurrection was fabricated by the disciples to counter their disappointment and to gain recognition in the world. Reimarus' arguments were published by Gotthold Ephraim Lessing (1729–81) with the (mistaken!) rationale that they would stimulate constructive discussion of the meaning of Christianity. Lessing's own position is summarized in his famous line: "The accidental truths of history can never be the proof for the necessary truths of reason." In other words, historical testimony of revelation cannot provide certainty of its truth. Historical religions, he argued, are stages of a divine process of education toward the true religion of love and reason. In Lessing's *Nathan the Wise* there is the parable of the ring where the true ring cannot be distinguished from two perfect imitations; hence each of the three heirs should live as if the father's true ring was given to him. The truth of real religion is manifest in its experience and practice.

The reduction of Christianity to morality "peaked" in Immanuel Kant. Nurtured in Pietism, he went off to a Pietist school at the age of eight. There he encountered Pietism's dark side: hypocrisy. It has been suggested that this context instilled in him such an abhorrence of religious emotion that he avoided church services altogether. A famous account relates that when made rector of the University of Königsberg he led the customary academic procession to the cathedral for the inauguration of rectors, but deserted the procession at the church. He was born and reared in Königsberg, attended the university there, became professor of philosophy there, and died there without ever going outside the borders of the province – clearly a challenge to the old adage that travel broadens the mind!

Kant provided the classic definition of the Enlightenment as the emergence from a self-inflicted state of minority. A minor is one who is incapable of understanding without guidance from someone else. This minority is self-inflicted whenever its cause lies in a lack of determination and courage to make use of one's reason without the supervision of another. Dare to use your own understanding is therefore the watchword of the Enlightenment. Kant championed autonomy, but did not mean doing whatever one pleases. Rather, true autonomy – self-law – is obedience to the universal law of reason. This is what makes Kant's age, as he says, the true age of criticism. Everything must be subjected to criticism. Every form of heteronomy (i.e., authorities external to the person that compromise autonomy, whether parents, society, state, church, or understandings of God) must be critiqued. Reason itself may not be excluded from criticism in order that in its critical use reason can be sure of itself.

Kant based religion as a moral system on his maxim "I ought, therefore I can." A person cannot be held responsible unless capable of doing something about his or her situation. Every sensible person will realize that the experience of oughtness leads to the moral mandates: "Treat every person as an end not as a means," and "Act solely on that principle which could become a universal law governing everyone's actions." The latter is known as the "categorical imperative." Faith is understood in terms of the duty to fulfill one's knowledge of the good. Pure religious faith, that is, morality, has no need for the church. The title of Kant's work on religion summarizes his viewpoint: *Religion within the Limits of Reason Alone.*

In limiting Christianity to reason, Kant inverted the order of the Reformation. Instead of good works flowing from grace, Kant begins with good works and reads all theological subjects in this light. Hence, Christ is viewed not as the Redeemer but as the moral archetype or model of the godly life to be imitated by humankind. Instead of God's descent to humankind, humankind is to ascend to God's commands. Autonomy is destroyed by anything applied from outside the self, including the grace of God. If God forgives; if God has mercy on whom he wills, then humankind is not free. Kant takes the side of Pelagius in the old battle over grace and free will. The one fly in Kant's ointment was the problem of "radical evil," which he acknowledged he could not resolve. But if evil is radical, it is also irrational, and there goes reason alone. This was shocking to Kant's Enlightenment contemporaries, whose optimistic rational concepts of God and humankind excluded sin and evil. Hence Goethe's pithy comment summarized the reaction of the day: in speaking of radical evil, Kant "slobbered" on his philosophical mantle.

The Catholic Church and the Enlightenment

In general, the Roman Catholic Church and its theologians were far less open to the Enlightenment than Protestant theologians. To the Roman Catholic Magisterium (teaching authority), in particular, the Enlightenment appeared as the destruction of Christendom. In the first half of the eighteenth century there were still a few late actions in the spirit of the Counter-Reformation: The "church of the wilderness" (Camisards or "French prophets," fanatical, ecstatic French Calvinists) was persecuted by Louis XIV in France, and evangelicals were expelled from the archbishopric of Salzburg in 1731. Also the Jansenist (a Catholic reforming movement) controversy broke out again, and led to another papal condemnation. Jesuit influences and pressures for orthodoxy unleashed such a storm of outrage in France, Portugal, and Spain that pope Clement XIV suspended the Jesuit order in 1773.

The concept of "Josephinism" showed however that the Enlightenment had also penetrated into the Catholic Church. The Austrian ruler Joseph II (r. 1780–90) attempted to bring the church under the rule of Enlightenment absolutism. This meant complete independence of the Austrian Catholic Church from Rome, reduction of the number of monasteries, reform of the theological formation of the clergy, and simplification of worship in the sense of a rational-ethical piety. Toleration (1781) gave Protestants the same civil rights as Catholics, as well as the right to exercise religion. This national church effort at reform was later withdrawn.

In Germany the bishoprics of the Rhine and Würzburg grasped the spirit of the Enlightenment and directed a popular reform Catholicism and an episcopacy independent of Rome. A book by the Trier suffragan bishop Johann Nikolaus von Hontheim (1701–90) under the pseudonym Justinius Febronius claimed that only the council of bishops, not the pope, is infallible; papal primacy is only a primacy of honor; and that the German Catholic Church should be independent of Rome. In 1786 the archbishop-electors summarized and again asserted these reform demands, but without success. Disunity among the bishops, lack of support from the Catholic state, and the outbreak of the French Revolution led to the victory of the papacy over Febronianism.

Chapter 10

Challenge and Response: The Church in the Nineteenth Century

Historians sometimes conceptualize the nineteenth century as the "long century" that begins with the French Revolution (1789) and concludes with the outbreak of World War I (1914). Parallel events in the history of theology are the Romantic affirmation of liberalism in Friedrich Schleiermacher's (1768–1834) *On Religion: Speeches to its Cultured Despisers* (1799) and the rejection of liberal theology in Karl Barth's (1886–1968) *Romans Commentary* (1918).

In general, nineteenth-century developments put the churches on the defensive. The Enlightenment and the rise of the natural sciences challenged biblical revelation and the foundations of the faith. Ludwig Feuerbach (1804–72) questioned the existence of God, and had the audacity to claim that theology, "the queen of the sciences," had no clothes when he stated that theology is anthropology. David Friedrich Strauss (1808–74) questioned the historicity of Jesus and described the Son of God as a myth. And for those who heeded Karl Marx's (1818–83) clarion call to socialism, that myth was not benign but an opiate that fogged the minds of the masses. In addition, the social consequences of the French and the industrial revolutions called into serious question the churches' relevance to society and culture.

It appeared to the churches that the barbarians were at the gates. In general, the Roman Catholic response was to lock the gates as securely as possible; to shut out the modern world if it could not be destroyed. The Protestant churches were not immune to this temptation – the rise of fundamentalism is a case in point – but also attempted to dialogue with the barbarians. These dialogical efforts became preoccupied with trying to ascertain the "essence" of Christianity in order to demonstrate that in its core the Christian faith was not antithetical to the modern world but rather supported the best it had to offer. On the social level, both the Catholic and Protestant churches promoted the faith through a variety of associations that ministered to the manifold needs of those wounded by the upheavals of the times.

The Churches and the French Revolution

The French Revolution promoted the ideas of popular sovereignty and democracy and the concepts of liberty, fraternity, and equality. People responded with either enthusiastic agreement or suffering dissent. On the one hand, political aspirations going back to medieval conciliarism sought political-social realization. On the other hand, the advance of the Revolution called forth multiple counter-reactions that pressed for the restoration of pre-revolutionary conditions. The Revolution furthermore accelerated the long history of criticism of the churches' influence. Pietism and the Enlightenment provided a strong practical and conceptual impetus for these developments, but it is in the nineteenth century that secularism proceeded beyond the upper middle class and created the modern context of the church.

Industrialization also profoundly changed the lives of people in the cities and the countryside. Charles Dickens vividly portrayed the degradation of urban living conditions in social novels such as *Oliver Twist* (1838) and *David Copperfield* (1850). The rise of a worker-proletariat and the rapid growth of cities created unimaginable problems, and consequently the modern mass collective that in socialist movements strove for power and its share of the communal pie.

The churches found themselves in a struggle to retain at least influence if not control over schools, marriage, public morality, nationalism, and science. By and large, nationalists and secularists did not desire to kill the churches but to conform them to the rationale of the state, and to establish reason over revelation for the common interest of society. Even those who emphasized churchly authority as the guarantee of tradition and legitimacy did so for reasons of state and strove to prohibit the churches from expressing political interests. Monarchs throughout Europe repeatedly emphasized that, as Wilhelm II of Prussia put it, "pastors ought to attend to the souls of the faithful and cultivate charity, but let politics alone for it does not concern them."

From the French Revolution to the Congress of Vienna

The Roman Catholic Church, profoundly tied to the old regime, shared to a great extent the fate of the absolute state in the French Revolution. For the first time in Europe the centuries-old connection of church and state was dissolved. The earlier American war of independence also separated church and state, but not by antagonism to the church. There Christianity and the free churches were rather an important factor for the people and politics.

The French National Assembly (1789–92) secularized church property, dissolved monasteries, and provided the "Civil Constitution for the Clergy." The latter subordinated church administration to the state; placed election of bishops and priests with the citizens; determined clerical income; released clergy from obedience to foreign authority (the papacy!); and demanded an oath of loyalty to the nation and constitution by all the clergy. During the Reign of Terror (1793–4) the government abolished the Christian calendar, prohibited Christian festivals, declared marriage a purely civil concern, pillaged and destroyed many churches, and set up the cult of reason in place of worship.

Napoleon Bonaparte restored the Catholic Church in the Concordat of 1801. The Catholic Church was recognized as the majority church of the French, but remained subordinate to state oversight. In 1804 Napoleon had pope Pius VII come to France to crown him emperor. At the ceremony, Napoleon overturned the tradition that had begun with the crowning of Charlemagne in 800 – he took the crown from the pope's hands and crowned himself! Popes no longer "made" emperors. In 1809 France incorporated the Papal States. Pius responded by excommunicating Napoleon, who then imprisoned the pope. Pius' resistance during these "troubles" contributed to the enhancement of papal prestige after the fall of Napoleon in 1815.

Prussia was drawn into the maelstrom of change through the coalition war against France, but was defeated at Jena and Auerstadt. French influence now led to the introduction of the Napoleonic Code, a collection of civil legislation that included civil equality, freedom of religion, equality of the confessions, and a non-confessional state. However, national and liberal reform movements were shoved aside by the new political order created at the Congress of Vienna (1815). State and church sought mutual support – the so-called alliance of "Throne and Altar" – and efforts were made to thwart constitutional and national aspirations. The repressed desires for reforms, however, broke out in numerous uprisings – the July Revolution in France in 1830 and the 1848 revolutions in Switzerland, France, and Prussia.

Church Reform in Germany: The Prussian Union and its Consequences

The cataclysms of the Revolution and the Napoleonic era forced continual reorganization of the churches. Prussia, predominantly

Lutheran, now also included a number of Reformed territories whose confessional commitments had to be taken seriously. On the personal level, the Reformed ruler Frederick Wilhelm III (1770–1840) was married to a Lutheran and wanted to share communion with her. The 300th anniversary of Luther's "Ninety-five Theses" in 1817 provided what the crown thought to be an appropriate occasion for uniting the two major Reformation churches. But widespread clergy opposition arose when the king intervened in affairs of the churches and mandated uniformity of worship according to his own liturgical creation. In opposition to the Prussian Union thousands of Lutherans emigrated to North America and Australia. A cabinet order of 1834 granted the Lutheran and Reformed churches continuing existence as specific confessions, and thus the Prussian Union brought forth three Protestant communities: Lutheran, Reformed, and United; a unified Union Church did not develop.

Inner Mission and the Social Question

The Francke Institutions at Halle, Pietism's efforts to transform the world by transforming individuals, were forerunners of nineteenth-century Protestant efforts to respond to social issues through the Inner Mission (i.e., service within the country in distinction from foreign mission) and the deaconess movements. These two movements soon became interrelated and addressed the same social miseries that called forth Marx's famous "Manifesto." The major figures of the Inner Mission and the development of the female diaconate are, respectively, Johann Hinrich Wichern (1808–81) and Theodore Fliedner (1800–64).

Wichern, a Hamburg pastor stunned by the impoverishment of the masses, began rescue homes for neglected and delinquent children. His initial effort, begun in 1833, emphasized education and job training in the context of God's forgiving grace. He then enlisted and trained assistants for this work, initiating what would become deacon and deaconess training institutes. In 1844 he began publishing a newspaper to arouse social conscience. Wichern was concerned that the future of both Christianity and society was jeopardized by the growing alienation of the urban masses from a seemingly uncaring state church. In 1848, some months after the appearance of Marx's "Communist Manifesto" and the outbreak of revolution in Berlin, Wichern issued a "Protestant Manifesto" at a meeting of the evangelical churches in Wittenberg.

In this long (2 hours!) rhetorical *tour de force*, Wichern proclaimed "love no less than faith is the church's indispensable mark." The church would have a future if it would only incarnate God's love in the industrialized cities. His forceful speech led to the formation of the Central Committee of Inner Missions of the German Evangelical Church.

"Redeeming love" was to awaken the whole society, and transform the church from an authoritarian establishment into a fellowship in which the laity would rediscover its mission as the universal priesthood to respond to the spiritual and social plight of society. The chief aims of the Inner Mission included reclaiming those who had left the church, and assisting the needy, sick, and poor. Wichern's initial advocacy for self-help associations broadened to include prison reform as well as care for the homeless, the mentally and physically disabled, immigrants, and seamen. The Inner Mission soon spread to other European countries and to America. It eventually became an umbrella agency for a wide variety of activities including social welfare work and services.

Wichern's work was not, of course, an isolated expression of Christian faith. Throughout Europe at this time religious renewal movements inspired social concern for the masses of people pauperized by industrialization. The Methodists in England had long been laboring at adult education, schooling, reform of prisons, abolition of slavery, and aid to alcoholics. Famous missions arose in Basel, London, and Paris. The YMCA (1844), YWCA

(1855), and Salvation Army (1865) were only some of the numerous Christian efforts to respond to the ills of modern society.

The revival of Christian service came not only through the Inner Mission, but also through the development of the deaconess movement by the German pastors Fliedner and Wilhelm Loehe (1808–72) who, among others, greatly desired the renewal of a women's ministry in the church.

In 1823 one of the precursors of the deaconess movement, Amalie Sieveking (1794–1859), began a sisterhood analogous to the Roman Catholic Sisters of Charity. During the 1831 Hamburg cholera epidemic she appealed to others to join her in nursing the sick. Undeterred by the lack of response, she carried on to become the director of the cholera hospital. In 1832 she organized a women's society for the care of the sick and the poor in Hamburg that served as an inspiration to Fliedner.

Fliedner's first steps toward the development of the female diaconate began with work on behalf of prisoners inspired by the English Quaker Elizabeth Fry (1780–1845) and the Mennonite deaconess movement he had observed in Holland. In 1833 a discharged woman prisoner came to the Fliedner parsonage in Kaiserswerth for help. The Fliedners lodged her in their garden house. Thus began the famous Kaiserswerth Institutions. Other discharged women prisoners as well as women in need began arriving, and the Fliedners trained them to serve others. The first Protestant deaconess motherhouse, established in Kaiserswerth in 1836, provided a structured environment of mutual support and a training center. Their ministry extended beyond helping released prisoners to serving the sick, orphans, and others at the margins of society. This is the origin of the Rhenish-Westphalian Deaconess Association, a model for dozens of similar associations that sprang up throughout Europe. By 1884 there were 56 deaconess communities with 5,653 deaconesses.

In addition to training deaconesses, the Fliedners also trained salaried Christian nurses. The experience of the pioneer English nurse Florence Nightingale (1820–1910) at Kaiserswerth informed her service in the Crimean War and the shape of her own school of nursing. By that time deaconesses from Kaiserswerth were serving in hospitals in England, America, Jerusalem, Constantinople, and Alexandria.

Loehe, Fliedner's contemporary, established a deaconess house in Neuendettelsau based on his conviction that Christian service flowed from fellowship grounded in the eucharistic liturgy. He organized a society for Inner Mission, and promoted foreign missions as well. The Neuendettelsau Foreign Mission Society trained people for work in America, Australia, and Brazil, and continues to this day.

The Inner Mission and diaconal movements increasingly came to understand the role that economic and social conditions such as work environments, unemployment, underemployment, and discrimination played among people the church sought to serve. Thus there was growing sensitivity to the view that diaconal work must encompass the political as well as the personal and congregational realms. One of the pastors who responded to these concerns was Rudolf Todt (1839–87). His *Radical German Socialism and Christian Society* agreed with the socialist analysis of class struggle, industrial exploitation of workers, social alienation, and mass poverty. He viewed proletarian revolt as legitimate emancipation from oppression, but advocated reform over revolution. Although he shocked many of his clerical contemporaries, and Bismarck considered banning his writings, Todt's National Association for Social Reform and its newspaper did help prepare the way for later social legislation.

Another challenge to the alliance of throne and altar came from a young pastor in an industrial parish in Saxony, Friedrich Naumann (1860–1919), who had worked with Wichern. Naumann and his colleagues opposed any form of Christian paternalism, and desired to work with social democrats to develop a party of radical reform. Bitter controversies resulted, and by the 1890s the Christian socialists of the Naumann school were denounced not only by Kaiser Wilhelm II but also by the Prussian Protestant church. Pastors were told to stay out of politics. Naumann himself resigned from the ministry, entered politics, and in 1919 participated in drafting the Weimar constitution as a member of the National Assembly.

Another pastor who entered politics to promote social reform was Friedrich von Bodelschwingh (1821–1910). In 1872 he accepted the directorship of the Rhenish-Westphalian home for epileptics and its deaconess home. Named Bethel, the center grew to include a training school for deacons, a theological school, and a home for destitute workers. Bodelschwingh's concern for the rehabilitation of the sick and the outcast led him to enter politics. Elected to the Prussian Diet in 1903, he secured passage of a law in 1907 that provided homes for itinerant workers. By this time the government began to favor such measures as means to undermine the socialist movement.

Bodelschwingh's son, of the same name (1877–1946), succeeded him as administrator of Bethel. The home was further enlarged, its medical facilities improved, and its research into the treatment of epilepsy expanded. At the beginning of the German church struggle against Hitler's effort to assimilate the church into the state, Bodelschwingh was elected national bishop, but the Nazi state nullified the election. He and his friends later led the opposition to the Nazi proposal to destroy all "life not worthy of living" and thereby protected the residents of Bethel and other institutions. Bethel continues to be a model of educational, therapeutic, and ecumenical diaconal work.

In spite of these and other exemplary efforts, evangelical social work in the nineteenth century remained a bourgeois concern; it gained little access to the industrial workers. The Inner Mission and diaconal movements were limited by their independence from the evangelical state churches, and by Protestant attachment to the government's opposition to socialism, communism, and democracy.

The response in America to comparable effects of industrialization and urbanization found voice and focus in the Social Gospel movement of the late nineteenth and early twentieth centuries. Washington Gladden (1836–1918), a Congregationalist minister, promoted the right of labor to organize. His many writings and hymns (e.g., "O Master, Let Me Walk with Thee") advocating Christian responsibility for social problems made him the "father" of the Social Gospel. The best known voice of the Social Gospel was the Baptist minister and professor Walter Rauschenbusch (1861–1918), whose *Christianity and the Social Crisis* (1907) gained international attention. He and his colleagues were oriented to a liberal Protestantism that stressed the realization of the Kingdom of God as the Christian goal. Their stress on social ethics modeled by Jesus is evident in the titles of some of Rauschenbusch's books (e.g., *Christianizing the Social Order* and *The Social Principles of Jesus*) as well as popular works directed toward the laity (e.g., William Stead's *If Christ Came to Chicago* and Charles Sheldon's immensely popular *In His Steps* – 25 million copies sold!). Rauschenbusch himself influenced progressive politics both at home and abroad; those who sought his advice included Theodore Roosevelt, Lloyd George, and Woodrow Wilson. However, World War I and then the Prohibition movement eroded the contributions of the Social Gospel.

The Catholic Church in the Nineteenth Century

After Napoleon's downfall, the Bourbons were restored to the French throne, and the papal states were restored to pope Pius VII. Conservatives presupposed that only a church supported by political authority could motivate and maintain the social bonds of society, and this stimulated a yearning for a unified Christian culture. The early Romantic movement transfigured the Middle Ages into such a culture. English Romanticism expressed the same fervor for Anglicanism as their French and German contemporaries did for Catholicism. A growing Catholic consciousness believed that only a strengthened papacy could renew the Catholic Church and thereby Western civilization.

Pius VII returned to Rome in 1814 after the abdication of Napoleon. The papacy regained its political freedom, and the Curia promoted the universal church against all tendencies toward national churches. The centralization of power in the papacy in opposition to national churches is known as ultramontanism (*ultra montes* – "beyond the mountains"). The restoration of the Papal States – a major thorn in the flesh of Italian aspiration for the unification of Italy – provided temporal security to a previously embattled papacy. In 1814 the pope reinstated the Jesuit order, whose influence continually increased in the course of the nineteenth century. The Jesuit ultramontanist offensive, abetted by an active Catholic press, expressed the anti-modernist spirit through revivals of medieval piety such as devotion to the Eucharist, the Sacred Heart, and Mary.

Pope Pius IX and Vatican I

Pius IX (r. 1846–78) focused the struggle against modernism. In 1854 he declared the first significant Marian dogma of the modern period: the Immaculate Conception of Mary. The dogma stated that Mary from the moment of her conception was free from all taint of original sin through a miraculous act of the Holy Spirit. Although a subject of medieval argument, this Marian dogma was proclaimed by Pius IX without consulting a council. The power of the pope to define dogma was a *fait accompli* even before it was justified by the dogma of papal infallibility.

In 1864 the "Syllabus of Errors" condemned rationalism, socialism, communism, Bible societies, and state independence in cultural and educational matters. Ultramontanist Catholicism rejected the separation of church and state, religious liberty, and public education without clerical control; and asserted the authority of the Catholic hierarchy to regulate public affairs. Civil legislation of marriage and divorce was not valid unless in conformity to canon law. The Catholic Church had the right to its own courts and police powers. The lasting impact of this upon the public imagination is exemplified by the specter of papal power raised during the election campaign of the American Catholic John F. Kennedy in 1960.

These developments culminated in the first Vatican Council (1869–70), which defined papal infallibility. The pope is infallible when he speaks "ex cathedra," that is, in the exercise of his teaching office on questions of faith and morals. Such infallible decisions must be made for the whole church and the foundation of faith "preserved holy and interpreted truly." Infallibility in doctrinal decisions was based in the papal decision not in the agreement of the church. Roman Catholicism became an absolute monarchy without constitutional restraints.

From Kulturkampf *to the Anti-Modernist Oath*

In general, the *Kulturkampf* refers to the clash of the Catholic Church with the spirit of liberalism and nationalism in the nineteenth century. In the narrower sense it was the struggle between the Prussian prime minister and chancellor Otto von Bismarck (1815–98) and the Roman Curia.

Bismarck wanted the churches, including the Protestant churches, out of state and political matters, and to confine them strictly to religious matters. Anti-Catholic legislation (1871–5) prohibited use of the pulpit for political agitation, expelled the Jesuits and related orders, and created state supervision of education. The so-called May Laws (1873) limited the disciplinary power of the church, instituted a Supreme Ecclesiastical Court, and mandated state control of all seminaries, including a state examination for all clergy. Pius IX condemned these laws in 1875 as subversive of the rights of the Church. Bismarck underestimated the strength of Catholic and Protestant opposition to these laws, and since he also desired Catholic support in his opposition to social democracy, he gradually reversed his policy.

Pope Leo XIII (r. 1878–1903) eased tensions with his encyclical *Rerum Novarum*, the so-called "Magna Carta" of Catholic social teaching. It began with a strong defense of private property and condemned socialism and anarchism, but it also endorsed the grievances of the working class against their employers. Leo laid the blame for the intolerable inequities of capitalism and the industrial age at the feet of the powerful and the rich. The state is to be responsible for the common good; no class is to be exploited for the advantage of another; and there should be appropriate state actions to alleviate child labor and excessive working hours. Workers should receive a just wage to support their families. Leo's application of "Christian principles" to capital –labor relations won him the title "the working man's pope."

Leo maintained many of Pius IX's antagonisms toward the modern world. Since the end of the nineteenth century, reform-minded Catholics had fought against reactionary curialism for greater freedom in theology. Pius X (1903–14) condemned these efforts as "modernism," and all Catholic theologians had to take the so-called "anti-modernist oath" (1910, abrogated in 1967) before receiving a church office.

Nineteenth-Century Theology

Nineteenth-century German evangelical theology was particularly rich and pluralistic. Variations of Orthodoxy, Pietism, and the Enlightenment continued to exert influence, but in competition with new developments such as "liberalism" and "culture-Protestantism." The towering figure of these developments was Friedrich Daniel Ernst Schleiermacher (1768–1834). His many theological works included his early apologetic masterpiece *On Religion: Speeches to its Cultured Despisers* and a comprehensive dogmatics, *The Christian Faith*, that ranks with Calvin's *Institutes*. His modern critic Karl Barth wrote: "The first place in a history of theology of the most recent times belongs and will always belong to Schleiermacher, and he has no rival."

Schleiermacher took seriously the Enlightenment critiques of religion in general and Christianity in particular. He was convinced that faith loses its life when it tries to protect itself through self-defensive strategies. Thus he prefaced his dogmatics with Anselm's famous lines: "Nor do I seek to understand, in order that I may believe, but I believe, in order that I may understand. For he who does not believe, does not experience, and he who does not experience, does not understand." For Schleiermacher, the Christian community had to express its faith as clearly as possible in its particular context.

The Enlightenment and its development in Idealism stressed human freedom and autonomy. In conjunction with the natural sciences, the philosophers' turn to empirical experience reduced talk about the supernatural to the natural. Schleiermacher met this challenge on its own ground. He too began with experience; but in contrast to his age's infatuation with freedom, he spoke of human dependence. The experience of God is not dependent upon either intellectual abstractions or compulsions to believe unbelievable things, but rather is rooted in human experience itself as dependent experience. Hence his famous description of faith as "the consciousness of being absolutely dependent, or, which is the same thing, of being in relation to God." The Christian faith is not believing certain doctrines, living a certain way, or having heart-warming experiences, but rather living in relationship with God. That relationship focuses on Jesus of Nazareth as the mediator of faith that becomes real in the fellowship of believers, the church.

The Awakening

The "Awakening Movements" were, like Pietism, transconfessional religious upheavals beginning in England and North America and moving to the European continent. Their common marks included opposition to the Enlightenment; the seriousness of human sin before God; the new life dependent only on the grace of Christ; individual personal experience of rebirth; the rebirth of the individual leading to the restructuring of society; increased social activity and missionary efforts to spread the Christian faith.

The Awakenings spread through preaching, revivals, camp meetings, tract literature, and Bible and mission societies. The many waves of Awakening in England and North America were about a century earlier than in Germany. The rigorous New England Calvinism of the First Great Awakening epitomized by Jonathan Edwards' (1703–58) sermon "Sinners in the Hands of an Angry God" (1741) gave way to a more Arminian theology in the later revivals of the Second Great Awakening at the end of the eighteenth century. The latter sense of personal initiation of the process of salvation carried over into the evangelical abolitionist, temperance, and suffragist-feminist movements. The English Awakening reached its high point in the rise of the Methodist movement founded by the Anglican clergyman John Wesley (1703–91), whose efforts to renew spiritual life among the people were supported by his hymn-writing brother Charles Wesley (1707–88) and the evangelist George Whitfield (1714–70).

Methodist preaching spread revival throughout England, Scotland, Ireland, and North America. It called for personal discipleship to Christ; aimed at conversion under penitential struggle and the experience of grace; and led to strong communal expressions. Wesley's lay preaching office is characteristic for the Methodist movement. After Wesley's death, Methodism separated from the Anglican state church.

The Oxford Movement (1833–45) in the Anglican Church responded to the decline in church life, the spread of "liberalism" in theology, growing interest in the early and medieval church stimulated by Romanticism, and anxiety that the Catholic Emancipation Act (1829) would facilitate conversions to Roman Catholicism. The Oxford Movement's defense of the Church of England as a divine institution, the doctrine of apostolic succession, and the Book of Common Prayer as a rule of faith have played important roles in Anglican theology and ecclesiology up to today.

The concerns of the Oxford Movement were expressed through its *Tracts for the Times*, of which one of the most famous authors was John Henry Newman (1801–90). His *Tract No. 90* (1841) caused a major controversy by interpreting the Thirty-nine Articles, the Reformation platform for the Church of England, in congruity with the decrees of the Roman Catholic Council of Trent. A few years later Newman was received into the Catholic Church, and in 1879 was made a cardinal by pope Leo XIII. Newman's life and writings have been very influential on both the Church of England and the restoration of Catholicism in England and elsewhere.

Theological Currents

The optimism of the nineteenth century that "man" (!) is the "captain of his ship" and "master of his destiny" – a hubris only slightly dampened by the sinking of the *Titanic* in 1912 – was shared by the major theological currents of the nineteenth century.

Georg Wilhelm Friedrich Hegel (1770–1831), the epitome of German Idealism, culminated an era of supreme confidence in human rational thought. He posited the dialectical nature of reality in which everything is taken up in its opposition: thesis, antithesis, synthesis. The synthesis itself becomes a new thesis that is opposed and transcended into a new synthesis, and on and on; reality is a historical process in which the Absolute ("God" for the theologians) comes to its self-realization in our (i.e., Hegel's) reason. History is read as a dialectical process, an evolution moving toward fulfillment. Boarding the train of history is to participate in its goal, whether it be the Prussian state, the classless society, or any number of ideas Hegel's students promulgated.

History then is an intelligible order: "Everything real is rational and everything rational is real." This may not be much comfort to those who suffer the antitheses of history, but life must "suffer wounds" to be reconciled to its unity, and that the Spirit may come to self-realization through the process of estrangement and reconciliation. The appeal to theologians was the application of this system to the biblical views of God's purposes in history, the problem of theodicy, and the overcoming of the modern gulf between reason and revelation.

Hegel's more interesting students turned him on his head by asserting that materialism not idealism is the locus of reality. Hence, Feuerbach's concise statement: "One is what one eats." Marx, Engels, and Lenin developed Hegel's ideas into dialectical materialism and applied it to society and politics with the motto that our task is not to understand history but to change it. And Søren Kierkegaard (1813–55), the "father of existentialism," vehemently rejected Hegel's system altogether for the sake of the solitary individual who stands before the infinitely qualitative Other, God.

Feuerbach and Strauss, the *enfants terribles* of theology, were not shy about expressing their views of the old guard. Strauss said of one of his professors that if Jesus Christ had studied theology with him, he would have abandoned Christianity before he ever started it. Feuerbach, who influenced such figures as Marx, Friedrich Nietzsche, Sigmund Freud, and Martin Buber, has been called the "grave-digger of theology" who killed God and divinized humankind. Feuerbach caused all this excitement by interpreting Christianity as the projection of human fears and hopes. In his *Essence of Christianity* he wrote: "The personality of God is nothing else than the projected personality of man" and "the beginning, middle, and end of religion is MAN." Having gained his contemporaries' attention, Feuerbach went on to assert that to negate the subject (God) does not mean to negate the predicates (wisdom, love, justice). The real atheist, he said, is the person who theoretically acknowledges God and then lives as if God did not exist.

Strauss also unleashed a storm of controversy with his *Life of Jesus*, which argued that the Christ figure of the Gospel accounts is not historical but mythological. This was a terribly cold bath to the contemporary quest for the historical Jesus that posited an end run around critiques of Christian doctrine by historical research. For Strauss, Jesus was a teacher of love to God and the neighbor, and the idea of the God-man was attached to the figure of Jesus by the church.

The neuralgic issue of the relationship of faith and history, so sharply put by Strauss, was addressed by a theologian who credited his conversion to the Awakening, Martin Kähler (1835–1912). In his *The So-Called Historical Jesus and the Historic Biblical Christ* Kähler argued that the foundation of the Christian faith is not the historical Jesus but rather the Christ preached by the community. The attempt to draw a picture of the historical Jesus is an error because the Gospels are sources of the church's preaching rather than historical sources for the biography of Jesus. Kähler argued that the Christian community does not focus on the departed Jesus, but on the present living Christ; and that the certainty of faith cannot rest upon the results of historical scholarship.

Liberal Theology

Kähler's effort to disentangle faith from historical-empirical research did not resolve the problem of faith in relation to science and history for everyone. How is Christianity possible when the telescope, microscope, and stethoscope found no evidence of God "in the starry skies above and the moral law within"? The liberal answer posited trust in God on the encounter with Jesus. But lacking home videos by Mary and Joseph, how do we know who Jesus was and what he said? The response was to claim that Jesus was accessible through historical research. Hence the promotion of historical study of the New Testament and its environment to find the "real" Jesus behind the accretions of centuries of dogmatic developments.

Among the many major influential figures in liberal theology, Adolf von Harnack (1851–1930) and Ernst Troeltsch (1865–1923) deserve special mention. Harnack, a scholar of the ancient church and the history of dogma, strove to set forth a non-dogmatic Christianity peeled clean of the doctrinal layers added through history. The development of doctrine, Harnack argued, shifted the religion *of* Jesus (his proclamation of the Kingdom of God's love) to a religion *about* Jesus (a preexistent divine being who vicariously atoned for sin). He attributed the conception and development of dogma as "a work of the Greek spirit on the soil of the Gospel." Harnack proposed then to distinguish the kernel of the gospel from the husk of Greek philosophy.

The "kernel–husk" theory of the development of the Christian faith found expression in numerous nineteenth-century searches for the "essence" of Christianity. Harnack's own expression of this quest, *What is Christianity?*, reduced faith to the fatherhood of God, the brotherhood of humankind, and the infinite worth of the human soul. Received as a liberation from an outmoded faith and a key for salvaging Christianity for the modern world, the book went through 14 editions and as many translations by 1927. Nevertheless, these efforts to bring biblical proclamation into the present became increasingly problematic as the foreignness of the biblical message in contrast to modern conceptions became clear.

The problem of the relationship of faith and history was reflected above all in the work of Troeltsch, whose impact continues into the present. He focused on the relationships of Christianity to modern culture, revelation to history, and personal freedom to social conditions. Troeltsch's major legacy is his vigorous historicizing of all thinking. Nothing lies outside historical conditioning. The liberal hope of finding the "kernel," the "essence of Christianity," became as suspect as the conservative claim of the absoluteness of dogma. There is no non-historical, eternal kernel under the husk; everything exists in historical conditions. Relativism had reared its head. Troeltsch's *The Absoluteness of Christianity* made it clear that historical work as such cannot claim the superiority of one religion over another. Troeltsch realized that the historical method is a new wine that when introduced to the old wineskins of biblical studies, church history, and theology will burst them apart. But at this very point, European civilization itself burst apart, as it descended into the unprecedented mutual slaughter of World War I.

Chapter 11

The Christian Churches
since World War I

World War I convulsed all areas of life. The breakdown of social and national order, the raging hatred among "civilized" nations of Europe, and the mass death upon the battlefields revealed the depths to which humankind can sink. The liberal optimism that had the temerity to think that this was the war to end all wars evaporated before the horrors of trench warfare and gas attacks. The "fatherhood of God, the brotherhood of humankind, and the infinite worth of the human soul" lost credibility as the "essence" of Christianity in view of the war between "Christian" nations.

The war's end did little to alleviate the nightmares of humankind's dark side, for it created conditions favorable to the rise of Hitler and World War II. Psychologically unable to acknowledge defeat and misled by their leaders about the realities of the Versailles Peace Treaty, the German population reacted against the onerous terms of reparations and the "war-guilt" clause that demanded Germany accept sole responsibility for the war. A German nationalist reaction, coupled with nostalgia for the monarchy and a proud Prussian military history, fueled widespread anti-democratic bias against the new Weimar Republic (1919–33) and set the stage for Adolf Hitler.

The churches did little to stem raging nationalism. Before the war, many pastors and theologians had actively fostered nationalism. Now they preached against the "war-guilt lie" and looked to a future divine vindication of the nation and the abolition of the Treaty of Versailles. As National Socialism appeared on the scene the danger of its ideology was not widely perceived.

The interwar years were in some respects not as difficult for the Catholic Church as for the Protestant ones. The end of the German monarchy left Catholicism undisturbed in its life under the pope. Furthermore, the Catholic Center Party, next to the Social Democrats one of the essential supporters of the new Weimar Republic, represented Catholic interests in opposition to the pretensions of Prussian Protestantism. Also, in the 1920s, Catholicism experienced fruitful developments in monastic and liturgical renewal.

New Formulations in Protestant Theology

In Germany the idealistic enthusiasm at the beginning of World War I awakened hopes of religious renewal. But the churches, filled in the first year of the war, were soon once again empty. The expectation that materialism and socialism would be overcome, and that people – especially the worker class – would return to the churches was disappointed. The "dechristianization" begun in the nineteenth century became "dechurchification" as the war promoted rather than halted alienation from the church. All too frequently after the war the pastors found themselves preaching to the choir of the conservative middle class and civil servants mourning the lost monarchy.

However, some voices began to pose striking alternatives to the contemporary throne and altar ideology of a synthesis of

Christianity and culture. Rudolf Otto's (1869–1937) *The Idea of the Holy* presented God not as the extension of humankind, but as the "totally other." The same year, Karl Holl's (1866–1926) *What did Luther Understand by Religion?* displaced liberal images of Luther as the hero and fighter for national liberty by presenting Luther's theology of sin, evil, and justification through the cross and suffering. Holl's work initiated the so-called Luther renaissance that also had great significance for the development of dialectical theology. A factor in the impact of this research was the theological and pastoral question of whether any other period in history had faced comparable religious and social crises.

The most important theological reorientation after World War I was the dialectical theology closely tied to Karl Barth. Barth, one of Harnack's prize students, became a pastor in 1911 in Safenwill, a worker community in his native Switzerland. Here Barth soon discovered that his vaunted education in liberalism had not prepared him for ministry in the context of the socioeconomic problems of his parish. Shocked by the low wages of the workers and disturbed that his wealthy parishioners saw no conflict between exploitation and the Christian faith, Barth became radicalized personally, politically, and theologically. He became a social democrat, that is, in his context a Marxist without communism, and earned the nickname "the red pastor." Required to preach, he discovered the Bible a "strange new world" rather than the blueprint for liberalism's great society. The next shock for Barth came with the outbreak of World War I when he saw, to his horror, that many of his learned professors signed the "Declaration of German Intellectuals" in support of "emperor and fatherland." It was now clear to him that liberalism was politically, socially, ethically, and religiously bankrupt.

Together with his friend and fellow-pastor Eduard Thurneysen (1888–1974), who mediated to him the writings of the Russian Orthodox novelist Fyodor Dostoyevski (1821–81), Barth turned his back on liberal theology and sought answers to his questions in the Bible. It is said that his *Commentary on Romans* (1918, second, reworked edition 1922) "fell like a bombshell on the playground of the theologians." Here the Bible is the address of the transcendent God who reveals himself in his judgment of the world in the death and resurrection of Christ. In this light all religion, including Christianity, is a human enterprise under God's judgment. Here, too, Barth echoed that great Dane, Søren Kierkegaard (1813–55), whose attack on both Hegel and bourgeois Christendom emphasized the "infinite qualitative difference" between God and humankind.

Barth and Thurneysen were soon joined by others: the Swiss Reformed theologian Emil Brunner (1889–1966), who blamed Schleiermacher for the misery of theology; the German Lutheran theologians Friedrich Gogarten (1887–1969), who came to similar insights through study of Luther, and Rudolf Bultmann (1884–1976), whose avenue to dialectical theology was through New Testament research and the rediscovery of Reformation theology. The German Lutheran theologian Paul Tillich (1886–1965) shared some of their concerns but was forced as a Religious Socialist to leave Germany in 1933; he then became a major theological voice in America. The movement of dialectical theology – shorthand for God's "no" to the world and sin which contained his "yes" of redemption – effectively spread its views through its own theological journal *Zwischen den Zeiten* (Between the Times) that lasted from 1923 to 1933.

Barth himself moved on to a series of German professorships until deported for criticism of the Nazis. At Bonn, Barth informed his students it would be in bad taste to begin a lecture on the Sermon on the Mount with "Heil Hitler." More forceful criticisms of National Socialism brought Barth before a Nazi court on the charge of seducing the minds of his students. His defense was to read Socrates' defense before the court of Athens. The judges were not amused, and Barth was expelled. He then became a professor at Basel.

The Churches during National Socialism

In 1933 Adolf Hitler and his National Socialist Party seized power. The Party program asserted its support for "positive Christianity," by which it meant churches in service to the state. But few at the time had any sense of Hitler's intention to replace the Christian faith with his own brand of brutal paganism of "blood and soil." In fact, during the 12 years of National Socialist rule only the first steps were enacted, mainly the co-option of the churches by state supervision and deconfessionalization. The "final solution" for the churches was to be completed after the war.

Nazi inroads into the churches were facilitated both by the churches' false sense of security concerning Nazi intentions, and by the enthusiastic reception of Hitler not only by many church members but also by many pastors. Before Hitler came to power, Catholic bishops warned of the dangers of National Socialism and forbade Catholics from joining the Party. Afterwards, however, the bishops muted their opposition. Catholics as well as Protestants were attracted to the new authoritarian regime by its rapid social accomplishments and suppression of communism. By the end of March 1933 the conference of German bishops declared their earlier warnings invalid. By the next July Hitler had removed potential problems with Catholicism by negotiating a Concordat with the Vatican. The regime promised to protect Catholic schools, institutions, and clergy in return for the cessation of all German Catholic political and social organizations. Soon, however, Nazi restrictions of the Catholic press, schools, and youth organizations created conflicts that were intensified by the church's condemnations of the paganism and totalitarian claims of National Socialism. In 1937 Pius XI's encyclical *Mit brennender Sorge* (With profound concern), strongly condemning National Socialism, was read from Catholic pulpits. Individual bishops and priests courageously opposed the Nazi programs to exterminate all Jews and all others deemed unworthy of life, such as the mentally and physically impaired. Consequently, numerous priests were imprisoned and murdered.

The Nazi program to domesticate the Protestant churches began with the proposal to unify the 28 "state" churches in a national Protestant Church. The churches' vulnerability to National Socialism related to the liberal theological heritage of "culture Protestantism" and the reactionary nationalist spirit following World War I that projected Germany's defeat upon evil foreign forces and internal atheistic subversion. Already in the 1920s there were voices scapegoating Jews and advocating purifying Christianity of its Jewish heritage. However, church authorities too frequently dismissed them as just the lunatic fringe of society.

The racist Protestants found a warm welcome in the Nationalist Socialist Party. In the spring of 1932 the National Socialists advanced the "German Christian Faith Movement" that vigorously promoted a nationalistic racism including the removal of all Jewish influences. The German Christians aroused an amazing response. People who had not darkened church doors in years now came out and darkened the church itself by electing German Christians to a third of the seats in the church government; by the summer of 1933 they were the majority.

The German Christians now openly attacked the churches. In order to safeguard the independence of the church, the evangelical state churches presented the highly respected Friedrich von Bodelschwingh as their own candidate for the office of Reichsbishof. Outside pressure and inner disunity led however to Bodelschwingh's resignation, and Hitler appointed an army chaplain, Ludwig Müller (1883–1945), national bishop. Supported by the full Nazi apparatus of press and radio propaganda, the German Christians proceeded to Nazify the church. Using the Civil Service Law (1933) that mandated the removal of all non-Aryan (that is, Jewish) officials from every level of government, the German Christians removed all clergy of Jewish descent and also all opponents of the Nazis.

The German Christians' effort to insert the non-Aryan paragraph into the constitution of the church precipitated the *Kirchenkampf* (church struggle). The World War I submarine hero and now pastor, Martin Niemöller (1892–1986), led the opposition. He founded the "Pastors' Emergency League," followed by "Councils of the Brethren," as alternative church authorities wherever the official church was ruled by the German Christians. These groups gained support from leading members of the theological faculties, including the not-yet expelled Karl Barth and the younger pastor Dietrich Bonhoeffer (1906–45), who was later executed for participating in the abortive plot to assassinate Hitler. Many of these pastors were later disposed of by conscripting them into the army, where they lost their lives. However, their revivifying of theology and their witness remained influential.

In May 1934 these pastors formed the "Confessing Church." Their Barmen Declaration rejected any and all synthesis of Christian faith and National Socialism, and proclaimed exclusive allegiance to the claims of biblical revelation. The authors made clear that if the German Christians succeeded, the church would cease to be the church. The Barmen Declaration thus witnessed to the importance of memory and history for the identity of the church and its confession. Barth, a major drafter of the Barmen Declaration, later regretted he had not made solidarity with the Jews a decisive feature of the text.

The one who made it crystal clear that racism denies the gospel was Dietrich Bonhoeffer, himself influenced by Barth. Bonhoeffer's essay "The Church and the Jewish Question" publicly stated that the Christian community is called "not just to bandage the victims under the wheel, but to put a spoke in the wheel itself. Such action would be direct political action." It is of interest that a couple of years before this Bonhoeffer had spent a year studying theology in New York City, and American racism had profoundly disturbed him.

In spite of persecution the clergy and laity of the Confessing Church continued to oppose the National Socialist regime until the outbreak of the war in 1939 ended public resistance. In this period conflicts within the Confessing Church over theological issues, above all the question of what makes the church the church, led Bonhoeffer to declare in 1936: "Whoever knowingly separates himself from the Confessing Church in Germany, separates himself from salvation."

The Confessing Church was also influential in Nazi-occupied territories such as the Netherlands, Norway, and France. As a European movement the Confessing Church contributed to the nascent ecumenical movement that blossomed after the war. The Barmen Confession remains a model statement of faith in areas of church–state confrontation and political oppression. It influenced the *Kairos* document (1985), a theological watershed of opposition to apartheid in South Africa, and the world confessional bodies of the World Alliance of Reformed Churches and the Lutheran World Federation in their condemnations of apartheid. The latter's position that apartheid ("apartness" – the South African National Party's platform of racial segregation to maintain white dominance) constitutes a confessional issue echoed Bonhoeffer's statement in 1938 that where the church is "subjected by outside force to a law which is alien to the church it may not yield, but must bear witness in word and deed to its freedom from the alien law and its sole obedience to Jesus Christ." When the integrity of the church is threatened, nothing is indifferent.

Bonhoeffer himself had ample opportunity for safety in a pastorate in London and offers of professorships in America, but was committed to serving his people in the Confessing Church. In *The Cost of Discipleship* he wrote: "When Christ calls a man, he bids him come and die." His emphasis upon "costly grace" critiqued what he called the "cheap grace" of all syntheses of Christ and culture. His emphasis "that a church without a confession is a church lost and defenseless, and that it is in its confession that a church has the only weapon that will not break," continues to be relevant to contemporary churches and the ecumenical movement.

National Socialism forced the Confessing Church underground. Niemöller, imprisoned at the Dachau concentration camp from 1938 to 1945, and Bonhoeffer, imprisoned in 1943 and executed in 1945, were among countless others, clergy and laity, Protestant and Catholic, who paid dearly to confess their faith. In the face of the Nazi pogrom against the Jews there were heroic actions by individual Christians, but there was no concerted public intervention. Immediately after the war, the Council of the German Protestant Churches acknowledged this in the "Stuttgart Declaration of Guilt" (October 1945) presented to the representatives of the Ecumenical Council of Churches: "We have for many years fought in the name of Jesus Christ against the spirit which in the name of National Socialism found terrifying expression; but we indict ourselves that we did not more courageously confess, more faithfully pray, more joyously believe, and more passionately love."

Developments in the Catholic Church after World War I

The pontificate of Pius XI (1922–39) was especially significant in directing the Catholic Church in opposing modern liberalism. He concluded many concordats, including that with Hitler in 1933. In 1929 the Lateran Treaty ended the long papal conflict with the Italian state and established the full sovereignty of the Vatican City. Among Pius XI's encyclicals were *Casti connubi* (1930) that condemned contraception and sought respect for married life, and *Quadragesimo Anno* (1931) that confirmed and elaborated the points of Leo XIII's *Rerum Novarum*, stressing the evils of both free capitalism and strict socialism. Pius XI was also called the "Pope of Catholic Action." Through activation of the laity under clerical leadership all social life should be filled with

Catholic impulses. Catholic Action testified to a self-conscious, powerfully active Catholicism after the war.

The activation of the laity was particularly evident in the religious renewal of youth. Catholic student and worker associations further promoted the mobilization of the laity. The living piety of modern Catholicism found expression in the renewal of monastic life, and in biblical and liturgical movements. In 1933 the Catholic Bible Work was founded to promote understanding of the Bible; and the Una Sancta movement continued this orientation while promoting understanding of other churches and seeking to soften the positions of the Counter-Reformation. The liturgical movement desired to move from modern subjectivism back to the treasures of the ancient church, including Gregorian chant and emphasis upon the communal character of the mass. Its main centers were the Benedictine cloisters of Beuron and Maria Laach, and it was closely tied to the Catholic youth movement.

Pius XII (r. 1939–58) remains controversial for dealing with National Socialism through traditional diplomacy, and for not publicly addressing the Nazi persecution of the Jews. He did continue his predecessors' condemnation of communism, and issued a blanket excommunication of members of communist parties and organizations. His more liberal tendencies supported the liturgical movement and biblical studies. *Divino afflante spiritu* (1943) allowed more liberty for scientific biblical study, and limited the normative character of the Vulgate Bible to the liturgy.

On the other hand, Pius XII condemned once again modernist theological movements, especially the "new theology" in France, in his *Humani generis* (1950). More noteworthy is the dogmatizing of the assumption of Mary in Pius XII's bull *Munificentissimus Deus* (1950). It concluded the development of Marian dogma since 1854, and underscored the great significance of Mariology in modern Catholicism. It was also the first use of the dogma of papal infallibility since Vatican I.

The most outstanding event in twentieth-century Catholicism is certainly the Second Vatican Council (1962–5). The largest council in church history, it began under pope John XXIII (r. 1958–63) and concluded under Paul VI (r. 1963–78). The council's achievements included renovation of the image of the church as "the people of God," a community of faith, sacrifice, prayer, and love; renewal of the liturgy by introduction of vernacular languages instead of mandatory Latin in worship; greater participation of the congregation, including allowing the cup to the laity at communion; strengthening the office of the bishop and the college of bishops so that in communion with the pope the bishops work together in leading the church, and presenting the papal office as service rather than rule; and the promotion of ecumenism and the desire for community with separated Christians.

The Ecumenical Movement

Rebuilding the European churches after World War II was closely connected to the most significant church historical event of the twentieth century, the ecumenical movement. It too had its roots in the nineteenth century through the cooperative work of the churches in mission fields and diaconal work. Although the Roman Catholic Church is not a member of the World Council of Churches, the relationships between the Catholic Church and the Protestant churches markedly improved in the late twentieth century.

Well before the first assembly of the World Council of Churches in Amsterdam in 1948, there had been proposals for an international Christian association. Joseph Oldham (1874–1969) had suggested to a meeting of mission leaders in 1920 that the coordination of Christian mission would probably have to develop into something like a world league of churches. Oldham, one of the chief architects of the ecumenical movement, was born in

Bombay, and planned to enter the Indian civil service after his education in Edinburgh and Oxford. A conversion experience at an Oxford meeting led by the American evangelist Dwight L. Moody radically altered his plans. Remaining a layman, he was active in the missionary struggle against racism in colonial Africa and he strove to assist the church in addressing the modern world.

Throughout the early history of the ecumenical movement lay leadership played an important role. One of Oldham's significant lay colleagues was the American Methodist John R. Mott (1865–1955). Converted while a student at Cornell, he was traveling secretary of the YMCA, and in 1895 participated in the founding meeting in Sweden of the World Student Christian Federation. Mott, like many of his contemporaries, saw students as the lever by which the world would be moved toward God. With his friend Nathan Söderblom, Mott saw the value of international Christian witness to issues of peace and justice. His many efforts in this direction led to the award of the Nobel Peace Prize in 1946.

Calls for ecumenical organization – including an encyclical letter in 1920 by the Ecumenical Patriarch of Constantinople – reflected the late nineteenth-century missionary activities and evangelical revivals in Europe and North America. In the 1890s the Student Volunteer Movement for Foreign Missions issued an urgent call to "evangelize the world in this generation." The tensions and divisions of confessional identities transplanted from Europe to America and to the mission fields had hampered such zeal, and were therefore addressed at the World Missionary Conference in Edinburgh (1910).

The delegates to the Edinburgh conference, mainly North Americans and Europeans, were from Protestant mission societies, not from the churches. But even with these limitations, the Edinburgh conference has been described as "one of the great landmarks in the history of the church" and the birthplace of the ecumenical movement. It was this meeting that led to the formation of the International Missionary Council, instrumental in forming local and national structures of ecumenism.

Charles Brent, an American Episcopalian and later bishop of the Philippines, and one of the missionaries at Edinburgh, was convinced that the divisive issues of doctrine and church order – deliberately not treated at Edinburgh – were crucial issues for the future of the churches. After years of labor and the intervention of World War I, his vision was realized at the 1927 World Conference on Faith and Order. Some 400 delegates, from over a hundred churches, met in Lausanne.

Two years earlier, in 1925, the Universal Christian Conference on Life and Work had met in Stockholm and encouraged the churches cooperatively to address social issues. All the delegates were official representatives of their own churches, and there was a strong Eastern Orthodox presence. The central figure was Nathan Söderblom (1866–1931), the archbishop of Stockholm, a historian of religions and a pioneer in bringing Orthodox and evangelical churches together. In 1930 he was awarded the Nobel Peace Prize for his initiatives for common Christian responsibility in international peace, freedom, and justice.

Some of the delegates at Lausanne were concerned that the Stockholm emphasis on "applied Christianity" would give precedence to interchurch collaboration on social issues over the search for church unity. The tension between these two concerns continued for many years, but the Life and Work movement itself began to realize that its slogan "doctrine divides and service unites" could not gloss over different theological understandings of the Kingdom of God. The growing tension over this issue led to a plan to merge Life and Work with Faith and Order. A 1938 conference in Utrecht made plans for a 1941 inaugural assembly of a World Council of Churches to incorporate this concern, but it had to be put on hold due to the outbreak of World War II.

At Utrecht, Willem A. Visser 't Hooft (1900–85) was invited to become general secretary of the World Council of Churches "in process of formation," a post he held until retirement in

1966. Visser 't Hooft had experienced ecumenism in the Student Christian Movement. After his theological studies he joined the Geneva staff of the YMCA. In this position he became involved with Christians from many churches, and then met John R. Mott. Visser 't Hooft expressed his unwavering commitment to church unity in his observation that Christ did not pray "that they may all enter into conversation with one another; he prayed that they all may be one."

The first assembly of the World Council of Churches (WCC) was held in Amsterdam in 1948. Its theme, "Man's Disorder and God's Design," reflected the disasters of World War II and acknowledged that the recent horrors testified in part to the churches' failures. The concern for international order reflected not only the recent past but also the steadily worsening relations between East and West. Hence the famous exchange between the American Presbyterian delegate John Foster Dulles, later the United States' Secretary of State, and the Czech theologian Josef Hromádka.

Dulles described communism as the greatest obstacle to world peace. Hromádka pleaded for a sympathetic understanding of communism as a force embodying much of the social impetus that the church and Western civilization should have been representing. In response to their sharp exchange, the assembly insisted that no civilization can escape the radical judgment of the Word of God, and explicitly rejected the assumption that capitalism and communism were the only available choices.

Future controversies were foreshadowed in the assembly's rejection in principle of war "as contrary to the will of God," while at the same time recognizing that this position was not accepted unanimously throughout Christendom. The assembly also stated that every kind of tyranny and imperialism calls for opposition and struggle to secure human rights and basic liberties. Ecumenical efforts to put these words into practice elicited strong reactions. In the 1980s both *Reader's Digest* and the *Sixty Minutes* television program claimed the WCC and the US National Council of Churches were supporting revolutionary and Marxist causes with money given by Christians. On the other hand, communist regimes attacked the WCC for its stand on human rights. The WCC's efforts for peace in the Middle East and the dismantling of apartheid also created what one observer called the "ecumenical character-assassination game." Conservative theological critics, reflecting the early twentieth-century fundamentalist–modernist conflict, have accused the WCC of being an exponent of "liberal theology."

The years following Amsterdam focused on responding to the vast human needs created by the war. Programs of interchurch aid, service to refugees and international affairs, loan funds, and reconstruction were major expressions of ecumenical life and work. The churches through the WCC would have to show, Visser 't Hooft stated, that their coming together "made a real difference."

In this light, the second assembly of the WCC (Evanston, 1954) met with the theme, "Christ – the Hope of the World." The assembly discussion became stormy as it became apparent that talk about hope raised a central theological issue: how does the Christian's hope for the coming of God's Kingdom relate to hopes for immediate improvements in people's lives? Those who emphasized the former tended to think of those who emphasized the latter as superficial optimists and activists, who in turn charged them with being out of touch with the "real world." The assembly itself could not agree on a formulation of how Christian hope here and now is related to ultimate hope. Nevertheless, priority was given to the problems of undeveloped regions, the arms race, and racism. The omnipresence of the Cold War was seen not only in these issues but also in the addresses by such public figures as US president Eisenhower and UN secretary general Dag Hammskjöld.

The WCC was slow to grasp the urgency of the socioeconomic problems facing the so-called "Third World," and like the UN was divided over how fast and far the decolonization process should go. Asian churches at a 1952 meeting in Lucknow, India, sponsored by the WCC, explicitly linked the Cold War and accelerating movements for independence. They insisted that the challenge of communism could be best met by a positive attitude to the social revolution taking place in East Asia. The Lucknow conference called for radical reform of land tenure systems, planned economic development, and church support for struggles for freedom and self-determination. A few months later the WCC Central Committee took up this challenge and launched national, regional, and global conferences and publications to support churches facing "rapid social change."

Succeeding assemblies of the WCC dealt with expanding ecumenical relationships as well as social ethical concerns. The affirmation of the uniqueness of Christ – an echo of the early church's Arian controversy – raised the issue of the relationship of Christianity to other religions. And pope John XXIII's invitation to the WCC to send observers to the sessions of the Second Vatican Council facilitated far-reaching changes in Roman Catholic–Protestant relations. One of the persistent social issues, however, was racism. Martin Luther King, Jr. was to address the WCC assembly in Uppsala in 1968, but was assassinated four months before the meeting. James Baldwin reminded the assembly of the long history of church involvement in racial injustice, and asked whether "there is left in Christian civilization the moral energy, the spiritual daring, to atone, to repent, to be born again." While insisting that proclamation of the gospel is essential, the assembly also insisted that Christian worship is ethical and that any segregation by race or class must be rejected. Future assemblies were marked by renewed commitments to human rights and the struggles for justice.

It should be noted that at the same time that the WCC was developing and growing, world communions of churches such as the Lutheran World Federation, the World Alliance of Reformed Churches, and the World Methodist Council among others, had begun and now continue to be involved in bilateral and multilateral dialogues among each other and with other churches, such as the Roman Catholic and Pentecostal churches.

The striving for reunion of separated confessions is one of the most significant aspects of modern church history. Rooted in the period of Pietism, it extended into the nineteenth-century Awakenings, and provided impulses to transconfessional and supranational connections in social and missionary endeavors. The ecumenical movement's conferences in the twentieth century provided many incentives to the rapprochement of the Christian churches, and essentially changed the climate between the churches in comparison to prior centuries.

Back to the Future: Christianity in Global Context

Our narrative of the history of Christianity now verges on journalism as we try to picture contemporary developments. It may well be that the most significant development in the modern story of Christianity is its remarkable shift from "Eurocentric" denominationalism to a truly global movement whose center of gravity is now the southern hemisphere of Latin America, sub-Saharan Africa, and Asia, and whose form is increasingly a trans-denominational Protestantism. In contrast to the efforts by the modern Western churches to adapt the faith to modern culture, the younger churches bear a stronger resemblance to the early churches' belief in prophecy, faith healing, exorcism, visions, and charismatic leadership. Like the early church, the younger churches confronted by pluralism and its concomitant relativism have embraced Christian identity, albeit in inculturated forms. The variety of new forms of churches as "community churches" also has a certain parallel to the early church in their decentralization. The old saying that all politics is local may perhaps be paraphrased to say that many churches are developing from the local context rather than depending upon denominational missions.

This by no means gainsays the contributions of historical missions from Paul onward. Jesuit missions reached Asia in the sixteenth century, and Protestant missions from Halle and then the major nineteenth-century British and American mission endeavors extended to the four corners of the world. What is noteworthy in the present is that the perceived and often all too actual relations between Christian missions and European exploration and empire building began to recede with the process of decolonization. As former colonies have gained their independence from imperial powers, so too have the mission churches. The consequent inculturation and indigenization of the local churches – phenomena evident also in the early churches' mission – are contributing a remarkable vitality to the so-called "younger churches."

Whatever the trends of the present, the old saw that the more things change the more they stay the same may prompt reflection on the development of Christian identity in history. What has stayed the same for the "one, holy, catholic church, the communion of saints" is *anamnesis* – Jesus' mandate to live "in remembrance" of him.

Appendix

Periodization

The memory and identity of the Christian community as it is handed on has influenced the understanding of the history of Christianity and the periodization of history in general. Until recently the collectors and tellers of the family conversations of Christianity were nearly all insiders. Thus the subject matter and the discipline of telling the gospel story were under the rubric of "church history." In modern times, for a variety of reasons, persons outside the Christian churches are also interested in presenting the history of Christianity. There is, to paraphrase the old saw, the sense that the telling of the story of the Christian contributions to contemporary identity is too important to be left to the Christians.

Since the eighteenth-century Enlightenment, there has been suspicion that the story of Christianity as told by its historians has been influenced by partisan polemics presented as objective truth. Thus a brief discussion of the distinct perspectives of church historians and historians of Christianity may be useful in reading both contemporary textbooks and historical sources. Some of the presuppositions that govern an author's interpretation of events and texts leap right off the page at us; others are more subtle and difficult to recognize – especially if we share the worldview of the authors. An example of the former are the miracle stories which lace one of our important sources for early medieval English history, the eighth-century *History of the English Church and People* by Bede. The two early church historians most influential upon the conceptualizing of the history of Christianity are Eusebius, bishop of Caesarea (ca. 260–ca. 339) and Augustine, bishop of Hippo (354–430). Eusebius is known as the "father of church history" because his *The History of the Church from Christ to Constantine* is the first history of the church outside the Book of Acts in the New Testament. Eusebius, by the way, was quite up front about his method of constructing his narrative: "From the scattered hints dropped by my predecessors I have picked out whatever seems relevant to the task I have undertaken, plucking like flowers in literary pastures the helpful contributions of earlier writers to be embodied in the continuous narrative I have in mind." Eusebius lived through the persecutions that accompanied the transition from the pagan to the Christian empire. Thus it is not surprising that the emperor Constantine, in his view God's agent for the church, plays a central role in this and his other historical work, the *Chronicle*, and that the unity of church and empire is God's plan. The *Chronicle* found numerous imitators and influenced medieval conceptions of world history as guided by the providence of God, bracketed by the creation and the Last Judgment. The classic expression of this genre is Augustine's *The City of God*, which presents history in terms of the people of God as pilgrims in an alien world traveling to the heavenly city. Augustine's eschatological orientation, conceived in the context of the fall of Rome and dominated by his understanding of the Bible, remained the basic orientation of history in the West until the Enlightenment. In contrast to Hellenistic views of history as cyclical, a repetitive "wheel," the biblical view of history is that it is linear, beginning with God's creation and progressing to its divine fulfillment. The basis of history for Augustine is not fate or human activity but the unfolding of God's plan. Augustine thus presented a theology of history.

In *The Myth of Christian Beginnings* Robert Wilken states: "Historical thinking is and should be selective" and "Christians, like others, cultivate the memory of the past for the uses of the present." The question of course is why historians select what they do for their narratives. The choice of miracle stories or divinely guided emperors clearly intends to advance the story of the Christian church. We are not surprised that in such examples the presuppositions are theological. As you are well aware, there are also other presuppositions active in historical studies, such as gender, race, and culture, that may not be so evident. As scholars in our own day struggle to bring awareness of the historical roles of women in the church, or slavery, or the once-dominant Eurocentric view of Christianity, there is recognition that the nineteenth-century historians' ideal of presenting the "facts" "exactly as they happened" has been undermined by our awareness of the role of the "self-evident" in history. This means that the profoundest mark of any age is what it accepts as self-evident, as the basic assumptions that tend to be held by everyone, friend and foe alike. It is difficult to assess the self-evident because it constitutes the very air an age breathes. Thus, for a modern culture fascinated by the "self-evident" value of innovation, it is difficult to appreciate the Eusebian concern for origins in the sense that "older is better." Other examples: prior to the modern ecumenical movement, historians tended to assume that schism in the Western church was the norm, and thus viewed the Protestant–Catholic colloquies of the sixteenth century differently than they do now; or, because the later church was patriarchal, historians tended to assume that women did not play significant leadership roles in the early church.

Historians no less than theologians are tempted to identify "history" as the actuality of the past with "history" as the construction they create from its records. For history as the actuality of the past, an "age" is simply a considerable span of time. For history as construction of the past, an "age" is a segment of the past on which the historian imposes some intelligibility. For example, the construction of history on the basis of the idea of progress, or human control over the course of history, creates the poignant predicament of choosing which myth is most useful to impose dramatic organization upon the data. This is a problem that pre-Renaissance historians, unfettered by belief in human freedom, did not have.

But let us go back to Eusebius and his influence upon the writing of histories of Christianity up to the modern period. The norm for Eusebius' church is the community of the first two centuries of the Christian era. From his time on, Christians would rationalize historical change and development as faithful expressions of early Christianity, and would so idealize the apostolic time, the time of origins, that even today theological curricula frequently separate biblical and historical studies, thus echoing the old conviction that the Bible, as the record of origins, precedes historical development. A century after Eusebius, Vincent of Lérins (d. ca. 450) provided a famous formula for true Christianity. The so-called Vincentian canon states that "the true faith is that which has been believed everywhere, always, and by all." In other words, the true and authentic teachings of the church had remained and will remain the same from the very beginning of Christianity. This formula, by the way, provided a simple means of determining who is a heretic: anyone who breaks this unity of doctrine, that is, who deviates from the tried and true, and innovates.

The Eusebian model that older is better continued to be influential into the early modern Renaissance (fourteenth to sixteenth centuries). The Humanists spoke of the roughly thousand-year period from the end of the classical Roman era to their own time as the "Middle Ages." They considered the Middle Ages as an intermediate period between what they perceived as the ideal classical period and their own time. They viewed their recovery of ancient literature and classical languages (Hebrew, Greek, and Latin) as the rebirth (hence, "Renaissance") of education, science, art, and the church. Their motto was *ad fontes* – back to the sources.

While *ad fontes* remains a watchword for historians, the Humanists gave it a pejorative slant. They regarded the Middle Ages as barbaric; it was the "gothic" (i.e., barbaric) age. This characterization was driven not just by aesthetic–philological criteria, but also by theological and religious criteria. The men and women of the Renaissance projected back into history their own reaction to what they regarded as the bigoted and narrow-minded authoritarianism and orthodoxy of their day. Their influence is evident in the continued usage of labels for the Middle Ages such as "Dark Ages" and "scholastic." Such value judgments received sharper edges by the continuation of the Renaissance in the seventeenth and eighteenth-century Enlightenment attacks upon the clergy as ignorant and superstitious, as well as the Enlightenment ideal of autonomy from all external authorities, including the church.

Even though the Reformations of the sixteenth century fragmented the medieval church, all parties continued to hold the Eusebian model of church history by claiming to be *the* faithful recovery or continuation of the early church, and by accusing all the other churches of being innovators. The Reformers urged people to judge all doctrines by scripture. And all the churches turned to studies of history to bolster their individual claims to be *the* community faithful to the tradition. Those convinced that the medieval church was nothing less than a total corruption of the primitive church developed martyrologies to support their view that in spite of corruption there continued to be faithful witnesses to the Jesus movement in history. In short, selective memories were at work in all parties.

The first comprehensive Protestant church history elaborated in great detail the claim that there had always been persons who had opposed the innovations and errors of the papacy. Under the leadership of the Lutheran Matthew Flacius Illyricus (1520–75), a group of scholars developed a history of the church from its beginning down to 1400 titled *Historia Ecclesia Christi*. Since this work divided the history of the church into centuries and was begun in the city of Magdeburg, it came to be known as the "Magdeburg Centuries." The Eusebian model of historical periodization remained effective in Flacius' argument that the Reformation was the restoration of the original purity of the church. Not surprisingly for a Lutheran apologist, the key to the faithfulness of the church was seen to be the doctrine of justification by grace alone. The original purity of the church lasted to about 300, and with some reservations perhaps even up to 600, but then there had been a falling away from the true faith due to the expansion of papal authority.

Not to be outdone, the Roman Catholic Church responded to the Magdeburg Centuries with the herculean efforts of Caesar Baronius (1538–1607). After thirty years of work in the Vatican archives, Baronius began publishing his study of the history of the church. In contrast to the Protestant chronology of centuries, Baronius proceeded year by year. By the time of his death, his *Annales Ecclesiastici* had reached the year 1198. No less partisan than Flacius, and equally subject to the Eusebian model, Baronius focused his study on the institution of the papacy rather than on the doctrine of justification.

In terms of periodization, the Magdeburg Centuries set forth the three periods of history now familiar to us: the ancient church, or time of origins up to about 300; the medieval period of decay, about 300 to 1500; and the new or modern period of recovery. The historical reality of this tripartite division of ancient–medieval–modern was little questioned, and passed into the schema of universal history by the end of the seventeenth century through the *Historia tripartita* of Christoph Cellarius (Keller; 1634–1707).

Cellarius divided history by monarchies, employing a periodization that went back to the vision of four beasts in Daniel 7:1–8 and their interpretation in ancient Christian historiography as four world empires on the basis of Daniel 7:17–27. For Cellarius, ancient history extended to the Roman emperor Constantine (ca. 288–337), the medieval period extended to the end of the Byzantine Empire (1453), and modern history was synchronized with the Reformation and its aftermath.

In the late seventeenth century a new historical perspective came to the fore in church historical writing. This new interpretive principle for history displaced the doctrinal and institutional principles running from the works of Eusebius and Augustine through those of Flacius and Baronius by that of religious experience, that is, personal piety and life. The work that uniquely and forcefully advocated this interpretation of history was by the radical Pietist Gottfried Arnold (1666–1714). His *Impartial History of the Church and of Heretics from the Beginning of the New Testament to the Year of Christ 1688* was of course no less "impartial" than its predecessors. But it did introduce a new perspective that with variations on the theme remains in vogue: history from the perspective of the marginalized. To Arnold, the essence of the Christian faith was not dogmatic, ecclesial, juridical, and cultic, but rather the personal piety of individuals. Thus to Arnold, the so-called heretics in the history of the church often handed on the faith of the church more authentically than the church's major theologians and institutions. For example, while both the Magdeburg Centuries and the *Annales* praised Athanasius (d. 373) as the great defender of Trinitarian doctrine, Arnold faulted Athanasius for his ruthless and vindictive church politics. What Athanasius thought about doctrine was less important, Arnold claimed, than the effect doctrine had on his life. From this point of view, those whom the church had persecuted as heretics were now seen as the true Christians who had faithfully followed Jesus in opposing the "Babel" of the established church and the world. The Pietist concern with individuals and their religious experience foreshadowed later interests in biographical and psychological studies of historical figures.

But Arnold also remained in debt to the Eusebian model. For Arnold the consummate epoch of church history was the first three centuries, a time of origins he saw filled with the spirit of freedom, living faith, and holy living. The corruption and decay of the responsible love of the early church, Arnold believed – in stark contrast to Eusebius – began under the emperor Constantine, whose legitimation of the church in the Roman Empire introduced it to the temptations of power and wealth. Here then is the oft-repeated claim that when the church became the established church of the Roman Empire it "fell" and initiated a long decline into the state church so sharply criticized by Søren Kierkegaard's nineteenth-century *Attack Upon "Christendom."*

The above brief sketch of historiography suggests that the periodization of history as ancient, medieval, and modern so ingrained in modern thought, is itself a construct. The effort in more recent studies to expand awareness of the history of Christianity beyond the history of doctrines, the ideas of the elite, and the institutions that shape and convey these ideas reflects the awareness that there is more than one memory and identity of the Christian community in history. These more comprehensive efforts indicate that much historical writing has lacked attention to the roles of the poor, the oppressed, and women in the church, as well as the explosive growth of Christianity in Asia, Africa, and Latin America. The newer histories may thus serve the present by not only recalling hitherto unnoticed aspects of the past, but also by strengthening people's awareness of their own cause by giving voice to the voiceless, that they may engage in the conversations forming personal and communal identities.

Glossary

adiaphora "Matters of indifference" in faith and practice because they are neither banned nor mandated by scripture. Adiaphorist controversies erupted in the Reformation over the doctrinal implications of liturgical ceremonies and vestments when mandated by the government. The issue was whether such elements (e.g., sign of the cross, limitation of ordination to bishops, baptism with exorcism, images, etc.) compromised an evangelical understanding of justification and Christian freedom.

Anabaptism Literally, "re-baptism," a pejorative designation of those in the Reformation period who rejected infant baptism in favor of a "believer's baptism." Because the first generation had been baptized as infants, they were "re-baptized" upon their adult confession of faith. Members of the Anabaptist communities promoted a "free church" principle of a voluntary church.

Apocalypticism Eschatological expectations of the end of history associated with the books of Daniel and Revelation that forecast great upheavals, the appearance of the Antichrist, and the Last Judgment. Apocalyptic prophecies intend to warn the evil of their coming cataclysmic judgment and to console the righteous with the promise of God's deliverance (cf. Mark 13:14–27).

Apocrypha Those books in the Septuagint and Vulgate Bibles excluded by Protestants as non-canonical; also known as the Deuterocanonical books.

apologetic theology Expositions that defend the faith, especially through its interpretation in relation to reigning cultural challenges (e.g., second-century Greco-Roman and nineteenth-century European philosophies).

Arianism Belief that Christ is a creation of the Father, having an origin and consequently neither eternal nor equal to the Father, who received the title Son of God due to his foreseen righteousness. A favorite biblical text of Arians was Proverbs 8:22ff.: "The Lord created me at the beginning of his work, the first of his acts of long ago. Ages ago I was set up, at the first, before the beginning of the earth." Arianism was condemned by the councils of Nicaea (325) and Constantinople (381).

benefice An endowed church office.

bull From Latin *bulla*, "seal"; a written papal mandate attested by the pope's seal.

canon law Legislation that governs the faith, morals, and organization of the Roman Catholic Church.

celibacy Unmarried state required of Western clergy and religious since the twelfth century; rejected by the Protestant Reformers. The Eastern Orthodox Church permits marriage of priests and deacons before ordination but not after; bishops must be celibate.

chiliasm Also, millennialism; a historical variation on the theme of a future thousand-year reign of Christ's saints based on readings of Revelation 20.

communicatio idiomatum The communication or exchange of attributes. Advanced by Cyril of Alexandria, among others, during the Christological controversies; posits that although the human and divine natures of Christ are distinct, the attributes of one may be predicated of the other due to their union in the one person of Christ.

conciliarism The vesting of church authority in a general or ecumenical council; promoted at the councils of Constance (1414–18) and Basel (1431–49); sought reform of church and papacy through church councils.

confession (1) Private or public acknowledgment of sin. (2) Public profession of the principles of faith subscribed to by its adherents (e.g., the Augsburg Confession of 1530).

council A formal church assembly convened to regulate matters of faith and discipline. A provincial council is a meeting of bishops with their archbishop; a diocesan synod is a meeting of a bishop with the clergy of his diocese; an ecumenical or general council is a meeting of all bishops of the church under the leadership of the pope or the emperor.

cuius regio, eius religio "Whose [the prince's] rule, his religion"; the formula later used to describe the Religious Peace of Augsburg (1555) by which rulers were permitted to decide whether their land would be Roman Catholic or Lutheran.

decretals Papal letters of advice with the force of law; also, collections of papal responses to questions.

docetism A heretical Christology related to Gnosticism that claimed Christ's body only appeared to be real, and that therefore at the crucifixion Christ only seemed to suffer and die. Docetism reflects Gnosticism's distrust of the material world.

Donatism A fourth-century schismatic renewal movement in northern Africa that stressed that the validity of Word and sacraments was contingent upon the moral purity of the priest. In general, the view that the message is dependent upon the messenger.

Ebionitism Early Jewish-Christian ascetic sect whose name derives from Hebrew for "poor men." Their teachings are obscure, but the name is associated with a reductionist Christology positing Jesus was the son of Joseph and Mary upon whom a heavenly archangel descended at his baptism. Basically held that Jesus was a true prophet, but the law of Moses remains the way to salvation, not Jesus himself.

ecumenical movement From Greek *oikumene*, "the whole inhabited world"; the efforts begun in the twentieth century among Christian churches seeking unity of ministry and worship; the main models for which, "conciliar fellowship" and "reconciled diversity," developed, respectively, from the World Council of Churches and the Christian World Communions.

encyclical A circular letter addressed to churches, initially by any bishop but now restricted to papal letters.

eschatology Doctrine of the "last things": death, resurrection, Last Judgment, end of the world, eternal life.

Eucharist From Greek *eucharistein*, "to give thanks;" the name for the central act of worship. Also termed communion, Lord's Supper, and mass.

evangelical From Greek *euangelion*, literally "good news" (i.e., the gospel). Historically, the term was used by Reformers as a self-designation in opposition to the papal church; modern usage often denotes those conservative Protestant groups that stress an experienced conversion and the centrality of a fundamentalist interpretation of scripture.

ex opere operantis The efficacy of the sacraments related to the receiver's subjective disposition.

ex opere operato Sacramental validity is due to the performance of the rite; posits the objective validity of the sacraments apart from the subjective attitude of the priest or recipient.

exegesis The methodology of the interpretation of texts. The specific principles used in the exegesis of scripture are often referred to as hermeneutics.

filioque Latin: "and the Son." The clause added to the Nicene creed in the West that states that the Holy Spirit proceeds from the Father and the Son.

fundamentalism Definition of the Christian faith by a list of specific necessary or fundamental doctrines; especially associated with claim for the inerrancy or infallibility of scripture promoted by conservative elements within many denominations from the last part of the nineteenth century in reaction to the biblical criticism and the theory of evolution. The term itself derives from a series of 12 tracts entitled *The Fundamentals* (ca. 1909).

glossalalia From Greek, *glossa*, "tongue" or "language"; speaking or praying in unknown tongues; a practice of Pentecostal churches and charismatic communities.

Gnosticism Greek *gnosis*, "secret knowledge" as the way of salvation; term applied to a variety of early Christian groups that held to a dualistic view of the cosmos that opposed the spiritual world and material world, matter being evil; since the creation is associated with evil, Gnostics rejected the God of Creation, and the Hebrew scriptures, and posited a Christology that denied the real humanity of Christ (docetism). The creeds respond specifically to Gnostic claims in their first article that professes God is the creator of heaven and earth (i.e., the material world) and in their second article that Jesus was born, died, and was buried (in opposition to the docetic claim that the Christ only appeared to be human).

Humanism Intellectual–cultural movement of the European Renaissance focused on classical culture as the resource for the renewal or "rebirth" of Western culture and Christianity.

Jansenism A French Catholic movement associated with Cornelius Jansen's revival of Augustinian theology and the convent of Port-Royal. Theologically, Jansenism claimed good works are impossible without special grace from God, and that grace is irresistible (a kind of determinism). Jansenist antagonism to the Jesuits was famously expressed in Pascal's *Provincial Letters*. The movement was condemned as heretical by the Sorbonne (1649) and pope Innocent X (1653).

liberal theology/liberalism An imprecise term for theological currents beginning with Schleiermacher which attempted to incorporate modern critical analysis of orthodox faith by reason and experience; tendency of some Protestant groups influenced by the Enlightenment; optimistic view of the human condition that affirms human freedom in faith and ethics to respond to God's will (e.g., Pelagianism). In Roman Catholic theology liberalism is usually termed modernism.

modernism Roman Catholic version of Protestant liberalism that was open to the application of modern science and philosophy to theology. Condemned by pope Pius X in 1907.

monophysitism View that there is one divine nature of the Christ; refused to accept Chalcedonian Christology because it was seen as Nestorian.

Nestorianism View that there were two subsistent beings in Christ united in one external undivided appearance. Condemned at the Council of Chalcedon (451).

Pelagianism Positive view of human capability to merit salvation through free will to choose and accomplish works pleasing to God; downplays divine grace.

pentecostalism Christian communities and churches marked by belief that the experience of the first Christians on the day of Pentecost (Acts 1–2) continues in the present, including the gifts of tongues (glossalalia), prophecy, healing, and exorcism. Rooted in the Holiness movement, the first "Spirit baptisms" began at Bethel College, Topeka Kansas, and spread to Houston, Texas, and then Los Angeles, where W. J. Seymour initiated the famous Azusa Street revival. Among the larger Pentecostal churches are the Assemblies of God, the Church of God in Christ, and the International Church of the Foursquare Gospel. Pentecostalism has spread widely in recent decades throughout Latin America.

Protestant Orthodoxy Characterization of the post-Reformation generation of Protestant efforts to define "correct doctrine" in conformity with their confessions and in opposition to alternative confessions; also referred to as Protestant Scholasticism because of the embrace of rational methodology, Aristotelian philosophy, and parallels to medieval efforts to develop theological systems.

soteriology Greek, *soteria*; theological treatment of salvation.

transubstantiation The doctrine that posits that the bread and wine in the Eucharist are transformed into the body and blood of Christ while retaining their outward appearance. Defined at the Fourth Lateran Council (1215).

Vulgate The Latin translation of the Bible, dependent to a great extent upon the work of Jerome (d. 420); criticized by Humanists and Reformers of the Reformation period for numerous inaccuracies.

Further Reading

General Reference

Barrett, David, ed., *World Christian Encyclopedia*, New York: Oxford University Press, 2000.
Bettenson, Henry and Chris Maunder, eds., *Documents of the Christian Church*, Oxford: Oxford University Press, 1999.
Bradley, James E. and Richard A. Muller, *Church History: An Introduction to Research, Reference Works, and Methods*, Grand Rapids, MI: Eerdmans, 1995.
Brauer, Jerald C., ed., *The Westminster Dictionary of Church History*, Philadelphia, PA: Westminster, 1971.
Brown, Raymond E., et al., eds., *The New Jerome Biblical Commentary*, Englewood Cliffs, NJ: Prentice-Hall, 1990.
Burgess, Stanley M. and Gary B. McGee, eds., *Dictionary of Pentecostal and Charismatic Movements*, Grand Rapids, MI: Zondervan, 1988.
Campbell, Ted A., *Christian Confessions: A Historical Introduction*, Louisville, KY: Westminster John Knox, 1996.
Chadwick, H. and G. R. Evans, *Atlas of the Christian Church*, London: Macmillan, 1987.
Cross, F. L. and E. A. Livingstone, eds., *The Oxford Dictionary of the Christian Church*, Oxford: Oxford University Press, 2002.

Dowley, Tim, ed., *The Baker Atlas of Christian History*, Grand Rapids, MI: Baker, 1997.

Fahlbusch, Erwin, et al., eds., *The Encyclopedia of Christianity*, 5 vols., Grand Rapids, MI: Eerdmans, 1999–.

Ferguson, Everett, ed., *Encylcopedia of Early Christianity*, 2nd edn., New York: Garland, 1997.

Fitzgerald, Allan D., gen. ed., *Augustine through the Ages: An Encyclopdia*, Grand Rapids, MI: Eerdmans, 1999.

Hillerbrand, Hans J., ed.-in-chief, *The Oxford Encyclopedia of the Reformation*, 4 vols., New York: Oxford University Press, 1996.

Hillerbrand, Hans J., ed., *The Encyclopedia of Protestantism*, 4 vols., New York: Routledge, 2004.

Langer, William L., ed., *The Encyclopedia of World History*, 6th edn., Boston, MA: Houghton Mifflin, 2001.

Leith, John, ed., *Creeds of the Churches*, 3rd edn., Atlanta, GA: John Knox, 1982.

Littell, Franklin H., *Historical Atlas of Christianity*, New York: Continuum, 2001.

Lohse, Bernhard, *A Short History of Christian Doctrine from the First Century to the Present*, Philadelphia, PA: Fortress, 1966.

Lossky, Nicholas, et al., eds., *Dictionary of the Ecumenical Movement*, Grand Rapids, MI: Eerdmans, 1991.

Metzger, Bruce and Michael D. Coogan, eds., *The Oxford Companion to the Bible*, New York: Oxford University Press, 1993.

Muller, Richard A., *Dictionary of Latin and Greek Theological Terms*, Grand Rapids, MI: Baker, 1985.

New Catholic Encyclopedia, 17 vols., New York: McGraw-Hill, 1967–79.

Noll, Mark, et al., eds., *Eerdmans Handbook to Christianity in America*, Grand Rapids, MI: Eerdmans, 1983.

Pelikan, Jaroslav, *The Christian Tradition: A History of the Development of Doctrine*, 5 vols., Chicago, IL: University of Chicago Press, 1971–89.

Sunquist, Scott W., ed., *A Dictionary of Asian Christianity*, Grand Rapids, MI: Eerdmans, 2001.

Walton, Robert C., *Chronological and Background Charts of Church History*, Grand Rapids, MI: Zondervan, 1986.

Comprehensive Histories of Christianity

Aland, Kurt, *A History of Christianity*, 2 vols., Philadelphia, PA: Fortress, 1985.

Duffy, Eamon, *Saints and Sinners: A History of the Popes*, New Haven, CT: Yale University Press, 1997.

González, Justo L., *The Story of Christianity*, 2 vols., San Francisco: Harper and Row, 1984–5.

Irvin, Dale T. and Scott W. Sunquist, *History of the World Christian Movement, I: Earliest Christianity to 1453*, New York: Orbis, 2001.

Jedin, Herbert and John Dolan, eds., *History of the Church*, 10 vols., New York: Crossroad, 1987.

Kee, Howard C., et al., *Christianity: A Social and Cultural History*, 2nd edn., Upper Saddle River, NJ: Prentice-Hall, 1998.

MacHaffie, Barbara J., *Her Story: Women in Christian Tradition*, Philadelphia, PA: Fortress, 1986.

McManners, John, ed., *The Oxford History of Christianity*, Oxford: Oxford University Press, 1993.

Miles, Margaret R., *The Word Made Flesh: A History of Christian Thought*, Oxford: Blackwell, 2005.

Noll, Mark, *Turning Points: Decisive Moments in the History of Christianity*, 2nd edn., Grand Rapids, MI: Baker, 2003.

Historiography

Cantor, Norman F., *Inventing the Middle Ages*, New York: Quill, 1991.

Chesnut, Glenn F., *The First Christian Histories: Eusebius, Socrates, Sozomen, Theodoret, and Evagrius*, 2nd revd. edn., Macon, GA: Mercer University Press, 1986.

Gay, Peter, Victor G. Wexler, and Gerald Cavenaugh, eds., *Historians at Work*, 4 vols., New York: Harper and Row, 1972–5.

Harvey, Van A., *The Historian and the Believer: The Morality of Historical Knowledge and Christian Belief*, New York: Macmillan, 1966.

Niebuhr, Reinhold, *Faith and History: A Comparison of Christian and Modern Views of History*, New York: Scribners, 1949.

Wengert, Timothy J. and Charles Brockwell, Jr., eds., *Telling the Churches' Stories: Ecumenical Perspectives on Writing Christian History*, Grand Rapids, MI: Eerdmans, 1995.

Wilken, Robert L., *The Myth of Christian Beginnings: History's Impact on Belief*, Garden City, NY: Anchor Books, 1972.

Early Christianity

Brown, Peter, *Augustine of Hippo: A Biography*, Berkeley: University of California Press, 1967.

Brown, Peter, *The Cult of the Saints: Its Rise and Function in Latin Christianity*, Chicago, IL: University of Chicago Press, 1981.

Brown, Peter, *The Body and Society: Men, Women, and Sexual Renunciation in Early Christianity*, New York: Columbia University Press, 1988.

Brown, Peter, *The Rise of Western Christendom: Triumph and Diversity AD 200–1000*, Oxford: Blackwell, 1996.

Burton-Christie, Douglas, *The Word in the Desert: Scripture and the Quest for Holiness in Early Christian Monasticism*, New York: Oxford University Press, 1993.

Davis, Leo Donald, *The First Seven Ecumenical Councils (325–787): Their History and Theology*, Collegeville, MN: Liturgical Press, 1990.

Edwards, Mark, ed. and trans., *Constantine and Christendom: The Oration to the Saints, The Greek and Latin Accounts of the Discovery of the Cross, The Edict of Constantine to Pope Silvester*, Liverpool: Liverpool University Press, 2003.

Ehrman, Bart D., *Lost Christianities: The Battles for Scripture and the Faiths We Never Knew*, New York: Oxford University Press, 2003.

Ehrman, Bart D., *Lost Scriptures: Books That Did Not Make It into the New Testament*, New York: Oxford University Press, 2003.

Eusebius, *The History of the Church from Christ to Constantine*, trans. by G. A. Williamson, London: Penguin Books, 1965, rep. 1981.

Evans, Craig A. and Donald A. Hagner, eds., *Anti-Semitism and Early Christianity: Issues of Polemic and Faith*, Minneapolis, MN: Fortress, 1993.

Evans, G. R., *A Brief History of Heresy*, Oxford: Blackwell, 2003.

Evans, G. R., ed., *The First Christian Theologians: An Introduction to Theology in the Early Church*, Oxford: Blackwell, 2004.

Frend, W. H. C., *The Rise of Christianity*, Philadelphia, PA: Fortress, 1984.

Gregg, R. and D. Groh, *Early Arianism: A View of Salvation*, Philadelphia, PA: Fortress, 1981.

Hall, Stuart G., *Doctrine and Practice in the Early Church*, Grand Rapids, MI: Eerdmans, 1991.

Herrin, Judith, *The Formation of Christendom*, Princeton, NJ: Princeton University Press, 1987.

Hofstadter, Richard, *The Progressive Historians*, New York, 1968.

Hultgren, Arland J., *The Rise of Normative Christianity*, Minneapolis, MN: Fortress, 1994.

Hultgren, Arland J. and Steven Haggmark, eds., *The Earliest Christian Heretics: Readings from Their Opponents*, Minneapolis, MN: Fortress, 1996.

Kraemer, Ross and Mary Rose d'Angelo, eds., *Women and Christian Origins*, New York: Oxford University Press, 1999.

Rusch, William, ed., *The Trinitarian Controversy*, Philadelphia, PA: Fortress, 1980.

Wilken, Robert L., *The Christians as the Romans Saw Them*, New Haven, CT: Yale University Press, 1984.

Wilken, Robert L., *Remembering the Christian Past*, Grand Rapids, MI: Eerdmans, 1995.

Wilken, Robert L., *The Spirit of Early Christian Thought: Seeking the Face of God*, New Haven, CT: Yale University Press, 2003.

Medieval Christianity

Atkinson, Clarissa, *The Oldest Vocation: Christian Motherhood in the Middle Ages*, Ithaca, NY: Cornell University Press, 1991.

Bynum, Caroline Walker, *Holy Feast and Holy Fast: The Religious Significance of Food to Medieval Women*, Berkeley: University of California Press, 1987.

Duby, Georges, *The Three Orders: Feudal Society Imagined*, trans. by Arthur Goldhammer, Chicago, IL: University of Chicago Press, 1980.

Evans, G. R., ed., *The Medieval Theologians: An Introduction to Theology in the Medieval Period*, Oxford: Blackwell, 2001.

Gurevich, Aaron, *The Origins of European Individualism*, Oxford: Blackwell, 1995.

Hinson, E. Glenn, *The Church Triumphant: A History of Christianity up to 1300*, Macon, GA: Mercer University Press, 1995.

Hodges, R. and D. Whitehouse, *Mohammed, Charlemagne and the Origins of Europe*, Ithaca, NY: Cornell University Press, 1983.

Hussey, J. M., *The Orthodox Church in the Byzantine Empire*, Oxford: Clarendon, 1986.

Leclercq, Jean, et al., *The Spirituality of the Middle Ages*, London: Burns and Oates, 1968.

Leclercq, Jean, *The Love of Learning and the Desire for God*, London: SPCK, 1978.

Le Goff, Jacques, *The Birth of Purgatory*, London: Scolar Press, 1984.

Le Goff, Jacques, *Intellectuals in the Middle Ages*, Oxford: Blackwell, 1993.

Little, Lester K., *Religious Poverty and the Profit Economy in Medieval Europe*, Ithaca, NY: Cornell University Press, 1978.

Little, Lester K. and Barbara H. Rosenwein, eds., *Debating the Middle Ages: Issues and Readings*, Oxford: Blackwell, 1998.

Lynch, Joseph H., *The Medieval Church: A Brief History*, London: Longman, 1992.

Moore, R. I., *The Formation of a Persecuting Society: Power and Deviance in Western Europe, 950–1250*, Oxford: Blackwell, 1987.

Radice, Betty, trans., *The Letters of Abelard and Heloise*, London: Penguin Books, 1974.

Riley-Smith, Jonathan, ed., *The Oxford History of the Crusades*, Oxford: Oxford University Press, 1999.

Shahar, Shulamith, *The Fourth Estate: A History of Women in the Middle Ages*, London: Routledge, 1991.

Southern, R. W., *Western Society and the Church in the Middle Ages*, London: Penguin Books, 1970.

Sumption, Jonathan, *Pilgrimage: An Image of Medieval Religion*, London: Faber and Faber, 1975.

Tierney, Brian, *The Crisis of State and Church, 1050–1300*, Englewood Cliffs, NJ: Prentice-Hall, 1964.

Ullmann, Walter, *A Short History of the Papacy in the Middle Ages*, London: Methuen, 1972.

Vauchez, André, *Sainthood in the Later Middle Ages*, New York: Cambridge University Press, 1997.

Reformation

Bossy, John, *Christianity in the West 1400–1700*, Oxford: Oxford University Press, 1985.

Brady, Thomas A., Jr., Heiko A. Oberman, and James D. Tracy, eds., *Handbook of European History 1400–1600. Late Middle Ages, Renaissance and Reformation*, 2 vols., Leiden: Brill, 1994.

Cameron, Euan, *The European Reformation*, Oxford: Clarendon, 1991.

Dickens, A. G. and John M. Tonkin with Kenneth Powell, *The Reformation in Historical Thought*, Cambridge, MA: Harvard University Press, 1985.

Dixon, C. Scott, ed., *The German Reformation: The Essential Readings*, Oxford: Blackwell, 1999.

Edwards, Mark U., Jr., *Printing, Propaganda, and Martin Luther*, Berkeley: University of California Press, 1994.

Gordon, Bruce, ed., *Protestant History and Identity in Sixteenth-Century Europe*, 2 vols., Aldershot: Scholar Press, 1996.

Greengrass, Mark, *The Longman Companion to the European Reformation c. 1500–1618*, London: Longman, 1998.

Gregory, Brad S., *Salvation at Stake: Christian Martyrdom in Early Modern Europe*, Cambridge, MA: Harvard University Press, 1999.

Hendrix, Scott, *Recultivating the Vineyard: The Reformation Agendas of Christianization*, Louisville, KY: Westminster John Knox Press, 2004.

Hsia, R. Po-chia, ed., *A Companion to the Reformation World*, Oxford: Blackwell, 2004.

Lindberg, Carter, *Beyond Charity: Reformation Initiatives for the Poor*, Minneapolis, MN: Fortress, 1993.

Lindberg, Carter, *The European Reformations*, Oxford: Blackwell, 1996.

Lindberg, Carter, ed., *The Reformation Theologians*, Oxford: Blackwell, 2001.

Muller, Richard A., *The Unaccommodated Calvin: Studies in the Foundation of a Theological Tradition*, New York: Oxford University Press, 2000.

Oberman, Heiko A., *Luther: Man between God and the Devil*, New Haven, CT: Yale University Press, 1990.

O'Malley, John W., *Trent and All That: Renaming Catholicism in the Early Modern Era*, Cambridge, MA: Harvard University Press, 2000.

Pettegree, Andrew, ed., *The Reformation World*, London: Routledge, 2000.

Pettegree, Andrew, *Europe in the Sixteenth Century*, Oxford: Blackwell, 2002.

Wiesner, Merry E., *Women and Gender in Early Modern Europe*, Cambridge: Cambridge University Press, 1993.

Wiesner-Hanks, Merry E., *Christianity and Sexuality in the Early Modern World: Regulating Desire, Reforming Practice*, London: Routledge, 2000.
Williams, George H., *The Radical Reformation*, 3rd edn. Kirksville, MO: Sixteenth Century Journal Publishers, 1992.

Modern

Ahlstrom, Sydney E., *A Religious History of the American People*, New Haven, CT: Yale University Press, 1972.
Barth, Karl, *Protestant Theology in the Nineteenth Century: Its Background and History*, Valley Forge, PA: Judson Press, 1973.
Bays, Daniel H., ed., *Christianity in China from the Eighteenth Century to the Present*, Stanford, CA: Stanford University Press, 1996.
Bediako, Kwame, *Christianity in Africa: The Renewal of a Non-Western Religion*, Maryknoll, NY: Orbis, 1995.
Berger, Peter L., *Questions of Faith: A Skeptical Affirmation of Christianity*, Oxford: Blackwell, 2004.
Bruce, Steve, *Fundamentalism*, Oxford: Blackwell, 2000.
Cameron, Euan, ed., *Early Modern Europe: An Oxford History*, Oxford: Oxford University Press, 1999.
Crowner, David and Gerald Christianson, eds., *The Spirituality of the German Awakening*, New York: Paulist, 2003.
Ford, David F., ed., *The Modern Theologians*, Oxford: Blackwell, 1997.
Hempton, David, *The Religion of the People: Methodism and Popular Religion c. 1750–1900*, London: Routledge, 1996.
Holifield, E. Brooks, *Theology in America: Christian Thought from the Age of the Puritans to the Civil War*, New Haven, CT: Yale University Press, 2003.
Holifield, E. Brooks, *A History of Pastoral Care in America: From Salvation to Self-Realization*, Nashville, TN: Abingdon, 1983.
Hollenweger, Walter, *Pentecostalism: Origins and Developments Worldwide*, Peabody, MA: Hendrickson Publishers, 1997.
Holtrop, Pieter and Huch McLeod, eds., *Missions and Missionaries*, Woodbridge: Boydall Press, 2000.
Jenkins, Philip, *The Next Christendom: The Coming of Global Christianity*, New York: Oxford University Press, 2002.
Lindberg, Carter, *The Third Reformation? Charismatic Movements and the Lutheran Tradition*, Macon, GA: Mercer University Press, 1983.

Lindberg, Carter, ed., *The Pietist Theologians*, Oxford: Blackwell, 2004.

McGrath, Alister, *The Future of Christianity*, Oxford: Blackwell, 2002.

McLeod, Hugh, *Religion and the People of Western Europe*, New York: Oxford University Press, 1981.

McLeod, Hugh, ed., *European Religion in the Age of the Great Cities 1830–1930*, London: Routledge, 1995.

McLeod, Hugh and Werner Ustof, eds., *The Decline of Christendom in Western Europe, 1750–2000*, Cambridge: Cambridge University Press, 2003.

Marsden, George, *Fundamentalism and American Culture: The Shaping of Twentieth Century Evangelicalism 1870–1925*, New York: Oxford University Press, 1980.

Martin, David, *Tongues of Fire: The Explosion of Protestantism in Latin America*, Oxford: Blackwell, 1990.

Noll, Mark, et al., eds., *Evangelicalism: Comparative Studies of Popular Protestantism in North America, the British Isles, and Beyond, 1700–1990*, New York: Oxford University Press, 1994.

Noll, Mark, *American Evangelical Christianity: An Introduction*, Oxford: Blackwell, 2001.

Noll, Mark, *America's God, from Jonathan Edwards to Abraham Lincoln*, New York: Oxford University Press, 2002.

Raboteau, Albert J., *A Fire in the Bones: Reflections on African-American Religious History*, Boston, MA: Beacon, 1995.

Robert, Dana, *American Women in Mission: A Social History of Their Thought and Practice*, Macon, GA: Mercer University Press, 1996.

Robert, Dana, ed., *Gospel Bearers, Gender Barriers: Missionary Women in the Twentieth Century*, Maryknoll, NY: Orbis, 2002.

Schleiermacher, Friedrich, *The Christian Faith*, 2 vols., New York: Harper Torchbooks, 1963.

Walls, Andrew F., *The Missionary Movement in Christian History: Studies in the Transmission of Faith*, Maryknoll, NY: Orbis, 1996.

Ward, W. R., *The Protestant Evangelical Awakening*, Cambridge: Cambridge University Press, 1992.

Ward, W. R., *Faith and Faction*, London: Epworth, 1993.

Williams, Peter W., ed., *Perspectives on American Religion and Culture*, Oxford: Blackwell, 1999.

Index

"Jesus," "God," and biblical names are not indexed

A Matter of Principle

A Matter of Principle

RONALD DWORKIN

HARVARD UNIVERSITY PRESS
Cambridge, Massachusetts

89-102

Library of Congress Cataloging in Publication Data

Dworkin, R. M.
  A matter of principle.

  Bibliography: p.
  Includes index.
  1. Political questions and judicial power—United
States. 2. Law—Philosophy. 3. Jurisprudence.
4. Law and politics. I. Title.
KF380.D85   1985   340′.1   84-25122
ISBN 0-674-55460-4 (alk. paper) (cloth)
ISBN 0-674-55461-2 (paper)

For My Mother

Contents

A Matter of Principle

Introduction

THIS IS A BOOK about fundamental theoretical issues of political philosophy and jurisprudence: about what liberalism is and why we still need it; whether we should be skeptical about law and morality; how collective prosperity should be defined; what interpretation is and how far law is a matter of interpretation rather than invention. It is also a practical book about urgent political issues. Is it fair to give blacks priority for jobs and university places? Can it ever be right to break the law? Is it uncivilized to ban dirty films; unfair to censor books to protect national security? What rights do suspects have when crime rates are rising? Does social justice mean economic equality? Should judges make political decisions? It is, above all, a book about the interplay between these two levels of our political consciousness: practical problems and philosophical theory, matters of urgency and matters of principle.

The essays were written separately over the last several years. The controversies they join are old; but history has given them fresh shape and importance. The ancient argument whether judges should and do make law is of more practical importance than ever before, at least in the United States. It seems very likely that the man now President will appoint enough Justices to the Supreme Court to set the character of that commanding institution for a generation, and people can review his choices intelligently only if they have a clear view about what adjudication is and what the Supreme Court is for. The development and deployment of atomic missiles has had powerful impact on people's attitudes about civil disobedience, and more generally about the connection between conscience and political obligation, in Western Europe as well as the United States and Britain. Affirmative action programs, seeking better racial relations through preferences and quotas, continue to divide people of conscience and to set one minority against another; recession and high unemployment make these arguments newly bitter. Old wars over pornography and censorship have new armies in radical feminists and the Moral Majority. The perennial conflict between

a free press, on the one hand, and privacy and security, on the other, seems sharper and more perplexing than ever.

Cases at law figure in much of the argument, not as an exercise in legal history or doctrine, but rather because law gives a special and illuminating shape to political controversy. When political issues come to court—as they always do, sooner or later, in the United States at least—then they plead for decision that is at once discrete and principled. They must be decided at retail, in their full social complexity; but the decision must be defended as flowing from a coherent and uncompromised vision of fairness and justice, because that, in the last analysis, is what the rule of law really means. Legal analysis, in this broad sense, is more concrete than classical political philosophy, more principled than political craft. It provides the right theater for philosophy of government.

PART ONE of the book studies the role political convictions should play in the decisions various officials and citizens make about what the law is, and when it should be enforced and obeyed. It rejects the popular but unrealistic opinion that such convictions should play no role in these decisions at all, that law and politics belong to wholly different and independent worlds. But it also rejects the opposite view, that law and politics are exactly the same, that judges deciding difficult constitutional cases are simply voting their personal political convictions as much as if they were legislators or delegates to a new constitutional convention. It rejects that crude view on two grounds, each of which furnishes a major theme for the rest of the book.

First, the crude view ignores a crucial constraint on adjudication. Judges should enforce only political convictions that they believe, in good faith, can figure in a coherent general interpretation of the legal and political culture of the community. Of course lawyers may reasonably disagree about when that test is met, and very different, even contradictory, convictions might all pass the test. But some could not. A judge who accepts this constraint, and whose own convictions are Marxist or anarchist or taken from some eccentric religious tradition, cannot impose these convictions on the community under the title of law, however noble or enlightened he believes them to be, because they cannot provide the coherent general interpretation he needs.

Second, the crude view obscures a distinction of capital importance to legal theory, a distinction that is the most immediate reference of the book's title. Our political practice recognizes two different kinds of argument seeking to justify a political decision. Arguments of policy try to show that the community would be better off, on the whole, if a particular program were pursued. They are, in that special sense, goal-based arguments. Arguments of principle claim, on the contrary, that particular programs must be

carried out or abandoned because of their impact on particular people, even if the community as a whole is in some way worse off in consequence. Arguments of principle are right-based. Because the simple view that law and politics are one ignores this distinction, it fails to notice an important qualification to the proposition that judges must and do serve their own political convictions in deciding what the law is. Even in hard cases, though judges enforce their own convictions about matters of principle, they need not and characteristically do not enforce their own opinions about wise policy.

I have discussed this distinction elsewhere, and it has been challenged in various ways. Some critics object to the distinction itself; others object to the claim I just made, that adjudication is characteristically a matter of principle rather than policy. Their arguments, and my replies, are collected in a recent volume which also includes critical comments on other essays reprinted in this book.[1] This book does not return to the argument. Instead it tries to exhibit the practical value of the distinction in various contexts. Chapter 4 argues, for example, that the case for civil disobedience must be differently constructed, and that it is subject to different forms of qualification, when the law or other official decision being challenged is seen as a serious mistake of policy than when it is seen as a grave mistake of principle. If protests against the deployment of atomic weapons in Europe, for example, are ordinarily challenges to policy rather than to principle, then civil disobedience is a very different matter from that directed, in earlier decades, against unjust wars and racial discrimination.

Part Two defends the claim I just mentioned, that legal analysis is fundamentally interpretive, and offers a general account of interpretation to describe the sense in which this is so. It also considers how this claim bears on an important theoretical issue in jurisprudence. Anglo-American lawyers have on the whole been skeptical about the possibility of a "right answer" in any genuinely hard case. If lawyers and judges disagree about what the law is, and no one has a knockdown argument either way, then what sense does it make to insist that one opinion is right and others wrong? Surely, so the common view runs, there are only different answers to the question of law and no one right or best answer. Some lawyers who hold that skeptical view draw what they take to be conservative conclusions: judges should defer to decisions made by more representative institutions like legislatures, and in the case of constitutional law to the decisions made by the Founders of the constitutional settlement long ago. Others find in this skepticism a kind of license: if there is no right answer in some lawsuit of constitutional magnitude, no one has a right that the courts decide in any particular way, and judges should therefore decide in whatever way seems to them best for the future of the nation. Part Two argues that this skeptical challenge is altered, and defused, once it is understood that legal argument and analysis is

interpretive in character. For the ways in which interpretive arguments may be said to admit of right answers are sufficiently special, and complex, as to call into question the familiar arguments for skepticism. Indeed, once law is seen in this way, there is little point in either asserting *or* denying an "objective" truth for legal claims.

Part Three turns from argument directly about law to issues of political theory that lie in the background. It explores the present state of liberal theory. Liberalism was once, not very long ago, almost a consensus political theory in Britain and the United States, at least among political and legal philosophers. They disagreed about a great deal, but they all seemed to accept, as close to axiomatic, a kind of egalitarian individualism. They believed, that is, that politics should have two general ambitions: first to improve the power of citizens, judged one by one, to lead the lives each thinks best for himself or herself; and second to reduce the great inequality in the resources different people and groups within the community have available for that purpose. But liberalism, so conceived, is no longer so popular; politicians now compete to disown various aspects of this ideal. It is said to have failed. It has proved, according to some critics, too generous and expensive, and, according to others, too divisive and mean-spirited. Part Three argues that the new consensus against liberalism is founded on muddled arguments, which have been encouraged by the failure of liberal political theorists to identify the constitutive principles of liberalism and to make plain the form of egalitarianism on which liberal ideals, properly understood, are based.

Part Four joins political and legal theory again. It considers a presently influential thesis about how judges should decide cases. This denies that judges should be concerned with moral standards, in the familiar sense, at all. Their decisions should be economic rather than moral; they should aim to make the community as a whole richer rather than in some different sense fairer. This attitude, often called the "economic" approach to law, has colonized a large part of American legal education and placed ambassadors in Britain and elsewhere. It is associated with conservative political positions and sometimes seems a cover for the renascent politics of self-interest that threatens to occupy the ground abandoned by liberalism. But it has intellectual appeal even for legal scholars and judges who are not committed to defending inequality, and law journals are now choked with its products. Part Four argues that the economic approach nevertheless lacks any defensible philosophical foundation.

Parts Five and Six are devoted to two complex and topical controversies. Each illustrates the practical value and importance of the distinction between arguments of principle and of policy. Part Five takes up the raging dispute about programs of positive discrimination in employment and admission to university and professional schools, programs designed to im-

prove the overall position of blacks and other minority groups. It argues that such programs are best justified not through arguments of principle, about the rights of the particular people they benefit, but rather on arguments of policy, about the general benefit they secure for the community as a whole. Then the crucial question is whether any argument of principle lies *against* a policy that seeks to benefit the community in that way. Chapter 13 inspects a variety of principles that might be thought to provide an argument of that character; it concludes that none does. If so, then the genuinely important issues in the debate about positive discrimination are entirely issues of policy. We must judge various programs of quota and preference one by one, by weighing practical costs and benefits, not altogether in some scale of principle.

Part Six is about censorship. It considers, first, the charged issue of sexually explicit books, films, and photographs. A case against censoring such material might be made out in two different ways. The first relies on an argument of policy; an excellent example is provided in the goal-based argument of the recent Williams Report, which claims that liberty of expression must be protected, at least to some degree, in order to promote the conditions of human flourishing. I describe that Report in Chapter 17; I argue that no justification of that kind will prove adequate to the degree of freedom the Report itself recommends. The second defense of liberty of expression relies instead on arguments of principle. I describe a defense of that kind, which appeals to a right people have to freedom of sexual choice, and more generally to moral independence, even if their choices will not make the community better as a whole even in the long run.

The last two essays take up freedom of the press. Much of the recent debate has been corrupted because those who support special privileges for the press offer, as arguments of principle, what are really arguments of policy. Chapter 18 discusses, for example, whether a reporter should be permitted to withhold information about his sources even when this information is needed by the defense in a criminal trial. Many reporters believe that if they are forced to reveal confidential sources, then such sources will "dry up" because informers will be reluctant to risk exposure. They claim that the question of requiring disclosure therefore presents a conflict of principle between two supposed rights: the right of someone accused of a crime to any information helpful to his defense, and the competing public "right to know" that the press will be unable to satisfy as fully if sources are revealed. I argue that this picture is mistaken, because the public's alleged right to know is not, properly speaking, a right at all. The argument for a free flow of information is an argument of policy: that the community will be improved in various ways if it is better informed. If this is correct, then the conflict between a fair trial and freedom of the press is not, in this instance, a conflict of principle, but rather a contest between a principle and policy.

They are both important, but except in extraordinary circumstances the contest must be settled in favor of principle, which means in favor of a fair trial for the accused.

The book's final essay expands this discussion into a warning. Though some defenders of the press blend policy into principle in order to expand freedom of speech, the confusion they create does disservice to their aim. It jeopardizes the central core of principle in the First Amendment, the genuine and fragile right of free speech. We stand in greater danger of compromising that right than of losing the most obvious policy benefits of powerful investigative reporting and should therefore beware the danger to liberty of confusing the two. The caution is general. If we care so little for principle that we dress policy in its colors when this suits our purpose, we cheapen principle and diminish its authority.

I HAVE REVISED the original essays, for this book, in minor ways; chiefly to eliminate temporal expressions no longer appropriate. I have not, however, made substantive changes or new arguments, because some of the original essays have been discussed and criticized by other writers, and it would be unfair to change my arguments in reprinting those essays in this collection. I leave these changes and further arguments, so far as they are about law, to a new book I am now writing about legal theory.

The Political Basis of Law

ONE

Political Judges and the Rule of Law

TWO QUESTIONS AND TWO IDEALS

This essay is about two questions, and the connections between them. The first is a practical question about how judges do and should decide hard cases. Do judges in the United States and Great Britain make political decisions? Should their decisions be political? Of course the decisions that judges make *must* be political in one sense. In many cases a judge's decision will be approved by one political group and disliked by others, because these cases have consequences for political controversies. In the United States, for example, the Supreme Court must decide important constitutional issues that are also political issues, like the issue whether accused criminals have procedural rights that make law enforcement more difficult. In Britain the courts must decide cases that demand an interpretation of labor legislation, like cases about the legality of secondary picketing, when the Trades Union Congress favors one interpretation and the Confederation of British Industries another. I want to ask, however, whether judges should decide cases on political *grounds,* so that the decision is not only the decision that certain political groups would wish, but is taken on the ground that certain principles of political morality are right. A judge who decides on political grounds is not deciding on grounds of party politics. He does not decide in favor of the interpretation sought by the unions because he is (or was) a member of the Labour party, for example. But the political principles in which he believes, like, for example, the belief that equality is an important political aim, may be more characteristic of some political parties than others.

There is a conventional answer to my question, at least in Britain. Judges should not reach their decisions on political grounds. That is the view of almost all judges and barristers and solicitors and academic lawyers. Some academic lawyers, however, who count themselves critics of British judicial practice, say that British judges actually do make political decisions, in spite of the established view that they should not. J. A. G. Griffiths of the

London School of Economics, for example, in a polemical book called *The Politics of the Judiciary*, argued that several recent decisions of the House of Lords were political decisions, even though that court was at pains to make it appear that the decisions were reached on technical legal rather than political grounds.[1] It will be helpful briefly to describe some of these decisions.

In *Charter*[2] and *Dockers*[3] the House of Lords interpreted the Race Relations Act so that political clubs, like the West Ham Conservative Club, were not obliged by the Act not to discriminate against coloured people. In *Tameside* the House overruled a Labour minister's order reversing a local Conservative council's decision not to change its school system to the comprehensive plan favored by the Labour government.[4] In the notorious *Shaw's Case*, the House of Lords sustained the conviction of the publisher of a directory of prostitutes.[5] It held that he was guilty of what it called the common law crime of "conspiracy to corrupt public morals," even though it conceded that no statute declared such a conspiracy to be a crime. In an older case, *Liversidge v. Anderson*, the House upheld the decision of a minister who, in the Second World War, ordered someone detained without trial.[6] Griffiths believes that in each of these cases (and in a great many other cases he discusses) the House acted out of a particular political attitude, which is defensive of established values or social structures and opposed to reform. He does not say that the judges who took these decisions were aware that, contrary to the official view of their function, they were enforcing a political position. But he believes that that was nevertheless what they were doing.

So there are those who think that British judges do make political decisions. But that is not to say that they should. Griffiths thinks it inevitable, as I understand him, that the judiciary will play a political role in a capitalist or semi-capitalist state. But he does not count this as a virtue of capitalism; on the contrary, he treats the political role of judges as deplorable. It may be that some few judges and academics—including perhaps Lord Justice Denning—do think that judges ought to be more political than the conventional view recommends. But that remains very much an eccentric—some would say dangerous—minority view.

Professional opinion about the political role of judges is more divided in the United States. A great party of academic lawyers and law students, and even some of the judges in the prestigious courts, hold that judicial decisions are inescapably and rightly political. They have in mind not only the grand constitutional decisions of the Supreme Court but also the more ordinary civil decisions of state courts developing the common law of contracts and tort and commercial law. They think that judges do and should act like legislators, though only within what they call the "interstices" of decisions already made by the legislature. That is not a unanimous view even among sophisticated American lawyers, nor is it a view that the public at large has

fully accepted. On the contrary, politicians sometimes campaign for office promising to curb judges who have wrongly seized political power. But a much greater part of the public accepts political jurisprudence now than did, say, twenty-five years ago.

My own view is that the vocabulary of this debate about judicial politics is too crude, and that both the official British view and the "progressive" American view are mistaken. The debate neglects an important distinction between two kinds of political arguments on which judges might rely in reaching their decisions. This is the distinction (which I have tried to explain and defend elsewhere) between arguments of political principle that appeal to the political rights of individual citizens, and arguments of political policy that claim that a particular decision will work to promote some conception of the general welfare or public interest.[7] The correct view, I believe, is that judges do and should rest their judgments on controversial cases on arguments of political principle, but not in arguments of political policy. My view is therefore more restrictive than the progressive American view but less restrictive than the official British one.

The second question I put in this essay is, at least at first sight, less practical. What is the rule of law? Lawyers (and almost everyone else) think that there is a distinct and important political ideal called the rule of law. But they disagree about what that ideal is. There are, in fact, two very different conceptions of the rule of law, each of which has its partisans. The first I shall call the "rule-book" conception. It insists that, so far as is possible, the power of the state should never be exercised against individual citizens except in accordance with rules explicitly set out in a public rule book available to all. The government as well as ordinary citizens must play by these public rules until they are changed, in accordance with further rules about how they are to be changed, which are also set out in the rule book. The rule-book conception is, in one sense, very narrow, because it does not stipulate anything about the content of the rules that may be put in the rule book. It insists only that whatever rules are put in the book must be followed until changed. Those who have this conception of the rule of law do care about the content of the rules in the rule book, but they say that this is a matter of substantive justice, and that substantive justice is an independent ideal, in no sense part of the ideal of the rule of law.

I shall call the second conception of the rule of law the "rights" conception. It is in several ways more ambitious than the rule-book conception. It assumes that citizens have moral rights and duties with respect to one another, and political rights against the state as a whole. It insists that these moral and political rights be recognized in positive law, so that they may be enforced *upon the demand of individual citizens* through courts or other judicial institutions of the familiar type, so far as this is practicable. The rule of law on this conception is the ideal of rule by an accurate public concep-

tion of individual rights. It does not distinguish, as the rule-book conception does, between the rule of law and substantive justice; on the contrary it requires, as part of the ideal of law, that the rules in the rule book capture and enforce moral rights.

That is a complex ideal. The rule-book conception of the rule of law has only one dimension along which a political community might fall short. It might use its police power over individual citizens otherwise than as the rule book specifies. But the rights conception has at least three dimensions of failure. A state might fail in the *scope* of the individual rights it purports to enforce. It might decline to enforce rights against itself, for example, though it concedes citizens have such rights. It might fail in the *accuracy* of the rights it recognizes: it might provide for rights against the state, but through official mistake fail to recognize important rights. Or it might fail in the *fairness* of its enforcement of rights: it might adopt rules that put the poor or some disfavored race at a disadvantage in securing the rights the state acknowledges they have.

The rights conception is therefore more complex than the rule-book conception. There are other important contrasts between the two conceptions; some of these can be identified by considering the different places they occupy in a general theory of justice. Though the two conceptions compete as ideals of the legal process (because, as we shall see, they recommend different theories of adjudication), they are nevertheless compatible as more general ideals for a just society. Any political community is better, all else equal, if its courts take no action other than is specified in rules published in advance, and also better, all else equal, if its legal institutions enforce whatever rights individual citizens have. Even as general political ideals, however, the two conceptions differ in the following way. Some high degree of compliance with the rule-book conception seems necessary to a just society. Any government that acts contrary to its own rule book very often—at least in matters important to particular citizens—cannot be just, no matter how wise or fair its institutions otherwise are. But compliance with the rule book is plainly not sufficient for justice; full compliance will achieve very great injustice if the rules are unjust. The opposite holds for the rights conception. A society that achieves a high rating on each of the dimensions of the rights conception is almost certainly a just society, even though it may be mismanaged or lack other qualities of a desirable society. But it is widely thought, at least, that the rights conception is not necessary to a just society, because it is not necessary, in order that the rights of citizens be protected, that citizens be able to demand adjudication and enforcement of these rights as individuals. A government of wise and just officers will protect rights (so the argument runs) on its own initiative, without procedure whereby citizens can dispute, as individuals, what these rights are. Indeed, the rights conception of the rule of law, which insists on the importance of

that opportunity, is often dismissed as legalistic, as encouraging a mean and selfish concern with individual property and title.

The two conceptions also differ in what might be called their philosophical neutrality. The rights conception seems more vulnerable to philosophical objections. It supposes that citizens have moral rights—that is, rights other than and prior to those given by positive enactment—so that a society can sensibly be criticized on the ground that its enactments do not recognize the rights people have. But many philosophers doubt that people have any rights that are not bestowed on them by enactments or other official decisions; or even that the idea of such rights makes sense. They doubt particularly that it is sensible to say that people have moral rights when (as the rights conception must concede is often the case) it is controversial within the community what moral rights they have. The rights conception must suppose, that is, that a state may fail along the dimension of accuracy even when it is controversial whether it has failed; but that is just what philosophers doubt makes sense. The rights conception therefore seems open to the objection that it presupposes a philosophical point of view that is itself controversial, and which will therefore not be accepted by all members of the community.

The last contrast I shall mention will join the two issues of this essay. For the two conceptions of the rule of law offer very different advice on the question of whether judges should make political decisions in hard cases— that is, cases in which no explicit rule in the rule book firmly decides the case either way. Though the two conceptions, as general political ideals, may both have a place in a full political theory, it makes a great difference which is taken to be the ideal of *law* because it is that ideal which governs our attitudes about adjudication. The rule-book conception has both negative and positive advice about hard cases. It argues, positively, that judges should decide hard cases by trying to discover what is "really" in the rule book, in one or another sense of that claim. It argues, negatively, that judges should never decide such cases on the ground of their own political judgment, because a political decision is not a decision about what is, in any sense, in the rule book, but rather a decision about what ought to be there. The rule-book conception supports the conventional British view about political judges.

I must now pause to explain the idea this positive advice uses: the idea that it makes sense to ask, in a hard case, about what is "really" in the rule book. In a modern legal system hard cases typically arise, not because there is nothing in the rule book that bears on the dispute, but because the rules that are in the book speak in an uncertain voice. *Charter,* for example, was a hard case because it was unclear whether the rule Parliament put in the rule book—the rule that organizations that serve "a section of the public" must not discriminate—forbade a political club to deny membership to blacks. It

is, in that sense, "unclear" what the rule book really, properly understood, provides. A lawyer who speaks this way treats the rule book as an attempt at communication and supposes that an unclear rule can be better understood by applying techniques that we use to improve our understanding of other sorts of communication.

Different generations of rule-book lawyers—and different lawyers within each generation—advocate different techniques for this purpose. Some prefer semantic questions. They argue in the following way. "The legislature uses words when it enacts a rule, and the meaning of these words fix what rules it has enacted. So any theory about the meaning of the phrase 'a section of the public' is a theory that makes the Race Relations Act more precise. The rule-book conception therefore directs judges to try to form semantic theories. They should ask, for example, what the phrase 'a section of the public' would be taken to mean in a similar context in ordinary discourse. Or what the most natural meaning of some component of the phrase, like the word 'public,' is. Or what similar phrases were taken to mean in other statutes. It is understood that different judges will give different answers to these semantic questions; no one answer will be so plainly right that everyone will agree. Nevertheless each judge will be trying, in good faith, to follow the rule-book ideal of the rule of law, because he will be trying, in good faith, to discover what the words in the rule book really mean."

These semantic questions are very popular in Britain. A different set of questions—group-psychological questions—are now more popular in the United States. Those who favor group-psychological questions rather than semantic questions take decisions rather than words to be the heart of the matter. "Why are the particular rules that a legislature enacts (rather than, for example, the rules that law professors prefer) the rules that form the rule book for law? Because legislators have been given authority by the community as a whole to *decide* what rules shall govern. The words they choose are normally the best evidence of what they have decided, because it is assumed that legislators use words in their standard meanings to report their decisions. But if, for some reason, the words used do not uniquely report a particular decision, then it is necessary to turn to whatever other evidence of what they intended to do we can find. Did the legislators—or some important group of them—suppose that their Race Relations Act would apply to political clubs so as to forbid racial discrimination there? If so, then the Act represents that decision, and it is that decision that is embedded in the rule book properly understood. But if they supposed that the Act would not apply to political clubs, then the rule book, properly understood, contains that decision instead."

Once again there is no assumption here that all reasonable lawyers will agree about what the legislators intended. On the contrary, defenders of the

rule-book model know that even skilled lawyers will disagree over infer-
ences of legislative intention drawn from the same evidence. They insist
that the question of intention is nevertheless the right question to ask, because each judge who asks it is at least doing his best to follow the rule-book
model and therefore (on this conception) to serve the rule of law.

The semantic and psychological questions these different groups propose
are historical rather than political. A third (and more sophisticated) set of
historical questions has recently gained in popularity. "Suppose a hard case
cannot be decided on semantic grounds. Perhaps the phrase 'a section of the
public' might just as properly be used to include as to exclude associations
like political clubs. Suppose it cannot be decided by asking what the legislators who enacted that statute intended to accomplish. Perhaps very few legislators had even thought of the question whether political clubs should be
included. We must then ask a question different from either the semantic or
the psychological question, which is this. What would the legislature have
decided if, contrary to fact, it *had* decided whether or not political clubs
were to be included?" Lawyers who want to answer this counterfactual
question might consider, for example, other decisions the same legislators
reached in other areas of law. Or they might consider more broadly the
pattern of legislation about race relations or freedom of association in recent years. They might use such evidence to argue, for example, that if Parliament had for some reason been forced to debate a clause explicitly
extending the acts to political clubs, it would have approved that clause.

It is even more obvious in the case of this counterfactual historical question than in the case of the semantic or psychological question that reasonable lawyers will disagree about the conclusions to be drawn from the same
evidence. But once again the rule-book conception deems it better that
they try to answer this question, even though they disagree, than that they
ask the different and political question, about which they will surely disagree, of what Parliament *should* have done. For the counterfactual question, like the semantic and psychological questions but unlike the political
question, is supported by a theory that also supports and explains the rule-
book conception itself. We follow the rule book, on this theory, because we
assign to a political institution the responsibility and the power to decide
how the police power of the state shall be used. If, on some occasion, that
institution has in fact not decided that question (because it did not realize
that a decision was necessary) but would have decided one way rather than
the other if it had, then it is more in keeping with the rationale of the rule
book that the power be used that way than the contrary way. If neither of
the two decisions that a court might reach is actually recorded in the rule
book, it is fairer, on this argument, to take the decision that would have
been in the rule book but for a historical accident.

This argument for the counterfactual question concedes that the rule that

is to be applied is not in the actual rule book. In this respect the counter-factual question is different from the semantic and psychological questions, each of which can more plausibly be said to reveal what is in the actual rule book "properly understood." But the three sorts of questions have a more fundamental unity. Each aims at developing what might be called a "recti-fied" rule book in which the collection of sentences is improved so as more faithfully to record the will of the various institutions whose decisions put those sentences into the rule book. The questions are all, in themselves, po-litically neutral questions, because they seek to bring to the surface a histor-ical fact—the will of responsible lawmakers—rather than to impose a distinct and contemporary political judgment upon that will. It is perfectly true—and conceded, as I said, by the rule-book model—that any particular judge's answer to these political neutral questions may well be different from another judge's answer. It is the virtue of the different historical ques-tions, not the certainty or predictability of the answer, that recommends these questions to the rule-book model. That conception of the rule of law opposes political questions, like the question of what the legislators should have done, not because these questions admit of different answers, but be-cause they are simply the wrong questions to ask.

The rights conception, on the other hand, will insist that at least one kind of political question is precisely the question that judges faced with hard cases must ask. For the ultimate question *it* asks in a hard case is the ques-tion of whether the plaintiff has the moral right to receive, in court, what he or she or it demands. The rule book is *relevant* to that ultimate question. In a democracy, people have at least a strong *prima facie* moral right that courts enforce the rights that a representative legislature has enacted. That is why some cases are easy cases on the rights model as well as on the rule-book model. If it is clear what the legislature has granted them, then it is also clear what they have a moral right to receive in court. (That statement must be qualified in a democracy whose constitution limits legislative power. It must also be qualified (though it is a complex question how it must be qualified) in a democracy whose laws are fundamentally unjust.

But though the rights model concedes that the rule book is in this way a source of moral rights in court, it denies that the rule book is the exclusive source of such rights. If, therefore, some case arises as to which the rule book is silent, or if the words in the rule book are subject to competing in-terpretations, then it is right to ask which of the two possible decisions in the case best fits the background moral rights of the parties. For the ideal of adjudication, under the rights model, is that, so far as is practicable, the moral rights that citizens actually have should be available to them in court. So a decision that takes background rights into account will be superior, from the point of view of that ideal, to a decision that instead speculates on, for example, what the legislation would have done if it had done anything.

It is important to notice, however, that the rule book continues to exert an influence on the question of what rights the parties have, under the rights model, even when background moral rights also exert an influence.[8] A judge who follows the rights conception of the rule of law will try, in a hard case, to frame some principle that strikes him as capturing, at the appropriate level of abstraction, the moral rights of the parties that are pertinent to the issues raised by the case. But he cannot apply such a principle unless it is, as a principle, consistent with the rule book, in the following sense. The principle must not conflict with other principles that must be presupposed in order to justify the rule he is enforcing, or any considerable part of the other rules. Suppose a judge himself approves what might be called a radical Christian principle: that each citizen is morally entitled that those who have more wealth than he does make available to him the surplus. He might wish to apply that principle to hard cases in tort or contract so as to refuse damages against a poor defendant, on the ground that the richer plaintiff's right to damages must be set off against the defendant's right to charity. But he cannot do so, because (for better or for worse) that principle is inconsistent with the vast bulk of the rules in the rule book. No adequate justification of what is in the rule book could be given, that is, without presupposing that the radical Christian principle has been rejected. The rights conception supposes that the rule book represents the community's efforts to capture moral rights and requires that any principle rejected in those efforts has no role in adjudication.

So a judge following the rights conception must not decide a hard case by appealing to any principle that is in that way incompatible with the rule book of his jurisdiction. But he must still decide many cases on political grounds, because in these cases contrary moral principles directly in point are each compatible with the rule book. Two judges will decide such a hard case differently because they hold different views about the background moral rights of citizens. Suppose a case applying a commercial statute requires a choice between a moral principle enforcing *caveat emptor* and a competing principle stressing the moral rights of contractual partners against each other, as members of a cooperative enterprise. It may well be—at a given stage of development of commercial law—that neither answer is in the sense described plainly incompatible with the British rule book taken as a whole. Each judge deciding that issue of principle decides as he does, not because all alternatives are excluded by what is already in the rule book, but because he believes his principle to be correct, or at least closer to correct than other principles that are also not excluded. So his decision is a political decision in the sense described. It is precisely that sort of political decision that the rule-book conception steadily condemns.

The two topics of this essay are in that way joined. The practical question, which asks whether judges should make political decisions in hard

cases, is joined to the theoretical question of which of two conceptions of the rule of law is superior. The connection is threatening to the rights conception, because many people are convinced that it is wrong for judges to make political decisions and they will be anxious to reject any theory about the ideals of law that recommends them. So I shall pursue the two topics, now joined, by asking whether the conviction that judges should stay out of politics is sound.

THE ARGUMENT FROM DEMOCRACY

Why is it wrong for judges to make political decisions of the sort I say the rights conception requires them to make? One argument will seem to many of you decisive against judicial political decisions. Political decisions, according to this argument, should be made by officials elected by the community as a whole, who can be replaced from time to time in the same way. That principle applies to all political decisions, including the decision what rights individuals have, and which of these should be enforceable in court. Judges are not elected or reelected, and that is wise because the decisions they make *applying* the rule book as it stands to particular cases are decisions that should be immune from popular control. But it follows that they should not make independent decisions about changing or expanding the rule book, because these decisions should be made in no way *other* than under popular control.

That is the familiar argument from democracy. There is a short answer to that argument, at least in Britain. If Parliament, which is elected by the people, is dissatisfied with a particular political decision made by judges, then Parliament can override that decision by appropriate legislation. Unfortunately that short answer is too short. Legislative time is a scarce resource, to be allocated with some sense of political priorities, and it may well be that a judicial decision would be overruled if Parliament had time to pass every law it would like to pass, but will not be overruled because Parliament does not. In some cases there is a further difficulty in the short answer. When an issue is the subject of great controversy, then Parliament may be disabled from changing a judicial decision, for practical political reasons, because any change would infuriate some powerful section of the community or alienate some parts of a governing coalition. It may be that the issue of whether the Race Relations Act should apply to certain sorts of clubs is an issue like that. Either decision would provoke such effective political opposition that Parliament is effectively saddled with whatever decision the courts reach.

So we cannot be content with the short answer to the argument from democracy. But there are more serious defects in that argument. It assumes, in the first place, that the rule-book solution to hard cases—which urges

judges to ask historical questions of the sort I described rather than political questions—does serve democracy in some way that the rights conception does not. It assumes that these historical questions do bring to the surface decisions that an elected legislature has actually made. But if we look more closely at the questions, we shall find that the assumption has no basis.

Suppose a statute can be interpreted in two ways, one of which requires one decision in a hard case and the other of which requires the other. The phrase "a section of the public," for example, may be interpreted so that the statute includes only facilities open to anyone who can afford them, in which case a political club which is not open to members of other parties does not fall within the statute. Or it may be interpreted so as to exclude only intimate or domestic occasions, like private parties, in which case a political club is covered by the statute. The semantic and group-psychological questions assume that Parliament decided to adopt one or the other of these two different statutes; they aim to provide techniques for deciding which of the two decisions it (probably) took.

The semantic questions argue that if the critical words of the statute are words more likely to be used by someone who has taken one of these decisions than someone who has taken the other, then that is evidence, at least, that the legislature has taken that decision. So if the words "the public or a section of the public" are more likely to be used by someone who had decided to exclude political clubs from the Act than by someone who has decided to include them, then Parliament probably took the former decision. But this is fallacious. For, though it is sensible to argue that if the legislature has taken one or other of these decisions, it is more likely to have taken the one more naturally expressed by the words it used, it is not sensible to argue in the other direction, that because it used these words it must have taken one or the other of these decisions. It may have taken neither. Indeed the fact that the words used are compatible with either decision makes it more likely that it has not taken either decision, unless there is some independent evidence that it has.

The group-psychological questions do not supply that independent evidence, except in very rare cases, because the strategy they recommend also presupposes, rather than shows, that the individuals whose intentions are in play had any pertinent intention at all. The rare exceptions are cases in which the legislative history contains some explicit statement that the statute being enacted had one rather than the other consequence, a statement made under circumstances such that those who voted for the statute must have shared that understanding. In most cases the legislative history contains nothing so explicit. The group-psychological questions then fix on peripheral statements made in legislative hearings, or on the floor of the legislature, or on other provisions of the statute in question, or on provisions of statutes in related areas, attempting to show that these statements or pro-

visions are inconsistent with an intention to create a statute under one interpretation of the unclear phrase, though consistent with an intention to
create a statute under the other interpretation. That is not an argument in
favor of the claim that key legislators intended to adopt that second statute,
unless it is assumed that these legislators must have intended to enact one or
the other. But they may not have intended to enact either; and the fact that
they did not enact their statute in words that clearly put either intention
into effect is a very strong argument that they did not.

We must be careful to avoid a trap here. We may be tempted to say, of
any particular legislator, that he either intended to enact a particular statute (that is, a particular interpretation of the words that form the bill he
votes for) or intended not to enact that statute. If that were so, then evidence that suggests that he did not intend to enact a statute that would include political clubs would suggest that he did intend to enact a statute that
did not include them. But it is not so. A legislator may vote with great enthusiasm for a bill because he knows that it will force hotels and restaurants
to cease discrimination without thereby having either the intention that the
same prohibition should apply to semipublic institutions like political clubs
or the intention that it should not. He may simply have failed to consider
the issue of whether it should. Or he may positively have intended that the
statute be inconclusive on whether such institutions should be covered, because either decision, if explicit, would anger an important section of the
public or otherwise prove impolitic.

In either case, the argument that it would be more consistent for him to
have had the intention to exclude political clubs than to include them—
more consistent with what he had voted for elsewhere in the present statute
or in other statutes, or more consistent with the arguments given in hearings
or on the legislative floor—is beside the point. That may be an argument
about what he *should* have intended on the question of political clubs. It is
no argument that he *did* so intend, because he may have been ignorant of,
or had good reason for ignoring, what consistency required.

The counterfactual questions I mentioned are not open to the same objection. They do not assume that particular members of the legislature took
a decision or had an intention one way or the other. They concede that no
one may even have thought of the relevant issue. They ask what legislators
would have decided or intended if, contrary to fact, they had been forced to
attend to the issue. They insist that that question admits of an answer in
principle, even though in particular cases it might be hard to discover what
the answer is, and even though any particular judge's answer will be controversial. The argument that counterfactual historical questions respect
democracy is therefore different from the argument that semantic and psychological questions do. It runs as follows. "Suppose we decide that it is
likely, on the balance of probabilities, that Parliament would have brought
political clubs within the statute if, for some reason, it had been forced to

decide whether they were to be within or without. Then it is just an accident that Parliament did not actually decide to include them. It is (we might say) the latent will of Parliament that they be within, and even though a latent will is not an actual will, it is nevertheless closer to the spirit of democracy to enforce the latent will of Parliament than to encourage judges to impose their own will on the issue."

This argument is unsound, for a number of reasons. First, it is at least arguable that in many cases there is no answer, even in principle, to a counterfactual historical question. Philosophers divide on whether it is necessarily true that if Parliament had been forced to vote on the issue of political clubs, it would either have voted to include them or not voted to include them. But let us set that philosophical point aside and assume that, in at least enough cases to support the argument from democracy, counterfactual historical questions have a right answer, even when it is controversial what that right answer is. It is nevertheless true that a great number of *different* counterfactual questions can be asked about any particular legislative decision, and the answers to these different questions will be different, because how Parliament would have decided if it had been forced to decide will depend on the way in which it was forced to decide.

It may be, for example, that if the Parliamentary draftsman had put a clause including political clubs into the first draft of the bill, that clause would have survived, because no amendment would have been proposed that would have succeeded; but also true that if the draftsman had included a clause excluding political clubs, *that* clause would have survived, again because no amendment would have been proposed that would have succeeded. What is the latent Parliamentary will then, assuming that neither clause was in fact put into the bill at any stage? The counterfactual technique cannot work unless it stipulates some canonical form of the counterfactual question. But why should one form of the question—one hypothesis about the conditions in which Parliament might have been forced to decide—be superior to another from the standpoint of the argument from democracy?

There is a further objection. *No* canonical form of the counterfactual question that makes that question genuinely historical would be acceptable to lawyers and judges in practice. For though counterfactual questions have found their way into legal practice, they are used as political rather than historical questions. The answer they would receive if they were really historical questions would be rejected by lawyers as irrelevant to adjudication. Consider the following (arbitrary) form for the counterfactual question: Suppose that just before the Race Relations Act had its final hearing one member of the Cabinet convinced his colleagues that the Act must take a position, one way or the other, on political clubs, and that in consequence Parliament finally took a position. What position would it have taken? If a historian were asked that question, he would reject any *a priori* restrictions

on the kind of evidence that would be relevant. Suppose he discovered that a Minister of the day had written a letter to his mistress on the subject of political clubs, describing the special vulnerability of one or the other of his colleagues to pressure from such clubs. Suppose he discovered that the party had commissioned a secret political poll on the public's attitudes on this or related issues. He would insist on seeing that letter or the results of that poll, if at all possible, and if he were fortunate enough to see these, he would insist that they were of dramatic relevance to the historical counterfactual question he had been asked. He would be right, if the question were really a historical one, because it is less likely that the Cabinet would have proposed including political clubs if some member were vulnerable or if the public strongly opposed their inclusion.

But a judge asking the question of what Parliament would have done had it attended to the problem of political clubs is distinctly not interested in letters to mistresses or in secret political polls. His argument is, not that Parliament would actually have taken the decision in question if it had taken any decision on the matter, but rather that Parliament would have taken that decision if it were acting consistently with some assumed justification for what it did do. That is a very different matter, and history has little to do with it. The argument I composed in favor of the counterfactual question insisted that, if Parliament would have included political clubs had it been forced to choose, then it is only an accident, from the standpoint of democracy, that political clubs are not explicitly included. But it does not follow, from the different claim that Parliament out of consistency should have included political clubs, that it is only an accident that it did not explicitly include them. Suppose it is true that Parliament should have included them out of consistency, but also true that for political reasons it would *in fact* have excluded them if it had done anything. Then the supposed theory of democracy, that decisions on political matters should be made by Parliament, hardly argues that political clubs should be included.

It might now be said, however, that a different theory of democracy does make relevant the question of what Parliament, in consistency, should have done. The legislature elected by the people does more (according to this theory) than enact the particular provisions that make up the statute books. It chooses the general policies the state is to pursue and the general principles it is to respect. If, in a hard case, one decision follows more naturally from the principles that the legislature served in enacting a statute, then the judges should take that decision, even though it is true that, as a matter of historical fact, the legislature itself would have taken the other one if it had taken either. The legislature endorses principles by enacting legislation these principles justify. The spirit of democracy is served by respecting these principles. It is not served by speculating whether the legislature itself, on some particular occasion, would have kept the faith.

This argument is meant to defend the counterfactual questions as they

are used in practice. It concedes that these questions are evaluative, at least in the sense described, rather than just historical, but argues that questions that are evaluative in that sense do serve democracy. Perhaps a similar argument could be made to justify the group-psychological questions. It might be said that these questions do not really suppose that individual legislators have an intention that the statute be construed one way rather than another. Instead they ask what principles a legislator who voted for the statute would be presumed to have thereby endorsed, so that the decision in a hard case may be governed by those principles. If the group-psychological questions are understood and defended in this way, then they are not after all different from the counterfactual questions. When a judge asks what the legislators must have intended to accomplish, he means to ask what policies or principles most naturally fit the statute they approved. When he asks what they would have done if required to answer the question before him, he means to ask what answer flows from policies or principles that most naturally fit the statute they approved. Neither question is really psychological or historical; they ask the same basic question in either a psychological or a historical disguise.

But if the psychological and counterfactual questions are understood in this way, then it is no longer plausible to suppose that a judge who puts these questions in order to decide a hard case is not making a political decision. For the evaluations these questions, so understood, require are not different in character from the evaluations recommended by the rights conception of the rule of law. If only one set of principles is consistent with a statute, then a judge following the rights conception will be required to apply these principles. If more than one is consistent, the question of which interpretation more "naturally" flows from the statute as a whole requires a choice among ways to characterize the statute that must reflect the judge's own political morality. That is the source of the complaint I mentioned at the outset of this essay, which is that British judges really make political judgments according to their own lights disguised as judgments about legislative intentions or history. This is true; though the suggestion of hypocrisy is, for the most part, unfair. If psychological or counterfactual questions are put as genuine historical questions, then they will supply no useful answers. If they are to be useful, then they must be understood as questions that call for the sort of political judgment that they, in practice, force from the judges who use them. Judges may not acknowledge these judgments, but that is a failure of recognition not a failure of integrity.

RIGHTS AND DEMOCRACY

The argument from democracy, therefore, does not provide an argument in favor of the rule-book conception of adjudication. So far I have not contested the root assumption of that argument, that it is offensive to democ-

racy if matters of political principle are decided by courts rather than elected officials. We must now ask whether that assumption is sound. Do judicial decisions on matters of principle (as distinct from policy) offend any plausible theory of democracy?

The argument that they do supposes that the decision of a legislature elected by the majority of the public is, in the last analysis, the best way of deciding questions about the rights that individual citizens have against each other and against the society as a whole. But this might be so for two different kinds of reasons, or some combination of the two. Legislation might be a more accurate procedure for deciding what people's rights are than alternative procedures, or it might be a better procedure for reasons other than accuracy. We rely, to some degree, on both sorts of justifications for other institutional theories, like the theory that a jury trial is a good method for testing accusations of crime. We think that trial by jury is a reasonably accurate method, but we also think that it is a good method for reasons that are not reasons of accuracy.

So we must consider the argument for democracy, as a strategy for deciding questions about rights, under two aspects. Are there, first, institutional reasons why a legislative decision about rights is likely to be more accurate than a judicial decision? It is difficult to assess the question of accuracy in the abstract, that is, apart from some particular theory of rights. But I cannot imagine what argument might be thought to show that legislative decisions about rights are inherently more likely to be correct than judicial decisions. Obviously, on any theory of rights, decisions about rights are better if they are based on more rather than less information about a variety of facts. But I know of no reason why a legislator is more likely to have accurate beliefs about the sort of facts that, under any plausible conception of rights, would be relevant to determining what people's rights are. On any plausible theory of rights, moreover, questions of speculative consistency—questions that test a theory of rights by imagining circumstances in which that theory would produce unacceptable results—are likely to be of importance in an argument about particular rights, because no claim of right is sound if it cannot stand the test of hypothetical counter-example. But the technique of examining a claim of right for speculative consistency is a technique far more developed in judges than in legislators or in the bulk of the citizens who elect legislators.

In some cases, moreover, the public that elects legislators will be in effect a party to the argument whether someone has a right to something, because that public's own interests oppose the concession of a right. That will typically be true when the argument lies in a politically sensitive area, like that of race relations. Politically powerful groups may prefer that political clubs discriminate, and no countervailing force, except the politically impotent minority itself, may very much care. It would be wrong to assume that in

such circumstances the legislators will lack the independent judgment to identify the right at stake or the courage to enforce it. But it is nevertheless true that in such cases legislators are subject to pressures that judges are not, and this must count as a reason for supposing that, at least in such cases, judges are more likely to reach sound conclusions about rights. I am now arguing only that legislators are not institutionally better placed to decide questions about rights than judges are. Someone might object that as things are, in Britain for example, judges will do a worse job because they hold worse theories about rights. They are drawn from a particular class, educated in a particular way, and members of a particular profession such that they are very likely not to appreciate the rights of people from very different classes. Nothing I have so far said meets that argument. I shall consider its force later.

Second, are there other reasons of fairness, apart from reasons of accuracy, why legislation should be the exclusive strategy for deciding what right people have? We must consider a familiar argument that appeals to the importance of respect for the law and other aspects of political stability. "Legislatures are unlikely to reach a decision about rights that will offend some powerful section of the community so much that it will shake the political order. If the legislature does make this mistake, the government will fall, and the orderly process of democracy will replace the foolish legislature with another. Courts have no similar built-in defense against very unpopular decisions, because judges have no direct fear of popular dissatisfaction with their performance. On the contrary, some judges may take pleasure in their freedom to disregard popular views. So if judges reach a political decision that is outrageous, the public will not be able to vindicate itself by replacing them. Instead it will lose a measure of its respect, not only for them, but for the institution and processes of the law itself, and the community will be less cohesive and less stable as a result. Surely that has been the consequence of the ill-judged experiment that brought courts into the political process through the Industrial Relations Act."

This argument urges that judges should not make political judgments, including political judgments about rights, because the effect of their being seen to make such judgments will lessen respect for the law. This particular argument, unlike the others I discuss, does not assume that the "historical" questions a judge might ask in lieu of political questions are nonpolitical. It assumes only that they will be *seen* to be nonpolitical. But that assumption is in fact equally dubious. For in all but a few of the cases in which a judicial decision has been widely and publicly criticized for being political, the judges set out historical rather than political grounds in their opinions. The law was brought into disrepect (whatever that means) by the content of the decision, not the character of the arguments provided. Political stability may argue against legislation that either deliberately or inadvertently

leaves politically sensitive issues open for judges to decide. It is not an argument that, if judges are in fact forced to decide such issues, they should decide them on historical rather than political grounds.

Moreover the factual basis of the argument is at best unproved. Groups of citizens who intensely dislike a judicial decision will complain, not only about the decision but also about the nature of the institution that produced it. They may even be moved to disobey the decision, particularly if they have the political power to do so with impunity. But there is so far no evidence that the inclination to disobey will be general rather than local. There were grave predictions, for example, that political hostility to the American war in Vietnam and the disobedience to laws pursuing that war would lead to a general breakdown of law and order. That danger was seen, by different groups, both as an argument against the war and an argument in favor of prosecuting dissidents. But though crime continues to rise in the United States at a depressingly orderly rate, there is no evidence whatsoever that these political events were in any way contributory.

In any case, if the argument is taken to be an argument specifically against frankly political decisions by courts, it fails for a reason I have so far not mentioned. For it assumes that the public discriminates between political decisions taken by legislatures and those taken by courts, and that the public believes that the former are legitimate and the latter are not. But even if this is so now, the public sense of illegitimacy would presumably disappear if it were recognized by lawyers and other officials that such decisions are consistent with democracy and recommended by an attractive conception of the rule of law. So the present argument begs the question whether lawyers and officials should embrace that conclusion. It provides only an argument that any professional endorsement of such decisions should be followed—as inevitably it would be followed—by a change in the public's attitudes toward the law as well.

I recognize that there are many differences between Britain and the United States (I shall mention some of these later) that make any quick comparison between public attitudes in the two countries suspect. But it is worth noticing that a shift in the Supreme Court's attitude toward constitutional interpretation a few decades ago—a shift from reliance on historical arguments toward political arguments—was not followed by any sharp loss in the public's respect for that Court's decisions, as measured by the public's disposition to comply. On the contrary, the Warren Court achieved almost miraculous compliance with extremely unpopular decisions when popular understanding of the Court's role still insisted on historical rather than political interpretation of the Constitution, certainly to a greater degree than it does now. Popular opinion, in this case, has followed the Court.

Political stability, however, is not the main reason—apart from reasons of accuracy—why most people want decisions about rights to be made by leg-

islatures. The reason is one of fairness. Democracy supposes equality of political power, and if genuine political decisions are taken from the legislature and given to courts, then the political power of individual citizens, who elect legislators but not judges, is weakened, which is unfair. Learned Hand gave this reason, in his famous Holmes lectures, for resisting political decisions by the Supreme Court. He said that he would not want to be ruled by "a bevy of Platonic Guardians," even if he knew how to choose them, which he did not.[9]

If all political power were transferred to judges, democracy and equality of political power would be destroyed. But we are now considering only a small and special class of political decisions. It is not easy to see how we are to test whether and how much individual citizens lose, in political power, if courts are assigned some of these decisions. But it seems plausible that— however gains or losses in political power are measured—some citizens gain more than they lose.

It is no doubt true, as a very general description, that in a democracy power is in the hands of the people. But it is all too plain that no democracy provides genuine equality of political power. Many citizens are for one reason or another disenfranchised entirely. The economic power of large business guarantees special political power for its managers. Interest groups, like unions and professional organizations, elect officers who also have special power. Members of entrenched minorities have, as individuals, less power than individual members of other groups that are, as groups, more powerful. These defects in the egalitarian character of democracy are well known and perhaps in part irremedial. We must take them into account in judging how much individual citizens lose in political power whenever an issue about individual rights is taken from the legislature and given to courts. Some lose more than others only because they have more to lose. We must also remember that some individuals gain in political power by that transfer in institutional assignment. For individuals have powers under the rights conception of the rule of law that they do not have under the rule-book conception. They have the power to demand, as individuals, a fresh adjudication of their rights. If their rights are recognized by a court, these rights will be enforced in spite of the fact that no Parliament had the time or the will to enforce them.

It may be a nice question whether any particular individual gains in power more than he loses when courts undertake to decide what political rights he has. Access to courts may be expensive, so that the right of access is in that way more valuable to the rich than the poor. But since, all else equal, the rich have more power over the legislature than the poor, at least in the long run, transferring some decisions from the legislature may for that reason be more valuable to the poor. Members of entrenched minorities have in theory most to gain from the transfer, for the majoritarian bias of

the legislature works most harshly against them, and it is their rights that are for that reason most likely to be ignored in that forum. If courts take the protection of individual rights as their special responsibility, then minorities will gain in political power to the extent that access to the courts is in fact available to them, and to the extent to which the courts' decisions about their rights are in fact sound. The gain to minorities, under these conditions, would be greatest under a system of judicial review of legislative decisions, such as holds in the United States and would hold in Britain under some versions of the proposed constitutional Bill of Rights. But it may nevertheless be substantial, even if the court's power to adjudicate political rights is limited to cases, like *Charter*, in which the legislature has not plainly settled the issue of what rights they shall be deemed to have. I assume, of course, favorable conditions that may not hold. But there is no reason to think, in the abstract, that the transfer of decisions about rights from the legislatures to courts will retard the democratic ideal of equality of political power. It may well advance that ideal.

CONSERVATIVE JUDGES

My argument thus far has been theoretical and institutional. Some will think it therefore beside the point, because they believe that the main arguments against encouraging judges to take political decisions are practical and personal. "British judges are intensely conservative and protective of established forms of authority. Perhaps that is only an accident of history, or perhaps it is the inevitable consequence of other institutional arrangements and traditions. But it is in any case a fact; and it would be perverse to ignore that fact in considering, for example, whether minorities and the poor would gain if judges were more explicitly political, or whether these judges are likely to do a better or worse job than Parliament in identifying genuine political rights."

I do not dispute that characterization of the present generation of judges in Great Britain. With some distinguished exceptions, it seems to me correct. But it does not follow that judges, however conservative, will reach less attractive decisions under a regime that encourages them to make political decisions about individual rights than a regime that obliges them to make "neutral" decisions by posing the "historical" questions I described. The various decisions cited by Griffiths and others to show the conservative character of British judges were all ostensibly justified on these "historical" grounds. Though critics suppose, for example, that the *Tameside* decision reflects the judge's disapproval of comprehensive education, and *Shaw's Case* shows their conviction that sexual license should be discouraged, each of these decisions reads as if the judges were obliged by neutral considerations of statutory construction and the interpretation of precedent to reach

the conclusions they did. It is therefore hard to see how the explicit direction to judges, to make decisions about rights on political grounds, would produce more "conservative" decisions. The point is not that judges deliberately ignore their duty to reach decisions on historical rather than political grounds. It is rather that "historical" decisions must in the nature of the case be political.

If the explicit direction had any effect on the decisions produced by conservative judges, it might well be to make these decisions *less* rather than more conservative. The obligation to show the political character of the decision as a decision about individual rights *rather than the general welfare* must act as a general liberal influence. In Shaw's case, for example, the House held itself obliged, by its view of the precedents, to consider whether the publication of Shaw's *Ladies Directory* tended to corrupt public morals. That is a question, considered in itself, about the character of the general welfare (Viscount Simonds called it the "moral welfare") of society, and conservative judges may naturally be expected to take a conservative view of the public's welfare. Suppose, however, that reigning legal theory required the House to ask itself first whether the precedents unambiguously required them to recognize such a crime, and, if not, whether the theory that such a crime existed was more consistent with Shaw's rights as an individual than the theory that it did not. It would then have been strenuously argued that individuals have a moral right, at least in principle, not to be punished except for committing a crime clearly published in advance, and that in virtue of that right it would be unjust to punish Shaw. I very much doubt that even "conservative" judges would wish to deny the inherent appeal of such a right or that any competent judge would argue that it would be incompatible with British legal and political practice to recognize it. But a judge asked to take the decision on grounds of political principle could not have jailed Shaw unless he rejected the right as a matter of moral principle or argued that British practice denied it.

The *Charter* case, which I have been using as my leading example, was decided in what might be called a conservative way, and that is why it is taken by critics to be a political decision. Certainly the opinions of the Law Lords do not describe their decision as political: these opinions apply semantic questions to the phrase "a section of the public." But it is no doubt a fair comment that less conservative judges might have assigned a more powerful meaning to that phrase, because they would have had a different opinion on the question whether it is in the public interest that semipublic institutions lose a measure of control over the character of their membership. Suppose, however, that their Lordships had put to themselves, instead of the semantic question that invites the influence of that judgment about the general welfare, an explicitly political question about the competing rights of members of minorities not to suffer from discrimination and of club

members to choose their own associates on criteria reasonable to them. The Race Relations Act embodies a compromise between those two rights: it holds that the right to be free from discrimination is sufficiently strong so that fully public institutions may not discriminate, but not so strong as to annihilate the competing right to choose associates in fully private settings like domestic entertainment or exclusive clubs. How should the balance be struck in intermediate cases not explicitly settled by the Act, like nonexclusive societies open in general to everyone with a particular political affiliation?

It is not inconceivable that a conservative judge would disagree with the initial judgment of the Act. He might think the Act undervalues freedom of association, or that it is bad policy to legislate morality in race relations (though it is sound to do so in sex). But if he is told he must decide a case like *Charter* on principles of political morality, compatible with the principles of the Act, he would be forced to set aside these convictions, because they are *not* compatible. He cannot hold that there is a morally relevant difference between the degree to which freedom of association is constrained by requiring Claridges not to discriminate and the degree to which that freedom is constrained by similar requirements on the West Ham Conservative Club. Even though he disapproves the way the balance was struck in the Act, he cannot plausibly suppose that a different political principle, striking the balance so as to couple the Conservative Club with private homes, is compatible with that Act. The more frankly political the subject matter of a case—the more that case is like *Charter* rather than the commercial case discussed abstractly earlier—then the more the explicitly political character of the statute or precedent in question will constrain the judge's own political morality in the way just described.

Here again the supposedly neutral semantic questions the House of Lords used permitted a decision that gave more effect to the judge's personal convictions than a frankly political jurisprudence would have allowed. The semantic questions, precisely because they are not political in form, do not discriminate among the kinds of political judgments that will, inevitably, influence the answers judges give them. They attract hidden political judgments that may be inconsistent in principle with the legislation supposedly being enforced. The political questions the rights model recommends, however, require that the political answers they receive be both explicit and principled, so that their appeal and their compatibility with principles more generally endorsed can be tested.

So even those who think that the political principles of the present judges are unsound do not have, in that belief, good reason to oppose the rights model and the style of adjudication it recommends. That model is likely to decrease the number of decisions they deplore. There is, however, a further and perhaps more important reason why we should reject the argument

that appeals to the conservative character of the present judges. For the character of judges is a consequence of the theory of adjudication in force; therefore it cannot reasonably be urged as a reason for not changing that theory. If the rights conception of the rule of law were to become more popular in this country than it has been, legal education would almost certainly become broader and more interesting than it is now, and men and women who would never think of a legal career, because they want a career that will make a difference to social justice, will begin to think differently. The profession would change, as it did dramatically in the United States earlier in this century, and the lawyers whom that profession values and sends to the bench would be different. The argument that political jurisprudence would be a misfortune in Britain because judges are too firmly welded to established order begs the question. If law had a different place here, different people would have a place in the law.

TWO IDEALS AND TWO COUNTRIES

Many people will resist the comparison I have made between Britain and the United States and argue that the role of law is so different in the two countries as to make comparisons unreliable. I agree with the spirit of the objection; but the differences do not touch the present point. I do not argue that it is likely that Britain will move toward a more openly political jurisprudence, but only that its judges and lawyers would be different if it did. I concede that the differences in legal culture reflect more fundamental differences that make the United States more fertile ground for the rights conception. Americans are still fascinated by the idea of individual rights, which is the zodiac sign under which their country was born. Their record in recognizing and protecting these rights has been less than spectacular. But public debate in the United States is dominated, to a degree British commentators find surprising, by discussion of what rights people have.

In Britain political debate centers on the different idea I have several times referred to, though not discussed, which is the nineteenth-century idea of the general welfare or collective good. When political debate talks of fairness, it is generally fairness to classes or groups within the society (like the working class or the poor), which is a matter of the collective welfare of these groups. American debate has insisted that rights belong to individuals rather than groups and has resisted measuring fairness by classes rather than people.

This difference in the vocabulary of political debate reflects and contributes to a difference in the general attitude toward lawyers and judges and their place in government. In the United States lawyers have often been scoundrels, and Americans give them no public honor, as they do give doctors and even some teachers. But America assigns lawyers, as a group,

power and influence in a wide variety of matters, notably including government. In Britain lawyers are treated very well. They are dressed up in costumes—though principally middle-aged drag—and when they become judges their dignity is protected by very wide powers of contempt. But they have very little real power.

I have so far said very little directly in support of the rights conception as a political ideal. I have been too occupied with its defense. The positive case for that conception is straightforward. I conceded that a society devoted to that conception of the rule of law may pay a price, certainly in efficiency and possibly in the communitarian spirit that too much concern with law is supposed to cripple. But that society makes an important promise to each individual, and the value of that promise seems to me worth the cost. It encourages each individual to suppose that his relations with other citizens and with his government are matters of justice, and it encourages him and his fellow citizens to discuss as a community what justice requires these relationships to be. It promises a forum in which his claims about what he is entitled to have will be steadily and seriously considered at his demand. It cannot promise him that the decision will suit him, or even that it will be right. But that is not necessary to make the promise and the sense of justice that it creates valuable. I may have made it seem as if democracy and the rule of law were at war. That is not so; on the contrary, both of these important political values are rooted in a more fundamental ideal, that any acceptable government must treat people as equals. The rule of law, in the conception I support, enriches democracy by adding an independent forum of principle, and that is important, not just because justice may be done there, but because the forum confirms that justice is in the end a matter of individual right, and not independently a matter of the public good.[10]

TWO

The Forum of Principle

TWO MISCHIEVOUS IDEAS

The Constitution is the fundamental law of the United States, and judges must enforce the law. On that simple and strong argument John Marshall built the institution of judicial review of legislation, an institution that is at once the pride and the enigma of American jurisprudence.[1] The puzzle lies in this. Everyone agrees that the Constitution forbids certain forms of legislation to Congress and the state legislatures. But neither Supreme Court justices nor constitutional law experts nor ordinary citizens can agree about just what it does forbid, and the disagreement is most severe when the legislation in question is politically most controversial and divisive. It therefore appears that these justices exercise a veto over the politics of the nation, forbidding the people to reach decisions which they, a tiny number of appointees for life, think wrong. How can this be reconciled with democracy? But what is the alternative, except abdicating the power Marshall declared? That power is now so fixed in our constitutional system that abdication would be more destructive of consensus, more a defeat for cultivated expectation, than simply going on as before. We seem caught in a dilemma defined by the contradiction between democracy and ancient, fundamental, and uncertain law, each of which is central to our sense of our traditions. What is to be done?

There may be a way out. We escape the dilemma if we can construct an apolitical program for deciding constitutional cases. A program that allows judges to decide, for example, whether statutes imposing a minimum wage or forbidding abortion are constitutional[2] without deciding for themselves whether minimum wage statutes are unfair or whether laws prohibiting abortion invade fundamental moral or political rights. But how can judges decide such cases apolitically if the text of the Constitution is not itself decisive? Two ideas are now prominent. One has been familiar for a long time, and though its appeal has waxed and waned, it has attracted a new generation of enthusiasts. This is the idea of a constitutional *intention*—often

called the "original" intention or the intention of the "Framers" of the Constitution. Suppose judges can discover how the Framers intended the uncertain provisions of the Constitution to be understood. If judges follow that original intention, they would not be making substantive choices themselves but only enforcing choices made long ago by others, choices that have been given authority by the people's ratification and acceptance of the Constitution.

The second strategy also has a long history, but it was given new life and direction in a famous footnote by Justice Harlan Stone and now, again, in an interesting book by John Ely.[3] This strategy relies not on the idea of an original intention, but rather on a sharp distinction between matters of substance and matters of process. Suppose judges take up the assignment not of reviewing the fairness or justice of substantive decisions made by those officials who enacted the statutes under review, but only of protecting the fairness of the process through which these statutes were made. Reasonable people can disagree whether particular processes are fair. But judges who follow their own convictions about the fairness of process will at least not be trespassing on substantive decisions. In any case, judicial review of the political process only polices democracy; it does not seek to override it as judicial review of substance does.

These are two ways of fleeing from substance in constitutional decisions. My point, in this essay, is that both ways end in failure, and in the same sort of failure. Judges cannot decide what the pertinent intention of the Framers was, or which political process is really fair or democratic, unless they make substantive political decisions of just the sort the proponents of intention or process think judges should not make. Intention and process are mischievous ideas because they cover up these substantive decisions with procedural piety, and pretend they have not been made. The old bodies are now buried here.

INTENTION

Interpretation and Constitutional Law

Before I begin my defense of these claims, however, I must raise a preliminary issue, in order to avoid a certain confusion. It has become common to distinguish "interpretive" from "noninterpretive" theories of judicial review.[4] Interpretive theories (according to this distinction) argue that judicial review of legislative decisions must be based on an interpretation of the Constitution itself. This might be a matter of construing the text, or determining the intention of the "Framers," or, more plausibly, some combination of both. Noninterpretive theories are said to suppose, on the contrary, that the Court is at least sometimes justified in holding legislative decisions

to standards taken from some source other than the text, like popular morality, or sound theories of justice, or some conception of genuine democracy.[5]

The putative distinction between these two types of theory provides not only a scheme of classification for theories of judicial review but also a scheme for argument about such theories. Constitutional lawyers write papers in which it is proposed, for example, that no noninterpretive theory is consistent with democracy.[6] Or that any noninterpretive theory must rest on a doctrine of natural law and so must be rejected.[7] Or that no interpretive theory can be correct, or adequate to sustain what almost everyone agrees are proper Supreme Court decisions, like the major decisions holding racial segregation in education unconstitutional.[8] In this way constitutional theories are studied and rejected at wholesale.

It is, of course, natural to look for schemes of classification that provide argumentative strategies. But this scheme is a poor one, for the following reason. Any recognizable theory of judicial review is interpretive in the sense that it aims to provide an interpretation of the Constitution as an original, foundational legal document, and also aims to integrate the Constitution into our constitutional and legal practice as a whole. No one proposes judicial review as if on a clean slate. Each theory claims to provide the most illuminating account of what our actual constitutional tradition, taken as a whole, really "comes to"—of the "point" or "best justification" of the constitutional system that has been developed in our own legal history. Each draws, from its interpretation of that system, a particular view of how best to interpret the Constitution as an original text. So the thesis, that a useful distinction can be made between theories that insist on and those that reject interpretation, either of the Constitution as a particular document or of our constitutional system as a whole, is more confusing than helpful.

The theories that are generally classed as "noninterpretive"—those that strike us as most activist or most liberated from the actual text of the Constitution—are plainly interpretivist in any plausible sense. They disregard neither the text of the Constitution nor the motives of those who made it; rather they seek to place these in the proper context. "Noninterpretive" theorists argue that the commitment of our legal community to this particular document, with these provisions enacted by people with those motives, presupposes a *prior* commitment to certain principles of political justice which, if we are to act responsibly, must therefore be reflected in the way the Constitution is read and enforced. That is the antithesis of a clean slate argument, and a paradigm of the method of interpretation. It disregards neither text nor original intention, but rather proposes a theory to teach us how to discover what the former means and what the latter is.

Indeed, it might seem that the theories most often called "interpretive"—the theories that strike us as most bound to the text of the Consti-

tution considered in isolation—are more likely to turn out to be noninterpretive in this broad sense. For they appear to pay very little attention to questions about the "point" of having a constitution or why the Constitution is the fundamental law. They seem to begin (and end) with the Constitution itself and suppose that constitutional theory need make no assumptions not drawn from within the "four corners" of that document. But this appearance is misleading. For "text-bound" theorists suppose that their disagreement with "noninterpretive" theories is a genuine disagreement. They suppose that they are right and that their opponents are wrong about how Supreme Court justices should go about judicial review. They therefore must have (or in any case acknowledge the desirability of having) reasons supporting their "four corners" theory. But these reasons cannot themselves be drawn from the text considered in isolation; that would beg the question. They must be taken from or defended as principles of political morality which in some way represent the upshot or point of constitutional practice more broadly conceived.

It is worth pursuing this point, because the alleged distinction between interpretive and noninterpretive theories is so popular. We might sharpen the issue by asking what reason a text-bound theorist would have for opposing a plainly outrageous example of what he detests. Suppose the Court held that the Senate was illegal, despite the clear provisions of the constitutional text as amended, because it is unrepresentative and therefore inconsistent with principles of democracy which must be assumed in order to give the Constitution any legitimacy at all. On what non-question-begging theory might the text-bound theorist object to that decision? He might say that the people would not accept such a decision. But this is not absolutely clear, and in any case he thinks the decision would be wrong even if it were (grudgingly) accepted in the end. But why?

A "textualist" cannot just say that it was the intention of those who wrote and ratified and accepted the Constitution that it be the highest law; still less that the Constitution itself so provides. For the question at issue is the force of the Constitution, and therefore the relevance of the intentions it might be said to embody. Begin at the beginning. A group of people met in Philadelphia and there wrote a document, which was accepted by the people in accordance with the procedures stipulated in the document itself, and has continued to be accepted by them in the way and to the extent that it has. If this makes that document law, it can only be because we accept principles of political morality having that consequence. But these principles might not only establish the Constitution as law but limit it as well. We cannot tell whether these principles do have this consequence, of course, until we decide what these principles are. Any answer to that question must take the form of a political theory showing why the Constitution should be treated as law, and certain plausible political theories at least raise the question whether the document must be limited in some way.

Suppose the textualist proposes, as the relevant theory, that legitimate government must enjoy the consent of the governed. This is a notoriously ambiguous proposition, and even the mythical decision holding the Senate illegal might be justified by some version of it. Someone supporting that decision might argue, for example, that the requisite consent must be more widespread than that gathered in the original ratification process, that it must, in any case, be contemporary, that it is far from clear that the unrepresentative Senate enjoys such consent, and that the availability of the amending process, particularly given the role of the Senate in the most feasible process, is no answer. This is not a silly argument; in any case it is not as silly as the mythical decision would be, and so we cannot explain our sense of the latter's absurdity by supposing that this interpretation of the consent of the governed is itself absurd.

Could the advocate of the "text" do better by appealing, not to political theory, but to the concept of law? None of the standing philosophical theories of law supplies the necessary arguments. Not even positivist theories, which seem the most likely. Neither Bentham's nor Austin's theory of positivism will do. Nor even Kelsen's.[9] Each has the consequence that if the Court's decision were accepted, this would show that the Court was sovereign. Hart's version of positivism might seem more promising.[10] But Hart's theory suggests that, since the Constitution was immediately accepted as law in virtue of the process of ratification, there must have been a rule of recognition—a generally accepted theory of the process through which legislation becomes law—in virtue of which the Constitution became law. But that rule is precisely the idea of a law behind the law to which the mythical decision appealed.

But I am wandering from my point. If the text-bound theorist appeals to some set of political principles as the principles truly embedded in the American tradition, in order to justify his reliance on the "four corners" of the Constitution, his theory becomes explicitly interpretive in the broad sense now in use. But this is also true if he appeals to a theory of law, because any theory of law is an interpretation, in this broad sense, of a social practice even more complex than, and including, constitutional practice. Any claim about the place the Constitution occupies in our legal structure must therefore be based on an interpretation of legal practice in general, not of the Constitution in some way isolated from that general practice. Those scholars who say they start from the premise that the Constitution is law underestimate the complexity of their own theories.

I am not suggesting that it is *not* obvious that the Constitution is the fundamental law. The weird decision I imagined holding the Senate illegal is preposterous exactly because the clear provisions of the Constitution are, for us, beyond legal challenge. But this is because, at least at this late date, no even minimally plausible interpretation of our legal practice as a whole could challenge the Constitution's fundamental place. Something like the

weird decision would have been somewhat more plausible at the beginning. (Just as *Marbury v. Madison*, plausible at the time, would have been implausible if it had not been decided until a century later.) The mythical decision is absurd now because its interpretation of legal practice is now absurd. The idea of the Constitution as fundamental law is so cemented into the common assumptions that constitute our legal order that an interpretation which denies it would be an interpretation of something else altogether, like an interpretation of architectural styles according to which Chartres turned out not to be Gothic, or an interpretation of Hamlet that ignored the Prince.

It will now be said, however, that even though all constitutional theories are interpretive in the broad sense I have been using, there is nevertheless an important distinction between those theories which interpret constitutional practice in such a way as to make the intention of the Framers of the Constitution decisive and those which do not. Some theories (the argument would run) hold that the best interpretation of our legal practice as a whole requires that legislative decisions be overturned by the Court only when it was the intention of the Framers that this should be done; while other theories believe, to the contrary, that the best interpretation permits Court intervention even when that was not the intention of the Framers. But we cannot tell whether this distinction is important, or even what it means, unless we achieve a better idea of what sort of thing the intention of the Framers is.

The Framers' Intention

"It is often problematical what a particular congressman or delegate to a constitutional convention intended in voting for a particular constitutional provision, especially one of the vaguer provisions, like the equal protection or due process clause. A particular delegate might have had no intention at all on a certain issue, or his intention might have been indeterminate. The difficulties obviously increase when we try to identify the intention of Congress or a constitutional convention as a whole, because that is a matter of combining individual intentions into some overall group intention. Even when each congressman or delegate has a determinate and ascertainable intention, the intention of the group might still be indeterminate, because there may not be enough delegates holding any particular intention to make it the intention of the institution as a whole."

This much is common ground between the rival schools on constitutional intention. They continue the argument in different ways. One side argues that in spite of the difficulties every effort must be made, with the resources of history and analysis, to discover what the collective intention of the constitutional Framers was on disputed matters of interpretation. They believe

that dogged historical study will reveal important and relevant original intentions. The effort is important in any case because, according to this school, judges can avoid making the substantive decisions that threaten democracy only by identifying the original constitutional intention in this way. The other side argues that any effort to discover the original collective intention of the Framers will turn out to be fruitless, or even perverse. It will end in the discovery that there are no, or very few, relevant collective intentions, or perhaps only collective intentions that are indeterminate rather than decisive one way or another, or perhaps intentions so contrary to our present sense of justice that they must in the end be rejected as a guide to the present Constitution.

Both sides to this debate suppose that the intention of the Framers, if it exists at all, is some complex psychological fact locked in history waiting to be winkled out from old pamphlets and letters and proceedings. But this is a serious common mistake, because there is no such thing as the intention of the Framers waiting to be discovered, even in principle. There is only some such thing waiting to be invented.

I shall begin my defense of this strong claim by setting out my understanding of how the concept of a "constitutional" intention actually functions in contemporary legal practice. We share the assumptions that when controversy breaks out whether the equal protection clause forbids segregated schools, for example, then it is relevant to ask about the purposes or beliefs that were in some sense "in the mind" of some group of people who were in some manner connected with the adoption of the Fourteenth Amendment, because these beliefs and purposes should be influential in some way in deciding what force the equal protection clause now has. We agree on that general proposition, and this agreement gives us what we might call the *concept* of a constitutional intention. But we disagree about how the blanks in the proposition should be filled in. We disagree in which sense some purpose must have been in the minds of particular people, in which sense these people must have been connected with the adoption of the constitutional provision, and so forth.

Different *conceptions* of constitutional intention give different answers to these questions. Brest's idea, that a group intention is the product of the "intention votes" of the members of the group, is (part of) one such conception. The idea of a "collective understanding," which I discuss in Chapter 16, could be used to construct another, and very similar, one. Each of these conceptions claims to give the "right" answer to the question of what a constitutional intention is. But this is a matter of filling in the blanks provided by the common concept through making political choices, not a matter of best capturing what a group intention, considered as a complex psychological fact, really is. There is no stubborn fact of the matter—no "real" intention fixed in history independent of our opinions about proper

legal or constitutional practice—against which the conceptions we construct can be tested for accuracy. The idea of an original constitutional understanding therefore cannot be the start or the ground of a theory of judicial review. At best it can be the middle of such a theory, and the part that has gone before is not philosophical analysis of the idea of intention, and still less detailed historical research. It is substantive—and controversial—political morality.

I must be careful not to overstate this point. I do not mean that we can sensibly state any political conclusion we choose in the language of intention, so that if we think the delegates to the original constitutional convention should have outlawed slavery, for example, we can say that they intended to do so, whatever they said or thought. The concept of constitutional intention is bounded by those aspects of the concept of intention that are not contested, as I suggested in my description of the common assumptions that provide us with the concept. Nevertheless, it is a concept open to many and different competing conceptions, as we shall see, and its uncontested contours do not determine which of these is the best to choose.

This is my understanding of how the concept of a constitutional intention functions in our jurisprudence. Many constitutional scholars seem to assume, to the contrary, that the idea of a legislative intention, including a constitutional intention, is so well defined in legal practice that once all the pertinent psychological facts are known there can be no room for doubt or debate about what the legislative or constitutional intention was. Brest, for example, in a recent and admirable article, assumes that our shared ordinary and legal language fixes the connection between a person's mental events or dispositions and his intentions sufficiently fully for legal purposes.[11] He raises various questions about the intentions of a mayor who enacts an ordinance forbidding vehicles from entering a park, and he discusses these on the assumption that we know the complete history of the mayor's mental events; that we know everything that went on in the mayor's mind. His answers to most of his own questions are confident and immediate. He says, for example, that if the mayor had never imagined that cars might be dropped into the park from a helicopter as a promotional stunt—if a picture of such a bizarre event never had flowed through his mind—then he certainly did not intend to ban cars entering in this way, even though he would have prohibited this means of entry if he had thought of it.

This is a claim about a single legislator's intention, and, as we shall see, such claims raise fewer problems than claims about the intentions of legislators as a group. But in fact there is no shared concept of even individual legislative intention that dictates either that the mayor had this intention or that he did not, or even that it is indeterminate whether he did. Suppose we are satisfied, for example, that if someone had called the mayor's attention

to the possibility of helicopters dropping cars from the sky after he had drafted his ordinance but before he had signed it, he would have expected that the language as drafted would certainly prohibit that stunt. But we are also satisfied that, since the mayor did not wish this result, he would then have changed the statute specifically to allow helicopter drops. Does this establish that his intention was to ban the helicopter drop after all? Or that this was not his intention? Or that his intention was in this respect indeterminate?

Consider the following three arguments: (1) The point of deferring to a lawgiver's intentions, when the words he used admit of different interpretations, is to insure that nothing be prohibited unless he desired to prohibit it, and we know, from the counterfactual evidence, that the mayor wanted not to prohibit the helicopter drop. (2) The point of deferring to a legislator's intentions, in such a case, is to insure that his words are read with the meaning or sense in which he used them and expected them to be understood, and the counterfactual evidence shows that the mayor used and meant these words in a sense that would prohibit the unorthodox entry. (3) The point of deferring to his intentions is complex; it includes both the goal that his words should be understood in the sense he meant, and that nothing should be prohibited that he wanted not to prohibit. Normally these two goals call for the same result, but the counterfactual evidence shows that here they argue for contrary results, and we should therefore say that the mayor's intention was indeterminate.

These three arguments propose three different (partial) theories of the legislative intention of a single legislator. The first proposes that legislative intention is a matter of what the legislator would have wanted the legal result of his act to be if he had thought of the troublesome case; the second that it is what he would have expected it to be in that case; and the third what he both would have expected and wanted it to be. None of these three is either established or ruled out by legal linguistic convention, still less by any ordinary language concept of intention. They are competing conceptions of that concept, in its legal use, and the choice among them depends, as the arguments for each suggest, on more general positions in legal and political theory. Brest is mistaken in supposing that there is only one plausible answer, demanded by some shared concept of intention, about what the mayor intended in these examples. (I use his argument as an example only because it is unusually discriminating and sophisticated. Nearly everyone writing about constitutional intention makes a similar fact-of-the-matter assumption.) Brest's various questions about the mayor teach us not, as he thinks, that our concept of intention has bizarre consequences when it is made the centerpiece of a theory of statutory or constitutional interpretation, but that we have no fixed concept capable of filling that role at all.

Brest's questions describe *choices* to be made in developing a concept of legislative or constitutional intention through political theory. Suppose the best theory of representative government holds that a statute covers all those cases which the enacting mayor would have wished it to cover if he had thought of them (even though he did not think of them all or even, in detail, of any), provided only that the language of the statute, as language, is arguably broad enough to embrace those cases. We might report this conclusion by adopting the first of the three conceptions of legislative intention just described. But it would be a mistake then to say that our theory about the proper reach of a statute follows from our independent theory of intention. The argument goes the other way around.

We have so far been considering only the question of individual intention. But constitutional theory requires the idea of a group, as distinct from an individual, intention, and it seems even plainer that we have no fixed concept of a group intention that makes what the Framers intended simply a matter of pure historical fact, a fact we discover simply in discovering everything that went on in their minds. In subsequent sections I shall try to support this claim by showing that there is no inevitable or natural answer to the question of which aspects of individual mental states are relevant to a group intention, or to the further question of how those mental states that are relevant should be combined to form a group intention.

But I should first recognize a final qualification to my general point. Even though the concept of constitutional intention is a contested concept, legal practice might nevertheless settle, by convention, some aspects of this concept which ordinary language leaves open, so that constitutional intention becomes partially a term of art. In Chapter 16 I suggest that our legal practice has actually narrowed a concept of legislative intention in this way. Legal convention stipulates, for example, that statements made in a committee report accompanying an ordinary congressional bill are in effect enacted, as a kind of official group intention, along with the bill itself. But I also emphasize that this convention leaves many issues about legislative intention open, and therefore subject to competing conceptions of that concept. In any case, there is plainly no equally elaborated convention about constitutional intention. There is no convention either tying various passages in the Federalist Papers to the Constitution itself or denying that connection, for example. On the contrary, constitutional practice in itself neither automatically excludes nor includes, as legislative practice does, matters that an historian might regard as pertinent to establishing the intention of those who made the Constitution. In any case, those who insist on the relevance of the original intention are hardly in a position to appeal to any such convention. They argue that the Supreme Court has consistently ignored the intention of the Framers, and so they cannot suppose that the practice of the Court has established a convention defining that intention.

Constructing an Original Intention

We must consider, in this section, the variety of choices available to a lawyer inventing or constructing a conception of constitutional intention. We might begin with a general distinction between pure psychological and what I shall call mixed conceptions. A pure psychological conception holds that a constitutional intention is constituted only by selected mental events or dispositions or other psychological states of identified individuals, like congressmen or delegates to a constitutional convention. A mixed conception, on the other hand, takes constitutional intention to be constituted in part by some more "objective" features; for example, the "natural" reading of the document. Or, differently, the set of values or purposes that the scheme of the document, taken as a whole, either assumes or promotes. Or the meaning that an intelligent and reflective member of the community would or should attach to the document. (These are merely examples of forms a mixed conception might take.) Psychological states will figure in a mixed conception, but they will not be the whole story.

My distinction between psychological and mixed conceptions of constitutional intention is very general; there are many different versions of both sorts, and any particular version must answer many questions left open by the general description. I shall try to indicate, in a general way, what these further questions are. I shall describe them as they would occur to someone trying to construct a psychological conception, though it will be obvious, I think, that the questions he would face in constructing a mixed conception would be no less numerous or difficult.

Who Counts? Psychological conceptions must identify, for a start, the individuals whose psychological states should count. In the constitutional case, are these the delegates to the original convention and the members of the congresses that proposed the various amendments? All the delegates or members, including those who voted against? Are the psychological states of some—for example, those who spoke, or spoke most often, in the debates—more important than those of others? What about the psychological states of those involved in the ratification process? Or the psychological states of the people as a whole, or those of them who participated in public debates or who read the pertinent documents when adopted? Do only psychological states at some particular moment in history count? Or is the process rather more dynamic, so that later psychological states should figure? If so, whose? Supreme Court Justices? Congressmen who might have pressed for amendments but, because they understood the Constitution in a certain way, did not? Segments of the public who formed certain views about the force of the Constitution to protect them in certain ways, and therefore took certain political decisions, perhaps including the decision not to cam-

paign for amendments? If any of these groups do not count, then why not? Shouting "democracy" is not, as we shall see, an answer. Or even muttering it.

Unfortunately, lawyers use various intellectual tranquilizers to convince themselves that they have answered at least some of these questions though they have not. These are generally personifications, as in, for example, the phrase "the intention of Congress." Constitutional lawyers have an even more dangerous personification at hand, in the terrible phrase, "the Framers." Strangers to constitutional law can have no idea how often constitutional lawyers rely on that phrase. I have read countless articles in which it is strenuously mooted for pages what the intention of "the Framers" was on some issue, without any attempt to indicate who in the world these people were—or are—and why.

What Psychological State: Hopes and Expectations?   Let us leave the question of who counts at that. There is next the question of what mental events or other psychological states are in play. We noticed a certain puzzle about individual intention in discussing Brest's ordinary-language assumptions about intention. Are we interested in a legislator's expectations about what a particular bill will do to the law, or are we interested in his attitudes about these expectations as well? Philosophers (particularly Paul Grice)[12] have developed an important analysis of "speaker's meaning," that is, what a speaker means in using a sentence as distinguished from what that sentence means in the more abstract. Speaker's meaning is determined by what the speaker expects the hearer to understand the speaker as intending him to understand. (This formulation of Grice's well-known analysis ignores important subtleties and complications.)

In the normal case, the speaker's expectations are also his hopes about how he will be understood. If I say that the moon is blue, expecting you to understand that I expect you to understand this in a certain way, I do so because I wish you to understand it that way. But someone may use words expecting them to be understood in a way that will have consequences he deplores. He might not have reflected, for example, on the full implications of the words being understood in just the sense he expected they would be. The mayor in my elaboration of Brest's example was in that position. I said, in discussing that example, that in such a case we might have to choose between a speaker's meaning, in the sense of his Gricean expectations, and his hopes.

In the more ordinary case, when a legislator votes as one member of a legislative body, his speaker's meaning and his hopes may come apart in ways he fully understands, not only later, like the mayor, but even as he votes. Suppose he votes for the Fourteenth Amendment as a whole, because he is offered only the choice to vote for or against it as a package. He ex-

pects that the amendment will be understood as abolishing school segregation, but he much regrets this and hopes that it will not be so understood. Or suppose he votes for it mainly because he hopes it will be understood as abolishing segregation, though he fears, and on balance, he thinks that it will not be. When we come to count his individual legislative intention, in determining the group intention as a whole, shall we look to his Gricean expectations about how the text will probably be construed? Or shall we look to his hopes, which might be different? Perhaps the whole legislature expected that the amendment would be understood in a certain way, but a majority (formed of those who voted against it and those who voted for it though they would have preferred it not do what they expected it would) hoped it would be understood otherwise. What is the legislative intention then?[13]

I do not mean to argue either that a congressman's expectations or his hopes should be given priority, when these come apart, but only that a choice must be made. Other choices, of a similar sort, must be made as well. Should we give different answers when the congressman (or other person) in question is someone who opposed the legislation, assuming that such people are to count at all? Do all of a congressman's expectations (or hopes or fears) count, or only those in some way institutionally expressed? Suppose the only evidence we have of what a congressman thought a particular bill would achieve is a breakfast conversation with his wife. Does this count? Why not? For evidentiary reasons? Or because we are interested only in what his psychological state was when in a certain building or when surrounded by colleagues? Or because it is not only his psychological state we are interested in after all? In the latter case our theory has become a mixed one.[14]

What Psychological State: Negation and Delegation?   Any useful conception of constitutional intention must take a position on the connected issues of negation and delegation. Of course there is a difference between a congressman's not intending that some piece of legislation have a particular effect, and intending that it not. But the difference is not fully appreciated in constitutional theory, because it is widely assumed that if some legislator has neither of these intentions, then he must have a third intention, which is that the matter be left for future determination by others, including, conspicuously, courts. Perry's statement of this assumption strikes me as representative. He says:

> If the Framers did contemplate P ... either they intended that the clause prohibit P or they did not. If they did not, either they left for resolution in the future the issue whether the clause should be deemed to prohibit P or they intended that the clause not prohibit P. But, again, there is no evidence

that the Framers of important power-limiting provisions intended them to serve as open-ended norms.[15]

This analysis of the structure of intention allows three values: a Framer can intend to prohibit, or not to prohibit, or to leave the matter open by delegating the decision to other institutions. Perry uses this three-valued structure to conclude that the Framers of the Fourteenth Amendment intended not to prohibit segregated public schools, because there is no evidence that they had either of the other two intentions.

But this analysis makes no allowance for the possibility that all three positive claims are false. Under many familiar conceptions of intention, they might well all be false, even when Perry's condition is satisfied, that is, even when the persons whose intentions are in issue "contemplated" (in some sense) the matter in hand, Perry assumes that the congressmen who considered the Fourteenth Amendment must have "contemplated" the question whether the amendment abolished segregated public schools, because there were segregated public schools around them as they debated. But suppose some congressman never even imagined that the amendment would have that effect; the thought never came to his mind. Is vacancy—not even recognizing an issue—a mode of contemplation? In any case, it surely does not follow, as we have already noticed, that the congressman who never imagined the amendment would strike down segregated schools intended that it not do so.

Suppose the congressman contemplated the possibility in a more active way. Suppose he spoke to himself in the following vein: "I wonder what the Supreme Court will do about segregated schools when the case comes up, as one day it must. There are, I suppose, the following possibilities. The justices may think that since we intended to forbid discrimination in matters touching fundamental interests, they are required to decide whether education is, in fact, a matter of fundamental interest. Or they may think that they should be guided by our more specific intentions about segregated schools, in which case they may try to decide whether the majority of us actively thought that the clause we were enacting would forbid segregation. Or they may think that the effect of what we did was to delegate the question to them as a fresh question of political morality, so that they have the power to decide for themselves whether, all things considered, it would be better to permit or forbid segregation. I hope they won't make the last of these choices, because I think that courts should decide what we've done, not what they want. But I don't know what the right answer is to the question of what we've done. That depends on the correct conception of constitutional intention to use, and, not being a constitutional lawyer, I haven't ever thought much about that. Nor do I, as it happens, have any particular preferences myself, either way, about segregated schools. I haven't thought much about that either."

This is a realistic description of the attitude of particular legislators about a great many issues. But the three-valued scheme proposed by Perry and assumed by many other commentators is simply inadequate in the face of that attitude. The legislator I describe has none of the intentions (using that word in any familiar sense) that Perry takes to be exhaustive.[16] But Perry is free to construct a conception of constitutional intention that does permit the inference he describes. He can introduce a kind of closure into his conception by making it a regulative principle that if some participant in the constitutional process did not intend to limit federal or state legislative power in some way, or intend to delegate this decision to others, then he will be taken as having intended not to limit that power. This closure insures that there are no "gaps" in any one person's scheme of intention about legislation. It is no objection that this departs from ordinary usage of "intention." We are, after all, constructing a conception for a particular use. But once again the choice needs a justification.

What Combination of Individual Intentions? These distinctions and comments have all been aimed at identifying the people whose psychological states are to count in a pure psychological conception of constitutional intention, and defining the psychological state of these people that is to count. But such a conception must also provide the function of these states that is to furnish the constitutional intention of the "Framers" as a group, because these psychological states will differ from person to person, in some cases radically. Shall we adopt what might be called a "majority intention" approach, which insists that the constitutional intention must be a set of intentions actually held by each member of a particular subclass defined (numerically but roughly) as the "bulk" or "majority" of the pertinent population? (That is the upshot of Brest's "intention-vote" theory of the way individual intentions combine in a group intention. But he is wrong, once again, to think that this choice is imposed on us by some fixed concept of what a group intention is.) In that case we might frequently expect to find no collective intention whatsoever on important issues, because even people whose psychological states face in the same direction on some issue may differ enough so that no concrete opinion of any particular person—about, for example, exactly what the equal protection clause should prohibit—will command the necessary number of assents. If we linked a majority intention conception to the closure stipulation on negation that I described, the total effect might well be that the original constitutional intention makes almost nothing unconstitutional.

Or shall we adopt some "representative intention" approach, according to which the constitutional intention is a kind of composite intention not too different from any one legislator's actual intention, but identical to the intention of no one at all? (We might think of this as the intention of some mythical average or representative legislator, in the same way that a sociol-

ogist constructing the "popular morality" of some community might describe a set of views held in total by no one.) Obviously more judgment
is required (and therefore more room for nonempirical disagreement is
provided) by this choice, but a larger positive intention would be provided, and less power therefore assigned to any closure rule that has been
included.

Abstract and Concrete Intentions

I will not pursue these various questions posed by the attempt to create a
constitutional intention: they are evident and of evident importance,
though they are rarely answered, or even recognized, in the recent academic debates. But I should discuss at greater length one special and perhaps less obvious problem. Imagine a congressman who votes for a statute
declaring combinations in restraint of trade illegal, and whose psychological state has the following character. He believes that combinations that restrain trade should be prohibited, and this is, in general, why he votes for
the bill. But he also believes that a forthcoming merger in the chemical industry does not restrain trade, and he expects that no court will decide that
it does. What is his "legislative" intention with respect to this merger?

We must distinguish between different levels of abstraction at which we
might describe that intention. We might say that he intends to prohibit
whichever combinations are in fact in restraint of trade, or that he intends
not to prohibit the chemical merger. The former is a relatively abstract
statement of his intention, which matches the words he voted for. (Or, to
put the same point differently, states his abstract intention.) The latter is a
much more concrete statement (or the statement of a much more concrete
intention) because it takes into account not only these words but his own
beliefs about their proper application.[17] It makes a difference which of the
two statements we regard as appropriate for our conception of legislative
intention. If we choose the abstract statement, then judges who believe that
the chemical merger does restrain trade will believe they are serving the
congressman's intentions by prohibiting it. If we choose the concrete statement, then prohibiting the merger will frustrate his intentions whether or
not that merger restrains trade. Which should we choose?

This issue arises in the constitutional context as well. Suppose a congressman votes for an amendment requiring "equal protection" because he
believes that government should treat people as equals, and that this means
not treating them differently with respect to their fundamental interests.
He believes that the clause he votes for would be violated by criminal laws
providing different penalties for black and whites guilty of the same crime,
for example, because he believes that liability to punishment touches a fundamental interest. But he also believes that separate and unequal public

schools would not violate the clause, because he does not consider education to be a fundamental interest. Once again we can distinguish an abstract and concrete formulation of his intention. Under the former he intends that whatever is in fact a fundamental interest be protected, so that if a court is itself convinced that education is (or perhaps has become) a fundamental interest, that court must believe it is serving his intention by outlawing segregation. But under the latter, concrete, formulation his intention is to protect what he himself understands to be a fundamental interest, and a court that abolishes segregation opposes rather than serves his intention.

One way to put the distinction, which I have used on other occasions, fits the constitutional but not the congressional example just used. When phrases like "due process" or "equal protection" are in play, we may describe a legislator's or delegate's intention either abstractly, as intending the enactment of the "concept" of justice or equality, or concretely, as intending the enactment of his particular "conception" of those concepts.[18] My earlier use of the distinction, in these terms, has drawn a considerable amount of criticism.[19] These critics make, I think, an important mistake; but it is perhaps one I encouraged by certain of the examples I gave of the way the distinction between concepts and conceptions works in ordinary language.[20] They suppose that any particular congressman who voted for the Fourteenth Amendment had either an abstract or a concrete intention—that he either intended to prohibit acts that treat people differently in what in fact are their fundamental interests or intended to prohibit acts that treat people differently in what he considered their fundamental interests—but not both, and that it is a matter of straightforward historical fact which of these intentions he had.[21] But both statements about his intention are true, though at different levels of abstraction, so that the question for constitutional theory is not which statement is historically accurate but which statement to use in constructing a conception of constitutional intention.

The choice is of devastating importance. If the abstract statement is chosen as the appropriate mode or level of investigation into the original intention, then judges must make substantive decisions of political morality not in place of judgments made by the "Framers" but rather in service of those judgments. The arduous historical research of the "intentionalists" into the concrete intentions of eighteenth- or nineteenth-century statesmen is then all wasteful irrelevance. The intentionalists might be able to defend their choice of the concrete intention by appealing to some controversial theory of representative democracy, or some other political theory, that makes legislators' concrete intentions decisive for interpretation. But that strategy would defeat their own claim that the content of the original intention is just a matter of history and not of political theory. Can they de-

fend the choice of the concrete intention in some more neutral, purely historical way, by collecting more information about the mental life of the delegates or congressmen? I think not, but I shall consider certain ways in which the attempt might be made.

Dominant Intention   We might be tempted to say that if someone has an abstract and a concrete intention one of these must be dominant—one must drive the other. There are certainly cases in which this distinction makes good sense. Suppose a delegate to a constitutional convention hates psychiatrists and believes that allowing psychiatrists to testify in criminal trials, from which practice they derive large fees, offends due process of law. If he votes for a due process clause, we may sensibly ask whether his dominant intention was to forbid violations of due process or to punish psychiatrists, and we may make progress in deciding which by deploying a counterfactual. If his conception of due process had been different, and he had believed that allowing psychiatrists to testify did not offend due process, would he still have voted for the clause? If not, then his reason for voting for it was to punish psychiatrists. His dominant intention was to attack psychiatrists by denying them fees; banning violations of due process was a derivative or instrumental intention only.

The distinction between dominant and derivative intentions must work differently, of course, when a legislator's concrete intention is the negative intention of not prohibiting something. The appropriate counterfactual question is then this one: if he had had a different belief, and believed that the provision in question would prohibit what he in fact thought it would not, would he nevertheless have voted for that provision? If our congressman had had a different conception of equality, for example, and thought that segregated schools would violate an equal protection clause, would he still have wanted to impose equality on government?

We may find reasons for thinking that some congressman would not have voted for an equal protection clause under those circumstances. These reasons might be as discreditable as the psychiatrist-hater's reasons. Perhaps he could not stand the idea of integrated schools as a matter of visceral reaction, and so would have voted against them even if he thought that justice demanded integration. In that case we might say that his intention that segregated schools not be prohibited was his dominant intention, not because his abstract intention was a means to that end but because the concrete intention would have trumped the abstract intention if he had been aware of the conflict. On the other hand, we might well discover positive evidence that a particular congressman would still have voted for the clause even if he thought that it did prohibit segregation. We might find a letter reporting that he personally favored integration on other grounds.

In the most interesting cases, however, the upshot of our counterfactual test would not be to establish either the abstract or the concrete intention as

dominant. For our counterfactual is a remarkably strong one. It requires us to imagine that our congressman's beliefs about equality were very different from what in fact they were—no counterfactual any less strong would serve the argument for dominant intention—and we must therefore suppose that the rest of his political theory suffered further changes that would make the beliefs we now suppose him to have natural for him. But this will have the effect of sharply reducing the amount of actual historical evidence that can be relevant to answering the counterfactual.

Suppose we found, for example, that our congressman considered liberty a much more important value than equality. We might be tempted to the conclusion that he would not have voted for the equal protection clause if he thought that a constitutional requirement of equality would strike down segregated schools, because this would be a substantial invasion of liberty. But this is an illegitimate conclusion, because someone's beliefs about the content and the importance of equality are mutually supportive, and we have no reason to think that if our congressman had thought equality more comprehensive than he did he would not also have thought it more important than he did. Our speculations, that is, must include not only the hypothesis that he thought differently about a particular issue of political morality, but that he therefore thought differently about political morality in general, and once we open the issue of how his more general political beliefs might have been different from what they actually were, we lose our moorings entirely. I do not mean that we are driven to the conclusion that if he had thought the clause would reach school segregation he would nevertheless have voted for it. Only that we are extremely unlikely to discover historical evidence that could support the opposite conclusion. Most of the evidence we might think relevant would have been swept away in the proper formulation of the counterfactual question. So we cannot find, in the counterfactual test, any general basis for the thesis that the Framers' concrete intentions must have been their dominant intentions.

Intention to Delegate   Now consider a different attempt to justify that thesis. Suppose we ask the following counterfactual question: if our congressman had imagined that some other official (a state legislator, perhaps, deciding whether to establish segregated schools, or a judge deciding whether segregated schools are unconstitutional) might hold a conception of equality different from his own, according to which segregation is a violation of equality, would he have wanted that other official to consider segregation unconstitutional? This is a very different counterfactual to the one considered in the last section, because now we understand our congressman to continue to believe that segregation does not violate equality. We ask whether, believing that, he would have wanted a judge or official to enforce (what he, the congressman, took to be) a mistaken view of equality.

Perhaps he would have, for the following sort of reason. He might have

thought that a constitution should reflect not the best standards of justice in some objective sense, but rather the conception of justice the citizens hold from time to time, and he might also have thought that the best means of realizing this ambition would be to encourage legislators and judges to employ their own conceptions. But though our congressman might have held such a view of proper constitutional practice, he probably did not. He probably would have wanted (what he thought to be) the correct standards of justice to be applied whether then popular or not. In that case, our present counterfactual would be answered: No. Our congressman would not have wanted a later judge, who disagreed with (what the congressman believed to be) the correct theory of equality, to apply the judge's own theory. But it would be a very grave mistake to report this conclusion by saying that the congressman's concrete intention that segregation not be abolished was his dominant intention and his abstract intention that equality be protected was only derivative. We are not entitled to that conclusion because our counterfactual did not discriminate the two intentions by supposing that he no longer held his permissive conception of equality.

Interpretive Intention   But this brings us to a third, and in many ways more interesting, argument that judges should look to the concrete rather than the abstract intentions of the Framers, which is just that the Framers intended they should. I do not know whether the Framers, as a group, had any particular view about the subjects we have been discussing. I do not know whether they themselves thought that judges construing a problematical text should look to the intentions of the legislators, or, if they did, how they would have answered the questions I raised about who counts as authors of the statute, or which psychological states of those authors count in fixing their intentions, whether abstract or concrete intentions count, and so forth. But suppose we were to find, through the appropriate research, that the Framers did have views on these issues, and that they thought the concrete rather than the abstract intentions of legislators should be decisive in interpreting problematical legislation. They would have thought, applying this thesis to their own work, that future officials faced with difficulties of interpreting their constitution should look to their own, the Framers', conceptions of justice and equality, even if later officials were convinced that these conceptions were poor ones. Would all this settle the question for us? Would it follow that this is the right conception of constitutional intention for our judges and other officials to use?

We might call the Framers' opinions about proper judicial performance their general "interpretive" intention.[22] In my earlier essay I suggested that most of the delegates and congressmen who voted for the "broad" provisions of the Constitution probably did not have an interpretive intention that favored concrete intentions. There is no reason to suppose they thought

that congressmen and state legislators should be guided by their, the Framers', conceptions of due process or equality or cruelty, right or wrong.[23] (I meant this as an argument *ad hominem* against the view that "strict" construction of the Constitution provided maximum deference to the wishes of the Framers.) The critics complain that I offered and had no evidence whatsoever for that opinion.[24] This is an overstatement. I had good evidence in the language in which the amendments were drafted. It is highly implausible that people who believe their own opinions about what counts as equality or justice should be followed, even if these beliefs are wrong, would use only the general language of equality and justice in framing their commands. They would not have been able to describe the applications of these clauses they intended in any detail, of course, but they could have found language offering more evidence of their own conceptions than simply naming the concepts themselves. It is hard to see what evidence, beyond the evidence of language, we should expect to find that would support my claim if it were true. Nor do my critics on this point suggest they have evidence in support of their rival claim.

So I hold to my opinion that, if those who voted for the due process and cruel and unusual punishment and equal protection clauses held any theories about how later officials should go about deciding what the Constitution required, they probably believed that their abstract intentions should be followed. But the mistake I believe my critics have made is a different one. They are wrong to think that the interpretive intention of the Framers matters one way or the other.

Brest agrees with the critics that, insofar as the Framers' intention is to be our general guide, their own interpretive intentions must be decisive of all questions about which conception of their intention we should use, including the question whether their abstract or concrete intentions are to count. He says that the first job of someone seeking to discover and enforce the intention of the Framers would be to discover their interpretive intent.[25] But why? Suppose we have decided (for reasons of legal or other political theory) that sound constitutional practice requires judges to look to and enforce the abstract intentions of the Framers, even though judges must make judgments of political morality in order to do this. Then we discover that the Framers themselves would have reached a different decision about that issue in our place. Why should this make a difference to us? Why is it not our view against theirs on a complex issue of political theory, so that if our reasons are good we should not abandon these reasons just because people in another age would have disagreed?

We might be seduced by the following answer: "We must accept their views on this matter because they made the Constitution and their intentions about how it should be interpreted should count, not our contrary views." But this is a very bad answer. Remember where the argument

stands. I argue that any conception of constitutional intention must be defended on political grounds, by deploying, for example, some theory of representative government as superior to other theories. The intentionalists reply that one conception can be defended as best on neutral grounds and, in particular, that the choice of concrete over abstract intentions can be defended in this way. But then the present argument—that we should look to concrete intentions if the Framers intended that we should—is circular in the following way.

We must be careful to distinguish the reasons we might have for looking to the intention of the Framers at all from the intentions we find when we look. Obviously we could not justify our initial general decision to look to their intention by saying they intended we should. That "argument" would obviously beg the question. But our present enterprise—trying to define a suitable conception of constitutional intention—is part of the project of justifying looking to intention, not part of the project of discovering what was intended. We are trying to state, more exactly than is usually done, the *sense* or *kind* of collective intention to which we have reasons to defer. But then we cannot, without begging the question in the same way, say that we should defer to one kind or sense of intention rather than another because those whose intentions are picked out in that description intended we should. If anyone argues that judges should look to abstract rather than concrete intention because the Framers intended this, then it would be pertinent, by way of objection, to point out that they did not. But this was not our reason. We are assuming, for the present purposes, that we found our reason in general arguments about just or wise constitutional practice. If so, the imagined fact that the Framers had other views on that score is not pertinent.

There is an important general point here.[26] Some part of any constitutional theory must be independent of the intentions or beliefs or indeed acts of the people the theory designates as Framers. Some part must stand on its own in political or moral theory; otherwise the theory would be wholly circular in the way just described. It would be like the theory that majority will is the appropriate technique for social decision because that is what the majority wants. For this reason a constitutional theory divides into two levels. At the first level the theory states whose beliefs and intentions and acts, of what character, make a constitution. Only at the second level does the theory look to the acts and intentions and beliefs described in the first level to declare what our own Constitution actually provides. If the first, independent level argues that the abstract intentions of the Framers count in determining what our Constitution is, we have no reason to withdraw that opinion if it is discovered that the Framers would have thought otherwise. The first level is for theory, not for them.

I labor this point because it is so widely assumed that the initial, broad

decision to look to the intentions of the Framers necessarily includes the decision to look to their interpretive intentions as well. In some circumstances this assumption would be even more obviously illegitimate or self-defeating. Suppose we had made an initial decision to look to the intention of the Framers, but found, when we investigated their own theories of constitutional intention, that they did not think their own intentions should matter at all, under any conception. They might all have thought, for example, that the Constitution should be interpreted according to the "plain meaning" of its words, with no reference to the intentions or other psychological states of the authors. Or suppose (to take another example) that we had decided, for our own reasons, that the intentions not only of delegates and congressmen but also of the state officials who were leaders in the process of ratification should count. But when we looked to the interpretive intention of the latter, we found that they, in our place, would have counted only the delegates and congressmen and would have ignored people like themselves. It would not then follow, in the case of either example, that we should then ignore the substantive intentions we had earlier resolved to consult. If the first level of our constitutional theory gives us good reasons to look to what the Framers intended in enacting the due process or equal protection or other clauses of the Constitution, it is no contrary argument that these would not have seemed good reasons to them. But we have no greater argument for referring the question of abstract against concrete intentions to the interpretive intentions of the Framers than we have for referring to them the question whether their intentions should count at all.

I shall summarize the argument of this section. The most important choice, in constructing a conception of constitutional intention, is the choice between an abstract and a concrete statement of that intention. This is not a matter of finding which of the two intentions a particular Framer had; he had them both. Nor can we establish, by historical evidence, that the concrete intentions of the Framers were dominant for them. We have good evidence, in the language of the Constitution, that the Framers did not themselves hold the interpretive opinion that only their concrete intentions should count. But that is not important, because the question of which of their intentions should count cannot itself be referred to their intentions.

Does It Matter?

This long catalog of problems and issues was meant to show that the idea of a legislative or constitutional intention has no natural fixed interpretation that makes the content of the Framers' intention just a matter of historical, psychological, or other fact. The idea calls for a construction which different lawyers and judges will build differently. Any justification for one con-

struction, and therefore for one view of what the Framers intended, must be found not in history or semantic or conceptual analysis, but in political theory. It must be found, for example, in an argument that one conception fits better with the most compelling theory of representative government. But then the idea with which we began, that judges can make apolitical constitutional decisions by discovering and enforcing the intention of the Framers, is a promise that cannot be redeemed. For judges cannot discover that intention without building or adopting one conception of constitutional intention rather than another, without, that is, making the decisions of political morality they were meant to avoid.

There is an obvious reply to that strong conclusion, which is this: "Your point is technically correct, but overblown. Perhaps it is true that the idea of an original constitutional intention is not, as it is often supposed to be, a neutral historical matter. Perhaps it is necessary to make political decisions in choosing one conception of that original intention rather than another. But these are not the kinds of political decisions that the 'original intention' school wants judges to avoid. They want judges to refrain from substantive political decisions, like the decision whether it is unjust to prohibit abortion or execute convicted murderers or interrogate suspected criminals without a lawyer. The choice of a conception of the Framers' intention depends, as you have several times suggested, not on substantive political decisions like these, but rather on decisions about the best form of representative democracy, and though this is a matter of political theory and may be controversial, it is not a matter of substantive political theory. So the 'original intention' school could accept all your arguments without surrendering its most important claims."

This reply is inadequate on its own assumptions. Even if judges need only look to issues of process in choosing a conception of constitutional intention, the conception they choose may nevertheless require them to decide issues of the plainest substantive character. This is obviously true, for example, of the point I discussed in most detail: the choice between an abstract and a concrete statement of intention. Perhaps the reason judges should look to abstract rather than concrete intentions (if they should) lies in some procedural theory about the proper level of abstraction for a democratic constitution. But judges who accept this view of constitutional intention must decide whether prohibiting abortion violates equality, or whether capital punishment is cruel and unusual, in order to enforce what they take the original intention to be.

But the reply I described is interesting because it shows how the two general topics of this essay—the flights from substance through the routes of intention and process—are connected. Intention could not even begin to provide a route from substance if the distinction between substance and process, the distinction on which the second route depends, were itself to

give way. If the "original intention" school were forced to concede not only that the consequences of certain conceptions of constitutional intention require judges to decide issues of substance, but that the choice among these conceptions is itself a matter of substance, then it would not be able to establish its position even by finding a good political argument for a conception that looks only to concrete intentions. The game would already have been lost.

In the next part of this essay we shall see that the distinction between substance and process on which the "original intention" school must rely is an illusion. But let me first end the present summary by picking up a thread left loose earlier. I asked whether the distinction between "interpretive" and "noninterpretive" constitutional theories was useful if we understood "interpretive" to mean relying on the Framers' intentions. I now suggest that it would not be useful, even so understood, for two reasons. First, almost any constitutional theory relies on some conception of an original intention or understanding. "Noninterpretive" theories are those that emphasize an especially abstract statement of original intentions (or could easily be revised so as to make that emphasis explicit with no change in the substance of the argument). Their argument is distorted by insisting that they do not rely on any conception of an original intention at all.

The second reason is more important. The distinction suggests, as I said, that illuminating arguments can be made for or against "interpretive" or "noninterpretive" theories as a class. But that now seems an unreasonable assumption. The important question for constitutional theory is not whether the intention of those who made the Constitution should count, but rather what should count as that intention. Any successful answer to that question will be complex, because a conception of constitutional intention is comprised of a great many discrete decisions, only some of which I described. We might want to say, for example, that the best answer is the answer given by the best conception of democracy. But that will not divide constitutional theories into two grand classes and provide a wholesale argument for one class and against another. It puts a question that we may hope will single out one theory from others both within and without any large class we might initially construct. Constitutional theory is not a wholesale trade.

PROCESS

Process and Democracy

"The United States is a democracy. The Constitution settles that, and no interpretation of our constitutional system that denies it could be plausible. This plain fact provides both a brake and a spur to judicial review. Democ-

racy means (if it means anything) that the choice of substantive political values must be made by representatives of the people rather than by unelected judges. So judicial review must not be based on the justices' opinions about whether, for example, laws prohibiting the sale of contraceptives violate rights to privacy. For that reason *Griswold* was wrong, as were *Roe v. Wade* and *Lochner*.[27] Liberals approve the first two of these decisions, and hate the third; conservatives vice versa. But a sound theory of judicial review—the only theory consistent with democracy—condemns them all, and condemns any other decision expressly or implicitly relying on the idea of substantive due process.

"But if our commitment to democracy means that the Court cannot make decisions of substance, it equally means that the Court must protect democracy. In particular, the Court must make democracy work by insuring, in the words of Justice Stone's famous footnote, that legislation not be permitted 'which restricts those political processes which can ordinarily be expected to bring about repeal of undesirable legislation,' and that 'prejudice against discrete and insular minorities' not be allowed 'to curtail the operation of those political processes ordinarily to be relied upon to protect minorities.'[28] So the Court must be aggressive in its protection of free speech, and sensitive to the consequences of prejudice, because these are the values of democracy itself."

This is (a paraphrase of) how Ely reads the *Carolene Products* footnote.[29] This is his theory of judicial review, his own route from substance. The argument contains a series of propositions: (1) Judicial review should be a matter of attending to the process of legislation rather than the outcome considered in isolation from that process. (2) It should test that process against the standard of democracy. (3) Process-based review is therefore consistent with democracy, while substance-based review, which looks to outcomes, is antagonistic to it. (4) The Court therefore errs when it cites a putatively fundamental substantive value to justify overturning a legislative decision. *Griswold* and *Roe v. Wade* were wrongly decided, and the Court should abstain from such adventures in the future. Ely defends each of these propositions; together they make up his book.

I think the first proposition is powerful and correct.[30] But the other three are in different ways wrong and in all ways misleading; they are mistakes that submerge and subvert the single insight. Judicial review should attend to process not in order to avoid substantive political questions, like the question of what rights people have, but rather in virtue of the correct answer to those questions. The idea of democracy is of very little help in seeking that answer. Nor does it follow, just from the commitment of judicial review to process rather than to outcomes isolated from process, that the so-called "substantive due process" decisions Ely and others deplore are automatically placed out of bounds. On the contrary, the commitment to process gives some of these decisions new and more powerful support.

In this section I argue that the abstract ideal of democracy, in itself, offers no greater support for a process-based than an outcome-based jurisprudence of judicial review. In the next section I try to develop a different basis for process-based review, in a theory of rights as trumps over the majority will, and then argue that Ely's argument, properly understood, is really that argument rather than the argument from democracy that lies in the title and on the surface of his book.

Ely insists that the proper role of the Supreme Court is to police the process of democracy, not to review the substantive decisions made through those processes. This might be persuasive if democracy were a precise political concept, so that there could be no room for disagreement whether some procedure was democratic. Or if the American experience uniquely defined some particular conception of democracy, or if the American people were now agreed on one conception. But none of this is true, as Ely recognizes.[31] His argument must therefore be read as supposing that one conception of democracy is the right conception—right as a matter of "objective" political morality—and that the job of the Court is to identify and protect this right conception. It is far from clear, however, that this assumption is consistent with Ely's argument against what he calls "fundamental value" theories of constitutional review. He says, as part of that argument, that there cannot be substantive political rights for the Court to discover because there is no consensus about what substantive political rights people have, or even whether they have any. Can he now suppose that there is a right answer to the question of what democracy really is, even though there is no consensus about what that answer is?

But I want to pursue a different issue now. In what sense is the concept of democracy a procedural as distinct from a substantive concept at all? I must be careful to avoid a certain confusion here. I am asking not about the *content* of a conception of democracy, but about the kind of *case* necessary to show that one conception of democracy is superior to another. Some theories of democracy put what we tend to regard as matters of substance into the very description of democracy. The theory of democracy celebrated in "peoples' democracies," for example, supposes that no society is democratic if its distribution of wealth is very unequal. Winston Churchill, relying on a very different idea, once said that democracy means that an early-morning knock on the door is the milkman.[32] Other theories insist that democracy is a process for reaching political decisions, a process that must be defined independently of any description of the decisions actually reached. They define democracy as a set of procedures governing the citizen's participation in politics—procedures about voting and speaking and petitioning and lobbying—and these procedures do not themselves include any constraints on what democratically elected officials can do or the reasons they can have for doing it. Even if we accept this view (it is plausible, I might add, only if we take a very generous view of process), the question

remains how to decide which procedures compose the best conception of democracy.

We might distinguish two general strategies for making this decision, two types of "cases" for democracy. Suppose we draw a line between "input" and "outcome" in the following way. Input cases for democracy are based entirely on some theory about the proper allocation of political power either between the people and the officials they elect, or among the people themselves, and make no reference to the justice or wisdom of the legislation likely to be the upshot of that allocation of power. Outcome cases, on the contrary, are based at least in part on predictions and judgments of this sort. The pure utilitarian case for democracy (to take a familiar example) is an outcome case. Utilitarians might agree that the *definition* of a democratic state consists in a set of procedures describing who can vote, how voting districts must be established, and so forth. But they would argue that democratic procedures are just because they are more likely than other procedures to produce substantive decisions that maximize utility. Any question about which of alternate procedures forms the best conception of democracy must therefore be submitted to the test of long-term utility, that is, to the test of outcomes.

The distinction between input and outcome cases for democracy is important in the constitutional context. If the Supreme Court must develop its own conception of democracy because it cannot find any sufficiently precise conception either in history or present consensus, then it must consider what counts as a good argument for one conception rather than another. If the Court can rely, for this purpose, on an input case, then it can avoid confronting the issues of substantive justice that Ely says it must avoid. But if it cannot—if the only plausible cases for democracy (and therefore the only plausible cases for one conception of democracy over another) are outcome cases—then the Court must face whatever issues of substance the best case makes pertinent. Ely's argument that the Court can avoid issues of substance by resting its decisions on the best conception of democracy would then be self-defeating. For once Ely concedes (as he must and has) that the Court must define the best conception of democracy for itself, and thus make fresh political judgments of some kind.[33] He has only two arguments in favor of the program he describes: that courts are well placed to make judgments about fair process, but very badly placed to make substantive political judgments, and that court-made judgments about process are consistent with democracy, while court-made judgments about substance are not. If the Court cannot make the judgments about process Ely recommends without making the judgments about substance he condemns, then his own arguments will subvert his own theory. Can Ely's argument (or any other version of a *Carolene Products* theory) survive this challenge by producing an input case for democracy?

It seems unlikely that there can be such a case, at least if we have in mind a case sufficiently powerful not merely to recommend democracy as a vague and general idea, but to supply reasons for choosing one conception of democracy over another. Outcome cases can easily be that powerful. Pure utilitarianism might turn out not only to recommend the general idea of majority rule, but also, as I suggested, to recommend extremely precise provisions about, for example, districting for representation, limiting the vote by age groups or in other ways, free speech, and the protection of minorities. But where would we turn for input theories this powerful? It seems, at first blush at least, that our ideas about the fair allocation of political power are exhausted by the general recommendation of some form of democracy, and are inadequate to discriminate which form.

We might test that initial intuition by studying the arguments that Ely himself makes for a particular version of democracy. He supposes that the best conception of democracy includes a scheme for the protection of free speech, which he describes as keeping open the channels of political change. Unfortunately, although Ely writes with great interest and power about freedom of expression, what he says is entirely by way of offering concrete advice about how the Court should decide free speech cases. He assumes rather than argues that his advice draws on considerations of process rather than substance.[34] Does it? Can Ely actually provide an input case for the proposition that democracy must include free speech?

There are a variety of theories in the field, each of which purports to explain the value of a rule prohibiting government from restricting what its citizens may say. Perhaps the best known is John Stuart Mill's theory which calls attention to the long-term value of such a rule to the community as a whole. Mill argues that truth about the best conditions of social organization—the conditions that will in fact improve the general welfare—is more likely to emerge from an unrestrained marketplace of ideas than from any form of censorship. But this is a utilitarian, outcome case for free speech, not an input, process-based case. (It is also a very doubtful case, but that is another matter.) Other theories defending free speech fall into the school that Ely calls "fundamental value" theories. Curiously, the best known of these theories also belongs to Mill. He argues that free speech is an essential condition of the development of individual personality; that the ability to speak out on matters of general concern is an ability of fundamental importance to people, without which they will not develop into the kinds of people they should be.

One other familiar argument for free speech might seem to provide an input case, at least at first sight. We might say, with Madison, that democracy is a sham (or, worse, self-defeating) unless the people are well informed, and that free speech is essential in order to give them the information necessary to make democracy a reality.[35] Justice Brennan re-

cently made a similiar argument from the structure of democracy the centerpiece of his case for free speech in *Richmond Newspapers.*[36] The Madisonian argument is not an argument for equality of political power, person by person. It is rather an argument for maximizing the political power of the people as a whole, the power of the populace to elect the right officials and control them once elected, so as to achieve what the people, as distinct from those actually in power, really want. It is an argument for improving the political power of the demos, not for equality of political power among the demos.

It is, moreover, a poor argument, at least when it is taken to justify the extensive freedom of speech that Ely and others understand the First Amendment to provide. I try to show why in the essay published as Chapter 19 in this book. Any constraint on the power of a democratically elected legislature decreases the political power of the people who elected that legislature. For political power is the power to make it more likely that political decisions will be made as one wishes. Suppose the majority wishes that no literature sympathetic to Marxism be published, but the Constitution denies it the power to achieve that goal through ordinary politics. The majority's political power surely is decreased by this constitutional prohibition. We may want to say that the majority has no right to protect (what it deems to be) its own interest through censorship, because this will prevent others from working to form a new majority dedicated to new values. But each member of the present democracy might prefer to accept less information for himself, and thus lower his own opportunity to change his mind, just because he does not want others, who now agree with him, to have a similar opportunity. So the argument that the present majority has no right to censor opinions is actually an argument for reducing the political power of any majority.

The Madisonian argument may be understood as pointing out that although a constitutional constraint on censorship decreases the political power of the people as a whole in this way, it also increases that power in a different way. It provides a larger base of information on which the people may act. At best, however, this shows only that any constitutional protection of free speech is likely to involve a trade-off in which a loss in political power in one sense is matched against a gain in another sense. There is no reason to think that political power as a whole is always on balance improved. If the population is generally well informed, or at least sufficiently well informed to have some general idea of what it might gain and lose by any piece of censorship, then the majority's political power will be decreased overall by the constitutional protection of speech. If this issue is even in doubt, then the general spirit of democracy would seem to argue that the choice, whether the gain in information is worth the loss in direct political power, is best made by a majority of the people from time to time.

So free speech cannot be justified by an input case addressed to maximiz-

ing the political power of the people as a whole. But it seems more sensible, in any case, to argue for free speech not from the goal of maximizing political power overall, but from the different goal of making political power more equal, person by person, across the population. A law prohibiting the publication of Marxist literature does seem to decrease equality of political power. If so, then a constitutional ban on such laws, even if it diminishes political power generally, distributes that power more equally. This suggests a different input case for free speech: democracy consists in providing as much political power in the people as a whole as is consistent with equality of such power, and free speech is necessary to provide that equality.

But now we need a metric of political power adequate to serve this egalitarian conception of democracy, and it is not clear which we should use. We might consider the following suggestion first: equality of political power consists in having the same opportunities for influencing political decisions as others have; the same opportunities to vote, write to congressmen, petition for grievances, speak out on political matters, and so forth. If there is a mechanism for influence available to some, it must be available to all. This immediately raises the question whether equality in these opportunities is imperiled when some, who are rich, may purchase ads in newspapers, promise substantial contributions to political campaigns, and so on, while others cannot afford to influence politics in any of these ways. We might try to set this difficult issue aside, however, by distinguishing between a right and the value of that right.[37] We might say, tentatively, that political equality requires at least that everyone have the same opportunity to influence political decisions, so that any legal barriers must apply to everyone, leaving aside whether political equality also requires that everyone's opportunities have the same value to him.

Does a law forbidding the expression of Marxist theories invade political equality so described? Suppose someone says that although the law does deny a certain opportunity to influence political decisions, it denies this opportunity to everyone. This sounds like Anatole France's observation that the laws of France are egalitarian because they forbid both rich and poor to sleep under the bridges.[38] But what is wrong with the argument? Is it a better argument in the *Cohen* (Fuck the Draft!) case?[39] A law forbidding people from wearing obscene messages on their backs prevents Cohen from making his political arguments in that way. But it also forbids his political rivals from wearing "Fuck Karl Marx!" messages stitched to the backs of their pinstripe suits. The Supreme Court protected Cohen on the argument, roughly speaking, that the medium, including the rhetorical style, is part of the message.[40] This is also Ely's argument in favor of the Court's decision.[41] But some people on any side of a political dispute would approve the opportunity to use Cohen's medium and rhetoric, and would therefore be equally constrained by an anti-*Cohen* rule.

If we want to say that an anti-*Cohen* rule would invade equality of politi-

cal power, therefore, we must bring back the idea we set aside, prematurely, a moment ago. We must say that equality in political power must take account not only of the opportunities people have if they want to use them, but of the value of these opportunities to them. On this account, those who object radically to the political structure must be permitted to make their protests in language appropriate to their sense of the occasion, if free speech is to have the same value to them as it has to a member of the bourgeois establishment. We must take value into account to defend free speech on the present grounds even in the easier classic case I set out first. A law prohibiting the publication of Marxist literature invades equality of political power because, though it leaves the Marxist free to say exactly what anyone else can say, it makes free speech much less valuable for him. Indeed it destroys its value for him, although it does not in any way diminish its value for others who will never be tempted by Marxism and will never want to hear what Marxists think.

Once we admit that a putatively input case for free speech must bring in the dimension of value, the danger is evident. For the most natural metric for the value of an opportunity lies in consequences, not in further procedures. Rights to participate in the political process are equally valuable to two people only if these rights make it likely that each will receive equal respect, and the interests of each will receive equal concern not only in the choice of political officials, but in the decisions these officials make. But then the case for free speech (or for any other feature distinguishing one conception of democracy from another) suddenly seems to be an outcome case. Whether the value of the political opportunities a system provides is equal will depend on whether the legislation likely at the end of the process treats everyone as equals.

But it is controversial what the correct standard is for deciding whether some piece of legislation treats people equally. If someone believes that legislation treats people as equals when it weighs all their utility prospects in the balance with no distinction of persons, then he will use what I earlier described as a pure utilitarian case for defending democracy and choosing among competing conceptions of democracy. If someone rejects this utilitarian account of treating people as equals in favor of some account that supposes that people are not treated as equals unless the legislative decisions respect certain fundamental rights, then this must inevitably affect his calculation of when a political process provides genuine equality of political power. But this means that judges charged with identifying and protecting the best conception of democracy cannot avoid making exactly the kinds of decisions of political morality that Ely is most anxious they avoid: decisions about individual substantive rights. Judges may believe that the utilitarian answer to the question of individual rights is the correct one— that people have no rights. But that is a substantive decision of political morality. And other judges will disagree. If they do, then the suggestion that

they must defend the best conception of democracy will not free them from having to consider what rights people have.

Equality and Process

Suppose we begin at the other end. Instead of asking what democracy requires, which leads to the question of what rights people have, let us ask the latter question directly. We might put the question, initially, in the context of Ely's other main topic of concern: racial justice. Assume that racial prejudice is so widespread in a community that laws enacted specifically for the purpose of putting the despised race at a disadvantage would satisfy the preferences of most people overall, even weighted for intensity and even in the long run. Pure utilitarianism (and pure majoritarianism) would then endorse these laws because they are laws that a legislature weighing the preferences of all citizens equally, with no regard to the character or source of these preferences, would enact. If a judge accepts the pure utilitarian account of treating people as equals, then he must conclude that in these circumstances laws deliberately designed to put blacks at an economic disadvantage (denying them access to certain jobs or professions, for example) treat blacks as equals. He cannot rely on equality or on any egalitarian theory of democracy to condemn such laws.

We know, however, that such laws do not treat blacks as equals. On what theory of equality must we then be relying? We have, I think, an initial choice here. We might argue, first, that these laws fail the test of equality because they offend some substantive interest of blacks which is in itself so important that it should not be left to the utilitarian calculation. This appeals to the consequences of the legislation as distinct from the legislators' reasons or grounds for enacting it. But we then need a theory that will tell us which interest is offended here and why it is fundamental. Is it an economic interest? An individual interest in having the same opportunities others have? A group interest in having the same opportunities as those of different races? Why is any of these a fundamental interest? We accept that many important interests people have may nevertheless be compromised for the sake of the general welfare; people in some businesses prosper while others go to the wall because of political decisions justified by the claim that the community is then better off overall. Why are the interests compromised by racially discriminatory legislation (whatever these are) different? It cannot be because people care more about these interests or suffer more pain when they are overridden by the claims of the general welfare. It is far from clear that people do, and in any case a pure utilitarian analysis will take account of this special suffering or specially strong preference in its calculations. If the interests are nevertheless overridden, why do they deserve the extraordinary protection of rights?

I do not think that questions like these can be answered satisfactorily. We

should therefore consider our second option. We might argue that racially discriminatory laws are inegalitarian not because they invade interests that are specially important but because it is unacceptable to count prejudice as among the interests or preferences government should seek to satisfy. In this case we locate the defect of the legislation in the nature of the justification that must be given for it, not in its consequences conceived independently of this justification. We concede that laws having exactly the same economic results might be justified in different circumstances. Suppose there were no racial prejudice, but it just fell out that laws whose effect was specially disadvantageous to blacks benefited the community as a whole. These laws would then be no more unjust than laws that cause special disadvantage to foreign car importers or Americans living abroad, but benefit the community as a whole. Racially discriminatory legislation is unjust in our own circumstances because no prejudice-free justification is available, or, in any case, because we cannot be satisfied that any political body enacting such legislation is relying on a prejudice-free justification.

I think this second argument is sound, and that it provides an adequate (if not necessarily exclusive) basis for judicial review.[42] It is, moreover, in one sense, a "process" or *"Carolene Products"* justification for that review. It holds that the rights created by the due process and equal protection clauses of the Constitution include rights that legislation not be enacted for certain reasons, rather than rights that legislation not be enacted with certain consequences. This is the theory on which Ely himself actually relies (in spite of much that he says).[43]

But it would be a mistake to suppose (as Ely does) that judges could either choose or apply this theory of judicial review without facing issues that are by any account substantive issues of political morality. Judges must decide that pure utilitarianism is wrong, for example, and that people do have rights that trump both the maximization of unrestricted utility and the majoritarian decisions that serve unrestricted utility. This is not a procedural decision of the sort that Ely thinks judges and lawyers make best. He says that democracy requires that the majority decide important issues of political principle, and that democracy is therefore compromised when these issues are left to judges. If that is right, then Ely's own arguments do condemn the only available "process" theory of judicial review, the very theory that he himself, properly construed, offers. If we want a theory of judicial review that yields acceptable results—that would permit the Court to strike down racially discriminatory laws even if they benefit the community as a whole, counting each person's interest as one—we cannot rely on the idea that the Supreme Court must be concerned with process *as distinct from* substance. The only acceptable version of "process" theory itself makes the correct process—the process the Court must protect—depend on deciding what rights people do or do not have. So I object to the characterization Ely gives of his own theory. He thinks it allows judges to avoid

issues of substance in political morality. But it does so only because the theory itself decides those issues, and judges can accept the theory only if they accept the decisions of substance buried within it.

We now reach a question more important than the issue of characterization. Ely thinks that a "process" theory of judicial review will sharply limit the scope of that review. He says, for example, that such a theory bars the Court from enforcing "the right to be different." [44] But this now seems arbitrary and in need of much more justification than Ely offers. Why is racial prejudice the only threat to treatment as an equal in the legislative process? If the Court should insure that people are treated as equals in that process, should it not, for that very reason, also strike down laws making contraceptives or homosexual practices illegal? Suppose the only plausible justification for these laws lies in the fact that most members of the community think that contraception or homosexuality is contrary to sound sexual morality. Or that the will of the majority is served by forbidding contraceptives and homosexual affairs. Or that long-term utility, taking into account the community's deep opposition to these practices, will be best served that way. If it is unfair to count racial prejudice as a ground for legislation, because this fails to treat people as equals, why is it not also unfair, and so also a denial of equal representation, to count the majority's moral convictions about how other people should live?

Some people think it is axiomatic that any legal distinction based on race is offensive to democracy, so that we need no more general explanation of why racial discrimination is unconstitutional. But this seems arbitrary, and the Supreme Court apparently has rejected it. So has Ely. [45] Ely therefore needs a more general explanation of why counting racial prejudice as a political justification violates equality. Once that more general explanation is provided, the question is raised whether the explanation reaches beyond race, and whether it reaches legislation based on popular opinions about sexual morality as well.

Ely discusses this problem only parenthetically, in the course of a footnote about legislation making homosexual practices a crime:

> Neither is there anything unconstitutional about outlawing an act due to a bona fide feeling that it is immoral: most criminal statutes are that at least in part. (Attempting to preclude the entire population from acting in ways that are perceived as immoral is not assimilable to comparatively disadvantaging a given group out of simple hostility to its members. . . . In raising my children not to act in ways I think are immoral, even punishing them when they do, I may incur the condemnation of some, but the sin is paternalism or some such, hardly that of leaving my children's interests out of account or valuing them negatively.) [46]

This will not do. Ely is wrong in thinking that legislation against homosexuals is typically motivated by concern for their interests. (Even if he were right, this would not provide the necessary distinction. Racial discrimina-

tion is often justified, sometimes sincerely, on the proposition that blacks are better off "in their place" or "with their own kind.") He is right, however, in supposing that a utilitarian justification of laws against homosexuals does not leave their interests "out of account" or value them negatively. It counts the damage to homosexuals at full value, but finds it outweighed by the interests of those who do not want to associate with practicing homosexuals or who find them and their culture and lives inferior. But a utilitarian justification of racial discrimination does not ignore the interests of blacks or the damage discrimination does to them. It counts these at full value and finds them outweighed by the interests of others who do not want to associate with blacks, or who find them and their culture and habits inferior or distasteful. The two utilitarian justifications are formally similar, and nothing in Ely's argument shows why it offends the proper conception of democracy to permit the one but does not offend it to permit the other.

Nor does his general distinction between process and substance provide the necessary distinction. We must ask why a process that counts racial prejudice as a ground of legislation denies equal representation, and then ask whether our explanation has the further consequence of also denying a role to popular convictions about private sexual morality. In various places I have argued, along the following lines, that the only adequate explanation does have that consequence. Legislation based on racial prejudice is unconstitutional not because any distinction using race is immoral but because any legislation that can be justified only by appealing to the majority's preferences about which of their fellow citizens are worthy of concern and respect, or what sorts of lives their fellow citizens should lead, denies equality.[47] If I am right, then constraints on liberty that can be justified only on the ground that the majority finds homosexuality distasteful, or disapproves the culture that it generates, are offensive to equality and so incompatible with a theory of representation based on equal concern and respect. It does not follow that no legislation about sexual behavior is permitted. Laws against rape, for example, can be justified by appealing to the ordinary interests of people generally through a theory of justice that does not rely on popular convictions. But I do not think that laws forbidding consensual homosexual acts can be justified in that way.

I do not propose to reargue my case for these various claims here.[48] But if Ely continues to reject my argument, he must provide a theory of equality that is superior. It remains to be seen what theory he can provide. But in any case, his theory must be based on some claim or assumption about what rights people have as trumps over an unrestricted utilitarian calculation, and what rights they do not have. So even if he is able to produce a theory justifying his distinction between racial prejudice and moral populism, he will have abandoned his main claim, that an adequate theory of judicial review need take no position about such rights.

My reservations extend, I should add, to Ely's paradigm example of improper judicial review, which is the case of *Roe v. Wade.*[49] But here the issue is more complex. What are the available justifications for prohibiting abortion in, say, the first trimester? If we rule out as medically unsound the idea that abortion is a threat to the mother, then two main justifications come to mind. The first appeals to the moral opinions of the majority, without assuming that these are sound. But if we believe that counting such preferences as a justification for constricting liberty denies equality, then our theory condemns this justification as unacceptable. The second appeals to the interests of the unborn. If unborn infants are people, whose interests may properly be counted by a legislature, then this second justification is sound and passes the test of equal representation. But the Court must decide that deep and undemonstrable issue for itself. It cannot refer the issue whether unborn infants are people to the majority, because that counts their moral opinions as providing a justification for legislative decisions, and this is exactly what our theory of equal representation forbids. (Nor, for the same reason, can it either delegate that question to the legislature or accept whatever answer the legislature itself offers.) I am not arguing (now) in favor of either view about abortion, or that *Roe v. Wade* was correctly decided. I insist only that incanting "process" or "democracy" or "representation" is neither here nor there. All the work remains to be done.

THE FORUM OF PRINCIPLE

We have seen an extraordinary amount of talent deployed to reconcile judicial review and democracy. The strategy is the same: to show that proper judicial review does not require the Supreme Court to displace substantive legislative judgments with fresh judgments of its own. The tactics are different. One program argues that the Court can achieve just the right level of constitutional supervision by relying on the "intention" of "the Framers." Another that the Court can avoid trespassing on democracy by policing the processes of democracy itself. Both these programs are self-defeating: they embody just the substantive judgments they say must be left to the people. The flight from substance must end in substance.

If we want judicial review at all—if we do not want to repeal *Marbury v. Madison*—then we must accept that the Supreme Court must make important political decisions. The issue is rather what reasons are, in its hands, good reasons. My own view is that the Court should make decisions of principle rather than policy—decisions about what rights people have under our constitutional system rather than decisions about how the general welfare is best promoted—and that it should make these decisions by elaborating and applying the substantive theory of representation taken from the root principle that government must treat people as equals. Whether I am

right in this, and what it means, are questions for legal and political theory, and it is these questions I think we should address.

Should we nevertheless accept all this with regret? Should we really be embarrassed that in our version of democracy an appointed court must decide some issues of political morality for everyone? Perhaps—but this is a much more complex matter than is often recognized. If we give up the idea that there is a canonical form of democracy, then we must also surrender the idea that judicial review is wrong because it inevitably compromises democracy. It does not follow that judicial review is right. Only that the issue cannot be decided by labels. Do the best principles of political morality require that the majority's will always be served? The question answers itself. But that is only the beginning of a careful study of the morality of judicial review.

If we undertake that study, we should keep steadily in mind what we have gained from the idea and the practice of that institution. I do not mean only the changes in our law and custom achieved by the Supreme Court. Every student of our legal history will find decisions to deplore as well as to celebrate. Judicial review insures that the most fundamental issues of political morality will finally be set out and debated as issues of principle and not political power alone, a transformation that cannot succeed, in any case not fully, within the legislature itself. That is important beyond the importance of the actual decisions reached in courts so charged.

Judicial review is a distinctive feature of our political life, envied and increasingly copied elsewhere. It is a pervasive feature, because it forces political debate to include argument over principle, not only when a case comes to the Court but also long before and long after. This debate does not necessarily run very deep, nor is it always very powerful. It is nevertheless valuable. In the last few decades Americans debated the morality of racial segregation, and reached a degree of consensus, at the level of principle, earlier thought impossible. That debate would not have had the character it did but for the fact and the symbolism of the Court's decisions. Nor is the achievement of consensus essential to the value I have in mind. American public officials—particularly the large number of them who have gone to law school—disagree about how far those accused of crimes should be protected at the cost of efficiency in the criminal process, and about capital punishment. They disagree about gender and other nonracial distinctions in legislation, about affirmative action, abortion, and the rights of school children to an equal public education whether they live in rich or poor districts of a state. But these officials are, as a group, extraordinarily sensitive to the issues of political and moral principle latent in these controversies; more so, I think, than even the brilliantly educated and articulate officials of Britain, for example. I do not mean that the Court has been their teacher. Many of them disagree profoundly with what the Court has said. But they would not

be so sensitive to principle without the legal and political culture of which judicial review is the heart. Nor would the public they represent read and think and debate and perhaps even vote as they do without that culture.

Learned Hand warned us that we should not be ruled by philosopher-judges even if our judges were better philosophers.[50] But that threat is and will continue to be a piece of hyperbole. We have reached a balance in which the Court plays a role in government but not, by any stretch, the major role. Academic lawyers do no service by trying to disguise the political decisions this balance assigns to judges. Rule by academic priests guarding the myth of some canonical original intention is no better than the rule by Platonic guardians in different robes. We do better to work, openly and willingly, so that the national argument of principle that judicial review provides is better argument for our part. We have an institution that calls some issues from the battleground of power politics to the forum of principle. It holds out the promise that the deepest, most fundamental conflicts between individual and society will once, someplace, finally, become questions of justice. I do not call that religion or prophecy.[51] I call it law.

THREE

Principle, Policy, Procedure

NOTHING is of more immediate practical importance to a lawyer than the rules that govern his own strategies and maneuvers; and nothing is more productive of deep and philosophical puzzles than the question of what those rules should be. One such puzzle is quickly stated. People have a profound right not to be convicted of crimes of which they are innocent. If a prosecutor were to pursue a person he knew to be innocent, it would be no justification or defense that convicting that person would spare the community some expense or in some other way improve the general welfare. But in some cases it is uncertain whether someone is guilty or innocent of some crime. Does it follow, from the fact that each citizen has a right not to be convicted if innocent, that he has a right to the most accurate procedures possible to test his guilt or innocence, no matter how expensive these procedures might be to the community as a whole?

Suppose (to put a crude case) that trials would be marginally more accurate if juries were composed of twenty-five rather than twelve jurors, though trials would then be much longer, retrials more frequent, and the whole process much more expensive. If we continue to use only twelve jurors in order to save the extra expense, that will result in some people being convicted though innocent. Is that decision an act of injustice to all those who are tried by a jury of twelve?

If so, then we must acknowledge that our criminal system—in both the United States and Great Britain as well as everywhere else—is unjust and systematically violates individual rights. For we provide less than the most accurate procedures for testing guilt or innocence that we could. We do this sometimes simply to save the public money and sometimes to secure some particular social benefit directly, like protecting the power of the police to gather information by not requiring the police to disclose the names of informers when the defense requests this information. If this is not systematic injustice, then why not?

If people are not entitled to the most accurate trials possible, hang the

cost, then to what level of accuracy are they entitled? Must we flee to the other extreme, and hold that people accused of crime are entitled to no particular level of accuracy at all? That would be our assumption if we chose trial procedures and rules of evidence entirely on the basis of cost-benefit calculations about the best interests of society as a whole, balancing the interests of the accused against the interests of those who would gain from public savings in a greatest-good-of-the-greatest-number way. Would that cool utilitarian approach be consistent with our fervent declaration that the innocent have a right to go free? If not, is there some middle ground available, between these two extreme claims, that an individual has a right to the most accurate procedures possible and that he has a right to nothing by way of procedures at all?

These are difficult questions. I am not aware of any systematic discussion of them in political philosophy. Instead they have been left to the simple formula that questions of evidence and procedure must be decided by striking "the right balance" between the interests of the individual and the interests of the community as a whole, which merely restates the problem. Indeed, it is worse than a mere restatement, because the interests of each individual are already balanced into the interests of the community as a whole, and the idea of a further balance, between their separate interests and the results of the first balance, is itself therefore mysterious. We must try to find more helpful answers to our questions, including, if possible, an explanation of why this talk of a "right balance" has seemed so appropriate. But it is worth stopping, first, to notice how our questions are connected to a series of apparently different issues, both theoretical and practical, in the law of evidence.

The puzzles about substance and procedure in the criminal law arise in the civil law as well, and though the conflict between issues of individual and public interest is perhaps less dramatic there, it is more complex. When a person goes to law in a civil matter he calls on the court to enforce his rights, and the argument, that the community would be better off if that right were not enforced, is not counted a good argument against him. We must be careful not to fall into a familiar trap here. Very often, when the plaintiff makes out his case by pointing to a statute that gives him the right he now claims, the statute was itself enacted, as a matter of history, because the legislature thought that the public would benefit as a whole, in a utilitarian sort of way, if people like the defendant were given a legal right to what the statute specifies. (The statute was enacted, that is, for reasons not of principle but of policy.) Nevertheless, the plaintiff's claim, based on that statute, is a claim of right.

Suppose, for example, that the plaintiff sues under a statute that awards him treble damages against a defendant whose business practices have reduced competition to the former's disadvantage. Suppose that the legisla-

ture enacted this statute only for economic reasons. It believed the statute would encourage investment, create jobs, reduce inflation, and otherwise contribute to the general good. Nevertheless, even in such a clear-cut case, the plaintiff is himself relying on an argument of principle when he sues in court, not an argument of policy. For he would still be entitled to win, under our legal practice, even if he conceded (and the court agreed) that the statute was unwise from the standpoint of policy and would not have the beneficial consequences supposed, so that the public welfare would gain from turning him away. It is not necessary, to make his claim a claim of principle rather than of policy, that anyone actually think that the statute is unwise as policy. All that is necessary is that his claim be independent of any assumptions about the wisdom of the statute, which it is. Until the statute is repealed he remains entitled to treble damages, whatever one might think of the policy grounds for making him so entitled.

So the same problem we saw in the structure of criminal procedure is raised in civil suits as well. For it is even plainer here than in the criminal case that trials provide less than the optimum possible guarantee of accuracy. And even plainer that the savings so achieved are justified by considerations of the general public welfare. The two questions we posed about the criminal law reappear here. Is the role of social welfare in fixing civil procedure consistent with our understanding that if the plaintiff or defendant has a legal right to win, he or she should win even though the public would then be worse off? If it is consistent, are the parties to a civil suit entitled to any particular level of accuracy? Or is it just a matter of what procedures and rules of evidence work in the overall public interest, all things considered?

These questions, as applied to civil cases, suggest a further puzzle about the law of evidence, a puzzle that belongs more generally to the theory of adjudication. It will take, I am afraid, somewhat longer to state. I just said that the plaintiff in a civil suit asserts a right to win, not merely an argument of policy that his winning would be in the general interest. That would, I think, be generally agreed about what we might call easy cases, that is, when the plaintiff's title to win is established uncontroversially by some doctrinal authority, like a statute or a prior court decision of a sufficiently elevated court. Everyone would agree that the plaintiff's argument—if just pointing at a statute can be considered an argument—is an argument of principle rather than policy.

This is less clear, however, in a hard case, that is, when competent lawyers are divided about which decision is required because the only pertinent statutes or precedents are ambiguous, or there is no doctrinal authority directly in point, or for some other reason the law is not, as lawyers say, settled. In such a case the plaintiff's lawyers will nevertheless present an argument as to why, all things considered, his case is stronger than the

defendant's, and the defendant's counsel will present a different argument to the opposite effect. At the end of the day the judge (perhaps a whole series of judges if the decision is appealed) will decide by preferring one of these two arguments, or perhaps by providing a different one of their own. I believe that even in hard cases like these the arguments that lawyers put forward and that judges accept are arguments of principle rather than arguments of policy, and that this is as it should be. Even in such a case, when the law is (depending on the metaphor you favor) either murky or unsettled or nonexistent, I believe that the plaintiff means to claim that he is entitled to win, all things considered, and not merely that the public would gain if he did win.

But I have not (to understate) persuaded everyone that this is so, and various critics have proposed a large number of counter-examples to my claim. Many of these are drawn from the law of procedure generally and the law of evidence in particular. A series of recent English decisions are thought to supply one such set of counter-examples. In *D v. National Society for the Prevention of Cruelty to Children*, for example, a woman, who had been falsely accused by an anonymous informer of cruelty to her children, sued the defendant agency and asked for the name of the informer.[1] The agency resisted, on the ground that it would receive less anonymous information, and so be in a worse position to protect children generally, if it became known that it might be forced to divulge the names of informers. The House of Lords said that though normally the courts would order the discovery of information of this sort in pretrial proceedings, the agency's argument was sound in this case, because it would be contrary to public policy for the informer's name to be disclosed.

The Court of Appeal reached the opposite result in a similar case, but through an argument that might seem to confirm the importance of policy arguments in cases like these.[2] An unknown employee of the British Steel Corporation delivered a confidential internal memorandum of that organization to Granada Television, which used the memorandum as the basis for a broadcast critical of the management. The corporation demanded the return of the document, and Granada complied, but only after defacing the document so as to remove all clues as to the identity of the (as the corporation deemed him) disloyal employee. The corporation then sued, relying on the discretionary remedy made available by the House of Lord's decision in *Norwich Pharmacal*, for the name of that employee.[3] Lord Justice Denning, in the Court of Appeal, suggested that, but for certain circumstances he thought affected the matter, he would have refused disclosure on the ground that the press can do a better job serving a vital public interest if it is not required to disclose the name of its informers. In fact, joined by his colleagues on the Court, he ordered disclosure, because Granada had, in his view, misbehaved. It had not told the corporation of its possession of the

memorandum soon enough, for example, and the television interview based on the memorandum was not conducted with suitable decorum.

That ground of decision is both silly and malign. Courts have no business reviewing either the editorial judgment or courtesy of the press, and any rule of law that makes the powers of the press turn on what judges think of their manners is a greater threat to their independence than a flat rule requiring them to name their informers. But the background judgment of the court—that the effect on the public's access to information must be taken into account in deciding what material may be discovered in pretrial proceedings in civil litigation—is of great importance.

For even if we say that in *D v. NSPCC* the court made the question of evidence, whether it would require production of the name of the informer, turn on the competing rights of children who would be protected less if such disclosure were ordered, we cannot take that view of *Granada*. No member of the public has a right to the information television companies would lose if they were forced to divulge the names of those who approach them in confidentiality. This obvious fact is sometimes obscured by the phrase, made popular by the press in recent years, that the public has what is called a "right to know." That phrase makes sense only if it is understood merely to claim that in general it is in the public interest to have more rather than less information about, for example, the internal management of state-owned industries. It does not mean that any individual member of the public has a right to this information in the strong sense that his right would provide an argument of principle requiring disclosure. It does not mean, that is, that it would be wrong to deny it to him even if the community would suffer overall by its disclosure. So the background assumption in *Granada*, that in the absence of the television company's indecorum the Steel Corporation's request would have been denied because of the public's interest in information, seems to rely on an argument of policy rather than an argument of principle to justify a judicial decision.[4]

But if that turns out to be so, then doubts must be raised about both the descriptive and normative sides of my claim about hard cases. The normative side argues that it would be wrong for judges to decide civil suits on grounds of policy. That is a claim about the final disposition of a case. It requires (put subjectively) that a judge not award damages to a plaintiff unless he believes that the plaintiff is entitled to that relief. It is not enough that he believe that the public interest would be served by creating a new right in the plaintiff. That says nothing, in itself, about how the judge should go about forming his belief *whether* the plaintiff is entitled to a given remedy. It does not say that he must not take the public interest into account in determining how he (or other triers of fact and law) should proceed to investigate that question. Therefore, the normative argument I makes does not in itself condemn judges who consider the social consequences of one rule of

evidence against another in deciding whether to require the NSPCC or Granada Television to make available particular information that will be used in determining their substantive legal rights.

Yet the normative force of my claim would surely be weakened—some would say extinguished—if judges were permitted to decide procedural issues on what we might call pure arguments of policy. If they were permitted, for example, to decide whether to require the NSPCC to furnish the names of informers simply by balancing the potential loss to plaintiffs against the potential gains to children in a standard cost-benefit calculation. For that would make the boast that society honors claims of right, even at the expense of the general welfare, an idle gesture easily subverted by denying the procedures necessary to enforce these rights for no better reason than that same public interest. So those who take pride in that boast have reason to see whether some middle ground can be found between the impractical idea of maximum accuracy and the submersive denial of all procedural rights.

Parallel threats are raised to the descriptive side of my claims about adjudication. Once again my claim is a claim about the final disposition of lawsuits. I say that judges adjudicate civil claims through arguments of principle rather than policy, even in very hard cases. I mean that they do not grant the relief the plaintiff demands unless satisfied that the plaintiff is entitled to that relief, or deny relief if they are satisfied that the plaintiff is so entitled. Once again that does not include, strictly speaking, any claim about how judges even characteristically decide how to decide whether the plaintiff is entitled or not. I do not argue, certainly, that judges never take considerations of social consequence into account in fixing rules of evidence or other procedural rules. So it is no counter-example to my claim when judges consider the public's interest in deciding whether a child protection agency or a branch of the press must disclose information bearing on adjudication before them.

But once again my descriptive claims would be jeopardized by any concession that these decisions were often purely matters of policy, that is, that they were often decided just by a routine utilitarianlike calculation pitting the damage to some litigant's financial position against the gains to society generally of some exclusionary rule. For since the sharp distinction between substantive and procedure is arbitrary from a normative standpoint, as we have just seen, any descriptive theory that relies so heavily on that distinction, even if factually accurate, cannot be a deep theory about the nature of adjudication but must be only a claim that happens to be true, perhaps for reasons of historical accident, about one part of adjudication and false about another.

So anyone who thinks, as I do, that adjudication of substantive issues at law is a matter of principle, and that this is an important claim both nor-

matively and theoretically, has a special interest in whether some middle ground can be found between the extravagant and the nihilistic claims about the rights people have to procedures in court. Before I turn at last to that issue, however, and to the other issues so far raised, I shall describe yet another legal controversy that raises many of these issues in a still different form.

The Court of Appeal and the House of Lords generated a fascinating discussion about the requirements of what in Britain is called natural justice and in the United States due process of law. In the case of *Bushell v. Secretary of State for the Environment,* for example, the question arose whether the department of the environment, which held hearings to determine whether a highway should be built through a part of the city of Birmingham, could properly exclude from the scope of those hearings an examination of its own "Red Book," a document setting out certain general predictions about traffic flow that the department had developed for the country as a whole.[5] The department did not allow the groups opposing the highway to contest the Red Book figures, which it proposed to use in connection with its decision, but instead limited the hearing to purely local issues. The department later conceded that the Red Book figures were inaccurate, because they did not take into account predicted reduction in highway use flowing from increased fuel costs, though it nevertheless argued that its decision, which was to build the highway, was the right decision anyway.

The opposing groups took the department to court, and the Court of Appeal, in a decision by Lord Denning, held that the denial of opportunity to contest the Red Book was a denial of natural justice and so rendered the hearings and the decision infirm. The House of Lords, in a divided opinion, reversed. The principal speech argued that the department was within its rights in limiting local hearings to issues that varied from locality to locality, excluding general predictions about traffic flow and other matters that must be decided centrally to govern all local decisions in a uniform manner.

Bushell presents the same problem we have been considering, about the connection between substantive and procedural political decisions, but in the reverse direction. For it is uncontroversial (I suppose) that the decision whether to build a highway in a particular direction is, absent of special circumstances I assume were not present here, a matter of policy. If it was in the public's overall interest to build the highway as the department wished to do, giving full weight, in that determination, to the adverse impact on those particularly inconvenienced by the decision, then the decision to build the highway was the right decision to take. No individual or group has a right in the strong sense against that decision. (It would not be wrong to build the highway over the objection of any particular person, that is, if building the highway were in fact in the general interest.) Of

course, if the highway seriously threatened the life or health of any particular individual, that might well make a difference. That person might well be thought to have a right against the highway in exactly that strong sense. But that is the kind of special circumstance that I am assuming was absent in the case.

If the question whether to build a highway in a particular direction is a question of policy, then is not the further question of what form and dimension of public hearings to hold in order to decide that question also a question of policy? The Court of Appeal, in effect, denied this connection. It held that considerations of "natural justice" apply even to hearings in service of policy decisions. We must therefore ask whether the commitment to procedural rights in the criminal and civil legal process, when we have further identified these rights, indeed do have that consequence.

WE HAVE IDENTIFIED a series of questions that I shall now restate, though in a slightly different order. (1) Is it consistent, with the proposition that people have a right not to be convicted of a crime if innocent, to deny people any rights, in the strong sense, to procedures to test their innocence? (2) If not, does consistency require that people have a right to the most accurate procedures possible? (3) If not, is there some defensible middle ground, according to which people have some procedural rights, but not to the most accurate procedures possible? How might such rights be stated? (4) Do our conclusions hold for the civil as well as the criminal law? (5) Are the decisions that courts make about procedure, in the course of a trial, decisions of policy or principle? Which should they be? (6) Do people have procedural rights with respect to political decisions of policy?

It will prove convenient to begin with the first of these questions. Imagine a society that establishes the right not to be convicted if innocent as absolute but denies, not only the right to the most accurate process conceivable, but any right to any particular process at all. This society (which I shall call the cost-efficient society) designs criminal procedures, including rules of evidence, by measuring the estimated suffering of those who would be mistakenly convicted if a particular rule were chosen, but would be acquitted if a higher standard of accuracy were established, against the benefits to others that will follow from choosing that rule instead of that higher standard.

It is not true that the right not to be convicted if innocent is a mere sham that has no value in the cost-efficient society. For the right protects people against deliberate prosecution by officials who know the accused to be innocent. Surely there is moral value, even in the cost-efficient society, in that prohibition. For there is a special injustice in knowingly and falsely claiming that someone has committed a crime. That is, among other things, a lie.

So there seems no logical inconsistency in a moral scheme that accepts the risk of innocent mistakes about guilt or innocence in order to save public funds for other uses, but will not permit deliberate lies for the same purpose.

But there is another kind of inconsistency, which will take a moment to explain. Political rights, like the right not to be convicted if innocent, have their main function as instructions to government; and we might therefore be tempted to think that nothing has gone wrong when government heeds the instruction and makes a blameless mistake. But this is wrong because the violation of a right constitutes a special kind of harm, and people may suffer that harm even when the violation is accidental. We must distinguish, that is, between what we might call the bare harm a person suffers through punishment, whether that punishment is just or unjust—for example, the suffering or frustration or pain or dissatisfaction of desires that he suffers just because he loses his liberty or is beaten or killed—and the further injury that he might be said to suffer whenever his punishment is unjust, just in virtue of that injustice. I shall call the latter the "injustice factor" in his punishment, or his "moral" harm. The harm someone suffers through punishment may include resentment or outrage or some similar emotion, and is more likely to include some emotion of this sort when the person punished believes his punishment to be unjust, whether it is unjust or not. Any such emotion is part of the bare harm, not the injustice factor. The latter is an objective notion which assumes that someone suffers a special injury when treated unjustly, whether he knows or cares about it, but does not suffer that injury when he is not treated unjustly, even though he believes he is and does care. It is an empirical question whether someone who is punished unjustly suffers more bare harm when he knows that the officials have made a mistake than when he knows that they have deliberately framed him. But it is a moral fact, if the assumption of the last paragraph is right, that the injustice factor in his injury is greater in the second case.

One can be skeptical about the idea of injustice factor, as a component of harm or injury, in the following way. The idea (it might be said) confuses the quantum of harm someone suffers from official decisions with the different issue whether that harm is just or unjust. Someone who suffers a certain degree of pain or frustration or incapacitation from a certain punishment— the "bare" harm—does not suffer *more* harm when he is innocent than when he is guilty. The harm he does suffer is unjust in the former case, whatever the amount of that harm is, but it only confuses that point to say that the injustice in some way adds to that harm. Nevertheless, we do feel more sympathy for someone when we learn that he has been cheated, even though we learn nothing more about his bare loss, and we do believe that someone suffers an injury when he is told a lie, even when he remains ignorant and suffers no bare harm in consequence.

But it is not important, for my present purpose, whether the idea of a distinct moral harm is accepted or rejected, for even if we abandon that idea we must still accept its substance in a different form. For surely we want to be able to say that the situation is worse when an innocent person is convicted, just because of the injustice, even if we balk at saying that that person is worse off; and in order to say even that we need a notion of a moral cost to or a moral loss in the worth of outcomes or situations. This notion will do the same work in my argument as the idea of a moral harm to an individual person, except that it treats the harm as general rather than as assigned. Suppose we discover that some person executed for murder several decades ago was in fact innocent. We shall want to say that the world has gone worse than we thought, though we may add, if we reject the idea of moral harm, that no one suffered any harm of which we were ignorant, or was in any way worse off than we believed. In the remainder of this essay I shall use the idea of moral harm to people, though nothing much in the arguments would be otherwise altered if I used the idea of a moral cost to situations, not assignable to people, instead.

We may now see why the behavior of our imaginary cost-efficient community, which recognizes an absolute right not to be convicted if innocent, but submits questions of evidence and procedure to an ordinary utilitarian cost-benefit analysis, seems so odd. For it makes no sense for our society to establish the right not to be convicted when known to be innocent as absolute, unless that society recognizes moral harm as a distinct kind of harm against which people must be specially protected. But the utilitarian calculus that the cost-efficient society uses to fix criminal procedures is a calculus that can make no place for moral harm. The injustice factor in a mistaken punishment will escape the net of any utilitarian calculation, however sophisticated, that measures harm by some psychological state along the pleasure-pain axis, or by the frustration of desires or preferences or as some function over the cardinal or ordinal preference rankings of particular people, even if the calculus includes the preferences that people have that neither they nor others be punished unjustly. For moral harm is an objective notion, and if someone is morally harmed (or, in the alternative language, if there is a moral loss in the situation) when he is punished though innocent, then this moral harm occurs even when no one knows or suspects it, and even when—perhaps especially when—very few people very much care.

So the practice of the cost-efficient society makes sense only if we accept that there is great distinct moral harm when someone is framed, but none whatsoever when he is mistakenly convicted. That is very implausible, and this explains, I think, why the combination of procedures strikes us as bizarre. We must ask how the procedures of the cost-efficient society must be changed so as to make place for the recognition of moral harm. It is neces-

sary—or possible—to insist on a right to the most accurate procedures imaginable? But first we must consider two possible objections to the argument I have just made, that the procedures of the cost-efficient society, as they stand, do show a kind of moral inconsistency.

I said that its endorsement of an absolute right not to be convicted if innocent shows that it recognizes moral harm as an independent and important sort of harm, while its acceptance of an ordinary utilitarian calculation about procedural issues denies that independence and importance. Someone might challenge each of these claims. He might say, first, that a society that rejected the idea of moral harm over and above bare harm, and aimed only to maximize utility on some ordinary conception (say maximizing the balance of pleasure over pain) would do well to adopt an absolute right not to be convicted of a crime if known to be innocent. He would argue that a society that allows officials even to toy with the idea of deliberately convicting an innocent person will generate more bare harm than a society that does not. This is the now familiar two-level utilitarian defense of ordinary moral sentiments. That defense seems to me, here as elsewhere, to run backward. Those who argue in this way have no direct evidence for their instrumental claims. (How could they know or even have good reason to believe that a society of intelligent act-utilitarian officials, who would consider convicting the innocent only on very special occasions, would do worse for long-term utility than a society that disabled its officials from ever taking that step?) Rather they argue backward from the fact that our moral intuitions condemn convicting the innocent to the conclusion that such a disability must be in the long-term utilitarian interests of any society.

But I do not need to rely on my general suspicions of arguments of this character. For the two-level justification of ordinary moral convictions, however persuasive or unpersuasive it might be in other contexts, is not in point here. The members of the cost-efficient society in my example suppose (as I think most of us do) that it would be wrong deliberately to convict the innocent, even if there were a long-term utilitarian benefit to be gained. They suppose, in other words, that the right not to be convicted if innocent is a genuine right, which trumps even long-term utility, not an instrumental or as-if right that serves it. It is that assumption that, I believe, presupposes the idea of moral harm.

Second, someone might say that the utilitarian test the cost-efficient society uses to fix procedures does not in fact reject that idea, or suppose that there is no moral harm when someone is mistakenly convicted, because even an ordinary utilitarian test will actually be sensitive to moral harm. For suppose we do discover that someone convicted and punished for murder long ago was innocent. We thereby discover that the bare harm done him, just considered in itself, was unnecessary, because the general utilitarian policies of the criminal law would have been advanced just as well—

perhaps even better—without punishing him. We discover, that is, that the bare harm, which is reflected in the utilitarian sum, was unjustified on the simple utilitarian test, and that gives us cause to regret the procedures that produced or allowed it. Of course, we might still conclude that these procedures nevertheless produced more net gain than more accurate procedures would have done, because the unnecessary bare harm was less, in total, than the added expense of the more accurate procedures would have been. But our test is nevertheless sensitive to moral harm, because it identified the bare harm associated with moral harm as unnecessary, and therefore as counting, just considered in itself, against the procedures that allowed it.

But this argument fails because it is not true, in any relevant sense, that the bare harm associated with moral harm was unnecessary. Convicting this particular person, though innocent, might for a vast variety of reasons have contributed especially efficiently to deterrence, or to another consequence of the criminal system of which utility approves. Indeed, if it might sometimes be in the long-term utilitarian interests of the community for officials deliberately to convict someone they thought to be innocent (and that possibility is the occasion for recognizing a right against this), then equally it might sometimes be in those long-term interests of the community that someone innocent be innocently convicted. It therefore does not follow that when we discover a past injustice we also discover an occasion when utility would have gained, even just considering the direct consequences of that injustice, had it been avoided. So the discovery of even a great number of such incidents would not automatically give us a utilitarian cost to set against the costs of having adopted more expensive procedures.

It seems even clearer that even when bare harm that is also moral harm is a mistake from the utilitarian point of view—when utility would have been advanced had that bare harm been avoided—the magnitude of the bare harm may be very different from the magnitude of the moral harm. When someone old, sick, and feeble is executed by a community that wrongly believes him guilty of treason, the bare harm, considered in cold utilitarian terms, might be very little, but the moral harm very great. The difference will be important when the question is raised whether the possibility of that harm justifies adopting expensive procedures that will reduce its chances. If the incident counts, in the grand calculation, only in the measure of the bare harm, then it may hardly advance the argument for more expensive procedures at all. But if it counts in the measure of its moral harm, it might count very heavily.

So these objections actually reinforce my suggestion that a society that submits questions of criminal procedure to an ordinary utilitarian calculus does not recognize the independence or importance of moral harm, or, if it does, does not recognize that even an accidental conviction of an innocent

person is an occasion of moral harm. The cost-efficient society I imagine does therefore act inconsistently. But this is only the end of the beginning. For we must now face the second question in our list. If the cost-efficient society is defective, must we substitute a practice under which all other social needs and benefits are sacrificed to producing the most elaborate and accurate criminal process the world has ever seen?

We might enforce that terrible requirement by ordering the avoidance of moral harm as lexically prior to all other needs. It would not quite follow from this lexical ordering that we would never have an excuse for choosing less than the most accurate criminal process, because there might be forms of moral harm other than innocent conviction of the innocent. Perhaps there is moral wrong, for example, not captured in any ordinary utilitarian calculation, when society neglects the education of the young, so that the provision of funds for public education would be competitive with funds for criminal trial accuracy even under the lexical ordering constraint. But a society governed by that constraint would be obliged to furnish the highest possible level of accuracy for the system (as we might call it) of avoiding moral harm altogether, and could never devote public funds to amenities like improvements to the highway system, for example, so long as any further expense on the criminal process could improve its accuracy. Our own society plainly does not observe that stricture, and most people would think it too severe.

NEVERTHELESS, we could not escape the severe requirement if we were forced to concede that accidentally convicting someone who is innocent is just as bad as framing him deliberately. Would we countenance framing someone for armed robbery if, for some reason, a hundred potential armed robberies would thereby be averted? If the gross national product would thereby be trebled? If a given amount of gain of that sort would not justify a single deliberate violation of the right not to be convicted if innocent, then that amount of gain could not justify adopting procedures that would increase the chance of a mistaken conviction by even one person over the pertinent period.

In the preceding section I denied the premise of this harsh syllogism. I said that it is morally worse deliberately to convict the innocent accidentally, because the deliberate act involves a lie and therefore a special insult to the dignity of the person. It is now important to see whether this is right—whether this is an available ground of distinction. Because if it is not, then we must accept lexical ordering of avoiding any risk of mistaken convictions over any amenity we might gain from less expensive procedures, however painful that seems.

I propose the following two principles of fair play in government. First, any political decision must treat all citizens as equals, that is, as equally en-

titled to concern and respect. It is not part of this principle that government may never deliberately impose a greater bare harm on some than others, as it does when, for example, it levies special import taxes on petrol or gasoline. It *is* part of the principle that no decision may deliberately impose on any citizen a much greater risk of moral harm than it imposes on any other. Moral harm is treated as special by this principle of equality. Second, if a political decision is taken and announced that respects equality as demanded by the first principle, then a later enforcement of that decision is not a fresh political decision that must also be equal in its impact in that way. The second principle appeals to the fairness of abiding by open commitments fair when adopted—the fairness, for example, of abiding by the result of a coin toss when both parties reasonably agreed to the toss.

These two principles each plays a role in fixing rules of criminal procedure. Under certain circumstances (I shall discuss these later) a decision to adopt a particular rule of evidence in criminal trials treats citizens as equals, because each citizen is antecedently equally likely to be drawn into the criminal process though innocent, and equally likely to benefit from the savings gained by choosing that rule of evidence rather than a socially more expensive rule. That decision therefore respects the first principle of fair play. When any particular citizen is accused of crime, the decision to enforce that rule of evidence in his trial, rather than to set it aside or repeal it, is a decision that may well work to that citizen's special disadvantage, because it may offer him a greater risk of moral harm than an alternative rule would, a greater risk not offered to those who have not been accused of a crime. But the second principle stipulates that the application of the rule to him is not a fresh political decision, but rather an unfolding of the earlier decision which was fair to him. So the second principle insists that trial under the established rule is not an instance of treating him other than as an equal.

These two principles of fair play, taken together, explain why deliberate conviction of someone known to be innocent is worse than a mistaken conviction under general though risky procedures fixed in advance. Framing someone is a case of a fresh political decision that does not treat him as an equal as required by the first principle. It is not (nor can it be) only the application to his case of open public commitments fixed in advance. (Framing would lose its point if there were a public commitment to frame people meeting a certain public test.) On the contrary, it is the decision to inflict on a particular person special moral harm, and that is true even when he is selected by lot from a group of candidates for framing. So a deliberate violation of the principle against convicting the innocent involves greater moral harm than an accidental mistaken conviction, because the former violates the equal standing of the victim in the special way condemned by the principles of fair play, as well as sharing in the residual moral harm of the latter.

But we have established only that risking accidental injustice, in the way

this is risked by rules of criminal procedure, is not as bad as inflicting deliberate moral harm. We are not much further along on deciding how bad the former is, and how, if at all, we are to balance the risk of accidental moral harm against the general social gains that are realized by accepting such a risk. We might consider looking for help in a different direction. I mean by capitalizing on the fact that we all, as individuals, in the various decisions we make about leading our own lives, both distinguish moral harm from bare harm, and accept some risk of moral harm in return for gains of different sorts.

Few of us would count it just as bad to be punished for a crime we did commit as for a crime we didn't but the community thought we did. Most of us dread injustice with a special fear. We hate to be cheated more than to be fairly defeated or found out. That is not because the bare harm is greater. On the contrary, if the bare harm is greater, this is because we believe that being cheated is worse, and we therefore feel anger and resentment that multiply the bare harm. Some of us also feel the self-loathing that is for them a paradoxical consequence of being treated with contempt by others.

It is not inevitable that we regard injustice as worse than our deserts. For guilt adds to the bare harm in the latter case, and newfound pride, at least for strong people, may reduce it in the former. But the normal phenomenology of guilt itself includes the idea of moral harm being a special harm to others, over and beyond the bare harm one causes them. For why else should we feel guilt for causing harm deliberately when we feel less guilt or even no guilt for causing the same harm accidentally? And perhaps the special pain of guilt is the recognition of Plato's claim, that when a man is unjust he inflicts moral harm upon himself.

So it is fair to say that we distinguish, in our own moral experience, between moral and bare harm, and at least often count an injury that includes moral harm as worse than one that does not. But we do not lead our lives to achieve the minimum of moral harm at any cost; on the contrary, we accept substantial risks of suffering injustice in order to achieve even quite marginal gains in the general course of our lives. We do this when we accept promises, enter into contracts, trust friends, and vote for procedural features of the criminal law that promise less than the highest levels of accuracy. Indeed under certain circumstances we might regard the design of criminal and civil procedures as a fabric woven from the community's convictions about the relative weight of different forms of moral harms, compared with each other, and against ordinary sacrifices and injuries.

I do not mean that the *correct* weighting of moral harms against bare harms, even for the purpose of a just assignment of risks, is constituted by a social decision. That would be to misunderstand the idea of moral harm and the contrast with bare harm. Bare harm is best understood, perhaps, in sub-

jective terms: someone suffers bare harm to the degree that the deprivation causes him pain or frustrates plans that he deems important to his life. But moral harm is, as I said, an objective matter; and whether someone suffers moral harm in some circumstances and the relative weight or importance of that harm as against what others save through the practices or events that produce it are moral rather than psychological facts. Our common moral experience shows only that we recognize moral harm but do not weigh it as lexically more important than bare harm or loss of various sorts. It does not show that we are right in either respect.

Nevertheless, our common experience does suggest a useful answer to the practical question of how a society should decide how important moral harm is. Under certain circumstances that issue should be left to democratic institutions to decide, not because a legislature or parliament will necessarily be correct, but because that is a fair way, in these circumstances, to decide moral issues about which reasonable and sensitive people disagree. It will be a fair way to decide when the decision meets the first principle of fair play I described, if the decision treats everyone as an equal because, whichever conception of the importance of different moral harms is chosen, that decision is equally in or against the antecedent whole interest of each person, by which I mean the combination of his or her moral and bare interests.

Suppose a society of people, each of whom is antecedently equally as likely to be charged with a crime, and each of whom would suffer the same bare harm from the same punishment if convicted. That society enacts, by majority decision, a criminal code defining crimes, attaching penalties, and stipulating procedures for trials for the different sorts and levels of crimes so defined. Everyone's whole interest is either threatened or advanced by that decision, and in equal degree. People will disagree about the wisdom of the decision. Members of the losing minority will think that the level of accuracy provided by the procedures for trying some crime is too low and so undervalues the moral harm of an unjust conviction for that crime, or that that level is too high and so overvalues that harm compared to the benefits forgone by using the society's funds in this way. But since moral harm is an objective matter and not dependent upon particular people's perception of moral harm, no one will think that the majority's decision is unfair in the sense that it is more in the interests of some than others. Majority rule therefore seems an especially appropriate technique for making this social decision.

It is never true, at any time, that all members of a society are equally likely to be accused of any particular crime. If there is economic inequality, the rich are more likely to be accused of conspiring to monopolize and the poor of sleeping under the bridges. If people differ in temperament the hot-blooded are more likely to be accused of some crimes and the greedy of

others. And so forth. So the constitution of a fair society might well insist that the punishments attached to various crimes must be consistent according to some reasonably objective theory of the importance of crimes, and that the assumed moral harm of an unjust conviction be correlated with the gravity of punishments on some uniform scale.

Even so, the circumstances we imagine for a fair majority decision will be compromised if some minority is more likely to be accused of crimes overall or of crimes carrying relatively serious punishments. That fact will not justify abandoning the majority decision procedure, however, unless the increased risk is great for particular individuals. It will also never be true in any actual society that different people will suffer exactly the same bare harm from any given punishment. But this fact provides even less of a reason to object to majority decision, because differences of that character are much less likely to be correlated with economic or social class and therefore less likely to provide systematic injustice. We should notice a third complexity here. In the actual world different people will gain differently through any alternative use of public funds saved by choosing less rather than more expensive criminal procedures. That will be true even when the saving takes the most abstract form, which is savings added to social funds available for general purposes. But society may save by sacrificing accuracy in the criminal process in much more concrete ways, as it does, for example, when it recognizes a privilege in the police (or in organizations like the National Society for the Prevention of Cruelty to Children or Granada Television mentionied earlier) not to furnish information about informers, or, more conventionally, if it recognizes a doctor-patient privilege so as to improve medical care. The justification for the sacrifice in trial accuracy in these latter cases is just as fully a justification of policy as when the gain is general money saved that might be used for highways or hospitals or a national theater. But the decision about who gains—children, for example, or that part of the public that takes an interest in politics—is part of the decision to reduce accuracy, rather than being, as in the general case, a decision that leaves the distribution of the gain to further political action. But once again the compromise with our imagined conditions is small if, as in these examples, the class that fails to benefit is not a class that is on general social or economic grounds distinct from the majority making the decision.

So even in the real world majoritarian decisions that fix a particular level of accuracy in criminal decisions in advance of particular trials, through the choice of rules of evidence and other procedural decisions, can be faulted for serious unfairness only if these decisions discriminate against some independently distinct group in one or another of the ways just canvassed. It is not enough, to make these decisions unfair, that they put one rather than another value on moral harm of different sorts, so long as this valuation is consistent and unbiased.

Antecedent decisions of this sort may show special concern for moral harm, not only by paying a high price for accuracy, but also, and especially, by paying a price *in* accuracy to guard against a mistake that involves greater moral harm than a mistake in the other direction. This is shown, for example, by the rule that guilt must be shown beyond a reasonable doubt, rather than on the balance of probabilities, and also by rules, like the rule that the accused may not be compelled to testify, whose complex justification includes weighing the scales in favor of the accused, at the cost of accuracy, as well as guarding the accused against certain kinds of mistakes and misimpressions that might compromise accuracy. Examples are rarer in the civil law, because it is generally assumed that a mistake in either direction involves equal moral harm. But when the burden of proving truth is placed on the defendant in a defamation suit, for example, after the plaintiff has proved defamation, this may represent some collective determination that it is a greater moral harm to suffer an uncompensated and false libel than to be held in damages for a libel that is in fact true.

THE IDEA of moral harm, coupled with the fact that a community's law provides a record of its assessment of the relative importance of moral harm, allows us to account for two different sorts of right that people might be said to have with respect to criminal procedure. First, people have a right that criminal procedures attach the correct importance to the risk of moral harm. In some circumstances it would be clear that this first right has been violated, as it would be if, for example, some community decided criminal cases by flipping a coin, or did not permit the accused to be present at this trial or to have a lawyer or to present evidence if he wished, or if it used only ordinary utilitarian calculations to choose criminal procedures as the cost-efficient society did. In other, closer cases it would be debatable whether the correct weight had been given to the risk of moral harm, and reasonable and sensitive people would disagree. The second right, which is the right to a consistent weighting of the importance of moral harm, is of great practical importance in these circumstances. For it enables someone to argue, even in cases in which the correct answer to the problem of moral harm is deeply controversial, that he is entitled to procedures consistent with the community's own evaluation of moral harm embedded in the law as a whole.

Both of these rights are rights in the strong sense of a right we identified earlier, because each of them acts as a trump over the balance of bare gains and losses that forms an ordinary utilitarian calculation. Once the content of the right is determined, then the community must furnish those accused of crime with at least the minimum level of protection against the risk of injustice required by that content, even though the general welfare, now conceived with no reference to moral harm but only as constituted by bare

gains and losses, suffers in consequence. But in each case the right is a right to that minimum of protection, not a right to as much protection as the community could provide were it willing to sacrifice the general welfare altogether. The second right, for example, holds the community to a consistent enforcement of its theory of moral harm, but does not demand that it replace that theory with a different one that values the importance of avoiding unjust punishment higher. So identifying and explaining these rights is a useful reply to the third question listed earlier. The content of these rights provides a middle ground between the denial of all procedural rights and the acceptance of a grand right to supreme accuracy.

The distinction between these two rights is not hard and fast. For the enterprise demanded by the second right—finding the account of moral harm that is embedded in the substantive and procedural criminal law as a whole—does not consist just in establishing a textual and historical record, though that is part of the job. It consists also in interpreting that record, and that means fitting a justification to it, a process that, as I have tried to explain elsewhere, draws upon though it is not identical with citation of principles that are taken to be independently morally correct.[6]

This connection between claims of consistency and claims of independent correctness is exhibited in the various attempts of the Supreme Court to interpret the due process clause of the Fourteenth Amendment, which is the constitutional home of these rights, at least for the criminal process. That clause has been said to protect, for example, "those fundamental principles of liberty and justice which lie at the base of all our civil and political institutions" (*Hurtado v. California* 110 US 516 (1884)), "ultimate decency in a civilized society" (*Adamson v. California* 332 US 45 (1947)), principles that are "basic in our system of jurisprudence" (*Re Oliver* 333 US 257 (1948)), and, in the most famous statement of the clause, "principle[s] of justice so rooted in the tradition and conscience of our people as to be ranked as fundamental" and for that reason "implicit in the concept of ordered liberty" (*Palko v. Connecticut* 302 US 319 (1937)). All these excerpts from constitutional decisions are taken by constitutional lawyers to be, roughly speaking, different statements of the same idea.

Nevertheless, history will play an important role in fixing the content of the second right, the right to consistency in procedure, and in some cases there can be no stronger argument for some particular institutional arrangement than the argument that it has always been so. It is hard to suppose, for example, that the criminal law would necessarily have been very different in other ways had its ancient practice required ten or fourteen jurors instead of twelve, though the former choice would have avoided many retrials and therefore saved a great deal of expense over the centuries, and the latter would have been correspondingly much more expensive. It is hard to resist supposing that the number actually chosen was in large part fortuitous. But the number of jurors is plainly so important a consideration in

guarding an accused against injustice, when a unanimous verdict is required to convict him, that any substantial change in that number for capital cases or cases threatening severe punishments—say reducing the number to six— would count as a violation of the rights of the accused just because it would be a substantial diminution in the level of safety provided at the center of the criminal process for so long. Dozens of Supreme Court decisions applying the due process clause against the states testify to the independent importance of what might be regarded as accidents of history, made into constitutional doctrine by the right to consistency, now conceived independently of the first or background right to a correct account of moral harm.

The second right therefore acts as a distinct conservative force protecting the accused from changes in the evaluation of moral harm. But it also acts as a lever for reform, by picking out even ancient procedures as mistakes— islands of inconsistency that cannot be brought within any justification that attaches the level of importance to the injustice factor in the mistaken conviction that is necessary to explain the rest of the law. This second, reforming function must be handled with great care, because it must respect the fact that criminal procedures provide protection as a system, so that the force of one rule of evidence, for example, may be misunderstood unless its effect is studied in combination with other aspects of that system. If the law does not provide a fund out of which indigent defendants might conduct expensive research relevant to the defense, that might show that little weight is put on the moral harm of an unjust conviction, unless the effect of that failure is measured as part of a system that places a great evidentiary burden on the prosecution and protects the defendant in other ways as well.

Nevertheless, it is not a sufficient answer to the objection that some feature of the criminal law puts an inconsistently low value on the importance of avoiding injustice, that other parts of the law of criminal procedure err in the opposite direction. For what must be shown is not that errors on each side of the established line will cancel each other out over the long run of criminal adjudication, but rather that a system of rules, taken together, provide no more than the established risk in each case, given the competing claims displayed in that case. The reforming function must also be sensitive (I should add) to the point we noticed in our discussion of the cost-efficient society. The value society puts on moral harm may be established elsewhere in its law or practices than in its criminal procedure, so that that procedure might be inconsistent with the remainder of legal and political practice beyond any internal inconsistency within the rules of procedure themselves.

With respect to both the checking and reforming functions of the second right, however, there is room for the skeptical claim that a principle that permits reasonable lawyers to differ provides no genuine protection. For (as

almost everywhere in legal analysis) the question of how much the law values avoiding moral harm, and which of two competing procedures comes closest to respecting that valuation, are not questions admitting of demonstration, and reasonable lawyers will disagree. Though the second right will not be so inherently controversial in its application as the first, it may be almost so. But (again here as elsewhere) it would be a mistake to take the skeptical claim as defeating the importance of a moral or legal principle, or as an excuse for refusing to deploy and defend as persuasive an application of that principle, in any particular case, as we can. For the practical importance of a contestable principle is not something that can be established *a priori*, in advance of our best attempts to see how far the principle takes us away from (what we take to be) injustice. This foolish form of skepticism is most often a self-fulfilling prophecy.

Where are we? We have seen that people drawn into the criminal process do not have a right to the most accurate possible procedures for testing the charges against them. But they do have two other genuine rights: the right to procedures that put a proper valuation on moral harm in the calculations that fix the risk of injustice that they will run; and the related and practically more important right to equal treatment with respect to that evaluation. It is that latter right that explains the due process cases in the Supreme Court, some of which I have mentioned, and which I soon shall consider in a slightly different context. I propose first, however, to apply the account of criminal procedure we have developed to the fourth and fifth of the questions I listed. These consist in the problem of civil procedure, and the issue of whether the law of evidence in civil cases shows an important defect or gap in the theory of adjudication that argues that civil cases should be and characteristically are decided on grounds of principle rather than policy.

PLAINLY, no one has a right to the most accurate possible procedures for adjudicating his or her claims in civil law. Nevertheless, someone who is held in tort for damage caused by negligently driving, when in fact he was not behind the wheel, or someone who is unable to pursue a genuine claim for damage to reputation, because she is unable to discover the name of the person who slandered her, or someone who loses a meritorious case in contract, because rules of evidence make the communication that would have established the claim privileged, has suffered an injustice, though the amount of the moral harm may well be different in these different cases. So civil litigants must have in principle the same two rights we found for those accused of crime. They have a right to procedures justified by the correct assignment of importance to the moral harm the procedures risk, and a related right to a consistent evaluation of that harm in the procedures af-

forded them as compared with the procedures afforded others in different civil cases.

The first of these two rights is a background and a legislative right. Everyone has a right that the legislature fix civil procedures that correctly assess the risk and importance of moral harm, and this right holds against the courts when these institutions act in an explicitly legislative manner, as when the Supreme Court enacts and publishes rules of civil procedure, for example, independently of any lawsuit. The second is a legal right. It holds, that is, against courts in their adjudicative capacity. It is a right to the consistent application of that theory of moral harm that figures in the best justification of settled legal practice. In the United States the comparable right in criminal trials is also a constitutional right, through the due process clause of the Fifth and Fourteenth amendments to the Constitution, as I said. That means that the courts have a duty to review procedures established by explicit legislation to see whether the historical theory of moral harm, embedded in traditions of criminal practice, has been sufficiently respected. There does not seem to be any similar general constitutional right on the civil side. The due process clauses have been interpreted to require at least a hearing and the form of adjudication in certain kinds of civil proceedings that might result in the deprivation of property broadly conceived.[7] But a legislature is not otherwise held, on the civil side, to any historical assessment of the risk worth running when it adopts some new rule of evidence designed to save money or to achieve some concrete benefit for society as a whole. Except through the operation of the equal protection clause and other provisions designed to insure that citizens are treated as equals in each of these decisions. In any case, it is the legal right *tout court*, quite apart from any constitutional right, that concerns us in this section.

I said, when I introduced this issue, that cases like *D v. NSPCC* and *Granada* pose an important problem for theories of adjudication, because in these cases arguments about what conduces to the general welfare seem to play a controlling role in civil litigation. The parties disagree, not only about the ultimate substantive rights in question, but about the legal mechanisms that will be used to decide that ultimate question, and judges take the impact of different mechanisms on the society as a whole as at least pertinent to their decision on that procedural issue. Does that practice call into question—or even provide an ungainly exception to—the general proposition that adjudication is a matter of principle rather than policy?

We should notice, first, that even if the procedural issues were decided as plain issues of policy, that would pose no flat contradiction to the claim that the underlying substantive issue is an issue of principle. This follows from the fact that the practices of the cost-efficient society we discussed, on the criminal side, were not logically contradictory. But there would be a kind of

moral inconsistency, parallel to the moral inconsistency we discovered in that society. For the idea that adjudication is a matter of principle—that someone is entitled to win a lawsuit if the law is on his side, even if the society overall loses thereby, and even if the law on which he relies was justified in the first instance on grounds of policy—presupposes that some distinct importance, at least, is attached to moral harm; and if that is so, then it is morally inconsistent to leave the procedures that protect against this moral harm to a utilitarian calculation that denies that presupposition.

But these reflections also show why the crude description, that procedural issues in cases like *D v. NSPCC* and *Granada* are decided on grounds of policy, is misleading. For the central question raised in such cases is the question whether the party claiming some procedural advantage or benefit is entitled to it as a matter of right, in virtue of his general right to a level of accuracy consistent with the theory of moral harm reflected in the civil law as a whole. The question is the question, that is, of the content of the second right we distinguished. That explains why the judges' calculations are not (as they would be if the crude description were satisfactory) calculations like those we imagined for fixing criminal procedures in the cost-efficient society. Judges deciding hard cases about evidence and procedure do not just balance the bare harm associated with an inaccurate decision against the social gains from procedures or rules that increase the risk of inaccurate decisions. On the contrary, once we have the distinctions we have brought to the surface in hand, we see that the calculations are rather those appropriate to a scheme of justice that recognizes the distinct procedural right that we have identified as a legal right.

This fact is sometimes obscured as much as revealed by judicial rhetoric. Rupert Cross cites, for example, the following statement by Lord Edmund Davies in *D v. NSPCC*:

> The disclosure of all evidence relevant to the trial of an issue being at all times a matter of considerable public interest, the question to be determined is whether it is clearly demonstrated that in the particular case the public interest would nevertheless be better served by excluding evidence despite its relevance. If, on balance, the matter is left in doubt, disclosure should be ordered.[8]

This seems like the language of ordinary cost-benefit balancing, topped up with a tie-breaker in favor of the disclosure of relevant information. But on a second look, it makes no sense read in that way.

It cannot sensibly be thought that the public has a "considerable" interest in learning the identity of the particular person who falsely accused D of cruelty to her children, or even in learning the particular identity of all persons who are accused of making such false accusations. It is hard to imagine any political decisions that the public could make more intelli-

gently if in possession of that information, for example. Perhaps there are people of morbid curiosity whose utility would rise if they could read the informer's name in the morning tabloids. But this utility gain could not be thought to outbalance the loss in utility to children if the Society's work stood any chance of suffering by disclosure, and would hardly justify the presumption in favor of disclosure in "doubtful" cases. Surely we must understand the reference to the public's interest in information to refer to its interest in justice being done, not to its interest in the information itself. But even this formulation would be misleading if it were taken to refer to the public's actual concern that justice be done in civil litigation, as this might be disclosed, for example, in a Gallup poll. For neither his Lordship nor anyone else has any accurate sense of how much the public cares about this—surely some care more than others and some not at all—and neither he nor anyone else would think that less material should be disclosed in litigation during those inevitable periods when the public as a whole cares less, perhaps because it is more occupied with seasonal matters of concern, like the World Series.

References to the public's interest in disclosure or in justice make sense only as disguised and misleading references to individual rights, that is, as references to the level of accuracy that litigants are entitled to have *as against* the public interest in, for example, the flow of information to useful public agencies or newspapers. For the public does have a straightforward interest, of the sort that might be captured in some utilitarian analysis, in the efficiency of these institutions. What is in question, in these cases, is whether the litigant is entitled to a level of accuracy, measured in terms of the risk of moral harm, that must trump these otherwise important and legitimate social concerns. That is a question of principle, not policy, though it is, as I hope the discussion of this essay makes plain, rather a special question of principle in various ways.

First, it is a question that requires, in the determination of the content of a right, attention to the social consequences of different rules and practices. I have tried, elsewhere, to distinguish questions of policy from questions of principle that involve consequential considerations, in order to guard against the unfortunate conflation of these two kinds of social questions.[9] Consequences enter into calculations enforcing the right under discussion, however, the right to a consistent assessment of the importance of moral harm, in a particularly intimate way. For our language does not provide us a metric for stating that content in sufficient detail to be helpful except comparatively, that is, by setting out the kinds of social gain that would or would not justify running a particular risk of a particular sort of moral harm. That is the consequence of something I have been at pains to emphasize, which is that the right in question is the right that a particular importance be attached to the risk of moral harm, not a right to a particular,

independently describable, overall level of accuracy in adjudication. If a particular rule of evidence will even marginally improve the accuracy of a trial and will cost society nothing either in general expense or in particular competing policies, then the court's failure to adopt that rule would show that it valued the risk of injustice at almost nothing. But if a rule would improve accuracy by a great deal but cost the community heavily, then a failure to adopt that rule would be consistent with valuing the risk of injustice very high indeed.

The plaintiff in *D v. NSPCC* argued that if the risk of civil injustice was given its normal force, the danger of that risk would be more important than the social loss that might follow disclosure of the informer's name. There was no way that the court could decide whether she was right without considering, not only the value put on the risk of injustice in civil cases generally—the value suggested in Lord Edmund Davies' remarks about doubtful cases—but also the complex value to society of the work of that agency. But it would be a mistake to conclude that because the court considered the latter issue in some detail the problem it faced was a problem of policy rather than principle.

Second, the play of principle in a court's decision about procedural issues may seem to leave room for judicial discretion, and therefore for genuine policy arguments of a sort that are normally out of place in substantive issues. When issues of substance are at stake, the defendant's rights begin where the plaintiff's leave off, so that once it is decided, for example, that the plaintiff has no right to damages for breach of contract, it follows that the defendant has a right that damages not be given. This is the consequence, as I have tried to explain elsewhere, not of any intrinsic logic in the grammar of rights and duties (quite the contrary, since that grammar is three-valued), but rather of the fact that substantive law is set out in what I called "dispositive" concepts, like the concept of liability in contract, whose function is precisely to bridge the gap between the failure of the plaintiff's right and the success of the defendant's.[10] But this connection between the two rights does not hold in the case of procedure, for it plainly does not follow from the fact that the plaintiff is not entitled to the admission of some document, for example, that the defendant is entitled that it be excluded.

We must be careful not to misunderstand this point. The basic procedural right in civil ligitation is the right that the risk of the moral harm of an unjust result be assessed consistently so that no less importance is attached to that risk by a court's procedural decisions than is attached in the law as a whole. Both parties have that procedural right, though in most cases only one will rely on that right to demand some procedural benefit. But neither party has any right *against* procedures *more* accurate than the accuracy required by that right. It might therefore *seem* that once it is clear that the

party contending for the admission of some evidence has no right to have it, a genuine policy issue is still presented whether, all things considered, the public would gain or lose more by permitting evidence of this character. For if the public would gain more from its disclosure, then the reason for disclosing it must be the public's interest rather than the procedural rights of either party, and that is just to say that the reason for admitting it must be policy rather than principle.

It should be clear from the preceding discussion, however, that this line of argument has gone wrong. It assumes that the procedural right is a right to a fixed level of accuracy rather than the right to a certain weight attached to the risk of injustice and moral harm. If the right were a right to a given level of accuracy, then the court's decision would be taken, as the argument assumes, in two steps: the first a judgment of principle asking whether the required level of accuracy would be achieved, as a matter of antecedent probability, even if the evidence were excluded; and the second a policy judgment whether, if so, to exclude it. But since the decision is a decision whether the risk of moral harm has been properly weighted, these two steps collapse into one. For if the "policy" calculations indicate that the public would not benefit from the exclusion of this evidence, or from a rule excluding evidence like this, then a decision nevertheless to exclude that evidence would indicate no concern with the risk of moral harm whatsoever, and would plainly violate the procedural right of the party seeking to admit it. So, though the reasons are different, the instrumental and consequential calculations associated with procedural decisions are just as thoroughly embedded in arguments of principle as such calculations are when they appear in substantive decisions. Consequences figure not in deciding whether to admit evidence to which no party is entitled, but in deciding whether one party is entitled to have that evidence.

The Court of Appeal's decision in *Granada*, though baroque, illustrates the principled character of the consequential arguments of procedure sufficiently well, though the case is complicated by the fact that British Steel sued for the information it wanted in an independent action, under the provision in *Norwich Pharmacal*, rather than as part of a larger substantive action against the television company. The Court of Appeal held that British Steel was not "in principle" entitled to the information, because the danger that it would suffer injustice for lack of that information was outweighed by the public interest in the free flow of information, which the Court believed would be to some extent cut off if potential informers knew that their names might be revealed in litigation. That was not a mere cost-benefit analysis, because it weighed the interests of potential plaintiffs in the position of British Steel much higher than these interests would rank in such an analysis. It ranked these interests as interests in avoiding moral harm. Nevertheless, it held that these interests, properly weighted, were

outbalanced by the public interest in news. But it then held that, in the particular circumstances of this case, taking into account the less than exemplary behavior of Granada, the public interest was not well served by protecting the confidentiality of the informer. (It is hard to see how Granada's conduct undercut the value of the news it gathered to the public, but that is nevertheless what the Court, if its decision is to be rational, must have supposed.) But in that case the threat of injustice to British Steel was not outweighed by the public interest on the special facts of the case. So failure to require disclosure would have violated that company's right to a proper concern for the threat of injustice to it.

THE SIXTH and last question I distinguished asks whether citizens can have any procedural rights to participate in what are plainly policy decisions (beyond their right to participate in the election of the government that decides these issues, in the way all citizens do) because these decisions in some way particularly affect them. That question is raised, as I said, by the *Bushell* decision in the House of Lords, which held that even though a hearing is required in connection with the government's decision to build a highway in a particular area as part of a national scheme, that hearing need not include any cross-examination by local residents on the question of whether the pertinent department's general assumptions about traffic flow in the nation are right. Lord Diplock, in the most thoughtful of their Lordships' speeches, said that whether fairness requires opportunity for such cross-examination depends "on all the circumstances," which include as "most important, the inspector's own views as to whether the likelihood that cross-examination will enable him to make a report which will be more useful to the minister in reaching his decision than it otherwise would, is sufficient to justify any expense and inconvenience to other parties to the inquiry which would be caused by any resulting prolongation of it." That language suggests that people particularly affected by a highway planning decision have no rights to any particular procedure in the conduct of any hearing at all, beyond what some statute might explicitly provide, so that the decision what procedures to provide is entirely a matter of cost-benefit policy considerations in the style of the cost-benefit society we imagined.

The argument of the preceding sections of this essay suggests no flaw in Lord Diplock's argument—unless we believe that if the government builds an unwise highway, because it relies on inaccurate predictions about traffic, it commits an act of injustice toward those who will be inconvenienced by that highway. Is an unwise highway an act of injustice? I assume that no one has a right not to have the highway built, in the strong sense that it would be wrong to build it even if it were wise policy to do so. Suppose we say, however, that since a deliberate decision to build a highway that is known

not to be justified on utilitarian grounds is an act of injustice and imposes moral harm on everyone who thereby loses, a mistaken decision to build a highway that is not justified on utilitarian grounds is also an act of injustice, though less serious injustice. That argument might seek to rely on some analogy to the proposition that a mistaken conviction of an innocent man is an act of injustice though not so serious as a deliberate framing. But the comparison is invalid, because it makes no sense to say that people have a right to what an accurate utilitarian calculation provides them, at least in the sense in which we can say that people have a right not to be punished for a crime they did not commit.

But the mistake in the present argument is deeper than that, because it fails even if we do assume that when the government makes a mistake in its policy calculations the government thereby violates each citizen's rights. Lord Diplock supposes that even if the public would lose overall by some highway decision, it may nevertheless gain by procedures that run a greater risk of allowing that mistake to be made than other, more expensive procedures would. Everything depends on whether the increased procedural costs of, for example, allowing local examination of every feature of the national program are worth the gains in the actual design of the program that would be *antecedently* likely to result. If they are not, then the fact, available only by hindsight, that the more expensive procedure would actually have produced a better program does not argue that the failure to follow that procedure deprived citizens of what utility would recommend. On the contrary, the best judgment of antecedent utility would then recommend the cheaper procedure followed by an increased risk of the worse program, rather than the more expensive procedure followed by a heightened chance of the better. In that case the decision not to allow cross-examination gave citizens what they were entitled, by the present hypothesis, to have: the decision that maximized average expected utility. So it did not mistakenly violate their alleged right to what utility would recommend, even if, in the event, it produced a highway that utility would condemn. Of course, the decision whether the more expensive procedures would be worth the cost is itself a policy decision. But the fact that the figures in the Red Book were actually wrong does not show, even in hindsight, that the more expensive procedures would have been better. Lord Diplock's point is precisely that the second-order policy decision should be made by the government, through the administrative agency in question, not by the courts.

It would seriously misunderstand this point, however, to conclude that the judgment about what procedures administrative agencies should follow is always or necessarily a second-order policy decision not to be taken by courts. In the controversial case of *Mathews v. Eldridge* (424 US 319 (1976)), the Supreme Court was asked to decide whether the United States Government could terminate someone's social security benefits without an

evidentiary hearing, consistently with the due process clause. The Court said that the decision whether a hearing was required depended on three factors:

> first, the private interest that will be affected by the official action; second, the risk of an erroneous deprivation of such interest through the procedures used, and the probable value, if any, of additional or substitute procedural safeguards; and finally, the government's interest, including the function involved and the fiscal and administrative burdens that the additional or substitute procedural requirement would entail.

The Court noticed, with respect to this third factor, that any additional expense the agency would be forced to incur, if the due process clause were interpreted to require hearings when benefits were canceled, would come from the funds available to other social security claimants. It decided, on the tests it proposed, that the Constitution does not require an adjudicative hearing before anyone's social security benefits are terminated.

Though it is hard to tell, from the surface of judicial rhetoric, whether a particular test is meant to be an ordinary cost-benefit calculation in the utilitarian style or not (as we saw when we studied, earlier, Lord Edmund Davies' speech in *D v. NSPCC*), the Supreme Court's language here does seem rather like Lord Diplock's in *Bushell.* And it has been interpreted by legal commentators to call for a straightforward utilitarian analysis.[11] If that is the correct interpretation, the Court has made a serious mistake in supposing that its test is the test the Constitution requires. For, once Congress has specified who is entitled to social security benefits, the people whom Congress has designated have a right to these benefits. It follows that there is an injustice factor in the harm done to these people when they are mistakenly deprived of their benefits, an injustice factor that cannot be captured in any utilitarian calculation, even a sophisticated one that brings the question of the antecedent value of expensive procedures into play. That is the important distinction between *Bushell* and *Mathews.* No one has a right that a highway not be built where it will spoil the landscape, but people do have a right to benefits that Congress (wisely or not) provides them. There is therefore a risk of moral as well as bare harm in any administrative judgment in the latter case, a risk not present in the former, and utility is out of place in the one though not the other.

I do not mean that the Court's decision in *Mathews* was necessarily wrong. For we are not faced here—any more than in the case of criminal procedure—with a stark choice between no procedural rights at all and a right to some particular procedure hang the cost. Participants in the administrative process have the same general procedural rights that litigants bring to court, because these rights are, in the first instance, political rights. People are entitled that the injustice factor in any decision that deprives

them of what they are entitled to have be taken into account, and properly weighted, in any procedures designed to test their substantive rights. But it does not automatically follow either that they do or do not have a right to a hearing of any particular scope or structure. That depends on a variety of factors, conspicuously including those the Court mentioned in *Mathews*. The Court was wrong, not in thinking those factors relevant, but in supposing that the claimant's side of the scales contained only the bare harm he would suffer if his payments were cut off—if that is the correct interpretation of what the Court said. The claimant's side must reflect the proper weighting of the risk of moral harm, though it might well be that the balance will nevertheless tip in the direction of denying a full adjudicative hearing anyway.

Because the question presented to a court in a case like *Mathews* is a question of principle, requiring a judgment about whether the right to a consistent assessment of the risk of moral harm has been met, it is a fit question for adjudication, and the Court would do wrong simply to defer to the agency's judgment on that question, though it may defer, on grounds of expert knowledge, to the agency's judgment on the consequentialist components of the question. Once again, that makes *Mathews* different from *Bushell*. In the latter case, the issue of procedure was itself integrated with other issues in an ordinary judgment of policy, with no distinct issue of entitlement. The general institutional scheme that assigns issues of policy to the executive rather than to the courts assigns the question of procedure to the agency. In *Mathews* there is a distinct issue of principle, and the courts cannot defer on that issue without cheating on their responsibility to say what people's constitutional rights are.

We must now ask, however, whether there are any other arguments—beyond the risk of substantive injustice which has been our principal concern in this essay—in favor of expensive procedures for administrative agencies or other bodies. In his recent and important treatise on constitutional law, Laurence Tribe suggests a distinction between two different grounds of principle for the due process requirements of the Constitution in cases like *Mathews*. He says that these requirements might be understood instrumentally, as stipulating procedures justified because they increase the accuracy of the underlying substantive judgments, or intrinsically, as something to which people are entitled when government acts in a way that singles them out, independently of any effect the procedure might have on the final outcome. The latter interpretation supposes, as he says, that both

> the right to be heard from, and the right to be told why, are analytically distinct from the right to secure a different outcome; these rights to interchange express the elementary idea that to be a *person*, rather than a *thing*, is at least to be *consulted* about what is done with one. . . . For when government acts in a way that singles out identifiable individuals—in a way that is

likely to be premised on suppositions about specific persons—it activates the special concern about being personally *talked to* about the decision rather than simply being *dealt with.*[12]

Tribe notes that the Court's actual decisions seem more consistent with the first of his two interpretations of the due process requirement than the second, perhaps, he suggests, because it has not noticed the distinction.

This analysis is of undeniable interest. But the reference to "special concern" requires some attention. It cannot mean to call attention simply to an aspect of bare harm that might be overlooked. For though it may be a psychological fact that people generally mind an adverse decision more if it is taken facelessly, without their participation, this is the sort of harm that figures in any decent utilitarian calculation, not a reason why the decision whether to hold a hearing should not be based on such a calculation. It is doubtful, in any case, whether that kind of bare harm would outweigh the loss to other social security claimants, or to other recipients of federal welfare programs, who would in the end bear the cost of expensive hearings.

So the "special concern" must be the fact or risk of some moral harm, not just a special kind of bare harm. But this cannot be only the risk of substantive injustice, for that is the harm contemplated by the instrumental interpretation of the procedural requirements. The intrinsic interpretation points to a different form of moral harm. But what? The language about talking to people rather than dealing with them, and about treating them as people rather than things, is of little help here, as it generally is in political theory. For it does not show why the undoubted harm of faceless decisions is not merely bare harm, and statements about what treatment treats a person as a person are at best conclusions of arguments, not premises. Nor is the reference to the fact that the decision is about particular individuals rather than large groups of people much help. We need to know why that makes a difference. The only suggestion in these passages is that a decision about a few people "is likely to be premised on suppositions about specific persons." But this brings us back to accuracy, because it suggests that the moral harm lies in being thought to have or not to have particular disabilities or qualifications, and that can be seen to be moral harm, without further argument, only if it is false.

So more work needs to be done to establish a relevant head of moral harm distinct from inaccuracy. Perhaps Tribe means only to suggest that the constitutional due process requirements are justified because inaccurate administrative decisions produce moral harm as well as bare harm, in which case his point does not require a distinction between instrumental and intrinsic aspects of due process, but rather a distinction within the instrumental aspect that calls attention to the importance of protecting against a kind of moral harm that falls outside cost-benefit, utilitarian calculations.

Yet we do have intuitions, at least, that more is at stake in procedural

issues than even that sort of moral harm. Suppose someone is punished for a crime we are absolutely certain he did commit, but with no trial whatsoever. We feel he has suffered an injustice, but it is artificial, I think, to suppose that this has much to do with the risk that he would be convicted though innocent. For we are certain that the risk was exactly nothing. No doubt our sense of injustice here is connected to the idea that people must be heard before society officially reaches certain sorts of conclusions about them. But these conclusions must be something to their discredit. It is perhaps not too strong to say that it must be something to their moral discredit, using morality here in the broader of the two senses John Mackie has usefully distinguished.[13] That would explain the idea and the law of bills of attainder, that is, laws that are unconstitutional because they are legislative rather than adjudicative determinations of the guilt of named individuals or groups.

It remains an open question what moral harm, distinct from the risk of substantive injustice, lies in these *ex parte* determinations of guilt that offer no role to the individual condemned. That is too big a question to begin here. But plainly there is no question of any such moral harm in highway hearings of the sort that figured in *Bushell*. There may be more room for argument in the case of a decision to terminate social security benefits, but that must surely depend on the kind of ground relied on or implicitly suggested for the termination.

FOUR

Civil Disobedience and
Nuclear Protest

THIS DISCUSSION of civil disobedience was prepared for a conference on that subject organized by the Social Democratic Party of Germany in Bonn. The idea is a new one for most German audiences. They know that civil disobedience has been much canvassed in what they call the Anglo-American tradition; accordingly, I was asked to describe the shape the discussion has taken in Britain and the United States. Actually the history of the idea has been somewhat different in those two countries. The United States suffered a long series of political divisions that made the dilemmas of legality particularly acute. Slavery was the first issue to produce a philosophical literature, a national debate. Before the American Civil War, Congress enacted the Fugitive Slave Act, which made it a crime for Northerners to help escaped slaves avoid the slavecatchers; many people violated that law because their consciences would not permit them to obey it. Religious sects generated a second and rather different crisis of compliance. Jehovah's Witnesses, for example, are forbidden by their faith to salute a flag, and the laws of many states required schoolchildren to begin each day by saluting the American flag. The refusal of the Witnesses to obey this law provoked some of the most important Supreme Court decisions in our constitutional history, but their acts were first seen, and judged, as acts of civil disobedience.

Europeans are certainly familiar with the more recent occasions of disobedience in the United States. Martin Luther King, Jr., is honored throughout the world. He led a campaign of disobedience against the Jim Crow laws that perpetuated, against his race, the badges of slavery a century after the Civil War had been won. This civil rights movement flowed into and merged with a great river of protest against the American involvement in Vietnam. The war provoked some of the most violent chapters of civil disobedience in American history and much of the most interesting philosophical literature on that subject.

The English history of civil disobedience in recent times is slimmer. One thinks of Bertrand Russell in jail for pacifism and, behind that, of the suf-

fragettes and the early days of the labor movement. But these did not provide any sustained national debate about the principles of civil disobedience; in any case, debates about principle are less common in Britain, less compatible with the temper of British life and politics. Just now, however, Britain, along with the rest of Western Europe and the United States as well, has a new occasion of civil disobedience in the vexed and frightening question whether American nuclear weapons should be deployed in Europe.

Much of the philosophical literature I just mentioned seems on the surface excessively terminological. Political philosophers have devoted a great deal of attention to the definition of civil disobedience, to the question of how it is different from other kinds of politically motivated criminal activity. These exercises are terminological only on the surface, however. They aim to discover differences in the moral quality of different kinds of acts in different kinds of situations. Distinctions are of the essence here; we will lose sight of them in the heat of practical decision and judgment unless they are etched in the theory through which we see the political world.

Civil disobedience, whatever further distinctions we might want to make within that general category, is very different from ordinary criminal activity motivated by selfishness or anger or cruelty or madness. It is also different—this is more easily overlooked—from the civil war that breaks out within a territory when one group challenges the legitimacy of the government or of the dimensions of the political community. Civil disobedience involves those who do not challenge authority in so fundamental a way. They do not think of themselves—and they do not ask others to think of them—as seeking any basic rupture or constitutional reorganization. They accept the fundamental legitimacy of both government and community; they act to acquit rather than to challenge their duty as citizens.

If we think of civil disobedience in that general way, abstracting from the further distinctions I am about to make, we can say something now we could not have said three decades ago: that Americans accept that civil disobedience has a legitimate if informal place in the political culture of their community. Few Americans now either deplore or regret the civil rights and antiwar movements of the 1960s. People in the center as well as on the left of politics give the most famous occasions of civil disobedience a good press, at least in retrospect. They concede that these acts did engage the collective moral sense of the community. Civil disobedience is no longer a frightening idea in the United States.

WHAT KIND of theory of civil disobedience do we want? If we want it to be robust rather than empty, we must avoid a tempting shortcut. Civil disobedience is a feature of our political experience, not because some people are

virtuous and other wicked, or because some have a monopoly of wisdom and others of ignorance. But because we disagree, sometimes profoundly, in the way independent people with a lively sense of justice will disagree, about very serious issues of political morality and strategy. So a theory of civil disobedience is useless if it declares only that people are right to disobey laws or decisions that are wicked or stupid, that the rightness of the disobedience flows directly from the wrongness of the law. Almost everyone will agree that *if* a particular decision is very wicked, people should disobey it. But this agreement will be worthless in particular, concrete cases, because people will then disagree whether the law *is* that wicked, or wicked at all.

We must accept a more difficult assignment. We must try to develop a theory of civil disobedience that can command agreement about what people should actually do, even in the face of substantive disagreement about the wisdom or justice of the law being disobeyed. But that means that we must be careful *not* to make the rightness of any decision about civil disobedience depend on which side is right in the underlying controversy. We must aim, that is, to make our judgments turn on the kinds of convictions each side has, rather than the soundness of these convictions. We might call a theory of that type a *working* theory of civil disobedience.

The key to our success lies in the following distinction. We must ask two different questions and insist on their independence. The first is this: What is the right thing for people to do *given* their convictions, that is, the right thing for people who believe that a political decision is wrong or immoral in a certain way? The second is: How should the government react if people do break the law when that is, given their convictions, the right thing to do, but the majority the government represents still thinks the law is sound? These questions have the formal structure we need to produce a robust theory, because people can, in principle, answer them the same way on any particular occasion even though they disagree about the merits of the underlying political controversy. Those in the majority can ask themselves, in the spirit of the first question, "What would be the right thing for us to do if we had their beliefs?" Those in the minority can ask, in the spirit of the second, "What would be the right thing for us to do if we had political power and the majority's beliefs?" So we can at least hope to find rough agreement about the best answers to these questions, even though we lack consensus about the substantive moral and strategic convictions in play.

WHEN WE TAKE up the first question—about the right thing for people to do who believe laws are wrong—everything depends on which general *type* of civil disobedience we have in mind. I have so far been speaking as if the famous acts of civil disobedience I mentioned all had the same motives and

circumstances. But they did not, and we must now notice the differences. Someone who believes it would be deeply wrong to deny help to an escaped slave who knocks at his door, and even worse to turn him over to the authorities, thinks the Fugitive Slave Act requires him to behave in an immoral way. His personal integrity, his conscience, forbids him to obey. Soldiers drafted to fight in a war they deem wicked are in the same position. I shall call civil disobedience by people in that circumstance "integrity-based."

Contrast the moral position of the blacks who broke the law in the civil rights movement, who sat at forbidden lunch counters seeking the privilege of eating greasy hamburgers next to people who hated them. It would miss the point to say they were there in deference to conscience, that they broke the law because they could not, with integrity, do what the law required. No one has a general moral duty to seek out and claim rights that he believes he has. They acted for a different reason: to oppose and reverse a program they believed unjust, a program of oppression by the majority of a minority.[1] Those in the civil rights movement who broke the law and many civilians who broke it protesting the war in Vietnam thought the majority was pursuing its own interests and goals unjustly because in disregard of the rights of others, the rights of a domestic minority in the case of the civil rights movement and of another nation in the case of the war. This is "justice-based" civil disobedience.

These first two kinds of civil disobedience involve, though in different ways, convictions of principle. There is a third kind which involves judgments of policy instead. People sometimes break the law not because they believe the program they oppose is immoral or unjust, in the ways described, but because they believe it very unwise, stupid, and dangerous for the majority as well as any minority. The recent protests against the deployment of American missiles in Europe, so far as they violated local law, were for the most part occasions of this third kind of civil disobedience, which I shall call "policy-based." If we tried to reconstruct the beliefs and attitudes of the women of Greenham Common in England, or of the people who occupied military bases in Germany, we would find that most—not all but most—did not believe that their government's decision to accept the missiles was the act of a majority seeking its own interest in violation of the rights of a minority or of another nation. They thought, rather, that the majority had made a tragically wrong choice from the common standpoint, from the standpoint of its own interests as much as those of anyone else.[2] They aim, not to force the majority to keep faith with principles of justice, but simply to come to its senses.

There is an obvious danger in any analytic distinction that rests, as this one does, on differences between states of mind. Any political movement or group will include people of very different beliefs and convictions. Nor will any one person's convictions necessarily fall neatly into a prearranged cate-

gory. Most of those who protested against the American war in Vietnam, for example, believed their government's policy was *both* unjust and stupid. Nevertheless, the distinction among types of civil disobedience (and the further distinctions I shall draw) are useful and important, because they allow us to ask hypothetical questions in something like the following way. We can try to identify the conditions under which acts of civil disobedience would be justified if the beliefs and motives of the actors were those associated with each type of disobedience, leaving as a further question whether the beliefs in play on a particular occasion might plausibly be thought to be or include beliefs of that sort.

Consider in that spirit the first type of civil disobedience, when the law requires people to do what their conscience absolutely forbids. Almost everyone would agree, I think, that people in this position do the right thing, given their convictions, if they break the law. Of course, violence and terrorism cannot be justified in this way. If someone's conscience will not let him obey some law, neither should it let him kill or harm innocent people. But it is hard to think of any other qualifications a working theory would have to recognize here. It could not, for example, add the further and tempting qualification that a citizen must have exhausted the normal political process so long as this offers any prospect of reversing the political decision he opposes. Integrity-based disobedience is typically a matter of urgency. The Northerner who is asked to hand over a slave to the slavecatcher, even the schoolchild asked once to salute the flag, suffers a final loss if he obeys, and it does not much help him if the law is reversed soon after. Another qualification is more plausible. A theory might insist that an actor must take consequences into account and not break the law if the likely result will be to make the situation not better but worse according to his own lights. But this consequentialist caution would be far from uncontroversial. Should someone kill innocent civilians in Vietnam or help return a slave to captivity just because, if he breaks the law instead, he will help produce a backlash that will kill more civilians and keep more people in slavery than if he had obeyed the law? Perhaps people have a moral privilege to refuse to do evil even when they know that as a result more evil will be done. This possibility is in fact now much discussed in moral philosophy.

Turn now, still with the first of our two main questions in mind, to justice-based disobedience, like the civil rights movement and many of the civilian protests against the war in Vietnam. When are people right to break the law in order to protest political programs they believe unjust? We should begin, once again, by conceding that civil disobedience is at least sometimes justified in these circumstances. But our conditions will now be much more stringent. We would certainly insist on the condition we rejected for integrity-based disobedience. People must exhaust the normal political process, seeking to have the program they dislike reversed by con-

stitutional means; they must not break the law until these normal political means no longer hold out hope of success. We would also insist on the further, consequentialist condition I said was problematic for integrity-based disobedience, which seems essential and straightforward now. Someone whose justification for breaking the law is, "But I'm doing it to reverse an immoral policy," has no good reply to the objection, "You're simply promoting that policy through what you do."

These two further conditions reflect an important difference between the first two types of disobedience. Integrity-based disobedience is defensive: it aims only that the actor not do something his conscience forbids. Justice-based disobedience is, in contrast, instrumental and strategic: it aims at an overall goal—the dismantling of an immoral political program. So consequentialist qualifications appear in our theory of the latter that are out of place in any theory of the former. And a new distinction becomes imperative. Justice-based disobedience might use two main strategies to achieve its political goals. We might call the first a persuasive strategy. It hopes to force the majority to listen to arguments against its program, in the expectation that the majority will then change its mind and disapprove that program. The second strategy, then, is nonpersuasive. It aims not to change the majority's mind, but to increase the cost of pursuing the program the majority still favors, in the hope that the majority will find the new cost unacceptably high. There are many different forms of nonpersuasive strategy—many different ways of putting up the price—and some of them are more attractive, when available, than others. A minority may put up the price, for example, by making the majority choose between abandoning the program and sending them to jail. If the majority has the normal sympathies of decent people, this nonpersuasive strategy may be effective. At the other extreme lie nonpersuasive strategies of intimidation, fear, and anxiety, and in between strategies of inconvenience and financial expense: tying up traffic or blocking imports or preventing official agencies or departments from functioning effectively or functioning at all.

Obviously, persuasive strategies improve the justification for justice-based disobedience. But they do so only when conditions are favorable for their success. Conditions were indeed favorable for the civil rights movement in the United States in the 1960s. The rhetoric of American politics had for some decades been freighted with the vocabulary of equality, and the Second World War had heightened the community's sense of the injustice of racial persecution. I do not deny that there was and remains much hypocrisy in that rhetoric and alleged commitment. But the hypocrisy itself provides a lever for persuasive strategies. The majority, even in the South, blushed when it was forced to look at its own laws. There was no possibility of a political majority saying, "Yes, that is what we're doing. We're treating one section of the community as inferior to ourselves." And then turning

aside from that with equanimity. Civil disobedience forced everyone to look at what the majority could no longer, for a variety of reasons, ignore. So minds were changed, and the sharpest evidence of the change is the fact that halfway through the battle the law became an ally of the movement rather than its enemy.

Sometimes, however, persuasive strategies offer no great prospect of success because conditions are far from favorable, as in, perhaps, South Africa. When, if ever, are nonpersuasive strategies justified in justice-based disobedience? It goes too far, I think, to say they never are. The following carefully guarded statement seems better. If someone believes that a particular official program is deeply unjust, if the political process offers no realistic hope of reversing that program soon, if there is no possibility of effective persuasive civil disobedience, if nonviolent nonpersuasive techniques are available that hold out a reasonable prospect of success, if these techniques do not threaten to be counterproductive, then that person does the right thing, given his convictions, to use those nonpersuasive means. This may strike some readers as excessively weak; but each of the qualifications I listed seems necessary.

I come finally to policy-based civil disobedience: when the actors seek to reverse a policy because they think it dangerously unwise. They believe the policy they oppose is a bad policy for everyone, not just for some minority; they think they know what is in the majority's own interest, as well as their own, better than the majority knows. Once again we can distinguish persuasive from nonpersuasive strategies in this new context. Persuasive strategies aim to convince the majority that its decision, about its own best interests, is wrong, and so to disfavor the program it formerly favored. Nonpersuasive strategies aim rather to increase the price the majority must pay for a program it continues to favor.

The distinction between persuasive and nonpersuasive strategies is even more important in the case of policy-based than justice-based disobedience, because it seems problematic that nonpersuasive strategies could ever be justified in a working theory of the former. In order to see why, we must notice a standing problem for any form of civil disobedience. Most people accept that the principle of majority rule is essential to democracy; I mean the principle that once the law is settled, by the verdict of the majority's representatives, it must be obeyed by the minority as well. Civil disobedience, in all its various forms and strategies, has a stormy and complex relationship with majority rule. It does not reject the principle entirely, as a radical revolutionary might; civil disobedients remain democrats at heart. But it claims a qualification or exception of some kind, and we might contrast and judge the different types and strategies of disobedience in combination, by asking what kind of exception each claims, and whether it is consistent to demand that exception and still claim general allegiance to the principle as a whole.

Persuasive strategies, whether they figure in justice-based or policy-based disobedience, have a considerable advantage here. For someone whose goal is to persuade the majority to change its mind, by accepting arguments he believes are sound arguments, plainly does not challenge the principle of majority rule in any fundamental way. He accepts that in the end the majority's will must be done and asks only, by way of qualification or annex to this principle, that the majority be forced to consider arguments that might change its mind even when it seems initially unwilling to do so. Nonpersuasive strategies lack this explanation, and that is why, particularly in a democracy, they are always inferior from a moral point of view. But when nonpersuasive strategies are used, subject to the conditions I listed, in justice-based disobedience, they can at least appeal to a standing and well-understood exception to the majority-rule principle, not only in the United States but in Germany and many other countries as well. I mean the exception assumed by the constitutional power of judges to hold acts of the majority's representatives void when, in the judge's view, these decisions outrage the principles of justice embedded in the Constitution. That power assumes that the majority has no right to act unjustly, to abuse the power it holds by serving its own interests at the expense of a minority's rights. I do not claim that judicial review by a constitutional court is a kind of nonpersuasive civil disobedience. But only that judicial review rests on a qualification to the principle of majority rule—the qualification that the majority can be forced to be just, against its will—to which nonpersuasive strategies might also appeal in order to explain why their challenge to majority rule is different from outright rejection of it.

Policy-based disobedience cannot make that appeal, because the standing qualification I just named does not extend to matters of policy. Once it is conceded that the question is only one of the common interest—that no question of distinct majority and minority interests arises—the conventional reason for constraining a majority gives way, and only very dubious candidates apply for its place. Someone who hopes not to persuade the majority to his point of view by forcing it to attend to his arguments, but rather to make it pay so heavily for its policy that it will give way without having been convinced, must appeal to some form of elitism or paternalism to justify what he does. And any appeal of *that* form does seem to strike at the roots of the principle of majority rule, to attack its foundations rather than simply to call for an elaboration or qualification of it. If that principle means anything, it means that the majority rather than some minority must in the end have the power to decide what is in their common interest.

So nonpersuasive means used in policy-based disobedience seems the least likely to be justified in any general working theory. I said earlier that most of those who sit in and trespass to protest the deployment of nuclear missiles in Europe have motives that make their disobedience policy-based. It is therefore important to consider whether they can plausibly consider

the means they use to be persuasive means, and this in turn depends on whether conditions are sufficiently favorable for success of a persuasive strategy. The contrast between the civil rights movement and the antinuclear movement is in this respect reasonably sharp. It was obvious early in the civil rights movement that the sit-ins and other techniques of disobedience had persuasive force, because it was obvious that the issue was an issue of justice and that the movement had rhetorical tradition as well as justice on its side. It was only necessary to force enough people to look who would be ashamed to turn away. The questions of policy at the bottom of the nuclear controversy are, by contrast, signally complex. It is plainly not obvious, one way or the other, whether deployment of missiles in Europe is more likely to deter or provoke aggression, for example, or even what kind of an argument would be a good argument for either view. It is hard to see in these circumstances how discussion could be illuminated or debate strengthened by illegal acts. On the contrary, such acts seem likely to make the public at large pay *less* attention to the complex issues on which any intelligent view must be based, because it will think it has at least one simple and easy-to-understand reason for sticking with the policy its leaders have adopted: that any change in that policy would mean giving way to civil blackmail.

If this is right, those who now support trespass and other illegal acts as protest against nuclear policy must, if they are honest with themselves, concede that they have in mind a nonpersuasive strategy. They aim to raise the price of a policy they believe a tragic mistake, to make that price so high that the majority will yield, though this means surrendering to minority coercion. So they must face the question I said is highly problematic, whether a robust working theory could justify that kind of disobedience. It might be helpful to consider whether we would think nonpersuasive means proper as acts of disobedience protesting other, non-nuclear policies many people think gravely mistaken. Would nonpersuasive disobedience be justified against bad economic policy? The governments of the United States and Britain are now following economic policies that I think unwise because they will work against the general interest in the long as well as the short run. I also think, as it happens, that these economic policies are unjust; even if they were in the best interests of the majority, they would still be unfair to a minority that has rights against that majority. But I mean to set that further claim of injustice aside for this argument and assume only that many people like me think monetarist policy bad from everyone's point of view. Would the fact that we believed this justify illegal acts whose point was to impose so high a price, in inconvenience and insecurity, that the majority would abandon its economic policy, though it remained convinced that it was the best policy?

I think the answer is no. But of course the risks of bad nuclear strategy are

vastly greater than the risks of mistaken economic policy. Does the fact that so much more is at stake destroy the analogy? Jürgen Habermas has argued that political legitimacy is threatened when decisions of enormous consequence are taken though only something like a bare or thin majority supports the decision.[3] Can we justify nonpersuasive civil disobedience against the decision to accept the missiles by appealing to that principle? The difficulty is evident. For exactly the same principle would argue against government's deciding *not* to deploy the missiles. That is as much a decision as the decision to adopt them, and it appears from recent polls that it would not command even a bare majority much less the extraordinary majority Habermas' principle would require. The present controversy, in short, is symmetrical in a way that undermines the value of his principle. Those who oppose the missiles believe that deployment will cause irreparable harm because it threatens the very existence of the community. But that is exactly what people on the other side—and we are assuming that there are slightly more of these—would think about a decision not to deploy the missiles. They think that this decision would make nuclear war more likely, and threaten the existence of the community. So no government violates any principle of legitimacy in accepting missiles that it would not have violated by rejecting them.

We cannot be dogmatic that no argument, better than I have been able to construct, will be found for civil disobedience in these circumstances. We are justified only in the weaker conclusion that those who advocate this form of disobedience now have the burden of showing how a working theory could accept it. They may say that this challenge is irrelevant; that nice questions about which justifications could be accepted by all sides to a dispute become trivial when the world is about to end. There is wisdom in this impatience, no doubt, which I do not mean to deny. But once we abandon the project of this essay, once we make the rightness of what we do turn entirely on the soundness of what we think, we cannot expect honor or opportunity from those who think it is we who are naive and stupid.

I HAVE BEEN SPEAKING, so far, entirely about the first of the two main questions I distinguished at the outset. When do people who oppose a political decision do the right thing, given their convictions, to break the law? I shall be briefer about the second question. Suppose we are satisfied, by our consideration of the first question, that someone has done the right thing, given his convictions, in acting illegally. How should the government react to what he has done? We must avoid two crude mistakes. We must not say that if someone is justified, given what he thinks, in breaking the law, the government must never punish him. There is no contradiction, and often much sense, in deciding that someone should be punished in spite of the fact

that he did exactly what we, if we had his beliefs, would and should have done. But the opposite mistake is equally bad. We must not say that if someone has broken the law, for whatever reason and no matter how honorable his motives, he must always be punished because the law is the law. Lawyers, even very conservative lawyers, rarely repeat that mindless maxim any more, because they know that in most countries people known to have committed a crime are sometimes, and properly, not prosecuted. The idea of prosecutorial discretion—across a wide range of crimes and sensitive to a wide variety of reasons for not prosecuting—is a fixture of modern legal theory.

When should the government stay its hand? Utilitarianism may be a poor general theory of justice, but it states an excellent necessary condition for just punishment. Nobody should ever be punished unless punishing him will do some good on the whole in the long run all things considered. Obviously that is not a sufficient condition for punishment. But it is a necessary condition, and it will sometimes condemn a decision to prosecute civil disobedience. I believe the German police made the right decision at Mitlangen, for example, when they ignored illegal acts of protest. It probably would have done more harm than good to arrest and prosecute the offenders.

Once we reject these two crude and mistaken claims—that it is always wrong to prosecute and always right to do so—we face a more difficult issue. Suppose it would do some good to punish someone who has broken the law out of conscience; suppose this would deter similar acts and so make life more peaceful and efficient for the majority. Could it nevertheless be proper not to punish him simply because his motives were better than the motives of other criminals? That suggestion sounds elitist to many people. But once we have answered our first question by acknowledging that someone does the right thing in breaking the law, given his conviction that the law is unjust, it seems inconsistent not also to acknowledge this as a reason that prosecutors may and should take into account in deciding whether to prosecute, even when the utilitarian test is met.[4] And as a reason for punishing someone more leniently who has been tried and convicted. It is a reason, that is, that can properly figure in the balance, along with the competing utilitarian reasons for punishing. These competing reasons may be very strong, and in that case they will outweigh the fact that the accused acted out of conscience. That is why it goes too far to say that people who do the right thing, given their convictions, should never be punished for doing it.

I have two final points. The first is the mirror image of the issue just discussed. Should people who act out of civil disobedience court punishment or even demand to be punished? My own view is very simple. I think Socrates was wrong in thinking that civil disobedience is incomplete, is in some way false, without punishment, without the actor presenting himself and

saying, "I have broken the law of our community; punish me." I see the appeal of that view, its dramatic appeal, but it seems to me mistaken and confused. It cannot be sound, for a start, when we are considering integrity-based disobedience. Someone who refused to aid slavecatchers or to fight a war he thinks immoral serves his purpose best when his act is covert and is never discovered. Punishment may of course be part of the strategy when disobedience is justice- or policy-based. Someone may wish to be punished, for example, because he is following the nonpersuasive strategy I mentioned, forcing the community to realize that it will have to jail people like him if it is to pursue the policy he believes wrong. But we should not confuse that instrumental argument for accepting punishment with any moral or conceptual requirement of submission to it. If an act of civil disobedience can achieve its point without punishment, then this is generally better for all concerned.

My final point is an important qualification to the argument as a whole. I have been assuming throughout this essay that the acts we all have in mind as acts of civil disobedience really are violations of the law of the pertinent jurisdiction properly understood. But it may turn out that on a more sophisticated and enlightened view of that law they are not. Habermas and others have stressed the ambiguity between legality and legitimacy, pointing out the ways in which these might be opposed ideas. In the United States and Germany, whose constitutions recognize abstract political rights as legal rights also, there will be an inevitable further area of ambiguity about what the law is. Several years ago I argued that the Constitution of the United States, properly understood, might actually sanction acts that were then generally considered acts in violation of law.[5] It would not surprise me if arguments of the same character were available about German law now, and I know that the constitutional lawyers of that country have considered the possibility. Nothing much will come of it, however, unless we are careful to notice one final distinction often overlooked in legal theory.

We must decide whether this argument, that acts considered acts of civil disobedience are actually protected by the Constitution, is still available once the courts have ruled that these acts are not, in their view, protected in that way. We are all too familiar with the aphorism that the law is what the courts say it is. But that might mean two very different things. It might mean that the courts are always right about what the law is, that their decisions create law so that, once the courts have interpreted the Constitution in a particular way, that is necessarily for the future the right way to interpret it. Or it might mean simply that we must obey decisions of the courts, at least generally, for practical reasons, though we reserve the right to argue that the law is not what they have said it is. The first view is that of legal positivism. I believe it is wrong, and in the end deeply corrupting of the

idea and rule of law. The argument I urge lawyers of Germany to take up, that the law properly understood might support what we call civil disobedience, can be an effective argument only when we reject this aspect of positivism and insist that, though the courts may have the last word in any particular case about what the law is, the last word is not for that reason alone the right word.

Law as Interpretation

FIVE

Is There Really No Right Answer in Hard Cases?

WHAT IS THE QUESTION?

When is there no right answer to a question of law? Suppose the legislature has passed a statute stipulating that "sacrilegious contracts shall henceforth be invalid." The community is divided as to whether a contract signed on Sunday is, for that reason alone, sacrilegious. It is known that very few of the legislators had that question in mind when they voted, and that they are now equally divided on the question of whether it should be so interpreted. Tom and Tim have signed a contract on Sunday, and Tom now sues Tim to enforce the terms of the contract, whose validity Tom contests. Shall we say that the judge must look for the right answer to the question of whether Tom's contract is valid, even though the community is deeply divided about what the right answer is? Or is it more realistic to say that there simply is no right answer to the question?

That issue is central to a large number of controversies about what law is. It has been debated under many titles, including the question of whether judges always have discretion in hard cases, and whether there are what some legal philosophers call "gaps" in the law. I now wish to defend the unpopular view—that in the circumstances just described, the question of Tom's contract may well have a right answer—against certain arguments on which its opponents knowingly or unknowingly rely. I shall also try to show what sense there is in the no-right-answer thesis, and why the occasions when a legal question has no right answer in our own legal system may be much rarer than is generally supposed. I shall begin, however, by insisting upon a clarification of the issue that removes a troublesome ambiguity.

Certain legal concepts, like the concept of a valid contract, of civil liability, and of a crime, have the following characteristic: If the concept holds in a particular situation, then judges have a duty, at least prima facie, to decide some legal claim one way; but if the concept does not hold, then judges have a duty, at least *prima facie*, to decide the same claim in the opposite way. I shall call such concepts "dispositive" concepts. Lawyers seem to as-

sume, in the way they talk and argue, that we might call the "bivalence thesis" about dispositive concepts: that is, that in every case *either* the positive claim, that the case falls under a dispositive concept, *or* the opposite claim, that it does not, must be true even when it is controversial which is true. Lawyers seem to assume, for example, that an exchange of promises either does or does not constitute a valid contract. If it does, then judges have at least a *prima facie* duty to enforce these promises if so requested within their jurisdiction; but if it does not, then they have at least a *prima facie* duty not to do so on contractual grounds. Lawyers seem to assume that a particular person is either liable in law for the damage his act has caused or he is not; if he is, then judges have a duty to hold him in damages, but if he is not, then they have a duty not to. They seem to assume that a particular piece of conduct, taking into account intention and circumstances, either constitutes a crime or it does not; if it does, and the actor has no other defense, then the judge (or jury) has a duty to hold him guilty; but if it does not, then the judge (or jury) has a duty to find him innocent.

If it is true that an exchange of promises either does or does not constitute a valid contract, and that someone sued in tort either is or is not liable in damages, and that someone accused of a crime either is or is not guilty, then at least every case in which these issues are dispositive has a right answer. It may be uncertain and controversial what that right answer is, of course, just as it is uncertain and controversial whether Richard III murdered the princes. It would not follow from that uncertainty that there is no right answer to the legal question, any more than it seems to follow from the uncertainty about Richard that there is no right answer to the question whether he murdered the princes. But is it true that an exchange of promises always either does or does not constitute a valid contract, or that someone always is either liable or not liable in tort, or guilty or not guilty of a crime?

I can now state the ambiguity latent in the thesis that in some cases a question of law has no right answer. We may distinguish two versions of that thesis. Both versions deny that the bivalence thesis holds for important dispositive concepts. They deny that an exchange of promises always either does or does not constitute a valid contract (and that a defendant always either is or is not liable in tort, and so forth). But they differ in the character of argument each makes. The first version argues that the surface linguistic behavior of lawyers just described is misleading because it suggests that there is no logical space between the proposition that a contract is valid and the proposition that it is not valid; that is, because it does not contemplate that both propositions may be false. In fact, however, if we look more deeply into the matter, we find that it might be false both that a contract is valid and that it is not valid, false both that a person is liable and that he is not liable for some act, and false both that a particular act constitutes a crime and that it does not. In each case both propositions may be false be-

cause in each case they do not exhaust the logical space they occupy; in each case there is a third independent possibility that occupies the space between the other two. On this first version of the thesis, the question "Is Tom's contract valid or invalid?" makes a mistake like the one that the question "Is Tom a young man or an old man?" makes. The latter question may have no right answer because it ignores a third possibility, which is that Tom is a middle-aged man. According to the first version, the legal question also ignores a third possibility, which is that an exchange of promises may constitute neither a valid contract, such that judges have a duty to enforce the exchange, nor a contract that is not valid, with the consequence that judges have a duty not to enforce it, but something else that might be called, for example, an "inchoate" contract.

The second version of the no-right-answer thesis, on the other hand, does not suppose that there is any logical space, in that sense, between the propositions that a contract is valid and that it is not valid, or that a person is liable or that he is not, or that an act is a crime or that it is not. It does not suppose that there is any third possibility, and yet it denies that one of the two available possibilities always holds, because it may not be true that either does. On this second version of the thesis, the question "Is Tom's contract valid or not valid?" is like the question "Is Tom middle-aged or not?" There may be no right answer to the latter question if Tom is of an age that lies on the border between youth and middle age, not because we recognize categories of age distinct from both middle age and non-middle age, but because, at the border, it is a mistake to say of someone either that he is or that he is not middle-aged.

I do not mean to suggest, by offering this comparison, that the second version of the thesis must suppose that the concepts of a valid contract, of legal liability, and of crime are vague like the concept of middle age. Though, as we shall see, some arguments for the second version are based on claims about vagueness, others are of the different character suggested by the following comparison. Some philosophers believe that there is no right answer to the question of whether Charles was brave if Charles is dead and never faced any occasion of danger during his lifetime, not because "brave" is vague but because it is wrong to say that a man was either brave or not brave if we could have no evidence bearing on the question of which he was.[1] The second version of the thesis may be defended, as we shall also see, in a manner that seems closer to this argument than to the argument from vagueness.

We may state the difference between the first and second version of the no-right-answer thesis more formally. Let $(\sim p)$ be defined as the logical negation of (p), so that if (p) is false $(\sim p)$ is true, and if $(\sim p)$ is false (p) is true. Let the proposition that Tom's contract is valid be represented by "p" and the proposition that his contract is not valid as "non-p." The bivalence the-

sis supposes that the question about Tom's contract must have a right answer, even if we are not sure what it is, because (non-p) is identical with ($\sim p$) and either (p) is true or ($\sim p$) is true because ((p) or ($\sim p$)) is necessarily true. Both versions of the no-right-answer thesis agree that this is a mistake, but they disagree about what kind of mistake it is. The first version argues that (non-p) is not identical to ($\sim p$); (non-p) should be represented as a proposition (r) that is not the logical negation of (p). (I do not mean, by the choice of "r" in that representation, to suggest that the first version must hold that (non-p) is unstructured, but only that it is not the negation of (p).) Plainly, ((p) or (r)) is not necessarily true; it does not allow for the possibility of (q) which is neither (p) nor (r) but something in between. The second version, on the other hand, does not deny that (non-p) is identical to ($\sim p$); instead it holds that in some cases neither (p) nor ($\sim p$) is true, that is, that in some cases bivalence does not hold.

If either version of the thesis is right, then there may be many lawsuits in which it would be wrong to say that either party is entitled to a decision, and right to concede that the judge has a discretion to decide either way. But there is this important difference. If the first version holds, then this discretion is affirmatively provided by law, because the law distinguishes circumstances in which exchanges of promises, for example, fall into a distinct category which has discretion as a consequence. If the second version holds, on the other hand, discretion follows, not by affirmative provision, but by default: since the law stipulates nothing, even discretion, the judge must do what he can on his own.

THE FIRST VERSION

We can easily imagine a legal system such that if anyone claimed that there is always a right answer to the question of whether judges have a duty to enforce an exchange of promises, or to refuse to enforce the exchange, he would be making a mistake of the sort the first version supposes. Even under our own law, after all, there are many decisions that a judge has no duty to make either way. That is so, for example, when the plaintiff requests an early adjournment on some particular day and the defendant asks that the request be denied. It is also so when the defendant has been convicted of a crime for which the statute provides a sentence of from three to five years, and the prosecution asks for the maximum, while the defense asks for the minimum, sentence. The concept of duty provides a space between the proposition that the judge has a duty to decide one way and the proposition that he has a duty to decide another way; this space is occupied by the proposition that he has no *duty* to decide one way or the other, but rather a permission or, as lawyers say, a "discretion," to decide either way.

That space might easily be exploited to introduce a form of contract that is neither valid nor invalid, as we now use those terms, but inchoate. The

law might provide, for example, that if a contract otherwise unobjectionable is entered into by two people each over twenty-one years of age the contract is "valid," and judges have a duty to enforce it; if either party is less than sixteen years of age, the contract is "invalid," and judges have a duty not to enforce it; but if the younger party is between sixteen and twenty-one years of age the contract is "inchoate," and the judge has a discretion to enforce it or not depending upon whether, all things considered, he thinks that the right thing to do. The law might stipulate, in a similar way, circumstances in which someone who has caused damage is neither liable nor not liable for that damage, but rather, as we might say, "vulnerable to liability," or circumstances in which a particular act is neither a crime nor not a crime but, perhaps, "criminous." In a legal system like that it would, of course, be wrong to translate "Tom's contract is valid" as "p" and "Tom's contract is not valid" as "$\sim p$," and therefore wrong to appeal to the bivalence thesis to argue that one of these propositions must be true.

The first version of the no-right-answer thesis argues that, contrary to how lawyers seem to talk, our own legal system is really like that; that is, that there is space between each dispositive concept and its apparent negation that is occupied by a distinct concept, like the concept of an inchoate contract, though, as it happens, we do not have a separate name for that distinct concept. But what argument is available to support that claim? It is a semantic claim, about the meaning of legal concepts, and it would therefore be natural to support the claim by some appeal to a linguistic practice that is decisive. But since lawyers do seem to treat "not valid" as the negation of "valid," "not liable" as the negation of "liable," and "is not a crime" as the negation of "is a crime," the argument cannot take that natural course. It cannot be like the argument that "old man" is not the true negation of "young man." That argument may proceed simply by calling attention to a widespread linguistic practice, or, more likely, simply by reminding the speaker who has made the mistake of how he, as a speaker of the language, ordinarily speaks. Since the legal argument cannot proceed in that direct way, it is unclear how it can proceed at all.

It would plainly be fallacious, for example, to argue for the first version in the following way: "There is logical space between the proposition that a judge has a duty to enforce the contract and the proposition that he has a duty not to. That space is occupied by the proposition that he has discretion to enforce it or not. Since it is a consequence of the proposition that the contract is valid that a judge has a duty to enforce it, and a consequence of the proposition that the contract is not valid that he has a duty not to enforce it, there must therefore be a parallel space between these two propositions about the contract, which is left available for the proposition that the contract is inchoate."

That would be a fallacious argument because it does not follow from the

fact that the concept of duty has, in this sense, three values, that the concepts used to define occasions of duty must also have three values. In tennis, for example, judges have a duty to call a fault if a serve falls wholly outside the service court, and a duty not to call a fault if it does not. There is space between the propositions that a judge has a duty to call a fault and that he has a duty not to, but it does not follow that there is space beween the propositions that the serve fell wholly without the service court and that it did not. Dispositive concepts are used to describe the occasions of official duty, but it does not follow that these concepts must themselves have the same structure as the concept of duty.

Someone who wishes to defend the first version of the thesis will properly object, however, to that analogy. He will rightly say that the concept of a valid contract does not simply describe the factual circumstances under which, as it happens, judges have a certain duty. We can easily imagine the rules of tennis being changed so that, for example, the judge will have a duty to call a fault if the ball lands on the service-court line. But we cannot imagine a change in the rules of law such that judges would no longer have even a *prima facie* duty to enforce a valid contract; in any case, if such a change were made, we should certainly say that the concept of contract had itself radically changed. For we use that concept (and the concepts of tort liability and crime) not simply to report in a neutral way that certain events, comparable to the ball landing in a certain area, have occurred, but as an argument in itself that certain legal consequences, including official duties, follow from these facts.

But though this is certainly right, it is unclear what useful conclusions a defender of the first version is able to draw. Suppose he were to take the point further, and say, not simply that statements about contracts always provide grounds for claims about official duty, but that such statements are indistinguishable from statements about duty. He might say, for example, that it means the same thing to say that a contract is valid as to say that a judge has a duty to enforce the promises that compose it, and the same thing to say that it is invalid as to say that he has a duty not to enforce these promises. If these equivalences in meaning hold, then the first version of the thesis follows in a straightforward way. Since there is space between the two propositions about judicial duty, and since the two propositions about contracts mean the same thing as the propositions about judicial duty, there must be space between the two latter propositions as well.

This argument would be impeccable if the semantic theory on which it is based, that propositions of law are equivalent in meaning to propositions about official duties, were sound. But that theory is not sound. There must be some differences in meaning between the proposition that a contract is valid and the proposition that judges have a duty to enforce the promises that compose the contract, because the former statement is ordinarily taken

as providing an argument for the latter, not merely as a question-begging restatement of it. If there is a conceptual, and not simply a contingent, connection between dispositive concepts and legal rights and duties, there is also a conceptual, and not merely a contingent, connection between such concepts and the types of events they report. If a lawyer says that his client has a right to win a judgment because the contract on which he sues is valid, or because the contract on which he is being sued is invalid, he indicates his readiness to make certain sorts of arguments rather than others, to point to facts having to do with offer, acceptance, capacity, illegality, or mistake rather than to other sorts of facts, to support his client's claim. The semantic theory which merely translates statements about contracts into statements about official duties therefore obscures the interesting and distinctive role of dispositive concepts in legal argument. These concepts provide a special kind of bridge between certain sorts of events and the conclusory claims about rights and duties that hold if these events can be demonstrated to have occurred. They both designate tests for conclusory claims and insist that if the tests they designate are not met, then the opposite conclusory claim, not only the denial of the first, holds instead. The need for concepts having that function in legal argument arises *because* the concepts of right and duty in which conclusory claims are framed are structured, that is, because there is space between the opposite conclusory claims. The function is the function of denying that the space thus provided may be exploited by rejecting both the opposing claims. Depositive concepts are able to fill this function just because the first version of the no-right-answer thesis is false; if there were space between the propositions that a contract is and is not valid, that concept could not close the space provided by the concepts of right and duty.

The correct analogy, on this account of the matter, is not between dispositive legal concepts and factual events in a game, like a ball landing within or without a physical area. The correct analogy is between these concepts and dispositive concepts that fulfill the same function within a game. The concept of a tennis serve being "in" or "out" *tout court*, rather than within or without a physical area, is a dispositive tennis concept. The events that make a serve "in" may change, within limits, as when the rules change so that a serve on the line is "out," but the dispositive concept nevertheless has the function of connecting whatever events do constitute a serve's being "in" to official duties in such a way as to close the space left open by the structure of claims of duty.

Someone who defends the first version of the no-right-answer thesis will, of course, challenge my description of the function of dispositive concepts. He will say that the function of these concepts is to enforce, rather than to suppress, the structure of claims of rights and duties. But he cannot win that dispute with me in advance; if he believes that the way lawyers use the

concept justifies his description of its function rather than mine, he must provide affirmative evidence drawn from their practice. I am able to point to the fact that lawyers treat the claim that a contract is not valid as the negation of the claim that it is valid, the claim that someone is not liable as the negation of the claim that he is, and so forth; and I am also able to show that lawyers do not use words of the sort his description suggests they would, like "inchoate" contracts or "vulnerability to liability" or "criminous" acts. These are powerful arguments in my favor against his account, and though they are not conclusive, I do not see any arguments that he might make on his own side.

One argument (which I have heard in various forms) at best begs the question. The argument is this: "An ordinary legal statement, like 'Tom's contract is valid,' is only a shorthand form of a longer and more accurate structured statement, namely, 'The law provides that Tom's contract is valid.' Similarly the statement, 'Tom's contract is not valid,' is only a shorthand form of the statement 'The law provides that Tom's contract is not valid.' But the two longer statements may plainly both be false. The law may simply stand silent, that is, provide nothing either way. But in that case, since the two shorter statements have the same meaning as the longer statements, the shorter statements are both false also, which is exactly what the first version of the no-right-answer thesis provides."

But we must ask what is meant by proposing that "Tom's contract is valid" has the same meaning as "The law provides that Tom's contract is valid." It might be meant that the latter is a redundant way of saying the former, just as "Legally, Tom's contract is valid" might be regarded as a redundant way of saying "Tom's contract is valid." But in that case no reason has been given to suppose that "The law provides that Tom's contract is valid" and "The law provides that Tom's contract is not valid" may both be false. It is not evident that "Legally, Tom's contract is valid" and "Legally, Tom's contract is not valid" may both be false. That is what the first version must prove, not presuppose. If it strikes someone as evident that "The law provides that the contract is valid" and "The law provides that the contract is not valid" may both be false, this is because he personifies "the law"; that is, he takes it to be like a person who may provide (p) or ($\sim p$) or neither. But the law is not a person.

Perhaps, however, the proposal is based, not on that redundancy, but on a more ambitious semantics, which holds that ordinary propositions of law have the same meaning as propositions about what some person or institution has said. "The law provides that Tom's contract is valid" may be read, on this understanding, as "Appropriate authorities have decreed some rule according to which contracts like Tom's must be enforced" or something of the sort. It may certainly be false that appropriate authorities have decreed either that rule or a rule requiring the opposite. But it is hardly evident that

"Tom's contract is not valid" means the same thing as "Authorities have enacted some rule according to which the contract is not valid" (or that "Tom is not guilty of a crime" means the same thing as "Authorities have decreed some rule according to which what Tom did is not a crime"). On the contrary, that seems wrong. One strong argument against it is just the fact that "Tom's contract is not valid" seems to be the negation of "Tom's contract is valid" (and "Tom is not guilty of a crime" the negation of "Tom is guilty of a crime"). So the argument under consideration (on this second interpretation as well as on the first) is not an argument for the first version of the no-right-answer thesis; it rather presupposes that thesis.

I shall mention one more apparent argument that the defender of the first version might urge, which we might call the argument from realism. He might say that my description of the function of dispositive concepts must be wrong, because if it were right, legal practice would be grossly unrealistic in the following way: If we look to the actual tests the law provides for claims about the validity of contracts, we see that in fact there is sometimes no right answer to the question of whether these tests are met in a particular case. Since there may be no right answer to the question whether an agreement is sacrilegious or not, for example, there can be no right answer to the question whether Tom's contract is valid or invalid, whether lawyers think there is a right answer or not. This kind of indeterminacy occurs with such frequency that it would be unrealistic and indeed perverse for lawyers to insist that there is nevertheless no logical space between the concept of a valid and an invalid contract. The frequency of such cases, that is, provides a strong motive for adjusting legal semantics to accommodate the case, and we should therefore expect that lawyers have already made that adjustment. They may not have actually developed separate names for each of the third categories they have been forced to acknowledge—perhaps they regret such third categories and wish to keep them secret from the public at large—but they nevertheless must recognize such cases as distinct. If we attend very carefully to the nuances of their arguments, therefore, we may expect to see traces of an unnamed concept actually in use.

I set out this argument from realism because I think it has been influential. We must now notice, however, that it is not an independent argument for the first version of the no-right-answer thesis; on the contrary, it assumes that the second version has already been made out. The common sense lawyers are supposed to have is the common sense necessary to accept the second version of the thesis, and therefore to adapt their semantics to its truth. We may therefore safely ignore the argument from realism, and turn instead to the second version of the no-right-answer thesis itself. If the second version fails, the argument from realism collapses; if the second version holds, the argument from realism is of no independent philosophical interest.

THE SECOND VERSION

I shall consider three arguments that might be thought to support the second version of the no-right-answer thesis. The first supposes that the inevitable vagueness or open texture of legal language sometimes makes it impossible to say that a particular proposition of law is either true or false.
The second supposes that propositions of law, like the proposition that
Tom's contract is valid, have a hidden structure, explicated by legal positivism, that explains how it may be true neither that Tom's contract is valid
nor that his contract is not valid. The third fixes on the fact that sometimes,
as in our example, a proposition of law is contested in such a way that neither side has any hope of proving that the other is wrong; this argument
supposes that propositions of law that are inherently controversial cannot
be either true or false.

The Argument from Vagueness

It is a very popular idea among lawyers that the vagueness of the language
they use guarantees that inevitably there will be no right answer to certain
legal questions. But the popularity of this idea is based on a failure to discriminate between the fact and the consequences of vagueness in canonical
legal language.

Consider the argument that since the word "sacrilegious" is vague there
can be no right answer to the question whether Tom's contract is valid. I
should want to insist that the argument makes one mistake not presently
important. It confuses the case in which a legislature uses a vague term, like
"middle-aged" or "red," with the different case in which it lays down a
concept that admits of different conceptions. I shall not press that distinction here, however, because someone who accepts the distinction might just
add that in either case what the legislature has said does not dictate a particular answer to the question of Tom's contract, either because it used a
vague term or, if I am right, for the different reason that it used a concept
that admits of different conceptions. I shall therefore assume, in this essay,
that "sacrilegious" is vague, and that the statute in question is therefore
vague in the way that a statute providing that contracts signed by people of
middle age are invalid would be vague.

In any case, the argument from vagueness makes a further mistake. It assumes that if a legislature enacts a statute, the effect of that statute on the
law is fixed by nothing but the abstract meaning of words it has used, so that
if these words are vague, it must follow that the impact of the statute on the
law must be in some way indeterminate. But that assumption is plainly
wrong, because a lawyer's tests for fixing the impact of a statute on the law
may include canons of statutory interpretation or construction which de-

termine what force a vague word must be taken to have on a particular occasion, or at least make its force depend upon further questions that in principle have a right answer. These tests may refer to matters of intention or other psychological facts. It is open for a lawyer to argue, for example, that the extension of "sacrilegious," on this occasion of its use, must be confined to cases which at least a majority of those who voted for the statute had in mind, or would have wished to embrace if the case had been put to them. But the tests may not rely on psychological facts. It is open for a lawyer to argue, as I have myself,[2] that the impact of the statute on the law is determined by asking which interpretation, of the different interpretations admitted by the abstract meaning of the term, best advances the set of principles and policies that provides the best political justification for the statute at the time it was passed. Or it is open for him to argue the much more conservative position that if a statute uses vague language it must be taken to have changed the legal *status quo ante* only to the extent justified by the indisputable core of the language employed.

This last suggestion is interesting, not because the recommendation to protect the *status quo* is either popular or attractive, but because it shows dramatically that vagueness in canonical legal language does not guarantee indeterminacy in propositions of law. But the suggestion is open to an apparent objection. Suppose I put the suggestion this way: (A) If the proposition that a particular contract is sacrilegious is not true, then the law must treat it as false, so that all propositions of law are true that would be true if it were false. It may be objected that, just as it may be indeterminate whether a contract is sacrilegious, it may also be indeterminate whether the proposition that it is sacrilegious is true. After all, someone seeking to apply (A) in practice may find that he is genuinely puzzled whether (A) requires him to treat a particular contract as sacrilegious or as not sacrilegious. Suppose all contracts are arranged on a spectrum from those clearly sacrilegious to those clearly not so. There will be a group at one end as to which the proposition, "This contract is sacrilegious," will be true and another group, around the middle, as to which that proposition will be neither true nor false. But there are still others (roughly one-third the way along) as to which it is unclear whether that proposition is true or neither-true-nor-false. So instructions like (A) cannot eliminate indeterminacy, though they may reduce it.

This objection raises interesting issues, but it does not succeed as a refutation of my present point. Let me recapitulate my argument with the Person (V) who urges that vagueness in legal language necessarily produces indeterminacy in propositions of law. V, who is pursuing the second version of the no-right-answer thesis, argues that if "ϕ" is a vague term, then there will be sentences of the form "x is ϕ" that are true, others that are false, and still others that are neither true nor false. (This is different from the claim, which

would be made by someone supporting the first version of the thesis, that in some cases "x is ϕ" and "x is not ϕ" are both false.) I reply (in this part of the argument) that if that is so, then indeterminacy will not result if a principle of legislation is adopted which requires that if "x is ϕ" is not true, it be treated as false. Now the present objector (R) replies that though this may reduce the indeterminacy, it cannot eliminate it; R moves up one level of language to assert that, if "ϕ" is vague, then there will be cases in which " 'x is ϕ' is true" will itself be neither true nor false. If I try to meet R by amending my recommended principle of legislation to provide that if " 'x is ϕ' is true" is not true, then it must be treated as false, I have achieved nothing. R may then move to a higher level of language still, and I shall be chasing him forever.

But is R's initial move sound? Can " 'x is ϕ' is true" itself be neither true nor false? Not if we hold to V's original scheme of three exhaustive truth values—true, false, and neither-true-nor-false. If "x is ϕ" is true, then " 'x is ϕ' is true" is true; but if "x is ϕ" is false *or* neither true nor false, then " 'x is ϕ' is true" is false. In none of the three possible cases is " 'x is ϕ' is true" itself neither true nor false. So R seems to be the victim of V's own formulation of his argument. V's argument assumes that propositions of law are indeterminate only when some proposition of the form "x is ϕ" is indeterminate in consequence of the vagueness of "ϕ," but it also assumes that whenever it is indeterminate whether "ϕ" holds, then the proposition that "x is ϕ" is not true.[3]

So the objection we have been discussing may be set aside. There is no reason to assume that no general theory of legislation can be found that will provide an answer to the question of what happens to the law when some institution has used vague language. It might now be said, however, that there is no such theory of legislation in general use. If we look at the decisions of courts called upon to interpret statutes containing vague terms, we find that the courts either disagree about techniques of statutory construction or agree only on canons that critically use terms like "intention" and "purpose" that are in their own way as vague as "sacrilegious." But what of that? Even if we treat these pronouncements by courts as canonical statements of law, like statutes, we still leave open the question of how the law is affected by the fact that courts, in *these* canonical statements, have used vague terms.

Suppose we put our question about Tom's contract, to which there is supposed to be no right answer, this way. Given that the legislature has enacted a statute which provides that "sacrilegious" contracts are void, given whatever we may suppose about the state of mind of the legislators who did this, given whatever we might suppose about the attitudes of the general public toward the Sabbath, and given whatever else may be relevant, is Tom's contract valid in law, so that he is entitled to have the exchange of promises enforced, or is the contract invalid, so that Tim is entitled not to

have the exchange enforced? The vagueness of the term "sacrilegious" and the vagueness inherent in any description the legislators might have given of their own state of mind, or members of the public of their own attitudes, are facts which our expanded question invites us to take into account. They do not mean that our question has no right answer. If someone now points out that the statements judges make about the construction of statutes themselves contain vague terms, he simply supplies a further fact. If we agree that that further fact is relevant to our question, as it plainly is, then we might add, to our list of considerations, that judges have made such statements. Nothing has yet been said, relying on the vagueness of the term "sacrilegious," to make us doubt that our question has an answer.

I emphasize that qualification because I think that the popular idea, that some legal questions have no right answer because legal language is sometimes vague, does not depend on any argument from vagueness after all, but rather on the different argument, which I describe later, that there can be no right answer to a legal question when reasonable lawyers disagree about what the right answer is. The concept of a valid contract is not itself vague like the concept of middle age, and it does not follow from the fact that some statutory language pertinent to the validity of a contract is vague that the question is also vague whether, given that language, the contract is valid. That fact does make it more likely, however, that lawyers will disagree about whether the contract is valid than if the statute contained no vague terms—not because the meaning of terms is decisive of questions of validity, but because lawyers do disagree about the techniques of interpretation and construction properly used to answer such questions.

The Argument from Positivism

Legal positivism has many different forms, but they all have in common the idea that law exists only in virtue of some human act or decision. In some forms of positivism, this act is the command of a person or group with actual political power; in other forms, it may be an act as passive as the general and casual acceptance of a customary rule; but in every form some set of acts is defined as necessary and sufficient. We may therefore state the structure of positivism, as a type of legal theory, this way. If "p" represents a proposition of law, and "$L(p)$" expresses the fact that someone or some group has acted in a way that makes (p) true, then positivism holds that (p) cannot be true unless $L(p)$ is true.

It might therefore seem that positivism, in any of its different forms, provides an argument for the second version of the no-right-answer thesis. Suppose (p) cannot be true unless $L(p)$ is true, and that $(\sim p)$ cannot be true unless $L(\sim p)$ is true. For any plausible value of "L," in some cases both $L(p)$ and $L(\sim p)$ are false. If "L" expresses the fact that a sovereign has issued a

particular command, for example, it might be false that he has commanded that act, and also false that he has commanded that the act not be done, that is, false that he has prohibited that act. But if $L(p)$ and $L(\sim p)$ are both false, then neither (p) nor $(\sim p)$ can be true, which is what the second version of the no-right-answer thesis holds.

Of course, the fact that legal positivism supports the second version of the no-right-answer thesis would not count as a complete proof of the second version without an independent proof that positivism is right. Nevertheless, since positivism in one form or another is a very popular legal theory, the apparent connection between that theory and the second version, if it can be sustained, would provide important support for the second version and also explain the great popularity of the no-right-answer thesis. It can quickly be shown, however, that none of the familiar forms of positivism does support the second version, and that the only form that might do so would support it only to a very limited degree.

We can distinguish types of positivism not only by distinguishing the different values given to "L" in the general structure I described, but also by distinguishing different relations supposed to hold between (p) and $L(p)$. Semantic positivism holds that (p) is identical in meaning to $L(p)$ so that, for example, "Tom's contract is valid" means the same thing as "A sovereign has commanded that contracts like Tom's be enforced" or something of the sort. Plainly, semantic positivism cannot offer an argument for the second version of the no-right-answer thesis. The second version concedes that "Tom's contract is not valid" is the logical negation of "Tom's contract is valid"; it concedes that if the latter proposition is represented as "p," the former must be represented as "$\sim p$." If a particular form of semantic positivism supplies a value of "L" such that $L(p)$ and $L(\sim p)$ cannot both be false, then the argument for the second version of the thesis just described does not, for this form of positivism, go through. But if it supplies some value for "L" such that $L(p)$ and $L(\sim p)$ may both be false (as the command form of semantic positivism does), then it contradicts itself, because, since (p) and $(\sim p)$ cannot both be false, it cannot be that (p) means the same as $L(p)$ and $(\sim p)$ means the same as $L(\sim p)$. Semantic positivism must therefore deny that "Tom's contract is not valid" is the negation of "Tom's contract is valid"; it is entitled to deny that, of course, only if it has already been shown that the surface linguistic behavior of lawyers is misleading in the way that the first version of the thesis claims.

There are, however, forms of positivism that do not claim that the relation between (p) and $L(p)$ is identity of meaning. Some forms of positivism claim only the relation of mutual logical entailment, so that it is logically necessary, for example, that Tom's contract is valid if a sovereign has commanded that contracts like his be enforced, and vice versa. Others claim only the still weaker relation of truth-functional equivalence, so that whenever Tom's contract is valid it will always also be true that some

sovereign has commanded judges to enforce contracts like his, and vice versa.

It is easy to show, however, that neither mutual-entailment positivism nor truth-functional-equivalence positivism can support the second version of the no-right-answer thesis. I will make the argument for the latter, weaker form of positivism; the same argument obviously holds for the stronger form. If (p) is truth-functionally equivalent to $L(p)$, then (p) is false, and not simply not true, when $L(p)$ is false. Therefore when $L(p)$ is false, $(\sim p)$, which is the logical negation of (p), must be true. Since $L(p)$ must be either true or false, then either (p) or $(\sim p)$ must be true, which is what the second version denies.

The argument from positivism I described earlier in this section is misleading, because it capitalizes on the supposed distinction between the internal negation of $L(p)$, which is $L(\sim p)$, and the external negation of $L(p)$, which is $\sim L(p)$. If (p) is truth-functionally equivalent to $L(p)$, then it seems naturally to follow that $(\sim p)$ is truth-functionally equivalent to $L(\sim p)$. That seems to leave $\sim L(p)$ equivalent to nothing, so that it seems plausible that neither (p) nor $(\sim p)$ is true when $\sim L(p)$ is true. But all that overlooks the fact that if $L(p)$ is indeed equivalent to (p) and $L(\sim p)$ is equivalent to $(\sim p)$, then it follows from the former equivalence that $\sim L(p)$ is equivalent to $(\sim p)$ and therefore that $L(\sim p)$ and $\sim L(p)$, being equivalent to the same thing, are equivalent to each other. Truth-functional positivism, if it concedes that the first version of the no-right-answer thesis is false, provides an argument against, not for, the second version.

That has the following interesting consequence. It has always been assumed that the values traditional forms of positivism assign to "L" use the ordinary meanings of the terms they employ; that the command theory uses, for example, the ordinary meaning of "command." But unless positivism maintains the first version of the no-right-answer thesis, that cannot be so. In the ordinary meaning of "command," the proposition that someone has commanded that a contract not be enforced is not equivalent to the proposition that he has not commanded that the contract be enforced. But if it is maintained that "Tom's contract is valid" is truth-functionally equivalent to "Lawmakers have commanded that such contracts be enforced" and that "Tom's contract is not valid" is the logical negation of "Tom's contract is valid," then it follows that "Lawmakers have commanded that the contract not be enforced" is equivalent to "Lawmakers have not commanded that the contract be enforced."[4]

In any case, no form of positivism that stipulates truth-functional equivalence or mutual entailment between every proposition of law and some proposition about lawmaking acts can support the second version of the no-right-answer thesis. If the argument from positivism is to be effective, some form of positivism must be found that makes the connection between these propositions a special one such that a proposition of law is true if and only if

a proposition about lawmaking acts is true, but is not false when that proposition about lawmaking acts is false. None of the orthodox forms of positivism seems to make that special and limited connection plausible. If a proposition of law is true when and only when a sovereign has issued a particular sort of command, then why should it not be false when he has not issued that command? If a proposition of law is true only when some rule from which the proposition follows has been enacted or adopted or accepted pursuant to some rule of recognition, why should it not be false when no such rule has been enacted or adopted or accepted?

I shall try to suggest, through an analogy, how a positivist might succeed in answering these difficult questions and thereby in making that special one-way connection more plausible than it might seem. Suppose a group of Dickens scholars proposes to discuss David Copperfield as if David were a real person. They propose to say, for example, that David attended Salem House, that he was industrious, and so forth. They might well develop the following ground rules governing these various assertions:

(1) Any proposition about David may be asserted as "true" if Dickens said it, or said something else such that it would have been inconsistent had Dickens denied it.

(2) Any proposition may be denied as "false" if Dickens denied it, or said something else such that it would have been inconsistent had Dickens said it.

The first version of the no-right-answer thesis would not hold in this enterprise. Consider any concept we use to describe real people such that if it is true that a person has the property in question it is false that he does not, and if it is false that he has the property it is true that he does not. That concept will have the same logical behavior in the literary discussion. If it is true that David attended Salem House, then it must be false, under the rules, that he did not, and vice versa. If it is true that David had an affair with Steerforth there, then it must be false, under the rules, that he did not, and vice versa. If it is true that David had type-A blood then it is false that he did not, and vice versa. We can even say, of David as of real people, that for any property it is true that either David had that property or not, because the law of the excluded middle is a necessary truth that it would have been inconsistent for Dickens to deny once he had said anything at all about David.

But the second version of the no-right-answer thesis would hold in the literary enterprise, for there would be many propositions about David that the participants would know were neither assertable as true nor deniable as false. Dickens never said that David had a homosexual affair with Steerforth, and it would not have been inconsistent with anything he did say if he had denied it. But he did not deny it, and it would not have been inconsistent with anything he said if he had asserted it. So the participants can nei-

ther assert nor deny the proposition, not because they lack sufficient information, but because they have sufficient information to be certain that, under their rules, the proposition is neither true nor false.

This story suggests a form of positivism that provides for the special connection I described between propositions of law and propositions about lawmaking acts. Law is an enterprise such that propositions of law do not describe the real world in the way ordinary propositions do, but rather are propositions whose assertion is warranted by ground rules like those in the literary exercise. A proposition of law will be assertable as true, under these ground rules, if a sovereign has issued a command of a certain sort, or if officials have adopted rules of a certain form in a certain way, or something of that sort. The same proposition will be deniable as false only if a sovereign has commanded to the contrary, or if officials have adopted a contrary rule, or something of that sort. This form of positivism does not presuppose the first version of the no-right-answer thesis, because it does not suggest that there is any conceptual space, within the institution of law, between any proposition and its apparent negation. It does not suppose that the proposition that a contract is valid and the proposition that it is not valid may both be false. But it does support the second version of the thesis, because it shows how a particular proposition may be neither true nor false, not because of some vagueness or open texture in canonical language, but because the ground rules of the legal enterprise, like the ground rules of the literary enterprise I described have that consequence.

We must now notice that this form of positivism differs from more familiar forms in one important respect. Orthodox positivism, in each of its forms, claims some sort of conceptual connection between law and the particular act or acts designated by the theory as the distinctive law-creating act. For an Austinian positivist, for example, the fact that law is the command of the sovereign is not simply the consequence of the particular legal practices in some countries. It is, on the contrary, constitutive of the very idea of law. But the new version of positivism I constructed, based on the analogy of the literary game, does not permit the positivist so global a claim. He must be content to say that (as it happens) the citizens and officials in a particular jurisdiction follow ground rules about the assertion and denial of legal propositions such that no such proposition may be asserted unless a sovereign has made the appropriate command, or denied unless he has made the contrary command, and that, for that reason, there are propositions of law that can neither be asserted nor denied. But then his claim is not that there must be, in any legal system, questions of law that have no right answer for that reason; but only that there are such questions, for that reason, in the legal system under consideration. He must concede the possibility, at least, of other legal systems which follow very different ground rules about the assertion and denial of propositions of law, and he must also

concede that questions of law that do not have right answers in the system he describes have right answers in those other systems, even though no further commands or other lawmaking acts have taken place there.[5] It is not difficult to imagine such other systems.

The participants in the literary game (to return to that analogy) might easily have chosen less ascetic ground rules for themselves. We might, in fact, distinguish a great many varieties of the literary exercise by progressively relaxing these ground rules. The second form of the exercise might provide, for example, that further propositions about David are assertable as true (or deniable as false) if it would be very likely indeed (or very unlikely indeed) that a real person having the properties true of David under the standard game would also have the properties asserted in the further propositions. The second version of the no-right-answer thesis would still hold for the second form of the literary exercise, but there would be many fewer cases of questions that have no right answer in the second form than in the first, not because the raw data of what Dickens said have changed, but because the ground rules now warrant the assertion or denial of much more. We can imagine a third form of the exercise in which the number of such questions would be reduced to very boring questions no one would wish to ask. The rules of this third form provide that a further proposition about David is assertable as true (or deniable as false) if that further proposition provides a better (or worse) fit than its negation with propositions already established, because it explains in a more satisfactory way why David was what he was, or said what he said, or did what he did, according to those already established propositions. In fact, literary criticism often takes the form of an exercise much closer to this third form of the exercise than to either of the other two.

We can imagine correspondingly different forms of the legal enterprise by supposing progressively less strict ground rules of assertion and denial for propositions of law. We can imagine an enterprise like the first form of the literary exercise, in which participants assert or deny propositions of law only if some stipulated lawmaker asserted or denied those very propositions, or propositions that entail these propositions. But we can also imagine an enterprise much more like the third form in which participants assert (or deny) propositions that provide a better (or worse) fit with the political theory that provides the best justification for propositions of law already established.

The issue of whether there is a right answer to any particular question of law will crucially depend upon which form of the legal enterprise is in play. If it is like the first form of the literary exercise, then the question of whether Tom's contract is valid will not have a right answer on the simple facts I stipulated at the start of the essay. But if it is like the third form, on the other hand, that question will almost certainly have a right answer, because, for reasons I consider more fully in the next section, it is very unlikely

that one answer will not provide a better fit in the sense just described. If a positivist wishes to argue that in cases like Tom's case there is no right answer, so that judicial discretion must be exercised willy-nilly, then he must show that our own legal practice is like the first form of the literary exercise and not like the third. (I leave aside the question of whether the latter would count as a positivistic account of law at all.) But whether our system is more like the first than the third form is a question of fact. So even if we accept the general account of law I described, which holds that legal propositions are not directly true or false of some external world, but are rather propositions whose assertion or denial is licensed by ground rules that vary with practice, nothing follows, from that general theory of law, about the extent, if any, to which the second version of the no-right-answer thesis is true of any particular legal jurisdiction.

The Argument from Controversy

I shall now consider what I think has been the most influential argument in favor of the second version of the no-right-answer thesis, even though this argument has not always been recognized or clearly set out in the thoughts of those whom it has influenced. The argument may be put in the form of a doctrine which I shall call the demonstrability thesis. This thesis states that if a proposition cannot be demonstrated to be true, after all the hard facts that might be relevant to its truth are either known or stipulated, then it cannot be true. By "hard facts" I mean physical facts and facts about behavior (including the thoughts and attitudes) of people. By "demonstrated" I mean backed by arguments such that anyone who understood the language in which the proposition is formed must assent to its truth or stand convicted of irrationality.

If the demonstrability thesis holds, then there must be legal questions to which no right answer can be given because neither the proposition that some dispositive concept holds nor the proposition that it does not hold can be true. If reasonable lawyers can disagree whether Sunday contracts are sacrilegious within the meaning of the statute, because they hold different views about how statutes containing vague terms should be interpreted or construed, then the proposition that Tom's contract is valid cannot be demonstrated to be true, even when all facts about what the legislators had in mind are known or stipulated. Therefore, on the demonstrability thesis, it cannot be true. But the same holds for the proposition that Tom's contract is not valid. Since neither of these propositions can be true, and since they are assumed to exhaust the range of possible answers, then there is no right answer to the question.

The demonstrability thesis therefore provides a conclusive argument for the second version of the no-right-answer thesis. But why should we accept the demonstrability thesis? Anyone will accept it, of course, who holds a

strict form of empiricism in metaphysics. If we believe that no proposition can be true except in virtue of some fact that makes it true, and that there are no facts in the world but hard facts, then the demonstrability thesis follows from that metaphysics. The proposition could rationally be believed to be true, even though its truth is not demonstrated when all the hard facts are known or stipulated, only if there were something else in the world in virtue of which it could possibly be true. But if there is nothing else, then the proposition cannot rationally be believed to be true; the failure of hard facts to make it true would have exhausted all hope of making it true.

But if, on the other hand, we suppose that there is something else in the world beside hard facts, in virtue of which propositions of law might be true, then the demonstrability thesis, in the form I set it out, must be false. Suppose, for example, there are moral facts, which are not simply physical facts or facts about the thoughts or attitudes of people. I do not mean that there are what are sometimes called "transcendent" or "Platonic" moral facts; indeed I do not know what these would be. I mean only to suppose that a particular social institution like slavery might be unjust, not because people think it unjust, or have conventions according to which it is unjust, or anything of the sort, but just because slavery is unjust. If there are such moral facts, then a proposition of law might rationally be supposed to be true even if lawyers continue to disagree about the proposition after all hard facts are known or stipulated. It might be true in virtue of a moral fact which is not known or stipulated.

The demonstrability thesis, therefore, seems to depend upon an answer to the question of what there is. I shall not, in this essay, try to make plausible the idea that moral facts exist, but I shall try to support the idea that some facts beside hard facts do. I wish, for this purpose, to consider again the third form of the literary exercise I described in the last section. Participants assert a proposition about David as true (or deny it as false) if that proposition provides a better (or worse) fit than its negation with propositions already established, because it explains in a more satisfactory way why David did what he did, or said what he said, or thought what he thought, according to the established propositions.

I do not mean to raise the question, through this story, of whether fictitious persons are in some sense real so that all these propositions may be said to be true of someone or something. I do not mean to suggest, that is, that in addition to hard facts there are facts like the fact that David Copperfield first read *Hamlet* at Salem House. The literary exercise I imagine does not require that assumption to make it a sensible exercise. But it does require the assumption, I think, that there are facts of narrative consistency, like the fact that the hypothesis that David had a sexual relationship with Steerforth provides a more satisfactory explanation of what he subsequently did and thought than the hypothesis that he did not.

That is not, I take it, a hard fact. It is not the sort of fact that is even in principle demonstrable by ordinary scientific methods. Since no one ever did have just the history and character Dickens said David did, we cannot provide ordinary arguments of probability, even when all the histories of real people are known, that would necessarily convince any rational man either to accept or reject the hypothesis. In some cases the argument will be so strong for a particular proposition, no doubt, that we should say that any participant who did not agree with that proposition was incompetent at the exercise. In other cases we should not say this at all; we should say that there is so much to be said on both sides that competent participants might reasonably disagree.

Suppose that the exercise proceeds with fair success. The participants often agree, and even when they disagree they understand the arguments on both sides well enough to rank each set, for example, in rough order of plausibility. Suppose now that an empiricist philosopher visits the proceedings of the group and tells them that there are no such things as facts of narrative consistency or that, in any case, there are no such facts when reasonable men can disagree about what they are. He adds that therefore no one can have any reason to think, in response to the terms of the exercise, that the argument that David had an affair with Steerforth is stronger than the argument that he did not. Why should they be persuaded by what he says? This case is not like Dummett's example of Charles's bravery I mentioned earlier. The participants do have reasons for preferring one proposition to another, or at least they think they do, and even when they disagree, each of them thinks he can distinguish cases when his opponents have genuine reasons on their side from cases when they do not. If they have all made a mistake, and no reasons exist, it is difficult to see why they think they do, and how their exercise can have had the success it has.

The philosopher's argument would be compromised, moreover, by the following consideration. It is very likely that if he is asked to take part in the exercise he will find, at least after listening to the group for a while, that he himself will have beliefs of narrative consistency, and that he will be able to provide arguments that others recognize as arguments, and so forth. But how can he say that he believes it is more likely that David had an affair with Steerforth, and offer reasons for that belief, and nevertheless maintain that no one can have reasons for such a belief, or that all such beliefs are illusions?

Suppose he says that while it is true that he and the other participants have such beliefs, they have these only as participants, so that it would be quite impossible for an independent observer or critic to say that one participant's beliefs are superior to another's. Would the independent observer or critic himself have beliefs, if he became a participant, even in controversial cases? If not, then the participants will properly doubt whether he has the capacity to judge their debates. But if so, then he does think, after re-

flection, that some of the participants have the better of the argument, namely those with whom he would agree. Why should he lose that belief, and whatever reasons he has to support it, when he steps back from the debate and reassumes the role of critic? Of course, he cannot demonstrate his beliefs, either as participant or critic, any more than the other participants can demonstrate their beliefs. But the fact that a critic is in that position offers no more argument for the demonstrability thesis than the fact that a participant is in the same position.

We might now assume the offensive against the philosopher and argue that the fact that the enterprise succeeds in the way it does is a reason for supposing that there are facts of narrative consistency about which the participants debate. He might oppose that argument in this way: He might try to show that the fact that a particular participant holds a particular belief of narrative consistency can be satisfactorily explained by considering only the participant's own personality and tastes and history, so that it is not necessary, to explain his beliefs, to suppose any objective fact to which he is responding, in the way in which we ordinarily suppose objective facts in explaining why people hold beliefs about hard facts. It is unclear how he might conceivably show this. Perhaps he might invent a machine which would be able to predict, with great accuracy, what a participant's belief would be with respect to any question about David that might be asked, once highly specific information about the participant's blood chemistry was programmed into the machine. It is, of course, very speculative that if such a machine were built it would yield such predictions in the case of this literary exercise, but not also in the case of, for example, astronomers who debate about the number of Jupiter's moons. If the demonstrability thesis depends on the speculation that the machine would yield positive results in the one case, but not in the other, then it rests on very shaky ground.

Let us assume, nevertheless, that such a machine could be built, and that it would yield that discriminatory information about the literary exercise. What follows? The philosopher might be justified in concluding that the literary exercise was special in the following sense: In many exercises, including the experimental sciences, participants are trained to respond to their observations of the external world in a way that, we suppose, increases our collective knowledge of the world. In the literary exercise, participants are trained to respond to certain questions of a highly specific form which, as the machine is supposed to have proved, cannot be said to be questions about the external world. They are trained to subject their responses to the disciplines of reflection and consistency, and then to make certain assertions that their training authorizes them to make on the authority of these responses so disciplined. The exercise, conducted by participants so trained, serves some purpose—perhaps recreational or cultural—other than to increase our collective knowledge of the external world.

Suppose the distinction, or some more sophisticated version, can in fact

be made out between enterprises like astronomy and enterprises like literary games. That would be an important discovery, and we should certainly wish to mark the distinction in some way. Suppose a philosopher argues that, in consequence of the distinction, we should not say that propositions asserted by participants in the literary exercise can be either true or false. If he explained that he wished to mark the important distinction in this way, we might or might not agree that the constraint he suggests is an appropriate way to do this. But we should be careful to stipulate what must not follow from the decision to restrict the use of "true" and "false" in that way.

It must not follow, for example, that the participants have no reason to think one judgment of narrative consistency superior to another when they disagree about which is superior. They still have just the reason the enterprise teaches them to recognize—the fact of their disciplined and reflective response to the distinct questions the enterprise requires them to ask. The philosopher might concede this, but then say that they must recognize that the enterprise that encourages them to make judgments of this sort is based on an illusion. But if the exercise serves its purpose, whatever that might be, what reform would be justified in consequence of what he says? If no reform would be justified, what is the illusion?

Our philosopher might say that the illusion is the supposition that facts about narrative consistency are part of the external world in the same sense in which facts about the weight of iron are part of the world. But the participants certainly do not think that narrative consistency is the same sort of thing as the weight of iron, or that it is part of the external world in anything like the way that the weight of iron is. The philosopher may say that they think that their judgments of narrative consistency are objective, whereas it has now been shown that they are merely subjective. But his own theory makes us lose our grip on that ancient distinction. Whatever sense statements about narrative consistency may have, they are given that sense by the enterprise that trains participants to make and respond to such statements. The philosopher's claim that the reasons of one are no better—provide no superior warrant for his assertion—than the reasons of another is a claim that can only be made from *within* the enterprise. From within the enterprise (except in certain circumstances I shall discuss in a moment) that claim is simply false, or, if we choose to avoid that word, simply not warranted. Our philosopher may, of course, say that an institution so contructed is a silly one, and that may or may not be so. Whether it is so will depend upon whether the enterprise, taken as a whole, serves some worthwhile purpose, and serves it better than a revised form of the enterprise would.

The third form of the literary exercise is therefore an enterprise that makes trouble for the demonstrability thesis. I suggested, in the preceding section, that our own legal system might resemble that form of the literary exercise. In fact, I have elsewhere offered a theory of adjudication which

supports the following description of our legal enterprise.[6] A proposition of law, like the proposition that Tom's contract is valid, is true if the best justification that can be provided for the body of propositions of law taken to be settled provides a better case for that proposition than for the contrary proposition that Tom's contract is not valid, but is false if that justification provides a better case for that contrary proposition. There are important differences between the idea of consistency used in this account of legal reasoning and the idea of narrative consistency used in the literary exercise. Legal reasoning makes use of the idea of normative consistency, which is plainly more complex than narrative consistency and may be thought to introduce new grounds for claims of subjectivism. Nevertheless, the comparison may help to explain why it is sensible to suppose that there might be a right answer to the question of whether Tom's contract is valid even when the answer cannot be demonstrated.

The comparison is useful in another way as well. It helps us to understand why, even though we reject the demonstrability thesis and therefore reject the idea that there is no right answer whenever the right answer is not demonstrable, it might nevertheless be sensible to say that there is no right answer to a question of law in certain very special cases. In certain circumstances, even in the third form of the literary exercise, it might be right for the participants to refuse to assert either that David had some property or that he did not. Suppose the question is raised whether David had type-A blood or not, and there is no reason to think that a boy with that blood type would be more likely to have had the history and character Dickens stipulates than a boy with any other blood type. The proposition that David had type-A blood is not vague; we can say that any historical boy would either have had type-A blood or not, and that there is a right answer to the question whether he did, even though we shall never know. But the assertion conditions of the literary exercise forbid saying that of David; it seems more sensible, given these conditions, to say that though the proposition that he had that blood type is not true, the proposition that he did not is not true either. In such a case the grounds for saying that there is no right answer to the question are not based on any external criticism of the enterprise, or on any external philosophical position like the demonstrability thesis. The grounds are simply that that is the right response *within* the terms of the enterprise itself. We may imagine a genuine controversy within the enterprise as to whether, in any particular case, that *is* the right response. One party may say that there is a reason for thinking that boys like David would for that reason have been more likely to have type-A blood and another that there is a reason for thinking that they would more likely not, and a third thinking either that there were no reasons either way, or that whatever reasons there were were so equally balanced that no sensible discrimination could be made.

The occasions on which the participants would be tempted to say that there was no right answer to some question about David would be a function of two considerations. The first is the length of the novel, or, rather, the density of the information that Dickens does in fact supply. The second is the character of the question. If it is a question about a feature that is randomly distributed throughout a population, so that the fact that a boy had the specific characteristics Dickens described, no matter how dense the description, can have little bearing on the question of whether he had the feature in question, then it is more likely that the question will have no right answer.

Can we imagine questions that might be raised within a legal system that would have no right answer for the same sort of reason? That must depend upon the legal system, of course, but it also depends upon how we understand and expand the claim, just mentioned, that a proposition of law is sound if it figures in the best justification that can be provided for the body of legal propositions taken to be settled. I argue that there are two dimensions along which it must be judged whether a theory provides the best justification of available legal materials: the dimension of fit and the dimension of political morality.[7] The dimension of fit supposes that one political theory is *pro tanto* a better justification than another if, roughly speaking, someone who held that theory would, in its service, enact more of what is settled than would someone who held the other. Two different theories may well provide equally good justifications, along that dimension, in immature legal systems with few settled rules, or in legal systems treating only a limited range of the conduct of their constituents. But in a modern, developed, and complex system, the antecedent likelihood of that kind of tie is very small. The tie result is possible in any system, but it will be so rare as to be exotic in these. I do not mean that it will be rare that lawyers disagree about which theory provides, even on that dimension, a better justification. It will be rare, I think, that many lawyers will agree that neither provides a better fit than the other.

The second dimension—the dimension of political morality—supposes that, if two justifications provide an equally good fit with the legal materials, one nevertheless provides a better justification than the other if it is superior as a matter of political or moral theory; if, that is, it comes closer to capturing the rights that people in fact have.[8] The availability of this second dimension makes it even less likely that any particular case will have no right answer. But the force of the second dimension—and the character of the indeterminacy it introduces—will be a matter of dispute, because lawyers who hold different types of moral theory will assess these differently. Straightforward moral skeptics will argue that the second dimension adds nothing, because no theory is superior, as a matter of political morality, to any other. If some case has no right answer taking into account the first di-

mension only, then that case has no right answer *tout court.* Someone who holds an old-fashioned pleasure-pain utilitarian theory of rights, on the other hand, will find it incredible that two theories distinct enough to require different decisions in any particular case will score equally on the second dimension. He will recognize the theoretical possibility that two distinct sets of moral rules would have exactly the same pleasure-pain consequences over the long run; but he will think that the possibility is so small that it may be ignored in practice.

In the case of some theories of rights, it will be problematic whether there is even the theoretical possibility of no-right-answer. Suppose a right-based theory of political morality that seeks to derive particular individual rights from some presumed absolute right to be treated as an equal, that is, with equal concern and respect. Two lawyers who accept that general theory may hold different conceptions of what counts as equal respect. May a third lawyer plausibly believe that neither is right, because one conception of respect is exactly as good as another? Once we grasp the ideas of the old-fashioned utilitarian, we can see what sense it makes to suppose a tie, within his system, between two acts or two rules or principles. They are tied if each would produce exactly the same positive pleasure balance. But it is not so easy to see how someone could accept the general idea of the equal respect theory and still maintain, not that he is uncertain which conception is superior, but that neither is. There seems to be no room here for the ordinary idea of a tie. If there is no right answer in a hard case, this must be in virtue of some more problematic type of indeterminacy or incommensurability in moral theory.

The question, therefore, of whether there are no-right-answer cases in a particular jurisdiction—and whether such cases are rare or numerous—is not an ordinary empirical question. I believe that such cases, if they exist at all, must be extremely rare in the United States and Great Britain. Someone who disputes this cannot, if the arguments of this essay are right, establish his case simply by relying on the demonstrability thesis or the other *a priori* arguments considered earlier. But nor is he likely to succeed by attempting to find actual examples of no-right-answer cases in a case-by-case search of the law reports. Each case report carries an opinion arguing that one side has, on balance, the better of the legal argument. Some cases carry a dissenting opinion as well, but this is also an argument that one side has the better case. Perhaps both the majority and minority opinions are wrong: Perhaps some combination of legal and philosophical analysis can show that, in this particular case, the arguments for neither side are on balance stronger than those for the other. But it is extremely unlikely that an argument that this is so in some particular case will convince all lawyers. Any case cited as an example by one scholar will be disputed by others.

The argument that I am wrong must therefore be a philosophical argu-

ment. It must challenge my assumption that in a complex and comprehensive legal system it is antecedently unlikely that two theories will differ sufficiently to demand different answers in some case and yet provide equally good fit with the relevant legal materials. It must provide and defend some idea of skepticism, or of indeterminacy in moral theory, which makes it plausible to suppose that neither of such theories can be preferred to the other on grounds of political morality. I do not think that any such argument has been provided, though I have certainly not shown that none could be.

SIX

How Law Is Like Literature

I SHALL ARGUE that legal practice is an exercise in interpretation not only when lawyers interpret particular documents or statutes but generally. Law so conceived is deeply and thoroughly political. Lawyers and judges cannot avoid politics in the broad sense of political theory. But law is not a matter of personal or partisan politics, and a critique of law that does not understand this difference will provide poor understanding and even poorer guidance. I propose that we can improve our understanding of law by comparing legal interpretation with interpretation in other fields of knowledge, particularly literature. I also expect that law, when better understood, will provide a better grasp of what interpretation is in general.

LAW

The central problem of analytical jurisprudence is this: What sense should be given to propositions of law? I mean the various statements lawyers make reporting what the law is on some question or other. Propositions of law can be very abstract and general, like the proposition that states of the United States may not discriminate on racial grounds in supplying basic services to citizens, or they can be relatively concrete, like the proposition that someone who accepts a check in the normal course of business without notice of any infirmities in its title is entitled to collect against the maker, or very concrete, like the proposition that Mrs. X is liable in damages to Mr. Y in the amount of $1,150 because he slipped on her icy sidewalk and broke his hip. In each case a puzzle arises. What are propositions of law really about? What in the world could make them true or false?

The puzzle arises because propositions of law seem to be descriptive—they are about how things are in the law, not about how they should be—and yet it has proved extremely difficult to say exactly what it is that they

describe. Legal positivists believe that propositions of law are indeed wholly descriptive: they are pieces of history. A proposition of law, in their view, is true just in case some event of a designated lawmaking kind has taken place, and otherwise not. This seems to work reasonably well in very simple cases. If the Illinois legislature enacts the words "No will shall be valid without three witnesses," then the proposition of law, that an Illinois will needs three witnesses, seems to be true only in virtue of that historical event.

But in more difficult cases the analysis fails. Consider the proposition that a particular affirmative action scheme (not yet tested in the courts) in constitutionally valid. If that is true, it cannot be so just in virtue of the text of the Constitution and the fact of prior court decisions, because reasonable lawyers who know exactly what the Constitution says and what the courts have done may yet disagree whether it is true. (I am doubtful that the positivists' analysis holds even in the simple case of the will; but that is a different matter I shall not argue here.)

What are the other possibilities? One is to suppose that controversial propositions of law, like the affirmative action statement, are not descriptive at all but are rather expressions of what the speaker wants the law to be. Another is more ambitious: controversial statements are attempts to decribe some pure objective or natural law, which exists in virtue of objective moral truth rather than historical decision. Both these projects take some legal statements, at least, to be purely evaluative as distinct from descriptive: they express either what the speaker prefers—his personal politics— or what he believes is objectively required by the principles of an ideal political morality. Neither of these projects is plausible, because someone who says that a particular untested affirmative action plan is constitutional does mean to describe the law as it is rather than as he wants it to be or thinks that, by the best moral theory, it should be. He might say that he regrets that the plan is constitutional and thinks that, according to the best moral theory, it ought not to be.

There is a better alternative: propositions of law are not merely descriptive of legal history, in a straightforward way, nor are they simply evaluative in some way divorced from legal history. They are interpretive of legal history, which combines elements of both description and evaluation but is different from both. This suggestion will be congenial, at least at first blush, to many lawyers and legal philosophers. They are used to saying that law is a matter of interpretation; but only, perhaps, because they understand interpretation in a certain way. When a statute (or the Constitution) is unclear on some point, because some crucial term is vague or because a sentence is ambiguous, lawyers say that the statute must be interpreted, and they apply what they call "techniques of statutory construction." Most of the literature assumes that interpretation of a particular document is a

matter of discovering what its authors (the legislators, or the delegates to the constitutional convention) meant to say in using the words they did. But lawyers recognize that on many issues the author had no intention either way and that on others his intention cannot be discovered. Some lawyers take a more skeptical position. They say that whenever judges pretend they are discovering the intention behind some piece of legislation, this is only a smoke screen behind which the judges impose their own view of what the statute should have been.

Interpretation as a technique of legal analysis is less familiar in the case of the common law, but not unfamiliar. Suppose the Supreme Court of Illinois decided, several years ago, that a negligent driver who ran down a child was liable for the emotional damage suffered by the child's mother, who was standing next to the child on the road. Now an aunt sues another careless driver for emotional damage suffered when she heard, on the telephone many miles from the accident, that her niece had been hit. Does the aunt have a right to recover for that damage? Lawyers often say that this is a matter of interpreting the earlier decision correctly. Does the legal theory on which the earlier judge actually relied, in making his decision about the mother on the road, cover the aunt on the telephone? Once again skeptics point out that it is unlikely that the earlier judge had in mind any theory sufficiently developed so as to decide the aunt's case either way, so that a judge "interpreting" the earlier decision is actually making new law in the way he or she thinks best.

The idea of interpretation cannot serve as a general account of the nature or truth value of propositions of law, however, unless it is cut loose from these associations with speaker's meaning or intention. Otherwise it becomes simply one version of the positivist's thesis that propositions of law describe decisions taken by people or institutions in the past. If interpretation is to form the basis of a different and more plausible theory about propositions of law, then we must develop a more inclusive account of what interpretation is. But that means that lawyers must not treat legal interpretation as an activity *sui generis*. We must study interpretation as a general activity, as a mode of knowledge, by attending to other contexts of that activity.

Lawyers would do well to study literary and other forms of artistic interpretation. That might seem bad advice (choosing the fire over the frying pan) because critics themselves are thoroughly divided about what literary interpretation is, and the situation is hardly better in the other arts. But that is exactly why lawyers should study these debates. Not all of the battles within literary criticism are edifying or even comprehensible, but many more theories of interpretation have been defended in literature than in law, and these include theories which challenge the flat distinction between description and evaluation that has enfeebled legal theory.

LITERATURE

The Aesthetic Hypothesis

If lawyers are to benefit from a comparison between legal and literary interpretation, however, they must see the latter in a certain light, and in this section I shall try to say what that is. (I would prefer the following remarks about literature to be uncontroversial among literary scholars, but I am afraid they will not be.) Students of literature do many things under the titles of "interpretation" and "hermeneutics," and most of them are also called "discovering the meaning of a text." I shall not be interested, except incidentally, in one thing these students do, which is trying to discover the sense in which some author used a particular word or phrase. I am interested instead in arguments which offer some sort of interpretation of the meaning of a work as a whole. These sometimes take the form of assertions about characters: that Hamlet really loved his mother, for example, or that he really hated her, or that there really was no ghost but only Hamlet himself in a schizophrenic manifestation. Or about events in the story behind the story: that Hamlet and Ophelia were lovers before the play begins (or were not). More usually they offer hypotheses directly about the "point" or "theme" or "meaning" or "sense" or "tone" of the play as a whole: that *Hamlet* is a play about death, for example, or about generations, or about politics. These interpretive claims may have a practical point. They may guide a director staging a new performance of the play, for example. But they may also be of more general importance, helping us to an improved understanding of important parts of our cultural environment. Of course, difficulties about the speaker's meaning of a particular word in the text (a "crux" of interpretation) may bear upon these larger matters. But the latter are about the point or meaning of the work as a whole, rather than the sense of a particular phrase.

Critics much disagree about how to answer such questions. I want, so far as is possible, not to take sides but to try to capture the disagreements in some sufficiently general description of what they are disagreeing about. My apparently banal suggestion (which I shall call the "aesthetic hypothesis") is this: an interpretation of a piece of literature attempts to show which way of reading (or speaking or directing or acting) the text reveals it as the best work of art. Different theories or schools of traditions of interpretation disagree on this hypothesis, because they assume significantly different normative theories about what literature is and what it is for and about what makes one work of literature better than another.

I expect that this suggestion, in spite of its apparent weakness, will be rejected by many scholars as confusing interpretation with criticism or, in any case, as hopelessly relativistic, and therefore as a piece of skepticism that really denies the possibility of interpretation altogether. Indeed the aes-

thetic hypothesis might seem only another formulation of a theory now popular, which is that since interpretation creates a work of art and represents only the fiat of a particular critical community, there are only interpretations and no best interpretation of any particular poem or novel or play. But the aesthetic hypothesis is neither so wild nor so weak nor so inevitably relativistic as might first appear.

Interpretation of a text attempts to show *it* as the best work of art *it* can be, and the pronoun insists on the difference between explaining a work of art and changing it into a different one. Perhaps Shakespeare could have written a better play based on the sources he used for *Hamlet* than he did, and in that better play the hero would have been a more forceful man of action. It does not follow that *Hamlet*, the play he wrote, really is like that after all. Of course, a theory of interpretation must contain a subtheory about identity of a work of art in order to be able to tell the difference between interpreting and changing a work. (Any useful theory of identity will be controversial, so that this is one obvious way in which disagreements in interpretation will depend on more general disagreements in aesthetic theory.)

Contemporary theories of interpretation all seem to use, as part of their response to that requirement, the idea of a canonical text (or score, in the case of music, or unique physical object, in the case of most art). The text provides one severe constraint in the name of identity: all the words must be taken account of and none may be changed to make "it" a putatively better work of art. (This constraint, however familiar, is not inevitable. A joke, for example, may be the same joke though told in a variety of forms, none of them canonical; an interpretation of a joke will choose a particular way in which to put it, and this may be wholly original, in order to bring out its "real" point or why it is "really" funny.) So any literary critic's style of interpretation will be sensitive to his theoretical beliefs about the nature of and evidence for a canonical text.

An interpretive style will also be sensitive to the interpreter's opinions about coherence or integrity in art. An interpretation cannot make a work of art more distinguished if it makes a large part of the text irrelevant, or much of the incident accidental, or a great part of the trope or style unintegrated and answering only to independent standards of fine writing. So it does not follow, from the aesthetic hypothesis, that because a philosophical novel is aesthetically more valuable than a mystery story, an Agatha Christie novel is really a treatise on the meaning of death. This interpretation fails not only because an Agatha Christie, taken to be a tract on death, is a poor tract less valuable than a good mystery, but because the interpretation makes the novel a shambles. All but one or two sentences would be irrelevant to the supposed theme; and the organization, style, and figures would be appropriate not to a philosophical novel but to an entirely different

genre. Some books originally offered to the public as mysteries or thrillers (and perhaps thought of by their authors that way) have indeed been "reinterpreted" as something more ambitious. The present critical interest in Raymond Chandler is an example. But the fact that this reinterpretation can be successful in the case of Chandler, but not Christie, illustrates the constraint of integrity.

There is nevertheless room for much disagreement among critics about what counts as integration, about which sort of unity is desirable and which irrelevant or undesirable. Is it really an advantage that the tongue of the reader, in reading a poem aloud, must "mime" motions or directions that figure in the tropes or narrative of the poem? Does this improve integrity by adding yet another dimension of coordination? Is it an advantage when conjunctions and line endings are arranged so that the reader "negotiating" a poem develops contradictory assumptions and readings as he goes on, so that his understanding at the end is very different from what it was at discrete points along the way? Does this add another dimension of complexity to unity, or does it rather compromise unity because a work of literature should be capable of having the same meaning or import when read a second time? Schools of interpretation will rise or fall in response to these questions of aesthetic theory, which is what the aesthetic hypothesis suggests.

The major differences among schools of interpretation are less subtle, however, because they touch not these quasi-formal aspects of art but the function or point of art more broadly conceived. Does literature have (primarily or substantially) a cognitive point? Is art better when it is in some way instructive, when we learn something from it about how people are or what the world is like? If so and if psychoanalysis is true (please forgive that crude way of putting it), then a psychoanalytic interpretation of a piece of literature will show why it is successful art. Is art good insofar as it is successful communication in the ordinary sense? If so, then a good interpretation will focus on what the author intended, because communication is not successful unless it expresses what a speaker wants it to express. Or is art good when it is expressive in a different sense, insofar as it has the capacity to stimulate or inform the lives of those who experience it? If so, then interpretation will place the reader (or listener or viewer) in the foreground. It will point out the reading of the work that makes it most valuable—best as a work of art—in that way.

Theories of art do not exist in isolation from philosophy, psychology, sociology, and cosmology. Someone who accepts a religious point of view will probably have a different theory of art from someone who does not, and recent critical theories have made us see how far interpretive style is sensitive to beliefs about meaning, reference, and other technical issues in the philosophy of language. But the aesthetic hypothesis does not assume that

anyone who interprets literature will have a fully developed and self-conscious aesthetic theory. Nor that everyone who interprets must subscribe
entirely to one or another of the schools I crudely described. The best critics, I think, deny that there is one unique function or point of literature. A
novel or a play may be valuable in any number of ways, some of which we
learn by reading or looking or listening, rather than by abstract reflection
about what good art must be like or for.

Nevertheless, anyone who interprets a work of art relies on beliefs of a
theoretical character about identity and other formal properties of art, as
well as on more explicitly normative beliefs about what is good in art. *Both*
sorts of beliefs figure in the judgment that one way of reading a text makes it
a better text than another way. These beliefs may be inarticulate (or
"tacit"). They are still genuine beliefs (and not merely "reactions") because
their force for any critic or reader can be seen at work not just on one isolated occasion of interpretation but in any number of other occasions, and
because they figure in and are amenable to argument.[1] (These weak claims
do not take sides in the running debate whether there are any necessary or
sufficient "principles of value" in art or whether a theory of art could ever
justify an interpretation in the absence of direct experience of the work
being interpreted.)[2]

None of this touches the major complaint I anticipated against the aesthetic hypothesis: that it is trivial. Obviously (you might say) different interpretive styles are grounded in different theories of what art is and what it
is for and what makes art good art. The point is so banal that it might as
well be put the other way around: different theories of art are generated by
different theories of interpretation. If someone thinks stylistics are important to interpretation, he will think a work of art better because it integrates pronunciation and trope; if someone is attracted by deconstruction,
he will dismiss reference in its familiar sense from any prominent place in
an account of language. Nor does my elaboration of the hypothesis in any
way help to adjudicate among theories of interpretation or to rebut the
charge of nihilism or relativism. On the contrary, since people's views about
what makes art good art are inherently subjective, the aesthetic hypothesis
abandons hope of rescuing objectivity in interpretation except, perhaps,
among those who hold very much the same theory of art, which is hardly
very helpful.

No doubt the aesthetic hypothesis is in important ways banal—it must be
abstract if it is to provide an account of what a wide variety of theories disagree about—but it is perhaps not so weak as all that. The hypothesis has
the consequence that academic theories of interpretation are no longer seen
as what they often claim to be—analyses of the very idea of interpretation—but rather as candidates for the best answer to the substantive question posed by interpretation. Interpretation becomes a concept of which

different theories are competing conceptions. (It follows that there is no radical difference but only a difference in the level of abstraction between offering a theory of interpretation and offering an interpretation of a particular work of art.) The hypothesis denies, moreover, the sharp distinctions some scholars have cultivated. There is no longer a flat distinction between interpretation, conceived as discovering the real meaning of a work of art, and criticism, conceived as evaluating its success or importance. Some distinction remains, because there is always a difference between saying how good a particular work can be made to be and saying how good that is. But evaluative beliefs about art figure in both these judgments.

Objectivity is another matter. It is an open question, I think, whether the main judgments we make about art can properly be said to be true or false, valid or invalid. This question is part of the more general philosophical issue of objectivity, presently much discussed in both ethics and the philosophy of language, and no one is entitled to a position who studies the case of aesthetic judgment alone. Of course no important aesthetic claim can be "demonstrated" to be true or false; no argument can be produced for any interpretation which we can be sure will commend itself to everyone, or even everyone with experience and training in the appropriate form of art. If this is what it means to say that aesthetic judgments are subjective—that they are not demonstrable—then they are subjective. But it does not follow that no normative theory about art is better than any other, nor that one theory cannot be the best that has so far been produced.

The aesthetic hypothesis reverses (I think to its credit) a familiar strategy. E. D. Hirsch, for example, argues that only a theory like his can make interpretation objective and particular interpretations valid.[3] This seems to me a mistake on two connected grounds. Interpretation is an enterprise, a public institution, and it is wrong to assume, *a priori*, that the propositions central to any public enterprise must be capable of validity. It is also wrong to assume much about what validity in such enterprises must be like—whether validity requires the possibility of demonstrability, for example. It seems better to proceed more empirically here. We should first study a variety of activities in which people assume that they have good reasons for what they say, which they assume hold generally and not just from one or another individual point of view. We can then judge what standards people accept in practice for thinking that they have reasons of that kind.

Nor is the point about reversibility—that a theory of art may depend upon a theory of interpretation as much as vice versa—an argument against the aesthetic hypothesis. I am not defending any particular explanation of how people come to have either theories of interpretation or theories of art but only a claim about the argumentative connections that hold between these theories however come by. Of course even at the level of argument these two kinds of theories are mutually reinforcing. It is plainly a reason

for doubting any theory of what an object of art is, for example, that that theory generates an obviously silly theory of interpretation. My point is exactly that the connection is reciprocal, so that anyone called upon to defend a particular approach to interpretation would be forced to rely on more general aspects of a theory of art, whether he realizes it or not. And this may be true even though the opposite is, to some extent, true as well. It would be a mistake, I should add, to count this fact of mutual dependence as offering, in itself, any reason for skepticism or relativism about interpretation. This seems to be the burden of slogans like "interpretation creates the text," but there is no more immediate skeptical consequence in the idea that what we take to be a work of art must comport with what we take interpreting a work of art to be than in the analogous idea that what we take a physical object to be must sit well with our theories of knowledge; so long as we add, in both cases, that the connection holds the other way around as well.

Author's Intention

The chief test of the aesthetic hypothesis lies, however, not in its resistance to these various charges but in its explanatory and particularly its critical power. If we accept that theories of interpretation are not independent analyses of what it means to interpret something but are rather based in and dependent upon normative theories of art, then we must accept that they are vulnerable to complaints against the normative theory in which they are based. It does seem to me, for example, that the more doctrinaire authors' intention theories are vulnerable in this way. These theories must suppose, on the present hypothesis, that what is valuable in a work of art, what should lead us to value one work of art more than another, is limited to what the author in some narrow and constrained sense intended to put there. This claim presupposes, as I suggested earlier, a more general thesis that art must be understood as a form of speaker-audience communication; but even that doubtful thesis turns out, on further inspection, not to support it.

The intentionalists would object to these remarks. They would insist that their theory of interpretation is not an account of what is valuable in a book or poem or play but only an account of what any particular book or poem or play means, and that we must understand what something means before we can decide whether it is valuable and where its value lies. And they would object that they do not say that only intentions of the author "in some narrow and constrained sense" count in fixing the meaning of his work.

In the first of these objections, the author's intention theory presents itself not as the upshot of the aesthetic hypothesis—not as the best theory of interpretation within the design stipulated by that hypothesis—but rather as

a rival to it, a better theory about what kind of thing an interpretation is. But it is very difficult to understand the author's intention theory as any sort of rival to the present hypothesis. What question does it propose to answer better? Not, certainly, some question about the ordinary language or even technical meaning of the words "meaning" or "interpretation." An intentionalist cannot suppose that all his critics and those he criticizes mean, when they say "interpretation," the discovery of the author's intention. Nor can he think that his claims accurately describe what every member of the critical fraternity actually does under the title "interpretation." If that were so, then his strictures and polemics would be unnecessary. But if his theory is not semantic or empirical in these ways, what sort of a theory is it?

Suppose an intentionalist replies: "It points out an important issue about works of literature, namely, What did the author of the work intend it to be? This is plainly an important question, even if its importance is preliminary to other equally or more important questions about significance or value. It is, in fact, what most people for a long time have called 'interpretation.' But the name does not matter, so long as the activity is recognized as important and so long as it is understood that scholars are in principle capable of supplying objectively correct answers to the question it poses."

This reply comes to this: we can discover what an author intended (or at least come to probabilistic conclusions about this), and it is important to do so for other literary purposes. But why is it important? What other purposes? Any answer will assume that value or significance in art attaches primarily to what the author intended, just because it is what the author intended. Otherwise, why should we evaluate what this style of interpretation declares to be the work of art? But then the claim that interpretation in this style is important depends on a highly controversial, normative theory of art, not a neutral observation preliminary to any coherent evaluation. No plausible theory of interpretation holds that the intention of the author is always irrelevant. Sometimes it is plainly the heart of the matter, as when some issue turns on what Shakespeare meant by "hawk" as distinguished from "handsaw." But it is nevertheless controversial that we must know whether Shakespeare thought Hamlet was sane or a madman pretending to be mad in order to decide how good a play he wrote. The intentionalist thinks that we do, and that is exactly why his theory of interpretation is not a rival to the aesthetic hypothesis but rather a suitor for the crown that hypothesis holds out.

The second objection to my charge against author's intention theories may prove to be more interesting. Intentionalists make the author's state of mind central to interpretation. But they misunderstand, so far as I can tell, certain complexities in that state of mind; in particular they fail to appreciate how intentions *for* a work and beliefs *about* it interact. I have in mind an

experience familiar to anyone who creates anything, of suddenly seeing something "in" it that he did not previously know was there. This is sometimes (though I think not very well) expressed in the author's cliché, that his characters seem to have minds of their own. John Fowles provides an example from popular fiction.

> When Charles left Sarah on her cliff edge, I ordered him to walk straight back to Lyme Regis. But he did not; he gratuitously turned and went down to the Dairy. Oh, but you say, come on—what I really mean is that the idea crossed my mind as I wrote that it might be more clever to have him stop and drink milk . . . and meet Sarah again. That is certainly one explanation of what happened; but I can only report—and I am the most reliable witness—that the idea seemed to me to come clearly from Charles, not myself. It is not only that he has begun to gain an autonomy; I must respect it, and disrespect all my quasi-divine plans for him, if I wish him to be real.[4]

Fowles changed his mind about how the story in *The French Lieutenant's Woman* "really" goes in the midst of writing it, if we are to credit this description. But he might also have changed his mind about some aspect of the novel's "point" years later, as he is rumored to have done after seeing the film made from his book. He might have come to see Sarah's motives very differently after reading Harold Pinter's screenplay or watching Meryl Streep play her: Pinter and Streep were interpreting the novel, and one or both of their interpretations might have led Fowles to change *his* interpretation once again. Perhaps I am wrong in supposing that this sort of thing happens often. But it happens often enough, and it is important to be clear about what it is that happens.

The intentionalist wants us to choose between two possibilities. Either the author suddenly realizes that he had a "subconscious intention" earlier, which he only now discovers, or he has changed his intention later. Neither of these explanations is at all satisfactory. The subconscious is in danger of becoming phlogiston here, unless we suppose some independent evidence, apart from the author's new view of his work, to suggest that he had an earlier subconscious intention. I do not mean that features of a work of art of which an author is unaware must be random accidents. On the contrary. If a novel is both more interesting and more coherent if we assume the characters have motives different from those the novelist thought of when he wrote (or if a poet's tropes and style tend to reinforce his theme in ways he did not appreciate at the time), the cause of this must in some way lie in the artist's talent. There are unsolved mysteries in the psychology of creation, but the supposition of subconscious *intentions,* unsupported by other evidence of the sort a psychoanalyst would insist on, solves no mysteries and provides no explanation. This is not crucial to the point, however, because whether or not Fowles had a subconscious intention to make Charles or Sarah different characters from the "quasi-divine plan" he thought he had,

his later decisions and beliefs neither consist in nor are based on any discovery of that earlier intention. They are produced by confronting not his earlier self but the work he has produced.

Nor is any new belief Fowles forms about his characters properly called (as in the intentionalist's second suggestion) a new and discrete intention. It is not an intention about what sort of characters to create because it is a belief about what sort of characters he has created; and it is not an intention about how others should understand the book, though it may or may not include an expectation of that sort. Fowles changed his view in the course of writing his book, but he changed it, as he insists, by confronting the text he had already written, by treating its characters as real in the sense of detachable from his own antecedent designs, in short, by interpreting it, and not by exploring the subconscious depths of some previous plan or finding that he had a new plan. If it is true that he changed his mind again, after seeing the film, then this was, once again, not a retrospective new intention or a rediscovered old one. It was another interpretation.

An author is capable of detaching what he has written from his earlier intentions and beliefs, of treating it as an object in itself. He is capable of reaching fresh conclusions about his work grounded in aesthetic judgments: that his book is both more coherent and a better analysis of more important themes read in a somewhat different way from what he thought when he was writing it. This is, I think, a very important fact for a number of reasons; but I want, for my present purpose, only to emphasize one. Any full description of what Fowles "intended" when he set out to write *The French Lieutenant's Woman* must include the intention to produce something capable of being treated that way, by himself and therefore by others, and so must include the intention to create something independent of his intentions. I quote Fowles once again, and again as a witness rather than for his metaphysics: "Only one reason is shared by all of us [novelists]: *we wish to create worlds as real as, but other than, the world that is.* Or was. That is why we cannot plan. . . . We also know that a genuinely created world must be independent of its creator."

I suspect that regarding something one has produced as a novel or poem or painting, rather than a set of propositions or marks, *depends* on regarding it as something that can be detached and interpreted in the sense I described. In any case this is characteristically how authors themselves regard what they have done. The intentions of authors are not simply conjunctive, like the intentions of someone who goes to market with a shopping list, but structured, so that the more concrete of these intentions, like intentions about the motives of a particular character in a novel, are contingent on interpretive beliefs whose soundness varies with what is produced and which might be radically altered from time to time.

We can, perhaps, isolate the full set of interpretive beliefs an author has

at a particular moment (say at the moment he sends final galleys to the printer) and solemnly declare that these beliefs, in their full concreteness, fix what the novel is or means. (These beliefs would inevitably be incomplete, but that is another matter.) But even if we (wrongly) call this particular set of beliefs "intentions," we are, in choosing them, ignoring another kind or level of intention, which is the intention to create a work whose nature or meaning is not fixed in this way, because it is a work of art. That is why the author's intention school, as I understand it, makes the value of a work of art turn on a narrow and constrained view of the intentions of the author.

LAW AND LITERATURE

The Chain of Law

These sketchy remarks about literary interpretation may have suggested too sharp a distinction between the role of the artist in creating a work of art and that of the critic in interpreting it later. The artist can create nothing without interpreting as he creates; since he intends to produce art, he must have at least a tacit theory of why what he produces is art and why it is a better work of art through this stroke of the pen or the brush or the chisel rather than that. The critic, for his part, creates as he interprets; for though he is bound by the fact of the work, defined in the more formal and academic parts of his theory of art, his more practical artistic sense is engaged by his responsibility to decide which way of seeing or reading or understanding that work shows it as better art. Nevertheless, there is a difference between interpreting while creating and creating while interpreting, and therefore a recognizable difference between the artist and the critic.

I want to use literary interpretation as a model for the central method of legal analysis, and I therefore need to show how even this distinction between artist and critic might be eroded in certain circumstances. Suppose that a group of novelists is engaged for a particular project and that they draw lots to determine the order of play. The lowest number writes the opening chapter of a novel, which he or she then sends to the next number, who adds a chapter, with the understanding that he is adding a chapter to that novel rather than beginning a new one, and then sends the two chapters to the next number, and so on. Now every novelist but the first has the dual responsibilities of interpreting and creating because each must read all that has gone before in order to establish, in the interpretivist sense, what the novel so far created is.[5] He or she must decide what the characters are "really" like; what motives guide them; what the point or theme of the developing novel is; how far some literary device or figure, consciously or unconsciously used, contributes to these, and whether it should be extended or refined or trimmed or dropped in order to send the novel further in one di-

rection rather than another. This must be interpretation in a non-intention-bound style because, at least for all novelists after the second, there is no single author whose intentions any interpreter can, by the rules of the project, regard as decisive.

Some novels have in fact been written in this way (including the softcore pornographic novel *Naked Came the Stranger*), though for a debunking purpose; and certain parlor games, for rainy weekends in English country houses, have something of the same structure. But in my imaginary exercise the novelists are expected to take their responsibilities seriously and to recognize the duty to create, so far as they can, a single, unified novel rather than, for example, a series of independent short stories with characters bearing the same names. Perhaps this is an impossible assignment; perhaps the project is doomed to produce not just a bad novel but no novel at all, because the best theory of art requires a single creator or, if more than one, that each have some control over the whole. But what about legends and jokes? I need not push that question further because I am interested only in the fact that the assignment makes sense, that each of the novelists in the chain can have some idea of what he or she is asked to do, whatever misgivings each might have about the value or character of what will then be produced.

Deciding hard cases at law is rather like this strange literary exercise. The similarity is most evident when judges consider and decide common law cases; that is, when no statute figures centrally in the legal issue, and the argument turns on which rules or principles of law "underlie" the related decisions of other judges in the past. Each judge is then like a novelist in the chain. He or she must read through what other judges in the past have written not only to discover what these judges have said, or their state of mind when they said it, but to reach an opinion about what these judges have collectively *done*, in the way that each of our novelists formed an opinion about the collective novel so far written. Any judge forced to decide a lawsuit will find, if he looks in the appropriate books, records of many arguably similar cases decided over decades or even centuries past by many other judges of different styles and judicial and political philosophies, in periods of different orthodoxies of procedure and judicial convention. Each judge must regard himself, in deciding the new case before him, as a partner in a complex chain enterprise of which these innumerable decisions, structures, conventions, and practices are the history; it is his job to continue that history into the future through what he does on the day. He *must* interpret what has gone before because he has a responsibility to advance the enterprise in hand rather than strike out in some new direction of his own. So he must determine, according to his own judgment, what the earlier decisions come to, what the point or theme of the practice so far, taken as a whole, really is.

The judge in the hypothetical case I described earlier, about an aunt's

emotional shock, must decide what the theme is not only of the particular precedent of the mother in the road but of accident cases, including that precedent, as a whole. He might be forced to choose, for example, between these two theories about the "meaning" of that chain of decisions. According to the first, negligent drivers are responsible to those whom their behavior is likely to cause physical harm, but they are responsible to these people for whatever injury—physical or emotional—they in fact cause. If this is the correct principle, then the decisive difference between that case and the aunt's case is just that the aunt was not within the physical risk, and therefore she cannot recover. On the second theory, however, negligent drivers are responsible for any damage they can reasonably be expected to foresee if they think about their behavior in advance. If that is the right principle, then the aunt may yet recover. Everything turns on whether it is sufficiently foreseeable that a child will have relatives, beyond his or her immediate parents, who may suffer emotional shock when they learn of the child's injury. The judge trying the aunt's case must decide which of these two principles represents the better "reading" of the chain of decisions he must continue.

Can we say, in some general way, what those who disagree about the best interpretation of legal precedent are disagreeing about? I said that a literary interpretation aims to show how the work in question can be seen as the most valuable work of art, and so must attend to formal features of identity, coherence, and integrity as well as more substantive considerations of artistic value. A plausible interpretation of legal practice must also, in a parallel way, satisfy a test of two dimensions: it must both fit that practice and show its point or value. But point or value here cannot mean artistic value because law, unlike literature, is not an artistic enterprise. Law is a political enterprise, whose general point, if it has one, lies in coordinating social and individual effort, or resolving social and individual disputes, or securing justice between citizens and between them and their government, or some combination of these. (This characterization is itself an interpretation, of course, but allowable now because relatively neutral.) So an interpretation of any body or division of law, like the law of accidents, must show the value of that body of law in political terms by demonstrating the best principle or policy it can be taken to serve.

We know from the parallel argument in literature that this general description of interpretation in law is not license for each judge to find in doctrinal history whatever he thinks should have been there. The same distinction holds between interpretation and ideal. A judge's duty is to interpret the legal history he finds, not to invent a better history. The dimensions of fit will provide some boundaries. There is, of course, no algorithm for deciding whether a particular interpretation sufficiently fits that history not to be ruled out. When a statute or constitution or other legal document is part of the doctrinal history, speaker's meaning will play a role. But the

choice of which of several crucially different senses of speaker's or legislator's intention is the appropriate one cannot itself be referred to anyone's intention but must be decided, by whoever must make the decision, as a question of political theory.[6] In the common law cases the question of fit is more complex. Any particular hypothesis about the point of a string of decisions ("these decisions establish the principle that no one can recover for emotional damage who did not lie within the area of physical danger himself") is likely to encounter if not flat counter-examples in some earlier case at least language or argument that seems to suggest the contrary. So any useful conception of interpretation must contain a doctrine of mistake—as must any novelist's theory of interpretation for the chain novel. Sometimes a legal argument will explicitly recognize such mistakes: "Insofar as the cases of *A v. B* and *C v. D* may have held to the contrary, they were, we believe, wrongly decided and need not be followed here." Sometimes the doctrine of precedent forbids this crude approach and requires something like: "We held, in *E v. F*, that such-and-such, but that case raised special issues and must, we think, be confined to its own facts" which is not quite so disingenuous as it might seem).

This flexibility may seem to erode the difference on which I insist, between interpretation and a fresh, clean-slate decision about what the law ought to be. But there is nevertheless this overriding constraint. Any judge's sense of the point or function of law, on which every aspect of his approach to interpretation will depend, will include or imply some conception of the integrity and coherence of law as an institution, and this conception will both tutor and constrain his working theory of fit—that is, his convictions about how much of the prior law an interpretation must fit, and which of it, and how. (The parallel with literary interpretation holds here as well.)

It should be apparent, however, that any particular judge's theory of fit will often fail to produce a unique interpretation. (The distinction between hard and easy cases at law is perhaps just the distinction betweeen cases in which they do and do not.) Just as two readings of a poem may each find sufficient support in the text to show its unity and coherence, two principles may each find enough support in the various decisions of the past to satisfy any plausible theory of fit. In that case substantive political theory (like substantive considerations of artistic merit) will play a decisive role. Put bluntly, the interpretation of accident law, that a careless driver is liable to those whose damage is both substantial and foreseeable, is probably a better interpretation, if it is, only because it states a sounder principle of justice than any principle that distinguishes between physical and emotional damage or that makes recovery for emotional damage depend on whether the plaintiff was in danger of physical damage. (I should add that this issue, as an issue of political morality, is very complex, and many distinguished judges and lawyers have taken each side.)

We might summarize these points this way. Judges develop a particular

approach to legal interpretation by forming and refining a political theory
sensitive to those issues on which interpretation in particular cases will depend; and they call this their legal philosophy. It will include both structural features, elaborating the general requirement that an interpretation
must fit doctrinal history, and substantive claims about social goals and
principles of justice. Any judge's opinion about the best interpretation will
therefore be the consequence of beliefs other judges need not share. If a
judge believes that the dominant purpose of a legal system, the main goal it
ought to serve, is economic, then he will see in past accident decisions some
strategy for reducing the economic costs of accidents overall. Other judges,
who find any such picture of the law's function distasteful, will discover no
such strategy in history but only, perhaps, an attempt to reinforce conventional morality of fault and responsibility. If we insist on a high order of
neutrality in our description of legal interpretation, therefore, we cannot
make our description of the nature of legal interpretation much more concrete than I have.

Author's Intention in Law

I want instead to consider various objections that might be made not to the
detail of my argument but to the main thesis, that interpretation in law is
essentially political. I shall not spend further time on the general objection
already noticed: that this view of law makes it irreducibly and irredeemably
subjective, just a matter of what particular judges think best or what they
had for breakfast. For some lawyers and legal scholars this is not an objection at all, but only the beginnings of skeptical wisdom about law. But it is
the nerve of my argument that the flat distinction between description and
evaluation on which this skepticism relies—the distinction between finding
the law just "there" in history and making it up wholesale—is misplaced
here, because interpretation is something different from both.

I shall want, therefore, to repeat the various observations I made about
subjectivity and objectivity in literary interpretation. There is no obvious
reason in the account I gave of legal interpretation to doubt that one interpretation of law can be better than another and that one can be best of all.
Whether this is so depends on general issues of philosophy not peculiar to
law any more than to literature; and we would do well, in considering these
general issues, not to begin with any fixed ideas about the necessary and sufficient conditions of objectivity (for example, that no theory of law can be
sound unless it is demonstrably sound, unless it would wring assent from a
stone). In the meantime, we can sensibly aim to develop various levels of a
conception of law for ourselves, to find the interpretation of a complex and
dramatically important practice which seems to us at once the right kind of
interpretation for law and right as that kind of interpretation.

I shall consider one further, and rather different, objection in more detail: that my political hypothesis about legal interpretation, like the aesthetic hypothesis about artistic interpretation, fails to give an adequate place to author's intention. It fails to see that interpretation in law is simply a matter of discovering what various actors in the legal process—constitutional delegates, members of Congress and state legislatures, judges and executive officials—intended. Once again it is important to see what is at stake here. The political hypothesis makes room for the author's intention argument as a conception of interpretation, a conception which claims that the best political theory gives the intentions of legislators and past judges a decisive role in interpretation. Seen this way, the author's intention theory does not challenge the political hypothesis but contests for its authority. If the present objection is really an objection to the argument so far, therefore, its claim must be understood differently, as proposing, for example, that very "meaning" of interpretation in law requires that only these officials' intentions should count or that at least there is a firm consensus among lawyers to that effect. Both of these claims are as silly as the parallel claims about the idea or the practice of interpretation in art.

Suppose, therefore, that we do take the author's intention theory, more sensibly, as a conception rather than an explication of the concept of legal interpretation. The theory seems on firmest ground, as I suggested earlier, when interpretation is interpretation of a canonical legal text, like a clause of the Constitution, or a section of a statute, or a provision of a contract or will. But just as we noticed that a novelist's intention is complex and structured in ways that embarrass any simple author's intention theory in literature, we must now notice that a legislator's intention is complex in similar ways. Suppose a delegate to a constitutional convention votes for a clause guaranteeing equality of treatment, without regard to race, in matters touching people's fundamental interests; but he thinks that education is not a matter of fundamental interest and so does not believe that the clause makes racially segregated schools unconstitutional. We may sensibly distinguish an abstract and a concrete intention here: the delegate intends to prohibit discrimination in whatever in fact is of fundamental interest and also intends not to prohibit segregated schools. These are not isolated, discrete intentions; our descriptions, we might say, describe the same intention in different ways. But it matters very much which description a theory of legislative intention accepts as canonical. If we accept the first description, then a judge who wishes to follow the delegate's intentions, but who believes that educaton is a matter of fundamental interest, will hold segregation unconstitutional. If we accept the second, he will not. The choice between the two descriptions cannot be made by any further reflection about what an intention really is. It must be made by deciding that one rather than the other description is more appropriate in virtue of the best

theory of representative democracy or on some other openly political grounds. (I might add that no compelling argument has yet been produced, so far as I am aware, in favor of deferring to a delegate's more concrete intentions, and that this is of major importance in arguments about whether the "original intention" of the Framers requires abolishing, for example, racial discrimination or capital punishment.)

When we consider the common law problems of interpretation, the author's intention theory shows in an even poorer light. The problems are not merely evidentiary. Perhaps we can discover what was "in the mind" of all the judges who decided cases about accidents at one time or another in our legal history. We might also discover (or speculate) about the psychodynamic or economic or social explanations of why each judge thought what he or she did. No doubt the result of all this research (or speculation) would be a mass of psychological data essentially different for each of the past judges included in the study, and order could be brought into the mass, if at all, only through statistical summaries about which proportion of judges in which historical period probably held which opinion and was more or less subject to which influence. But this mass, even tamed by statistical summary, would be of no more help to the judge trying to answer the question of what the prior decisions, taken as a whole, really come to than the parallel information would be to one of our chain novelists trying to decide what novel the novelists earlier in the chain had collectively written. That judgment, in each case, requires a fresh exercise of interpretation which is neither brute historical research nor a clean-slate expression of how things ideally ought to be.

A judge who believed in the importance of discerning an author's intention might try to escape these problems by selecting one particular judge or a small group of judges in the past (say, the judges who decided the most recent case something like his or the case he thinks closest to his) and asking what rule that judge or group intended to lay down for the future. This would treat the particular earlier judges as legislators and so invite all the problems of statutory interpretation including the very serious problem we just noticed. Even so it would not escape the special problems of common law adjudication after all, because the judge who applied this theory of interpretation would have to suppose himself entitled to look only to the intentions of the particular earlier judge or judges he had selected, and he could not suppose this unless he thought that it was the upshot of judicial practice as a whole (and not just the intentions of some *other* selected earlier judge) that this is what judges in his position should do.

POLITICS IN INTERPRETATION

If my claims about the role of politics in legal interpretation are sound, then we should expect to find distinctly liberal or radical or conservative opin-

ions not only about what the Constitution and laws of our nation should be but also about what they are. And this is exactly what we do find. Interpretation of the equal protection clause of the United States Constitution provides especially vivid examples. There can be no useful interpretation of what that clause means which is independent of some theory about what political equality is and how far equality is required by justice, and the history of the last half-century of constitutional law is largely an exploration of exactly these issues of political morality. Conservative lawyers argued steadily (though not consistently) in favor of an author's intentions style of interpreting this clause, and they accused others, who used a different style with more egalitarian results, of inventing rather than interpreting law. But this was bluster meant to hide the role their own political convictions played in their choice of interpretive style, and the great legal debates over the equal protection clause would have been more illuminating if it had been more widely recognized that reliance on political theory is not a corruption of interpretation but part of what interpretation means.

Should politics play any comparable role in literary and other artistic interpretation? We have become used to the idea of the politics of interpretation. Stanley Fish, particularly, has promoted a theory of interpretation which supposes that contests between rival schools of literary interpretation are more political than argumentative: rival professoriates in search of dominion.[7] And of course it is a truism of the sociology of literature, and not merely of the Marxist contribution to that discipline, that fashion in interpretation is sensitive to and expresses more general political and economic structures. These important claims are external: they touch the causes of the rise of this or that approach to literature and interpretation.

Several of the papers delivered at the conference for which this essay was first prepared discuss these issues.[8] But we are now concerned with the internal question, about politics in rather than the politics of interpretation. How far can principles of political morality actually count as arguments for a particular interpretation of a particular work or for a general approach to artistic interpretation? There are many possibilities and many of them are parasitic on claims developed or mentioned in these essays. It was said that our commitment to feminism, or our fidelity to nation, or our dissatisfaction with the rise of the New Right ought to influence our evaluation and appreciation of literature. Indeed it was the general (though not unanimous) sense of the conference that professional criticism must be faulted for its inattention to such political issues. But if our convictions about these particular political issues count in deciding how good some novel or play or poem is, then they must also count in deciding, among particular interpretations of these works, which is the best interpretation. Or so they must if my argument is sound.

We might also explore a more indirect connection between aesthetic and political theory. Any comprehensive theory of art is likely to have, at its

center, some epistemological thesis, some set of views about the relations that hold among experience, self-consciousness, and the perception or formation of values. If it assigns self-discovery any role in art, it will need a theory of personal identity adequate to mark off the boundaries of a person from his or her circumstances, and from other persons, or at least to deny the reality of any such boundaries. It seems likely that any comprehensive theory of social justice will also have roots in convictions about these or very closely related issues. Liberalism, for example, which assigns great importance to autonomy, may depend upon a particular picture of the role that judgments of value play in people's lives; it may depend on the thesis that people's convictions about value are beliefs, open to argument and review, rather than simply the givens of personality, fixed by genetic and social causes. And any political theory which gives an important place to equality also requires assumptions about the boundaries of persons, because it must distinguish between treating people as equals and changing them into different people.

It may be a sensible project, at least, to inquire whether there are not particular philosophical bases shared by particular aesthetic and particular political theories so that we can properly speak of a liberal or Marxist or perfectionist or totalitarian aesthetics, for example, in that sense. Common questions and problems hardly guarantee this, of course. It would be necessary to see, for example, whether liberalism can indeed be traced, as many philosophers have supposed, back into a discrete epistemological base, different from that of other political theories, and then ask whether that discrete base could be carried forward into aesthetic theory and there yield a distinctive interpretive style. I have no good idea that this project could be successful; I only report my sense that politics, art, and law are united, somehow, in philosophy.

SEVEN

On Interpretation and Objectivity

TWO OBJECTIONS

I have been engaged in a running discussion about Chapter 6, "How Law Is Like Literature," since it was first published.[1] I shall use this essay to add some comments inspired by that discussion. One reader of the original essay, at least, thought that in spite of my many disclaimers, I was committed to a silly metaphysical theory of interpretation, according to which meanings are "just there" in the universe, literary genres are "self-announcing," texts act as a "self-executing constraint" on any interpretation, and interpretation is therefore the discovery of brute, noninterpretive, and recalcitrant facts. Of course I never said any of these things, and denied them all, but I was supposed nevertheless to be committed to them by what I did say. For I did say, among other things, that interpreting was different from inventing, and that certain interpretations of an Agatha Christie mystery would be wrong because they would make a shambles of her novel. According to the argument I am now reporting, these propositions presuppose the silly "just there," view I said I reject.

That, I believe, is a serious confusion worth taking some care to repair. It rests on a mistaken assumption about the *sense* of interpretive claims, that is, about what people mean when they endorse or reject a particular interpretation of a character or a play or a line of precedent cases at law. It assumes that people who make interpretive judgments think that the meanings they report are "just given" in the universe as a hard fact everyone can see and must acknowledge. But it is a question of semantics whether this is true—whether this is what people think when they make interpretive claims—and when we look twice we discover that it is not, for the following decisive reason. People who make these judgments do not believe any of this nonsense about brute facts (I doubt there is anything there to believe), and yet they continue to make and argue about their interpretive claims in a critical and judgmental way, supposing that some claims are better than others, that some are right and others wrong.

My essay was an attempt to improve on the mistaken "just there" theory of the sense of interpretive judgments. We can make sense of interpretive claims and arguments about literature only if we stop treating them as doomed attempts to report ontologically independent meanings scattered among the furniture of the universe. We should understand them, instead, as special and complex aesthetic claims about what makes a particular work of art a better work of art. Interpretive claims are interpretive, that is, and so dependent on aesthetic or political theory all the way down. But that means, as I took pains to emphasize, that the distinction between interpreting and inventing is itself the product of an interpretive judgment, because we have to rely on one kind of interpretive conviction or instinct—about which readings would destroy the artistic integrity of a text—in order to set aside as ineligible readings that, if they were eligible, would make the work very good indeed. We need that dimension of interpretive judgment in order to explain why, for example, we do not think (as most of us do not) that a meaning-of-death interpretation is a good interpretation of a Christie mystery, even though we do think the meaning of death is a noble theme.

So the complaint that my essay contemplates "just there" meanings is a comprehensive misunderstanding. My substitute account of the sense of interpretive judgments, however, might provoke two very different and much more important objections. The first is this: interpretation, on my account, really is no different from invention. The distinction between these two activities presupposes that in the case of interpretation a text exercises some *constraint* on the result. But on my account the text itself is the product of interpretive judgments. There can be no more constraint in that story than in Wittgenstein's example of the man who doubted what he read in the newspaper and bought another copy to check it.

The second objection is even more fundamental. It insists that an interpretation, on my account, cannot really be true or false, good or bad, because I make the soundness of an interpretation turn on the question of which reading of a poem or novel or series of cases makes it best aesthetically or politically, and there can be no objective "fact of the matter" about a judgment of that sort, but only different "subjective" reactions. This objection presupposes an argument familiar to students of moral philosophy, which is sometimes called the argument from diversity. People disagree about aesthetic value, and so about which works of art are better than others. They disagree about justice and other political virtues, and so about which political decisions are better and which worse. These are not disagreements one side can win by some knockdown argument everyone must accept. So people continue to disagree, even when argument has been exhausted. In these circumstances, according to the second objection, no one can sensibly think that his own views about the best interpretation are "really" true. So my recommendations, about how chain novelists and

judges ought to make their decisions, advise them to act on beliefs that are absurd.

THEORY DEPENDENCE

Is the first objection right? It declares that if all parts of an interpretation are theory-dependent in the way I say they are, then there can be no difference between interpreting and inventing because the text can exercise only an illusory constraint over the result. I anticipated this objection in my argument that interpretive convictions can act as checks *on one another* in the way necessary to avoid this circularity and give bite to interpretive claims. I divided interpretive convictions into two groups—convictions about form and about substance—and suggested that in spite of the obvious interactions these two groups were nevertheless sufficiently disjoint to allow the former to constrain the latter in the way I used the chain novel example to suggest.

The first objection might challenge my argument at wholesale or retail. It might deny the very possibility that different parts of a general theoretical structure could ever act as constraints of checks on one another. Or it might accept this possibility but deny its application to the case of literary or legal interpretation. If the challenge is wholesale, denying the possibility of internal theoretical constraint, it contradicts an important theme in contemporary philosophy of science. For it is a familiar thesis in that discipline that none of the beliefs we have, about the world and what is in it, is forced upon us by a theory-independent recalcitrant reality; that we have the beliefs we do only in consequence of having accepted some particular theoretical structure. According to one prominent version of this view, the entire body of our convictions about logic, mathematics, physics, and the rest confronts experience together, as one interdependent system, and there is no part of this system which could not, in principle, be revised and abandoned if we were willing and able to revise and adjust the rest. If we held very different beliefs about the theoretical parts of physics and the other sciences, we would, in consequence, divide the world into very different entities, and the facts we "encountered" about these different entities would be very different from the facts we now take to be unassailable.

Now suppose we accepted this general view of knowledge and drew from it the startling conclusion that discrete scientific hypotheses cannot be tested against facts at all, because once a theory has been adopted there are no wholly independent facts against which to test that theory. We would have misunderstood the philosophical thesis we meant to apply. For the point of that thesis is not to deny that facts constrain theories but to explain how they do. There is no paradox in the proposition that facts both depend on and constrain the theories that explain them. On the contrary, that prop-

osition is an essential part of the picture of knowledge just described, as a complex and interrelated set of beliefs confronting experience as a coherent whole.

So the first objection is more striking if we read it to challenge, not the overall possibility of theory-dependent knowledge, but its possibility in the case of literature and art. Facts check theories in science because the over-all theoretical apparatus of science is complex enough to allow internal tensions, checks, and balances. This would be impossible if there were no functional distinctions within the system of scientific knowledge among various kinds and levels of belief. If we did not have special and discrete opinions about what counts as an observation, for example, we could not disprove established theories by fresh observations. The first objection should be read as complaining that our interpretive systems are in this way much less complex than our scientific systems, that the former lack the requisite internal structure to allow the internal constraint that is a feature of the latter.

It is, I think, an insight that the distinction between judgment and taste often turns on the complexity or simplicity of theoretical apparatus. It would be silly to claim that our preferences for chocolate over vanilla, for example, were judgments constrained by facts about the ice cream itself. The obvious "subjectivity" of this kind of taste is often taken as an opening wedge for general aesthetic and even moral skepticism. But it is easy enough to explain the ice cream case in a way that distinguishes rather than implicates more complex judgments. Ice cream opinions are not sufficiently interconnected with and dependent upon other beliefs and attitudes to allow a taste for chocolate, once formed, to conflict with anything else. So the question raised by the first objection, taken in the more interesting way, can be stated bluntly: are interpretive claims of the sort critics and lawyers make more like scientific claims, in this respect, or more like tastes in ice cream? Do they have or lack the necessary structure to permit a useful degree of internal constraint?

"How Law Is Like Literature" tried to show that they do have the necessary structure, and there is no point in repeating my arguments. I emphasized the difference between what I called convictions about integrity, pertinent to the dimensions of fit, and convictions about artistic merit, pertinent to the dimensions of value. I tried to show how each interpreter finds, in the interaction between these two sets of attitudes and beliefs, not only constraints and standards for interpretation but the essential circumstance of that activity, the grounds of his capacity to give discrete sense to interpretive judgments. It is true that these two departments of interpretive convictions are not wholly insulated from one another; my claim is rather that they are, for each person, sufficiently insulated to give friction and therefore sense to anyone's interpretive analysis. It is a further question how

far interpretive convictions of either sort are—or must be—shared within a community of people who talk and argue about interpretation among themselves. Some overlap is certainly necessary in order for one person even to understand another's judgment as interpretive; but it would be a mistake to think that the overlap must be even so complete as it is in ordinary science. For we know that it is not, among us, anywhere near so complete, and we seem to have succeeded in giving sense to both agreement and disagreement about interpretation. I do not mean this last remark to be facetious. In the end we can make no better answer, to the first objection, than to point to our own practices of interpretation. For we could have no reason to accept a test, for what is necessary to give interpretation sense, that our own practices would not pass, until of course we had some other reason to disown them.

OBJECTIVITY

My interest in the question of objectivity raised by the second objection I described is entirely negative. I see no point in trying to find some general argument that moral or political or legal or aesthetic or interpretive judgments *are* objective. Those who ask for an argument of that sort want something different from the kind of arguments I and they would make for particular examples or instances of such judgments. But I do not see how there could be any such different arguments. I have no arguments for the objectivity of moral judgments except moral arguments, no arguments for the objectivity of interpretive judgments except interpretive arguments, and so forth.

I believe, for example, that slavery is unjust in the circumstances of the modern world. I think I have arguments for this view, though I know that if these arguments were challenged I would in the end have to rest on convictions for which I had no further direct argument. I say "I think" I have arguments not because I am worried about the philosophical standing of the arguments I have but because I know that others have taken a contrary view, that I might not be able to convince them, and that they might, in fact, be able to convince me if I gave them a decent opportunity to do so. But now suppose someone, having heard my arguments, asks me whether I have any different arguments for the further view that slavery is objectively or really unjust. I know that I do not because, so far as I can tell, it is not a further claim at all but just the same claim put in a slightly more emphatic form.

Of course someone might stipulate a sense for the word "objectively" that would make the "further" proposition really different. He might say that the further question, about whether slavery is objectively unjust, asks whether everyone agrees that it is, for example, or would agree under fa-

vorable conditions for reflection. In that case I would say that I do not believe slavery is objectively unjust. But this would in no way affect or qualify my original judgment, that slavery is unjust. I never thought everyone did or would agree.

So I have no interest in trying to compose a general defense of the objectivity of my interpretive or legal or moral opinions. In fact, I think that the whole issue of objectivity, which so dominates contemporary theory in these areas, is a kind of fake. We should stick to our knitting. We should account to ourselves for our own convictions as best we can, standing ready to abandon those that do not survive reflective inspection. We should make such arguments to others, who do not share our opinions, as we can make in good faith and break off arguing when no further argument is appropriate. I do not mean that this is all we can do because we are creatures with limited access to true reality or with necessarily parochial viewpoints. I mean that we can give no sense to the idea that there is anything else we could do in deciding whether our judgments are "really" true. If some argument should persuade me that my views about slavery are not really true, then it should also persuade me to abandon my views about slavery. And if no argument could persuade me that slavery is not unjust, no argument could persuade me that it is not "really" unjust.

But I am not allowed to turn my back on the problem of objectivity in the way I would like, and Fish's essay shows why not. People like Fish say there is something radically wrong with what I and others think about law and morality and literature. Our arguments assume, they say, that judgments in these enterprises can be objectively right and wrong, but in fact they cannot be. Since I take the view I do about what the claim of objectivity in these disciplines can mean, I am tempted to reply by arguing in favor of the judgments they say cannot be objective. I want to meet the claim that moral judgments cannot be objective by repeating my arguments why slavery is unjust, for example. But they do not mean their arguments to be taken in this spirit. A moral philosopher who denies that slavery can be really or objectively unjust does not wish to be understood as holding the same position as a fascist who argues that there is nothing wrong with slavery. He insists that his arguments are not moral arguments at all but philosophical arguments of a very different character to which I must respond in a very different way.

I cannot do this, however, until I understand the difference between the proposition that slavery is unjust, which the fascist denies, and the proposition that slavery is really or objectively unjust, which the skeptical philosopher denies. The philosopher says: the latter proposition is different because it claims that the injustice of slavery is part of the furniture of the universe, that it is really "out there" in some way. We are back in the land of the incomprehensible metaphors. I do think that slavery is unjust, that

this is not "just my opinion," that everyone ought to think so, that everyone has a reason to oppose slavery, and so forth. Is this what it means to think that the injustice of slavery is part of the furniture of the universe? If so, then I do think this, but then I cannot see the difference between the proposition that slavery is unjust and the proposition that the injustice of slavery is part of the furniture of the universe. The proposition about furniture, interpreted in this way, has become a moral proposition about what I and others should believe and do, and I do not see how there can be any argument against that moral proposition which is not a moral argument. What other kind of argument could possibly persuade me to abandon these claims about what others should think and do?

But the philosopher will insist that I am missing the point. When it comes to moral opinions, he will say, he has the same ones I do. He also thinks that slavery is unjust. He disagrees with me not *within* morality but *about* morality. How is this possible? How can he believe that slavery is unjust and also believe that no propositions of political morality can be really or objectively true? For some decades one explanation was very popular. Skeptical philosophers said that what seem to be moral beliefs are not really beliefs at all but only emotional reactions. So when a philosopher says, off duty, that slavery is unjust, he is only reporting or expressing his own subjective reaction to slavery, and there is no inconsistency when he confirms, back on duty, that no moral propositions can be true. But this explanation will not work because the convictions philosophers try to explain away in this fashion do not function, on their own mental stage, as emotional reactions. They entertain arguments, take up or abandon different positions in response to arguments, see and respect logical and other connections among these positions, and otherwise behave in a style appropriate to belief rather than mere subjective reaction. So the redescription of their moral beliefs as emotional reactions is just bad reporting. The fact is: they think that slavery is unjust.

Now consider a more contemporary explanation of how it is possible to think this and yet be a skeptic. Suppose we distinguish between truth within a special game or enterprise and real or objective truth outside it. Taking fiction as a model, we might say that within the enterprise of a certain story someone killed Roger Ackroyd. But in the real world, outside that enterprise, Roger Ackroyd never existed, so that it cannot be true that anyone killed him. We might want to conceive the social practices of morality, art, law, and interpretation in some such way. Within the enterprise we make arguments and have beliefs of a certain sort—that slavery is unjust, for example, or that Christie novels display a certain view of evil. But when we stand outside the enterprise we know that no such proposition can be really or objectively true.

This strategy is appealing because, as I just said, skeptics not only have

moral or interpretive opinions but also treat these as beliefs, and this new picture explains how and why. When people make interpretive or moral or legal judgments, it says, they are playing a certain game of make-believe, asking themselves which interpretation would be better if any really could be better, or what would be morally right if anything really could be morally right, and so forth. There is no reason why skeptical philosophers themselves should not "play the game," even though they know it is really, objectively speaking, all nonsense.

But now we are back at the beginning, and my initial problem, that I do not see what difference could be made by the word "objectively," remains. For this explanation supposes that we can distinguish between the game and the real world, that we can distinguish between the claim that slavery is unjust, offered as a move in some collective enterprise in which such judgments are made and debated, and the claim that slavery is really or objectively unjust in the actual world; or that we can distinguish between the claim that Christie novels are about evil, offered as a move in a different kind of enterprise, and the claim that they are really about evil, offered as a claim about how things really are. It supposes that we can distinguish these as two different kinds of claims the way we distinguish claims about Roger Ackroyd as a character in a novel from claims about Roger Ackroyd as a historical character. And this is exactly what we cannot do, because the words "objectively" and "really" cannot change the sense of moral or interpretive judgments. If moral or aesthetic or interpretive judgments have the sense and force they do just because they figure in a collective human enterprise, then such judgments cannot have a "real" sense and a "real" truth value which transcend that enterprise and somehow take hold of the "real" world.

I have yet been given no reason to think that any skeptical argument about morality can be other than a moral argument, or skeptical argument about law other than a legal argument, or skeptical argument about interpretation other than an interpretive argument. I think that the problem of objectivity, as it is usually posed, is a fake because the distinction that might give it meaning, the distinction between substantive arguments within and skeptical arguments about social practices, is itself a fake. I must now take some care, however, to guard against misunderstandings of what I have said. Someone might say that my position is the deepest possible form of skepticism about morality, art, and interpretation because I am actually saying that moral or aesthetic or interpretive judgments cannot possibly describe an independent objective reality. But that is not what I said. I said that the question of what "independence" and "reality" are, for any practice, is a question within that practice, so that whether moral judgments can be objective is itself a moral question, and whether there is objectivity in interpretation is itself a question of interpretation. This threatens to make skepticism not inevitable but impossible.

SKEPTICISM

It threatens to make skepticism impossible becauses it seems to deny that someone can criticize morality, for example, without himself taking up the moral point of view. Skepticism, on this account, would be self-defeating, for if the skeptic must make moral arguments in order to challenge morality, he must concede the sense and validity of arguments whose sense and validity he wants to deny. But this, too, is an overstatement because it ignores what I tried to stress throughout my original essay, which is the complexity of the moral and interpretive practices skeptics want to challenge. My arguments about objectivity leave even very general skepticism possible as a position *within* the enterprise it challenges.

I have already pointed out one kind of skeptical argument about interpretive judgments. Someone might try to show that interpretive judgments are too unstructured and disconnected to be checked by other judgments in the way the enterprise of interpretation supposes such judgments to be checked—too unstructured to count as beliefs even within that enterprise. This form of skepticism does require taking up some minimal position, which might nevertheless be controversial among interpreters, about the point and value of interpretation. It seems to rest, in fact, on exactly the view I urged in my essay—that plausible interpretations must be connected to normative aesthetic or political theories that are themselves plausible. It uses that very general assumption about the point of interpretation to argue for the impossibility of successful interpretations, and that should be sufficiently skeptical for anyone. (It also assumes a false psychology of interpretation, and that is why it fails.) This kind of skepticism, however, while very general, is nevertheless internal in the sense I am now assuming. No one who accepts this argument could then add that, in his personal opinion, a Christie novel is really an exploration of the nature of evil.

There are many other, and more plausible, possibilities for skepticism within interpretation. An interpreter might accept some theory about the point or value of art according to which certain interpretive questions (or even all of them) simply have no answer, because no answer to these questions could make any difference to the value of a work of art. Someone might well think, for example, that the old question whether Hamlet and Ophelia were lovers has no answer because neither answer would intersect any criterion of value in drama. The play could not be read better one way rather than the other. Almost any theory of art would have that consequence for some issues—whether Hamlet slept on his side, for example. But some would have it for most of the questions that exercise critics, and these theories would furnish very skeptical accounts of interpretation.

We can even imagine a skeptical argument rising from the issues that seem important to Fish and his skeptical colleagues. They dwell on the fact that two interpreters will often disagree about the correct characterization

of a work of fiction because characterizations are so theory-dependent. That is apparently what they mean to argue in those unfortunate metaphors about meanings not being "just there." If someone thinks that the point of interpretation is to secure a large measure of interpersonal agreement, he will notice that interpretation as presently practiced offers no such prospect, and he will draw the appropriate global and skeptical conclusions. But his arguments will then depend on the plausibility of that view of the point of the enterprise.

These different forms of skepticism about interpretation are all internal to that enterprise. They adopt some controversial view about the point or nature of interpretation, as do positive theories, but they adopt a view that has skeptical consequences. We can easily construct parallel examples of internal skepticism about the value of art and about political morality. No problem of consistency arises for this sort of skepticism because we are no longer dealing with the myth of two standpoints, an internal standpoint from which an interpreter has his own answer to interpretive questions, and an external standpoint from which he acknowledges that such questions can have no answers. No one who says there is no answer to the question about Hamlet and Ophelia, because neither answer makes the play better or worse than the other, will go on to say that in his personal opinion they were lovers.

If we abandon that myth, we threaten not the impossibility of skepticism but the impossibility of what we might call, in contrast to the kinds of skepticism we have recognized, external skepticism. The external skeptic supposes he can check all interpretive judgments against some external reality whose content is not to be determined by arguments of the sort made familiar by the practice but which is to be apprehended in some other way. He supposes that he can step wholly outside the enterprise, give some different sense to interpretive judgments from the sense they have within it, test these judgments so conceived in some way different from confronting the arguments deployed for and against them in the ordinary practice of interpretation, and find them all false or senseless when measured against this supposedly more objective standard. If we reject external skepticism of this sort, then we shall say, to Fish and other would-be skeptics, that the only way they can make good their extravagant claim—that any text allows any interpretation whatsoever—is to make a genuine argument to that effect, by setting out some appealing normative theory of artistic integrity that has that consequence. If Fish wishes us to entertain such an argument, he must begin by assuring us of his own good faith. If he really does hold such a theory himself, he must abandon, as inconsistent, his own favorite interpretations of texts, including, for example, his interpretation of *Paradise Lost*, not to mention *Peril at End House*.

Of course if he did make such an argument he might end by convincing

us. We cannot say for certain, in advance, that he would not. The only kind of skepticism that is ruled out by my earlier observations is skepticism brought to an enterprise from the outside, skepticism which engages no arguments of the sort the enterprise requires, skepticism which is simply tacked on at the end of our various interpretive and political convictions, leaving them all somehow unruffled and in place. This kind of skepticism can make no difference to our own efforts to understand and improve interpretation, art, and law. What do we lose in giving it up?

Liberalism and Justice

EIGHT

Liberalism

IN THIS ESSAY I shall propose a theory about what liberalism is. But I face an immediate problem. My project supposes that there is such a thing as liberalism, and the opinion is suddenly popular that there is not. Sometime before the Vietnam war, politicians who called themselves "liberals" held certain positions that could be identified as a group. Liberals were for greater economic equality, for internationalism, for freedom of speech and against censorship, for greater equality between the races and against segregation, for a sharp separation of church and state, for greater procedural protection for accused criminals, for decriminalization of "morals" offenses, particularly drug offenses and consensual sexual offenses involving only adults, and for an aggressive use of central government power to achieve all these goals. These were, in the familiar phrase, liberal "causes," and those who promoted these causes could be distinguished from another large party of political opinion that could usefully be called "conservative." Conservatives tended to hold the contrary position to each of the classical liberal causes.

But a series of developments in the 1960s and 1970s called into question whether liberalism was a distinct political theory after all. One of these was the war. John F. Kennedy and his men called themselves liberals; so did Johnson, who retained the Kennedy men and added liberals of his own. But the war was inhumane and discredited the idea that liberalism was the party of humanity. It would have been possible to argue, of course, that the Bundys and McNamaras and Rostows were false liberals, who sacrificed liberal principles for the sake of personal power, or incompetent liberals, who did not understand that liberal principles prohibited what they did. But many critics drew the different conclusion that the war had exposed hidden connections between liberalism and exploitation. Once these supposed connections were exposed, they were seen to include domestic as well as external exploitation, and the line between liberalism and conservatism was then thought to be sham.

Second, politics began to produce issues that seemed no longer to divide into liberal and conservative positions. It was not clear, for example, whether concern for protecting the environment from pollution, even at the cost of economic growth that might reduce unemployment, was a liberal cause or not. Consumer protection appealed equally to consumers who called themselves liberal and those who said they were conservative. Many different groups—not only environmentalists and consumer protectionists—opposed what they called the growth mentality, that is, the assumption that it should be an important aim of government to improve the total wealth or product of the country. It became fashionable to ask for more local control by small groups over political decisions, not so much because decisions made locally are likely to be better, but because personal political relationships of mutual respect and cooperation, generated by local decisions, are desirable for their own sake. Opposition to growth for its own sake and opposition to the concentration of power seem liberal in spirit because liberals traditionally opposed the growth of big business and traditionally supported political equality. But these positions nevertheless condemn the strategies of central economic and political organization that have, certainly since the New Deal, been thought to be distinctly liberal strategies.

Third, and in consequence, politicians became less willing than before to identify themselves as "liberal" or "conservative," and more likely to combine political positions formerly thought liberal with those formerly thought conservative. President Carter, for example, professed what seemed to be "liberal" positions on human rights with "conservative" positions on the importance of balancing the national budget even at the expense of improved welfare programs, and many commentators attributed his unanticipated nomination to his ability to break through political categories in this way. In Britain as well, new combinations of old positions appeared: the last Labour government seemed no more "liberal" than the Tories on matters of censorship, for example, and scarcely more liberal on matters of immigration or police procedures.

Reagan's presidency and Thatcher's administration arrested this process, and revived their nations' sense of an important line between liberalism and conservatism. Issues that cut across that distinction in the seventies have now receded; arguments over economic justice and national defense are now more prominent and divisive, and it is easier to assign politicians to liberal and conservative sides on these issues. But a new debate has emerged between "old" and "neo" liberals. In the contest for the Democratic nomination Walter Mondale was called an old-fashioned liberal, committed to a large supervisory role for government in economic affairs; Gary Hart, on the contrary, was said to speak for the new liberals who reject New Deal attitudes as inappropriate to a nation needing a more flexible and discriminating approach to industrial policy. The Labour Party, in Britain, has

moved to the left; many of the most prominent "liberals" in that party have deserted it to form the Social Democratic Party, which, they claim, now carries the banner of genuine liberalism.

I want to argue that a certain conception of equality, which I shall call the liberal conception of equality, is the nerve of liberalism. But that supposes that liberalism is an authentic and coherent political morality, so that it can make sense to speak of "its" central principle, and the history just described may be taken to suggest that that is not. They may seem to support the following skeptical thesis instead. "The word 'liberalism' has been used, since the eighteenth century, to describe various distinct clusters of political positions, but with no important similarity of principle among the different clusters called 'liberal' at different times. The explanation of why different clusters formed in various circumstances, or why they were called 'liberal,' cannot be found by searching for any such principle. It must be found instead in complicated accidents of history, in which the self-interest of certain groups, the prevalence of certain political rhetoric, and many other discrete factors played different parts. One such cluster was formed, for such reasons, in the period of the New Deal: it combined an emphasis on less inequality and greater economic stability with more abundant political and civil liberty for the groups then campaigning for these goals. Our contemporary notion of 'liberal' is formed from that particular package of political aims."

"But the forces that formed and held together that package have now been altered in various ways. Businessmen, for example, have now come to see that various elements in the package—particularly those promoting economic stability—work very much in their favor. White working men have come to see that certain sorts of economic and social equality for racial minorities threaten their own interests. Political liberties have been used, not merely or even mainly by those anxious to achieve the limited economic equality of the New Deal, but also by social rebels who threaten ideals of social order and public decency that the old liberal did not question. The question of Israel and Soviet violations of the rights of intellectuals have led the old liberal to withdraw his former tolerance for the Soviet Union and the expansion of its power. So New Deal 'liberalism,' as a package of political positions, is no longer an important political force. Perhaps a new cluster of positions will form which will be called 'liberal' by its supporters and critics. Perhaps not. It does not much matter, because the new cluster, whether it is called liberalism or not, will bear no important connections of principle to the old liberalism. The idea of liberalism, as a fundamental political theory that produced a package of liberal causes, is a myth with no explanatory power whatsoever."

That is the skeptic's account. There is, however, an alternative account of the breakup of the liberal package of ideas. In any coherent political pro-

gram there are two elements: constitutive political positions that are valued for their own sake, and derivative positions that are valued as strategies, as means of achieving the constitutive positions.[1] The skeptic believes that the liberal package of ideas had no constitutive political morality at all; it was a package formed by accident and held together by self-interest. The alternate account argues that the package had a constitutive morality and has come apart, to the extent it has, because it has become less clear which derivative positions best serve that constitutive morality.

On this account, the breakup of New Deal liberalism was the consequence, not of any sudden disenchantment with that fundamental political morality, but rather of changes in opinion and circumstance that made it doubtful whether the old strategies for enforcing that morality were right. If this alternate account is correct, then the ideal of liberalism as a fundamental political morality is not only a myth, but is an idea necessary to any adequate account of modern political history, and to any adequate analysis of contemporary political debate. That conclusion will, no doubt, appeal to those who continue to think of themselves as liberals. But it must also be the thesis of critics of liberalism, at least of those who suppose that liberalism, in its very nature, is exploitative, or destructive of important values of community, or in some other way malign. For these comprehensive critics, no less than partisans, must deny that the New Deal liberal settlement was a merely accidental coincidence of political positions.

But of course we cannot decide whether the skeptical account or this alternative account is superior until we provide, for the latter, some theory about which elements of the liberal package are to be taken as constitutive and which derivative. Unfortunately liberals and their critics disagree, both between and within the two groups, about that very issue. Critics often say, for example, that liberals are committed to economic growth, to the bureaucratic apparatus of government and industry necessary for economic growth, and to the form of life in which growth is pursued for its own sake, a form of life that emphasizes competition, individualism, and material satisfactions. It is certainly true that politicians whom we consider paradigmatic liberals, like Hubert Humphrey and Roy Jenkins, emphasized the need for economic growth. But is this emphasis on growth a matter of constitutive principle because liberalism is tied to some form of utlitarianism that makes overall prosperity a good in itself? If so, then the disenchantment of many liberals with the idea of growth argues from the skeptical view that liberalism was a temporary alliance of unrelated political positions that has now been abandoned. Or is it a matter of derivative strategy within liberal theory—a debatable strategy for reducing economic inequality, for example—and therefore a matter on which liberals might disagree without deep schism or crisis? This question cannot be answered merely by pointing to the conceded fact that many who call themselves liberals once

supported economic development more enthusiastically than they do now, any more than it can be shown that there is a connection of principle between imperialism and liberalism simply by naming men who called themselves liberals and were among those responsible for Vietnam. The vital questions here are questions of theoretical connection, and simply pointing at history, without at least some hypothesis about the nature of those connections, is useless.

The same question must be raised about the more general issue of the connection between liberalism and capitalism. Most of those who have called themselves liberals, both in the United States and Britain, have been anxious to make the market economy more fair in its workings and results, or to mix a market and collective economy, rather than to replace the market economy altogether with a plainly socialist system. That is the basis for the familiar charge that there is no genuine difference, within the context of Western politics, between liberals and conservatives. But once again different views about the connection between capitalism and liberalism are possible. It may be that the constitutive positions of New Deal liberalism must include the principle of free enterprise itself, or principles about liberty that can only be satisfied by a market economy for conceptual reasons. If so, then any constraints on the market the liberal might áccept, through redistribution or regulation or a mixed economy, would be a compromise with basic liberal principles, perhaps embraced out of practical necessity in order to protect the basic structure from revolution. The charge that the ideological differences between liberalism and conservatism are relatively unimportant would be supported by that discovery. If someone was persuaded to abandon capitalism altogether, he would no longer be a liberal; if many former liberals did so, then liberalism would be crippled as a political force. But perhaps, on the contrary, capitalism is not constitutive but derivative in New Deal liberalism. It might have been popular among liberals because it seemed, rightly or wrongly, the best means of achieving different and more fundamental liberal goals. In that case, liberals can disagree about whether free enterprise is worth preserving under new circumstances, again without theoretical crisis or schism, and the important ideological difference from conservatives may still be preserved. Once again we must give attention to the theoretical question in order to frame hypotheses with which to confront the political facts.

These two issues—the connection of liberalism with economic growth and with capitalism—are especially controversial, but we can locate similar problems of distinguishing what is fundamental from what is strategic in almost every corner of the New Deal liberal settlement. The liberal favors free speech. But is free speech a fundamental value, or is it only a means to some other goal, such as the discovery of truth (as Mill argued) or the efficient functioning of democracy (as Michaeljohn suggested)? The liberal dis-

approves of enforcing morality through the criminal law. Does this suggest that liberalism opposes the formation of a shared community sense of decency? Or is liberalism hostile only to using the criminal law to secure that shared community sense? I must say, perhaps out of unnecessary caution, that these questions cannot be answered, at the end of the day, apart from history and developed social theory; but it does not contradict that truism to insist that philosophical analysis of the idea of liberalism is an essential part of that very process.

So my original question—what is liberalism?—turns out to be a question that must be answered, at least tentatively, before the more clearly historical questions posed by the skeptical thesis can be confronted. For my question is just the question of what morality is constitutive in particular liberal settlements like the New Deal package.

My project does take a certain view of the role of political theory in politics. It supposes that liberalism consists in some constitutive political morality that has remained roughly the same over some time and that continues to be influential in politics. It supposes that distinct liberal settlements are formed when, for one reason or another, those moved by that constitutive morality settle on a particular scheme of derivative positions as appropriate to complete a practical liberal political theory, and others, for their own reasons, become allies in promoting that scheme. Such settlements break up, and liberalism is accordingly fragmented, when these derivative positions are discovered to be ineffective, or when economic or social circumstances change so as to make them ineffective, or when the allies necessary to make an effective political force are no longer drawn to the scheme. I do not mean that the constitutive morality of liberalism is the only force at work in forming liberal settlements, or even that it is the most powerful, but only that it is sufficiently distinct and influential to give sense to the idea, shared by liberals and their critics, that liberalism exists, and to give sense to the popular practice of arguing about what it is.

The argument so far has shown that the claim that a particular position is constitutive rather than derivative in a political theory will be both controversial and complex. How shall I proceed? Any satisfactory description of the constitutive morality of liberalism must meet the following catalog of conditions. (1) It must state positions that it makes sense to suppose might be constitutive of political programs for people in our culture. I do not claim merely that some set of constitutive principles could explain liberal settlements if people held those principles, but that a particular set does help to explain liberal settlements because people actually have held those principles. (2) It must be sufficiently well tied to the last clear liberal settlement—the political positions I described at the outset as acknowledged liberal "causes"—so that it can be seen to be constitutive for that entire scheme, so that the remaining positions in the scheme can be seen, that is,

to be derivative given that constitutive morality. (3) It must state constitutive principles in sufficient detail so as to discriminate a liberal political morality from other, competing political moralities. If, for example, I say only that it is constitutive of liberalism that the government must treat its citizens with respect, I have not stated a constitutive principle in sufficient detail, because, although liberals might argue that all their political schemes follow from that principle, conservatives, Marxists, and perhaps even fascists would make the same claim for their theories. (4) Once these requirements of authenticity, completeness, and distinction are satisfied, then a more comprehensive and frugal statement of constitutive principles meeting these requirements is to be preferred to a less comprehensive and frugal scheme, because the former will have greater explanatory power and provide a fairer test of the thesis that these constitutive principles both precede and survive particular settlements.

The second of these four conditions provides a starting point. I must therefore repeat the list of what I take to be the political positions of the last liberal settlement, and I shall, for convenience, speak of "liberals" as these who support those positions. In economic policy, liberals demand that inequalities of wealth be reduced through welfare and other forms of redistribution financed by progressive taxes. They believe that government should intervene in the economy to promote economic stability, to control inflation, to reduce unemployment, and to provide services that would not otherwise be provided, but they favor a pragmatic and selective intervention over a dramatic change from free enterprise to wholly collective decisions about investment, production, prices, and wages. They support racial equality and approve government intervention to secure it, through constraints on both public and private discrimination in education, housing, and employment. But they oppose other forms of collective regulation of individual decision: they oppose regulation of the content of political speech, even when such regulation might secure greater social order, and they oppose regulation of sexual literature and conduct, even when such regulation has considerable majoritarian support. They are suspicious of the criminal law and anxious to reduce the extension of its provisions to behavior whose morality is controversial, and they support procedural constraints and devices, like rules against the admissibility of confessions, that makes it more difficult to secure criminal convictions.

I do not mean that everyone who holds any of these positions will or did hold them all. Some people who call themselves liberal do not support several elements of this package; some who call themselves conservative support most of them. But these are the positions that we use as a touchstone when we ask how liberal or conservative someone is; and indeed on which we now rely when we say that the line between liberals and conservatives is more blurred than once it was. I have omitted those positions that are only

debatably elements of the liberal package, like support for military intervention in Vietnam, or the present campaign in support of human rights in Communist countries, or concern for more local participation in government, or for consumer protection against manufacturers, or for the environment. I have also omitted debatable extension of liberal doctrines, like busing and quotas that discriminate in favor of minorities in education and employment. I shall assume that the positions that are uncontroversially liberal positions are the core of the liberal settlement. If my claim is right, that a particular conception of equality can be shown to be constitutive for that core of positions, we shall have, in that conception, a device for stating and testing the claim that some debatable position is also "really" liberal.

Is THERE a thread of principle that runs through the core liberal positions, and that distinguishes these from the corresponding conservative positions? There is a familiar answer to this question that is mistaken, but mistaken in an illuminating way. The politics of democracies, according to this answer, recognizes several independent constitutive political ideals, the most important of which are the ideals of liberty and equality. Unfortunately, liberty and equality often conflict: sometimes the only effective means to promote equality require some limitation of liberty, and sometimes the consequences of promoting liberty are detrimental to equality. In these cases, good government consists in the best compromise between the competing ideals, but different politicians and citizens will make that compromise differently. Liberals tend relatively to favor equality more and liberty less than conservatives do, and the core set of liberal positions I described is the result of striking the balance that way.

This account offers a theory about what liberalism is. Liberalism shares the same constitutive principles with many other political theories, including conservatism, but is distinguished from these by attaching different relative importance to different principles. The theory therefore leaves room, on the spectrum it describes, for the radical who cares even more for equality and less for liberty than the liberal, and therefore stands even farther away from the extreme conservative. The liberal becomes the man in the middle, which explains why liberalism is so often now considered wishy-washy, an untenable compromise between two more forthright positions.

No doubt this description of American politics could be made more sophisticated. It might make room for other independent constitutive ideals shared by liberalism and its opponents, like stability or security, so that the compromises involved in particular decisions are made out to be more complex. But if the nerve of the theory remains the competition between liberty and equality as constitutive ideals, then the theory cannot succeed. In the first place, it does not satisfy condition (2) in the catalog of conditions

I set out. It seems to apply, at best, to only a limited number of the political controversies it tries to explain. It is designed for economic controversies, but is either irrelevant or misleading in the case of censorship and pornography, and indeed, in the criminal law generally.

But there is a much more important defect in this explanation. It assumes that liberty is measurable so that, if two political decisions each invades the liberty of a citizen, we can sensibly say that one decision takes more liberty away from him than the other. That assumption is necessary, because otherwise the postulate, that liberty is a constitutive ideal of both the liberal and conservative political structures, cannot be maintained. Even firm conservatives are content that their liberty to drive as they wish (for example, to drive uptown on Lexington Avenue) may be invaded for the sake, not of some important competing political ideal, but only for marginal gains in convenience or orderly traffic patterns. But since traffic regulation plainly involves some loss of liberty, the conservative cannot be said to value liberty as such unless he is able to show that, for some reason, less liberty is lost by traffic regulation than by restrictions on, for example, free speech, or the liberty to sell for prices others are willing to pay, or whatever other liberty he takes to be fundamental.

That is precisely what he cannot show, because we do not have a concept of liberty that is quantifiable in the way that demonstration would require. He cannot say, for example, that traffic regulations interfere less with what most men and women want to do than would a law forbidding them to speak out in favor of Communism, or a law requiring them not to fix their prices as they think best. Most people care more about driving than speaking for Communism, and have no occasion to fix prices even if they want to. I do not mean that we can make no sense of the idea of fundamental liberties, like freedom of speech. But we cannot argue in their favor by showing that they protect more liberty, taken to be an even roughly measurable commodity, than does the right to drive as we wish; the fundamental liberties are important because we value something else that they protect. But if that is so, then we cannot explain the difference between liberal and conservative political positions by supposing that the latter protect the commodity of liberty, valued for its own sake, more effectively than the former.[2]

It might now be said, however, that the other half of the liberty–equality explanation may be salvaged. Even if we cannot say that conservatives value liberty, as such, more than liberals, we can still say that they value equality less, and that the different political positions may be explained in that way. Conservatives tend to discount the importance of equality when set beside other goals, like general prosperity or even security; while liberals value equality relatively more, and radicals more still. Once again, it is apparent that this explanation is tailored to the economic controversies,

and fits poorly with the noneconomic controversies. Once again, however, its defects are more general and more important. We must identify more clearly the sense in which equality could be a constitutive ideal for either liberals or conservatives. Once we do so, we shall see that it is misleading to say that the conservative values equality, in that sense, less than the liberal. We shall want to say, instead, that he has a different conception of what equality requires.

We must distinguish between two different principles that take equality to be a political ideal.[3] The first requires that the government treat all those in its charge *as equals*, that is, as entitled to its equal concern and respect. That is not an empty requirement: most of us do not suppose that we must, as individuals, treat our neighbor's children with the same concern as our own, or treat everyone we meet with the same respect. It is nevertheless plausible to think that any government should treat all its citizens as equals in that way. The second principle requires that the government treat all those in its charge *equally* in the distribution of some resource of opportunity, or at least work to secure the state of affairs in which they all are equal or more nearly equal in that respect. It is conceded by everyone that the government cannot make everyone equal in every respect, but people do disagree about how far government should try to secure equality in some particular resource, for example, in monetary wealth.

If we look only at the economic–political controversies, then we might well be justified in saying that liberals want more equality in the sense of the second principle than conservatives do. But it would be a mistake to conclude that they value equality in the sense of the first and more fundamental principle any more highly. I say that the first principle is more fundamental because I assume that, for both liberals and conservatives, the first is constitutive and the second derivative. Sometimes treating people equally is the only way to treat them as equals; but sometimes not. Suppose a limited amount of emergency relief is available for two equally populous areas injured by floods; treating the citizens of both areas as equals requires giving more aid to the more seriously devastated area rather than splitting the available funds equally. The conservative believes that in many other, less apparent, cases treating citizens equally amounts to not treating them as equals. He might concede, for example, that positive discrimination in university admissions will work to make the two races more nearly equal in wealth, but nevertheless maintain that such programs do not treat black and white university applicants as equals. If he is a utilitarian, he will have a similar, though much more general, argument against any redistribution of wealth that reduces economic efficiency. He will say that the only way to treat people as equals is to maximize the average welfare of all members of community, counting gains and losses to all in the same scales, and that a free market is the only, or best, instrument for achieving that goal. This is not (I think) a good argument, but if the conservative who makes it is sin-

cere, he cannot be said to have discounted the importance of treating all citizens as equals.

So we must reject the simple idea that liberalism consists in a distinctive weighting between constitutive principles of equality and liberty. But our discussion of the idea of equality suggests a more fruitful line. I assume (as I said) that there is broad agreement within modern politics that the government must treat all its citizens with equal concern and respect. I do not mean to deny the great power of prejudice in, for example, American politics. But few citizens, and even fewer politicians, would now admit to political convictions that contradict the abstract principle of equal concern and respect. Different people hold, however, as our discussion made plain, very different conceptions of what that abstract principle requires in particular cases.

WHAT DOES it mean for the government to treat its citizens as equals? That is, I think, the same question as the question of what it means for the government to treat all its citizens as free, or as independent, or with equal dignity. In any case, it is a question that has been central to political theory at least since Kant.

It may be answered in two fundamentally different ways. The first supposes that government must be neutral on what might be called the question of the good life. The second supposes that government cannot be neutral on that question, because it cannot treat its citizens as equal human beings without a theory of what human beings ought to be. I must explain that distinction further. Each person follows a more-or-less articulate conception of what gives value to life. The scholar who values a life of contemplation has such a conception; so does the television-watching, beer-drinking citizen who is fond of saying "This is the life," though he has thought less about the issue and is less able to describe or defend his conception.

The first theory of equality supposes that political decisions must be, so far as is possible, independent of any particular conception of the good life, or of what gives value to life. Since the citizens of a society differ in their conceptions, the government does not treat them as equals if it prefers one conception to another, either because the officials believe that one is intrinsically superior, or because one is held by the more numerous or more powerful group. The second theory argues, on the contrary, that the content of equal treatment cannot be independent of some theory about the good for man or the good of life, because treating a person as an equal means treating him the way the good or truly wise person would wish to be treated. Good government consists in fostering or at least recognizing good lives; treatment as an equal consists in treating each person as if he were desirous of leading the life that is in fact good, at least so far as this is possible.

This distinction is very abstract, but it is also very important. I shall now argue that liberalism takes, as its constitutive political morality, the first conception of equality. I shall try to support that claim in this way. In the next section of this essay I shall show how it is plausible, and even likely, that a thoughtful person who accepted the first conception of equality would, given the economic and political circumstances of the United States in the last several decades, reach the positions I identified as the familiar core of liberal positions. If so, then the hypothesis satisfies the second of the conditions I described for a successful theory. I shall later try to satisfy the third condition by showing how it is plausible and even likely that someone who held a particular version of the second theory of equality would reach what are normally regarded as the core of American conservative positions. I say "a particular version of" because American conservatism does not follow automatically from rejecting the liberal theory of equality. The second (or nonliberal) theory of equality holds merely that the treatment government owes citizens is at least partly determined by some conception of the good life. Many political theories share that thesis, including theories as far apart as, for example, American conservatism and various forms of socialism or Marxism, though these differ in the conception of the good life they adopt, and hence in the political institutions and decisions they endorse. In this respect, liberalism is decidedly not some compromise or halfway house between more forceful positions, but stands on one side of an important line that distinguishes it from all competitors taken as a group.

I shall not provide arguments in this essay that my theory of liberalism meets the first condition I described—that the theory must provide a political morality that it makes sense to suppose people in our culture hold—though I think it plain that the theory does meet this condition. The fourth condition requires that a theory be as abstract and general as the first three conditions allow. I doubt there will be objections to my theory on that account.

I NOW DEFINE a liberal as someone who holds the first, or liberal, theory of what equality requires. Suppose that a liberal is asked to found a new state. He is required to dictate its constitution and fundamental institutions. He must propose a general theory of political distribution, that is, a theory of how whatever the community has to assign, by way of goods or resources or opportunities, should be assigned. He will arrive initially at something like this principle of rough equality: resources and opportunities should be distributed, so far as possible, equally, so that roughly the same share of whatever is available is devoted to satisfying the ambitions of each. Any other general aim of distribution will assume either that the fate of some people should be of greater concern than that of others, or that the ambitions or

talents of some are more worthy, and should be supported more generously on that account.

Someone may object that this principle of rough equality is unfair because it ignores the fact that people have different tastes, and that some of these are more expensive to satisfy than others, so that, for example, the man who prefers champagne will need more funds if he is not to be frustrated than the man satisfied with beer. But the liberal may reply that tastes as to which people differ are, by and large, not afflictions, like diseases, but are rather cultivated, in accordance with each person's theory of what his life should be like.[4] The most effective neutrality, therefore, requires that the same share be devoted to each, so that the choice between expensive and less expensive tastes can be made by each person for himself, with no sense that his overall share will be enlarged by choosing a more expensive life, or that, whatever he chooses, his choice will subsidize those who have chosen more expensively.[5]

But what does the principle of rough equality of distribution require in practice? If all resources were distributed directly by the government through grants of food, housing, and so forth; if every opportunity citizens have were provided directly by the government through the provisions of civil and criminal law; if every citizen had exactly the same talents; if every citizen started his life with no more than what any other citizen had at the start; and if every citizen had exactly the same theory of the good life and hence exactly the same scheme of preferences as every other citizen, including preferences between productive activity of different forms and leisure, then the principle of rough equality of treatment could be satisfied simply by equal distributions of everything to be distributed and by civil and criminal laws of universal application. Government would arrange for production that maximized the mix of goods, including jobs and leisure, that everyone favored, distributing the product equally.

Of course, none of these conditions of similarity holds. But the moral relevance of different sorts of diversity are very different, as may be shown by the following exercise. Suppose all the conditions of similarity I mentioned did hold except the last: citizens have different theories of the good and hence different preferences. They therefore disagree about what product the raw materials and labor and savings of the community should be used to produce, and about which activities should be prohibited or regulated so as to make others possible or easier. The liberal, as lawgiver, now needs mechanisms to satisfy the principles of equal treatment in spite of these disagreements. He will decide that there are no better mechanisms available, as general political institutions, than the two main institutions of our own political economy: the economic market, for decisions about what goods shall be produced and how they shall be distributed, and representative democracy, for collective decisions about what conduct shall be prohibited or

regulated so that other conduct might be made possible or convenient. Each of these familiar institutions may be expected to provide a more egalitarian division than any other general arrangement. The market, if it can be made to function efficiently, will determine for each product a price that reflects the cost in resources of material, labor, and capital that might have been applied to produce something different that someone else wants. That cost determines, for anyone who consumes that product, how much his account should be charged in computing the egalitarian division of social resources. It provides a measure of how much more his account should be charged for a house than a book, and for one book rather than another. The market will also provide, for the laborer, a measure of how much should be credited to his account for his choice of productive activity over leisure, and for one activity rather than another. It will tell us, through the price it puts on his labor, how much he should gain or lose by his decision to pursue one career rather than another. These measurements make a citizen's own distribution a function of the personal preferences of others as well as of his own, and it is the sum of these personal preferences that fixes the true cost to the community of meeting his own preferences for goods and activities. The egalitarian distribution, which requires that the cost of satisfying one person's preferences should as far as is possible be equal to the cost of satisfying another's, cannot be enforced unless those measurements are made.

We are familiar with the anti-egalitarian consequences of free enterprise in practice; it may therefore seem paradoxical that the liberal as lawgiver should choose a market economy for reasons of equality rather than efficiency. But, under the special condition that people differ only in preferences for goods and activities, the market is more egalitarian than any alternative of comparable generality. The most plausible alternative would be to allow decisions of production, investment, price, and wage to be made by elected officials in a socialist economy. But what principles should officials use in making those decisions? The liberal might tell them to mimic the decisions that a market would make if it was working efficiently under proper competition and full knowledge. This mimicry would be, in practice, much less efficient than an actual market would be. In any case, unless the liberal had reason to think it would be much more efficient, he would have good reason to reject it. Any minimally efficient mimicking of a hypothetical market would require invasions of privacy to determine what decisions individuals would make if forced actually to pay for their investment, consumption, and employment decisions at market rates, and this information gathering would be, in many other ways, much more expensive than an actual market. Inevitably, moreover, the assumptions officials make about how people would behave in a hypothetical market reflect the officials' own beliefs about how people should behave. So there would be, for the liberal,

little to gain and much to lose in a socialist economy in which officials were asked to mimic a hypothetical market.

But any other instructions would be a direct violation of the liberal theory of what equality requires, because if a decision is made to produce and sell goods at a price below the price a market would fix, then those who prefer those goods are, *pro tanto*, receiving more than an equal share of the resources of the community at the expense of those who would prefer some other use of the resources. Suppose the limited demand for books, matched against the demand for competing uses for wood pulp, would fix the price of books at a point higher than the socialist managers of the economy will charge; those who want books are having less charged to their account than the egalitarian principle would require. It might be said that in a socialist economy books are simply valued more, because they are inherently more worthy uses of social resources, quite apart from the popular demand for books. But the liberal theory of equality rules out that appeal to the inherent value of one theory of what is good in life.

In a society in which people differed only in preferences, then, a market would be favored for its egalitarian consequences. Inequality of monetary wealth would be the consequence only of the fact that some preferences are more expensive than others, including the preference for leisure time rather than the most lucrative productive activity. But we must now return to the real world. In the actual society for which the liberal must construct political institutions, there are all the other differences. Talents are not distributed equally, so the decision of one person to work in a factory rather than a law firm, or not to work at all, will be governed in large part by his abilities rather than his preferences for work or between work and leisure. The institutions of wealth, which allow people to dispose of what they receive by gift, means that children of the successful will start with more wealth than the children of the unsuccessful. Some people have special needs, because they are handicapped; their handicap will not only disable them from the most productive and lucrative employment, but will incapacitate them from using the proceeds of whatever employment they find as efficiently, so that they will need more than those who are not handicapped to satisfy identical ambitions.

These inequalities will have great, often catastrophic, effects on the distribution that a market economy will provide. But, unlike differences in preferences, the differences these inequalities make are indefensible according to the liberal conception of equality. It is obviously obnoxious to the liberal conception, for example, that someone should have more of what the community as a whole has to distribute because he or his father had superior skill or luck. The liberal lawgiver therefore faces a difficult task. His conception of equality requires an economic system that produces certain inequalities (those that reflect the true differential costs of goods and oppor-

tunities) but not others (those that follow from differences in ability, inherit-ance, and so on). The market produces both the required and the forbidden inequalities, and there is no alternative system that can be relied upon to produce the former without the latter.

The liberal must be tempted, therefore, to a reform of the market through a scheme of redistribution that leaves its pricing system relatively intact but sharply limits, at least, the inequalities in welfare that his initial principle prohibits. No solution will seem perfect. The liberal may find the best answer in a scheme of welfare rights financed through redistributive income and inheritance taxes of the conventional sort, which redistributes just to the Rawlsian point, that is, to the point at which the worst-off group would be harmed rather than benefited by further transfers. In that case, he will remain a reluctant capitalist, believing that a market economy so re-formed is superior, from the standpoint of his conception of equality, to any practical socialist alternative. Or he may believe that the redistribution that is possible in a capitalist economy will be so inadequate, or will be pur-chased at the cost of such inefficiency, that it is better to proceed in a more radical way, by substituting socialist for market decisions over a large part of the economy, and then relying on the political process to insure that prices are set in a manner at least roughly consistent with his conception of equality. In that case he will be a reluctant socialist, who acknowledges the egalitarian defects of socialism but counts them as less severe than the practical alternatives. In either case, he chooses a mixed economic sys-tem—either redistributive capitalism or limited socialism—not in order to compromise antagonistic ideals of efficiency and equality, but to achieve the best practical realization of the demands of equality itself.

Let us assume that in this manner the liberal either refines or partially retracts his original selection of a market economy. He must now consider the second of the two familiar institutions he first selected, which is repre-sentative democracy. Democracy is justified because it enforces the right of each person to respect and concern as an individual; but in practice the de-cisions of a democratic majority may often violate that right, according to the liberal theory of what the right requires. Suppose a legislature elected by a majority decides to make criminal some act (like speaking in favor of an unpopular political position, or participating in eccentric sexual prac-tices), not because the act deprives others of opportunities they want, but because the majority disapproves of those views or that sexual morality. The political decision, in other words, reflects not just some accommodation of the *personal* preferences of everyone, in such a way as to make the opportu-nities of all as nearly equal as may be, but the domination of one set of *ex-ternal* preferences, that is, preferences people have about what others shall do or have.[6] The decision invades rather than enforces the right of citizens to be treated as equals.

How can the liberal protect citizens against that sort of violation of their fundamental right? It will not do for the liberal simply to instruct legislators, in some constitutional exhortation, to disregard the external preferences of their constituents. Citizens will vote these preferences in electing their representatives, and a legislator who chooses to ignore them will not survive. In any case, it is sometimes impossible to distinguish, even by introspection, the external and personal components of a political position: this is the case, for example, with associational preferences, which are the preferences some people have for opportunities, like the opportunity to attend public schools—but only with others of the same "background."

The liberal, therefore, needs a scheme of civil rights whose effect will be to determine those political decisions that are antecedently likely to reflect strong external preferences and to remove those decisions from majoritarian political institutions altogether. The scheme of rights necessary to do this will depend on general facts about the prejudices and other external preferences of the majority at any given time, and different liberals will disagree about what is needed at any particular time.[7] But the rights encoded in the Bill of Rights of the United States Constitution, as interpreted (on the whole) by the Supreme Court, are those that a substantial number of liberals would think reasonably well suited to what the United States now requires (though most would think that the protection of the individual in certain important areas, including sexual publication and practice, are much too weak).

The main parts of the criminal law, however, present a special problem not easily met by a scheme of civil rights that disable the legislature from taking certain political decisions. The liberal knows that many of the most important decisions required by an effective criminal law are not made by legislators at all, but by prosecutors deciding whom to prosecute for what crime, and by juries and judges deciding whom to convict and what sentences to impose. He also knows that these decisions are antecedently very likely to be corrupted by the external preferences of those who make these decisions because those they judge, typically, have attitudes and ways of life very different from their own. The liberal does not have available, as protection against these decisions, any strategy comparable to the strategy of civil rights that merely remove a decision from an institution. Decisions to prosecute, convict, and sentence must be made by someone. But he has available, in the notion of procedural rights, a different device to protect equality in a different way. He will insist that criminal procedure be structured to achieve a margin of safety in decisions, so that the process is biased strongly against the conviction of the innocent. It would be a mistake to suppose that the liberal thinks that these procedural rights will improve the *accuracy* of the criminal process, that is, the probability that any particular decision about guilt or innocence will be the right one. Procedural rights

intervene in the process, even at the cost of inaccuracy, to compensate in a rough way for the antecedent risk that a criminal process, especially if it is largely administered by one class against another, will be corrupted by the impact of external preferences that cannot be eliminated directly. This is only the briefest sketch of how various substantive and procedural civil rights follow from the liberal's initial conception of equality; it is meant to suggest, rather than demonstrate, the more precise argument that would be available for more particular rights.

So the liberal, drawn to the economic market and to political democracy for distinctly egalitarian reasons, finds that these institutions will produce inegalitarian results unless he adds to his scheme different sorts of individual rights. These rights will function as trump cards held by individuals; they will enable individuals to resist particular decisions in spite of the fact that these decisions are or would be reached through the normal workings of general institutions that are not themselves challenged. The ultimate justification for these rights is that they are necessary to protect equal concern and respect; but they are not to be understood as representing equality in contrast to some other goal or principle served by democracy or the economic market. The familiar idea, for example, that rights of redistribution are justified by an ideal of equality that overrides the efficiency ideals of the market in certain cases, has no place in liberal theory. For the liberal, rights are justified, not by some principle in competition with an independent justification of the political and economic institutions they qualify, but in order to make more perfect the only justification on which these other institutions may themselves rely. If the liberal arguments for a particular right are sound, then the right is an unqualified improvement in political morality, not a necessary but regrettable compromise of some other independent goal, like economic efficiency.

I SAID THAT the conservative holds one among a number of possible alternatives to the liberal conception of equality. Each of these alternatives shares the opinion that treating a person with respect requires treating him as the good man would wish to be treated. The conservative supposes that the good man would wish to be treated in accordance with the principles of a special sort of society, which I shall call the virtuous society. A virtuous society has these general features. Its members share a sound conception of virtue, that is, of the qualities and dispositions people should strive to have and exhibit. They share this conception of virtue not only privately, as individuals, but publicly: they believe their community, in its social and political activity, exhibits virtues, and that they have a responsibility, as citizens, to promote these virtues. In that sense they treat the lives of other members of their community as part of their own lives. The conservative position is

not the only position that relies on this ideal of the virtuous society (some forms of socialism rely on it as well). But the conservative is distinct in believing that his own society, with its present institutions, is a virtuous society for the special reason that its history and common experience are better guides to sound virtue than any nonhistorical and therefore abstract deduction of virtue from first principles could provide.

Suppose a conservative is asked to draft a constitution for a society generally like ours, which he believes to be virtuous. Like the liberal, he will see great merit in the familiar institutions of political democracy and an economic market. The appeal of these institutions will be very different for the conservative, however. The economic market, in practice, assigns greater rewards to those who, because they have the virtues of talent and industry, supply more of what is wanted by the other members of the virtuous society; and that is, for the conservative, the paradigm of fairness in distribution. Political democracy distributes opportunities, through the provisions of the civil and criminal law, as the citizens of a virtuous society wish it to be distributed, and that process will provide more scope for virtuous activity and less for vice than any less democratic technique. Democracy has a further advantage, moreover, that no other technique could have. It allows the community to use the processes of legislation to reaffirm, as a community, its public conception of virtue.

The appeal of the familiar institutions to the conservative is, therefore, very different from their appeal to the liberal. Since the conservative and the liberal both find the familiar institutions useful, though for different reasons, the existence of these institutions, as institutions, will not necessarily be a point of controversy between them. But they will disagree sharply over which corrective devices, in the form of individual rights, are necessary in order to maintain justice, and the disagreement will not be a matter of degree. The liberal, as I said, finds the market defective principally because it allows morally irrelevant differences, like differences in talent, to affect distribution, and he therefore considers that those who have less talent, as the market judges talent, have a right to some form of redistribution in the name of justice. But the conservative prizes just the feature of the market that puts a premium on talents prized in the community, because these are, in a virtuous community, virtues. So he will find no genuine merit, but only expediency, in the idea of redistribution. He will allow room for the virtue of charity, for it is a virtue that is part of the public catalog; but he will prefer private charity to public, because it is a purer expression of that virtue. He may accept public charity as well, particularly when it seems necessary to retain the political allegiance of those who would otherwise suffer too much to tolerate a capitalist society at all. But public charity, justified either on grounds of virtue or expediency, will seem to the conservative a compromise with the primary justification of the market,

rather than, as redistribution seems to the liberal, an improvement in that primary justification.

Nor will the conservative find the same defects in representative democracy that the liberal finds there. The conservative will not aim to exclude moralistic or other external preferences from the democratic process by any scheme of civil rights; on the contrary, it is the pride of democracy, for him, that external preferences are legislated into a public morality. But the conservative will find different defects in democracy, and he will contemplate a different scheme of rights to diminish the injustice they work.

The economic market distributes rewards for talents valued in the virtuous society, but since these talents are unequally distributed, wealth will be concentrated, and the wealthy will be at the mercy of an envious political majority anxious to take by law what it cannot take by talent. Justice requires some protection for the successful. The conservative will be (as historically he has been) anxious to hold some line against extensions of the vote to those groups most likely to be envious, but there is an apparent conflict between the ideals of abstract equality, even in the conservative conception, and disenfranchisement of large parts of the population. In any case, if conservatism is to be politically powerful, it must not threaten to exclude from political power those who would be asked to consent, formally or tacitly, to their own exclusion. The conservative will find more appeal in the different, and politically much more feasible, idea of rights to property.

These rights have the same force, though of course radically different content, as the liberal's civil rights. The liberal will, for his own purposes, accept some right to property, because he will count some sovereignty over a range of personal possessions essential to dignity. But the conservative will strive for rights to property of a very different order; he will want rights that protect, not some minimum dominion over a range of possessions independently shown to be desirable, but an unlimited dominion over whatever has been acquired through an institution that defines and rewards talent.

The conservative will not follow the liberal in the latter's concern for procedural rights in the criminal process. He will accept the basic institutions of criminal legislation and trial as proper; but he will see, in the possible acquittal of the guilty, not simply an inefficiency in the strategy of deterrence, but an affront to the basic principle that the censure of vice is indispensable to the honor of virtue. He will believe, therefore, that just criminal procedures are those that improve the antecedent probability that particular decisions of guilt or innocence will be accurate. He will support rights against interrogation or self-incrimination, for example, when such rights seem necessary to protect against torture or other means likely to elicit a confession from the innocent; but he will lose his concern for such rights when noncoercion can be guaranteed in other ways.

The fair-minded conservative will be concerned about racial discrimination, but his concern will differ from the concern of the liberal, and the remedies he will countenance will also be different. The distinction between equality of opportunity and equality of result is crucial to the conservative: the institutions of the economic market and representative democracy cannot achieve what he supposes they do unless each citizen has an equal opportunity to capitalize on his genuine talents and other virtues in the contest these institutions provide. But since the conservative knows that these virtues are unequally distributed, he also knows that equality of opportunity must have been denied if the outcome of the contest is equality of result.

The fair conservative must, therefore, attend to the charge that prejudice denies equality of opportunity between members of different races, and he must accept the justice of remedies designed to reinstate that equality, so far as this may be possible. But he will steadily oppose any form of "affirmative action" that offers special opportunities, like places in medical school or jobs, on criteria other than some proper conception of the virtue appropriate to the reward.

The issue of gun control, which I have thus far not mentioned, is an excellent illustration of the power of the conservative's constitutive political morality. He favors strict control of sexual publication and practice, but he opposes parallel control of the ownership or use of guns, though guns are more dangerous than sex. President Ford, in the second Carter–Ford debate, put the conservative position of gun control especially clearly. Sensible conservatives do not dispute that private and uncontrolled ownership of guns leads to violence, because it puts guns in circulation that bad men may use badly. But (President Ford said) if we meet that problem by not allowing good men to have guns, we are punishing the wrong people. It is, of course, distinctive to the conservative's position to regard regulation as condemnation and hence as punishment. But he must regard regulation that way, because he believes that opportunities should be distributed, in a virtuous society, so as to promote virtuous acts at the expense of vicious ones.

IN PLACE of a conclusion, I shall say something, though not much, about two of the many important questions raised by what I have said. The first is the question posed in the first section of this essay. Does the theory of liberalism I described answer the skeptical thesis? Does it explain our present uncertainty about what liberalism now requires, and whether it is a genuine and tenable political theory? A great part of that uncertainty can be traced, as I said, to doubts about the connections between liberalism and the suddenly unfashionable idea of economic growth. The opinion is popular that some form of utilitarianism, which does take growth to be a value in itself, is con-

stitutive of liberalism; but my arguments, if successful, show that this opinion is mistaken. Economic growth, as conventionally measured, was a derivative element in New Deal liberalism. It seemed to play a useful role in achieving the complex egalitarian distribution of resources that liberalism requires. If it now appears that economic growth injures more than it aids the liberal conception of equality, then the liberal is free to reject or curtail growth as a strategy. If the effect of growth is debatable, as I believe it is, then liberals will be uncertain, and appear to straddle the issue.

But the matter is more complicated than that analysis makes it seem, because economic growth may be deplored for many different reasons, some of which are plainly not available to the liberal. There is a powerful sentiment that a simpler way of life is better, in itself, than the life of consumption most Americans have recently preferred; this simpler life requires living in harmony with nature and is therefore disturbed when, for example, a beautiful mountainside is spoiled by strip mining for the coal that lies within it. Should the mountainside be saved, in order to protect a way of life that depends upon it, either by regulation that prohibits mining or by acquisition with taxpayers' money for a national park? May a liberal support such policies, consistently with his constitutive political morality? If he believes that government intervention is necessary to achieve a fair distribution of resources, on the ground that the market does not fairly reflect the preferences of those who want a park against those who want what the coal will produce, then he has a standard, egalitarian reason for supporting intervention. But suppose he does not believe that, but rather believes that those who want the park have a superior conception of what a truly worthwhile life is. A nonliberal may support conservation on that theory; but a liberal may not.

Suppose, however, that the liberal holds a different, more complex, belief about the importance of preserving natural resources. He believes that the conquest of unspoiled terrain by the consumer economy is self-fueling and irreversible, and that this process will make a way of life that has been desired and found satisfying in the past unavailable to future generations, and indeed to the future of those who now seem unaware of its appeal. He fears that this way of life will become unknown, so that the process is not neutral amongst competing ideas of the good life, but in fact destructive of the very possibility of some of these. In that case, the liberal has reasons for a program of conservation that are not only consistent with his constitutive morality, but sponsored by it.

I raise these possible lines of argument, not to provide the liberal with an easier path to a popular political position, but to illustrate the complexity of the issues that the new politics has provided. Liberalism seems precise and powerful when it is relatively clear what practical political positions are derivative from its fundamental constitutive morality; on these occasions poli-

tics allows what I called a liberal settlement of political positions. But such a settlement is fragile, and when it dissolves liberals must regroup, first through study and analysis, which will encourage a fresh and deeper understanding of what liberalism is, and then through the formation of a new and contemporary program for liberals. The study and theory are not yet in progress, and the new program is not yet in sight.

The second question I wish to mention, finally, is a question I have not touched at all. What is to be said in favor of liberalism? I do not suppose that I have made liberalism more attractive by arguing that its constitutive morality is a theory of equality that requires official neutrality amongst theories of what is valuable in life. That argument will provoke a variety of objections. It might be said that liberalism so conceived rests on skepticism about theories of the good, or that it is based on a mean view of human nature that assumes that human beings are atoms who can exist and find self-fulfillment apart from political community, or that it is self-contradictory because liberalism must itself be a theory of the good, or that it denies to political society its highest function and ultimate justification, which is that society must help its members to achieve what is in fact good. The first three of these objections need not concern us for long, because they are based on philosophical mistakes which I can quickly name if not refute. Liberalism cannot be based on skepticism. Its constitutive morality provides that human beings must be treated as equals by their government, not because there is no right and wrong in political morality, but because that is what is right. Liberalism does not rest on any special theory of personality, nor does it deny that most human beings will think that what is good for them is that they be active in society. Liberalism is not self-contradictory: the liberal conception of equality is a principle of political organization that is required by justice, not a way of life for individuals, and liberals, as such, are indifferent as to whether people choose to speak out on political matters, or to lead eccentric lives, or otherwise to behave as liberals are supposed to prefer.

But the fourth objection cannot so easily be set aside. There is no easy way to demonstrate the proper role of institutions that have a monopoly of power over the lives of others; reasonable and moral men will disagree. The issue is at bottom the issue I identified: what is the content of the respect that is necessary to dignity and independence?

That raises problems in moral philosophy and in the philosophy of mind that are fundamental for political theory though not discussed here; but this essay does bear on one issue sometimes thought to be relevant. It is sometimes said that liberalism must be wrong because it assumes that the opinions people have about the sort of lives they want are self-generated, whereas these opinions are actually the products of the economic system or other aspects of the society in which they live. That would be an objection

to liberalism if liberalism were based on some form of preference-utilitarianism which argued that justice in distribution consists in maximizing the extent to which people have what they happen to want. It is useful to point out, against that preference-utilitarianism, that since the preferences people have are formed by the system of distribution already in place, these preferences will tend to support that system, which is both circular and unfair. But liberalism, as I have described it, does not make the content of preferences the test of fairness in distribution. On the contrary, it is anxious to protect individuals whose needs are special or whose ambitions are eccentric from the fact that more popular preferences are institutionally and socially reinforced, for that is the effect and justification of the liberal's scheme of economic and political rights. Liberalism responds to the claim that preferences are caused by systems of distribution, with the sensible answer that in that case it is all the more important that distribution be fair in itself, not as tested by the preferences it produces.

NINE

Why Liberals Should Care about Equality

THOUGH LIBERALISM is often discussed as a single political theory, there are in fact two basic forms of liberalism and the distinction between them is of great importance. Both argue against the legal enforcement of private morality—both argue against the Moral Majority's views of homosexuality and abortion, for example—and both argue for greater sexual, political, and economic equality. But they disagree about which of these two traditional liberal values is fundamental and which derivative. Liberalism based on neutrality takes as fundamental the idea that government must not take sides on moral issues, and it supports only such egalitarian measures as can be shown to be the result of that principle. Liberalism based on equality takes as fundamental that government treat its citizens as equals, and insists on moral neutrality only to the degree that equality requires it.

The difference between these two versions of liberalism is crucial because both the content and appeal of liberal theory depends on which of these two values is understood to be its proper ground. Liberalism based on neutrality finds its most natural defense in some form of moral skepticism, and this makes it vulnerable to the charge that liberalism is a negative theory for uncommitted people. Moreover it offers no effective argument against utilitarian and other contemporary justifications for economic inequality, and therefore provides no philosophical support for those who are appalled at the Reagan administration's economic program. Liberalism based on equality suffers from neither of these defects. It rests on a positive commitment to an egalitarian morality and provides, in that morality, a firm contrast to the economics of privilege.

In this essay I shall set out what I believe are the main principles of liberalism based on equality.[1] This form of liberalism insists that government must treat people as equals in the following sense. It must impose no sacrifice or constraint on any citizen in virtue of an argument that the citizen could not accept without abandoning his sense of his equal worth. This abstract principle requires liberals to oppose the moralism of the New Right,

because no self-respecting person who believes that a particular way to live is most valuable for him can accept that this way of life is base or degrading. No self-respecting atheist can agree that a community in which religion is mandatory is for that reason finer, and no one who is homosexual that the eradication of homosexuality makes the community purer.

So liberalism as based on equality justifies the traditional liberal principle that government should not enforce private morality of this sort. But it has an economic as well as a social dimension. It insists on an economic system in which no citizen has less than an equal share of the community's resources just in order that others may have more of what he lacks. I do not mean that liberalism insists on what is often called "equality of result," that is, that citizens must each have the same wealth at every moment of their lives. A government bent on the latter ideal must constantly redistribute wealth, eliminating whatever inequalities in wealth are produced by market transactions. But this would be to devote *unequal* resources to different lives. Suppose that two people have very different bank accounts, in the middle of their careers, because one decided not to work, or not to work at the most lucrative job he could have found, while the other single-mindedly worked for gain. Or because one was willing to assume especially demanding or responsible work, for example, which the other declined. Or because one took larger risks which might have been disastrous but which were in fact successful, while the other invested conservatively. The principle that people must be treated as equals provides no good reason for redistribution in these circumstances; on the contrary, it provides a good reason *against* it.

For treating people as equals requires that each be permitted to use, for the projects to which he devotes his life, no more than an equal share of the resources available for all, and we cannot compute how much any person has consumed, on balance, without taking into account the resources he has contributed as well as those he has taken from the economy. The choices people make about work and leisure and investment have an impact on the resources of the community as a whole, and this impact must be reflected in the calculation equality demands. If one person chooses work that contributes less to other people's lives than different work he might have chosen, then, although this might well have been the right choice for him, given his personal goals, he has nevertheless added less to the resources available for others, and this must be taken into account in the egalitarian calculation. If one person chooses to invest in a productive enterprise rather than spend his funds at once, and if his investment is successful because it increases the stock of goods or services other people actually want, without coercing anyone, his choice has added more to social resources than the choice of someone who did not invest, and this, too, must be reflected in any calculation of whether he has, on balance, taken more than his share.

This explains, I think, why liberals have in the past been drawn to the

idea of a market as a method of allocating resources. An efficient market for investment, labor, and goods works as a kind of auction in which the cost to someone of what he consumes, by way of goods and leisure, and the value of what he adds, through his productive labor or decisions, is fixed by the amount his use of some resource costs others, or his contributions benefit them, in each case measured by their willingness to pay for it. Indeed, if the world were very different from what it is, a liberal could accept the results of an efficient market as *defining* equal shares of community resources. If people start with equal amounts of wealth, and have roughly equal levels of raw skill, then a market allocation would ensure that no one could properly complain that he had less than others, over his whole life. He could have had the same as they if he had made the decisions to consume, save, or work that they did.

But in the real world people do not start their lives on equal terms; some begin with marked advantages of family wealth or of formal and informal education. Others suffer because their race is despised. Luck plays a further and sometimes devastating part in deciding who gains or keeps jobs everyone wants. Quite apart from these plain inequities, people are not equal in raw skill or intelligence or other native capacities; on the contrary, they differ greatly, through no choice of their own, in the various capacities that the market tends to reward. So some people who are perfectly willing, even anxious, to make exactly the choices about work and consumption and savings that other people make end up with fewer resources, and no plausible theory of equality can accept this as fair. This is the defect of the ideal fraudulently called "equality of opportunity": fraudulent because in a market economy people do not have equal opportunity who are less able to produce what others want.

So a liberal cannot, after all, accept the market results as defining equal shares. His theory of economic justice must be complex, because he accepts two principles which are difficult to hold in the administration of a dynamic economy. The first requires that people have, at any point in their lives, different amounts of wealth insofar as the genuine choices they have made have been more or less expensive or beneficial to the community, measured by what other people want for their lives. The market seems indispensable to this principle. The second requires that people not have different amounts of wealth just because they have different inherent capacities to produce what others want, or are differently favored by chance. This means that market allocations must be corrected in order to bring some people closer to the share of resources they would have had but for these various differences of initial advantage, luck, and inherent capacity.

Obviously any practical program claiming to respect both these principles will work imperfectly and will inevitably involve speculation, compromise, and arbitrary lines in the face of ignorance. For it is impossible to

discover, even in principle, exactly which aspects of any person's economic position flow from his choices and which from advantages or disadvantages that were not matters of choice; and even if we could make this determination for particular people, one by one, it would be impossible to develop a tax system for the nation as a whole that would leave the first in place and repair only the second. There is therefore no such thing as the perfectly just program of redistribution. We must be content to choose whatever programs we believe bring us closer to the complex and unattainable ideal of equality, all things considered, than the available alternatives, and be ready constantly to reexamine that conclusion when new evidence or new programs are proposed.[2]

Nevertheless, in spite of the complexity of that ideal, it may sometimes be apparent that a society falls far short of any plausible interpretation of its requirements. It is, I think, apparent that the United States falls far short now. A substantial minority of Americans are chronically unemployed or earn wages below any realistic "poverty line" or are handicapped in various ways or burdened with special needs; and most of these people would do the work necessary to earn a decent living if they had the opportunity and capacity. Equality of resources would require more rather than less redistribution than we now offer.

This does not mean, of course, that we should continue past liberal programs, however inefficient these have proved to be, or even that we should insist on "targeted" programs of the sort some liberals have favored—that is, programs that aim to provide a particular opportunity or resource, like education or medicine, to those who need it. Perhaps a more general form of transfer, like a negative income tax, would prove on balance more efficient and fairer, in spite of the difficulties in such schemes. And whatever devices are chosen for bringing distribution closer to equality of resources, some aid undoubtedly goes to those who have avoided rather than sought jobs. This is to be regretted, because it offends one of the two principles that together make up equality of resources. But we come closer to that ideal by tolerating this inequity than by denying aid to the far greater number who would work if they could. If equality of resources were our only goal, therefore, we could hardly justify the present retreat from redistributive welfare programs.

WE MUST THEREFORE consider a further and more difficult question. Must liberals insist on equality of resources no matter what the cost to the national economy as a whole? It is far from obvious that treating people as equals forbids any deviation from equality of resources for any reason whatsoever. On the contrary, people with a lively sense of their own equal worth, and pride in their own convictions, can nevertheless accept certain

grounds for carrying special burdens for the sake of the community as a whole. In a defensive war, for example, we expect those who are capable of military service to assume a vastly greater share of danger than others. Nor is inequality permissible only in emergencies when the survival of the community is at stake. We might think it proper, for example, for the government to devote special resources to the training of exceptionally talented artists or musicians, beyond what the market would pay for the services these artists produce, even though this reduces the share others have. We accept this not because we think that the life of an artist is inherently more valuable than other lives, but because a community with a lively cultural tradition provides an environment within which citizens may live more imaginatively, and in which they might take pride. Liberalism need not be insensitive to these and similar virtues of community. The question becomes not whether any deviation is permitted, but what reasons for deviation are consistent with equal concern and respect.

That question is now pressing for this reason. Many economists believe that reducing economic inequality through redistribution is damaging to the general economy and, in the long run, self-defeating. Welfare programs, it is said, are inflationary, and the tax system necessary to support them depresses incentive and therefore production. The economy, it is claimed, can be restimulated only by reducing taxes and adopting other programs that will, in the short run, produce high unemployment and otherwise cause special damage to those already at the bottom of the economy. But this damage will only be temporary. For a more dynamic economy will produce prosperity, and this will in the end provide more jobs and more money for the handicapped and others truly needy.

Each of these propositions is doubtful, and they may well all be wrong. But suppose we were to accept them. Do they make a case for ignoring those in the economic cellar now? The argument would be unanswerable, of course, if *everyone* who lost because of stringent policies now would actually be better off in the long run. But though this is often suggested in careless supply-side rhetoric, it is absurd. People laid off for several years, with no effective retraining, are very unlikely to recoup their losses later, particularly if their psychological losses are counted. Children denied adequate nutrition or any effective chance of higher education will suffer permanent loss even if the economy follows the most optimistic path of recovery. Some of those who are denied jobs and welfare now, particularly the elderly, will in any case not live long enough to share in that recovery, however general it turns out to be.

So the currently popular argument, that we must reduce benefits now in order to achieve general prosperity later, is simply a piece of utilitarianism, which attempts to justify irreversible losses to a minority in order to achieve gains for the large majority. (One report of Reagan's Council of Economic

Advisers was quite explicit in embracing that utilitarian claim: it argued that his economic policies were required in order to avoid treating the very poor, who will permanently lose, as a special interest!) But this denies the principle fundamental to liberalism based on equality, the principle that people must be treated with equal concern. It asks some people to accept lives of great poverty and despair, with no prospect of a useful future, just in order that the great bulk of the community may have a more ample measure of what they are forever denied. Perhaps people can be forced into this position. But they cannot accept it consistently with a full recognition of their independence, and their right to equal concern on the part of their government.

But suppose the case for the administration's policies is put differently, by calling attention to the distinct social dangers of continuing or expanding past programs of redistribution. We might imagine two arguments of this sort. The first calls attention to the damage inflation does, not simply to the spending power, savings, and prospects of the majority, as individuals, but also to the public environment in which all citizens must live and in which all might take either pride or shame. As society becomes poorer, because production falls and wealth decays, it loses a variety of features we cherish. Its culture fails, its order declines, its system of criminal and civil justice becomes less accurate and less fair; in these and other ways it steadily recedes from our conception of a good society. The decline cannot be arrested by further taxation to support these public goods, for that will only shrink production further and accelerate the decline. According to this argument, those who lose by programs designed to halt inflation and reinvigorate the economy are called upon to make a sacrifice, not just in order to benefit others privately, but out of a sense of loyalty to the public institutions of their own society.

The second argument is different because it calls attention to the interests of future generations. It asks us to suppose that if we are zealous for equality now, we will so depress the wealth of the community that future Americans will be even less well off than the very poor are now. Future Americans will have no more, perhaps, than the citizens of economically depressed third world countries in the present world. The second argument comes to this: the present poor are asked to sacrifice in favor of their fellow citizens now, in order to prevent a much greater injustice, to many more citizens, later.

Neither of these two arguments plainly violates the liberal's axiomatic principle of equal concern and respect. Each can be offered to people who take pride in their equal worth and in the value of their convictions. But only in certain circumstances. Both arguments, though in different ways, appeal to the idea that each citizen is a member of a community, and that he can find, in the fate of that community, a reason for special burdens he can accept with honor rather than degradation. This is appropriate only

when that community offers him, at a minimum, the opportunity to develop and lead a life he can regard as valuable both to himself and to it.

We must distinguish, that is, between passive and active membership in a community. Totalitarian regimes suppose that anyone who is present in their community, and so is amenable to its political force, is a member of the community from whom sacrifice might fairly be asked in the name of that community's greatness and future. Treating people as equals requires a more active conception of membership. If people are asked to sacrifice for their community, they must be offered some reason why the community which benefits from that sacrifice is their community; there must be some reason why, for example, the unemployed blacks of Detroit should take more interest in either the public virtue or the future generations of Michigan than they do in those of Mali.

We must ask in what circumstances someone with the proper sense of his own independence and equal worth can take pride in a community as being his community, and two conditions, at least, seem necessary to this. He can take pride in its present attractiveness—in the richness of its culture, the justice of its institutions, the imagination of its education—only if his life is one that in some way draws on and contributes to these public virtues. He can identify himself with the future of the community and accept present deprivation as sacrifice rather than tyranny, only if he has some power to help determine the shape of that future, and only if the promised prosperity will provide at least equal benefit to the smaller, more immediate communities for which he feels special responsibilities, for example, his family, his descendants, and, if the society is one that has made this important to him, his race.

These seem minimal conditions, but they are nevertheless exigent. Together they impose serious restraints on any policy that denies any group of citizens, however small or politically negligible, the equal resources that equal concern would otherwise grant them. Of course no feasible program can provide every citizen with a life valuable in his own eyes. But these constraints set a limit to what a government that respects equality may deliberately choose when other choices are available. People must not be condemned, unless this is unavoidable, to lives in which they are effectively denied any active part in the political, economic, and cultural life of the community. So if economic policy contemplates an increase in unemployment, it must also contemplate generous public provision for retraining or public employment. The children of the poor must not be stinted of education or otherwise locked into positions at the bottom of society. Otherwise their parents' loyalty to them acts not as a bridge but as a bar to any identification with the future these parents are meant to cherish.

If this is right, then it suggests an order of priorities which any retrenchment in welfare programs should follow. Programs like food stamps, Aid to

Families with Dependent Children, and those using federal funds to make higher education available for the poor are the last programs that should be curtailed, or (what amounts to the same thing) remitted to the states through some "new federalism." If "targeted" programs like these are thought to be too expensive, or too inefficient, then government must show how alternative plans or programs will restore the promise of participation in the future that these programs offered. In any case, cutbacks in the over-all level of welfare provided to the poor should be accompanied by efforts to improve the social integration and political participation of blacks and other minorities who suffer most, in order to assure them a more prominent role in the community for which they sacrifice. Reductions in welfare should not be joined to any general retreat from affirmative action and other civil rights programs, or to any effort to repeal or resist improvements in the Voting Rights Act. That is why the economic and social programs so far proposed or enacted by the present administration seem so mean-spirited and cynical. Taken together, they would reduce rather than enlarge the political participation and social mobility of the class from which they demand the greatest sacrifice.

These observations offer only rough guidelines to the necessary conditions for asking people to sacrifice equal resources for the sake of their community. Different people will interpret these guidelines differently, and disagree about when they have been violated. But they may nevertheless serve as the beginning of an overdue development of liberal theory. During the long period of liberal ascendancy, from the New Deal through the 1960s, liberals felt confident that the immediate reduction of poverty was in every way good for the larger community. Social justice would, in Lyndon Johnson's phrase, make the society great. Liberals thus avoided the question of what liberalism requires when prosperity is threatened rather than enhanced by justice. They offered no coherent and feasible account of what might be called economic rights for hard times: the floor beneath which people cannot be allowed to drop for the greater good.

If liberals remember the counsel of equal concern, they will construct such a theory now, by pointing to the minimal grounds on which people with self-respect can be expected to regard a community as their community, and to regard its future as in any sense their future. If government pushes people below the level at which they can help shape the community and draw value from it for their own lives, or if it holds out a bright future in which their own children are promised only second-class lives, then it forfeits the only premise on which its conduct might be justified.

We need not accept the gloomy predictions of the New Right economists that our future will be jeopardized if we try to provide everyone with the means to lead a life with choice and value, or if we continue to accept mobility as an absolute priority and try to provide appropriate higher educa-

tion for everyone qualified. But if these gloomy predictions were sound, we should simply have to tailor our ambitions for the future accordingly. For society's obligation runs first to its living citizens. If our government can provide an attractive future only through present injustice—only by forcing some citizens to sacrifice in the name of a community from which they are in every sense excluded—then the rest of us should disown that future, however attractive, because we should not regard it as our future either.

TEN

What Justice Isn't

In *Spheres of Influence,* Michael Walzer proposes a pluralistic theory of social justice that aims at what he calls "complex" equality. He rejects the goals of "simple" egalitarians who want to make people as equal as possible in their *overall* situation. He thinks they ignore the fact that the conventions and shared understandings that make up a society do not treat all goods as subject to the same principles of distribution. Our conventions, he argues, assign different kinds of resources and opportunities to different "spheres" of justice, each of which is governed by its own distinct principle of fairness. These conventions provide what Walzer calls the "social meaning" of different goods; for us it is part of social meaning, he says, that medicine and other necessities of a decent life should be distributed according to need, punishment and honors according to what people deserve, higher education according to talent, jobs according to the needs of the employer, wealth according to skill and luck in the market, citizenship according to the needs and traditions of the community, and so forth.

The theory of complex equality consists in two ideas. Each kind of resource must be distributed in accordance with the principle appropriate to its sphere, and success in one sphere must not spill over to allow domination in another. We must not allow someone who achieves great wealth in the market, for example, to buy votes and so control politics. But if we keep the boundaries of the spheres intact, then we need no overall comparison of individuals across the spheres; we need not worry that some people have yachts and others not even a rowboat, or that some are more persuasive in politics than others, or that some win prizes and love while others lack both.

This is a relaxed and agreeable vision of social justice: it promises a society at peace with its own traditions, without the constant tensions, comparisons, jealousies, and regimentation of "simple" equality. Citizens live together in harmony, though no one has exactly the wealth or education or opportunities of anyone else, because each understands that he has received what justice requires within each sphere, and does not think that his self-

respect or standing in the community depends on any overall comparison of his overall situation with that of others. Unfortunately, Walzer offers no comprehensive description of what life in such a society would be like, of who would have what share of the different types of resources he discusses. Instead he offers anecdotal and historical examples of how different societies, including our own, have developed distinct principles for distribution in different spheres.

His aim in providing these examples is not only practical. He hopes to break the grip that the formal style has lately had on Anglo-American political philosophy. Such philosophers try to find some inclusive formula that can be used to measure social justice in any society, and that can therefore serve as a test rather than only an elaboration of our own conventional social arrangements. John Rawls argues, for example, that no inequality in what he calls "primary goods" is justified unless it improves the overall position of the worst-off class, and this formula takes no account of which of Walzer's spheres such goods are drawn from. Utilitarians insist, on the contrary, that whatever social arrangement will produce the greatest long-term happiness of the greatest number is just, and this means that justice might conceivably recommend violating one of Walzer's spheres by selling political offices at auction, for example, even though our conventions condemn this. "Simple" egalitarians argue that justice lies in everyone's having the same resources overall, which might mean abandoning prizes and badges of honor, and "libertarians" argue that it lies in allowing people to buy whatever others rightfully own and are willing to sell, whether this is corn or labor or sex.

Theories like these ignore the social meanings of the goods they try to distribute. So they will inevitably be arid, unhistorical, and above all abstract. We can test them only against our private "intuitions" of what would be just in this or that circumstance, not by asking how they would strike most members of our own community, and we can argue them only through highly artificial examples tailored to bring out some stark contrast between isolated abstract principles. Such theories seem more at home with mathematics than with politics.

Walzer shows us how different, and how much more concrete, political analysis can be. His historical examples are often fascinating, and this, along with his clear prose, makes his book a pleasure to read. The examples are nicely judged to illustrate the characteristic features of each of his spheres of justice, and the persistence yet diversity of certain themes in the social meanings people give to their experience. The Greeks provided free public drama because they saw this as a social need, but they made the most rudimentary provision for the poor; the Middle Ages offered welfare for the soul but not for the body. Earlier communities provided everyone with holidays that guaranteed a public life; we have switched to vacations whose social

meaning is private variety and choice. Some of Walzer's examples have a different function: they illustrate the dangers of failing to protect the boundaries between spheres. George Pullman, who invented Pullman cars, built a town around his factory and tried to own his employees' lives as he owned the machines at which they worked. He tried to use his success in the market to dominate the different spheres of politics and citizenship, and this explains why society and the courts checked his ambitions. Walzer's range is admirable: we are encouraged to consider the meritocracies of China under the dynasties, a cooperative garbage-collecting firm in San Francisco, the *Kula* practice of gift exchange among the Trobriand Islanders, and education among the Aztecs.

Nevertheless, his central argument fails. The ideal of complex equality he defines is not attainable, or even coherent, and the book contains very little that could be helpful in thinking about actual issues of justice. It tells us to look to social conventions to discover the appropriate principles of distribution for particular goods, but the very fact that we debate about what justice requires, in particular cases, shows that we have no conventions of the necessary sort. In the United States we sponsor medical research through taxes, and after long political struggles we offer Medicare to the old and Medicaid to the poor, though the latter remains very controversial. Walzer thinks these programs demonstrate that our community assigns medical care to a particular sphere, the sphere of needs that the state must satisfy. But the brutal fact is that we do not provide anything like the same medical care for the poor that the middle classes can provide for themselves, and surely this also counts in deciding what the "social meaning" of medicine is for our society. Even those who agree that some medical care must be provided for everyone disagree about limits. Is it part of the social meaning of medicine that elective surgery must be free? That people "need" heart transplants?

Our political arguments almost never begin in some shared understanding of the pertinent principles of distribution. Every important issue is a contest between competing models. Nor do we accept that everything we find valuable must be wholly subject to a single logic of distribution: if we recognize spheres of justice, we also recognize the need for interaction between them. The most important way in which wealth influences politics, for example, is by buying not votes but television time. Those who favor restricting campaign expenses say that money should not buy office. But their opponents reply that such restrictions would violate rights to property as well as free speech, so the issue belongs to no settled sphere of justice, but is rather the subject of bargaining and compromise endlessly debated.

Walzer's response to these plain facts about political argument shows how feeble his positive theory of justice really is: "A given society is just if its substantive life is lived in a certain way—that is, in a way faithful to the

shared understandings of the members. (When people disagree about the meaning of social goods, when understandings are controversial, then justice requires that the society be faithful to the disagreements, providing institutional channels for their expression, adjudicative mechanisms, and alternative distributions.)"

This passage confirms Walzer's deep relativism about justice. He says, for example, that a caste system is just in a society whose traditions accept it, and that it would be unjust in such a society to distribute goods and other resources equally. But his remarks about what justice requires in a society whose members disagree about justice are mysterious. Does "alternative distributions" mean medical care for the poor in some cities but not in others? How can a society that must make up its mind whether to permit political action committees to finance election campaigns really be "faithful" to disagreement about the social meaning of elections and political speech? What would "being faithful" mean?

If justice is only a matter of following shared understandings, then how can the parties be debating about justice when there is no shared understanding? In that situation no solution can *possibly* be just, on Walzer's relativistic account, and politics can be only a selfish struggle. What can it mean even to say that people disagree about social meanings? The fact of the disagreement shows that there is no shared social meaning to disagree about. Walzer has not thought through the consequences of his relativism for a society like ours, in which questions of justice are endlessly contested and debated.

Why does Walzer not recognize that his theory must be irrelevant in such a society? He does discuss a number of contemporary political issues in some detail, and these discussions suggest an explanation. He takes no position of his own about some of the issues he describes, and when he does express his own opinion he sometimes provides no argument at all for it. But when he does argue for his own views, by trying to show how these follow from the general scheme of complex equality, he reveals that he is actually relying on a hidden and mystical premise that plays no part in his formal statements of that scheme, but that helps to explain why he thinks that it can give practical advice for people in our circumstances.

What is this premise? He tacitly assumes that there are only a limited number of spheres of justice whose essential principles have been established in advance and must therefore remain the same for all societies. He also assumes that, though any particular community is free to choose whether to assign some type of resource to one or another of these fixed spheres, by developing the appropriate conventions, it must do so on an all-or-nothing basis. It cannot construct new patterns of distribution that have elements drawn from different spheres. So, if a community recognizes medicine as something people need, or establishes political offices, or develops

institutions of specialized higher education, or recognizes some group of people as citizens, it is thereby committed to every feature of the spheres of social welfare or merit or education or citizenship as Walzer understands these. A caste system is not in itself unjust, but if it develops an official bureaucracy of civil servants, it may not restrict offices within that bureaucracy to higher castes, because the concept of bureaucracy belongs, according to Walzer, to its own sphere, the sphere of merit. A capitalist society, he argues, may, with perfect justice, assign medical care wholly to the market. Or (perhaps) it may assign only a fixed, minimum level of care to the sphere of need. But "so long as communal funds are spent . . . to finance research, build hospitals, and pay the fees of doctors in private practice, the services that these expenditures underwrite must be equally available to all citizens," and there is then "no reason to respect the doctor's market freedom."

Once the hidden assumption—that a community must accept a preestablished sphere on an all-or-nothing basis—is exposed, the fallacy in these arguments becomes clear. We cannot just rule out in advance the possibility that though justice requires the state to intervene in the market for medicine in order to ensure that the poor have some care, it does not require that the poor be provided the same medical care the rich are able to buy. Walzer takes the contrary view that justice demands a full national health service. We may find this attractive, but we need an argument for it, and merely constructing an ideal sphere and calling it the sphere of need, provides no argument. The point is a crucial one, because it might be that any genuine argument for a national health service would contradict Walzer's relativism. It might show that a rich society that leaves medical care entirely to the market would not be a just society, as he thinks, but would in fact be even more unjust than a society, like ours, that provides some but not enough free medical care.

Walzer relies even more heavily on the idea of fixed, preordained spheres in his discussion of university admission programs that give some preference to minority applicants. "In our culture," he says, "careers are supposed to be open to talents," and "just as we could not adopt a system of preventive detention without violating the rights of innocent people, even if we weighed fairly the costs and benefits of the system as a whole, so we can't adopt a quota system without violating the rights of candidates." He knows, of course, that many people "in our culture" do not think that the affirmative action programs he has in mind violate the rights of candidates. They reject the analogy to punishing the innocent. They deny that there is some canonical set of qualities, fixed in advance, such that people are entitled to be admitted to medical schools on the basis of these qualities alone, no matter what special needs a society might have for doctors or what larger needs might also be served through professional education. Walzer, on the con-

trary, believes that a certain conception of talent is automatically assigned to certain university places or professional offices, no matter how thoroughly the community is divided about this. So he says that any racial preference corrupts one of the spheres he has constructed—the sphere of "office"—in order to serve the sphere of welfare, and thinks he needs no better argument than that. He is bewitched by the music of his own Platonic spheres.

Criticism of Walzer's idea of complex equality must not end here, however, because his theory is not only unhelpful but finally incoherent. It ignores the "social meaning" of a tradition much more fundamental than the discrete traditions it asks us to respect. For it is part of our common political life, if anything is, that justice is our critic not our mirror, that any decision about the distribution of any good—wealth, welfare, honors, education, recognition, office—may be reopened, no matter how firm the traditions that are then challenged, that we may always ask of some settled institutional scheme whether it is fair. Walzer's relativism is faithless to the single most important social practice we have: the practice of worrying about what justice really is.

So a theory that ties justice to conventions would not be acceptable even if it were available to us. Walzer sometimes seems to suggest that the only alternative is the "simple" equality he dismisses, which requires that everyone have exactly the same share of everything. But no one argues for that: no one suggests that punishments or Nobel prizes should be distributed by lot. Few egalitarians would even accept simple equality in income or wealth. Any defensible version of equality must be much more subtle; it must permit inequalities that can be traced to the choices people have made about what kind of work to do, what kinds of risks to take, what kind of life to lead.[1]

But we need to argue for any theory of justice of that kind, by finding and defending general, critical principles of the appropriate sort. So Walzer's book provides a wholly unintended defense of the style of philosophy he wants to banish. His failure confirms the instinct that drives philosophers to their formulas and artificial examples and personal intuitions. Perhaps we have gone too far in that direction. Mathematical preference functions, fictitious social contracts, and the other paraphernalia of modern political theory do sometimes blind us to the subtle distinctions Walzer teases out of history. Political philosophers who reflect on his historical studies—particularly his demonstration of how different societies have conceived very different resources as needs—will be more imaginative about the possibilities of social arrangements in our own society.

In the end, however, political theory can make no contribution to how we govern ourselves except by struggling, against all the impulses that drag us back into our own culture, toward generality and some reflective basis

for deciding which of our traditional distinctions and discriminations are genuine and which spurious, which contribute to the flourishing of the ideals we want, after reflection, to embrace, and which serve only to protect us from the personal costs of that demanding process. We cannot leave justice to convention and anecdote.

ELEVEN

Can a Liberal State Support Art?

My topic in this essay is art and the humanities and how far the public should support these to make them excellent and fecund. People have discussed this subject endlessly, and discussion always begins by opposing two methods of study: the economic and the lofty approaches to the matter.

The economic approach—I use a rather generous definition—takes as its premise that a community should have the character and quality of art that it wishes to buy at the price necessary to secure it. The lofty approach, in contrast, turns its back on what the people think they want; it concentrates instead on what it is good for people to have. It insists that art and culture must reach a certain degree of sophistication, richness, and excellence in order for human nature to flourish, and that the state must provide this excellence if the people will not or cannot provide it for themselves.

These two approaches are generally thought to be opposed as well as different, because it seems at first blush that the economic approach would commend either no public support for the arts, or very little. The argument goes this way. The *market* is the most effective instrument for deciding how much and what kind of culture people want at the necessary price. Would people contemplate Aristotle contemplating Homer if they had to pay the full cost of that opportunity, including their share of the cost of maintaining a museum, buying that painting from foreign owners, insuring and guarding it, and paying taxes on the property on which the museum sits? There is only one way to discover this. Let a museum charge people an admission price that reflects all these costs; then we shall see whether the museum was right in thinking that this is what enough of the people wanted badly enough. If art is left to the market in this way—and the same holds for universities providing courses in the humanities—then the public automatically will have exactly the art it really does want at the price it is willing to pay. But if public support enters this picture—if the public treasury subsidizes part of the true cost of space in front of a Rembrandt so that the museum's admission charges do not reflect the true cost—then this means that

the public as a whole is spending more on art than it wishes to spend, at the expense of whatever the funds would otherwise have provided. The economic approach thus seems to rule out public subsidy almost by definition.

The lofty approach seems a much more promising avenue to pursue if we begin, as many of us do, by wanting to find some justification for a generous level of state support. We should decide how much collectively to spend on art by asking how much is necessary to make our culture excellent. The economic approach seems too mundane, almost Philistine, in contrast.

But before embracing the lofty approach, we must at least pause to notice its warts. First, experience teaches that those who would benefit most from subsidies to universities and museums and other cultural institutions are, on the whole, people who are already very well off, because they have been taught how to use and enjoy art. It seems unfair to provide, under the cover of some ideal of human flourishing, further and special benefits to those who already flourish more than most. Would it not be better to divert funds from rich museums to poor clinics and subsidized medical care? Second, the lofty approach seems haughtily paternalistic. Orthodox liberalism holds that no government should rely, to justify its use of public funds, on the assumption that some ways of leading one's life are more worthy than others, that it is more worthwhile to look at Titian on the wall than watch a football game on television. Perhaps it is more worthwhile to look at Titian; but that is not the point. More people disagree with this judgment than agree with it, so it must be wrong for the state, which is supposed to be democratic, to use its monopoly of taxing and police power to enforce judgments only a minority accepts.

These difficulties in the lofty approach send us back to the economic approach, this time to study it more sympathetically and carefully. Perhaps it can furnish some support for state aid to the arts after all. I suggested that the economic approach must reject subsidy because only a market uncontaminated by subsidy can discover the public's true preferences about how its funds should be spent. But that was a simplification: the connections between market prices and people's true preferences are not always so tight. What someone is willing and able to spend on something depends on how much he has to spend altogether. If wealth is very unequally distributed in a community, then the fact that a rich man buys caviar while a poor man goes without bread does not mean that the community as a whole values the caviar more than the bread. For this reason, market prices and transactions will not always be a fair measure of what the community as a whole really wants.

I offer this only as a reasonably clear qualification of my original dictum about the market; unfortunately it offers no help in using the economic approach to justify subsidy to the arts. It can furnish an argument for a sub-

sidy—for bread, for example—only if those who lack what is to be subsidized are relatively poor. But this is not true (or so it seems) of those who could not afford to go to the opera unless the opera were subsidized, but could afford it and would go if it were. They belong for the most part to the middle classes; indeed that was the basis of one of my initial objections to the lofty approach.

There is, however, another well-known qualification to the dictum that the market is a fair test of what the community wants for what it has to spend. This one is much more promising, for it might support an argument that art and the humanities, properly understood, are what the economists call "public goods" and for that reason must be supported from the public treasury rather than only from private purses.

Public goods are those whose production cannot efficiently be left to the market because it is impossible (or very difficult or expensive) to exclude those who do not pay from receiving the benefit and so riding free. People have no incentive to pay for what they will receive anyway if others buy it. Military defense is a common and useful example. Suppose an army could be raised only by private subscription. If I think my neighbors will purchase, together, an army large enough to repel an invasion, then I have no incentive to pay my share, because they cannot exclude me from the benefit they have bought. There is no way their army can protect them without also protecting me. Environmental benefits provide another example. If my neighbors spend enough to purify the air they breathe, they will also purify the air I breathe; they cannot exclude me from that benefit if I have not paid my share. So even though I might be anxious to pay my fair share of the cost of an army or of clean air if this were necessary in order for me to have these benefits, I nevertheless have a strong reason not to pay my share in the hope that others will buy the army or clean the air. But since everyone else will have the same reason, there is a lively danger that we will not, collectively, spend the sum we would be willing to spend if we each thought this necessary; so we will, perversely, end by not spending what we collectively want to spend.

In these circumstances, according to orthodox economic theory, the best remedy is for the state to calculate what the public would be willing to spend if necessary, and to spend that sum itself, gathered from taxes which the public is required by law to pay. Notice that the lofty approach plays no role in this kind of argument for state support. There is no assumption that the people should have military security or fresh air whether they want it or not; but just the very different assumption that they do want it, at the price that will provide it, so that state intervention is merely a tactical solution to a technical problem.

Such an analysis assumes that public officials can know, or at least have a respectable opinion about, how much the people would spend collectively

if this were necessary. Economists have puzzled a great deal not only about how the state could discover this information but also about the more fundamental question of what exactly it means to say, of someone, that he would pay a particular price for something under circumstances that in fact never arise. They have offered various theories of what this should be taken to mean and of how the state can form some idea of what that hypothetical price is. All these theories are complex, and several are ingenious. But the important point here is that the usefulness of the public-goods approach depends on the availability of a reasonably plausible device for deciding what the public really wants to pay for whatever it is that the market, for technical reasons, cannot provide.

Particular cultural experiences, like the opportunity to hear a particular performance of a particular opera, are not public goods because it is easy to exclude those who will not pay. But the public-goods problem can arise in a partial or mixed way when private transactions have spillover effects which others value and from which they cannot be excluded. Consider vaccination. If someone pays the price necessary to be vaccinated, he secures for himself a special kind of protection from which those who do not pay are excluded; but if enough people are vaccinated, then even those who are not themselves vaccinated will benefit to a lesser degree because the risk of disease will be reduced for them. This "free-clinger" problem may also produce the perverse result, if production were left to the market, that society will not have what it wants at the price it would be willing to pay. Enough people might decide not to buy vaccination, in the hope of having much of the benefit anyway, so that overall protection drops below the level the community as a whole really wants. Once again state provision of vaccination in one form or another, rather than leaving vaccination to the market, would be justified on that ground, as wholly compatible with the economic approach to the matter.

Perhaps art should be regarded as at least a mixed public good, like vaccination, and some state subsidy justified on that ground. This suggestion assumes that when some people buy art and culture—by buying books or visiting fee-charging museums or attending concerts or studying in universities—other people who do not engage in these transactions benefit to a significant degree. Plainly that assumption is justified to some degree, but the power of the suggestion turns on the character and significance of the free-rider benefit. How do transactions in culture benefit those who are not parties? A sizable economic literature has been devoted to that question. Most of it considers a kind of free-rider benefit we might call "extrinsic" because it is not of the same aesthetic or intellectual character as the benefits parties to the transactions receive. For example, New Yorkers who never use the Metropolitan Museum benefit financially when tourists come to their city to visit the museum—and remain to spend money elsewhere.

These New Yorkers may benefit in another way: through the pride they may feel when their community's culture is celebrated and renowned.

My sense of the literature, however, is that the sum of the extrinsic benefits of this sort, even generously defined, would not be high enough to justify any substantial level of public support for that reason alone. I also have a sense that any attempt to justify art as a public good by appealing to this extrinsic kind of benefit demeans the suggestion that art is a public good. The initial appeal of that suggestion, I believe, lies in our sense that art makes a general contribution to the community as a whole, not just to those who enter into special commercial transactions to enjoy it, a contribution that is not extrinsic to aesthetic and intellectual experience, but one that, on the contrary, is exactly of that character.

The sense I report—that art and culture have intrinsic benefits for the public as a whole—rests on an assumption that is familiar and sound: that culture is a seamless web, that high culture and popular culture are not distinct but influence one another reciprocally. By general culture I do not just mean, though I mean to include, popular novels and plays and music. I mean also the whole range of diction and trope and style available within a community, as these are displayed in every aspect of communication from reporting and televizing public and athletic events to advertising campaigns. I mean, in short, the general intellectual environment in which we all live.

The influence of high culture on general or popular culture is reciprocated; but we should concentrate on the influence the former exerts on the latter and notice the various dimensions of that influence. High culture provides popular culture with form: musical comedy and television thrillers alike exploit genres first developed in opera and novel. It provides popular culture with reference: the working vocabulary of our community is saturated with specific reference to Oedipus, Hamlet, Carmen. (Hair-curling equipment is called "Carmen," for example, and decorated with a rose and advertised on television through the Toreador Song.) As a complement, high culture provides general culture with resonance. Specific references, such as the reference to Carmen, supply not just a convenient set of ideas easily invoked, but a set of ideas valuable exactly because they are identified as belonging to high culture and therefore as having a distinct aesthetic value.

All this might be summarized in the familiar phrase: spillover. It seems an encouraging start to an argument whose end may be the justification of state support for high culture. Because high culture, like vaccination, provides spillover benefits to the public at large, most of whom do not engage in the specific commercial transactions that finance it, state support is necessary to prevent the community's having less than it really wants of high culture because of the free-rider (or free-clinger) problem. Unfortunately

there are grave flaws in this argument, which are, taken together, fatal to it in this original form.

The first is the problem of time lag. In the standard examples of public goods, like clean air and military defense, the people who will pay for these goods through their taxes, if the state supplies them, are for the most part the very people who will benefit. If the state supports high culture in order to secure spillover benefits for the general intellectual culture of the community as a whole, on the other hand, we cannot be confident that those who will pay the cost will reap the benefit, for the impact may be long enough delayed so that the main beneficiaries belong to a different generation of taxpayers. This objection, by itself, need not be fatal to our argument. It might be countered by using the public-good argument to support, not a one-time state contribution to art, paid for by those who do not receive the major benefit, but a continuing program of contribution, so that each generation might be said to pay for benefits to the next, and each will both give and receive.

The second problem compounds the first, however. This is the problem of indeterminacy. Public officials can predict, perhaps with some confidence, how any particular level of public expense on military defense will improve security and so give the public what collectively it wants, and how any particular device or program for combating pollution will affect the quality of the air people breathe. But though we know that a decision to have a great many more productions of grand opera or larger collections of Renaissance paintings or more advanced university courses in classical literature will affect the general intellectual climate a generation hence, we have no way of predicting, even roughly, what genres or tropes or references it will add to that climate. It is in the nature of the transfer from high to general culture that such effects depend on judgments and reactions and developments that would be worthless because mechanical if they could be predicted. This fact weakens my original public-good argument for state support for the arts in a fundamental way. If we cannot predict what impact a public program will have on people's lives in the future, how can we justify that program as helping to give them what they really want?

The third difficulty is more fundamental yet. Any public-good argument requires some degree of information about what the public would be willing to spend to secure the benefit in question. In conventional examples—military defense and clean air—economists have difficulty devising techniques for identifying this sum once the market has been dismissed as inaccurate. But they are encouraged to search for these techniques because they assume, reasonably enough, that the community as a whole does want military security and clean air at *some* substantial price. The difficulty is one of accuracy and refinement. The parallel assumption needed for a public-good argument for art—that the community wants a popular or

general culture of a certain character—is not only problematical; it may well be incoherent.

The intellectual culture of a community exerts such a profound influence over the preferences and values of its members that the question of whether and how much they would prefer a different culture to the one they have becomes at best deeply mysterious. I can explain why by beginning with a dramatic and improbable example. Imagine some cultural tragedy in which whole types of aesthetic experience familiar to us have wholly disappeared: no one has any idea, for example, of combining music and drama in the form we call opera. We could not say that people living in that culturally impoverished state would mind. They could not, after all, miss opera or regret not having it. Part of their situation, an aspect of their impoverished culture, would be that they would not have the capacity to mind, miss, or regret. What sense does it make, then, to say that if we do not preserve opera for them, we would be denying them something they want?

We would certainly want to say that they are missing something, that their lives are impoverished in some way compared to ours. But that is very different. It is not their judgment about their lives, which is what the economic approach in general and the public-goods argument in particular requires, but rather *our* judgment about their lives. We might want to say: If they knew what they were missing, they would miss it. But that is saying that if they did want it, they would want it—which is true but unhelpful. Someone may say: They would in any case want pleasure, and they would have more pleasure if they had opera. But this won't do. Set aside the thorny question whether it is always (or ever) right to say that people want pleasure. Set aside the question whether we can measure pleasure in the way this suggestion assumes. How can we say that people whose culture has developed without opera, and is therefore different from ours in countless other ways, would have less pleasure from what their culture does provide than we have from our own? We, who know opera, take pleasure in it—or some of us do—and we would be pained at suddenly finding it unavailable. But this is because the structure of our culture has that consequence for people fully immersed in it, and we can draw no conclusions about the hedonic states of people whose culture is entirely different. A taste for opera is in this way unlike some raw material—oil—that future generations might have to do without. If we assume their desires are much like our own—they want heat and light and transportation—we can say that not having oil gives them less of what they want, even if they have never heard of oil. But we cannot make a parallel assumption about people whose culture is unlike ours: we cannot say their desires are otherwise like our own, because the desires now in question are those produced by and bound up in the culture we assume they do not have.

Nor does it help if we abandon speculating about future generations and

simply ask whether we ourselves would be willing collectively to pay any particular price to retain some valued part of our culture. For very much the same problem arises anyway. Suppose we ask, for example, whether our community would rather have the present richness and diversity of its general culture or more and better public parks. We have no way of approaching this question intelligently. The value public parks have for us and the ways in which we find value in them depend greatly on our culture. Parks would have very different meaning and value for us if we had no cultural tradition of romantic landscape, for example, a tradition that began in high culture, though it is now carried largely by general culture, including advertising. So the choice just offered is spurious: we would be assuming our present culture in valuing something we could only have, by hypothesis, by giving that culture up. Since our intellectual environment provides the spectacles through which we identify experiences as valuable, it cannot sensibly be put on the scales as one of the experiences it identifies, to be weighed against others and found more or less valuable than they.

These are dramatic examples, but the point also holds when the aspects or features of culture supposedly being valued are less comprehensive, more a matter of tone or degree. Imagine opera, not disappearing entirely without a trace, but losing its edge and excellence and general seriousness, no longer being performed well or in state, no longer being thought a matter of the highest art worth enormous sacrifice to perfect, in short, no longer being taken so seriously. This would be at once a change in the quality of an art and also a change in how much people want quality in that art, and these would not be separate and distinct changes. We are no more able, just because the stakes are not so high, to separate what is being valued from the social and personal apparatus being used to value it. This is the final blow to efforts to construct a public-good argument on the spillover effects of high culture. That argument cannot work without some way to identify, or at least make reasonable judgments about, what people—in the present or future—want by way of culture; and culture is too fundamental, too basic to our schemes of value, to make questions of that kind intelligible. Our problem is not one of discovery but of sense.

This essay began with the familiar story of opposition between the economic approach and the lofty approach as alternate ways to puzzle about public support for the arts. I said that the economic approach, at first glance, seemed to argue against public support; but I undertook to consider whether, on a closer look, the economic approach might favor it instead. That hope was encouraged by an apparent analogy between the public benefits of private transactions in art and familiar examples of public goods like military defense and clean-air campaigns. The analogy failed, but not in a way that reinstates the economic approach as the opponent of public support. On the contrary, all the difficulties in the claim that economics

smiles on public support are equally difficulties in the opposing claim, with which we began, that economics frowns on it. The difficulties are symmetrical for both the positive and the negative claim. Nothing I said about the three problems of time lag, indeterminacy, and incoherence indicates that the public does not want what it would receive through public support. Or that the market, uncontaminated by any subsidy, is the best test of what the public does want at the price. My argument, if sound, justifies a much more radical and interesting conclusion, which is that the economic approach is simply unavailable either way as a test of whether art should be publicly supported or at what level. The issue of public support lies beneath or beyond the kinds of tastes, preferences, and values that can sensibly be deployed in an economic analysis.

Where, then, do we stand? We began with two approaches, the economic and the lofty; the first is now deemed unavailable, so presumably we are left with the second. But my argument, particularly with respect to the indeterminacy of prediction, seems to challenge the usefulness of the lofty approach as well. Once we acknowledge that the main impact of any program of aid to high culture will be, for most people and in the long run, its impact on general culture, and also that it is next to impossible to predict the details of that impact, the argument that we must aid culture to make people's lives better lives seems a shot in the dark, an article of faith. It suddenly appears that we have no argument at all, either way, and it is time to regroup. It is time to notice a distinction I have so far left latent: the distinction between two consequences our culture has for us. It provides the particular paintings, performances, and novels, designs, sports, and thrillers that we value and take delight in; but it also provides the structural frame that makes aesthetic values of that sort possible, that makes them values for us. We can use this distinction to define an approach to the problem of public support for the arts that is not the economic, and yet is different from the more unattractive versions, at least, of the lofty.

My suggestion is this. We should identify the structural aspects of our general culture as themselves worthy of attention. We should try to define a rich cultural structure, one that multiplies distinct possibilities or opportunities of value, and count ourselves trustees for protecting the richness of our culture for those who will live their lives in it after us. We cannot say that in so doing we will give them more pleasure, or provide a world they will prefer as against alternative worlds we could otherwise create. That is the language of the economic approach, and it is unavailable here. We can, however, insist—how can we deny this?—that it is better for people to have complexity and depth in the forms of life open to them, and then pause to see whether, if we act on that principle, we are open to any objection of elitism or paternalism.

Now let me concentrate on the structure of culture, the possibilities it

allows, rather than on discrete works or occasions of art. The center of a community's cultural structure is its shared language. A language is neither a private nor a public good as these are technically defined; it is inherently social, as these are not, and as a whole it generates our ways of valuing and so is not itself an object of valuation. But language has formal similarities to what I called a mixed public good. Someone can exclude others, by relatively inexpensive means, from what he or she writes or says on any particular occasion. People cannot, however, be excluded from the language as a whole; at least it would be perverse to exclude them because, from the point of view of those who use a language, free riders are better than no riders. And the private transactions in language—the occasions of private or controlled speech—collectively determine what the shared language is. The books that we write and read, the education we provide and receive, the millions of other daily transactions in language we conduct, many of them commercial, all of these in the long run determine what language we have. We are all beneficiaries or victims of what is done to the language we share.

A language can diminish; some are richer and better than others. It barely makes sense to say that people in later generations would prefer not to have had their language diminished in some particular way, by losing some particular structural opportunity. They would lack the vocabulary in which to express—that is to say, have—that regret. Nor does it make much more sense to say that they would prefer to have a language richer in opportunities than they now have. No one can want opportunities who has no idea what these are opportunities of. Nevertheless, it is perfectly sensible to say that they would be worse off were their language to lack opportunities that ours offers. Of course, in saying this, we claim to know what is in their interest, what would make their lives better.

Is this paternalism? Now we need more distinctions. Paternalism is primitive when those in charge act in defiance of the preferences of those they govern, though supposedly in their interests. The police make people wear seat belts or avoid unorthodox sexual associations, in spite of their driving or sexual tastes. Paternalism is more sophisticated when those in charge try, not to oppose preferences already established, but to create preferences they think desirable and avoid those they think harmful. This is the paternalism of much moral education, for example, and the justification of much censorship. Protecting language from structural debasement or decay is paternalism of neither of these sorts. It does not, like primitive paternalism, oppose anyone's preferences. Nor does it, like sophisticated paternalism, aim to create or forestall preferences identified in advance as good or bad. On the contrary, it allows a greater rather than a lesser choice, for that is exactly the respect in which we believe people are better off with a richer than a poorer language. Our dislike of paternalism furnishes a reason for,

rather than against, naming ourselves trustee of the structure of linguistic opportunity.

The connection between these observations about language and our problem about art and the humanities is obvious. For the structural aspect of our artistic culture is nothing more than a language, a special part of the language we now share. The possibilities of art, of finding aesthetic value in a particular kind of representation or isolation of objects, depend on a shared vocabulary of tradition and convention. This part of our language could have been much poorer. Suppose no one had ever found value in narrative invention, that is, in a story. Our language would not then have had the complex resources it does to distinguish between a novel and a lie. Then no one could suddenly, just out of creative inspiration, write a novel. There would be no resources available for him to recognize value in a false narrative, for others to receive what he offered them in this mode. The same point, obviously enough, can be made about painting and sculpture and music and painting. And, for that matter, about history and philosophy and other humane studies as well.

Though we cannot imagine our culture losing any of the basic vocabulary of art entirely—we can scarcely imagine losing the power to distinguish fiction from lie—we can all too easily imagine less dramatic adverse change. For example, we now have the conceptual equipment to find aesthetic value in historical and cultural continuity. We can, and do, find various forms of quotation from the history of our culture exciting; we find value in the idea that contemporary art reworks themes or styles of other ages or is rich in allusion to them, that the past is with us, reworked, in the present. But this complex idea is as much dependent on a shared practice as is the idea of narrative fiction. It can be sustained only so long as that practice continues in a lively form, only so long the past is kept alive among us, in the larger culture that radiates out from the museum and university into concentric circles embracing the experience of a much larger community. The very possibility of finding aesthetic value in continuity depends on our continuing to achieve success and interest in continuity; and this in turn may well require a rich stock of illustrative and comparative collections that can only or best be maintained in museums and explored in universities and other academies. If it is right that the community as a whole, and not just those who use these institutions directly, shares and employs the structural possibilities of continuity and reference, something like the public-good argument for state support of such institutions is rehabilitated.

The language of culture can grow impoverished in a second way, not by losing particular dimensions of value, like continuity, but by becoming less innovative, by ceasing to develop or elaborate new dimensions. Our own culture has had moments of particular originality, when a use of language or a kind of presentation is suddenly claimed for art, as valuable in the aes-

thetic dimension, and the claim succeeds. Our ability to innovate is based on tradition in two ways, or on two levels. We must have a tradition *of* innovation, and we must have particular forms of art sufficiently open-ended and amenable to reinterpretation so that continuity can be preserved *through* innovation, so that people can see what is new as nevertheless sufficiently connected to what they already regard as a mode of art, sufficiently connected to be embraced as falling within the same overall mode of experience. These traditions can languish into an academic or conventionalist settlement when the boundaries of what can count as art are drawn too tightly, and art degenerates into what is merely familiar or only pretty or, worse still, what is useful for some nonaesthetic goal. The state of art in some tyrannies is a depressing reminder of what is possible by way of degeneration.

We have much less difficulty in imagining changes that count as the decay rather than the extinction of some main branch of culture. Our question was, Can there be any objection, in principle, to accepting the postulate and the program I have described: that people are better off when the opportunities their culture provides are more complex and diverse, and that we should act as trustees for the future of the complexity of our own culture? We have seen, but it bears repeating, that the economic approach and the democratic values that approach represents offer no objection. Using state funds in that way does not deny the future public what it wants. I noted two standing objections to the lofty approach to state support for the arts: paternalism and elitism. If state subsidy has as its purpose protecting structure rather than providing particular aesthetic events, the charge of paternalism is defused. So is the charge of elitism, because structure affects almost everyone's life, and in such fundamental and unpredictable ways that we lack the conceptual equipment to measure who benefits most from the various possibilities and ideas they generate.

Once, long ago in this argument, it looked black for state support for the arts. Now it suddenly looks too rosy. Can we really end the argument simply by announcing that the point of state support is to protect the structure of our intellectual culture? No, of course not. We must earn, not just claim, the structural description, then show what kind and level of support that description justifies in the circumstances. We have changed the terms of the argument, but not won it in advance.

How much state support can be justified in this way? One point needs to be made at once. The argument at best justifies public officials' placing the protection of culture among their goals; it does not justify their making it the main or most pressing goal. They must still fix priorities about how much to spend for art and the humanities as against competing claims that will include, for some, military defense and, for others, social justice. It is far beyond my subject to consider how these priorities should be arranged. But

the choice between art and the rest is not the choice between luxury and necessity, grandeur and duty. We inherited a cultural structure, and we have some duty, out of simple justice, to leave that structure at least as rich as we found it.

My argument, however, is meant to show that art qualifies for state support, not to set floors or ceilings to that support. But art qualifies only on a certain premise: that state support is designed to protect structure rather than to promote any particular content for that structure at any particular time. So the ruling star of state subsidy should be this goal: it should look to the diversity and innovative quality of the culture as a whole rather than to (what public officials take to be) excellence in particular occasions of that culture. The rest is strategy and tactics: maxims and rules-of-thumb made to be broken. In general, aid should be given in the form of indiscriminate subsidies, such as tax exemptions for donations to cultural institutions rather than as specific subsidies to particular institutions, though not when private donation turns out to work against rather than for diversity and innovation. When discriminations are made, they should favor forms of art that are too expensive to be sustained by wholly private, market transactions. If these include (as I think they do) expensive comprehensive collections of paintings or comprehensive studies that the market would not support, like much of the programs of great universities, then it can be no objection that only a relatively few people who are already privileged in various ways will benefit directly and immediately. I do not mean that we should be insensitive to the appeal of programs with other aims, in particular, programs that try to secure a wider audience for the arts and scholarship. That ambition remains important and urgent. It can be defended in many ways, including pointing out how this, too, helps protect the fragile structure of our culture.

The Economic View of Law

TWELVE

Is Wealth a Value?

IN THIS ESSAY I consider and reject a political theory about law often called the economic analysis of law. (That name is the title of an extended book by Richard Posner,[1] and I shall be concerned largely, though not entirely, with arguments that Posner has himself presented.) The economic analysis of law has a descriptive and a normative limb. It argues that common law judges, at least, have on the whole decided hard cases to maximize social wealth, and that they ought to decide such cases in that way. I shall discuss the normative limb of the theory mainly, although at the end of the essay I shall argue that the normative failures of the theory are so great that they cast doubt on its descriptive claims, unless these descriptive claims can be embedded within a very different normative theory.

The concept of wealth maximization is at the center of both the descriptive and normative aspects of the theory. But it is a concept that is easily misunderstood, and it has been misunderstood, in a certain way, by its critics. "Wealth maximization" is a term of art within the theory, and is not intended to describe the same thing as "Pareto efficiency." In this introductory section, I shall try to explain each of these terms, to show why it misunderstands the economic analysis of law to suppose, as critics have, that the lawyer's definition of the former is a botched attempt to capture the meaning of the latter.

Wealth maximization, as defined, is achieved when goods and other resources are in the hands of those who value them most, and someone values a good more only if he is both willing and able to pay more in money (or in the equivalent of money) to have it. An individual maximizes his own wealth when he increases the value of the resources he owns; whenever he is able, for example, to purchase something he values for any sum less than the most he would be willing to pay for it. Its value to him is measured by the money he would pay if necessary; if he is able to pay, say $4, for what he would pay $5 to have if necessary, his wealth has been increased by $1. Society maximizes its wealth when all the resources of that society are so distributed that the sum of all such individual valuations is as high as possible.

There are many conceptual difficulties in this idea of individual and social wealth maximization. Some of these will emerge in the course of our discussion, but one is sufficiently isolable that it can be disposed of now. For most people there is a difference between the sum they would be willing to pay for something that they do not have and the sum they would take in exchange for it if they already had it. Sometimes the former sum is greater—the familiar "grass is greener" phenomenon that leads someone to covet his neighbor's property more than if it were his own. If many people were often in that position, then social wealth maximization would be inherently unstable. Social wealth would be improved by a transfer of some property from A to B, but then improved by a retransfer from B to A, and so on. In these circumstances, that is, wealth maximization would be a cyclic standard—a very disagreeable property in a standard of social improvement. The second case is perhaps more common (although not either more or less rational): someone will ask more for something he owns than he would pay to acquire it. When I am lucky enough to be able to buy Wimbledon tickets in the annual lottery for £5, I will not sell them for, say, £50, although I will certainly not pay £20 to buy them when I lose in the lottery. If many people are in that position with respect to many goods, then wealth maximization will not be path-independent; the final distribution that achieves a wealth maximization will be different, even given the same initial distribution, depending upon the order in which intermediate transfers are made. Path-dependency is not so serious a flaw as cyclicity, but does nevertheless introduce an element of arbitrariness into any scheme of transfers designed to promote social wealth maximization.

Neither Posner nor other proponents of economic analysis of law seem much bothered by either possibility. They assume, perhaps, stipulations of rationality that preclude differences in pay-or-take value of this sort. Or perhaps they are concerned principally with the behavior of commercial firms where such stipulations would not seem so arbitrary. It will do no harm, however, to tighten their definitions. We may say that the goal of wealth maximization is served by a particular transfer or distribution only when that transfer would increase social wealth measured by what the person into whose hands the good falls would pay if necessary to acquire it, and *also* by what he would take to part with it. In cases where the two tests disagree, the standard of social wealth maximization is indeterminate. Indeterminacy in some cases is no great objection to any standard for social improvement, provided that such cases are not disagreeably numerous.

The familiar economist's concept of Pareto efficiency (or Pareto optimality) is a very different matter. A distribution of resources is Pareto efficient if no change in that distribution can be made that leaves no one worse off and at least one person better off. It has often been pointed out that almost any widespread distribution of resources meets that test. Even willing

trades that improve the position of both parties may adversely affect some third party by, for example, changing prices. It would be absurd to say that judges should make no decision save those that move society from a Pareto-inefficient to a Pareto-efficient state. That constraint is too strong, because there are few Pareto-inefficient states; but it is also too weak because, if a Pareto-inefficient situation does exist, any number of different changes would reach a Pareto-efficient situation and the constraint would not choose among these.

Suppose no court has decided, for example, whether a candy manufacturer is liable to a doctor if the manufacturer's machine makes it more difficult to practice medicine in an adjacent building.[2] The doctor does not have a recognized legal right to damages or an injunction, but neither does the manufacturer have a recognized right to run his machine without paying such damages. The doctor sues the candymaker, and the court must decide which of these two rights to recognize. Neither decision will be Pareto-superior to the situation before the decision, for either decision will improve the position of one party at the expense of the other. Both decisions will reach a Pareto-efficient result, for no further change in the legal position would benefit one without hurting the other. So the requirement, that the court should decide in favor of a Pareto-superior rule, if one is available, would be useless in such a case.

But the different advice, that the court should choose the rule that maximizes social wealth, is far from useless. R. H. Coase has argued that, if transaction costs were zero, it would make no difference to that goal which of the two decisions the court made.[3] If the decision did not in itself maximize wealth, then the parties would negotiate a solution that did. But since transaction costs are always positive, it will in practice make a difference. If the candymaker would lose $10 by not running his machine, and the doctor would lose only $9 if the machine were run, then social wealth would not be maximized by a rule giving the doctor a right to prevent the running of the machine, if transaction costs would exceed $1. The judge should, therefore, choose so that goods (in this case the right to practice medicine free from noise or the right to make candy free from injunction) are given directly, by his decision, to that party who would purchase the right if not assigned it, and would not sell it if assigned it, in both cases assuming that transaction costs were zero. In many cases this requirement, unlike the requirement of Pareto superiority, would dictate a unique solution. If the candy manufacturer makes enough through his noisy machine to compensate fully the doctor for his lost practice and still have profit left over, as he does on the figures just assumed, then the right to make the noise without compensation should be assigned to the candymaker. Of course, that will not produce the *distribution* that would have been achieved if the right had been assigned to the doctor and there were no transaction costs. In that case the doctor

would have had something over $9 and the candymaker something less than $1. Now the candymaker will have $10 and the doctor nothing. But that produces more total *social* wealth than the only actual alternative, given the transaction cost, which is that the candymaker have nothing and the doctor $9.

So the theory of wealth maximization is both different from the theory of Pareto efficiency and more practical. The economic analysis of law, which makes the concept of wealth maximization central, must therefore be distinguished from the economists' analysis of law, that is, from the application to legal contexts of the economists' notion of efficiency, which is Pareto efficiency. When an economist asks whether a rule of law is efficient, he usually means to ask whether the situation produced by the rule is Pareto-efficient, not whether it is wealth maximizing. Much confusion could have been avoided if Posner and others had not used the words "economic" or "efficient" in their description of their own work. Economists would not have been so concerned to point out that these words are obviously not used in their normal professional sense. They would not then have supposed that Posner and his colleagues had made some simple conceptual mistakes.

BUT NOW COMES the nerve of the problem. Economic analysis holds, on its normative side, that social wealth maximization is a worthy goal so that judicial decisions should try to maximize social wealth, for example, by assigning rights to those who would purchase them but for transaction costs. But it is unclear *why* social wealth is a worthy goal. Who would think that a society that has more wealth, as defined, is either better or better off than a society that has less, except someone who made the mistake of personifying society, and therefore thought that a society is better off with more wealth in just the way any individual is? Why should anyone who has not made this mistake think social wealth maximization a worthy goal?

There are several possible answers to this question, and I shall start by deploying a number of distinctions among them. (1) Social wealth may be thought to be itself a component of social value—that is, something worth having for its own sake. There are two versions of this claim. (a) The immodest version holds that social wealth is the *only* component of social value. It argues that the only respect in which one society may be better or better off than another is that it may have more social wealth. (b) The modest version argues that social wealth is one component of social value among others. One society is *pro tanto* better than another if it has more wealth, but it might be worse overall when other components of value, including distributional components, are taken into account.

(2) Social wealth may be thought to be, not a component, but an instrument of value. Improvements in social wealth are not valuable in them-

selves, but valuable because they may or will produce other improvements that are valuable in themselves. Once again, we may distinguish different versions of the instrumental claim. (a) The causal claim argues that improvements in social wealth themselves cause other improvements: improvements in wealth, for example, improve the position of the worst-off group in society by alleviating poverty through some invisible hand process. (b) A second claim argues that improvements in social wealth are ingredients of social value, because although they do not work automatically to cause other improvements, they provide the material for such improvements. If a society has more wealth, it is better off because it is in a position to use that increased wealth to reduce poverty. (c) A third claim holds that social wealth is neither a cause nor an ingredient of social value, but a surrogate for it. If society aims directly at some improvement in value, such as trying to increase overall happiness among its members, it will fail to produce as much of that goal than if it instead aimed at improving social wealth. Social wealth is, on this "false-target" account, a second-best goal, valued not for its own sake, nor because it will cause or can be used to bring about other improvements, but because there is a sufficiently high correlation between improvements in social wealth and such other improvements to make the false target a good target.

Another distinction cuts across these. Each of these modes of social wealth claims, except the immodest version of the component-of-value claim, may be combined with some functional claim of institutional responsibility which argues that it is the special function of courts to pursue social wealth single-mindedly, although it is not necessarily the function of, for instance, legislatures to do so. It might be said, for example, that although wealth maximization is only one among several components of social value, it is nevertheless a component that courts should be asked single-mindedly to pursue, leaving other components to other institutions. Or that although social wealth is only an ingredient of social value it should be left to courts to maximize that ingredient, on the understanding that the further use of the ingredient is the province of other institutions. Or that social wealth is a value surrogate for courts, because courts cannot for some reason pursue the true target directly, though other institutions can and therefore need no surrogate or perhaps need a different surrogate. I shall call a theory of this sort a strong institutional theory—"institutional" because it specifies reasons why one institution should pursue social wealth maximization, and "strong" because it requires that those institutions do so single-mindedly.

The normative claim of economic analysis, then, admits of many variations. Calabresi, Posner, and other advocates of that analysis have not been as clear as they might be about which variation they wish to promote, so any thorough discussion of their claims must consider different possibilities and paint on a reasonably wide canvas. I shall begin by considering whether

the claim that social wealth is a component of value, in either the immodest or the modest versions of that claim, is a defensible idea.

I THINK it is plain it is not. Perhaps no one thinks it is, although there has been much careless rhetoric on this score.[4] Before I provide an illustration that seems to me decisive against the component-of-value theory, however, I shall try to clarify the point at issue. If economic analysis argues that lawsuits should be decided to increase social wealth, defined in the particular way described, then it must show why a society with more wealth is, for that reason alone, better or better off than a society with less. I have distinguished, and now propose to consider, one form of answer: social wealth is in itself a component of value. That answer states a theory of value. It holds that if society changes so that there is more wealth then that change is in itself, at least *pro tanto*, an improvement in value, even if there is no other change that is also an improvement in value, and even if the change is in other ways a fall in value. The present question is not whether a society that follows the economic analysis of law will produce changes that are improvements in wealth with nothing else to recommend them. The question is whether such a change would be an improvement in value. That is a question of moral philosophy, in its broadest sense, not of how economic analysis works in practice. If the answer to my question is no—a bare improvement in social wealth is not an improvement in value—the claim that social wealth is a component of value fails, and the normative claim of economic analysis needs other support.

Consider this hypothetical example. Derek has a book Amartya wants. Derek would sell the book to Amartya for $2 and Amartya would pay $3 for it. T (the tyrant in charge) takes the book from Derek and gives it to Amartya with less waste in money or its equivalent than would be consumed in transaction costs if the two were to haggle over the distribution of the $1 surplus value. The forced transfer from Derek to Amartya produces a gain in social wealth, even though Derek has lost something he values with no compensation. Let us call the situation before the forced transfer takes place "Society 1" and the situation after it takes place "Society 2." Is Society 2 *in any respect* superior to Society 1? I do not mean whether the gain in wealth is overridden by the cost in justice, or in equal treatment, or in anything else, but whether the gain in wealth is, considered in itself, any gain at all. I should say, and I think most people would agree, that Society 2 is not better in any respect.[5]

It may be objected that in practice social wealth would be maximized by rules of law that forbid theft and insist on a market exchange, when it is feasible, as it is in my imaginary case. It is true that Posner and others recommend market transactions except in cases in which the transaction costs

(the costs of the parties identifying each other and concluding an agreement) are high. But it is crucial that they recommend market transactions for their *evidentiary* value. If two parties conclude a bargain at a certain price, we can be sure that wealth has been increased (setting aside problems of externalities), because each has something he would rather have than what he gave up. If transaction costs are "high" or a transaction is, in the nature of the case, impossible, Posner and others recommend what they call "mimicking" the market, which means imposing the result they believe a market would have reached. They concede, therefore, or rather insist, that information about what parties would have done in a market transaction can be obtained in the absence of the transaction, and that such information can be sufficiently reliable to act on.

I assume, therefore, that we have that information in the book case. We know that there will be a gain in social wealth if we transfer the book from Derek to Amartya. We know there will be less gain (because of what either or both might otherwise produce) if we allow them to "waste" time haggling. We know there can be no more gain in social wealth if we force Amartya to pay anything to Derek in compensation. (Each would pay the same in money for money.) If we think that Society 2 is in no respect superior to Society 1, we cannot think that social wealth is a component of value.

It may now be objected, however, that wealth maximization is best served by a legal system that assigns rights to particular people, and then insists that no one lose what he has a right to have except through a voluntary transaction. Or (if his property has been damaged) in return for appropriate compensation ideally measured by what he would have taken for it in such a transaction. That explains why someone who believes that wealth maximization is a component of value may nevertheless deny that Society 2 is in any way better than Society 1. If we assume that Derek has a right to the book under a system of rights calculated to maximize wealth, then it offends, rather than serves, wealth maximization to take the book with no compensation.

I shall discuss later the theory of rights that is supposedly derived from the goal of maximizing wealth. We must notice now, however, that the goal justifies only instrumentally rights, like Derek's right to the book. The institution of rights, and particular allocations of rights, are justified only insofar as they promote social wealth more effectively than other institutions or allocations. The argument for these rights is formally similar to the familiar rule-utilitarian account of rights. Sometimes an act that violates what most people think are rights—such as taking Derek's book for Amartya—improves total utility. Some rule utilitarians argue that such rights should nevertheless be respected, as a strategy to gain long-term utility, even though utility is lost in any isolated case considered by itself.

This form of argument is not to the point here. I did not ask whether it is a wise strategy, from the standpoint of maximizing social wealth in the long run, to allow tyrants to take things that belong to one person and give them to others. I asked whether, in the story of Amartya and Derek, Society 2 is in any respect superior to Society 1. The utilitarian, assuming that Amartya would get more utility than Derek would lose, might reply that it is. He might say that, if we confine our attention only to this case, Society 2 is in every way better because there is more happiness, or less suffering, or whatever. He would add, however, that we should nevertheless impose on the tyrant a rule forbidding the transfer, because, although the act makes the immediate situation better, its consequences will make the situation in the future much worse. This distinction is important, because a utilitarian who takes this line must concede that, if the tyrant's act would not have the long-term adverse utility consequences he supposes (because the act could be kept secret, or because a suitably limited exception to the general rule he endorses could be carved out and maintained), then the tyrant *should* so act. Even if the utilitarian insists that a rule forbidding the transfer in all cases will improve long-term utility, he still concedes that something of value is lost through the rule, namely, the utility that would have been gained but for the rule.

The wealth maximizer's answer to my question about Amartya and Derek—that economic analysis would not recommend a set of legal rules permitting the tyrant to transfer the book without compensation—is simply an evasion. Like the reply that market exchanges provide the most reliable information about value, it misunderstands the force of my story. I still ask whether the situation is in any respect better if the transfer is made. If Society 2 is not in any way superior to Society 1, considered in themselves, then social wealth is not even one among several components of social value.

I have assumed so far, however, that you will agree with me that Society 2 is not superior. Perhaps I am wrong. You may wish to say that a situation is better, *pro tanto*, if goods are in the hands of those who would pay more to have them. If you do, I suspect it is because you are making a further assumption, which is this: if Derek would take only $2 for the book and Amartya would pay $3, then the book will provide more satisfaction to Amartya than it does to Derek. You assume, that is, that the transfer will increase overall utility as well as wealth. But Posner, at least, is now explicit that wealth is conceptually independent of utility. He now allows that interpersonal comparisons of utility make sense and holds that increases in wealth may produce decreases in utility and vice versa.[6] (He relies on cases in which this is so as part of his argument that economic analysis is superior to utilitarianism as a moral theory.)

I must thus make my example more specific. Derek is poor and sick and

miserable, and the book is one of his few comforts. He is willing to sell it for
$2 only because he needs medicine. Amartya is rich and content. He is will-
ing to spend $3 for the book, which is a very small part of his wealth, on the
odd chance that he might someday read it, although he knows that he probably will not. If the tyrant makes the transfer with no compensation, total
utility will sharply fall. But wealth, as specifically defined, will improve. I
do not ask whether you would approve the tyrant's act. I ask whether, if the
tyrant acts, the situation will be in any way an improvement. I believe it
will not. In such circumstances, the fact that goods are in the hands of those
who would pay more to have them is as morally irrelevant as the book's
being in the hands of the alphabetically prior party.

Once social wealth is divorced from utility, at least, it loses all plausibility
as a component of value. It loses even the spurious appeal given to utilitarianism by the personification of society. It is sometimes argued by utilitarians that, since an individual is necessarily better off if he has more total
happiness in his entire life, even though less on many particular days, so a
society must be better off if it has more total happiness distributed across its
members even though many of these members have less. That is, I think, a
bad argument in two different ways. First, it is not true that an individual is
necessarily better off if he has more total happiness over his life without regard to distribution. Someone might well prefer a life with less total pleasure than a life of misery with one incredibly ecstatic month, and perjured
Clarence would not have relived the agony of his dream "Though 'twere to
buy a world of happy days."[7] Second, society is not related to individual citizens as an individual is related to the days of his life. The analogy is, therefore, one way of committing the ambiguous sin of "not taking seriously the
difference between people."

The parallel argument on behalf of social wealth maximization is, however, much worse. It is false that even an individual is necessarily better off
if he has more wealth, once having more wealth is taken to be independent
of utility information. Posner concedes that improvements in wealth do not
necessarily lead to improvements in happiness. He should also concede that
they sometimes lead to a loss in happiness because, as he says, people want
things other than wealth, and these further preferences may be jeopardized
by more wealth. That is, after all, a staple claim of sentimental fiction and
quite unsentimental fairy tales. Suppose, therefore, that an individual faces
a choice between a life that will make him happier (or more fulfilled, or
more successful in his own lights, or whatever) and a life that will make him
wealthier in money or the equivalent of money. It would be irrational of
him to choose the latter. Nor, and this is the crux, does he lose or sacrifice
anything of value in choosing the former. It is not that he should, on balance, prefer the former, recognizing that in the choice he sacrifices something of value in the latter. Money or its equivalent is useful so far as it

enables someone to lead a more valuable, successful, happier, or more moral life. Anyone who counts it for more than that is a fetishist of little green paper.

It is important to notice that the Derek-Amartya story shows the failure not only of the immodest but also of the modest version of the theory that social wealth is a component of value. For the story shows not merely that a gain in wealth may be outweighed by losses in utility or fairness or something else. It shows that a gain in social wealth, considered just in itself and apart from its costs or other good or bad consequences, is no gain at all. That denies the modest as well as the immodest theory. I shall therefore take this opportunity to comment on a familiar idea that, on its most plausible interpretation, presupposes the modest theory, that is, that social wealth is one among other components of social value.

This is the idea that justice and social wealth may sensibly be traded off against each other, making some sacrifice in one to achieve more of the other. Guido Calabresi, for example, begins *The Costs of Accidents* by noticing that accident law has two goals, which he describes as "justice" and "cost reduction," and notices also that these goals may sometimes conflict so that a "political" choice is needed about which goal should be pursued.[8] The same point is meant to be illustrated by the indifference curves I have seen drawn on countless blackboards, on space defined by axes one of which is labeled "justice" (or sometimes "morality") and the other "social wealth" (or sometimes "efficiency").

Whose indifference curves are supposed to be drawn on that space? The usual story speaks of the "political" or "collective" choice in which "we" decide how much justice we are willing to give up for further wealth or vice versa. The suggestion is that the curves represent individual choices (or collective functions of individual choices) over alternative societies defined as displaying different mixes of justice and wealth. But what sort of choice is the individual, whose preferences are thus displayed, supposed to have made? Is it a choice of the society in which he would like to live, or the choice of the society he thinks best from the standpoint of morality or some other normative perspective? We shall have to consider these two interpretations in turn.

If the former, self-interest might be thought to enter directly in a way antagonistic to justice, as in the case of an individual deciding whether to lead a perfectly just life that will leave him poor, or a life in which he sometimes acts unjustly but in which he is richer, or a life of many very unjust acts in which he is richer still. Since I believe that people can (and often do) act in a way they know is unjust, I acknowledge that individuals "trade off" justice against personal welfare in their own lives. But what sense does it make to

suppose that they trade off justice against, not welfare in their own lives, but wealth over the society as defined by economic analysis?

Perhaps the point is that an individual chooses a society that has more rather than less wealth as a whole because the antecedent probability is that he will have more wealth personally in a richer society. This makes the supposed preferences something like those displayed in Rawls's original position. Individuals choose a mix of justice and efficiency with an eye to maximizing their individual utility under conditions of dramatic uncertainty; or, rather, trading off gains in their prospects, so conceived, against losses in the just character of the society. (This is very different from the choice made in Rawls's own version of the original position, in which people maximize their antecedent self-interest not as some trade-off against justice, but as part of a demonstration—by Rawls, not them—of what principles constitute justice.)

Individuals in this exercise would be ill-advised to take gains in social wealth as some index to gains in their own antecedent welfare, even under conditions of uncertainty about the role they will occupy. Just under those conditions, they will use a very different index. Which index they will use will depend upon whether they decide to draft their preferences over society in the language of utility or the language of wealth. Which language they use—the language of utility or the language of individual wealth—will depend upon calculations about which vocabulary will, in practice, maximize antecedent welfare. If they choose the language of utility, then, as Hirsanyi and Mackie and others argue, they will choose, as the surrogate for maximizing their own antecedent welfare, average utility. If they choose (as I think they should) the language of individual wealth, they will certainly not choose, as that surrogate, that function of individual wealth constituted by social wealth as defined by the economic analysis of law. That would be crazy. Nor will they choose, for that surrogate, average individual wealth, because of the effects of marginal utility. They would be better advised to choose something much closer to maximin of individual wealth, for example, which is Rawls's second principle. I do not think that they would choose only maximin—they would allow some gains for those better off, if sufficiently large, to outweigh small losses to those worse off. But if their only choice were maximin or highest social wealth, they would certainly choose the former.

But surely this is all irrelevant. Calabresi and others contemplate actual political choices—they suppose that the economic analysis of law is useful because it shows how much wealth is lost if some other value is chosen. But in that case we cannot understand the axis of wealth or efficiency, in the indifference curves as generally offered, as a surrogate for judgments about antecedent individual welfare under conditions of uncertainty. We must understand the axis as representing judgments about individual welfare, to

be traded off against justice, as things actually stand. *No* particular individual will, then, be concerned about social wealth (or, indeed, about Pareto efficiency). It makes no sense for him to trade off anything, let alone justice, for *that.* He will be concerned with his individual fate, and since, by hypothesis, he now knows his actual position, he can choose among societies by trading off justice against increases in his individual welfare in these different societies. *Social* wealth (or Pareto efficiency) plays no role in these calculations.

Let us turn to the second interpretation of the supposed trade-off choice. An individual is supposed to be choosing which mix of justice and wealth represents, not the society in which he, as an individual with both moral and self-interested motives, would prefer to live, but the morally best society, all things considered. The very idea of a trade-off between justice and wealth now becomes mysterious. If the individual is to choose the morally best society, why should not its justice alone matter?

We might expect one of two replies to that question. It might be said, first, that justice is not the only virtue of a good society. It surely makes sense, from a normative perspective, to speak of the trade-off between justice and culture, and also to speak of the trade-off between justice and social wealth, as two distinct, sometimes competing social virtues. The second reply is different in form but similar in spirit. It suggests that, when people speak of a trade-off between justice and social wealth, they use "justice" to refer to only part of what that word means in ordinary language and in political philosophy—that is, they use it to refer to the distributional and meritocratic or desert features of justice in the wider sense. They mean the trade-off between those specific aspects of justice and other aspects that are comprehended under "wealth maximization."

These two replies are similar in spirit because they both assume that wealth maximization is a component of social value. In the first, wealth maximization is treated as a component competitive with justice and, in the second, as a component of justice but competitive with other components of that concept. Both replies fail, for that reason. It is absurd to consider wealth maximization to be a component of value, within or without the concept of justice. Remember Derek and Amartya.

Of course, if someone denies that wealth is a component of value, but argues that it is sometimes instrumental in achieving value, in one of the senses we distinguished earlier in this essay, he would not speak of a trade-off between justice and wealth. Or rather he would be confused if he did. It makes no sense to speak of trading off means against ends, or of people being indifferent about different mixes of a particular means and the end it is supposed to serve. Someone who speaks this way must have in mind an entirely different point. He might mean, for example, that sometimes we achieve more of the desired end if we aim only at what is (in this sense) a

means. That is the "false-target" instrumental theory I mentioned before and will discuss later. It entirely distorts that theory to describe it as requiring some trade-off between justice and anything else.

But suppose I was wrong to take the trade-off described in the familiar indifference curves, or in texts like Calabresi's, to be a matter of individual preferences, or some collective function of individual preferences. Perhaps the choice *is* meant to be the choice of society as a whole, conceived as a composite entity. I think that the choice is mentally represented this way, although not reflectively, by many of those who speak of trade-offs between justice and wealth. They have a personified community in mind, as the reference of the "we" in the proposition that "we" want a society of such-and-such sort. That picture must be disowned when made explicit. It is a silly and malign personification.

Even if society is personified in this silly way, it remains mysterious why society so conceived would want a trade-off between justice and wealth. First, the choice of wealth, taken to be independent of utility information, would make no more sense for society as a composite person than it does for individuals as actual people. Second, and more interesting, the reference of "justice" would be lost. Justice (at least when the trade-off is in question) is a matter of distribution—of the relation among individuals who make up the society, or between the society as a whole and these individuals. Once we personify the society so as to make the social choice an individual choice, there is no longer anything to be considered under the aspect of justice. Society personified can, of course, still be concerned about questions or ordering or distribution among its members. But the dimensions of such orderings do not include that of justice. An individual cares about the distribution of benefits or experiences over the days of his life. But he does not care under the aspect of justice.

None of these interpretations of the trade-off between justice and wealth makes sense. I hope the idea, however familiar, soon disappears from economic and political theory. My present point is more basic. The argument thus far is as destructive of modest normative claims for economic analysis, such as those Calabresi suggests, as it is of the most full-blown immodest claims of Posner.

I NOW TURN to the claim that a society with more wealth is better because wealth bears some important instrumental connection—whether as cause, as ingredient, or as false-target—to some independent component of value. I characterized certain versions of the instrumental claim as "strong," and we must be careful to distinguish these from weaker claims. A weak instrumental claim argues merely that sometimes improvements in social wealth cause improvements of other sorts. That is plainly sometimes so, for a vari-

ety of reasons. If, for example, judges are able to increase wealth dramatically by some decision they reach, then in, perhaps, a quarter-century everyone then alive may be better off than he would have been if the gain had not been made, either because the increased wealth will be distributed by political action so that even the poor benefit, or because the same result is reached by some invisible hand mechanism with no direct political action. But the weak instrumental claim—that sometimes this will be so—is insufficient to argue that judges should accept wealth maximization as the single test for change in the common law, or even in some particular branch or division of the common law. That argument requires the strong thesis that judges who accept such a single test will produce more of what is independently valuable, like the amelioration of poverty, than if they were to adopt a more discriminating test and try to maximize wealth only in those cases in which they have some special reason to think that they would thereby increase the independent value.

This is an important point. The difference between a strong and a weak instrumental claim is not only measured in scope. A strong theory need not claim that judges must pursue wealth maximization as the only standard of their decisions in all cases at law, or even in all common law cases or all tort cases—although the more scope the claim has, the more interesting it is. But the theory must claim that judges should pursue wealth single-mindedly over some class of cases specified independently of the instrumental claim itself—that is, specified other than as "the cases in which maximizing wealth will in fact produce the true goal." If the normative limb of economic analysis does not include at least some strong instrumental claim of that sort—if it rests only on the weak and unelaborated claim that sometimes pursuing wealth will lead to other good results—then the normative limb of the theory is boring and misleading: boring because no one will dispute the claim, and misleading because the theory should then be named, not after wealth, but after the so-far unspecified true goal that wealth is taken sometimes to serve.

I shall assume, therefore, that if economic analysis rejects wealth as a component of value and argues only that wealth maximization is instrumental toward some other conceptually independent goal or value, it argues for that instrumental connection in some strong form, though I shall not assume that the strong claim it makes has any particular scope. The strong thesis need not suppose (of course, it need not deny) that in every case a judicial decision that maximizes social wealth will improve the true goal. But it must show why, if in some cases wealth maximization will not have that desirable effect, it is nevertheless wise strategy to pursue wealth maximization in all cases within the scope of the claim.

Any strong claim, even of limited scope, must specify the independent goal or value that it supposes is advanced instrumentally by maximizing social wealth. Supporters of economic analysis might have any number of in-

dependent values in mind, or some structured or intuitionistic mix of different independent values. We cannot test the instrumental claim for wealth maximization until the independent value or mix of these is at least roughly specified.

It is surprising that, in spite of the supposed popularity of economic analysis, there have been few attempts to do this. This failure supports my view that many lawyers have uncritically assumed that wealth is at least a component of value. But in a recent article, and much more clearly in remarks prepared for a recent conference, Posner suggests different instrumental claims that he, at least, might be tempted to make.[9] He suggests that wealth maximization is a value because a society that takes wealth maximization to be its central standard for political decisions will develop other attractive features. In particular, it will honor individual rights, encourage and reward of variety of "Protestant" virtues, and give point and effect to the impulses of people to create benefits for each other. Posner believes that it will do better in promoting these attractive traits and consequences than a society that takes, as its central standard for political decisions, either utilitarianism or some "Kantian" position.[10]

The argument has the form of a strong instrumentalist claim of the causal variety. It has very wide scope. It specifies a set of features of society—individual rights, agreeable virtues, and humane instincts—that can plausibly be taken to be components of value. It then suggests that the "right" mix of these will be best obtained by a single-minded attention to wealth maximization as a standard for political decisions, including judicial decisions. The trouble begins, however, when we ask what arguments he might offer to support this strong and wide instrumentalist claim.

We may begin with the claim that wealth maximization will encourage respect for individual rights. A society that sets out to maximize social wealth will require some assignment of rights to property, labor, and so forth. That is a conceptual requirement, because wealth is measured by what people are willing to pay, in money or its equivalent, but no one can pay what he does not own, or borrow if he has nothing to pledge or if others have nothing to lend. Society bent on maximizing wealth must specify what rights people have to money, labor, or other property so that it can be determined what is theirs to spend and, in this way, where wealth is improved. A society is, however, not a better society just because it specifies that certain people are entitled to certain things. Witness South Africa. Everything depends on which rights society recognizes, and on whether those rights should be recognized according to some independent test. It cannot, that is, provide an instrumental claim for wealth maximization that it leads to the recognition of certain individual rights, if all that can be said, in favor of the moral value of these rights, is that these are the rights that a system of wealth maximization would recognize.

There is, however, a danger that Posner's argument will become circular

in that way. According to the economic analysis of law, rights *should* be assigned instrumentally, in such a way that the assignment of rights will advance wealth maximization. That is the principal use of the standard of wealth maximization in the judicial context. Recall the case of the doctor and the candymaker. The question put to the court was whether the doctor should be recognized to have the right to stop the noisy machine. Economic analysis does not suppose that there is some independent moral argument in favor of giving or withholding that right. So it *cannot* be claimed, in favor of economic analysis, that it points to what is independently, on moral grounds, the right answer. On the contrary, it claims that the right answer is right only because the answer increases social wealth.

Nor does Posner limit the scope of that argument—that assignments of rights must be made instrumentally—to what might be called less important rights, like the right to an injunction in nuisance or to damages in negligence. On the contrary, he is explicit that the same test must be used in determining the most fundamental human rights of citizens, including their right to life and to control their own labor rather than be slaves to others. He counts it an important virtue of wealth maximization that it explains why people have those rights. But if wealth maximization is only to be an instrumental value—and that is the hypothesis now being considered—then there must be some independent moral claim for the rights that wealth maximization recommends. These rights cannot have a moral claim on us simply because recognizing those rights advances wealth.

Let us, therefore, suppose that Posner believes people have a right to their own bodies, and to direct their own labor as they wish, for some independent moral reason. Suppose he also argues that wealth maximization is of instrumental value because a society that maximizes wealth will recognize just those rights. There remains a serious conceptual difficulty. The argument supposes that a social order bent only on wealth maximization, which makes no independent judgments about the fairness of distributions of resources, will recognize the rights of the "natural" owner to his own body and labor. That is true only if the assumption of those rights can be justified by the wealth maximization test, which requires that if rights to the "natural owner's" body or labor are assigned to someone else, he will nevertheless be willing and able to purchase these rights, at least, if we assume no transaction costs.

We cannot, however, speculate intelligibly about whether someone would purchase the right to his own labor unless we make some assumptions about the distribution of wealth. Posner acknowledges this. Indeed, he uses this example—someone's ability to purchase the right to his own labor if he is made a slave—to make the point that whether someone can purchase that right depends on his and others' wealth, and in particular how large a share of that wealth is that right. He says that in such a case "eco-

nomic analysis does not predict a unique allocation of resources unless the initial assignment of rights is specified."[11] If A is B's slave he may not be able to buy back the right to his labor; although if he were not B would not be able to buy that right from him. If economic analysis makes someone's initial right to his own labor depend upon whether he would purchase the right if assigned to another, that right cannot be "derived" from economic analysis unless we already know who initially has the right. This appears to be a serious circle. We cannot specify an initial assignment of rights unless we answer questions that cannot be answered unless an initial assignment of rights is specified.

Can we break out of this circle? We might, for example, stipulate that we are to ask our question about who would purchase what in a state of nature when no one has any rights to anything. I assume that means not only that no one already owns his own labor, but also that no one has any money, the equivalent of money, or anything else. In that case, the question is without meaning, or, if it has meaning, the answer is that no one would purchase anything.

We might more plausibly stipulate that we are to ask the question *now*, that is, at a moment when *other* rights, including wealth, are in place (which does not preclude asking it again later when we suspect that a different answer might be available). There is, perhaps, a determinate answer to the question of who values the right more under these circumstances. In order to test the claim—that wealth maximization would (determinately) assign the right to labor to the "natural owner"—we suppose that the right to the labor of a certain easily distinguished group of people (say those with IQs over 120) is taken from them (perhaps by some anti-emancipation proclamation) and assigned to others. The present wealth of those who have lost these rights (as well as the present wealth of those who have gained them) is not otherwise disturbed. Can we say that at least most of those who have lost their rights would now repurchase them or would but for transaction costs?

We must remind ourselves that willingness to purchase these rights supposes ability to purchase them—the ability to pay what those who have the rights would ask in the market. It may be—it would be for most people today—impossible to repurchase the right to their labor, because the value of that labor represents more than half of their present wealth. Could they borrow, in the money market, the necessary funds? Posner speaks to this possibility. He says, "No doubt the inherent difficulties of borrowing against human capital would defeat some efforts by the natural owner to buy back the right of his labor . . . even from someone who did not really value it more highly than he did—but that is simply a further reason for initially vesting the right in the natural owner."[12] These "inherent difficulties" must be transaction costs or other market imperfections, because Posner is very

strict about how economic analysis must understand the verb "to value." Someone values something more than someone else (and the system of economic analysis depends on this) only if he is willing (and able) to pay more for it. If (for reasons other than market imperfections) the natural owner is unable to pay what the owner of the right would take, then he does *not* value it more.

So let us assume that the "inherent difficulties" can be overcome, so that someone who has lost the right to his labor can borrow against the discounted value of his future labor. Will he thereby gain enough capital so that we can be confident that he (or most people in his position) will be able to purchase the right to his labor back from someone else? Almost certainly not, because the *monetary* value of his future labor is unlikely to be worth more to him, for this purpose, than it is to someone else.

Suppose someone called Agatha who is poor but who can write detective stories so brilliantly that the public will relish and pay for as many books as she can possibly write. Suppose the right to Agatha's labor is assigned to Sir George. That means that Sir George can direct the way Agatha's labor is to be used: she is his slave. Sir George will, of course, be an enlightened slave-holder, in the sense that he will not work Agatha so hard that the total value of what she produces declines. But he will work her just short of that point. Suppose that Agatha, if she had the right to her own labor, would work as an interior designer, at which work she would make much less money but find her life more satisfying. Or suppose that she would write many fewer detective stories than she could, sacrificing the additional income to spend time at her garden. At *some* point she would rather stop writing to enjoy what she has made, rather than make marginally more money, but have no time to enjoy anything. She may, perhaps, work somewhat more effectively while she works if she is her own master—but she will probably work at a less lucrative job, and almost certainly will work less.

If she tells the bank manager that she intends to design interiors, or to work at her garden, she will not be able to borrow anywhere near the funds necessary to buy the right to her own labor from Sir George. If she does not, but leads her life that way anyway, she will soon be in default on debt service. She can borrow enough money, even to make Sir George indifferent about selling her the right to her labor, only by undertaking to lead a life as distasteful to her as the life she would have led under Sir George. She will have to perform almost exactly the labors that he, as a master of enlightened self-interest, would prescribe. She will cease to be his slave only by becoming the slave of the First National Bank (of Chicago, of course).

Indeed, her situation is even worse than that, because I have ignored the interest the bank will take. (The rate may be high if others are at the same time trying to find capital to buy back the right to *their* labor.) So her ability to borrow enough to make Sir George indifferent will depend upon his other investment opportunities, and (if he is confident about her abilities)

his risk aversion. Nor is it by any means plain that, if she could borrow enough, she would. She gains very little actual control over the conduct of her life, as we have seen, and she loses a considerable degree of security. The main value of freedom is the value of choice and self-direction, and if she starts her career a slave she will never be able to recapture more than a token amount to these. We cannot be confident (to understate) that a thorough analysis would justify the conclusion that Agatha either could or would buy back the right to her labor. We therefore cannot claim that economic analysis supports giving her that right in the first place.

Readers will no doubt think that I have gone mad some time ago. They will think that the character of the arguments I have been making demeans the case against the normative aspect of the economic analysis of law. Many will think it more important to say that a theory that makes the moral value of slavery depend on transaction costs is grotesque. They are right. But my present point is not that wealth maximization, taken seriously, may lead to grotesque results. It is the more limited point that this particular effort to show that wealth maximization has strong instrumental value wholly fails.

Posner has another argument we should notice here. He gives some place to a different instrumental claim: wealth maximization has value because a society that seeks only social wealth maximization will encourage attractive personal virtues, particularly the virtue of beneficence. This is not an unfamiliar argument. Defenders of capitalism often call attention to how the "Protestant" virtues of industry and self-reliance thrive in a capitalist system, but they do not give prominence to specifically altruistic virtues. It is this feature of the claim that makes Posner's account so paradoxically attractive.

Posner's argument is straightforward: in a society dedicated to wealth maximization, people can improve their position only by benefiting others, because when someone produces goods and services others buy, he must be producing some benefit for them as well as for himself. The argument does not specify the metric it assumes for testing whether a society bent on wealth produces more beneficial-for-others activity than a society that encourages a more direct altruism. It is not easy to see which metric would be appropriate. Even if wealth-produced-for-others is taken as the measure, with no allowance for distribution, it is far from clear that more wealth will be produced by people for other people, as distinct from themselves, under wealth maximization that under a system of taxation and redistribution, even though the latter produced less wealth altogether. Surely, welfare-for-others is a better measure of moral achievement than simply wealth-for-others, and, because of marginal utility, welfare-for-others is a standard that includes distributional requirements. It is far from plain that wealth maximization will produce more total welfare-for-others activity than other, more compromising, economic and political structures.

But that is an empirical question. We need not pursue it here, moreover,

because of a more fundamental flaw in Posner's argument that wealth maximization is of instrumental value because it produces people who benefit others. For the moral value of beneficial activity, considered in itself, consists in the will or intentions of the actor. If he acts out of a desire to improve the welfare of others, his act has inherent moral value even if he does not benefit others. But it has no inherent moral value if he acts with the intention of benefiting only himself. Posner makes plain that his production-for-others claims have nothing to do with the other-regarding intentions of actors in the economic process. He supposes, on the contrary, that they will act to maximize benefit to themselves, benefiting others only through their inability to absorb every last bit of the consumer surplus, as they would like to do for themselves. The better someone is at personal wealth maximization—the more he displays the skills and talents to be rewarded in the system—the less his acts will benefit others, because the more of the surplus will he be able to retain from each transaction or enterprise. Any benefit to others comes from the invisible hand not good will. It cannot be the intrinsic value of wealth-producing acts that recommends wealth maximization.

IT IS, PERHAPS, the consequences of these acts. Perhaps the individuals seeking wealth only for themselves will produce a distribution that is just. This suggestion, in its widest scope, supposes that a society pursuing wealth maximization will achieve a closer approximation to ideals of distributive justice, for some reason, than a society not single-mindedly pursuing that goal. These ideals of distributive justice must be specified, or at least conceived, independently of wealth maximization. It will not do to say that distributive justice is whatever state of affairs is produced by wealth maximization. For then the claim that wealth maximization leads to distributive justice would be merely tautology.

So this new interpretation of the instrumental account must be completed by at least a rough specification of justice. It would be natural for an economic analyst to choose one of the several accounts of justice already in the traditions of political philosophy—highest total or average utility, for example, or equality, or maximin over welfare or wealth, or some meritocratic theory. The theory selected must be a patterned rather than a historical theory, to use Robert Nozick's useful distinction.[13] Historical theories argue that a distribution is just, whatever inequalities or other features it displays, if it is reached in accordance with correct principles of justice in acquisition and transfer. Patterned theories argue that a distribution is just only if it conforms to some pattern that can be specified apart from the history of how that distribution occurred. Wealth maximization specifies a patterned rather than a historical test for the assignment of rights: the decision whether the doctor or the candymaker has the right each seeks is to be

made with a pattern in view—goods should be in the hands of those who would pay most to have them. It is almost incoherent to propose that a patterned distribution might be instrumental in achieving a historically contingent distribution.

The defender of wealth must thus choose some patterned conception of justice, like highest utility, equality, maximin, meritocracy, or desert. Posner disclaims the first three of these specifically. Merit or desert theories are more congenial to his spirit, so we will consider these first.

Meritocratic theories hold that justice consists in that distribution in which people are rewarded in accordance with their merits. We now suppose that wealth maximization might be said to be of strong instrumental value, because (through an invisible hand or false-target mechanism) a society whose laws seek only wealth maximization will produce the required meritocratic distribution, or come closer to it than any alternative system. But we must now distinguish between two conceptions of merit such an argument might employ. The first we might call an independent conception of merit. It requires that we be able to state what counts as merit independently of the wealth maximization process, so that it becomes an empirical hypothesis that wealth maximization rewards merit so stated. But for *any* list of independent merits that empirical hypothesis must fail, because which abilities or traits will be rewarded in any particular community at any particular time is a matter of technology, taste, and luck. Consider that set of talents necessary consistently to hit a breaking pitch. If any list of independent merits does not include that set, then it will be false that in our society wealth maximization rewards merits better than alternatives. Ted Williams will be rewarded, in such a system, much more highly than almost everyone else who ranks higher in the set of merits we do list.

If, however, we list that set of talents as merits, it will be false that wealth maximization characteristically rewards merits. That set of talents was not rewarded before baseball developed as it has, is not now rewarded where baseball has not so developed, and will not be rewarded if baseball declines and disappears. We can generalize: since which talents are rewarded by the market is highly contingent on a variety of factors, the pursuit of efficiency cannot be relied on to reward any particular set of these fixed as independent merits over time. But neither can it be relied on to disregard any particular set.

I shall call the second conception of merit the dependent conception. It holds that merit is constituted by the set of talents that enables one to succeed in the market from time to time. Some of these talents are relatively fixed, such as industry, shrewdness, and, perhaps, greed. Typically, although not inevitably, one does better with industry or shrewdness than without it. Other talents become merits only by virtue of transient tastes and luck; they are merits for a time because they enable one to produce what others take

to be benefits to themselves and are willing and able to buy. Under the dependent conception of merit, it *is* true that a market economy geared to wealth maximization will reward merits. It is too true, for under the dependent conception the instrumental claim has collapsed into tautology.

At least for Posner, therefore, we cannot find any suitable independent conception of justice in the literature of political philosophy. He makes a wide claim for wealth maximization, but he has rejected all the conceptions that do not make that wide claim either plainly false or trivial. What about pluralistic conceptions of justice? I mean theories that disclaim any single value, like utility or equality or merit, as making up all of justice in distribution, but instead argue that a truly just distribution will achieve a sensible mix of several of these values. The just distribution, on a pluralistic conception, will be one in which the average level of welfare is reasonably high, in which there is not too much inequality, and in which what people have is at least roughly related to how hard they have worked or how much they have produced. It may not be possible to specify the exact mix of the different components of the just society. But someone may claim to know it when he sees it. Is it sensible to say that wealth maximization is instrumentally related, in the strong sense, to some such pluralistic conception of justice?

The danger is evident enough. The instrumental claim completed in this way is in danger of becoming a tautology once again, unless the pluralistic conception is stated clearly enough to allow that claim to be tested empirically. That is close to impossible. Let us suppose that single-minded wealth maximization, in a particular society, would produce a certain precise cardinal level of average utility, a specific inequality factor (measured, for example, in Gini coefficients), and a determinate correlation between merit, somehow defined, and wealth. A critic now proposes a compromise with wealth maximization—for example, by a piece of redistribution that lowers the total wealth of the community. That compromise would produce slightly less average utility, slightly less inequality, and a different correlation between merit and wealth. Each of these factors, that is, becomes somewhat, but not radically, different from the result under single-minded wealth maximization. Now the partisan of wealth maximization on this instrumental argument must suppose that the original mix of these different components of social value is better than the new mix. It is not enough for him to suppose that the original mix is better than the maximand of any of the three components: better than the society in which average utility is as high as possible, or inequality as low as possible, or people are never rewarded except in proportion to merit. He must also believe it better than the different mixes of these three desiderata that would be achieved under political and economic systems less uncompromising than his single-minded wealth production.

His belief is implausible. It is highly indeterminate, *ex ante*, which car-

dinal level of average utility, which coefficient of inequality, and which correlation of wealth to merit (on any nontautologous definition of merit) will be produced by a program of wealth maximization. It is also highly indeterminate which mix of these putative desiderata would be achieved by any discrete compromise with wealth maximization. It is, therefore, implausible that a particular mix exists such that it is *both* independently preferable, on moral grounds, to possible alternatives, and also antecedently more likely to be secured by wealth maximization than by discrete compromises. My point is not that it is impossible antecedently to *describe* the "best" mix of components, other than in the I-know-it-when-I-see-it fashion—although that is a bad sign. But rather that, at the level of fine tuning necessary to distinguish the results of wealth maximization from the results of compromises, there simply *is* no one "best" mix antecedently more likely to be produced by one rather than the other of these social techniques. The pluralistic instrumental account is weaker than a straightforward hitching of wealth maximization to a traditional theory—for example, utilitarianism—might be. In the latter case the goal that different instrumental theories compete to maximize is at least specifiable.

There is an important and more general point here. Even patterned theories of justice are likely to leave something to the contingencies of history. At a certain level of fine tuning, for example, even a strict egalitarian will admit that the result of a trade between equals respects equality just because it is a trade among equals, rather than because its results are those specifically demanded by equality. I suspect that partisans of wealth maximization also believe that a particular distribution is just because it is the distribution achieved by wealth-maximizing rules, and not vice versa. Surely that suspicion is supported by the great bulk of writing exploring the economic analysis of law. But of course that judgment takes us back to wealth as a component of value. It cannot be supported by any instrumental defense of wealth maximization. It supposes, instead, that wealth maximization is a fair procedure whose results are just, as an egalitarian supposes that a trade between equals is an inherently fair procedure. So a wealth maximizer who holds that a distribution is just if it is the product of wealth-maximizing rules cannot rely on *any* instrumental justification of at least that aspect of his theory.

WE HAVE BEEN considering how the various forms of the instrumental claim for wealth maximization might be completed by specifying an independent conception of social value that wealth maximization promotes. I first set aside the utilitarian conception of justice because Posner explicitly rejects that conception. But Posner's own suggestions—individual rights, individual virtue, and some impressionistic mix of different values—all fail, and al-

though he has been the most explicit and extreme wealth maximizer among lawyers, his rejection of utilitarianism is not binding on the others. Does the utilitarian tradition offer a way of completing the instrumental defense of wealth?

I do not mean, in raising that question, to endorse utilitarianism in any of its various forms. On the contrary, it seems to me that utilitarianism, as a general theory of either value or justice, is false, and that its present unpopularity is well-deserved. It is not, however, a theory that can be rejected out-of-hand, by any argument as simple as the argument I used to dispose of the theory that wealth is a value in itself. It has enjoyed the support of a large number of sophisticated and sensitive philosophers. It is, therefore, worth asking whether a thoroughgoing utilitarian might be led to support wealth maximization on an instrumental basis.

Once again we must be sensitive to the different types of instrumental theory. There are invisible-hand, ingredient, and false-target versions of the instrumental thesis available, and also versions of wider and narrower scope. The versions share, however, a common conceptual problem. Utilitarianism supposes that individual welfare levels are at least sometimes comparable, so that total or average utility levels can be ordered over various choices of social programs. Economists as a group have been skeptical about interpersonal comparisons of utility. If utilitarianism is to be the motor of wealth maximization, then wealth maximizers must forego that skepticism and move even further from present orthodoxy in economics. But when we admit generalizations about comparisons of welfare within large communities—like the generalization that the marginal utility of wealth declines—then any broad version of the utilitarian-instrumentalist theory becomes immediately implausible. It is implausible to think that a society that seeks wealth maximization single-mindedly will achieve more total utility than a society that seeks wealth maximization but puts an upper bound on the level of inequality it will tolerate in the name of social wealth.

So any plausible utilitarian-instrumentalist theory of wealth maximization must be a reasonably narrow theory. Let us construct a sample narrow theory tied to adjudication. This holds that a society whose judges decide hard cases at common law by choosing the rule expected to maximize social wealth will achieve more total utility in the long run than a society that chooses another discrete program for deciding such cases, including a society whose judges decide such cases by choosing the rule that can be expected to maximize total utility in the long run. This is a strong instrumentalist theory; it defines a group of political decisions (hard common law cases) such that officials are required to decide all such cases to maximize wealth, rather than to ask, in each case, whether maximizing wealth in that case would promote utility. What sort of empirical evidence, or set of correlative assumptions, would support that theory?

The most eligible assumption considers selective wealth maximization as an ingredient rather than as a cause or false target of value. It supposes that if judges decided such cases so as to increase the total wealth, other institutions—perhaps legislatures—would then redistribute the increased total wealth to improve average or total utility. That chain of events is, no doubt, conceivable, once we accept that interpersonal comparisons of individual utility make sense in principle. It is not, however, inevitable. The political process might, for a variety of reasons, leave those who gain most from wealth maximization with their gains intact. We should, therefore, ask whether the utilitarianism-instrumental theory requires that legislatures actually redistribute to improve total utility, or whether it is sufficient, to support that theory, simply that they might do so.

Consider the following elaboration of the theory. Judges decide discrete common law cases against the background of a given distribution of wealth and legal rights. No decision a judge makes in a particular case will significantly affect that distribution. The best a judge bent on improving total utility can do is to improve the total supply of wealth. If the legislature finds some way to redistribute the increased wealth so as to optimize utility, well and good. If not, nothing has been lost. It is better to provide the legislature with an opportunity to improve utility, even if the opportunity may not be taken, than to do nothing.

Is this a good defense of our narrow theory? It rests on a large assumption: that there is nothing that judges can ever do directly to advance utility more than they can do simply by maximizing wealth, even when they know that the legislature will do nothing further to advance that goal itself. It assumes that judges would promote utility less overall, even in those circumstances, if they sometimes asked whether a less single-minded, more discriminating approach would improve utility in particular cases. It rests on the assumption that wealth maximization is a good false target for utility even when it is not a useful ingredient of utility. We may test that assumption in this way. Suppose someone suggests the following alternative program for adjudication. Judges should reach that decision, in hard cases at common law, that will promote utility better than any alternative decision. In some cases, perhaps most, that will be the wealth-maximizing decision and in some not. Everything depends on circumstances, and it is impossible to say in advance how often this theory will recommend non-wealth-maximizing decisions.

That is (in the sense defined) a weak instrumental theory of wealth maximization. Two questions arise. Will the weak theory ever recommend a judicial decision the narrow strong theory would not? Will a society whose judges follow the weak theory produce more utility in the long run than a society that follows the strong one? The answer to the first of these questions will depend on a variety of issues, but is almost certainly, yes. Pater-

nalism will provide occasions when the utility-maximizing rule differs from the wealth-maximizing rule. Suppose, for example, that the community will pay more for candy than for medical care lost through the noise of a candy machine, but the candy will be bad for its health and therefore its long-term utility. Future generations provide other occasions: once the utility of future generations is taken into account, even common law decisions—like those affecting the environment—may injure utility if they promote wealth in its present distribution. Quite apart from these factors, some common law decisions are potentially redistributive. Suppose a decision might either protect the workers of an ailing and, possibly, noncompetitive industry or hasten their unemployment by structuring rights in favor of a developing new industry? The wealth-maximizing decision might be the latter; the utility-promoting decision nevertheless the former.

If there are many occasions on which the two theories—weak and strong—would recommend different decisions, the answer to the second question is probably, no. It is true that false targets are sometimes good targets: we sometimes gain more by aiming slightly away from what we want, as a man bent on pleasure would do well not to aim directly at it. But that is not always or even usually so, and there seems, *a priori*, no more reason why it should hold in the case of courts than in the case of legislatures. If it is sometimes true that a legislature should choose a decision that does not maximize wealth, because it will nevertheless improve utility, there seems no reason why a court should not do so as well. The occasions on which a court has that choice are, perhaps, fewer, but that is plainly a different matter.

So the utilitarian-instrumental theory does seem to depend on some judgment that the legislature will act in cooperation with courts to redistribute, so as to produce more utility from the wealth the court provides. But if that is so, then the theory is seriously incomplete, because, so far as I know, that case has never been made. Nor is it immediately plausible. On the contrary, if the familiar assumption is right, that optimal utility would require much more equality of wealth than now exists in our country, the hypothesis that the legislatures, federal and state, have been busy redistributing in search of utility seems embarrassingly disconfirmed.

Even if that hypothesis were sound, much more would be needed to defend judicial wealth maximization in this way. We should still have to show why, when more utility could be produced by a decision aiming directly at utility, the court should aim instead at wealth. The hypothesis, that the legislature will concern itself with utility, is not in itself a satisfactory answer. Would the gains in utility not be provided sooner and more securely in one step rather than two? There seems no reason not to prefer a weak instrumental theory: courts should decide to maximize utility, recognizing that the existence of legislatures ready to redistribute might mean that on some

occasions wealth improvements might be the best means of improving utility in the long run. If any strong theory is preferred to that weak theory, it must, once again, rest on the (unsupported) false-target theory.

I have considered, in this part of the essay, whether a strong instrumental theory can defend wealth maximization, taken as the single-minded goal for at least a discrete part of adjudication, on the assumption that total utility is a value in itself. I argue that the hypothesis that it can seems weak, and is far from demonstrated. The same arguments apply, I think, against any strong instrumental claim for wealth maximization that takes maximin (on either the wealth or the utility space) rather than total utility to be a social value in itself. Once again, the question is raised why a weak theory, which encourages judges to seek maximin solutions directly, taking due account of the potential instrumental role of wealth maximization, would not be superior. No answer to that question has been provided, and it is not clear that there is a good one.

I should close this section, however, by noticing what I hope has been apparent in the discussion so far. The instrumental claims for wealth maximization are more plausible if they are harnessed to one of the nonmeritocratic-patterned theories of justice, such as utility or maximin, than to anything else. They cannot then be ruled out conceptually as, for example, Posner's instrumental claims can be. But they are still—certainly in the present state of play—claims with almost no foundation.

ECONOMIC ANALYSIS of law is a descriptive and a normative theory. Does the failure of the normative limb impair the descriptive limb? The latter offers an explanation of one aspect of human behavior, namely, the decisions of common law judges in the cases economic analysis purports to explain. There are several modes (or, as some would say, levels) of explanation of human behavior. Some of these are nonmotivational. These include genetic or chemical or neurological accounts of either reflex or reflective behavior. The motivational modes of explanation may also be of different forms. The most straightforward is explanation from the agent's point of view, an explanation that cites the agent's goals or intentions and his belief about appropriate means. But there are more complex forms of motivational explanation. Invisible hand explanations, for example, suppose that people act out of certain motives, and explain why, that being so, they collectively achieve something different from what they aim at individually. One class of Freudian explanations also assumes that people act out of motives, but holds that these motives are unconscious. These Freudian explanations are, nevertheless, motivational because their explanatory power hinges on the claim that people whose behavior is so explained are acting in a way best expressed by analogy to the behavior of people who hold such

motives consciously. The theory is therefore dependent on an understanding of that straightforward motivational claim.

The argument of economic analysis, that judges decide hard cases so as to maximize social wealth, is not a genetic, chemical, neurological, or any other form of nonmotivational explanation. Nor is it an invisible hand explanation. It is true that something like an invisible hand explanation of why common law decisions promote social wealth has been offered,[14] but this is not part of the claims of Posner, Calabresi, or other proponents of economic analysis. To my knowledge, economic analysis has never been presented as a Freudian analysis. But even if it had, that analysis would presuppose the sense of a straightforward claim. So economic analysis, in its descriptive limb, seems to rest on the sense and the truth of a straightforward motivational claim, which is that judges decide cases with the intention of maximizing social wealth.

But my arguments against the normative limb of economic analysis also call any such motivational claim into question. I did not argue that maximizing social wealth is only one among a number of plausible social goals, or is a mean, unattractive, or unpopular social goal. I argued that it makes no sense as a social goal, even as one among others. It is preposterous to suppose that social wealth is a component of social value, and implausible that social wealth is strongly instrumental toward a social goal because it promotes utility or some other component of social value better than would a weak instrumental theory. It is, therefore, bizarre to assign judges the motive either of maximizing social wealth for its own sake or pursuing social wealth as a false target for some other value. But a straightforward motivational explanation makes no sense unless it makes sense to attribute the motive in question to the agents whose behavior is being explained.

It follows that the descriptive claims of economic analysis, as they have so far been presented, are radically incomplete. If they are to have descriptive power, they must be recast. They might be recast, for example, in some way appropriate to a weak instrumental claim. The arguments must then become more discriminating. They must pick out particular classes of judicial decisions and explain why it was plausible for judges to suppose that a rule improving social wealth was likely, for that reason, to advance some independent social goal these judges valued—utility, maximin, the relief of poverty, the economic power of the country in foreign affairs, or some other goal. That becomes a claim of great complexity, for it involves not only a detailed causal account but detailed intellectual history or sociology. Did judges who developed the fault system in negligence or the system of strict liability suppose that their decisions would advance average total utility? Were these judges uniformly utilitarians, who would therefore count that an advantage? Does this explanation hold good only for a certain group of cases at a particular point in the development of the common law? Is it

plausible to suppose that judges throughout some extended period held the same theory of social value? Is it plausible to suppose, for example, that they were utilitarians indifferently before, during, and after the academic popularity of that theory of social justice? That only scratches the surface of the kind of account that would be needed to give a weak instrumental explanation of judicial behavior along wealth maximization lines, but it is enough perhaps to suggest how far short the present literature falls. It has not achieved the beginning of a beginning.

It may now be objected, however, that I am asking for far too much, and unfairly discounting what has been done already. Suppose that the economic analysts have established an important correlation between the decisions that common law judges have reached in some particular area—say nuisance or negligence or contract damages—and the decisions that would have been taken by judges explicitly seeking to maximize social wealth. Suppose that, although not every decision actually made is the decision such a judge would reach, the great majority are. (I know this putative correlation is contested, and I assume it in this section *arguendo*.) It seems silly, not to say churlish, to turn our backs on all this information. We may hold the following attitude. No doubt it would be better still if an intellectual historical account could explain why actual judges acted in this way, either by showing that they took wealth maximization itself to be a component of value, or because they held a strong instrumental theory of wealth maximization, or a weak instrumental theory that had the consequences discovered. But the correlation, in and of itself, advances our understanding of the legal process to an important degree.

I think this attitude is wrong. It is wrong because a correlation of this sort has no explanatory power unless it is backed by some motivational hypothesis that makes independent sense. Suppose the following exercise. Let us construct a binary alphabetical priority sequence for all cases ever decided by the highest court in Illinois. (We take 1 if the winning party's name is alphabetically prior to the loser's; 0 otherwise. Forget complications or ties.) Call the sequence Arthur. We would not say that Arthur explains the judicial decisions in these cases, although Arthur is in fact a perfect correlation. Arthur has indefinitely many projections into the future. Suppose each academic lawyer in the United States were to project Arthur to a further 100 places at random. We would then have a very large variety of further sequences (Arthur Posner, Arthur Michelman, Arturo Calabresi, and so on), one of which would predict the results of the next, say, 100 decisions on the Illinois court better than any other, and, quite likely, very well indeed. But we would not say that, for example, Arthur Michelman had great predictive power or was a better theory of judicial decision making in Illinois on that account.

The point is both evident and important. Our standards for the explana-

tion of human behavior require, in order for some account even to be a candidate for an explanation, that it bring to bear either a biological or a motivational account. If a correlation, however secure, cannot promise even the prospect of such a connection—if these connections cannot sensibly be taken even as mysteries waiting to be solved—then it becomes coincidence only. The claims for astrological and other occult explanations of behavior are problematical in this way. It strikes many people that both a motivational and a biological account are excluded by positive conclusions of physics that are beyond reexamination; but it strikes others that Hamlet's warning to Horatio is sound and pertinent.

We have three choices. We may disregard the putative correlation between actual and wealth-maximizing decisions as coincidental and attempt to construct theories of adjudication that ignore it. That seems wasteful and perverse, for the correlation, if it exists, is different from the correlation between Arthur and the cases from which Arthur was constructed in one important respect. In the case of Arthur, the method of construction guarantees that the correlation is coincidental rather than explanatory. In the case of economic analysis, coincidence is one hypothesis only.

Second, we may pursue the enterprise I suggested earlier in this section. We may try to construct a weak instrumental theory of wealth maximization showing why, in just the areas of law where the correlation holds, the weak instrumental theory, harnessed to some conventional idea of social value like utility, would recommend the wealth-maximizing strategy as a good means, and why it is plausible that judges realized this, in at least a rough and inarticulate way. That enterprise would carry economic analysis into layers of detail of both political theory and intellectual history it has not yet even begun to reach. But the enterprise cannot be dismissed in advance.

There is a third choice. We may try to embed the correlation in a radically different sort of analysis and explanation. We may try to show that the decisions that seem to maximize wealth are required, not as instrumental decisions seeking to produce a certain state of affairs, of social wealth, utility, or any other goal of policy, but rather as decisions of principle enforcing a plausible conception of fairness. We might aim, that is, at an explanation of principle, instead of an explanation of policy. I have, on various occasions, tried to show why an account of judicial decisions on grounds of principle should always be preferred to one on grounds of policy, for normative and positive reasons. I have also illustrated a strategy for a principled account of judicial decisions that look to consequences, including third-party consequences.[15] This strategy of principle seems to me much more promising than the weak instrumental program of policy just described.[16] But I have not yet provided any compelling reasons why you should join me in that confidence.

THIRTEEN

Why Efficiency?

CALABRESI'S RIGHT MIX

Guido Calabresi challenges my description of how his theory relates justice and efficiency.[1] But the example he gives from his book, *The Costs of Accidents*, confirms that description instead.[2] For he reminds me that he argues that justice should be a veto on the pursuit of efficiency, so that no scheme for reducing the overall costs of accidents should be accepted if it is really unjust. I agree that it is misleading to describe this picture as calling for a trade-off between justice and efficiency. It calls for a trade-off only in a limiting (indeed Pickwickian) sense of a lexical ordering of one over the other, which is better described as denying a trade-off. But this veto power or lexical ordering nevertheless supposes that a trade-off is in question—that it is, that is, conceptually on the cards. So it provides a particularly sharp version of the mistaken theory about efficiency that I said Calabresi holds, along with other economists of law who contemplate trade-offs but do not give justice the dominant power it enjoys in Calabresi's version.

This is the theory that social wealth is worth pursuing for some reason distinct from justice. When Calabresi insists that the goals of cost reduction may conflict with principles of justice, in which case the latter principles have a veto power, he must be relying on exactly that theory. For unless social wealth is taken to be desirable in itself, as what I called a component of value, or as instrumental toward something else that is a component of value, it makes no sense to say that justice must operate as a veto over the pursuit of social wealth.

Calabresi speaks of a trade-off or mix, not between justice and cost reduction, but between total wealth and its distribution. But it is doubtful that he has altogether abandoned the mistaken idea latent in the earlier distinction, that total wealth is of value in itself. In order to expose the problem I must make a further distinction. Whenever the idea of a "right mix" is in play two senses of that idea must be distinguished. The first is the idea of a trade-off or compromise between two goods or qualities independently desired. Someone who likes both parkland and crops, for example,

must think about the best mix of park and cultivated fields on his property. He wants as much as he can have of each, but since the total property is limited these desires conflict, so he must sacrifice some of what he wants to have more of something else he wants. If he has chosen a particular mix as the "right" mix and subsequently discovers a way to produce more crops from the land he has cultivated, he will regard this as an obvious and unqualified improvement. (He may or may not now alter the mix so as to leave more land as park.)

This "compromise" sense of a trade-off or right mix must be distinguished from the "recipe" sense, in which some mix of ingredients is the right mix only because it will produce the best final product. Someone making a cake may be concerned about the right mix of flour and eggs, not because he independently values each and wants as much as he can have of both, but because a particular mix is better than any other mix for making cakes. Suppose the right mix is two eggs to a cup of flour. A baker who is told that he can add three eggs without thereby decreasing the flour he may add will not think that this suggestion points the way to an improvement in his situation, but only the way to disaster.

Calabresi speaks of a trade-off or mix of wealth and distribution. Does he mean "right mix" in the compromise or the recipe sense? In my article, to which he refers, I supposed that he meant the compromise sense. I pointed out that in that case he must be assuming what I was in train of denying, which is that wealth is a component of value. For, if an egalitarian distribution is in itself a component of value—something worth having for its own sake—it makes no sense to compromise that value for something else unless that something else is also a component of value. If crops are taken to be of value, it makes no sense to have less crops for more parkland unless parkland is also something of value.

But Calabresi says that he agrees with me that social wealth is not a component of value. There seem to be two ways left to interpret his position. He might mean by the right mix a recipe rather than a compromise. Or he might mean a compromise, but a compromise not between an egalitarian pattern of distribution and wealth as a component of value, but between that pattern and wealth as a surrogate for something else.

Does he mean a recipe? The story might go this way. Maximum utility is the only thing valuable in itself. The highest possible total utility will be produced by a recipe that combines something less than the highest total wealth with something less than the most egalitarian possible pattern; and that is the *right* mix of wealth and distribution. Now this is a recipe story because neither wealth nor an egalitarian pattern is valued for its own sake. They are treated as the baker who wants only cake treats eggs and flour. But that is just why I doubt that this story is Calabresi's story. He seems to me to want to say that a more egalitarian distribution *is* something to be valued

for its own sake. So that it might be worth having less overall total utility to have a much more egalitarian distribution. That is in the spirit of his agreeable pluralism—indeed he expressly disclaims a monistic interest in utility. So I assume that his story is not the straightforward utility-recipe story—at least until he advises me otherwise.

I come therefore to the more complex case, that is, I suppose him to have in mind a compromise rather than a recipe, but a compromise between an egalitarian pattern valued for its own sake and social wealth valued as a surrogate (or as a "false target") for something else that is valued for its own sake. But now what is the something else for which social wealth is a surrogate? He might wish to say: total utility. The underlying compromise is between total utility and an egalitarian distribution; this becomes, on the surface, for practical purposes, the compromise between total wealth and an egalitarian distribution. Calabresi is not a monistic or absolute utilitarian, but he may be a partial, compromising one.

Is this his story? Before we decide that it is, I want to construct a different story to offer him. This is a recipe story. But it is an equality-recipe rather than a utility-recipe story. Before I describe this equality-recipe story I must say something about equality as a political ideal. I assume that we both accept, as fundamental, the principle that people should be treated *as equals* in the matter of distribution. But we know that it is a hard question just what that principle means. In the following section I shall describe one plausible interpretation of the equal-treatment principle—one interpretation of equality.

An Interpretation of Equal Treatment

If a fixed sum of identical goods is to be distributed, our treatment-as-equals principle requires that each must have an equal share of those goods. But in all but the crudest societies, different forms of goods fail to be distributed, because different forms of goods can be produced and because rights and opportunities must be distributed as well as other forms of property. In an actual community it is very much an open question, about which reasonable people may differ, just what a truly egalitarian distribution is. Suppose, for example, that we can distribute rights in nuisance or negligence in such a way that people hold either more nearly equal shares of a lower total production of goods or less equal shares of a larger total production. If the second state-of-affairs is Pareto superior to the first, then we will have no difficulty in saying that the first does not treat people as equals. For it shows contempt for people to refuse them benefits in deference only to others' external preferences. (I am assuming that the second state-of-affairs really is Pareto superior, so that no one is worse off even when any possible damage to self-respect that results from relative deprivation is taken into account.)

But if the second state-of-affairs is not Pareto superior, because some people would have absolutely higher welfare in the first, then a different problem is posed. It is then necessary to discover why total wealth is increased in the second situation.

Sometimes a wealth-inegalitarian distribution is the product of a political or economic system that patently does not treat people as equals. Suppose, to take a blatant case, the distribution is the result of political decisions that give one group legal rights denied to another. But sometimes it is at least arguable that it is a wealth-egalitarian distribution that denies deep equality—that is, that wealth equality does not treat people as equals. Suppose, for example, a community each of whose members has roughly the same abilities and talents, but who have very different conceptions of how best to lead their lives. They have different preferences, in particular, over forms of labor and over the best mix of labor and leisure. But each is paid the same total wage for whatever work he does, and wealth is equal.

We may want to make two complaints about this situation. First, it may be wealth inefficient, because a different set of wages—those fixed in a market for labor—would in the circumstances provide more incentives for production and increase total wealth. Second, it may be unfair, because wages do not reflect the true costs to others of each person's indulging his own preference over forms of labor. A different set of wages—those fixed in a market for labor—would more nearly treat people as equals because it would require each to take responsibility for the true costs of his own choices. If we hold a theory of how to treat people as equals that includes the principle that people must take that responsibility, we can therefore object to the arrangement on grounds of equality as well as grounds of efficiency. Our two objections may then be identical: the arrangement is unfair (on this conception of equality) just in the way it is inefficient. We repair our distributional as well as our wealth complaints by moving away from wealth equality.

My example is artificial because it assumes that people are alike in talents, so that different choices of occupation represent only different preference sets. In the real world different choices reflect different talents and initial opportunities as well. But even in the real world different choices of occupation depend in part on differences in preference sets, so that a wealth-inefficient wage scheme might be objectionable from the standpoint of equality because it came too close to providing equality of wages, even though the most wealth-efficient wage scheme would also be objectionable from the same standpoint. In the real world it would be a matter of judgment which degree of wealth efficiency in the wage structure came closest to achieving the demands of equality, all things considered. But it would presumably be a point somewhere between total wage equality and total wealth efficiency.

In many cases, moreover, equality would demand social arrangements that maximize wealth efficiency without regard to the independent distributional consequences of these arrangements themselves. Suppose, as Richard Posner argues, a system of negligence in tort law is more wealth efficient than a system of strict liability,[3] but (contrary to his further assumption) this endures to the benefit of a class of persons—call them inveterate pedestrians—who are not, however, distinct otherwise as forming a worse-off economic group. Strict liability is, we might say, distortive but not redistributive toward a more attractive pattern of distribution. (I am assuming all this only *arguendo*, because I know others would disagree.) In that case, strict liability would be, from the standpoint of the deeper principle, inegalitarian, because the pedestrians would be purchasing their activity at too low a price measured against an ideal egalitarian auction, and the mark and measure of the inequality would be just the wealth inefficiency. Equality would require, once again, a move toward the wealth-efficient regime of negligence.

A Recipe Theory for Equality

Someone who holds this theory of deep equality does not think that either total wealth or total utility, on the one hand, or wealth equality, on the other, is valuable in itself. He does believe that on some occasions genuine equality requires a move toward wealth equality, and on other occasions a move toward wealth efficiency. But he does not mean that, when these demands of justice are correctly assessed and met, something valuable has been sacrificed. Suppose deep equality calls for abandoning strict liability even though this means that some pedestrians will therefore have less welfare. If all were equally rich before—or even closer to being equally rich—then wealth equality has declined. But this is not a matter of regret as such, because in this case wealth equality would be unfair, and it is absurd to regret not having more of what, in the circumstances, we do not wish to have. That would be like regretting that one cannot put more eggs into the cake with the flour. Someone holding this second theory would regret that pedestrians cannot have what they want. But that is regretting the loss that these people suffer, which he would regret whether or not others gain, and that is a different story. He does not regret the loss in wealth equality itself if he believes that deep equality does not require, but instead condemns, that form of equality.

Suppose, on the other hand, that deep equality requires an improvement in wealth equality that will have the consequence of decreasing total wealth. That decline in total wealth must mean that someone will have less than he otherwise would, and that may be a cause for regret. We regret, that is, our inability to make a Pareto improvement on a fair distribution,

which we would certainly make if we could. But that does not mean that we regret sacrificing a higher aggregate level of wealth (or utility) for a lower in order to achieve justice, or even that we regard this exchange as a sacrifice at all. Someone who holds the deep-equality theory will deny that there is even *pro tanto* a loss in justice when total utility declines, if the higher utility was produced by a distribution that did not treat people as equals.

So the story of deep equality is at bottom very different from the story of a compromise between wealth equality and the highest possible utility, even though the operational recommendations of the two theories may in some circumstances be much the same. Even though, that is, they will both pay attention to both wealth equality and wealth efficiency and call for a "right mix" between them. For the deep-equality theory is a recipe theory: It holds that justice consists in that distribution in which people are treated as equals (or, if this is different, in Pareto improvements on that distribution) and denies that there is any independent value, apart from the play of that calculation, in either wealth equality or highest aggregate wealth or utility. The compromise story takes wealth equality and total utility to be of independent moral value, so that a decline in either, even if required to improve the other, is *pro tanto* a loss in justice. On the compromise theory, that is, the "right mix" is of derivative or parasitic importance: It is valuable as the right compromise between two goals of dominant or primary value. But on the deep-equality theory the "right mix" is dominant and primary, and that is why it is misleading, though comprehensible, for a deep egalitarian to speak of any "trade-off."

A second important difference between the theories is consequent upon this first one. For the compromise theory the question of justice is a question of balance, and the balance is both impersonal and intuitive. Impersonal because individuals become the instruments of achieving aggregate quantities—of equality as much as of utility. Intuitive because the correct balance must be a matter of inarticulate "feel." For the egalitarian theory, on the other hand, the question of justice is a matter of fairness person-by-person rather than fairness of aggregate sums—and one's judgment about fairness to persons depends on judging arguments for a particular result, not on striking intuitive and indeterminate aggregate balances.

These are, I think, important theoretical differences between the compromise and the deep-egalitarian theory. How important these differences are in practice will depend on the theory of deep equality one holds. The principle that people must be treated as equals admits, as I said, of different interpretations or conceptions. That principle, one might say, is only a schema for different theories of equality—different theories about what treating people as equals requires. Suppose one holds the following theory of equality: "People are treated as equals when they are made equal in welfare—except when differences in welfare will produce very much more

welfare overall. No flat principle can be stated governing the operation of that proviso; everything will depend on intuitionistic judgments made in particular cases." On this theory the difference between the compromise theory and the deep-equality theory all but disappears, for the compromise has simply been embedded in the definition of deep equality.

But there are better and more precise accounts of deep equality than that. The utilitarian account of equality is certainly more precise. It holds that people are treated as equals when goods and opportunities are so distributed as to maximize average utility among them. Now if a compromise theory is conceived as requiring a compromise between equality of welfare and highest total welfare, then a utilitarian theory of deep equality will plainly yield different results, because it will deny that it is ever fair to compromise total welfare, over a given group, for equality of welfare within that group.

I prefer a different and more complex account of deep equality than the utilitarian account, which is the theory I relied on in the brief sketch of the last section. This argues that individuals are treated as equals when an equal share of the resources of the community measured abstractly—that is, before these resources are committed to any particular production route—is devoted to the life of each. I doubt that this description makes much sense put so briefly, and I have tried to describe the theory and its consequences at some length elsewhere.[4] My present purpose is not to persuade you of the merits of this (or any other) account of deep equality, but only to illustrate my claim that, under some such accounts, the compromise theory and the deep-equality theory will yield very different results, though neither requires that society be committed to either total wealth equality or total maximization of wealth.

A Polemical but Powerful Point

I hope to persuade Calabresi to embrace some deep-equality recipe theory rather than the compromise theory, and therefore to give up all talk of a "trade-off" between distribution and wealth, conceived either as valuable in themselves or as surrogates for equality of welfare and maximization of welfare. What arguments should I use? My strongest positive argument would be the development of a compelling deep-egalitarian theory. We shall see about that. In the meantime I offer the following polemical, negative but nevertheless powerful point. I doubt that he will find a compromise theory appealing when he examines the foundations of any such theory.

The compromise theory I described—the compromise between equality of welfare and highest possible aggregate welfare—requires that one accept what might be called pluralistic utilitarianism. This theory holds that aggregate welfare is not the only good, but is at least one good to be compro-

mised against both distributional and what Calabresi calls "other justice" considerations. The compromiser must, that is, be partly a utilitarian, because otherwise he could not take wealth maximization to be valuable as a surrogate for aggregate utility; but only partly a utilitarian, because otherwise he could not allow rights and other nonutilitarian factors to feature as he says he wishes them to do.

Utilitarianism is really two different theories; or, rather, there are two different ways of being a utilitarian. One holds that total utility is a value because pleasure (or happiness on some more sophisticated conception) is good in itself, so that the more of it the better, quite apart from its distribution. This is teleological utilitarianism. The other holds that goods should be distributed so as to produce the highest average utility over some stipulated population, because only a distribution of that sort treats people as equals. That is the egalitarian utilitarianism I mentioned earlier in this essay—I called it the utilitarian theory of equality. The well-known classical utilitarian philosophers, like Bentham, seem to me to be egalitarian utilitarians, though this is perhaps arguable. Certainly the modern defense of utilitarianism, in the spirit of Harsanyi[5] and Hare,[6] for example, is explicitly egalitarian utilitarianism. Teleological utilitarianism seems to make very little sense. As Rawls (and many others) have pointed out, it recommends a world of teeming population each of whose lives is barely worth living so long as the aggregate happiness is larger than a world with less people whose average happiness is much larger.[7]

Now even a partial utilitarian must choose between these two ways of being a utilitarian. If he is an egalitarian utilitarian—if he holds that the right way to treat people as equals is to count each for one and only one in a Benthamite calculation—then he can nevertheless compromise highest average welfare for a variety of reasons—in order better to serve God, for example, or advance culture, or improve the genetic stock. But he cannot coherently offer to compromise highest average welfare over a given population in the name of simple wealth or welfare equality. Treating people as equals, on the utilitarian's conception of equality, demands the highest aggregate welfare, and one cannot coherently treat people other than as equals in the name of some deeper conception of equality. (One can *refine* the utilitarian conception of equality—for example, by disregarding external preferences[8]—so that treating people as equals is not quite maximizing average welfare. But this abandons a compromise in favor of a recipe theory.)

So if Calabresi holds to the compromise theory I offered, he must be a teleological utilitarian. It is not logically incoherent to believe that pleasure (or some other concept of utility) is a good in itself, apart from distribution, so that the world is *pro tanto* better the more pleasure there is, no matter how miserable people then are. But it is not sensible, because teleological utilitarianism is not a sensible theory. It is not sensible to believe that plea-

sure in itself is a good, apart from distribution, no matter how miserable everyone is. That is pleasure fetishism, which is just as silly as wealth fetishism. Wouldn't Calabresi rather give up the idea of a trade-off between distribution and wealth?[9]

POSNER'S WRONG START

Richard Posner believes that agencies of government, and particularly courts, should make political decisions in such a way as to maximize social wealth.[10] In "The Ethical and Political Basis of the Efficiency Norm in Common Law Adjudication" he narrows his claim and offers a new argument.[11] He wishes to show, not as before why society as a whole should seek wealth maximization in every political decision, but only why common law judges should decide cases so as to maximize wealth. He offers two arguments meant to be connected (or perhaps even to be only one argument).[12] First, everyone (or at least almost everyone) may be deemed to have consented in advance to the principles or rules that judges who seek to maximize wealth will apply. Second, the enforcement of these principles and rules is in the interest of everyone (or almost everyone), including those who thereby lose lawsuits. The first—the argument from consent—is supposed to introduce the idea of autonomy (and therefore a strain of Kant) to the case for wealth. The second—the argument from universal interest—insists in the continuing relevance of welfare to justice, and therefore is supposed to add a dose of utilitarianism. The combined arguments, Posner suggests, show that wealth maximization—at least by judges—provides the best of both these traditional theories of political morality and avoids their famous problems.

Posner illustrates the second claim by showing why, if negligence rules are superior from the standpoint of wealth maximization to rules of strict liability, it follows that all those who benefit from reduced driving costs— almost everyone—would be better off under a regime of negligence than a regime of strict liability. The first claim—about consent—is then supposed to follow directly: If it is in fact true that almost everyone would be better off under a regime of negligence than strict liability, then it is fair to assume that almost everyone would have chosen negligence if offered the choice between these two regimes at a suitably early time, and therefore fair to deem almost everyone to have consented to negligence even though no one has actually done so.

The Argument from Consent

These arguments are more complex and I think more confused than first appears. (I discussed both at length several years ago.[13]) It is important to remember, first, that consent and self-interest are independent concepts

that have independent roles in political justification. If I have consented in advance to governance by a certain rule, then this counts as some reason for enforcing against me the rule to which I have consented. Of course, in determining how much reason my actual consent provides we must look to the circumstances of my consent, in particular to see whether it was informed and uncoerced. In this latter investigation the question of whether it was in my self-interest to have consented may figure only as evidence: if it was plainly not in my self-interest, this might suggest, though it does not prove, that my consent was either uninformed or coerced. But the bare fact that my consent was against my own interest provides no argument in itself against enforcing my consent against my later wishes.

Conversely, the fact that it would have been in my self-interest to have consented to something is sometimes evidence that I did consent, if the question of whether I did actually consent is for some reason in doubt. But only evidence: the fact of self-interest in no way constitutes an actual consent. In some circumstances, however, the fact of self-interest is good evidence for what we might call a counterfactual consent: that is, the proposition that I would have consented had I been asked. But a counterfactual consent provides no reason in itself for enforcing against me that to which I would have (but did not) consent. Perhaps the fact of my earlier self-interest does provide an argument for enforcing the principle against me now. I shall consider that later. But the counterfactual consent, of which the self-interest is evidence, can provide no further argument beyond whatever argument the self-interest itself provides. Since Posner's argument from consent depends entirely on counterfactual consent, and since counterfactual consent is in itself irrelevant to political justification, the argument from consent wholly fails. Posner's appeal to "autonomy"—and his associated claim to have captured what is most worthwhile in "Kantian" theories—is wholly spurious.

Autonomy is, I agree, a different concept from consent. It contemplates what is sometimes called—perhaps misleadingly—authentic consent, meaning the consent of the true or genuine person. That dark idea is often elaborated as a kind of hypothetical or counterfactual consent. But then the authenticity is provided by—and everything turns on—the way the conditions of the counterfactual consent are specified. Kant himself deployed a complex metaphysical psychology to identify the consent of the genuine person counterfactually. Rawls constructs an elaborate "original position" for an arguably similar purpose. But Posner's argument lacks any comparable structure, and so provides no reason to think that the counterfactual consent he describes has more claim to authenticity—and hence to autonomy—than any other choice people might have, but did not, make.

Why has Posner confused self-interest and consent in this apparently elementary way? His article provides a variety of clues. Consider this extraordinary passage:

The notion of consent used here is what economists call ex ante compensation. I contend, I hope uncontroversially, that if you buy a lottery ticket and
lose the lottery . . . you have consented to the loss. Many of the involuntary,
uncompensated losses experienced in the market, or tolerated by the institutions that take the place of the market where the market cannot be made to
work effectively, are fully compensated ex ante and hence are consented
to.[14]

This passage confuses two questions: Is it fair that someone should bear
some loss? Has he consented to bear that loss? If I buy a lottery ticket
knowing the odds, and was uncoerced, it is perhaps fair that I bear the loss
that follows, because I received a benefit ("compensation") for assuming the
risk. But it hardly follows, nor is it true, that I have consented to that loss.
What, indeed, would that mean? (Perhaps that I agreed that the game
should be rigged so that I must lose.)

In some circumstances it may be said that I consented to the *risk* of loss,
which is different, though even this stretches a point and in many cases is
just false. Suppose (with no question of fraud or duress) I wildly overesti-
mated my chance of winning—perhaps I thought it a sure thing. It may
nevertheless be fair that I lose, if the ticket was fairly priced, even though I
would not have bet if I had accurately assessed my chances of winning. All
this—the importance of distinguishing between fairness and consent—is
even clearer in the case of the "entrepreneurial risks" Posner discusses. He
imagines a case in which someone buys land which then falls in value when
the biggest plant in town unexpectedly moves. He says that the loss was
compensated *ex ante* (and hence "consented to"), because "[t]he probability
that the plant would move was discounted in the purchase price that they
paid."[15] The latter suggestion is mysterious. Does it assume that the price
was lower because both parties to the sale expected the move? But then the
plant's move would not have been unexpected. Or does it mean only that
anyone buying or selling anything knows that the unexpected may happen?
In either case the argument begs the question even as an argument that it is
fair that the buyer bear the loss. For it assumes that it has already been established and understood by the parties that the buyer must bear the loss—
otherwise the price would not have reflected just the risk that the plant
would move, but also the risk that the buyer would be required to bear the
loss if it did move.

But in any event it is just wrong to say, in either case, that the buyer consented to the loss. Perhaps, though the buyer knew that the plant would
very likely move and that he was getting a bargain price because the seller
expected that the buyer would bear the loss if the plant did move, the buyer
hoped that he might be able to persuade some court to rescind the sale if
the feared move did take place or to persuade some legislature to bail him
out. It would be fair, in these circumstances, for the court to refuse rescis-
sion, but dead wrong to say that the buyer had consented to bear the loss.

The argument of fairness must stand on its own, that is, and gains nothing from any supposition about consent. Autonomy is not a concept here in play.

So Posner may have conflated interest and consent because he has conflated consent more generally with the grounds of fairness. A second clue is provided by his remarks about what he calls "implied consent."[16] He acknowledges that plaintiffs in negligence suits cannot be said to have consented expressly to rules of negligence rather than strict liability—even in the way he believes buyers of lottery tickets have consented to losing. But he says that courts can *impute* consent to such plaintiffs the way courts impute intentions to parties to a contract who have not spelled out every term, or to legislatures whose statutes are dark with ambiguity. Once again Posner's analogy betrays a confusion; in this case it is a confusion between unexpressed and counterfactual consent.

Lawyers disagree about how best to describe contractual or statutory interpretation. According to one theory, the court takes what the parties or the legislators say expressly as evidence—as clues to the existence of some individual or group psychological state which is an actual intention, though one that is never expressed formally in the requisite document. According to the competing theory, the court does not purport to discover such a hidden psychological state, but rather uses the fiction of an unexpressed psychological state as a vehicle for some argument about what the parties or the legislature would have done (or, perhaps, should have done) if they had attended to the issue now in question. These are different and competing theories of constructive intention, precisely because they describe very different justifications for a judicial decision. If a judge really has discovered a hidden but actual psychological state—some common understanding of parties to a contract or of members of a legislative group—then the fact of that common understanding provides a direct argument for his decision. But if the putative psychological state is fiction only, then the fiction can provide no argument in itself. In that case it is the arguments the judge himself deploys, about what the parties or the legislature would or should have done, that do all the work, and the idea of consent plays no role whatsoever. When Posner says that the courts might impute consent to plaintiffs in automobile-accident cases, there can be no doubt which kind of description he means to suggest. He does not suppose that plaintiffs have really but secretly consented to negligence rules, taking a silent vow to that effect each morning before breakfast. He means that the imputed consent would be a fiction. He has in mind only counterfactual, not unexpressed, consent. But a counterfactual consent is not some pale form of consent. It is no consent at all.

The third clue Posner offers us is more interesting. He notices that Rawls (and Harsanyi and other economists) have built elaborate arguments for

theories of justice that are based on counterfactual consent.[17] He means to make the same sort of argument, though, as he makes plain, he has in mind a different basis for counterfactual consent and a different theory of justice. He asks himself, not what parties to some original position would consent to under conditions of radical uncertainty, but what actual people, each of whom knows his particular situation in full detail, would consent to in the fullness of that understanding. He answers that they would consent, not to principles seeking maximin over wealth or even average utility, but to just those rules that common law judges concerned about maximizing social wealth would employ.

But Posner ignores the fact that Rawls's (and Harsanyi's) arguments have whatever force they do have just because the questions they describe must be answered under conditions of radical uncertainty. Indeed (as I have tried to make plain elsewhere[18]) Rawls's original position is a powerful mechanic for thinking about justice because the design of that position embodies and enforces the theory of deep equality described in the last part of this essay. It embodies that theory precisely through the stipulation that parties consent to principles of justice with no knowledge of any qualities or attributes that give them advantages over others, and with no knowledge of what conception of the good they hold as distinct from others.

Posner says that his own arguments improve on Rawls because Posner is concerned with actual people making choices under what he calls "natural" ignorance—he means, I suppose, ignorance about whether they will actually be unlucky—rather than under what he calls Rawls's "artificial" and more radical ignorance.[19] But this "improvement" is fatal. Posner does not contemplate, as we saw, actual consent. If he did, then the degree of "natural" ignorance to attribute to the choosers (or, what comes to the same thing, the date at which to define that ignorance) would be given. It would be the date of the actual, historical choice. But since Posner has in mind a counterfactual rather than an actual choice, any selection of a degree or date of ignorance must be wholly arbitrary, and different selections would dictate very different rules as fair. It would plainly be arbitrary, for example, to construct "natural" ignorance so that no one knew whether he was one of the few inveterate pedestrians whose expected welfare would be improved by strict liability rather than negligence rules for automobile accidents. But if natural ignorance does not exclude such self-knowledge, then Posner cannot claim that even the counterfactual consent would be unanimous. It must be a matter of the counterfactual choice of most people and that provides, as we shall see, not an improved version of a Rawlsian argument, but a utilitarian argument only.

The situation is worse even than that. For if only "natural" ignorance is in play, then there is no nonarbitrary reason to exclude the knowledge of those who know that they have already been unlucky—that is, the plaintiffs

of the particular lawsuits the judge is asked to decide by imposing a wealth-maximizing rule. After all, at any moment some people are in that position, and their consent will not be forthcoming then, even counterfactually. Posner plainly wants to invite consent under what turns out to be, not natural ignorance, but a tailored ignorance that is even more artificial than Rawls's original position. For any particular plaintiff, he wants to invite consent at some time after that person's driving habits are sufficiently well formed so that he is a gainer from reduced driving costs, but before the time he has suffered an uninsured nonnegligence accident. What time is that? Why is that time decisive? Rawls chose his original position, with its radical ignorance, for reasons of political morality: the original position, so defined, is a device for enforcing a theory of deep equality. Posner seems to be able to define his conditions of counterfactual choice only so as to reach the results he wants.

The Argument from Interest

Posner's second main argument, as I said earlier, is an argument from the self-interest of most people. He offers to show that it is in the interest of almost everyone that judges decide common law cases by enforcing those rules that maximize social wealth. Even those people who do not drive, he notices, use motor vehicles—they take buses or are driven by others—and so gain from reduced driving costs. If a regime of negligence rules, rather than rules of strict liability, would reduce driving costs, and if nearly everyone would benefit overall from that reduction, then something very like a Pareto justification on the welfare space is available for negligence. Almost everyone is better off and almost no one is worse off. Of course not absolutely everyone will be better off—we can imagine someone who is always a pedestrian and never even a passenger—but "only a fanatic" would insist on complete unanimity when a Pareto justification is in play.[20]

This is Posner's argument from nonfanatical Paretianism, shorn of its autonomy or consent claims. What are we to make of it? We must first of all try to become clearer about whom the "almost everyone" proviso leaves out. Suppose I am an automobile driver who benefits steadily over my whole life from the reduced driving costs made possible by the institution of negligence. One day I am run down (on one of my rare walks around the block) by a non-negligent driver, and I suffer medical and other costs far in excess of the amount I formerly saved from reduced driving costs, and will save from reduced ambulance charges and motorized wheelchair costs in the future. In what sense do I benefit from a regime of negligence, which denies me recovery, over a regime of strict liability? Only in the sense of what might be called my antecedent self-interest. I was better off under the system of negligence before I was run down, at least on the reasonable assumption that I had no more chance of being run down than anyone else.

After all (by hypothesis), I could have bought insurance against being run down with part of what I saved, as a motorist, from the lower driving costs. But *after* the accident (if I have not in fact bought such insurance) I would be better off under a system of strict liability. The difference can also be expressed not temporally, but as a difference in expected welfare under different states of knowledge. When I do not know that it is I who will be run down, my expected welfare is higher under negligence. When I do know that, my expected welfare is higher under strict liability.

But what is the appropriate point (expressed either temporally or as a function of knowledge) at which to calculate my expected welfare? Suppose my case is a hard case at law because it has not yet been decided in my jurisdiction whether negligence or strict liability governs cases like mine. (It is, after all, just in such hard cases that we need a theory of adjudication like the one Posner proposes.) Now the fact that I would have been better off, before my accident, under a system of negligence seems irrelevant. I did not in fact have the benefits of a negligence rule. In such a case the question— under which rule will everyone be better off—must look to the future only. And I, for one, will not be better off under negligence. I will be better off under strict liability.

But suppose it is said that at least everyone else—or everyone else except the few who walk and never drive or are driven—will be better off. Only I and these inveterate pedestrians will be worse off. Is that true? It is true that (ignoring these inveterate pedestrians) everyone else's expected welfare, fixed at the time of my lawsuit, will be improved. But it is not true that everyone's actual welfare will be improved. For there will be some who will not take out the appropriate insurance, and who will be unlucky. They will suffer so much uncompensated loss from nonnegligent accidents that they would have been better off, *ex post*, had the court laid down a regime of strict liability in my case, even when their reduced driving costs in the meantime, and their reduced ambulance costs thereafter, have been taken into account. Suppose you are one of these unlucky people. You sue. You cannot say that you have had no benefit from the system of negligence, but you nevertheless suggest that the system of negligence be abandoned now and strict liability instituted, starting with your case.

It cannot be said, as a reason for refusing your request, that you gained more than you lost from the decision in my case. You did not—you lost more than you gained. But suppose it were true that you gained more than you lost. Let me change the facts once again so that that is so. Suppose that your present accident arises near the end of your expected life and that you did arrange insurance after the decision in my case so that you will now suffer only a short-lived increase in your premium if you lose your case. You have gained more in reduced driving costs in the meantime than you will lose even if you lose your case. Nevertheless, it is not true that you will gain more *in the future* if the judge in your case refuses your request and

maintains the system of negligence. Even under the new set of facts you will gain more if strict liability is now instituted, starting with your case. Otherwise (being rational) you would not have made the request that you did.

I hope the point is now clear. If we set out to justify any particular common law decisions on Pareto grounds, then the class of exceptions—the class of those worse off through the decision—must include, at a minimum, those who lose the lawsuit and others in like cases. It does not improve the Pareto justification that the rule now imposed would have increased the expected welfare of the loser had it been imposed earlier. Nor that the rule was in fact imposed earlier so that his expected welfare was actually increased at some earlier date. Nor that, because the rule was imposed earlier, the loser in the present suit gained more from that past rule than he now loses. Each of these is irrelevant because a Pareto justification is a forward-looking, not a backward-looking, justification. It proposes that a decision is right because no one is worse off through *that* decision being taken. But then all those who are worse off from a forward-looking point of view must stand as counter-examples to a proposed Pareto justification. These different *backward*-looking considerations might well be relevant to a different kind of justification of a judicial decision. They might, in particular, be relevant to a familiar sort of argument from fairness. (I shall consider that argument later.) But they are not relevant to a Pareto justification, which justification Posner is at pains to supply.

Is Posner saved here by his caveat, that only a fanatic would insist on absolute unanimity? Perhaps it does sound fanatical to insist that every last person must benefit—or at least not lose—before any social decision is taken. If we accepted that constraint, almost no social decision would be justified. Nevertheless, that is exactly what the Pareto criterion requires. It insists that no one be worse off, and if anyone is, then the Pareto justification is not simply weakened; it is destroyed. Pareto is all or nothing, like pregnancy and legal death.

Why? Because unless the Pareto criterion is treated as all or nothing, as fanatical in this way it collapses into the utilitarian criterion. In particular, it assumes the burden of both the conceptual and the moral defects of utilitarian theories. Suppose we state the Pareto criterion in the following, non-fanatical way: "A political (including a judicial) decision is justified if it will make the vast bulk of people better off and only a relatively few people worse off." Surely we must interpret this test so as to take account of the quantity of welfare gained or lost as well as the numbers who gain or lose. Otherwise it might justify devastating losses to a few in exchange for such trivial gains to the many that the sum of the latter, on any reckoning, falls short of the sum of the former. But when we do introduce the dimension of quantity of welfare gained and lost we also introduce the familiar problems of interpersonal comparisons of utility. One important claim for the Pareto

criterion is that it avoids such comparisons; if it turns out not to avoid them after all, then this claim must be withdrawn.

A second claim for the Pareto criterion is a claim of political morality. Utilitarianism faces the problem of explaining to someone who loses in a Benthamite calculation why it is fair to make him suffer so that others may prosper. Critics of utilitarianism hold that any Benthamite justification offered to him will commit what I have called the ambiguous sin of ignoring the difference between people.[21] Now if a fanatical Pareto justification is available for a given political decision, then this problem—explaining why someone must be worse off in order that others be better off—is avoided. I do not mean that Pareto justifications are wholly unproblematical. Someone who holds a deep-egalitarian theory of absolute equality of welfare will object to a decision that makes some better off and no one worse off if that decision destroys a preexisting absolute equality of welfare. But fanatical Pareto justifications do avoid the obviously more serious problem of justifying losses to some so that others may gain.

It is important to see, moreover, that this is not a problem of the numbers of who lose. Suppose only one person loses in a Benthamite calculation. If the fact that the gain to others outweighs, in total, the loss to that one person provides a justification for the loss to him, then that same justification must obviously be available when the number of losers increases to any number, provided that the aggregate gain still exceeds the aggregate loss. The issue of principle is raised, decisively, in the individual case. That is the eye of the needle; if utility can pass through that eye it gains heaven. So our relaxed Pareto criterion can have no advantage of political morality over straightforward Benthamism. Nonfanatical Paretianism is utilitarianism merely.

It is time for a reckoning. Posner is pleased to claim that wealth maximization combines the most appealing features of both the Kantian concern with autonomy and the utilitarian concern with individual preferences, while avoiding the excesses of either of these traditional theories. His argument from counterfactual consent is meant to supply the Kantian features. But this is spurious: The idea of consent does no work at all in the theory and the appeal to autonomy is therefore a facade. His argument from the common interest is meant to supply the utilitarian features. But it does this too well. He cannot claim a genuine Pareto justification for common law decisions, in either hard or easy cases. His relaxed version of Paretianism is only utilitarianism with all the warts. The voyage of his essay ends in the one traditional theory he was formerly most anxious to disown.

Beyond Consent and Interest

Can we discover, in Posner's various discussions, some more attractive argument of fairness than those he makes explicitly? The following general

principle (we may call it the antecedent-interest principle) seems somehow in play. If a rule is in everyone's antecedent interest at the time it is enacted, then it is fair to enforce that rule even against those who turn out, in the event, to lose by its adoption, provided that they were, in advance, no more likely to lose by it than others were. That is not, as we have seen, the Pareto criterion, nor will everyone agree that it is a fair principle. Indeed I shall provide reasons to doubt it. But it has enough initial appeal for us to ask whether it provides a base for Posner's arguments for wealth maximization in adjudication.

The antecedent-interest principle cannot be used directly in favor of any particular wealth-maximizing rule a judge might adopt, for the first time, in a hard case. For any particular rule will fail the test the principle provides: It will not be in the interest of the party against whom it is used at the time of its adoption, because the time of its adoption is just the time at which it is used against him. But the antecedent-interest principle does seem to support a *meta*-rule of adjudication (call it alpha) which provides that in a hard case judges should choose and apply that rule, if any, that is in the then antecedent interests of the vast bulk of people though not in the interests of the party who then loses. Once alpha has been in force in a community for some time, at least, alpha itself meets the antecedent-interest-principle test. For each individual, alpha may unhappily make it more likely that some rule will be adopted that will work against his interests. For inveterate pedestrians, for example, alpha may make it more likely that the negligence rule will be adopted. But since each individual will gain through the adoption of other rules in virtue of alpha—inveterate pedestrians will gain through all manner of common law rules that work in their benefit as well as the benefit of most others—it may plausibly be said that alpha *itself* is in the antecedent interest of absolutely everyone. But even if it turns out that this is wrong—that a certain economic or other minority exists such that that minority characteristically loses by a wide range of particular rules meeting the test of alpha—then alpha can be suitably amended. Let us therefore restate alpha this way: In a hard case, judges should choose that rule, if any, that is in the then antecedent interests of the vast bulk of people and not against the interests of the worst-off economic group or any other group that would be generally and antecedently disadvantaged, as a group, by the enforcement of this principle without this qualification.

Now Posner believes that alpha (taken hereafter to be amended in this way) would require judges to adopt a wealth-maximizing test for common law adjudication, at least in general. If this is so, then the combination of the antecedent-interest rule and alpha might seem to provide an argument of fairness in favor of (at least general) wealth-maximizing adjudication at common law. That would be an important conclusion and, in my opinion, a clear advance over previous attempts to justify wealth maximization as a

standard for adjudication. It is more convincing to argue that, under the conditions of common law adjudication, wealth-maximizing rules are fair, than to say either that wealth is good in itself or that it is causally related to other, independently stated, goods in such a way as to justify instrumentally the doctrine that society should single-mindedly pursue wealth.

So we have good reason to ask whether the antecedent-interest principle is fair. We should notice that if that principle could be sensibly applied by the parties to Rawls's original position, and if they chose to apply it, then they would select the principle of average utility as the fundamental principle of justice rather than the principles Rawls says they would select. (Harsanyi and others, as Posner reminds us, have argued for average utility in just this way.) We can immediately see one reason, however, why parties to the original position, under one description of their interests, would not accept the antecedent-interest principle. If they were conservative about risks and adopted a maximin strategy for that reason, they would avoid the principle, because it works against those who in one way or another have very bad luck.

We have already seen why this is so. Suppose alpha has been in force for generations. But the question of whether negligence or strict liability holds for automobile accidents has never been settled. Some person who is injured by a nonnegligent driver, and is uninsured, finds that a court, responding to alpha, chooses a negligence rule, and he is therefore ruined by medical expenses. He argues that this is unfair. It is not an appealing reply that the economic group to which he belongs gains along with everyone else under a regime of negligence. He loses. Nor is it necessarily true that, as things turned out, he gained more than he lost from alpha's being accepted in his community. It is hard to guess at how much he gained. We should have to ask what other arguments were in favor of the rules that were adopted earlier in virtue of alpha in order to decide whether the same rules would have been adopted even if alpha had been rejected from the outset. But if he is absolutely ruined by his uncompensated accident, he might well be better off, *ex post*, had alpha never been recognized.

Suppose we say to him, in reply to his complaint, that he should have known that alpha would settle any case testing negligence against strict liability for accidents, should have calculated that alpha required negligence, and should have purchased appropriate insurance against nonnegligent injury. He will answer, with some force, that we have begged every important question. First, it does not follow, from the fact that alpha recommends negligence, that the argument that it does was, in the appropriate sense, publicly available. That argument might rest on reasonably recondite economic analysis developed and worked through for the first time in connection with this litigation. Second, our reply assumes that alpha is fair, so that he should have made provisions for insurance in its light, though that is just

what he questions. We cannot say that he consented to alpha just because it was in his antecedent interest when established—that claim would repeat Posner's initial mistake. Nor will he accept that it is fair to impose some standard on him just because he has had some benefit from it in the past, particularly if he had no choice whether to accept that benefit.[22] We must show that the principle of antecedent interest is fair, not just assume it.

We shall clarify these objections, I think, if we construct a different principle (call it beta). Beta is not, in its basic formulation, a principle for adjudication, as alpha is, but it furnishes one. Beta is basically a theory of social responsibility. We might formulate it in its most abstract form this way. People should take responsibility for such costs of accidents (defined, as elsewhere in this essay, broadly) if responsibility for such costs would be assigned to them by legislation in an ideal community in which everyone acted and voted with a sense of justice and with mutual and equal concern and respect, based on information that is also easily, publicly, and reliably available to the actor. Beta (stated at that level of abstraction) might well be said to be only a schema for a principle of responsibility not a principle itself. Reasonable people who accept it will nevertheless disagree about what it requires because they disagree about how just people would act and vote. (Beta, we might say, admits of different interpretations or conceptions.) But even put so abstractly, beta is far from empty. On the contrary, it is very demanding—perhaps too demanding—because it proposes to enforce legislation that would be adopted in certain unlikely circumstances but in fact has not yet been. Beta is a strong theory of responsibility because it is a theory of natural responsibility tied to counterfactual propositions about legislation. Someone might intelligibly believe that beta requires people to take responsibility themselves for the costs of nonnegligent accidents, and yet deny that they should do so until and unless the legislation described in beta is actually in force. He accepts, that is, that beta requires some particular assumption of responsibility, but rejects beta.

Though beta is a theory of natural responsibility, it furnishes a recommendation for adjudication, particularly against the background of a general theory of adjudication, which argues that, in principle, natural rights and duties should be enforced in court. Suppose someone now says, however, that beta is nothing but alpha. Or (perhaps a bit more plausibly) that alpha is one interpretation or conception of beta. Either would be a mistake, and a serious confusion. For alpha will, under certain circumstances all too familiar, recommend judicial decisions that no plausible interpretation of beta could countenance. Suppose, as we just imagined, that a particular rule meets the requirements of alpha, but for reasons that are neither familiar nor generally available but are developed in adjudication in just the way in which recondite economic data or analysis might properly be developed looking toward legislation. Alpha will insist that that rule must be ap-

plied to someone who, even though aware of alpha, could not reliably have anticipated the rule. Beta will not eliminate all surprises: If people disagree radically about what it requires, because they disagree about the underlying moral issues, then someone may indeed be surprised by its application. But the grounds and incidents of this surprise differ greatly between the two principles.

A second difference seems to me more important. Consider the following familiar argument about the consequences of a principle like alpha. Suppose considerations of fairness recommend that members of some group— the poor, for example, or the uneducated—should have certain contractual privileges or immunities, either through special rules or through general rules that will have special importance for people in their situation. But if a court adopts such a rule, members of that group will suffer in the long run, because merchants or other contractors will be less likely to contract with them, or will insist on compensatory price increases or other conditions, or will in some other way thwart the purpose of the rule in question. Alpha now argues against the immediately protective rule. If alpha is followed, someone loses in the present case who is told that, although fairness would justify a decision for him if his case could be considered on its own merits, he must lose in order to protect others in his economic class in the future. Beta, on the other hand, argues the other way. It regards the fact that others would act so as to undermine the requirements of fairness as irrelevant to the question of natural responsibility, and so irrelevant to the question put for adjudication. The merchants who will ignore the claims of the disadvantaged group, claims we assume *arguendo* to be required by justice, are not behaving as they would in the counterfactual conditions stipulated for fixing natural responsibility.

Legislators would be wiser, no doubt, to consider the real world rather than these counterfactual conditions, and so to prefer alpha to beta as a guide for forward-looking legislation about contractual immunities, responsibility for accidents, and so forth. Some people might think that judges deciding hard cases at law should also prefer alpha to beta, though others, perhaps more sensitive to the differences between the questions put to the two institutions, will disagree. My point is only that beta is different from alpha, both in what it requires and in its philosophical basis.

But beta will require much of what alpha requires. If Posner is right about the fact and the distribution of the cost savings under a negligence rule, for example, both beta and alpha will recommend a regime of negligence rather than strict liability over a certain range of cases. Under even more plausible assumptions, beta as well as alpha will recommend some version of the Hand test as the basis for computing negligence.[23] Perhaps beta as well as alpha would characteristically recommend wealth-maximizing rules for the sorts of disputes that come to adjudication under common

law. (Perhaps beta would recommend the wealth-maximizing rule in more of such cases than alpha would.)

What conclusions should we draw? Beta seems to me inherently more attractive as a guide to adjudication than alpha does. Beta is itself a principle about natural responsibility, and so, as a guide for adjudication, unites adjudication and private morality and permits the claim that a decision in a hard case, assigning responsibility to some party, simply recognizes that party's moral responsibility. Alpha is not itself a principle of responsibility at all, but only a guide to wise forward-looking legislation. It must rely on the antecedent-interest principle to supply an argument of fairness in adjudication, and that principle (as we noticed in considering the complaints of someone who loses when alpha is applied) is seriously flawed.

In any case, however, there is a fatal objection to relying on the combination of alpha and the antecedent-interest principle to justify wealth-maximizing decisions in our own legal system. I skirted over this problem in explaining the argument for alpha, but must confront it now. The antecedent-interest principle could never justify introducing alpha itself in a hard case, for if some member of the then community loses who would not otherwise have lost—either the losing party in that case or someone else—then the antecedent-interest principle is violated. It is only after alpha has been in force for some time that it could be in the antecedent interests of every *then* member of the community to *have* introduced it. It can never be fair to introduce alpha for the first time (if the fairness of doing so depends on the antecedent-interest principle), though the unfairness of having introduced it may disappear over time.

Is this a boring technical point, calling attention only to some presumed unfairness in a past long dead, or something of practical importance? That depends on what is taken to be the adoption of alpha. Can we say that alpha has already been adopted as a principle of adjudication within a legal system when the decisions the courts have reached (or tended to reach) are the same as the decisions that alpha would have required had it been expressly adopted? Or only when alpha has been expressly adopted and relied on in reaching those decisions? The antecedent-interest principle supports alpha only after alpha has been adopted in the second sense. That principle supposes a moment at which people's antecedent or expected welfare is improved by a social decision to adjudicate in a certain way, and that moment is not supplied simply by a set of decisions that would have been reached by an institution that had taken that decision. For no one's expected welfare would be improved in the way alpha promises just by a course of decisions, however consistent with alpha, that did not carry a commitment to enforce alpha generally, and this is true even if that course of decisions worked to enforce alpha not by coincidence, but through some invisible hand, or even by the subconscious motivation of judges. What is essential is a commitment, and that can be achieved only by adoption in the second sense.

But since that is so, alpha has never been adopted in our own legal system in the pertinent sense, even if the positive claims of Posner and others about the explanatory power of wealth maximization are accepted in full. So we cannot rely on alpha to show that wealth-maximizing decisions in the past were fair through some combination of alpha and the antecedent-interest principle. Nor can we rely on that combination to justify any wealth-maximizing decisions in the future. On a more careful look, that is, alpha drops away as a candidate for the basis of a normative theory of wealth maximization.

We might well be left with beta. Beta does not rely on the antecedent-interest principle in the way alpha did. Beta is itself a principle of fairness—it is, as I said, a principle of natural responsibility—and though it will seem to some too demanding, it requires no help from the antecedent-interest principle to count as an argument of fairness in adjudication. So it is irrelevant that beta has never been expressly recognized as a commitment of our legal system. It carries, as it were, its own claims to be a principle of fairness. If it can be shown that past decisions were those that beta would have justified, that does count as an argument that these decisions were fair. If the same can be shown for future decisions, that, without more, recommends these decisions as fair.

So it would be well to carry further than I have here the possibility that beta requires common law decisions that (at least over a certain range of cases) are just those decisions that maximize wealth. If beta does have that consequence, then a Kantian justification of wealth maximization may indeed be available. Posner's long search for a philosophical basis for his normative theory of adjudication may therefore end in what seemed, at the beginning, unlikely territory for him. For the roots of Kantian morality (as beta practically shouts) are deeply egalitarian.

Reverse Discrimination

FOURTEEN

Bakke's Case: Are Quotas Unfair?

ON OCTOBER 12, 1977, the Supreme Court heard oral argument in the case of *The Regents of the University of California v. Allan Bakke.* No lawsuit has ever been more widely watched or more thoroughly debated in the national and international press before the Court's decision. Still, some of the most pertinent facts set before the Court have not been clearly summarized.

The medical school of the University of California at Davis has an affirmative action program (called the "task force program") designed to admit more black and other minority students. It sets sixteen places aside for which only members of "educationally and economically disadvantaged minorities" compete. Allan Bakke, white, applied for one of the remaining eighty-four places; he was rejected but, since his test scores were relatively high, the medical school has conceded that it could not prove that he would have been rejected if the sixteen places reserved had been open to him. Bakke sued, arguing that the task force program deprived him of his constitutional rights. The California Supreme Court agreed, and ordered the medical school to admit him. The university appealed to the Supreme Court.

The Davis program for minorities is in certain respects more forthright (some would say cruder) than similar plans now in force in many other American universities and professional schools. Such programs aim to increase the enrollment of black and other minority students by allowing the fact of their race to count affirmatively as part of the case for admitting them. Some schools set a "target" of a particular number of minority places instead of setting aside a flat number of places. But Davis would not fill the number of places set aside unless there were sixteen minority candidates it considered clearly qualified for medical education. The difference is therefore one of administrative strategy and not of principle.

SO THE CONSTITUTIONAL question raised by *Bakke* is of capital importance for higher education in the United States, and a large number of universities

and schools have entered briefs *amicus curiae* urging the Court to reverse the California decision. They believe that if they are not free to use explicit racial criteria in their admissions programs, they will be unable to fulfill what they take to be their responsibilities to the nation.

It is often said that affirmative action programs aim to achieve a racially conscious society divided into racial and ethnic groups, each entitled as a group to some proportionable share of resources, careers, or opportunities. That is a perverse description. American society is currently a racially conscious society; this is the inevitable and evident consequence of a history of slavery, repression, and prejudice. Black men and women, boys and girls, are not free to choose for themselves in what roles—or as members of which social groups—others will characterize them. They are black, and no other feature of personality or allegiance or ambition will so thoroughly influence how they will be perceived and treated by others, and the range and character of the lives that will be open to them.

The tiny number of black doctors and other professionals is both a consequence and a continuing cause of American racial consciousness, one link in a long and self-fueling chain reaction. Affirmative action programs use racially explicit criteria because their immediate goal is to increase the number of members of certain races in these professions. But their long-term goal is to *reduce* the degree to which American society is overall a racially conscious society.

The programs rest on two judgments. The first is a judgment of social theory: that the United States will continue to be pervaded by racial divisions as long as the most lucrative, satisfying, and important careers remain mainly the prerogative of members of the white race, while others feel themselves systematically excluded from a professional and social elite. The second is a calculation of strategy: that increasing the number of blacks who are at work in the professions will, in the long run, reduce the sense of frustration and injustice and racial self-consciousness in the black community to the point at which blacks may begin to think of themselves as individuals who can succeed like others through talent and initiative. At that future point the consequences of nonracial admissions programs, whatever these consequences might be, could be accepted with no sense of racial barriers or injustice.

IT IS THEREFORE the worst possible misunderstanding to suppose that affirmative action programs are designed to produce a balkanized America, divided into racial and ethnic subnations. They use strong measures because weaker ones will fail; but their ultimate goal is to lessen not to increase the importance of race in American social and professional life.

According to the 1970 census, only 2.1 percent of American doctors were

black. Affirmative action programs aim to provide more black doctors to serve black patients. This is not because it is desirable that blacks treat blacks and whites treat whites, but because blacks, through no fault of their own, are now unlikely to be well served by whites, and because a failure to provide the doctors they trust will exacerbate rather than reduce the resentment that now leads them to trust only their own. Affirmative action tries to provide more blacks as classmates for white doctors, not because it is desirable that a medical school class reflect the racial makeup of the community as a whole, but because professional association between blacks and whites will decrease the degree to which whites think of blacks as a race rather than as people, and thus the degree to which blacks think of themselves that way. It tries to provide "role models" for future black doctors, not because it is desirable for a black boy or girl to find adult models only among blacks, but because our history has made them so conscious of their race that the success of whites, for now, is likely to mean little or nothing for them.

The history of the campaign against racial injustice since 1954, when the Supreme Court decided *Brown v. Board of Education,* is a history in large part of failure. We have not succeeded in reforming the racial consciousness of our society by racially neutral means. We are therefore obliged to look upon the arguments for affirmative action with sympathy and an open mind. Of course, if Bakke is right that such programs, no matter how effective they may be, violate his constitutional rights, then they cannot be permitted to continue. But we must not forbid them in the name of some mindless maxim, like the maxim that it cannot be right to fight fire with fire, or that the end cannot justify the means. If the strategic claims for affirmative action are cogent, they cannot be dismissed on the ground that racially explicit tests are distasteful. If such tests are distasteful, it can only be for reasons that make the underlying social realities the programs attack more distasteful still.

It is said that, in a pluralistic society, membership in a particular group cannot be used as a criterion of inclusion or exclusion from benefits. But group membership is, as a matter of social reality rather than formal admission standards, part of what determines inclusion or exclusion for us now. If we must choose between a society that is in fact liberal and an illiberal society that scrupulously avoids formal racial criteria, we can hardly appeal to the ideals of liberal pluralism to prefer the latter.

ARCHIBALD COX of Harvard Law School, speaking for the University of California in oral argument, told the Supreme Court that this is the choice the United States must make. As things stand, he said, affirmative action programs are the only effective means of increasing the absurdly small num-

ber of black doctors. The California Supreme Court, in approving Bakke's claim, had urged the university to pursue that goal by methods that do not explicitly take race into account. But that is unrealistic. We must distinguish, Cox said, between two interpretations of what the California Court's recommendation means. It might mean that the university should aim at the same immediate goal, of increasing the proportion of black and other minority students in the medical school, by an admissions procedure that on the surface is not racially conscious.

That is a recommendation of hypocrisy. If those who administer the admissions standards, however these are phrased, understand that their immediate goal is to increase the number of blacks in the school, then they will use race as a criterion in making the various subjective judgments the explicit criteria will require, because that will be, given the goal, the only right way to make those judgments. The recommendation might mean, on the other hand, that the school should adopt some non-racially conscious goal, like increasing the number of disadvantaged students of all races, and then hope that that goal will produce an increase in the number of blacks as a by-product. But even if that strategy is less hypocritical (which is far from plain), it will almost certainly fail because no different goal, scrupulously administered in a non-racially conscious way, will significantly increase the number of black medical students.

Cox offered powerful evidence for that conclusion, and it is supported by the recent and comprehensive report of the Carnegie Council on Policy Studies in Higher Education. Suppose, for example, that the medical school sets aside separate places for applicants "disadvantaged" on some racially neutral test, like poverty, allowing only those disadvantaged in that way to compete for these places. If the school selects those from that group who scored best on standard medical school aptitude tests, then it will take almost no blacks, because blacks score relatively low even among the economically disadvantaged. But if the school chooses among the disadvantaged on some basis other than test scores, just so that more blacks will succeed, then it will not be administering the special procedure in a non-racially conscious way.

So Cox was able to put his case in the form of two simple propositions. A racially conscious test for admission, even one that sets aside certain places for qualified minority applicants exclusively, serves goals that are in themselves unobjectionable and even urgent. Such programs are, moreover, the only means that offer any significant promise of achieving these goals. If these programs are halted, then no more than a trickle of black students will enter medical or other professional schools for another generation at least.

If these propositions are sound, then on what ground can it be thought

that such programs are either wrong or unconstitutional? We must notice an important distinction between two different sorts of objections that might be made. These programs are intended, as I said, to decrease the importance of race in the United States in the long run. It may be objected, first, that the programs will harm that goal more than they will advance it. There is no way now to prove that that is not so. Cox conceded in his argument that there are costs and risks in these programs.

Affirmative action programs seem to encourage, for example, a popular misunderstanding, which is that they assume that racial or ethnic groups are entitled to proportionate shares of opportunities, so that Italian or Polish ethnic minorities are, in theory, as entitled to their proportionate shares as blacks or Chicanos or American Indians are entitled to the shares the present programs give them. That is a plain mistake: the programs are not based on the idea that those who are aided are entitled to aid, but only on the strategic hypothesis that helping them is now an effective way of attacking a national problem. Some medical schools may well make that judgment, under certain circumstances, about a white ethnic minority. Indeed it seems likely that some medical schools are even now attempting to help white Appalachian applicants, for example, under programs of regional distribution.

So the popular understanding is wrong, but so long as it persists it is a cost of the program because the attitudes it encourages tend to a degree to make people more rather than less conscious of race. There are other possible costs. It is said, for example, that some blacks find affirmative action degrading; they find that it makes them more rather than less conscious of prejudice against their race as such. This attitude is also based on a misperception, I think, but for a small minority of blacks at least it is a genuine cost.

In the view of the many important universities which have such programs, however, the gains will very probably exceed the losses in reducing racial consciousness overall. This view is hardly so implausible that it is wrong for these universities to seek to acquire the experience that will allow us to judge whether they are right. It would be particularly silly to forbid these experiments if we know that the failure to try will mean, as the evidence shows, that the status quo will almost certainly continue. In any case, this first objection could provide no argument that would justify a decision by the Supreme Court holding the programs unconstitutional. The Court has no business substituting its speculative judgment about the probable consequences of educational policies for the judgment of professional educators.

So THE ACKNOWLEDGED uncertainties about the long-term results of such programs could not justify a Supreme Court decision making them illegal.

But there is a second and very different form of objection. It may be argued that even if the programs *are* effective in making our society less a society dominated by race, they are nevertheless unconstitutional because they violate the individual constitutional rights of those, like Allan Bakke, who lose places in consequence. In the oral argument Reynold H. Colvin of San Francisco, who is Bakke's lawyer, made plain that his objection takes this second form. Mr. Justice White asked him whether he accepted that the goals affirmative action programs seek are important goals. Colvin acknowledged that they were. Suppose, Justice White continued, that affirmative action programs are, as Cox had argued, the only effective means of seeking such goals. Would Colvin nevertheless maintain that the programs are unconstitutional? Yes, he insisted, they would be, because his client has a constitutional right that the programs be abandoned, no matter what the consequences.

Colvin was wise to put his objections on this second ground; he was wise to claim that his client has rights that do not depend on any judgment about the likely consequences of affirmative action for society as a whole, because if he sustains that claim, then the Court must give him the relief he seeks.

But can he be right? If Allan Bakke has a constitutional right so important that the urgent goals of affirmative action must yield, then this must be because affirmative action violates some fundamental principle of political morality. This is not a case in which what might be called formal or technical law requires a decision one way or the other. There is no language in the Constitution whose plain meaning forbids affirmative action. Only the most naive theories of statutory construction could argue that such a result is required by the language of any earlier Supreme Court decision or of the Civil Rights Act of 1964 or of any other congressional enactment. If Colvin is right, it must be because Allan Bakke has not simply some technical legal right but an important moral right as well.

WHAT could that right be? The popular argument frequently made on editorial pages is that Bakke has a right to be judged on his merit. Or that he has a right to be judged as an individual rather than as a member of a social group. Or that he has a right, as much as any black man, not to be sacrificed or excluded from any opportunity because of his race alone. But these catch phrases are deceptive here, because, as reflection demonstrates, the only genuine principle they describe is the principle that no one should suffer from the prejudice or contempt of others. And that principle is not at stake in this case at all. In spite of popular opinion, the idea that the *Bakke* case presents a conflict between a desirable social goal and important individual rights is a piece of intellectual confusion.

Consider, for example, the claim that individuals applying for places in

medical school should be judged on merit, and merit alone. If that slogan means that admissions committees should take nothing into account but scores on some particular intelligence test, then it is arbitrary and, in any case, contradicted by the long-standing practice of every medical school. If it means, on the other hand, that a medical school should choose candidates that it supposes will make the most useful doctors, then everything turns on the judgment of what factors make different doctors useful. The Davis medical school assigned to each regular applicant, as well as to each minority applicant, what it called a "benchmark score." This reflected not only the results of aptitude tests and college grade averages, but a subjective evaluation of the applicant's chances of functioning as an effective doctor, in view of society's present needs for medical service. Presumably the qualities deemed important were different from the qualities that a law school or engineering school or business school would seek, just as the intelligence tests a medical school might use would be different from the tests these other schools would find appropriate.

There is no combination of abilities and skills and traits that constitutes "merit" in the abstract; if quick hands count as "merit" in the case of a prospective surgeon, this is because quick hands will enable him to serve the public better and for no other reason. If a black skin will, as a matter of regrettable fact, enable another doctor to do a different medical job better, then that black skin is by the same token "merit" as well. That argument may strike some as dangerous; but only because they confuse its conclusion—that black skin may be a socially useful trait in particular circumstances—with the very different and despicable idea that one race may be inherently more worthy than another.

CONSIDER the second of the catch phrases I have mentioned. It is said that Bakke has a right to be judged as an "individual," in deciding whether he is to be admitted to medical school and thus to the medical profession, and not as a member of some group that is being judged as a whole. What can that mean? Any admissions procedure must rely on generalizations about groups that are justified only statistically. The regular admissions process at Davis, for example, set a cutoff figure for college grade-point averages. Applicants whose averages fell below that figure were not invited to any interview, and therefore rejected out of hand.

An applicant whose average fell one point below the cutoff might well have had personal qualities of dedication or sympathy that would have been revealed at an interview, and that would have made him or her a better doctor than some applicant whose average rose one point above the line. But the former is excluded from the process on the basis of a decision taken for administrative convenience and grounded in the generalization, un-

likely to hold true for every individual, that those with grade averages below the cutoff will not have other qualities sufficiently persuasive. Even the use of standard Medical College Aptitude Tests (MCAT) as part of the admissions procedure requires judging people as part of groups, because it assumes that test scores are a guide to medical intelligence, which is in turn a guide to medical ability. Though this judgment is no doubt true statistically, it hardly holds true for every individual.

Allan Bakke was himself refused admission to two other medical schools, not because of his race but because of his age: these schools thought that a student entering medical school at the age of thirty-three was likely to make less of a contribution to medical care over his career than someone entering at the standard age of twenty-one. Suppose these schools relied, not on any detailed investigation of whether Bakke himself had abilities that would contradict the generalization in his specific case, but on a rule of thumb that allowed only the most cursory look at applicants over (say) the age of thirty. Did these two medical schools violate his right to be judged as an individual rather than as a member of a group?

The Davis medical school permitted whites to apply for the sixteen places reserved for members of "educationally or economically disadvantaged minorities," a phrase whose meaning might well include white ethnic minorities. In fact several whites have applied, though none has been accepted, and the California Court found that the special committee charged with administering the program had decided, in advance, against admitting any. Suppose that decision had been based on the following administrative theory: it is so unlikely that any white doctor can do as much to counteract racial imbalance in the medical professions as a well-qualified and trained black doctor can do that the committee should for reasons of convenience proceed on the presumption no white doctor could. That presumption is, as a matter of fact, more plausible than the corresponding presumption about medical students over the age of thirty, or even the presumption about applicants whose grade-point averages fall below the cutoff line. If the latter presumptions do not deny the alleged right of individuals to be judged as individuals in an admissions procedure, then neither can the former.

COLVIN, in oral argument, argued the third of the catch phrases I mentioned. He said that his client had a right not to be excluded from medical school because of his race alone, and this as a statement of constitutional right sounds more plausible than claims about the right to be judged on merit or as an individual. It sounds plausible, however, because it suggests the following more complex principle. Every citizen has a constitutional right that he not suffer disadvantage, at least in the competition for any public benefit, because the race or religion or sect or region or other natural

or artificial group to which he belongs is the object of prejudice or contempt.

That is a fundamentally important constitutional right, and it is that right that was systematically violated for many years by racist exclusions and anti-Semitic quotas. Color bars and Jewish quotas were not unfair just because they made race or religion relevant or because they fixed on qualities beyond individual control. It is true that blacks or Jews do not choose to be blacks or Jews. But it is also true that those who score low in aptitude or admissions tests do not choose their levels of intelligence. Nor do those denied admission because they are too old, or because they do not come from a part of the country underrepresented in the school, or because they cannot play basketball well, choose not to have the qualities that made the difference.

Race seems different because exclusions based on race have historically been motivated not by some instrumental calculation, as in the case of intelligence or age or regional distribution or athletic ability, but because of contempt for the excluded race or religion as such. Exclusion by race was in itself an insult, because it was generated by and signaled contempt.

Bakke's claim, therefore, must be made more specific than it is. He says he was kept out of medical school because of his race. Does he mean that he was kept out because his race is the object of prejudice or contempt? That suggestion is absurd. A very high proportion of those who were accepted (and, presumably, of those who run the admissions program) were members of the same race. He therefore means simply that if he had been black he would have been accepted, with no suggestion that this would have been so because blacks are thought more worthy or honorable than whites.

That is true: no doubt he would have been accepted if he were black. But it is also true, and in exactly the same sense, that he would have been accepted if he had been more intelligent, or made a better impression in his interview, or, in the case of other schools, if he had been younger when he decided to become a doctor. Race is not, in *his* case, a different matter from these other factors equally beyond his control. It is not a different matter because in his case race is not distinguished by the special character of public insult. On the contrary, the program presupposes that his race is still widely if wrongly thought to be superior to others.

In the past it made sense to say that an excluded black or Jewish student was being sacrificed because of his race or religion; that meant that his or her exclusion was treated as desirable in itself, not because it contributed to any goal in which he as well as the rest of society might take pride. Allan Bakke is being "sacrificed" because of his race only in a very artificial sense of the word. He is being "sacrificed" in the same artificial sense because of his level of intelligence, since he would have been accepted if he were more clever than he is. In both cases he is being excluded not by prejudice but

because of a rational calculation about the socially most beneficial use of limited resources for medical education.

IT MAY NOW be said that this distinction is too subtle, and that if racial classifications have been and may still be used for malign purposes, then everyone has a flat right that racial classifications not be used at all. This is the familiar appeal to the lazy virtue of simplicity. It supposes that if a line is difficult to draw, or might be difficult to administer if drawn, then there is wisdom in not making the attempt to draw it. There may be cases in which that is wise, but those would be cases in which nothing of great value would as a consequence be lost. If racially conscious admissions policies now offer the only substantial hope for bringing more qualified black and other minority doctors into the profession, then a great loss is suffered if medical schools are not allowed voluntarily to pursue such programs. We should then be trading away a chance to attack certain and present injustice in order to gain protection we may not need against speculative abuses we have other means to prevent. And such abuses cannot, in any case, be worse than the injustice to which we would then surrender.

WE HAVE NOW considered three familiar slogans, each widely thought to name a constitutional right that enables Allan Bakke to stop programs of affirmative action no matter how effective or necessary these might be. When we inspect these slogans, we find that they can stand for no genuine principle except one. This is the important principle that no one in our society should suffer because he is a member of a group thought less worthy of respect, as a group, than other groups. We have different aspects of that principle in mind when we say that individuals should be judged on merit, that they should be judged as individuals, and that they should not suffer disadvantages because of their race. The spirit of that fundamental principle is the spirit of the goal that affirmative action is intended to serve. The principle furnishes no support for those who find, as Bakke does, that their own interests conflict with that goal.

It is regrettable when any citizen's expectations are defeated by new programs serving some more general concern. It is regrettable, for example, when established small businesses fail because new and superior roads are built; in that case people have invested more than Bakke has. And they have more reason to believe their businesses will continue than Bakke had to suppose he could have entered the Davis medical school at thirty-three, even without a task force program.

There is, of course, no suggestion in that program that Bakke shares in any collective or individual guilt for racial injustice in the United States; or

that he is any less entitled to concern or respect than any black student accepted in the program. He has been disappointed, and he must have the sympathy due that disappointment, just as any other disappointed applicant—even one with much worse test scores who would not have been accepted in any event—must have sympathy. Each is disappointed because places in medical schools are scarce resources and must be used to provide what the more general society most needs. It is not Bakke's fault that racial justice is now a special need—but he has no right to prevent the most effective measures of securing that justice from being used.

FIFTEEN

What Did *Bakke* Really Decide?

THE DECISION of the Supreme Court in *Bakke* was received by the press and much of the public with great relief, as an act of judicial statesmanship that gave to each party in the national debate what it seemed to want most. Such a sense of relief, however, hardly seems warranted, and it is important to explain why it does not.

Everyone knows something of the facts of the case. The University of California medical school at Davis administered a two-track admission procedure, in which sixteen of a hundred available places were in effect set aside for members of "minority" groups. Allan Bakke, a white applicant who had been rejected, sued. The California Supreme Court ordered the medical school to admit him, and forbade California universities to take race into account in their admissions decisions.

The United States Supreme Court's decision affirmed the California Court's order that Bakke himself be admitted, but reversed that court's prohibition against taking race into account in any way. So opponents of affirmative action plans could point to Bakke's individual victory as vindication of their view that such plans often go too far; while proponents were relieved to find that the main goals of affirmative action could still be pursued, through plans more complex and subtle than the plan that Davis used and the Supreme Court rejected.

But it is far too early to conclude that the long-awaited *Bakke* decision will set even the main lines of a national compromise about affirmative action in higher education. The arithmetic of the opinions of various justices, and the narrow ground of the pivotal opinion of Mr. Justice Powell, mean that *Bakke* decided rather less than had been hoped, and left more, by way of general principle as well as detailed application, to later Supreme Court cases that are now inevitable.

BAKKE'S LAWYERS raised two questions against the Davis quota plan. They argued, first, that the plan was illegal under the words of the Civil Rights

Act of 1964, which provides that no one shall "on the ground of race . . . be excluded from participation in, be denied the benefits of, or be subjected to discrimination under any program" receiving federal aid. (Davis, like all medical schools, receives such aid.) They argued, second, that the plan was unconstitutional because it denied Bakke the equal protection guaranteed by the Fourteenth Amendment.

Five out of nine Justices—Justices Brennan, White, Marshall, Blackmun, and Powell—held that Bakke had no independent case on the first ground—the 1964 Civil Rights Act—and that the case therefore had to be decided on the second—the Constitution. They said that the language of the Civil Rights Act, properly interpreted, was meant to make illegal only practices that would be forbidden to the states by the equal protection clause itself. They decided, that is, that it is impossible to decide a case like *Bakke* on statutory grounds without reaching the constitutional issue, because the statute does not condemn the Davis program unless the Constitution does. The remaining four Justices—Chief Justice Burger, and Justices Stewart, Rehnquist, and Stevens—thought that Bakke was right on the first ground, of the Civil Rights Act, and that they therefore did not have to consider the second, the Constitution itself, and they did not do so.

Of the five Justices who considered the second, constitutional argument, four—Brennan, White, Marshall, and Blackmun—held that Bakke had no case under the Constitution either. Mr. Justice Powell held otherwise. He held that the equal protection clause forbids explicit quotas or reserved places unless the school in question can show that these means are necessary to achieve goals of compelling importance, and he held that Davis had not met that burden of proof. But he also held that universities may take race into account explicitly as one among several factors affecting admission decisions in particular cases, in order to achieve racial diversity in classes. (He cited the Harvard undergraduate admissions program as an example.) He said that the Constitution permits this use of race and, since the California Supreme Court had held otherwise, he voted to reverse that court on this point. So a majority of those considering the matter voted against Bakke on *both* of his arguments; but Bakke nevertheless won, because five justices thought he should win on some ground even though they disagreed on which ground.

WHAT DOES all this mean for the future? The Supreme Court has now decided, by a vote of five to four, that the Civil Rights Act does not in and of itself bar affirmative action programs, even those, like Davis', that use explicit quotas. It has decided, by a vote of five to none, that the Constitution permits affirmative action plans, like the Harvard undergraduate plan, that allow race to be taken into account, on an individual-by-individual basis, in order to achieve a reasonably diverse student body.

Both of these decisions are important. The Civil Rights Act issue was, in my opinion, not a difficult issue, but it is useful that it is now removed from the argument. The argument of the California Supreme Court—that racially conscious admissions programs are always unconstitutional—would have been disastrous for affirmative action had it prevailed in the United States Supreme Court, and it is therefore of great importance that it was rejected there. It is also important that at least five Justices are agreed that a program like the Harvard undergraduate plan is constitutional. The Harvard model provides a standard; if the admissions officers of other universities are satisfied that their plan is like the Harvard plan in all pertinent respects, they can proceed in confidence.

It is equally important to emphasize, however, that the Supreme Court has *not* decided that only a program such as Harvard's is constitutional. It has not even decided that a program with a rigid quota such as the one Davis used is unconstitutional. Mr. Justice Powell drew the line that way in his opinion: he said that a quota-type program is unconstitutional, and his arguments suggest that only something very like the Harvard program is constitutional. But his opinion is only one opinion; no other Justice agreed, and four other Justices expressly disagreed with him on both points. So Powell's line will become the Supreme Court's line only if not a single one of the four Justices who remained silent on the constitutional issue takes a position less restrictive than Powell's on that issue. In these circumstances it seems premature to treat Powell's opinion, and the distinction he drew, as the foundation of the constitutional settlement that will eventually emerge.

THERE SEEMS little doubt that the four Justices who remained silent on the constitutional issue will have to break that silence reasonably soon. For there are a variety of affirmative action cases likely to confront the Court soon in which no statute can provide a reason for avoiding the constitutional issue. The Court has now remanded a case, for example, which challenges the provision of the Public Works Employment Act of 1977 that at least 10 percent of funds disbursed under the act be applied to "minority" businesses. Since Congress enacted this statute, there can be no argument that its provisions violate congressional will, and the four Justices will have to face the question of whether such quota provisions are unconstitutional when this case (or, if it is moot, when some similar case) finally arrives before them. Of course these will not be education cases, and Powell's opinion is carefully tailored to education cases. But the arguments of principle on which he relied, in taking a more restrictive view of what the equal protection clause permits than did the other Justices who spoke to that issue, are equally applicable to employment and other cases.

Indeed, it is arguable that, in strict theory, the four Justices who remained silent would have to speak to the constitutional issue even if another education case, like the *Bakke* case, were for some reason to come before the Court. Suppose (though this is incredible) that some university that administers a quota-type system like the Davis system were to refuse to dismantle it in favor of a more flexible system, and the Supreme Court were to review the inevitable challenge. Since *Bakke* decides that the Civil Rights Act is no more restrictive than the Constitution, the four Justices might well consider this point foreclosed by that decision in any future case, in which event they would have to face the constitutional issue they avoided there.

(Anthony Lewis, in *The New York Times,* said that it was surprising that these Justices did not give their opinion on the Constitution even in *Bakke,* since they knew that the Court as a whole rejected their argument that the case could be decided under the statute. Lewis speculates that one of the five Justices who rejected the statutory argument might have held the contrary view until just before the decision was released, and so left the four little time to address the constitutional issue.

He may be right, but there is at least another possibility. Supose at least one of the four believed that even the Davis quota-type plan was constitutional. If he had said so, but nevertheless voted in favor of Bakke on the statutory issue, then the Court would have ordered Bakke admitted even though a majority of the full Court, and not simply a majority of those speaking to each issue, was against Bakke on both grounds, and even though the Court would have been constrained, by precedent, to approve a quota-type program in the future. That would have been even more bizarre and confusing than the present decision. But all this is simply guesswork squared.)

Is THERE any point (other than as an academic exercise) in these speculations about the position that members of the silent four would take on the constitutional issue? Some practical lawyers have already said that the main goals of affirmative action programs, at least in university and professional school education, can be served by programs that fall comfortably within what Mr. Justice Powell expressly permitted. If that is so, then it might be wise to proceed as if the Powell opinion, even though the opinion of only one Justice, states constitutional law for university educational programs, and then try to work out a similar settlement for other areas, like employment, in other cases. But I am not so sure that it is so, because the Powell opinion, at least until clarified by later decisions, is less coherent and may well be less permissive than it has widely been taken to be.

Powell expressly ruled out admissions programs, like the Davis program,

that reserve certain places for minority members only. He approved programs, like the Harvard undergraduate program he cited, that do not even set target numbers for minority acceptance. Such programs are aimed at diversity in the student body. They recognize that racial diversity is as important as geographical diversity or diversity in extracurricular talents and career ambitions, and so take race into account in such a way that the fact that an applicant is black may tip the balance in his favor just as the fact that another applicant is an accomplished flutist may tip the balance in his.

But a great many affirmative action admissions programs fall between these two extremes. They do not expressly reserve a set number of places for which only minority applicants compete, but they nevertheless do set rough "target" figures representing a general decision about the proportion of the class that should on general principles be filled by minority applicants. The number of such applicants accepted will vary from year to year but will hover within a range that will be less varying than the proportion of accomplished musicians, for example, or of applicants from a particular section of the country. In most cases, the admissions committee will report the number of minority applicants selected to the faculty at large, as a separate statistic, and will attempt to explain a particularly low percentage in any particular year. Minority applications will in this way be treated very differently from applications of musicians or West Coast residents. Do such rough "targets," used in this way, make a program unconstitutional under the analysis Powell proposed?

THE ANSWER may depend on the goal or purpose of the "target." Powell considered a number of goals that affirmative action programs in a medical school might be expected to achieve, and he said that some goals were constitutionally permitted, while others were not. He rejected, in particular, "the purpose of helping certain groups whom the faculty . . . perceived as victims of 'societal discrimination.' " (He said that this goal must not be pursued by any classification that imposes disadvantages on others who had no responsibility for the earlier discrimination.) He accepted as permissible the goal of supplying more professional people for under-served communities, but denied that Davis had shown that a program "must prefer members of particular ethnic groups" in order to achieve that goal. He also accepted the goal of educational diversity, which in his opinion justified the flexible Harvard plan though not the Davis quota plan.

The constitutionality of an affirmative action plan therefore depends, according to Powell, on its purpose as well as its structure. It is not altogether plain how courts are to decide what the purpose of a racially conscious admissions program is. Perhaps they should not look behind an official institutional statement that the plan seeks educational diversity, if such a statement seems plausible.

But in the case of some professional schools it may not be plausible, and Powell says, in this connection, that "good faith" should be presumed only "absent a showing to the contrary." Perhaps the motives of individual members of the admissions committee or of the faculty as a whole are not relevant. It is nevertheless true that many faculty members, particularly of professional schools, support racially conscious admissions programs because they do believe that such programs are necessary to provide more professional people for the ghettos. Even more support them because they are anxious that their school help groups that have been disadvantaged by discrimination, by providing models of successful professional men and women from these groups, for example.

The leaders of many institutions are now on record, in fact, that these are their goals. (They may or may not also believe that the level of diversity in their classes that would be reached without racially conscious programs is unsatisfactory for purely educational reasons.) May disappointed applicants to such institutions now sue, placing in evidence statements faculty members have made about the purposes of racially conscious plans, or subpoenaing officers of admission to examine their motives under oath?

POWELL'S OPINION raises these questions, but it does little to help answer them, even in principle, because the argumentative base of his opinion is weak. It does not supply a sound intellectual foundation for the compromise the public found so attractive. The compromise is appealing politically, but it does not follow that it reflects any important difference in principle, which is what a constitutional, as distinct from a political, settlement requires.

There are indeed important differences between the "quota" kind of affirmative action program—with places reserved for "minorities" only—and more flexible plans that make race a factor, but only one factor, in the competition for all places. But these differences are administrative and symbolic. A flexible program is likely to be more efficient, in the long run, because it will allow the institution to take less than the rough target number of minority applicants when the total group of such applicants is weaker, and more when it is stronger. It is certainly better symbolically, for a number of reasons. Reserving a special program for minority applicants—providing a separate door through which they and only they may enter—preserves the structure, though of course not the purpose, of classical forms of caste and apartheid systems, and seems to denigrate minority applicants while helping them. Flexible programs emphasize, on the other hand, that successful minority candidates have been judged overall more valuable, as students, than white applicants with whom they directly competed.

But the administrative and symbolic superiority of the flexible programs, however plain, cannot justify a constitutional distinction of the sort Powell

makes. There should be no constitutional distinction unless a quota program violates or threatens the constitutional rights of white applicants *as individuals* in some way that the more flexible programs do not.

Powell does not show any such difference, and it is hard to imagine how he could. If race counts in a flexible program, then there will be some individual white applicant who loses a place but who would have gained one if race did not count. However that injury is described it is exactly the same injury—neither more nor less—that Bakke suffered. We cannot say that in a flexible system fewer whites lose places because race figures in the decision; that will depend on details of the flexible and quota programs being compared, on the nature of the applicants, and on other circumstances. But even if it could be shown that fewer whites would lose in a flexible plan, it would not follow that the rights of those individuals who did lose were different or differently treated.

Powell argues that in a flexible plan a marginal white applicant is at least in a position to try to show that, in spite of his race, he ought to be taken in preference to a black applicant because he has some special contribution that the black applicant does not. His race does not rule him out of even part of the competition automatically.

This argument may be based on an unrealistic picture of how admissions committees must deal with a vast volume of applications even under a flexible plan. An individual admissions officer will use informal cutoff lines, no matter how flexible the program is in principle, and a majority applicant with a low test score may be cut off from the entire competition with no further look to discover whether he is a good musician, for example, though he would have been rescued for a further look if he were black.

But even if Powell's sense of how a flexible plan works is realistic, his argument is still weak. An individual applicant has, at the start of the competition for places, a particular grade record, test score average, personality, talents, geographical background, and race. What matters, for a white applicant, is the chance these give him in the competition, and it does not make any difference to him in principle whether his race is a constant small handicap in the competition for all the places, or no handicap at all in the competition for a slightly smaller number of places. His fate depends on how much either the handicap or the exclusion reduces his overall chances of success; and there is no reason to assume, *a priori*, that the one will have a greater or lesser impact than the other. That will depend on the details of the plan—the degree of handicap or the proportion of exclusion—not which type of plan it is.

Powell sees an important difference between a handicap and a partial exclusion. He says that in the former case, but not the latter, an applicant is

treated "as an individual" and his qualifications are "weighed fairly and competitively." (He chides Justices Brennan, White, Marshall, and Blackmun for not speaking to the importance of this "right to individualized consideration.") But this seems wrong. Whether an applicant competes for all or only part of the places, the privilege of calling attention to other qualifications does not in any degree lessen the burden of his handicap, or the unfairness of that handicap, if it is unfair at all. If the handicap does not violate his rights in a flexible plan, a partial exclusion does not violate his rights under a quota. The handicap and the partial exclusion are only different means of enforcing the same fundamental classifications. In principle, they affect a white applicant in exactly the same way—by reducing his overall chances—and neither is, in any important sense, more "individualized" than the other. The point is not (as Powell once suggests it is) that faculty administering a flexible system may covertly transform it into a quota plan. The point is rather that there is no difference, from the standpoint of individual rights, between the two systems at all.

THERE IS a second serious problem in Powell's opinion which is more technical, but in the end more important. Both Powell and the other four Justices who reached the constitutional issue discussed the question of whether racial classifications used in affirmative action programs for the benefit of minorities are "suspect" classifications which the Supreme Court should subject to "strict scrutiny." These are terms of art, and I must briefly state the doctrinal background.

Legislatures and other institutions that make political decisions must use general classifications in the rules they adopt. Whatever general classifications they use, certain individuals will suffer a disadvantage they would not have suffered if lines had been differently drawn, sometimes because the classifications treat them as having or lacking qualities they do not. State motor codes provide, for example, that no one under the age of sixteen is eligible to drive an automobile, even though some people under that age are just as competent as most over it. Ordinarily the Supreme Court will not hold such a general classification unconstitutional even though it believes that a different classification, which would place different people at a disadvantage, would be more reasonable or more efficient. It is enough if the classification the legislature makes is not irrational; that is, if it could conceivably serve a useful and proper social goal. That is a very easy test to meet, but if the Court used a more stringent test to judge all legislation, then it would be substituting its judgment on inherently controversial matters for the judgment reached by a democratic political process.

There is, however, an important exception to this rule. Certain classifications are said to be "suspect," and when a state legislature employs these

classifications in legislation, the Supreme Court will hold the legislation unconstitutional unless it meets a much more demanding test which has come to be called the test of "strict scrutiny." It must be shown, not simply that the use of this classification is not irrational, but that it is "necessary" to achieve what the Court has called a "compelling" governmental interest. Obviously it is a crucial issue, in constitutional litigation, whether a particular classification is an ordinary classification, and so attracts only the relaxed ordinary scrutiny, or is a suspect classification which must endure strict scrutiny (or, as some Justices have sometimes suggested, falls somewhere between these two standards of review).

Racial classifications that *disadvantage* a "minority" race are paradigm cases of suspect classifications. In the famous *Korematsu* case the Supreme Court said that "[All] legal restrictions which curtail the rights of a single racial group are immediately suspect. That is not to say that all such restrictions are unconstitutional. It is to say that courts must subject them to the most rigid scrutiny." But what about racial classifications that figure in a program designed to *benefit* a group of disadvantaged minorities? It had never been decided, prior to *Bakke*, whether such "benign" classifications are suspect.

The four Justices who voted to uphold the Davis plan did not argue that "benign" racial classifications should be held only to the weak ordinary standard—that is, that it could conceivably serve a useful social goal. But neither did they think it appropriate to use the same high standard of strict scrutiny used to judge racial classifications that work against minorities. They suggested an intermediate standard, which is that remedial racial classifications "must serve important governmental objectives and must be substantially related to achievement of those objectives." They held that the Davis medical school's purpose of "remedying the effects of past societal discrimination" was sufficiently important, and that the racial classification Davis used was "substantially related" to that objective.

BUT Mr. Justice Powell disagreed. He held that "benign" racial classifications should be held to the same extremely strict scrutiny that is applied to racial classifications that disadvantage a minority. He therefore required that the Davis classification be "necessary" to a "compelling" purpose, and he held that it was not. He argued that no distinction should be made between the test applied to racial classifications that benefit and those that disadvantage an established minority for two reasons. First, because any such distinction would rest on judgments, like judgments about what groups are, in the relevant sense, minorities, and which classifications carry a "stigma," that Powell called "subjective" and "standardless." Second, because constitutionally important categories would then be constantly

changing as social or economic conditions (or the perception of Supreme Court justices of such conditions) changed, so that yesterday's disadvantaged minority became a member of today's powerful majority, or yesterday's helping hand became today's stigma.

There is plainly some force in this argument. All else being equal, it is better when constitutional principles are such that reasonable lawyers will not disagree about their application. But often the political and moral rights of individuals do depend on considerations that different people will assess differently, and in that case the law would purchase certainty only at the price of crudeness and inevitable injustice. American law—particularly constitutional law—has refused to pay that price, and it has become in consequence the envy of more formalistic legal systems.

It is easy, moreover, to exaggerate the "subjectivity" of the distinctions in play here. Once the distinction is made between racial classifications that disadvantage an "insular" minority, like the detention of Japanese Americans in the *Korematsu* case, and those that are designed to benefit such a minority, then reasonable men cannot sincerely differ about where the racial classification of the Davis medical school falls. Nor is the social pattern of prejudice and discrimination the Davis program attacked either recent or transient. It is as old as the country, tragically, and will not disappear very soon.

My present point, however, is a different one. Powell's argument in favor of strict scrutiny of all racial classifications, which is that the putative distinction between benign and malignant classifications relies on "subjective" and "standardless" judgments, is not and cannot be consistent with the rest of his judgment, because his approval of flexible admissions programs, like the Harvard undergraduate program, presupposes exactly the same judgments. Powell begins his defense of flexible but racially conscious admissions programs with the following exceptionally broad statement of a constitutionally protected right of universities to choose their own educational strategies:

> Academic freedom, though not a specifically enumerated constitutional right, long has been viewed as a special concern of the First Amendment. The freedom of a university to make its own judgments as to education includes the selection of its student body. Mr. Justice Frankfurter summarized the "four essential freedoms" that comprise academic freedom: "It is an atmosphere in which there prevail the four essential freedoms of a university—to determine for itself on academic grounds who may teach, what may be taught, how it shall be taught, and who may be admitted to study."

Diversity is the "compelling" goal that Powell believes universities may seek through flexible (but not crude) racially conscious policies. But what if a law school faculty, in the exercise of its right to "determine for itself . . .

who shall be admitted to study," decided to count the fact that an applicant is Jewish as a negative consideration, though not an absolute exclusion, in the competition for all its places? It might decide that it is injurious to "diversity" or to the "robust exchange of ideas" that Jews should form so large and disproportionate a part of law school classes as they now do. Or what if a Southern medical school one day found that a disproportionately large number of black applicants was being admitted on racially neutral tests, which threatened the diversity of its student body, to the detriment, as it determined, of its educational process? It might then count being white as a factor beneficial to admission, like being a musician or having an intention to practice medicine in a rural area.

THE FOUR Justices who voted to uphold the Davis program as constitutional would have no trouble distinguishing these flexible programs that count being Jewish as a handicap or being white as a beneficial factor. Neither of these programs could be defended as helping to remedy "the effects of past societal discrimination." They could argue that, on the contrary, since these programs put at a disadvantage members of races that have been and remain the victims of systematic prejudice, the programs must for that reason be subject to "strict scrutiny" and disallowed unless positively shown to be both "necessary" and compelling.

Mr. Justice Powell did not, of course, have any such programs in mind when he wrote his opinion. He surely could not accept them as constitutional. But he, unlike the four Justices, could not consistently distinguish such programs on their grounds, since the judgments I just described involve precisely the "subjective" and "standardless" judgments about "stigma" that he rejected as inappropriate to constitutional principles.

The point is, I think, a simple one. The difference between a general racial classification that causes further disadvantage to those who have suffered from prejudice, and a classification framed to help them, is morally significant, and cannot be consistently denied by a constitutional law that does not exclude the use of race altogether. If the nominal standard for testing racial classifications denies the difference, the difference will nevertheless reappear when the standard is applied because (as these unlikely hypothetical examples show) our sense of justice will insist on a distinction. If that is so, then the standard, however it is drafted, is not the same, and will not long be thought to be.

I raise these objections to Powell's opinion, not simply because I disagree with his arguments, but to indicate why I believe that the compromise he fashioned, though immediately popular, may not be sufficiently strong in principle to furnish the basis for a coherent and lasting constitutional law of affirmative action. Later cases will, of course, try to absorb his opinion into

a more general settlement, because it was the closest thing to an opinion of the Court in the famous *Bakke* case, and because it is the creditable practice of the Court to try to accommodate rather than to disown the early history of its own doctrine. But Powell's opinion suffers from fundamental weaknesses and, if the Court is to arrive at a coherent position, far more judicial work remains to be done than a relieved public yet realizes.

SIXTEEN

How to Read the Civil Rights Act

WHEN *Steelworkers v. Weber* began its way through the federal courts in 1976, it was widely thought that the case would prove an even more important challenge to affirmative action programs than the famous *Bakke* case. *Bakke* tested affirmative action programs in universities and professional schools. But *Weber* tested the legality of programs giving blacks advantages in training programs for industry, programs that would benefit more blacks directly and might be expected to have an earlier impact on economic racial inequality.

Blacks were seriously underrepresented in the work force of the Kaiser Aluminum Company's plant in Gramercy, Louisiana, where Brian Weber, a white laborer, was employed. Blacks held hardly any of the plant's craft or skilled jobs. Kaiser agreed with its union to establish a training program for craft jobs, to which current employees would be admitted in order of seniority, that is, in the order in which they had entered the plant—except that one black employee would be admitted for each white employee until the number of blacks in skilled jobs formed the same proportion of all skilled workers as blacks formed of the labor force in the Gramercy area.

Weber applied for the program but was insufficiently senior to obtain a "white" place, though he was more senior than applicants who received "black" places. He sued Kaiser, arguing that the program used a racial quota system and so was illegal under the Civil Rights Act of 1964, which provides in Section 703(a) of Title VII that it is unlawful for an employer:

> (1) to fail or refuse to hire or discharge any individual or otherwise to discriminate against any individual with respect to his compensation, terms, conditions, or privileges of employment, because of such individual's race, color, religion, sex, or national origin; or,
> (2) to limit, segregate, or classify his employees or applicants for employment in any way which would deprive any individual of employment opportunities or otherwise adversely affect his status as an employee, because of such individual's race, color, religion, sex, or national origin.

Five Justices—Brennan, Marshall, White, Stewart, and Blackmun—held that Weber was wrong, and that this statute did not outlaw the Kaiser plan. They said that Congress did not intend to outlaw affirmative action plans of this sort, and that if a court interpreted the statute as Weber wished, the statute's "purpose" would be frustrated. Chief Justice Burger and Justice Rehnquist dissented. The two other Justices—Powell and Stevens—took no part in the case.

In the *Bakke* case Powell had held that the admissions program of the Davis medical school was unconstitutional because it set aside a fixed number of places for minority applicants. The Kaiser training plan also set aside a fixed number of places for blacks, but it could not be said to be unconstitutional. The equal protection clause of the Constitution requires states (and therefore state university professional schools) to treat people as equals, but imposes no such requirement on private institutions, unless "state action" is involved in what these private institutions do. The Court assumed that the voluntary decision of Kaiser did not constitute state action, and that the case therefore did not present any constitutional issue. The question raised in *Weber*, therefore, was only the question whether the Kaiser plan was made illegal by the Civil Rights Act.

That might seem a less important question than the question whether the plan is constitutional. If Congress disapproves a court decision interpreting a congressional statute, it can always reverse the decision by changing the statute. It cannot reverse a decision that interprets the Constitution. In the present circumstances, however, a Supreme Court decision on the statutory legality of affirmative action programs is, as a practical matter, almost as irreversible as a decision on their constitutional validity. It seems unlikely that Congress would now pass legislation either explicitly condoning or explicitly forbidding affirmative action in employment, at least so long as that issue remains politically as volatile as it is now. So the Court's decision about the legal consequences of what Congress has already done is likely to remain in force for some time, whatever that decision is.

Weber was not a simple case to decide. The Civil Rights Act is explicit, in Section 703(j), that the government may not *order* private institutions to adopt affirmative action plans. But Kaiser's program was not ordered by the Justice Department or any other government agency; it was agreed between the company and the union. The case would have been easier if Kaiser had admitted that it had discriminated against blacks in the past. If it had said that its previous hiring policies had been in some way discriminatory, so as to violate Title VII, and if that had been proved, then its affirmative action program would have been justified as a self-imposed remedy of the sort that a court might have ordered. The trial judge said that it was "arguable" that Kaiser had violated Title VII in the past. But Kaiser certainly did not concede that it had—that admission would have opened it to

a large number of private suits by blacks. And no other private party to the suit had any interest in even raising the issue.

Burger and Rehnquist thought that the language of 703(a) of Title VII was so precise and unambiguous that there was no need for the Court to do more than read the statute. Burger said that if he had been in Congress in 1964, he would have voted against outlawing plans like Kaiser's, but he thought there could be no doubt that the words of the section quoted above did just that. That view of the statute is unpersuasive. Against the background of centuries of malign racial discrimination, phrases like "discriminate against someone because of race" or "deprive someone of an opportunity because of race" may be used in a neutral (or, as Brennan put it in his opinion, in a "literal") sense, so that *any* racial classification whatsoever is included. Or they may be used (and I think typically are used) in an evaluative way, to mark off racial classifications that are invidious, because they reflect a desire to put one race at a disadvantage against another, or arbitrary, because they serve no legitimate purpose, or reflect favoritism, because they treat members of one race with more concern than members of another. In the former sense, choosing a black actor over a white one to play Othello or instituting an affirmative action plan to help establish genuine racial equality both count as discrimination against whites and depriving whites of opportunities because of race. But in the latter, evaluative, sense neither does. It is a difficult question which sense to assign to Title VII.

Of course, in either sense, the provisions of Title VII would apply to racial discrimination against whites as well as against blacks. In an earlier case, *McDonald v. Santa Fe Trail Transportation Co.*, the Supreme Court held that it was illegal for a truck company arbitrarily to fire a white employee when black employees guilty of the same offense were retained. That was as explicit a case of favoritism—as unrelated to any legitimate established program of affirmative action—as the reverse would have been. But in that case the Court explicitly and carefully left open the question whether the statute outlawed affirmative action programs "which do not involve discrimination against any race, white or black, but are rather designed to compensate for the past racial discrimination."

Weber required the Court to decide the question it had left open in *McDonald*. If it were clear that "discriminate . . . because of . . . race" was used in the neutral sense, it would have made no sense for the Court to leave open the question of whether it applied to affirmative action. The majority in *Weber* was right, both as a matter of ordinary language and precedent: the question of how Title VII should be interpreted cannot be answered simply by staring at the words Congress used.

This is obviously a question of cardinal importance. The majority and dissenting opinions describe two very different conceptions of the Civil Rights Act, and it is important to decide which version is part of the law of

the United States. According to Brennan, who wrote for the majority, the act represents a decision by Congress to advance racial equality in education, employment, and other areas, and to end an economic era in which those blacks not wholly unemployed are largely restricted to lower paying and less interesting jobs. It would therefore be inconsistent with the underlying policy of the act to construe it to forbid voluntary industrial plans aimed at these goals.

Rehnquist disagrees, savagely. He said that the majority acted like the tyranny of Orwell's *1984,* reaching the conclusion it wanted in an intellectually dishonest way in spite of what Rehnquist considered devastating and conclusive arguments to the contrary. According to Rehnquist, the act embodies a conception of equality that prohibits any distinctions based on race whatsoever, so that the decision of the majority, far from promoting the policy of the act, "introduces into Title VII a tolerance for the very evil that the law was intended to eradicate." If Rehnquist is right, then the *Weber* decision, though much celebrated by civil rights groups now, may well be limited sharply or even overruled by related cases in the future.

THE TWO OPINIONS—majority and dissenting—take competing positions on the question of what procedures the Court should use to interpret an act of Congress, and we cannot understand or evaluate these opinions without discussing that jurisprudential question. It is necessary, first, to distinguish between a statute, which is a canonical set of sentences enacted by Congress, and the legislation created by that statute, that is, the set of legal rights, duties, powers, permissions, or prohibitions the statute brings into existence or confirms. In the United States (as in every mature legal system) there are strict and precise rules, agreed on by everyone, that determine what counts as the statute. It is the set of sentences before Congress when it votes, as certified by a clerk, and thereafter signed by the president. But it is highly controversial what principles fix the legislation that a particular statute creates. When two conditions are met—when the words in the statute unambiguously require a certain decision about legal rights and duties, and when that decision is sensibly related to some widely supported political aim— then it is uncontroversial that the legislation includes that decision, and judges are bound to enforce it, whether they themselves approve it or not, unless they believe it unconstitutional.

When either of these conditions fails—when, for example, the words used might be used to express either of two decisions—then an argument must be provided establishing which decision, if either, does form part of the legislation. Any such argument will assume what might be called a theory of legislation, that is, a theory of how to determine which legal rights and duties Congress has established when it enacts a particular set of sentences.

There is no agreement about theories of legislation among American

judges, or indeed among judges of any developed legal system. On the contrary, the concept of legislation figures in jurisprudence as what philosophers call a "contested" concept. Theories of legislation are not themselves set out in statutes or even fixed by judicial precedent; each judge must himself apply a theory whose authority, for him as for others, lies in its persuasive force.

Rehnquist's dissenting opinion has the virtue of setting out his own theory of legislation in a reasonably clear way. "Our task in this case, like any other case involving the construction of a statute," he said, "is to give effect to the intent of Congress. To divine that intent, we traditionally look first to the words of the statute and, if they are unclear, then to the statute's legislative history." (Lawyers use the phrase "legislative history" to refer to the records of congressional consideration of a bill that ultimately becomes a statute, including committee reports and debates on the floor.) Rehnquist believes that, on this theory of legislation, which takes legislation to be fixed only by what he calls the "intent" of the legislature, plans like the Kaiser plan are plainly outlawed. His contempt for the majority opinion shows that he thinks that this theory of legislation is not just the best theory, but the only conceivable theory, so that the majority was not only wrong but intellectually dishonest in applying, as it did, a different theory.

It is true that Rehnquist's intent-of-Congress theory is a popular one. It has two apparent and related advantages. First, it seems to enforce the general principles of democracy: since the legislature is entrusted with making law, the legislature should be taken to have done what it intended to do, at least if the words it used are capable of bearing that interpretation. Second, it seems to make the Court's decision a politically neutral decision: the Court is supposed to answer a historical question—what did the legislature intend the statute to do—rather than to make its own political judgment. In fact, however, both appeals are in large part illusory, and the theory of legislative intent turns out to be, on examination, much less useful than it seems.

The theory seems useful only because it exploits an ambiguity in the idea of a legislative intention. Two different concepts have been described by that phrase, and legal scholarship and practice has not sufficiently attended to the difference. The first is the idea of an *institutionalized intention,* a policy or principle, or some set of these, that is in some way *enacted* so that it becomes part of the legislation by express legislative decision. Statutes sometimes contain explicit declarations of purpose, set out in what are called "preambles," though this was once more common in the United States than it is now. If the Civil Rights Act had contained a preamble, reciting that its intention was to ensure that no person gained any advantage by any racial classification whatsoever, that understanding would thereby have been made part of the legislation, and the rules described by the rest of the statute would have been properly interpreted only in that light.

Though preambles are now rare, convention has established other methods through which purposes are enacted as part of statutes. The most commonly used, I think, is the method of committee report: if the appropriate committee of Congress has considered a bill, and published an extended report recommending it, then convention now treats any understanding of what that bill will accomplish that is set out in that report as if the understanding were attached to the statute. If the bill is enacted, that statement is understood to be enacted as well, as an institutionalized account of its purpose.

It is only through convention that this association of a committee report with a statute is achieved, and it is only through that convention that the association is justified. Since members of Congress understand the convention, and have the committee report before them as a part of the institutional material on which they vote, it is fair to take any statement in the report as part of what they vote to enact, unless, of course, as sometimes happens, the statute is deliberately amended in order to override some statement of the report.

Preambles and committee reports do not exhaust the mechanisms of institutionalized intention. Such intentions may also be created by statements of congressmen on the floor in debate over the bill, though the details of this convention cannot be stated so crisply. If a prominent spokesman for a bill proposes a general understanding about what the bill will do, and if this is accepted by other congressmen as a kind of official clarification or informal amendment, then his statement will have that force, and it is now common for courts to attend to such statements. But the qualification—that the statement must be accepted as understood to form part of the statute—is essential. If even a leading spokesman's statement of what the bill will do is contradicted by other legislators, then that statement becomes simply a report of his own belief, different ɪrom theirs, of how the statute should or will be interpreted by agencies and courts, not an institutionalized intention at all.

This first concept of legislative intention—the concept of institutionalized intention—is in no sense a psychological concept. A preamble, or an explicit statement in a committee report, or an uncontradicted proposed understanding is taken to be part of what is enacted, not because of any assumption about the hopes or motives or beliefs or other mental state of any particular congressman, but because the convention that attaches the statement to the statute is now part of the institution of legislation in the United States. The convention has the same logical standing (though of course it is neither so explicit nor so secure) as the fixed constitutional rules that provide for the form in which a statute must be enacted.

The concept of institutionalized intention must therefore be sharply distinguished from the second concept of legislative intent, which I shall call the concept of collective understanding, and which is distinctly a psycho-

logical concept. This second concept takes a legislative intention to be some combination—which combination is a matter of dispute—of the beliefs of particular congressmen who draft, advocate, oppose, lobby for or against, and vote to pass or reject a particular statute. Of course the senators or representatives who are in this way part of the legislative process, and their staffs, and other government agencies or personnel do act on the basis of some beliefs about what legislation the statute will in fact enact. A congressman may have voted for the Civil Rights Act, for example, precisely because he thought that it would prohibit affirmative action programs of a certain type; another may have voted for it only because he thought it would not. This psychological concept of legislative intention supposes that some combination or function of these individual beliefs constitutes the collective understanding of the institution as a whole, so that, if, for example, that combination existed in favor of the understanding that affirmative action was outlawed, then this was the intention of the legislature itself.

This concept of legislative intention is useless unless the combination of individual understandings necessary to constitute the collective intention is at least roughly specified. Lawyers who seem to rely on this concept of legislative intention are rarely explicit on this matter and assume that the necessary combination can be formed in different ways. If the theory of legislative intent is to remain faithful to democratic principles, however, a minimum requirement must be met: a sufficient number of those who voted for a statute must have an understanding in common, so that that number alone could have passed the statute even if everyone else—all those who did not share that understanding—had voted against.

The idea of a collective legislative understanding is therefore of limited use. Some of its limitations have been noticed often in the extensive legal literature on statutory interpretation. Lawyers know, for example, that it is very difficult for a court to discover, years after the event, what understanding any particular legislator had, and therefore difficult to know what the composite understanding was. This is an epistemological difficulty that Rehnquist himself concedes, because he acknowledges that in some cases it may be difficult to say what the legislature's intention was, though he thinks that this is not so in the case of the Civil Rights Act.

There are other, less familiar, difficulties with the idea. Let us assume, for a moment, that every congressman who voted on the Civil Rights Act had some belief about whether that statute would ban affirmative action. Suppose that of one hundred senators, sixty voted for the act, but only forty-nine of these believed it would outlaw plans like Kaiser's. In that case, there could be no collective understanding either way, even if all those who voted against the act also had the same belief, making a total of eighty-nine who held it. And in fact the assumption we have made is almost always unjustified. It is wrong to assume that every legislator who votes on a bill has an

understanding one way or the other about every consequence that bill might have. It seems quite likely, for example, that some of the senators and representatives who voted on the Civil Rights Act paid no attention at all to the problem of whether the act would forbid voluntary programs like Kaiser's. It seems equally likely that many of those who did consider this were genuinely uncertain whether the act would, and either had no motive for attempting to clarify the matter or a strong motive for not doing so. If a significant number of congressmen had no firm understanding either way, or if the majority that passed the statute was divided in its opinion, then once again the collective understanding is not simply difficult to discover. It does not exist.

Even when a sufficient number of congressmen do share a belief about what a statute will do, moreover, that agreement might not constitute a collective understanding of the sort that a court should enforce. For we must be careful to distinguish among different sorts of belief a congressman might have about a vague or uncertain provision in a statute on which he must vote. He might assume that the language of the provision itself does determine some controversial issue, or that some preamble or unchallenged statement constitutes an institutionalized intention one way or the other. If the text is genuinely unclear, however, and if there has been no statement forming an institutionalized intention, he is more likely to think that the text of the statute leaves the issue open as an issue of interpretation for the courts to decide.

In that case, any belief he might hold or express about the consequences of the statute would be a matter of predicting the decision the courts will reach. The decision he predicts might be the decision he prefers, and would have enacted explicitly if he had been able to do so. It might, that is, represent his hopes. If so, and if a sufficient number of other congressmen express the same hope, that would represent the will of Congress. But a congressman's prediction might represent not his hopes but simply his expectations or even his fears. In that case, it would be a grave confusion to suppose that if a court fulfills his prediction, it enforces his will. If the idea of a collective understanding is to play any useful role in a theory of legislation, it must be defined so that only evidence of the legislators' hopes, not of their bare predictions, however confidently these are made, count as evidence of a collective understanding.[1] But that makes it less likely still that a collective understanding will exist either way in any particular case, and more likely that a court's "discovery" of such an understanding would be only an invention.

Nothing illustrates the need for these distinctions better than the congressional debates of 1964 leading to the Civil Rights Act. Opponents repeatedly argued that Title VII would allow federal agencies to impose racial quotas on private industry. They detested such interference, and they

hoped to enlist the aid of others who also did. In the event, the statute was amended, by adding Section 703(j) to Title VII, which expressly declared that nothing in the act should be construed to allow such imposed quotas. But if the act had not been amended, it would have been perverse to cite these statements of opponents to prove that the statute did accomplish what they feared. It would have been equally perverse to cite those proponents of the bill who argued that the statute did *not* allow compulsory quotas as evidence of any congressional will that such quotas be prohibited. Several of the act's sponsors thought that it would be interpreted to prohibit such imposed quotas even before the amendment—that is certainly what they said—but it was not necessarily what even they wanted. Many backbenchers who favored the bill even before the amendment might have done so fearing that these leaders were right, but hoping that they were wrong, and that the act would be interpreted to license exactly the sort of government-supervised integration of industry that they wanted.

WE MUST NOW examine Rehnquist's argument to see which of the two concepts of legislative intent we have distinguished he himself had in mind. He builds his argument around the debate I have already described: between opponents of the Civil Rights Act in the 1964 congressional debates, who said that as drafted the act would authorize federal agencies to dictate that private industries hire according to racial quotas, and proponents who replied that it would not. Several of these proponents went further and declared that the bill would not permit *any* employment decisions, even voluntary decisions, to be taken on the basis of race. Senator Humphrey, for example, argued that Title VII "says that race, religion, and national origin are not to be used as the basis for hiring and firing. Title VII is designed to encourage hiring on the basis of ability and qualifications, not race or religion."

Senators Joe Clark and Clifford Case, who were designated the bipartisan "captains" of the bill, submitted what they called an "interpretative memorandum" addressed to the problem of imposed quotas, which said: "There is no requirement in Title VII that an employer maintain a racial balance in his work force. On the contrary, any deliberate attempt to maintain a racial balance . . . would involve a violation of Title VII because maintaining such a balance would require an employer to hire or to refuse to hire on the basis of race . . . He would not be obliged—or indeed permitted—to fire whites in order to hire Negroes, or to prefer Negroes for future vacancies, or, once Negroes are hired, to give them special seniority rights at the expense of the white workers hired earlier."

None of these statements satisfied opponents who feared government orders making racial quotas or racial balance mandatory. In the end it was necessary to introduce an amendment explicitly prohibiting such orders.

This was Section 703(j), which said that nothing in Title VII "shall be interpreted to require any employer . . . to grant preferential treatment to any individual or to any group" in order to reduce racial imbalance in the work force. Mr. Justice Brennan, writing for the majority in *Weber*, emphasized that this new provision said only that affirmative action was not required, not that voluntary affirmative action was prohibited. But Rehnquist emphasized instead the previous history, and the many congressional statements he had discovered, arguing that the new provision was not necessary, because the act, by itself, without the new provision, barred any form of race-conscious employment or promotion program.

What does Rehnquist take these statements to show? Did they constitute an institutionalized intention, so that the statute should be construed as if these statements were formally a part of it, like an oral preamble? That is extremely implausible. There is no legislative convention that automatically turns the statements even of key leaders, even of "bipartisan captains," into preambles. If there were such a convention, it would not have been appropriate for opponents of the bill to voice fears after the reassuring statements had been made. On the contrary, it would have been preposterous. Nor would it have been necessary to add Section 703(j). That would have been redundant, merely repeating what Senators Humphrey, Clark, Case, and others had already added to the bill.

The fact that Congress added 703(j) shows that congressmen do not acknowledge a convention that turns the statements of important senators into amendments. Of course these statements *might* have been offered and taken by everyone to constitute an institutionalized intention. But plainly they were not. The leaders Rehnquist quoted offered their own opinions about the effect of the bill simply *as* their opinions, which continued to be contested by others, so that it was necessary to resolve the matter by formal amendment. A backbench senator or representative voting for the Civil Rights Act need not have supposed that he was bound by what Humphrey or the Clark-Case memorandum said the Civil Rights Act would do, and it is unfair—and contrary to democracy—to insist that he was.

Does Rehnquist think, on the contrary, that the statements of the leaders he quoted are evidence of some shared psychological state, some collective understanding of the legislators as a whole? If so, then the evidence is very thin indeed. Rehnquist is able to cite the remarks of only a relatively few congressmen, whom he interprets as holding the opinion that the act would forbid affirmative action plans like the Kaiser plan. He cites several who thought that until the act was amended it would have authorized mandatory government racial quotas based on percentages of blacks in the labor force, and who must therefore have held the contrary opinion on affirmative action plans, that is, that the act would permit industry to do voluntarily what the government could order it to do.

Nothing suggests that most of the legislators—or enough of those who

voted for the act to pass it unaided—accepted either of these two opinions, or if so which, or indeed that they had any opinion at all. But even if we assume that they did, and that they agreed with Rehnquist's interpretation, it hardly follows that that was their will. Many might seriously have regretted that they must enact a statute that would block affirmative action (assuming they thought that they were doing so) in order to prevent outright racial discrimination in employment. They would have been pleased to be persuaded that their judgment of how the act would be interpreted was wrong.

The only remarks in either house that said directly that it would be illegal under the act for a black employer to prefer black employees so as to improve the economic condition of blacks stated that this was a matter of great regret. (This was a staged dialogue between Senators Curtis and Cotton, opponents of the bill, whose sympathy for the black employer might have been diplomatic.) If Rehnquist means to use the psychological concept of a composite intention, then, his use displays every one in the long catalog of flaws in that misunderstood concept. It is not just that we need more evidence to discover what the collective understanding was. Rather the evidence we have suggests that there was none to discover.

So Rehnquist's argument fails, whether we take it to rely on the institutional or the psychological concept of legislative intent. Its appeal to him might have come from a failure to distinguish these two concepts, so that he could take arguments for the psychological branch as arguments for the warrant of the institutional branch. He should not have taken this occasion so violently to tax his colleagues with using slipshod arguments to cover a purely political judgment, for his own arguments were much weaker than he thought.

WE MUST ASK, however, whether the majority had better arguments than Rehnquist had. For his charge that their decision was based on purely personal political convictions is not answered simply by showing that his own arguments are poor. The opinion for the majority was written by Mr. Justice Brennan. It contains two different arguments, one of them explicit, and one that must be reconstructed from independent remarks. The explicit argument is the mirror image of Rehnquist's opposing argument and suffers from the same defects. It uses general remarks about the purpose of the Civil Rights Act, together with the fact of Section 703(j), to establish a legislative intention to exempt affirmative action from Title VII. Brennan is not explicit whether this is an institutionalized intention or a collective understanding.

If Congress did not intend to permit voluntary affirmative programs, he argues, it would have stated in 703(j) that such programs were neither re-

quired nor permitted; but it said only that they were not required. "The natural inference is that Congress chose not to forbid all voluntary race-conscious affirmative action." That inference is not natural but fallacious. The argument shows that Congress did not choose to outlaw affirmative action, but it does not follow that Congress chose not to do so. Personifying the Congress encourages the mistake (Brennan's opinion is full of phrases like "Congress' primary concern," "Congress feared," and so on). But it is not true even in the case of an individual that he either chooses to permit something or chooses not to permit it. He may have chosen neither.

Brennan's second argument is much more successful. If made more explicit, it would take something like the following form.

(1) We can identify an uncontroversial political policy that fully supports the main provisions of Title VII of the Civil Rights Act. This is the policy of ameliorating the economic inferiority of blacks and other minorities. Many members of both houses expressly endorsed that policy, and no one contested it.

(2) That policy will be advanced by permitting plans like Kaiser's. It would be sharply arrested by making such plans illegal.

(3) Section 703(j) is supported by a different, and to some degree competing, political principle, which is that it is wrong for the government to intervene in private hiring and personnel policy just to secure a racial balance. Even though such intervention would advance the main policy of achieving greater economic racial equality, it is wrong because it abrogates what Brennan calls "traditional management prerogatives." Though this principle is not uncontroversial, there is no dissent from it in the legislative history either.

(4) A rule forbidding voluntary affirmative action would certainly constitute an intervention in traditional management decisions, therefore violating the principle supporting Section 703(j), and it would be, moreover, not an intervention advancing the core policy of economic equality but one impeding that policy, and so condemned by that principle *a fortiori*. For all these reasons, the statute should not be construed to forbid the Kaiser plan.

Is this a good argument? It does not in any way personify Congress or presuppose a congressional intention, in either sense, to exempt private and voluntary race-conscious employment plans from the act. So it does not suffer from the mistakes of Brennan's first argument or of Rehnquist's opinion. It rests instead on a different theory of legislation, which we might call the coherence theory. This supposes that a statute should be interpreted to advance the policies or principles that furnish the best political justification for the statute.

It may, of course, be controversial which principles or policies supply the best justification for a particular statute, or for some particular provision or

limitation of that statute. Nor is it possible to state any mechanical formula for determining the answer to that question. A proposed justification cannot be accepted, unless it is consistent with the provisions of the statute and finds substantial support in the political climate of the time. The justification Brennan provided for Title VII of the Civil Rights Act—the policy of promoting economic inequality between the races, subject to the principle that private employers should not be forced to maintain a racial balance—meets that test of consistency. The main provisions of Title VII, which forbid traditional discrimination against blacks, could be expected to reduce economic inequality, and though the various speeches Brennan cited, which include a statement by President Kennedy as well as statements by various senators, do not establish that all the congressmen had this justification in mind, they do establish that the justification had wide currency and political appeal.

But though Brennan's proposed justification does meet this test of consistency, other, different justifications might meet the test as well. It is easy to construct a different justification, according to which the coherence theory of legislation would support not the decision of the majority in favor of affirmative action but Rehnquist's opinion condemning it. We might say that Title VII is justified, not by a policy of promoting economic equality, but by the principle that any use of race-conscious criteria in hiring or promoting employees is unfair. That principle also fits the central provisions of the statute, and it is also supported by a substantial section of political opinion. But if *that* principle is taken to be the justification of Title VII, rather than the policy of promoting racial equality, then it is a decision for Weber, rather than a decision in favor of the Kaiser plan, that is most consistent with the statute so justified.

How is a court to choose between two justifications for a statute, each of which fits the statute and finds a basis in political opinion? If one of these justifications has been attached to the statute as an institutionalized intention, through some legislative convention of the sort described earlier, then the court must apply that justification even though it prefers another. If the legislative history shows that while one justification had great support among a number of legislators, the other went unnoticed or was rejected by all who noticed it, then that might well be some evidence that the second does not, after all, reflect any widespread political opinion. But in most hard cases testing whether a statute applies in controversial circumstances, when there are two justifications available that point in opposite directions, both justifications will fit well enough both the text of the statute and the political climate of the day, and neither will be attached to the statute by convention.

Weber was such a case. In these cases I see no procedure for decision—no theory of legislation—other than this: one justification for a statute is better

than another, and provides the direction for coherent development of the statute, if it provides a more accurate or more sensitive or sounder analysis of the underlying moral principles. So judges must decide which of the two competing justifications is superior as a matter of political morality, and apply the statute so as to further that justification. Different judges, who disagree about morality, will therefore disagree about the statute. But that is inevitable, and if each judge faces the moral decision openly, an informed public will be in a better position to understand and criticize them than if the moral grounds of decision lie hidden under confused arguments about nonexistent legislative intents.

It is no use protesting that this procedure allows judges to substitute their own political judgment for the judgment of elected representatives of the people. That protest is doubly misleading. It suggests, first, that the legislators have in fact made a judgment so that it is wrong for the judges to displace that judgment. But if there is no institutionalized intention, no pertinent collective understanding, and two competing justifications, there is no such judgment. Second, the protest suggests that judges have some way to decide such a case that does *not* require them to make a political judgment. But there is no such procedure, except a method that leaves the decision to chance, like flipping a coin.

The jurisprudential point at stake here can be put two different ways. We can say that the legislation a statute produces, when the words of the statute are indecisive and there is no institutionalized intention, directly depends upon political morality. When a court asks, for example, whether Congress outlawed affirmative action in Title VII, the court must ask, as part of *that* question, whether affirmative action is unfair, because if it is, then Congress did. Or we can say that, in such a case, what Congress has done is not uncertain, but rather indeterminate: it has neither outlawed affirmative action nor not done so, so that when a court decides on the basis of a judgment about the fairness of affirmative action, it cannot be displacing a congressional judgment either way. It must be supplementing that judgment in the only rational way available to it. I believe that the first of these two descriptions is more accurate: it reflects a deeper understanding of the complex idea of legislation. But the second may seem more sensible to lawyers who favor more traditional theories of that institution. The difference is not important in the present context, because under *either* interpretation the objection to the majority's decision in *Weber*—that that decision is based on the judges' own beliefs about the fairness and wisdom of affirmative action—is no objection at all.

We can now see why Rehnquist's bitter condemnation of the majority was so misguided. *Weber* offered the Supreme Court not an exercise in reconstructing the mental states of a variety of senators and congressmen but a serious and complex issue about the nature of discrimination and the fair-

ness of affirmative action. It was, in fact, the same issue that the Court faced
in *Bakke,* but did not, as a Court, answer. Discrimination of the conventional sort, practiced against blacks in the United States for centuries, is
wrong. But why? Is it wrong because any race-conscious distinction is always and inevitably wrong, even when used to redress inequality? If so,
then it would be correct, under the coherence theory of legislation, to interpret Title VII as outlawing all such distinctions in employment. Or is
traditional discrimination wrong because it reflects prejudice and contempt
for a disadvantaged group, and so increased the disadvantage of that group?
In that case, it would be sounder to attribute to Title VII the different program of outlawing such malign discrimination, and seeking to remove its
inegalitarian consequences, and it would be perverse, rather than sensible,
to understand the statute to bar private efforts in that direction.[2]

Either decision in the case—the decision of the minority as well as that of
the majority—must be supported by some answer to these questions if it is
to be supported at all. Chief Justice Burger's remark—that he would vote to
permit plans like Kaiser's if he were in Congress, but nevertheless believed
that Congress had made them illegal—is therefore more perplexing than it
first appears. If Burger's interpretation of Title VII can be supported only
by supposing that affirmative action is wrong as a matter of moral principle,
and if he does not think it wrong, because he would have voted to permit it
if he were in Congress, he cannot continue in his opinion of the law. If he
accepted the jurisprudential argument of this essay, that is, he would have
to switch his vote in *Weber* and later cases.

We cannot make the same assumption about Rehnquist's dissenting vote.
He argued, as I said, that he was forced to his vote by neutral arguments of
statutory construction. But even if he accepted that no such arguments are
available, and that any decision in the case must reflect some answer to the
question of political morality, he might still answer that affirmative action is
unfair and that Kaiser's plan is for that reason barred by the statute. Nothing in his opinion suggests or assumes the contrary.

What of the five judges who made up the majority? Four of them—Justices Brennan, Blackmun, Marshall, and White—voted in *Bakke* to uphold
the constitutionality even of the quota plan used by the Davis medical
school to assure a fixed proportion of minority students. Their votes assumed that even a quota plan did not invade the fundamental political
rights of white students who were thereby denied places. So their votes in
Weber are consistent with their votes in *Bakke,* even if we assume that their
Weber votes were based on Brennan's second and more successful argument. The fifth Justice forming the majority was Mr. Justice Stewart, and
that fact is, I think, of some importance.

The *Bakke* decision was indecisive because the four Justices who held
that the Davis plan was illegal under Title VI of the Civil Rights Act ex-

pressed no opinion on whether it was unconstitutional, and therefore no explicit opinion on the underlying issue: the moral issue of the fairness of affirmative action. Stewart was one of these, and his present vote with the majority in *Weber* is especially important if it does signal his acceptance of Brennan's second argument, because that would establish a clear majority in favor of the principle that affirmative action of the sort used in *Weber*—a race-conscious policy aimed at improving racial equality and not subjecting anyone to disadvantage because his or her race is disfavored—offends no one's political rights.

I put this point in a guarded way, because my argument does not supply any firm basis for predictions about future affirmative action cases. Stewart may have joined the majority because he accepted some argument about legislative intent, like Brennan's first argument. In any case, the majority opinion Stewart joined is carefully limited in various ways. It emphasizes, for example, that the Kaiser plan was limited to securing rather than also maintaining a racial balance, and though that distinction is irrelevant as a matter of moral principle, it might be used to limit the impact of the decision for the future.

The opinion stresses, moreover, that it is an interpretation of one title of the Civil Rights Act only, and does not speak to any constitutional issue. Nevertheless, the development of constitutional law is governed more by the latent moral principles that are presupposed by a good justification of Supreme Court decisions than by the more technical arguments and limitations set out in the discrete opinions, and this is especially true when, as in *Weber*, these more technical points do not withstand close analysis. The Court's decision in *Weber* is of great importance, and not only because it permitted valuable programs developed by private initiative to go forward. For all its careful limitations, the case marks another step in the Court's efforts to develop a new conception of what equality requires in the search for racial justice. In retrospect, that step will seem more important than the Court's hesitant shuffle in *Bakke.*

Censorship and a Free Press

SEVENTEEN

Do We Have a Right to Pornography?

GOALS

The Williams Strategy

It is an old problem for liberal theory how far people should have the right to do the wrong thing. Liberals insist that people have the legal right to say what they wish on matters of political or social controversy. But should they be free to incite racial hatred, for example? British and American law now give different answers to that specific question. The United Kingdom Race Relations law makes it a crime to advocate racial prejudice, but the First Amendment to the United States Constitution forbids Congress or any of the states from adopting any such law.

Pornography in its various forms presents another instance of the same issue. The majority of people in both countries would prefer (or so it seems) substantial censorship, if not outright prohibition, of "sexually explicit" books, magazines, photographs, and films, and this majority includes a considerable number of those who are themselves consumers of whatever pornography is on offer. (It is part of the complex psychology of sex that many of those with a fixed taste for the obscene would strongly prefer that their children, for example, not follow them in that taste.) If we assume that the majority is correct, and that people who publish and consume pornography do the wrong thing, or at least display the wrong sort of character, should they nevertheless have the legal right to do so?

Some lawyers and political philosophers consider the problem of pornography to be only an instance of the first problem I mentioned, the problem of freedom to speak unpopular or wicked thoughts. But we should be suspicious of that claim, because the strongest arguments in favor of allowing *Mein Kampf* to be published hardly seem to apply in favor of the novel *Whips Incorporated* or the film *Sex Kittens*. No one, I think, is denied an equal voice in the political process, however broadly conceived, when he is forbidden to circulate photographs of genitals to the public at large, or denied his right to listen to argument when he is forbidden to consider these

photographs at his leisure. If we believe it wrong to censor these forms of pornography, then we should try to find the justification for that opinion elsewhere than in the literature celebrating freedom of speech and press.

We should consider two rather different strategies that might be thought to justify a permissive attitude. The first argues that even if the publication and consumption of pornography is bad for the community as a whole, just considered in itself, the consequences of trying to censor or otherwise suppress pornography would be, in the long run, even worse. I shall call this the "goal-based" strategy. The second argues that even if pornography makes the community worse off, even in the very long run, it is nevertheless wrong to censor or restrict it because this violates the individual moral or political rights of citizens who resent the censorship. I shall call this the "rights-based" strategy.

Which of these strategies, if either, does the 1979 Report of the Committee on Obscenity and Film Censorship[1] (the Williams Report) follow? The Report recommends that the present law on obscenity be revised radically and provides an important distinction as the centerpiece of the new legal scheme it suggests. Certain forms of pornography are to be prohibited altogether. These include live sex shows (actual rather than merely simulated copulation, fellatio, and the like performed live before an audience) and films and photographs produced through the exploitation of children. Other forms of pornography are to be, not prohibited, but restricted in various ways. These restrictions include rules about offensive displays or advertising in public places, limitation of the sale of pornography to special shops, and an elaborate scheme of previewing and licensing of films. I shall later discuss whether these admirably clear recommendations can all be justified in a coherent way. I want first to identify the justification the Report offers.

It sets out and endorses what it calls the harm condition, that "no conduct should be suppressed by law unless it can be shown to harm someone." It notes the popularity of that condition, but rightly adds that either the popularity or the power of the condition evaporates when it is made less ambiguous. Everything turns on what "harm" is taken to be. If "harm" includes only direct physical damage to particular people, or direct damage to their property or financial interests, then the condition is much too strong, since it would condemn a large part of standing British and American law. It would forbid regulating the commercial development of certain parts of cities, or restricting the private use of natural resources like the seashore. Almost everyone would reject the harm condition interpreted in that way. But if "harm" is broadened to include mental distress or annoyance, then the condition becomes much too weak to be of any use in political theory, since any kind of conduct likely to be made criminal in a democracy, at least, is conduct that causes annoyance or distress to someone. Suppose "harm" is taken to exclude mental distress, but to include

damage to the general social and cultural environment. Then the harm condition is in itself no help in considering the problem of pornography, because opponents of pornography argue, with some force, that free traffic in obscenity does damage the general cultural environment.

So the harm condition does not in itself recommend a permissive attitude toward pornography, except in a form much too strong to be accepted, and the Report places little weight on that condition. Its argument begins instead in a special and attractive theory about the general value of free expression. John Stuart Mill suggested, in *On Liberty,* that society has most chance to discover truth, not only in science but about the best conditions for human flourishing as well, if it tolerates a free marketplace of ideas. The Report rejects Mill's optimistic (not to say complacent) ideas about the conditions most propitious for the discovery of truth. But it nevertheless accepts something close to Mill's position in the following important passage.

> The more basic idea, to which Mill attached the market-place model, remains a correct and profound idea: that we do not know in advance what social, moral or intellectual developments will turn out to be possible, necessary, or desirable for human beings and for their future, and free expression, intellectual and artistic—something which may need to be fostered and protected as well as merely permitted—is essential to human development, as a process which does not merely happen (in some form or another, it will happen anyway) but so far as possible is rationally understood. It is essential to it, moreover, not just as a means to it, but as part of it. Since human beings are not just subject to their history but aspire to be conscious of it, the development of human individuals, of society and of humanity in general, is a process itself properly constituted in part by free expression and the exchange of human communication.[2]

This account of the value of free expression requires some supplement before it can provide a justification for much of contemporary pornography, because the offerings of Soho and Eighth Avenue—close-up glossies and *Beyond the Green Door*—are not patently expressions about desirable human development. The Report finds that supplement in the topology of the slippery slope.[3] It is difficult, if not impossible, to devise a form of words that we can be confident will in practice separate useless trash from potentially valuable contributions. Any form of words will be administered by prosecutors, jurors, and judges with their own prejudices, their own love or fear of the new, and, in the case of prosecutors, their own warm sense of the political advantages of conformity. In any case, writers and publishers, anxious to avoid risk and trouble, will exercise a self-censorship out of abundant caution, and themselves extend the constraint of any words we find. If we recognize the general value of free expression, therefore, we should accept a presumption against censorship or prohibition of any activity when that ac-

tivity even arguably expresses a conviction about how people should live or feel, or opposes established or popular convictions. The presumption need not be absolute. It might be overcome by some showing that the harm the activity threatens is grave, probable, and uncontroversial, for example. But it should nevertheless be a strong presumption in order to protect the long-term goal of securing, in spite of our ignorance, the best conditions that we can for human development.

This general strategy, which I shall sometimes call the "Williams strategy," organizes the more specific arguments and distinctions of the Report. The Committee concedes, for example, the relevance of the question whether an increase in the amount of pornography in circulation in the community is likely to produce more violence or more sexual crimes of any particular sort. If harm of this sort can be demonstrated, then the presumption can be overcome. But the Committee finds no persuasive evidence of this causal influence. The same strategy supports the crucial distinction between outright prohibition and various forms of restriction of pornography. Restriction does not so severely curtail the contribution that pornography might make to the exchange of ideas and attitudes, though it will change the character of that contribution. So the slippery slope is not so much of a threat when the question is whether some book must be sold only in special shops as it is when the question is whether it can be published at all.

The Williams strategy is a version of the goal-based strategy that I earlier distinguished from the rights-based strategy. It does not define the goal it seeks to promote as the crude Benthamite might, as the outcome that produces the highest surplus of pleasure over pain, or even as a more sophisticated utilitarian would, perhaps as the outcome in which more people have more of what they want to have. The Report speaks instead of human development, and insists that some social, moral, and intellectual developments are more "desirable" than others. We would not go far wrong, I think, to summarize the Report's conception of the best society as the society that is most conducive to human beings' making intelligent decisions about what the best lives for them to lead are, and then flourishing in those lives. The Williams strategy emphasizes, however, an important idea latent in that description. It would be wrong to think of social and political decisions as aimed only at producing the best society at some particular (and therefore arbitrary) future time, so that the acts and forbearances of people now are merely parts of a development to be judged for its instrumental value in producing the best society then. How a society develops is itself an important part of the value of that society, now conceived in a longer perspective that includes the present and the indefinite future as well. In particular, the social development of ideals of human flourishing must be "conscious" and "rationally understood," and "a process itself properly constituted in part

by free expression and the exchange of human communication." Human development must be self-development or its value is compromised from the start.

Live Sex

This is in many ways a more attractive picture of the good society than either the crude or the more sophisticated utilitarian can provide. But it is nevertheless a theory (as these less attractive pictures are theories) about what outcomes are good as a whole, rather than a theory about what rights must be recognized even at the cost of accepting less than the best outcome on the whole. I want now to ask whether the Report's attractive goal-based theory justifies its recommendations about pornography. I shall begin with a fairly specific and limited question. Does the Williams strategy support the recommendation that live sex shows be prohibited altogether, rather than simply being restricted in their advertising, or in the location or outside display of the theater in which they take place, or in the age of those who may be admitted? In that way live shows with unfeigned sex are treated more stringently than live shows with simulated sex or films with actual sex. Can the goal-based Williams strategy show why?

We might, by way of preparation for this question, compose a list of possible justifications for treating different forms of pornography differently. I assume that we do not have any good reason to believe that any of the pornography we are now considering does make a positive and valuable contribution to the free exchange of ideas about human flourishing. (The Report considers the claim that some does, and seems to reject it as humbug. It recommends only that we accept the presumption that some pornography might make such a contribution.) So we cannot discriminate between different forms on the basis of our present beliefs that the positive contributions of some is greater than that of others, that the positive contribution of the film *Deep Throat* is greater, for example, than a cabaret re-enactment of the main events of that film. We may, however, be able to justify discrimination between different forms of pornography, conformably with the Williams strategy, in some other way. After all, if we do think that pornography appeals to the less attractive aspects of human personality, we may very well think that the unrestrained publication and consumption of pornography is very much a wrong turn in human flourishing. We may be persuaded, by the Williams strategy, that the damage to human development might be greater still if all pornography were prohibited, because we cannot be sure about our views of human flourishing, because the slippery slope argument warns us that we may prohibit too much, and because in any case any restraint just in itself damages the process of social development because it makes that process less a matter of rational and deliberate

choice. But this is very much a question of balancing, and we may be prepared to restrain some form of pornography rather more than other forms,
in spite of these competing arguments of the Williams strategy, if (1) we
believe that that form does present a special danger of personal harm narrowly conceived, or (2) we believe that that form presents some special danger of cultural pollution that will, we believe, do more damage to the
prospects for human flourishing than other forms, or (3) we think that we
can be more secure of our footing on the slippery slope in prohibiting that
form; that is, that we can draft legislation specifically aimed at that form
that will not in practice carry away anything valuable with the dross.

The Report says that live shows are different from films because the former involve the spectator "being in the same space" as "people actually
engaged in sexual activity." It is "from this relationship between actual
people that arises the peculiar objectionableness that many find is the idea
of the live sex show, and the sense that the kind of voyeurism involved is
especially degrading to both audience and performers."[4] This last suggestion might be thought ambiguous. It might mean that the justification for
prohibiting live sex shows lies in the fact that so many people object to
others performing or watching them, that so many others believe that this is
degrading. In that case the argument is of the first sort we just distinguished: the harm in question is direct personal harm in the form of the
mental suffering or pain of those who know that others are behaving in a
degrading way. But the Report cannot consistently appeal to that sort of
harm as the justification of a prohibition, because it elsewhere explicitly rejects the idea that that kind of harm can count. "If one accepted, as a basis
for coercing one person's actions, the fact that others would be upset even
by the thought of his performing those actions, one would be denying any
substantive individual liberty at all."[5]

So we should take the other interpretation of the remarks about live sex
shows, which is that they should be prohibited not because many people
believe that they are degrading, but just because they are degrading. This
must then be understood as an appeal to the second sort of justification for
restraint: the strong presumption in favor of freedom of expression must
yield to prohibition here, because the cultural pollution that would be inflicted by live sex shows, and hence the setback to the achievement of the
best conditions for human development, is too great to keep such shows
within the presumption of the Williams strategy. This is, however, an extraordinary justification for singling out live sex shows in this way. For the
Report emphasizes that live sex shows will in any case be so rare, will appeal to so limited an audience, and will be relatively so expensive, that the
impact that they could have on the general environment must be very small
whether it is for good or bad. Live shows would be very unlikely to offer
more of an overall threat of cultural pollution than the all too lifeless and

depressingly obscene photographs and films that the Report allows though restricts, each of which can be duplicated and distributed to millions.

Does the third sort of argument just listed provide a better argument here? Is the slippery slope less of a danger in the case of live sex? The Report does say that "it seems to us, in fact, that the presentation of actual sex on the stage immediately introduces a presumption that the motives no longer have any artistic pretension."[6] But that seems an ill-considered remark. I am not aware of any serious dramatic presentation that uses "actual sex." But that is, apart from obvious casting problems, because it would not now be permitted. Certainly serious dramatic work uses simulated sex, as the Report recognizes, and it can hardly be maintained that a passion for realism on the stage is inconsistent with "artistic pretension." An entire school of dramatic theory argues just the contrary. At one point the Report, apparently as an argument for prohibition, observes that "the live show is a contemporary happening with an unknown future end, which the audience may be capable of influencing or in which they might participate."[7] But that passage might have been lifted from an essay on the aims of Arthauld or Genet or even Brecht or dozens of other ambitious playwrights, and any director who was wholly indifferent to that conception of theater would probably be a boring hack. The slippery slope argument seems especially strong rather than especially weak in the case of live sex on the stage. The continuing flat prohibition of actual copulation undoubtedly limits the drama in its examination of the relation between art and taboo; and the assumption that the consequences of live sex in serious theater are both predictable and very bad betrays, I think, exactly the claim to omniscience that the Williams strategy deplores. It is not my present purpose to suggest that the ban should be relaxed, but only that the strategy of the Report provides no very clear or very effective argument why it should not be.

Why Restrict?

We must not make too much of the Report's difficulties in disposing of live sex shows. Though the Report is an outstanding example of a political argument, it is a political argument nevertheless, both in the sense that it hopes to encourage legislation and in the different sense that it is the joint product of many people with diverse points of view. Perhaps the members of the Committee felt that live sex shows, even in a restricted form, were intolerable, good arguments or not. But the point is important because it illustrates the great force of the different assumptions embedded in the Williams strategy, and how difficult it is to justify, within that strategy, any exception to the permissive policy it generally recommends.

We might therefore turn to a much more important part of the Report's recommendations, which is the distinction it draws between the restriction

and the prohibition of pornography. If the Williams strategy argues against the outright prohibition of pornographic pictures and films, except in very limited cases, can it consistently accept the restrictions the Report commends? The Report offers different arguments proposing to justify the distinction. These arguments fall into groups rather like the different kinds of arguments we considered justifying the special treatment of live sex shows. It argues in favor of the restrictions it urges on the open display and advertising of pornography, for example, (1) that the personal harm caused by such display is much greater than the harm caused by private consumption alone, (2) that the cultural pollution is also greater, and (3) that the slippery slope is less of a danger in the case of restriction because if genuinely valuable material is caught by the restriction it is nevertheless still allowed to enter the exchange of ideas in a sufficiently effective way. We must look at each of these claims, and I shall consider them in reverse order.

The Report argues, in favor of the last claim, that restricting a pornographic publication to a volunteer audience does not defeat the aims of the publication, as distinct perhaps from the aims of its author who may make less money. But this personification takes a rather narrow view of the aims of publication, a view that does not sit comfortably with the Williams strategy. From the standpoint of that strategy, which emphasizes the contribution that expression may make to the reflective search for new possibilities of social and cultural practice, the manner in which pornography is presented to the public may be equally important as its content. Though pornography may not itself be a form of art (the Report speaks instructively to that troublesome issue), the analogy is appropriate here. When Duchamp hung a urinal on the wall of an art gallery, he made a claim about the nature of art—a claim that was to engage critics for many years—that he could not have made by inviting a volunteer audience to view the same object in a public convenience. His medium was certainly his message. If we attend only to the immediate purpose of pornography, and we take that purpose to be the gratification of those who are willing to take trouble and risk embarrassment to secure it, then restricted publication may serve that purpose. But if we are concerned—as the Williams strategy says we must be—with the consequences of publication for the exploration of forms of life, then restricted publication is not simply less publication. It is publication of something different. Restricted publication leaves a certain hypothesis entirely unmade: the hypothesis that sex should enter all levels of public culture on the same standing as soap opera romance or movie trivia, for example, and play the role in day-to-day life that it then would. There may be good reason for not allowing that hypothesis to be presented in the most natural and effective way. But this cannot be the reason now given, that those who are already converted may not complain so long as their own needs are (perhaps inconveniently) met.

Is there more power in the second kind of argument, that even though the danger of cultural pollution is not strong enough to justify prohibition it is nevertheless strong enough to justify restriction? The argument here is contained, I think, in the following comments of the Report:

> One witness whom we saw made it clear that she looked forward to a society in which nothing one saw going on in the park would be more surprising than anything else, except perhaps in the sense of being more improbable. Most of us doubt whether this day will come, or that nothing would have been lost if it did. Still less do we look forward to a world in which sexual activity is not only freely conducted in public and can be viewed, but is offered to be viewed, copulating parties soliciting the interest of the passer-by. But this is, in effect, what publicly displayed pornography does . . . The basic point that pornography involves by its nature some violation of lines between public and private is compounded when the pornography not only exists for private consumption, but is publicly displayed.[8]

The "basic point" of this last sentence suggests that public display threatens to break down the culturally important distinction between public and private activity. But that seems an overstatement. It would be more accurate, I think, to say that public display of pornography trades on that distinction—what it displays would not be shocking or (to those who might find it so) attractive without that distinction—but that it trades on it in a way that might (or might not) rearrange the boundaries, so that people used to (perhaps we should say hardened by) public display of pictures of copulation would no longer think that such displays were wholly inappropriate to the public space. It does not follow that if the boundaries were rearranged in that way they would be rearranged further, so that people would take the same attitude to copulation in the open spaces of parks. The Report itself, as we noticed, insists on the special character of live sex just because being "in the same space" as people actually copulating is so different from looking at pictures of such people. But suppose that the public display of photographs would bring the day nearer in which the boundaries were further rearranged so that copulation itself became much more a public activity than now it is. That does not mean that the distinction between public and private, which is certainly of great cultural importance, would itself fall. We have seen great rearrangements of these boundaries even in recent years. People now eat in public streets, kiss and embrace in public, and play naked on at least certain public beaches, and these activities belonged much more firmly to the private space not long ago. The boundaries culture sets on what is public have in other ways contracted in the same period: people are much less likely now than once to pray in public, for example, because the attitude that prayer is a more private than a public activity, limited to the home or special places of worship, has become much more widespread. Surely the dimensions and contours of the public space prop-

erly belong to the dialogue through example about the possibilities of human development, the dialogue the Williams strategy wishes to protect. The vitality and character of the basic distinction, the basic idea that there must be a private space, is more threatened by any legally enforced freeze on the boundaries set at any particular time than by allowing the market of expression constantly to reexamine and redraw those boundaries. The Committee says that it would not like to see a world in which the contours of the private were set in the particular way it describes and fears. But that seems exactly the sort of opinion which the Williams strategy argues should be treated with respectful skepticism. It is not plain why it deserves to be enforced through law any more than the opinion of others who dread a world in which their children will be free to fantasize over obscene photographs in private.

What of the first kind of reason that might support the central distinction between prohibition and restriction? This appeals to greater personal harm. The Report argues that if pornography were not restricted in the way it suggests, then the personal harm it would cause would be much greater, or would be of a character that the law should attend to more, than the personal harm that pornography restricted and made essentially a private activity would cause. If this is correct, then it might indeed supply an argument for restriction that does not hold for outright prohibition. If it can be shown that the public display of pornography in the form of advertisements, for example, causes special or great harm to passersby, then even though the presumption of the Williams strategy is strong enough to defeat arguments of prohibition it might fall before the claims for restriction. But what is this special or serious harm that public display might cause? It is not the danger of violent assault or sexual abuse. The Report rejects the evidence offered to it, that even unrestricted pornography would cause an increase in such crimes, as at best inconclusive. The harm is rather of the sort suggested by the word the Report adopts: "offensiveness."

Once again it is worth setting out the clear and concise language of the Report itself:

> Laws against public sex would generally be thought to be consistent with the harm condition, in the sense that if members of the public are upset, distressed, disgusted, outraged or put out by witnessing some class of acts, then that constitutes a respect in which the public performance of those acts harms their interests and gives them a reason to object . . . The offensiveness of publicly displayed pornography seems to us . . . to be in line with traditionally accepted rules protecting the interest in public decency. Restrictions on the open sale of these publications, and analogous arrangements for films, thus seem to us to be justified . . . If one goes all the way down this line, however, one arrives at the situation in which people objected to even knowing that pornography was being read in private; and if one accepted as

a basis for coercing one person's actions, the fact that others would be upset even by the thought of his performing these actions, one would be denying any substantive liberty at all. Any offence caused by such shops would clearly be much less vivid, direct and serious than that caused by the display of the publications, and we do not accept that it could outweigh the rights of those who do wish to see this material, or more generally the argument in favour of restricting, rather than suppressing, pornography.[9]

The last sentence, if I understand it correctly, raises one argument distinct from the others, which is that the disgust or other offense likely to be caused to people who are affected just by the knowledge that pornography exists will be "less vivid, direct and serious" than the disgust caused by directly encountering indecent displays. But this seems far from clear, particularly if we take the numbers likely to suffer these different injuries into account. Everything depends, of course, on how much display the market would bear, and where the market would put that display, if pornography were wholly unrestricted. But if we take the present situation in New York City as a useful guide, then only a very small part of the population of Britain would often be forced to encounter displays if they did exist or have to adjust their lives much to avoid them altogether. No doubt a much larger part of the population would be very upset just by the fact that public displays of pornography existed, even though not in their ordinary paths; but this would be an instance of being upset by knowledge of what others were doing, not by the sight of it. Even if my guess is wrong (as it well might be) and the misadventure of actually stumbling on pornography would in fact be a great source of mental distress in a society that permitted pornography without restriction, this is hardly so obvious and so readily predictable as to justify the Report's crucial distinction without a good deal more empirical evidence.

But it is wrong to pursue this point, because the Report plainly places more weight on the preceding point, that the distress of those who are disgusted by the bare knowledge of pornography should not be counted at all in any overall calculation of the personal harm pornography does. But why should it not be counted? The Report says only that if this kind of harm was allowed to count, one would be denying all individual liberty. We might well ask why, if this observation makes sense, it argues only against counting disgust-harm arising from the bare knowledge of what is thought disgusting. Why does it not argue instead against counting any disgust-harm at all, including disgust-harm from actual sighting of the allegedly disgusting act? The point seems to be that we must stop somewhere short of counting all disgust-harm; but this does not justify the particular stopping point the Report chooses.

But I shall not pursue this issue either, because I cannot make much sense of the Report's initial claim. Of course individual liberty would be

very restricted if no one was allowed to do anything that any single other person found offensive. But the suggestion now in question, which the Committee believes would deny "any substantive liberty," is very much weaker than that.[10] The suggestion is only that the disgust that people feel when they learn that others are doing what they regard as offensive should figure along with other kinds of mental and physical distress in the calculation whether the presumption in favor of liberty should be overturned. So the question is whether the harm to those who find offense would outweigh the desire of all those who wish to do what would offend them. If only one or a few people took offense there would be little danger of that. It would be different if a large majority found some activity disgusting. But whether the majority's outrage would then leave much substantive individual liberty would depend on what that majority found outrageous. If the majority found it disgusting that anyone practice a religion other than the established religion, then liberty would be invaded in a way that we have independent reasons for thinking grave. (That is why we speak of a right to religious freedom.) But suppose the majority merely thinks it disgusting if people read or contemplate pornography in private. The slippery slope argument calls our attention to the fact that if the majority is allowed to have its way, individuals might be prevented from reading some things that are valuable for them to read. But even so it would surely overstate the facts to say that if people were not allowed any sexually explicit literature or art at all, they would lose their liberty altogether.

The Report may mean to say something different from this. It may mean that if the suggestion were adopted, that people may not do whatever the majority finds deeply disgusting, even in private, then people would have lost their *right* to liberty—because they may no longer insist that it is always wrong for the majority to restrict them for that reason—even if their actual loss of liberty turns out not to be very great. I agree that some such right is important (even though I would hesitate to call it a right to liberty as such).[11] But whether people have that right, as a matter of principle, is exactly what is now in dispute. Lord Devlin, for example, and presumably Mrs. Whitehouse, Lord Longford, and the other members of the putative "Moral Majority" as well, may be understood as challenging the proposition that they do. In any case, if it is some right to liberty, rather than liberty itself, that is in play here, then the Report has departed from the Williams strategy, unless it can be shown that that right, and not merely a large area of liberty, is essential to reflective social development. The Report does not provide arguments why this is so. In the next section I shall argue that that idea is antagonistic to the Williams strategy's goal-based character. But even if we assume that such a right can be extracted from that strategy, then the question I set aside a moment ago reappears. If the right to liberty is the right not to be limited in one's freedom simply because others are

disgusted by what one proposes to do, why does that right not include the right to do what one wants in public free from the majority's possible offense at actually viewing it? Nothing, I think, in the subjective character of the harm the majority suffers from seeing what it finds disgusting can provide the necessary distinction here. For the offense in question is not just offense to the majority's aesthetic tastes, like the offense people might find in a pink house in Belgravia. The offense is freighted with moral convictions, particularly with convictions about what kinds of sights are indecent rather than only regrettable in the public space, so that people would be offended by a pornographic billboard among the already ugly and cheap displays of Piccadilly or Times Square. The Report does not explain why allowing moral convictions to count in this way, through the offense that people suffer in public displays because of their moral beliefs, does not invade the individual right that is, however, invaded when the majority protects itself from being offended, perhaps more painfully, through its knowledge of what happens behind closed doors.

Why Not Prohibit?

So the Williams strategy does not offer very persuasive grounds for the operating distinction the Report makes fundamental to its recommendations, the distinction between prohibition and restriction. But the situation is, I think, even worse than that, because it is unclear that the strategy even provides a good argument for the generally permissive recommendations of the Report about the use of pornography in private. The strategy adopts an attitude of tolerant skepticism on the question of which "social, moral or intellectual developments" will turn out to be "most desirable" for human flourishing. It urges something like a free market in the expression of ideas about what people should be like and how they should live, not because freedom of expression is a good in itself, but because it enables a variety of hypotheses about the best developments to be formulated and tested in experience. But does this strategy leave sufficient room for the hypothesis that now has (or seems to have) the widest appeal? This is the hypothesis that humans will develop differently and best, and find the most suitable conditions for their own flourishing, if their law cultivates an ennobling rather than a degrading attitude toward their sexual activity by prohibiting, even in private, practices that are in fact perversions or corruptions of the sexual experience. We cannot be sure that this hypothesis, which I shall call the enforcement hypothesis, is sound. Many of us may believe that it is unsound. But can we be sure of that? The Report sometimes suggests that only those who "think that fundamental human moral truths have been laid down unchangeably for all time, for instance in religious terms"[12] will wish to urge the enforcement hypothesis. But I do not see why that must be so.

Those who find the enforcement hypothesis plausible may say that it represents their best judgment, though of course they might be wrong, just as those who reject the hypothesis should concede that they might be wrong.

Suppose we reply that prohibition freezes the market in expression, so that the enforcement hypothesis is the one view that should not be allowed to be tested, because it will then make itself immune to reexamination. Experience hardly supports this claim, at least in democracies. For though the law of obscenity in Great Britain has been relatively repressive since Victorian times, it has become steadily more liberal, on the whole, in practice if not in text, as the result of nonpornographic political debate about pornography, and also as a result of the acts of those who feel strongly enough about the principle, or are greedy enough, to break the law. In any case, this is a compliment that can easily be returned. Perhaps a society dulled by conformity in matters of sexual practice and expression would become a society in which more liberal attitudes are less likely to find a voice or a hearing in politics. But a society weakened by permissiveness is correspondingly a society less likely to attend to the advantages of a public and publicly enforced morality.

This is not an argument that the Williams strategy actually recommends prohibition; but rather that it should be neutral between prohibition and permissiveness. Skepticism about the most desirable developments for human beings, or about the most desirable conditions for their flourishing, should not rule out a set of conditions that a great many people believe to be the most promising of all. It does recommend an open political process, with no substantive part of the criminal law, for example, privileged against change. But that, as I just said, does not argue for present permissiveness any more than present prohibition. Skepticism may perhaps provide an argument for giving the present advantage to one rather than another hypothesis through something like Louis Brandeis' "fifty laboratories" theory. That famous Justice proposed that the different states (and territories) of the United States experiment with different economic and social models so that the best system might emerge by comparison. But no particular country need now, I think, eschew prohibition of pornography for that reason. There is already enough experimentation in the level of permissiveness the Report recommends, if not in more radical alternatives, in other countries.

But I have so far ignored the Williams strategy's insistence that cultural development must be conscious and reflective, must be, that is, self-development. That might be thought to suggest that cultural development should be the product of individuals deciding for themselves what form of life best suits their own condition or, if that seems too grand, what shoe seems to fit; and therefore to rule the enforcement hypothesis out of order from the start. But it is hard to see why the admittedly attractive idea, that society's search for the best conditions for fulfillment must be reflective and

self-conscious, demands this particular form of individualism. For in a democracy politics is an appropriate (some would say the appropriate) vehicle through which people strive to determine the circumstances of their situation and to give effect to their own convictions about the conditions of human flourishing. It is only in politics, for example, that people can express in any effective way their sense of justice, or of conservation of the art of the past, or of the design of the space in which they will live and work, or the education their children will, at least for the most part, receive. There are losers in politics, but we cannot say that a society's development of its own culture is unreflective or unconscious or otherwise not self-development just because the convictions of some people do not triumph.

Once we admit that political activity is part of the idea of social self-determination, then we cannot draw, from the idea that human beings should be conscious actors in the process of developing their own culture, any disqualification of the enforcement hypothesis as a theory about human flourishing to be given equal room with other theories. The Report states, as I said earlier, that it follows from this idea that human development is "a process itself properly constituted in part by free expression and the exchange of human communication."[13] But it is suddenly unclear what this means. This inference is unexceptionable, I think, if it means only that free speech as conventionally defined should be protected. But the inference does not hold if it means that people must have a right to privacy that prevents the majority from achieving the cultural environment that it, after full reflection, believes best. Suppose that the community is persuaded such a right exists, and that in consequence it would be wrong to forbid the use of pornography in private. That decision would sharply limit the ability of individuals consciously and reflectively to influence the conditions of their own and their children's development. It would limit their ability to bring about the cultural structure they think best, a structure in which sexual experience generally has dignity and beauty, without which structure their own and their families' sexual experience are likely to have these qualities in less degree. They would not be free to campaign for the enforcement hypothesis in politics on the same basis as others would be free to campaign, for example, for programs of conservation or of state aid to the arts; that is, simply by providing their reasons for believing that enforcement provided the best conditions for human fulfillment. They would meet the reply that a society that chose enforcement would become, for that reason, a society of automatons led by blind forces rather than a society in charge of its own affairs. But that reply is wrong. If we are concerned only with the power of individuals to influence the conditions in which they must try to thrive, any theory of self-development that forbids the majority the use of politics and the law, even the criminal law, is at least *prima facie* self-defeating.

All this points up the importance of not conflating the argument of the

Williams strategy, that people should be in charge of the development of the social conditions in which they try to flourish, rather than the unknowing objects of social forces, with the very different argument that each person, for some other reason, should have some sphere private to himself in which he is solely responsible, answerable only to his own character, about what he does. These two ideas are not (as is sometimes thought) two sides of the same coin, but are antagonistic ideas, because the protection of a private sphere, the recognition of an individual right to privacy of that sort, reduces the power of people generally to put into play their own ideas about the best circumstances for human flourishing. Their power to do this is reduced whether this right is given legal standing, through incorporation in some constitution like that of the United States, or just accepted as part of a moral constitution. The concept of a right to privacy therefore belongs not to the class of goal-based strategies for defending a permissive attitude to pornography, but to the very different class of right-based strategies, because that concept argues that people should have a private sphere even if this damages rather than advances society's long-term goals, and therefore gives most people less rather than more actual control over the design of their environment. The right to privacy cannot be extracted from even the sophisticated Williams version of a goal-based strategy, at least as it now stands.

So the main point remains. The Williams strategy should be as hospitable to the enforcement hypothesis as to the more permissive scheme of the Report. I must be careful not to misdescribe this point. I am not arguing (in the spirit of those who make this argument against liberalism) that the strategy is circular or self-contradictory. It is not my point, for example, that the strategy must apply the same skepticism to itself that it applies to theories about the desirable conditions for human development. Any political theory is entitled—indeed obliged—to claim truth for itself, and so to exempt itself from any skepticism it endorses. My point instead depends on distinguishing the content from the consequences of the Williams strategy. Those who favor the outright prohibition of pornography might, I agree, put their position on the same level as, and in flat opposition to, that strategy. They might argue that we can be certain that the best possibility for human development lies in a society that forbids all pornography everywhere, so that we should not allow even political discussion of alternatives. But they *need* not defend prohibition in that way. They might accept the Williams strategy, and appeal to it as warrant for political action aimed at testing their own convictions about the best developments for human flourishing (in which of course they believe though they cannot be certain). If they pitch their argument on this level, it is no answer that if they succeed they make the campaign for opposing views much more difficult or much less effective. For they can answer that any political decision, including the decision that

prohibition is wrong in principle, will have exactly that consequence for other views.

Opponents of prohibition would then be remitted to one or another of two substantive arguments the Report recognizes as possible arguments but does not itself make. They may make the heroic claim that a society in which people actually do read pornography in private will for that reason provide more desirable conditions for human excellence. The Report steadily and deliberately avoids that claim. Or they may make the different and perhaps more plausible claim that a society in which people are legally free to read pornography in private, even if some people actually do so, provides better conditions than a society in which no one does because no one can. This claim goes far beyond the argument of the Williams strategy, that different theories about the best conditions should be free to compete, because it argues that one such theory is better than other theories, not just that it might be. No doubt some members of the Committee do believe this, but the Report offers no grounds. We need a positive argument that freedom of individual choice whether or not to read sadistic novels or study photographs of oral sex is an essential or highly desirable condition for human flourishing. Or at least that it is an undesirable condition that people who want to do these things should be told that they cannot. The general skepticism of the Williams strategy does not even begin to make out such an argument, even as bolstered by the proposition that human development should be self-conscious rather than automatic.

A New Start

I hope it is now clear what fish I am trying to fry. I am not arguing that the Report's conclusions are too conservative, and certainly not that they are too liberal. But only that the goal-based strategy the Report uses is inadequate to support its conclusions. It does not follow from this that no better, more refined goal-based strategy could do so. But we should remember that the Committee included several members of great intellectual and practical ability, and that it had as its chairman a famous philosopher of unusual power and subtlety. It is evident why a goal-based strategy, which promises that things will go better for everyone in the long run if we accept what we do not like now, would seem an attractive premise for a political document. But it does not seem likely that any committee could extract much better arguments from that premise than this committee was able to do.

In any case, my arguments point up a general weakness of goal-based arguments that may be especially evident when these arguments are used to defend a liberal attitude toward pornography, but which is latent even when they are used to defend the protection of other unpopular activities like, for example, bogus or hateful political speech. Most of us feel, for rea-

sons we perhaps cannot fully formulate, that it would be wrong to prevent Communists from defending the Russian invasion of Afghanistan on Hyde Park soapboxes, or neo-Nazis from publishing tracts celebrating Hitler. The goal-based justification of these convictions proposes that even though we might be worse off in the short run by tolerating distasteful political speech, because it distresses us and because there is always some chance that it will prove persuasive to others, there are reasons why we shall nevertheless be better off in the long run—come nearer to fulfilling the goals we ought to set for ourselves—if we do tolerate that speech. This argument has the weakness of providing contingent reasons for convictions that we do not hold contingently. For the story usually told about why free speech is in our long-term interests is not drawn from any deep physical necessity like the laws of motion, or even deep facts about the genetic structure or psychic constitution of human beings; the argument is highly problematical, speculative and in any case marginal. If the story is true, we might say, it is only just true, and no one can have any overwhelming ground for accepting it. But our convictions about free speech are not tentative or halfhearted or marginal. They are not just barely convictions. We can easily construct a goal-based *explanation* of why people like us would develop convictions we thought deep and lasting, even though the advantages to us of having these convictions were both temporary and contingent. But that is beside the present point, which is rather that these explanations do not provide a *justification* of the meaning these convictions have for us.

This problem in all goal-based justifications of fundamental political convictions is aggravated, in the case of liberal convictions about pornography, because the goal-based story seems not only speculative and marginal, but implausible as well. In the case of free political speech, we might well concede, to the goal-based theory, that each person has an important interest in developing his own independent political convictions, because that is an essential part of his personality, and because his political convictions will be more authentically his own, more the product of his own personality, the more varied the opinions of others he encounters. We might also concede that political activity in a community is made more vigorous by variety, even by the entry, that is, of wholly despicable points of view. These are decent arguments why both individuals and the community as a whole are at least in certain respects better off when the Nazi has spoken his piece; they are arguments not only for liberty of political expression but also for more political speech rather than less. But the parallel arguments in the case of most pornography seem silly, and very few of those who defend peoples' right to read pornography in private would actually claim that the community or any individual is better off with more pornography rather than less. So a goal-based argument for pornography must do without what seem the strongest (though still contingent) strands in the goal-based argument for free speech. The Williams strategy ingeniously ignores that defect

by providing an argument for tolerance of pornography that, unlike the standard arguments for tolerance of speech, does not suppose that more of what is to be tolerated is better for everyone. But that argument fails, as we have seen, precisely because it does not include that supposition or anything like it. Its claim of skepticism toward the value of pornography (even assisted by the slippery slope) produces nothing stronger than impartial skepticism about the value of prohibiting it.

I want to consider what sort of an argument might be found in the other kind of strategy I mentioned at the outset, the rights-based strategy. Do people have moral or political rights such that it would be wrong to prohibit them from either publishing or reading or contemplating dirty books or pictures or films even if the community would be better off—provide more suitable conditions within which its members might develop—if they did not? Would these rights nevertheless permit the limited sorts of prohibitions that the Report accepts? Would these rights also permit restrictions like those the Report recommends on the public display of pornography that it does not prohibit altogether? I want to take the occasion of the Report, not only to ask these special questions about the proper attitude of the law toward pornography, but also to ask something more general, about what questions like these mean, and how they might even in principle be answered.

RIGHTS

Consider the following suggestion. People have the right not to suffer disadvantage in the distribution of social goods and opportunities, including disadvantage in the liberties permitted to them by the criminal law, just on the ground that their officials or fellow-citizens think that their opinions about the right way for them to lead their own lives are ignoble or wrong. I shall call this (putative) right the right to moral independence, and in this part I shall consider what force this right would have on the law of pornography if it were recognized. In the next part I shall consider what grounds we might have to recognize it.

The right to moral independence is a very abstract right (or, if you prefer, the statement of the right I gave is a very abstract statement of the right) because this statement takes no account of the impact of competing rights. It does not attempt to decide whether the right can always be jointly satisfied for everyone, or how conflicts with other rights, if they arise, are to be settled. These further questions, along with other related questions, are left for more concrete statements of the right. Or (what comes to the same thing) for statements of the more concrete rights that people have in virtue of the abstract right. Nevertheless, the questions I wish to put may usefully be asked even about the abstract statement or the abstract right.

Someone who appeals to the right of moral independence in order to jus-

tify a permissive legal regime of obscenity does not suppose that the community will be better off in the long run (according to some description of what makes a community better off like, for example, the description offered in the Williams strategy) if people are free to look at obscene pictures in private. He does not deny this. His argument is in the conditional mood: even if conditions will not then be so suitable for human flourishing as they might be, for example, nevertheless the right must be respected. But what force does the right then have? When does the government violate that right?

It violates the right, we may say, at least in this case: when the only apparent or plausible justification for a scheme of regulation of pornography includes the hypothesis that the attitudes about sex displayed or nurtured in pornography are demeaning or bestial or otherwise unsuitable to human beings of the best sort, even though this hypothesis may be true. It also violates that right when that justification includes the proposition that most people in the society accept that hypothesis and are therefore pained or disgusted when other members of their own community, for whose lives they understandably feel special responsibility, do read dirty books or look at dirty pictures. The right is therefore a powerful constraint on the regulation of pornography, or at least so it seems, because it prohibits giving weight to exactly the arguments most people think are the best arguments for even a mild and enlightened policy of restriction of obscenity. What room is left, by the apparently powerful right, for the government to do anything at all about pornography?

Suppose it is discovered that the private consumption of pornography does significantly increase the danger of crimes of violence, either generally or specifically crimes of sexual violence. Or suppose that private consumption has some special and deleterious effect on the general economy, by causing great absenteeism from work, for example, as drink or breakfast television is sometimes said to do. Then government would have, in these facts, a justification for the restraint and perhaps even for the prohibition of pornography that does not include the offending hypothesis either directly, by the assumption that the hypothesis is true, or indirectly, in the proposition that many people think it true. After all (as is often pointed out in discussions of obscenity, including the Williams Report), the Bible or Shakespeare might turn out to have these unfortunate consequences, in which case government would have a reason for banning these books that did not require a comparable hypothesis about them.

This possibility raises a slightly more subtle point. Suppose it were discovered that all forms of emotionally powerful literature (including Shakespeare, the Bible, and many forms of pornography) contributed significantly to crime. But the government responded to this discovery selectively, banning most examples of pornography and other literature it considered worthless, but allowing Shakespeare and the Bible nevertheless, on the

ground that these were of such literary and cultural value that it was worth the crime they caused to preserve them. Nothing in this selection and discrimination (as so far stated) violates the right to moral independence. The judgment in question—that pornography does not in fact contribute enough of literary value, or that it is not sufficiently informative or imaginative about the different ways in which people might express themselves or find value in their lives, to justify accepting the damage of crime as the cost of its publication—is not the judgment that those who do enjoy pornography have worse character on that account. Any judgment of literary or cultural value will be a judgment about which honest and reasonable people will disagree. But this is true of many other kinds of judgments that government must nevertheless make. The present judgment is no doubt special because it may be used as a screen to hide a different judgment that would offend the right to independence, the judgment that pornography should be treated differently from the Bible because the people who prefer it are worse people. That danger might be sufficiently strong so that a society jealous of the right of moral independence will, for prophylactic reasons, forbid officials to make the literary judgment that would distinguish *Sex Kittens* from *Hamlet* if both were found to provoke crime. That does not touch the present point, that the literary judgment is different, and does not itself threaten the right of independence; and it is worth adding that very few of the people who do admit to enjoying pornography claim distinct literary merit for it. They claim at most the kind of merit that others, with more conventional ideas about amusement, claim for thrillers.

But this is, in any case, only academic speculation, because there is no reason to suppose a sufficiently direct connection between crime and either *Sex Kittens* or *Hamlet* to provide a ground for banning either one as private entertainment. But what about public display? Can we find a plausible justification for restricting the display of pornography that does not violate the right of moral independence? We can, obviously, construct a certain argument in that direction, as follows. "Many people do not like to encounter genital displays on the way to the grocer. This taste is not, nor does it necessarily reflect, any adverse view of the character of those who do not mind such encounters. Someone who would not like to find pornography in his ordinary paths may not even object to finding it elsewhere. He may simply have tastes and preferences that reject certain combinations in his experience, like someone who likes pink sunsets but not pink houses in Belgravia, who does not object to neon in Leicester Square but would hate it in the Cotswolds. Or he may have a more structured or more consequentialist scheme of preferences about his environment. He may find or believe, for example, that his own delight in other peoples' bodies is lessened or made less sharp and special if nakedness becomes either too familiar to him or less peculiar to those occasions in which it provides him special pleasure, which

may be in museums or his own bedroom or both. Or that sex will come to be different and less valuable for him if he is too often or too forcefully reminded that it has different, more commercial or more sadistic, meaning for others. Or that his goal that his children develop certain similar tastes and opinions will be thwarted by the display or advertising that he opposes. None of these different opinions and complaints *must* be the product of some conviction that those with other opinions and tastes are people of bad character, any more than those who hope that state-supported theater will produce the classics exclusively must think that those who prefer experimental theater are less worthy people."

This picture of the motives people might have for not wanting to encounter pornography on the streets is a conceivable picture. But I suspect, as I suggested earlier, that it is far too crude and one-dimensional as a picture of what these motives actually are. The discomfort many people find in encountering blatant nudity on the hoardings is rarely so independent of their moral convictions as these various descriptions suggest. It is at least part of the offense, for many people, that they detest themselves for taking the interest in the proceedings that they do. It is a major part of the offense, for others, that they are so forcefully reminded of what their neighbors are like and, more particularly, of what their neighbors are getting away with. People object to the display of naked men and women in erotic poses, that is, even when these displays occur (as for commercial reasons they inevitably do) in those parts of cities that would be in no sense beautiful or enlightening even without the pornography. Even if we took the descriptions of peoples' motives in the argument I set out at face value, moreover, we should be forced to recognize the substantial influence of moral convictions just in those motives, for someone's sense of what he wants his own attitudes toward sex to be, and certainly his sense of what attitudes he hopes to encourage in his children, are not only influenced by, but constitute, his moral opinions in the broad sense.

We therefore encounter, in peoples' motives for objecting to the advertising or display of pornography, at least a mix and interaction of attitudes, beliefs, and tastes that rule out any confident assertion that regulation justified by appeal to these motives would not violate the right to moral independence. We do not know whether, if we could disentangle the different strands of taste, ambition, and belief, so as to winnow out those that express moral condemnation or would not exist but for it, the remaining strands would justify any particular scheme of regulation of display. This is not just a failure of information that would be expensive to obtain. The problem is more conceptual than that: the vocabulary we use to identify and individuate motives—our own as well as those of others—cannot provide the discrimination we need.

A society anxious to defend the abstract right to moral independence in

the face of this complexity, has two options at least. It might decide that if popular attitudes toward a minority or a minority practice are mixed in this way, so that the impact of adverse moral convictions can be neither excluded nor measured, then these attitudes should all be deemed to be corrupted by such convictions, and no regulation is permissible. Or it might decide that the case of mixed attitudes is a special kind of case in the administration of the abstract right, so that more concrete statements of what people are entitled to have under the right must take the fact of mixed attitudes into account. It might do this, for example, by stipulating, at the more concrete level, that no one should suffer *serious* damage through legal restraint when this can only be justified by the fact that what he proposes to do will frustrate or defeat preferences of others that we have reason to believe are mixed with or are consequences of the conviction that people who act in that way are people of bad character. This second option, which defines a concrete right tailored to the problem of mixed preferences, is not a relaxation or compromise of the abstract right, but rather a (no doubt controversial) application of it to that special situation. Which of the two options (or which further option) provides the best response to the problem of mixed motives is part of the more general problem of justification that I postponed to the next section. The process of making an abstract right successively more concrete is not simply a process of deduction or interpretation of the abstract statement but a fresh step in political theory.

If society takes the second option just described in the case of pornography (as I think it should, for reasons I describe later), then its officials must undertake to decide what damage to those who wish to publish or read pornography is serious and what is trivial. Once again reasonable and honest officials will disagree about this, but we are trying to discover, not an algorithm for a law of obscenity, but rather whether a plausible concrete conception of a plausible abstract right will yield a sensible scheme of regulation. We should therefore consider the character of the damage that would be inflicted on consumers of pornography by, say, a scheme of zoning that requires that pornographic materials be sold and films shown only in particular areas, a scheme of advertising that prohibits in public places advertisements that would widely be regarded as indecent, and a scheme of labeling so that those entering cinemas or shops whose contents they might find indecent would be warned. There are three main heads of damage that such a regime might inflict on consumers: inconvenience, expense, and embarrassment. Whether the inconvenience is serious will depend on the details of, for example, the zoning. But it should not be considered serious if shoppers for pornography need travel on average only as far as, say, shoppers for stereo equipment or diamonds or secondhand books need travel to find the centers of such trade. How far this scheme of restriction would increase the price of pornography is harder to predict. Perhaps the constraint

on advertising would decrease the volume of sales and therefore increase unit costs. But it seems unlikely that this effect would be very great, particularly if the legal ban runs to the character not to the extent of the advertising, and permits, as it should, not only stark "tombstone" notices, but the full range of the depressingly effective techniques through which manufacturers sell soap and video cassette recorders.

Embarrassment raises a more interesting and important question. Some states and countries have required people to identify themselves as belonging to a particular religion or holding certain political convictions just for the sake of that identification, and for the sake of the disadvantage it brings in its train. The Nazi's regime of yellow armbands for Jews, for example, or the registry of members of civil rights groups that some southern states established and the Supreme Court ruled unconstitutional in *NAACP v. Alabama ex rel Patterson*.[14] Since in cases like these identification is required just as a mark of public contempt, or just to provide the social and economic pressure that follows from that contempt, these laws are ruled out by even the abstract form of the right. But the situation is rather different if identification is a by-product rather than the purpose of a scheme of regulation, and is as voluntary as the distinct goals of regulation permit. It would violate the right of moral independence, plainly, if pornography houses were not allowed to use plain-brown-wrapper mail for customers who preferred anonymity, because embarrassment would be the point of that restriction, not a by-product. Also, I think, if the law forbade pornography shops from selling anything but pornography, so that a shy pornographer could not walk out of the shop with a new umbrella as well as a bulge in his coat pocket. But the right of moral independence does not carry with it any government obligation to insure that people may exercise that right in public places without its being known by the public that they do. Perhaps the government would be obliged to take special measures to guard against embarrassment in a society in which people actually were likely to suffer serious economic harm if they were seen leaving a shop carrying the wrong sign. But that is unlikely to be true about shy pornographers in this country now, who might sensibly be required to bear the social burden of being known to be the kind of people they are.

I conclude that the right to moral independence, if it is a genuine right, requires a permissive legal attitude toward the consumption of pornography in private, but that a certain concrete conception of that right nevertheless permits a scheme of restriction rather like the scheme that the Williams Report recommends. It remains to consider whether that right and that conception can themselves be justified in political theory. But I might first observe that nothing in my conclusion collides with my earlier claim that the Williams strategy, on which the Report relies, cannot support either its permissive attitude or its restrictive scheme. For I did not

argue, in support of that claim, that the restrictive scheme would impose great damage on individuals. I said only that the Williams strategy as a whole, which based its arguments not on the interests of pornographers but on the contribution they might make to a beneficial exchange of communication, failed to provide the necessary distinction. Nor do I now appeal to the ideal that is the nerve of that strategy—that the community be free to develop the best conditions for human flourishing—in support of my own conclusions about the law of pornography. I argue rather that, whether or not the instrumental claims of the Williams Report are sound, private liberty is required and public constraint permitted by an appealing conception of an important political right.

EQUALITY

A *Trump over Utility*

The rest of this essay considers the question of how the right to moral independence might be defended, both in its abstract form and in the more concrete conception we discussed in considering public display of pornography. This question is important beyond the relatively trivial problem of obscenity itself: the right has other and more important applications, and the question of what kinds of arguments support a claim of right is an urgent question in political theory.

Rights, I have argued elsewhere,[15] are best understood as trumps over some background justification for political decisions that states a goal for the community as a whole. If someone has a right to moral independence, this means that it is for some reason wrong for officials to act in violation of that right, even if they (correctly) believe that the community as a whole would be better off if they did. There are many different theories in the field about what makes a community better off on the whole; many different theories, that is, about what the goal of political action should be. One prominent theory (or rather group of theories) is utilitarianism in its familiar forms, which suppose that the community is better off if its members are on average happier or have more of their preferences satisfied. Another, and in certain ways different, theory is the theory we found in the Williams strategy, which argues that the community is better off if it provides the most desirable conditions for human development. There are of course many other theories about the true goal of politics, many of them much more different from either of these two theories than these are from each other. To some extent, the argument in favor of a particular right must depend on which of these theories about desirable goals has been accepted; it must depend, that is, on what general background justification for political decisions the right in question proposes to trump. In the following discus-

sion I shall assume that the background justification with which we are concerned is some form of utilitarianism, which takes, as the goal of politics, the fulfillment of as many of peoples' goals for their own lives as possible. This remains, I think, the most influential background justification, at least in the informal way in which it presently figures in politics in the Western democracies.[16]

Suppose we accept then that, at least in general, a political decision is justified if it promises to make citizens happier, or to fulfill more of their preferences, on average, than any other decision could. Suppose we assume that the decision to prohibit pornography altogether does meet that test, because the desires and preferences of publishers and consumers are outweighed by the desires and preferences of the majority, including their preferences about how others should lead their lives. How could any contrary decision, permitting even the private use of pornography, then be justified?

Two modes of argument might be thought capable of supplying such a justification. First, we might argue that, though the utilitarian goal states one important political ideal, it is not the only important ideal, and pornography must be permitted in order to protect some other ideal that is, in the circumstances, more important. Second, we might argue that further analysis of the grounds that we have for accepting utilitarianism as a background justification in the first place—further reflection of why we wish to pursue that goal—shows that utility must yield to some right of moral independence here. The first form of argument is pluralistic: it argues for a trump over utility on the ground that though utility is always important, it is not the only thing that matters, and other goals or ideals are sometimes more important. The second supposes that proper understanding of what utilitarianism is, and why it is important, will itself justify the right in question.

I do not believe that the first, or pluralistic, mode of argument has much prospect of success, at least as applied to the problem of pornography. But I shall not develop the arguments now that would be necessary to support that opinion. I want instead to offer an argument in the second mode, which is, in summary, this. Utilitarianism owes whatever appeal it has to what we might call its egalitarian cast. (Or, if that is too strong, would lose whatever appeal it has but for that cast.) Suppose some version of utilitarianism provided that the preferences of some people were to count for less than those of others in the calculation how best to fulfill most preferences overall either because these people were in themselves less worthy or less attractive or less well loved people, or because the preferences in question combined to form a contemptible way of life. This would strike us as flatly unacceptable, and in any case much less appealing than standard forms of utilitarianism. In any of its standard versions, utilitarianism can claim to provide a conception of how government treats people as equals, or, in any

case, how government respects the fundamental requirement that it must treat people as equals. Utilitarianism claims that people are treated as equals when the preferences of each, weighted only for intensity, are balanced in the same scales, with no distinctions for persons or merit. The corrupt version of utilitarianism just described, which gives less weight to some persons than to others, or discounts some preferences because these are ignoble, forfeits that claim. But if utilitarianism in practice is not checked by something like the right of moral independence (and by other allied rights), it will disintegrate, for all practical purposes, into exactly that version.

Suppose a community of many people including Sarah. If the Constitution sets out a version of utilitarianism which provides in terms that Sarah's preferences are to count for twice as much as those of others, then this would be the unacceptable, nonegalitarian version of utilitarianism. But now suppose that the constitutional provision is the standard form of utilitarianism, that is, that it is neutral toward all people and preferences, but that a surprising number of people love Sarah very much, and therefore strongly prefer that her preferences count for twice as much in the day-to-day political decisions made in the utilitarian calculus. When Sarah does not receive what she would have if her preferences counted for twice as much as those of others, then these people are unhappy, because their special Sarah-loving preferences are unfulfilled. If these special preferences are themselves allowed to count, therefore, Sarah will receive much more in the distribution of goods and opportunities than she otherwise would. I argue that this defeats the egalitarian cast of the apparently neutral utilitarian Constitution as much as if the neutral provision were replaced by the rejected version. Indeed, the apparently neutral provision is then self-undermining because it gives a critical weight, in deciding which distribution best promotes utility, to the views of those who hold the profoundly un-neutral (some would say anti-utilitarian) theory that the preferences of some should count for more than those of others.

The reply that a utilitarian anxious to resist the right to moral independence would give to this argument is obvious: utilitarianism does not give weight to the truth of that theory, but just to the fact that many people (wrongly) hold that theory and so are disappointed when the distribution the government achieves is not the distribution they believe is right. It is the fact of their disappointment, not the truth of their views, that counts, and there is no inconsistency, logical or pragmatic, in that. But this reply is too quick. For there is a particularly deep kind of contradiction here. Utilitarianism must claim (as I said earlier, any political theory must claim) truth for itself, and therefore must claim the falsity of any theory that contradicts it. It must itself occupy, that is, all the logical space that its content requires. But neutral utilitarianism claims (or, in any case, presupposes) that no one is, in principle, any more entitled to have any of his preferences ful-

filled than anyone else is. It argues that the only reason for denying the fulfillment of one person's desires, whatever these are, is that more or more intense desires must be satisfied instead. It insists that justice and political morality can supply no other reason. This is, we might say, the neutral utilitarian's *case* for trying to achieve a political structure in which the average fulfillment of preferences is as high as possible. The question is not whether a government can achieve that political structure if it counts political preferences like the preferences of the Sarah-lovers[17] or whether the government will then have counted any particular preference twice and so contradicted utilitarianism in that direct way. It is rather whether the government can achieve all this without implicitly contradicting that case.

Suppose the community contains a Nazi, for example, whose set of preferences includes the preference that Aryans have more and Jews less of their preferences fulfilled just because of who they are. A neutral utilitarian cannot say that there is no reason in political morality for rejecting or dishonoring that preference, for not dismissing it as just wrong, for not striving to fulfill it with all the dedication that officials devote to fulfilling any other sort of preference. For utilitarianism itself supplies such a reason: its most fundamental tenet is that peoples' preferences should be weighed on an equal basis in the same scales, that the Nazi theory of justice is profoundly wrong, and that officials should oppose the Nazi theory and strive to defeat rather than fulfill it. A neutral utilitarian is barred, for reasons of consistency, from taking the same politically neutral attitude to the Nazi's political preference that he takes toward other sorts of preferences. But then he cannot make the case just described in favor of highest average utility computed taking that preference into account.

I do not mean that endorsing someone's right to have his preference satisfied automatically endorses his preference as good or noble. The good utilitarian, who says that the pinball player is equally entitled to satisfaction of that taste as the poet is entitled to the satisfaction of his, is not for that reason committed to the proposition that a life of pinball is as good as a life of poetry. Only vulgar critics of utilitarianism would insist on that inference. The utilitarian says only that nothing in the theory of justice provides any reason why the political and economic arrangements and decisions of society should be any closer to those the poet would prefer than those the pinball player would like. It is just a matter, from the standpoint of political justice, of how many people prefer the one to the other and how strongly. But he cannot say that about the conflict between the Nazi and the neutral utilitarian opponent of Nazism, because the correct political theory, his political theory, the very political theory to which he appeals in attending to the fact of the Nazi's claim, does speak to the conflict. It says that what the neutral utilitarian prefers is just and accurately describes what people are, as a matter of political morality, entitled to have, but that what the Nazi

prefers is deeply unjust and describes what no one is entitled, as a matter of political morality, to have. But then it is contradictory to say, again as a matter of political morality, that the Nazi is as much entitled to the political system he prefers as is the utilitarian.

The point might be put this way. Political preferences, like the Nazi's preference, are on the same level—purport to occupy the same space—as the utilitarian theory itself. Therefore, though the utilitarian theory must be neutral between personal preferences like the preferences for pinball and poetry, as a matter of the theory of justice, it cannot, without contradiction, be neutral between itself and Nazism. It cannot accept at once a duty to defeat the false theory that some people's preferences should count for more than other people's and a duty to strive to fulfill the political preferences of those who passionately accept that false theory, as energetically as it strives for any other preferences. The distinction on which the reply to my argument rests, the distinction between the truth and the fact of the Nazi's political preferences, collapses, because if utilitarianism counts the fact of these preferences, it has denied what it cannot deny, which is that justice requires it to oppose them.

We could escape this point by distinguishing two different forms or levels of utilitarianism. The first would be presented simply as a thin theory about how a political constitution should be selected in a community whose members prefer different kinds of political theories. The second would be a candidate for the constitution to be so chosen; it might argue for a distribution that maximized aggregate satisfaction of personal preferences in the actual distribution of goods and opportunities, for example. In that case, the first theory would argue only that the preferences of the Nazi should be given equal weight with the preferences of the second sort of utilitarian in the choice of a constitution, because each is equally entitled to the constitution he prefers, and there would be no contradiction in that proposition. But of course the neutral utilitarian theory we are now considering is not a thin theory of that sort. It proposes a theory of justice as a full political constitution, not just a theory about how to choose one, and so it cannot escape contradiction through modesty.

Now the same argument holds (though perhaps less evidently) when the political preferences are not familiar and despicable, like the Nazi theory, but more informal and cheerful, like the preferences of the Sarah-lovers who think that her preferences should be counted twice. The latter might, indeed, be Sarahocrats who believe that she is entitled to the treatment they recommend by virtue of birth or other characteristics unique to her. But even if their preferences rise from special affection rather than from political theory, these preferences nevertheless invade the space claimed by neutral utilitarianism and so cannot be counted without defeating the case utilitarianism provides. My argument, therefore, comes to this. If utilitari-

anism is to figure as part of an attractive working political theory, it must be qualified so as to restrict the preferences that count by excluding political preferences of both the formal and informal sort. One very practical way to achieve this restriction is provided by the idea of rights as trumps over unrestricted utilitarianism. A society committed to utilitarianism as a general background justification which does not in terms disqualify any preferences might achieve that disqualification by adopting a right to political independence: the right that no one suffer disadvantage in the distribution of goods or opportunities on the ground that others think he should have less because of who he is or is not, or that others care less for him than they do for other people. The right of political independence would have the effect of insulating Jews from the preferences of Nazis, and those who are not Sarah from the preferences of those who adore her.

The right of moral independence can be defended in a parallel way. Neutral utilitarianism rejects the idea that some ambitions that people might have for their own lives should have less command over social resources and opportunities than others, except as this is the consequence of weighing all preferences on an equal basis in the same scales. It rejects the argument, for example, that some people's conception of what sexual experience should be like, and of what part fantasy should play in that experience, and of what the character of that fantasy should be, are inherently degrading or unwholesome. But then it cannot (for the reasons just canvassed) count the moral preferences of those who do hold such opinions in the calculation whether individuals who form some sexual minority, including homosexuals and pornographers, should be prohibited from the sexual experiences they want to have. The right of moral independence is part of the same collection of rights as the right of political independence, and it is to be justified as a trump over an unrestricted utilitarian defense of prohibitory laws against pornography, in a community of those who find offense just in the idea that their neighbors are reading dirty books, in much the same way as the latter right is justified as a trump over a utilitarian justification of giving Jews less or Sarah more in a society of Nazis or Sarah-lovers.

It remains to consider whether the abstract right to moral independence, defended in this way, would nevertheless permit restriction of public display of pornography in a society whose preferences against that display were backed by the mixed motives we reviewed in the last part. This is a situation in which the egalitarian cast of utilitarianism is threatened from not one but two directions. To the extent to which the motives in question are moral preferences about how others should behave, and these motives are counted, then the neutrality of utilitarianism is compromised. But to the extent to which these are the rather different sort of motives we reviewed, which emphasize not how others should lead their lives, but rather the char-

acter of the sexual experience people want for themselves, and these motives are disregarded, the neutrality of utilitarianism is compromised in the
other direction, for it becomes unnecessarily inhospitable to the special and
important ambitions of those who then lose control of a crucial aspect of
their own self-development. The situation is therefore not an appropriate
case for a prophylactic refusal to count any motive whenever we cannot be
sure that that motive is unmixed with moralism, because the danger of unfairness lies on both sides rather than only on one. The alternative I described in the preceding section is at least better than that. This argues that
restriction may be justified even though we cannot be sure that the preferences people have for restriction are untinged by the kind of preferences we
should exclude, provided that the damage done to those who are affected
adversely is not serious damage, even in their own eyes. Allowing restrictions on public display is in one sense a compromise; but it is a compromise
recommended by the right of moral independence, once the case for that
right is set out, not a compromise of that right.

Hart's Objections

There are, then, good grounds for those who accept utilitarianism as a general background justification for political decisions also to accept, as part of
the same package, a right of moral independence in the form that I have
just argued, would support or permit the major recommendations of the
Williams Report. I shall end this essay by considering certain objections
that H. L. A. Hart made, in 1980,[18] to a similar argument that I made some
years ago about the connection between utilitarianism and these rights.[19]
Hart's objections show what I think is a comprehensive misunderstanding of
this argument, which my earlier statement, as I now see, encouraged; it
might therefore be helpful, as insurance against a similar misunderstanding
now, to report these objections and my reasons for thinking that they mis-
conceive my argument.

I suggested, in my earlier formulation of the present argument, that if a
utilitarian counts preferences like the preferences of the Sarah-lovers, then
this is a "form" of double-counting because, in effect, Sarah's preferences
are counted twice, once on her own account, and once through the second-
order preferences of others that incorporate her preferences by reference.
Hart says that this is a mistake, because in fact no one's preferences are
counted twice, and it would *under*count the Sarah-lovers' preferences, and
so fail to treat them as equals, if their preferences in her favor were discarded. There would be something in this last point if votes rather than
preferences were in issue, because if someone wished to vote for Sarah's
success rather than his own, his role in the calculation would be exhausted
by this gift, and if his vote was then discarded, he might well complain that

he had been cheated of his equal power over political decision. But preferences, as these figure in utilitarian calculations, are not like votes in that way. Someone who reports more preferences to the utilitarian computer does not (except trivially) diminish the impact of other preferences he also reports; he rather increases the role of his preferences overall, compared with the role of other people's preferences, in the giant calculation. So someone who prefers Sarah's success to the success of people generally, and through the contribution of that preference to an unrestricted utilitarian calculation secures more for her, does not have any less for himself—for the fulfillment of his more personal preferences—than someone else who is indifferent to Sarah's fortunes.

I do not think that my description, that counting his preferences in favor of Sarah is a form of double-counting, is misleading or unfair. But this description was meant to summarize the argument, not to make it, and I will not press that particular characterization. As Hart notices, I made it only about some of the examples I gave in which unrestricted utilitarianism produced obviously inegalitarian results.) Hart makes more substantial points about a different example I used, which raised the question of whether homosexuals have the right to practice their sexual tastes in private. He thinks I want to say "that if, as a result of [preferences that express moral disapproval of homosexuals] tipping the balance, persons are denied some liberty, say to form some sexual relations, those so deprived suffer because by this result their concept of a proper or desirable form of life is despised by others, and this is tantamount to treating them as inferior to or of less worth than others, or not deserving of equal concern and respect."[20]

But this misstates my point. It is not the result (or, as Hart later describes it, the "upshot") of the utilitarian calculation that causes or achieves the fact that homosexuals are despised by others. It is rather the other way round: if someone is denied liberty of sexual practice in virtue of a utilitarian justification that depends critically on other people's moralistic preferences, then he suffers disadvantage in virtue of the fact that his concept of a proper life is already despised by others. Hart says that the "main weakness" in my argument—the feature that makes it "fundamentally wrong"—is that I assume that if someone's liberty is restricted, this must be interpreted as a denial of his treatment as an equal. But my argument is that this is not inevitably or even usually so, but only when the constraint is justified in some way that depends on the fact that others condemn his convictions or values. Hart says that the interpretation of denial of liberty as a denial of equal concern is "least credible" in exactly the case I discuss, that is, when the denial is justified through a utilitarian argument, because, he says, the message of that justification is not that the defeated minority or their moral convictions are inferior, but only that they are too few to outweigh the preferences of the majority, which can only be achieved if the

minority is denied the liberty it wishes. But once again this ignores the distinction I want to make. If the utilitarian justification for denying liberty of sexual practice to homosexuals can succeed without counting the moralistic preferences of the majority in the balance (as it might if there was good reason to believe what is in fact incredible, that the spread of homosexuality fosters violent crime), then the message of prohibition would be only the message Hart finds, which might be put this way: "It is impossible that everyone be protected in all his interests, and the interests of the minority must yield, regrettably, to the concern of the majority for its safety." There is, at least in my present argument, no denial of treatment as an equal in that message. But if the utilitarian justification cannot succeed without relying on the majority's moralistic preferences about how the minority should live, and the government nevertheless urges that justification, then the message is very different and, in my view, nastier. It is exactly that the minority must suffer because others find the lives they propose to lead disgusting, which seems no more justifiable in a society committed to treating people as equals, than the proposition we earlier considered and rejected as incompatible with equality, that some people must suffer disadvantage under the law because others do not like them.

Hart makes further points. He suggests, for example, that it was the "disinterested" political preferences of liberals that tipped the balance in favor of repealing laws against homosexual relationships in 1967 in England, and he asks how anyone could object that counting *those* preferences at that time offended anyone's right to be treated as an equal. But this question misunderstands my point in a fundamental way. I do not argue—how could anyone argue?—that citizens in a democracy should not campaign and vote for what they think is just. The question is not whether people should work for justice, but rather what test we and they should apply to determine what is just. Utilitarianism holds that we should apply this test: we should work to achieve the maximum possible satisfaction of the preferences we find distributed in our community. If we accepted this test in an unrestricted way, then we would count the attractive political convictions of the 1960s liberals simply as data, to be balanced against the less attractive convictions of others, to see which carried the day in the contest of number and intensity. Conceivably the liberal position would have won this contest. Probably it would not have.

But I have been arguing that this is a false test, which undermines the case for utilitarianism, if political preferences of either the liberals or their opponents are counted and balanced to determine what justice requires. That is why I recommend, as part of any overall political theory in which utilitarianism figures as a background justification, rights to political and moral independence. But the liberals who campaigned in the interests of homosexuals in England in the 1960s most certainly did not embrace the

test I reject. They *expressed* their own political preferences in their votes and arguments, but they did not *appeal to* the popularity of these preferences as providing an argument in itself for what they wanted, as the unrestricted utilitarian argument I oppose would have encouraged them to do. Perhaps they appealed instead to something like the right of moral independence. In any case they did not rely on any argument inconsistent with that right. Nor is it necessary for us to rely on any such argument to say that what they did was right, and treated people as equals. The proof is this: the case for reform would have been just as strong in political theory even if there had been very few or no heterosexuals who wanted reform, though of course reform would not then have been practically possible. If so, then we cannot condemn the procedure that produced reform on the ground that that procedure offended anyone's right to independence.

Hart's misunderstanding here was no doubt encouraged by my own description of how rights like the right to moral independence function in a constitutional system, like that of the United States, which uses rights as a test of the legality of legislation. I said that a constitutional system of this sort is valuable when the community as a whole harbors prejudices against some minority or convictions that the way of life of that minority is offensive to people of good character. In that situation the ordinary political process is antecedently likely to reach decisions that would fail the test we have constructed, because these decisions would limit the freedom of the minority and yet could not be justified, in political theory, except by assuming that some ways of living are inherently wrong or degrading, or by counting the fact that the majority thinks them so as itself part of the justification. Since these *repressive* decisions would then be wrong, for the reasons I offer, the constitutional right forbids them in advance.

The decision for reform that Hart describes would not—could not—be a decision justified only on these offending grounds. Even if the benign liberal preferences figured as data rather than argument, as I think they should not, no one would be in a position to claim the right to moral or political independence as a shield against the decision that was in fact reached. But someone might have been led to suppose, by my discussion, that what I condemn is any political process that would allow any decision to be taken if people's reasons for supporting one decision rather than another are likely to lie beyond their own personal interests. I hope it is now plain why this is wrong. *That* position would not allow a democracy to vote for social welfare programs, or foreign aid, or conservation for later generations. Indeed, in the absence of an adequate constitutional system, the only hope for justice is precisely that people will vote with a disinterested sense of fairness. I condemn a political process that assumes that the fact that people have such reasons is itself part of the case in political morality for what they favor. Hart's heterosexual liberals may have been making the following ar-

gument to their fellow-citizens. "We know that many of you find the idea of homosexual relationships troubling and even offensive. Some of us do as well. But you must recognize that it would deny equality, in the form of moral independence, to count the fact that we have these feelings as a justification for penal legislation. Since that is so, we in fact have no justification for the present law, and we ought, in all justice, to reform it." Nothing in this argument counts the fact that either the liberals or those they address happen to have any particular political preferences or convictions as itself an argument: the argument is made by appeal to justice not to the fact that many people want justice. There is nothing in that argument that fails to treat homosexuals as equals. Quite the contrary. But that is just my point.

I shall consider certain of the remaining objections Hart makes together. He notices my claim, that the rights people have depend on the background justification and political institutions that are also in play, because the argument for any particular right must recognize that right as part of a complex package of other assumptions and practices that it trumps. But he finds this odd. It may make sense to say, he remarks, that people *need* rights less under some forms of government than others. But does it make sense to say that they *have* less rights in one situation rather than another? He also objects to my suggestion (which is at the center of the argument I made in the last section) that rights that have long been thought to be rights to liberty, like the right of homosexuals to freedom of sexual practice or the right of pornographers to look at what they like in private, are really (at least in the circumstances of modern democracies) rights to treatment as an equal. That proposition, which Hart calls "fantastic," would have the consequence, he says, that a tyrant who had forbidden one form of sexual activity or the practice of one religion would actually eliminate the evil rather than increase it if he broadened his ban to include all sex and all religions, and in this way removed the inequality of treatment. The vice in prohibitions of sexual or religious activity, he says, is that these diminish liberty, not equal liberty; adding a violation of equality to the charge makes equality an empty and idle idea with no work to do.

These different objections are plainly connected, because they suppose that whatever rights people have are at least in large part timeless rights necessary to protect enduring and important interests fixed by human nature and fundamental to human development, like interests in the choice of sexual partners and acts and choice of religious conviction. That is a familiar theory of what rights are and what they are for, and I said that I would not give my reasons, in this essay, for thinking that it is in the end an inadequate theory of rights. I did say that this theory is unlikely to produce a defense of the right I have been considering, which is the right of moral independence as applied to the use of pornography, because it seems im-

plausible that any important human interests are damaged by denying dirty books or films. But that is not much of an argument against the general fundamental-interests theory of rights, because those who accept that theory might be ready to concede—perhaps even to insist—that the appeal to rights in favor of pornographers is an error that cheapens the idea of rights, and that there is nothing in political morality that condemns the prohibition of pornography altogether if that is what will best fulfill the preferences of the community as a whole.

My aim is to develop a theory of rights that is relative to the other elements of a political theory, and to explore how far that theory might be constructed from the exceedingly abstract (but far from empty) idea that government must treat people as equals. That theory makes rights relative in only one way. I am anxious to show how rights fit into different packages, so that I want to see, for example, which rights should be accepted as trumps over utility if utility is accepted, as many people think it should be accepted, as the proper background justification. That is an important question because, as I said, at least an informal kind of utilitarianism has for some time been accepted in practical politics. It has supplied, for example, the working justification of most of the constraints on our liberty through law that we accept as proper. But it does not follow from this investigation that I must endorse (as I am sometimes said to endorse)[21] the package of utilitarianism together with the rights that utilitarianism requires as the best package that can be constructed. I do not. Though rights are relative to packages, one package might still be chosen over others as better, and I doubt that in the end any package based on any familiar form of utilitarianism will turn out to be best. Nor does it follow from my argument that there are no rights that any defensible package must contain— no rights that are in this sense natural rights—though the argument that there are such rights, and the explanation of what these are, must obviously proceed in a rather different way from the route I followed in arguing for the right to moral independence as a trump over utilitarian justifications.

But if rights figure in complex packages of political theory, it is both unnecessary and too crude to look to rights for the only defense against either stupid or wicked political decisions. No doubt Hitler and Nero violated whatever rights any plausible political theory would provide; but it is also true that the evil these monsters caused could find no support even in the background justification of any such theory. Suppose some tyrant (an Angelo gone even more mad) did forbid sex altogether on penalty of death, or banned all religious practice in a community whose members were all devout. We should say that what he did (or tried to do) was insane or wicked or that he was wholly lacking in the concern for his subjects which is the most basic requirement that political morality imposes on those who gov-

ern. Perhaps we do not need the idea of equality to explain that last requirement. (I am deliberately cautious here.) But neither do we need the idea of rights.

We need rights, as a distinct element in political theory, only when some decision that injures some people nevertheless finds *prima facie* support in the claim that it will make the community as a whole better off on some plausible account of where the community's general welfare lies. But the most natural source of any objection we might have to such a decision is that, in its concern with the welfare or prosperity or flourishing of people on the whole, or in the fulfillment of some interest widespread within the community, the decision pays insufficient attention to its impact on the minority; and some appeal to equality seems a natural expression of an objection from that source. We want to say that the decision is wrong, in spite of its apparent merit, because it does not take the damage it causes to some into account in the right way and therefore does not treat these people as equals entitled to the same concern as others.

That charge is never self-validating. It must be developed through some theory about what equal concern requires, or, as in the case of the argument I offered, about what the background justification itself supposes that equal concern requires. Others will inevitably reject any such theory. Someone may claim, for example, that equal concern requires only that people be given what they are entitled to have when their preferences are weighed in the scales with the preferences, including the political and moral preferences, of others. In that case (if I am correct that the right to sexual freedom is based in equality), he would no longer support that right. But how could he? Suppose the decision to ban homosexuality even in private is the decision that is reached by the balance of preferences that he thinks respects equality. He could not say that, though the decision treats homosexuals as equals, by giving them all that equal concern for their situation requires, the decision is nevertheless wrong because it invades their liberty. If some constraints on liberty can be justified by the balance of preferences, why not this one?[22] Suppose he falls back on the idea that sexual freedom is a fundamental interest. But does it treat people as equals to invade their fundamental interests for the sake of minor gains to a very large number of other citizens? Perhaps he will say that it does, because the fundamental character of the interests invaded have been taken into account in the balancing process, so that if these are outweighed the gains to others, at least in the aggregate, were shown to be too large in all fairness to be ignored. But if this is so, then deferring to the interests of the outweighed minority would be giving the minority more attention than equality allows, which is favoritism. How can he then object to the decision the balancing process reached? So if anyone really does think that banning homosexual relationships treats homosexuals as equals, when this is the decision reached by an unrestricted

utilitarian balance, he seems to have no very persuasive grounds left to say that that decision nevertheless invades their rights. My hypothesis, that the rights which have traditionally been described as consequences of a general right to liberty are in fact the consequences of equality instead, may in the end prove to be wrong. But it is not, as Hart says it is, "fantastic."

EIGHTEEN

The Farber Case:
Reporters and Informers

IN 1978 Dr. Mario Jascalevich went on trial in New Jersey, for the murder, by curare poisoning, of a number of hospital patients in 1965 and 1966. His indictment was the direct result of a series of articles about the deaths of these patients written by a reporter for *The New York Times*, Myron Farber. Jascalevich's lawyer, Raymond Brown, asked the trial judge to order Farber and the *Times* to turn over to the defense all the notes, memoranda, interview records, and other material Farber had compiled during his investigation. Judge Arnold ordered, instead, that all such material be delivered to him, so that he himself could determine whether any of it was sufficiently relevant that it should be given to Brown. Farber refused this order, and was jailed for contempt, though he was subsequently released. The *Times* at first refused to deliver any material in its control, and was also cited for contempt, and forced to pay large daily fines. It later handed over certain files, but the judge who imposed the fines, Judge Trautwein, charged that these files had been "sanitized," and did not cure the contempt.

Farber and the *Times* appealed to the New Jersey Supreme Court, claiming that Judge Arnold's order was illegal on two different grounds. They argued that the order violated the New Jersey "Shield Law," which provides that in any legal proceeding a journalist "has a privilege to refuse to disclose" any "source" or "news or information obtained in the course of pursuing his professional activity." They also argued that, quite apart from the Shield Law, the order violated their rights under the First Amendment to the United States Constitution, which provides for freedom of the press.

EACH of these legal arguments is controversial. It is arguable that the Shield Law, insofar as it grants reporters a privilege not to disclose information that might tend to prove an accused criminal innocent, is unconstitutional because it denies the accused a right to a fair trial guaranteed by the Sixth Amendment. If so, then Judge Arnold acted properly in asking

that Farber's notes and material be furnished to him privately so that he could determine whether any of them might tend to support Dr. Jascalevich's innocence.

The First Amendment argument is weaker still. The Supreme Court in a 1972 decision, *Branzburg v. Hayes*, denied that the First Amendment automatically grants journalists a privilege to withhold sources and other information in legal proceedings. Four of the five majority Justices stated categorically that journalists have no special privilege under the First Amendment beyond those of ordinary citizens. Mr. Justice Powell agreed that the reporters in the cases the Court was considering did not have the privileges they asserted. But he added, in a short and cryptic concurring opinion, that in some circumstances the First Amendment might require courts to protect reporters from disclosure orders which serve no "legitimate need of law enforcement." He spoke of the need to strike "a proper balance between freedom of the press and the obligation of all citizens to give relevant testimony with respect to criminal conduct."

I do not interpret Powell's opinion as recognizing a First Amendment privilege against disclosure ordered at the request of a criminal defendant, which is a very different matter from disclosure requested by the prosecution or other law enforcement agencies. State courts have disagreed about the correct interpretation of Powell's opinion, however, and some have recognized a reporter's privilege to withhold information requested by the defense when it appears that that information would be at best only tangentially relevant to the defense's case. But even if this interpretation of Powell's opinion is correct, Judge Arnold acted properly in ordering the material furnished to him privately, so that he could determine its relevance and importance to the defense, and the extent to which "freedom of the press" would be compromised by its public disclosure.

So it is at least doubtful that the legal arguments on which Farber and the *Times* relied are sound. The affair has been debated publicly, however, not as a technical legal issue but as an event raising important questions of political principle. Commentators say that the dispute is a conflict between two fundamental political rights, each of which is protected by the Constitution. Farber and the *Times* (supported by many other newspapers and reporters) appealed to the right of free speech and publication; they claimed that this right, crucial in a democracy, is violated when the press is subjected to orders that impede its ability to gather information.

Those who supported Judge Arnold argued that the right of free speech and publication, though of fundamental importance, is not absolute, and must sometimes yield to competing rights. They therefore appealed to the principle, which they took to be paramount, that a criminal defendant has a

right to a fair trial, which right, they said, includes the right to use any material that he might reasonably think supports his innocence. Both sides shared the assumption that in these circumstances one or both of two important civil rights must be compromised to some degree, though they disagreed where the compromise should be struck.

But the assumption they shared is wrong. The privilege claimed by Farber has nothing to do with the political right to speak or publish free from censorship or constraint. No official had ordered him not to investigate or publish what he wanted, or threatened him with jail for what he did publish. Judge Arnold's subpoena was very different from the government's attempts to stop *The New York Times* from publishing the Pentagon Papers or from the prosecution of Daniel Ellsberg or even the civil actions against Frank Snepp. It is, no doubt, valuable to the public that reporters have access to confidential information. But this is not a matter of anyone's right. The question raised by the *Farber* case is not the difficult question of how to compromise competing rights, but the different question of how much the efficiency of reporters, valued by the public, must nevertheless be sacrificed in order to ensure that the right to a fair trial is not compromised at all.

THE PUBLIC argument over the *Farber* case failed to notice an important distinction between two kinds of arguments that are used to justify a legal rule or some other political decision. Justifications of *principle* argue that a particular rule is necessary in order to protect an individual right that some person (or perhaps group) has against other people, or against the society or government as a whole. Antidiscrimination laws, like the laws that prohibit prejudice in employment or housing, can be justified on arguments of principle: individuals do have a right not to suffer in the distribution of such important resources because others have contempt for their race.

Justifications of *policy*, on the other hand, argue that a particular rule is desirable because that rule will work in the general interest, that is, for the benefit of the society as a whole. Government subsidies to certain farmers, for example, may be justified, not on the ground that these farmers have any right to special treatment, but because it is thought that giving subsidies to them will improve the economic welfare of the community as a whole. Of course, a particular rule may be justified by both sorts of arguments. It may be true, for example, both that the very poor have a right to free medical treatment and that providing treatment for them will work for the general interest because it will provide a healthier labor force.

But the distinction is nevertheless of great importance, because sometimes principle and policy argue in opposite directions, and when they do (unless the considerations of policy are of dramatic importance, so that the community will suffer a catastrophe if they are ignored) policy must yield to

principle. It is widely thought, for example, that crime would decrease, trials be less expensive, and the community better off as a whole if strict rules of criminal procedure that guard against the conviction of the innocent, at the inevitable cost of some acquittal of the guilty, were abandoned. But that is an argument of policy against these procedural rules, and so it would not justify relaxing the rules if those who are accused of crime have a right (as most liberals think they do) to the protection the rules provide.

THE DISTINCTION between principle and policy is relevant to the *Farber* case because the arguments Farber and the *Times* made, in defense of a special reporter's privilege to withhold information, were arguments of policy not principle. I do not mean that classical First Amendment arguments are arguments of policy; on the contrary, the core of the First Amendment is a matter of principle. Individual citizens have a right to express themselves free from government censorship; no official may limit the content of what they say, even if that official believes he has good policy reasons for doing so, and even if he is right. Many Americans thought that it was in the national interest to censor those who opposed the war in Vietnam. No doubt it was in the interest of the community of Skokie, Illinois, that the American Nazi Party be forbidden to march through that town. But as a matter of principle the war protesters had a right to speak and the Nazis a right to march, protected by the Constitution, and the courts so decided.

Reporters, columnists, newscasters, authors, and novelists have the same right of free expression as other citizens, in spite of the great power of the press. Peter Zenger, the colonial publisher with whom Farber was sometimes compared, was jailed because he attacked the governor in print, and it was the object of the press clause of the First Amendment to prohibit that form of censorship. But journalists do not, as a matter of principle, have any greater right of free speech than anyone else.

There are, however, reasons of policy that may justify special rules enhancing the ability of reporters to investigate. If their confidential sources are protected from disclosure, more people who fear exposure will talk to them, and the public may benefit. There is a particular need for confidentiality, for example, and a special public interest in hearing what informers may say, when the informer is an official reporting on corruption or official misconduct, or when the information is information about a crime.

This is the argument of policy that justifies the Shield laws many states have enacted, like the New Jersey law described earlier, and that justifies a variety of other special privileges journalists enjoy. The Justice Department has adopted guidelines, for example, instructing its agents not to seek confidential information from reporters unless the information is crucial and unavailable from other sources. The special position of the press is justified, not because reporters have special rights, but because it is thought that the

community as a whole will benefit from their special treatment, just as wheat farmers might be given a subsidy, not because they are entitled to it, but because the community will benefit from that.

THE *Times*'s own arguments confirmed that the privilege it sought is a matter of policy not principle. It argued that important sources would "dry up" if Judge Arnold's order were upheld. It is hard to evaluate that argument, though it does not seem powerful, even as an argument of policy. The Supreme Court's decision in *Branzburg v. Hayes,* though its full force is debatable, plainly held that a reporter may be forced to reveal his sources when that information would be crucial to a defendant's case, as determined by a trial judge. So even now reporters cannot, or should not, flatly promise an informer confidentiality. Any such promise must be qualified, if the reporter is scrupulous, by the statement that under certain circumstances, not entirely defined by previous court decisions, and impossible to predict in advance, a court may legally compel disclosure.

Judge Arnold's order in Farber's case—that he be allowed to review a reporter's notes to determine whether any material there would be important to the defendant's case, even though the defense had not demonstrated the probability of such material—arguably extended the *Branzburg* limitations on confidentiality. But it is unclear how much the extension, if any, increased the risk that public disclosure would finally be made, and unclear whether many informers not already deterred by *Branzburg* would be deterred by the additional risk of disclosure to a judge alone. It is therefore entirely speculative how far the general welfare would suffer if the information that might be provided by informers of that special sort were lost.

In any event, however, this argument of policy, however strong or weak as an argument of policy, must yield to the defendant's genuine rights to a fair trial, even at some cost to the general welfare. It provides no more reason for overriding these rights than the policy argument in favor of convicting more guilty criminals provides for overriding the rights of those who might be innocent. In both cases there is no question of competing rights, but only the question of whether the community will pay the cost, in public convenience or welfare, that respect for individual rights requires. The rhetoric of the popular debate over *Farber,* which supposed that the press has rights that must be "balanced" against the defendant's rights, was profoundly misleading.

It is also dangerous because this rhetoric confuses the special privileges newspapers seek, justified on grounds of policy, with genuine First Amendment rights. Even if this special privilege has some constitutional standing (as the four dissenting Justices in *Branzburg* suggest), it has been and will continue to be sharply limited to protect a variety of other principles and policies. It would be unfortunate if these inevitable limitations were under-

stood to signal a diminished concern for rights of free speech generally. They might then be taken as precedents for genuine limitations on that fundamental right—precedents, for example, for censorship of political statements on grounds of security.

It is both safer and more accurate to describe the privilege of confidentiality the press claims not as part of a constitutional right to freedom of expression or publication but as a privilege frankly grounded in efficiency, like the privilege the FBI claims not to name its informers, or the executive privilege Nixon claimed not to turn over his tapes. In *Rovario v. United States,* the Supreme Court held that neither the FBI nor its informers have any right (even a *prima facie* right) to secrecy, although it conceded that, for reasons of policy, it would be wise for courts not to demand disclosure in the absence of some positive showing that the information would be important to the defense.

A President's executive privilege is, as the Court emphasized in the Nixon case, not a matter of his right, or the right of the government as a whole. It is a privilege conferred for reasons of policy, in order that the executive may function efficiently, and it must therefore yield when there is reason to believe that a different public interest—the public's interest in guarding against executive crime—demands constraint on the privilege. If the strong policy arguments in favor of executive privilege must yield when that privilege would jeopardize the prosecution of a crime, then *a fortiori* a reporter's privilege, supported by weaker policy arguments, must yield when it opposes a defendant's right to gather material that might prove him innocent.

So the question raised by *Farber* is simply the question of how far the defendant's moral and constitutional right to information extends, not just against reporters, but against anyone who has the information he wants. Several shrewd commentators, who do not dispute that the journalist's privilege must give way if the information in question is vital to the defense, nevertheless argue that Judge Arnold's order was wrong in this case because Brown, the defense lawyer, had not shown any reasonable prospect that Farber's notes were important to his case. They point out that it would be intolerable if every criminal defendant was able to subpoena all the notes and files of any newspaper which had reported on his case, in the thin hope that something unexpected might turn up. Lawyers call that sort of investigation a "fishing expedition"; and courts have always refused defendants an opportunity to fish in anyone's files.

Indeed, it has been suggested that Brown made his request not because he believed he would discover anything useful to his client but because he hoped the request would be refused, so that he could later claim, on appeal, that the trial was unfair. (It has also been suggested that Judge Arnold or-

dered the material requested to be shown to him privately, instead of rejecting the request outright, to frustrate this supposed strategy.) It would have been better, these commentators suggest, for the judge to require some initial showing by the defense why it was reasonable to suppose that the files would contain relevant material, before ordering the files to be shown to him alone.

EVEN THIS MORE moderate position seems wrong on the facts of this particular case, however. Farber's investigations were responsible for the police reopening a murder case years after their own investigation had been suspended. He accumulated a great deal of information not previously available, and it is not disputed that this information was the proximate cause of the indictment. In particular, Farber discovered and interviewed witnesses who now appear to be vital to the prosecution and who might have made statements to him that either amplified or contradicted their testimony or the accounts he published. There is, of course, no suggestion here that Farber deliberately withheld anything that would be helpful to the defense. But he, like any other reporter, exercised editorial judgment, and he should not, in any case, be expected to be sensitive to the same details that would interest a good lawyer whose client is on trial for murder.

These facts are sufficient to distinguish Farber's case from imagined cases in which the newspaper has done not much more than report on facts or proceedings developed or initiated by others. Judge Arnold held that Farber's unusual role in the case in itself *constituted* a showing of sufficient likelihood that his files contain material a competent defense lawyer should see; sufficient at least to justify the judge's own preliminary examination of the file. Perhaps he would have required a further showing of probable relevance, or a more precise statement of the material sought, if the trial were not a trial for murder. Perhaps another judge would have required some further precision even in a murder case. No doubt Judge Arnold should have held a hearing at which lawyers for Farber and the *Times* could have put their legal objections and asked for greater specificity before they were found in contempt. (The New Jersey Supreme Court held that in the future such a hearing must be held if requested.) Nevertheless, Judge Arnold's decision, that the facts of this case in themselves constituted the necessary demonstration, showed commendable sensitivity to the problems of a defendant faced with an investigation whose very secrecy deprived him of the knowledge he needed to show his need to know.

BUT IT WAS NOT, I should add, reasonable to order Farber to jail or to order the *Times* to pay punitive daily fines while their legal arguments were

pending before appellate courts. They relied in good faith on their under-standing of the Shield Law and the First Amendment.[1] It is useless to say that they should have complied with Judge Arnold's order and contested its legality later. They believed that their rights would have been violated and the principles at stake compromised, even by an initial compliance with the judge's order. They were wrong, but our legal system often gains when people who believe that law and principle are on their side choose not to comply with orders they believe illegal, at least until appellate courts have had a chance to consider their arguments fully, and it served no purpose to jail Farber or fine the *Times* before their arguments were heard. Certainly it was not necessary to defend the dignity of Judge Arnold's court or of the criminal process.

The courts must at all costs secure a criminal defendant's right to a fair trial. But within that limit they should show, not outrage, but courtesy and even gratitude to people like Myron Farber, who act at personal sacrifice to provide the constant judicial review of principle that is the Constitution's last protection.

NINETEEN

Is the Press Losing the First Amendment?

THE PRESS has had an up and down time in the courts recently. Several decisions excited its fear that the protection of the First Amendment of the Constitution was shrinking. One low point was the Supreme Court's decision in 1980 in the amazing case of *United States v. Snepp*, in which the Supreme Court ordered an author to turn over all his profits to the government without even holding a hearing on the issue. But the press has also won what it regards as important victories. One was the 1980 *Richmond Newspapers* case, in which the Court reversed its decision in an earlier case and held that reporters, at least in principle, have a right to attend criminal trials even when the defendant wishes to exclude them.[1]

United States v. Snepp is much the more important of the two cases. Frank Snepp signed a contract when he joined the CIA, promising to submit to it before publication anything he later wrote about it. The CIA argues that that agreement, which it obtains from every agent, is necessary so that it can make its own judgment in advance about whether any of the material an author proposes to publish is classified, and take legal action to enjoin what it does consider classified if the author does not accept its judgment. Snepp wrote a book called *Decent Interval*, after leaving the agency, in which he sharply criticized the CIA's behavior in Vietnam during the final months of the war.[2] He feared that the agency would use its right to review his manuscript to delay and harass him by claiming that matters of no importance to security were classified, as the agency had certainly done in the case of Victor Marchetti, another former agent who had written and submitted a book.[3] After much indecision, Snepp decided to publish his book without submitting it to the CIA first.

The agency sued him under the contract. Snepp argued that the First Amendment made his contractual agreement null and void because it was a form of censorship. But neither the federal district court nor the Circuit Court of Appeals, to which Snepp appealed, accepted that claim. The district court ordered Snepp, by way of remedy, to hand over to the govern-

ment all his profits on the book—his only earnings for several years of work—but the Circuit Court did reverse the district court on this point. It said that the government must be content with such actual financial damages as it could prove it suffered because Snepp had broken his contract, which is the normal remedy in breach of contract cases.

Snepp appealed to the Supreme Court on the First Amendment point. The government asked the Court *not* to take the case for review, and said that it was satisfied under the circumstances with the damage remedy the Circuit Court had ordered. But it added that if the Court did take the case, it would like the opportunity to argue that the Court should reinstate the district court's much more onerous remedy. In the end the Court did accept the case, against the government's wishes, but, as it turned out, only for the purpose of reinstating the harsher penalty. The Court did that, contrary to all traditions of judicial fairness, without offering opportunity for argument to anyone. A court that is supposedly dominated by the ideal of judicial restraint twisted principles of procedural fairness to reach a result for which no party had asked.

Some journalists speculate that the Court is furious with the press over *The Brethren,* Woodward and Armstrong's "inside story" of the Court published in 1980, and took this opportunity for revenge.[4] But many First Amendment lawyers take the more worrying view that the case is only the latest and most dramatic example of the decline of free speech in the United States.

It is worth describing the evidence for this gloomy opinion in some detail. No leading constitutional lawyer (except Mr. Justice Black) has ever thought that the First Amendment bars the government from any conceivable regulation of speech. It has always been possible for people to sue one another in American courts for libel and slander, for example, and even the most famous defenders of free speech have conceded that no one has a constitutional right to cry "fire" in a crowded theater or publish information about troop movements in time of war. Nevertheless, there have been tides in the Court's concern for speech as against other interests, and the present moment strikes many commentators as very low tide indeed.

The Warren Court moved very far, for example, toward protecting pornography from the censor, on the ground that it is not part of the state's concern to decide what people, in private, should or should not find tasteless or embarrassing. But the Burger Court endorsed the idea of censorship in accordance with local standards of decency, and though this test has posed no problems for the pornographers of Times Square, it has made many movie theaters in small towns very cautious. Defamation suits brought by public figures against newspapers provide another example. The Warren Court, in its famous decision in *Times v. Sullivan,* held that a public figure could not sue a paper for libel, even if what that paper had published was

both false and damaging, unless the public figure succeeded in showing that the paper had been not merely wrong but either malicious or reckless in what it published. The Court held that public figures must be supposed to have waived their common law right to sue for ordinary misrepresentation.

The Burger Court has not overruled the *Sullivan* decision, but it has narrowed the class of people who count as public figures for this purpose, and in the recent case of *Herbert v. Landau* it held that even when a public figure sues, reporters may be examined, under oath, about their methods of investigation and editorial judgment, in an effort to show their malice or recklessness. The Court rejected the protests of newspapers and television networks that the threat of such examinations, in which reporters would be forced to defend largely subjective judgments, would inhibit reporters' freedom of inquiry and so make them less effective servants of the public.

Two of the most important recent judicial decisions involving First Amendment claims never reached the Supreme Court. The first of these was the much publicized case of the *New York Times* reporter Myron Farber, which I discussed in the preceding essay. The New Jersey courts held that Farber could be jailed for contempt because he refused to turn over his files, which might well have contained information useful to a defendant accused of murder, to defense attorneys. The *Times* (supported by other papers) argued that unless reporters are able to promise confidentiality to informers, for example, their sources will disappear and the public will lose an important source of its information. But the courts did not accept that argument.[5]

The second was the case of *The Progressive*, which ended in comedy, but was nevertheless the occasion for the first preliminary injunction ever granted in the United States against publication in advance. That magazine proposed to publish an article entitled "The H-Bomb Secret: How We Got It—Why We're Telling It," and submitted it to the Atomic Energy Commission for informal clearance. The author had in fact used only public and legally available information. But the Commission, relying on its claim that all information relating to atomic weapons is "born classified" under the Atomic Energy Act, and cannot be published unless it is affirmatively cleared for publication by the Commission, refused to pass the article and sued to enjoin it. The Commission persuaded a district court judge, who listened to government testimony in secret, that publication would be damaging to national security, because it might enable a smaller nation (Idi Amin's Uganda was the example of the day) to construct a hydrogen bomb.

The Progressive appealed the district court's injunction to the Circuit Court, but before that Court acted it became apparent that all the information the author used was available at a public library maintained by the Commission, and several newspapers then published the contents of the proposed article without seeking clearance. The government withdrew in

some embarrassment, and *The Progressive*'s article was finally published. Nevertheless, it was ominous that the First Amendment provided so little protection in this case. The Commission's "born classified" argument—that it is illegal to publish any information about atomic weapons that it has not specifically cleared—is absurdly overbroad, and would not have been sustained, I think, by higher courts. But the courts might well have sustained a procedure that allows a judge to decide particular censorship cases in secret proceedings where the judge may be unduly impressed by government technical "experts." The Atomic Age is not a healthy environment for free speech.

Not all the evidence of the present decline of free speech is drawn from judicial decisions. The Freedom of Information Act, which was strengthened by Congress after the Watergate scandal, provides that anyone can obtain any information in the hands of the federal government, with certain exceptions to protect personal privacy, trade secrets, national security, and the like. We owe much valuable information—for example, parts of William Shawcross' book on Cambodia—to that Act. But pressure has been building for substantial amendment. Doctors point out that double-blind experiments testing new drugs and procedures are ruined when reporters discover information that destroys the confidentiality that makes the experiments statistically significant. Scientists argue that the incentive to carry on research may be jeopardized when newspapers publish details of interesting grant applications. The National Disease Control Center finds that hospitals will not seek its aid in locating hospital infections when journalists can make the Center's reports to the hospitals available to potential litigants.

The press has not, as I said, lost all its battles. The Burger Court unanimously rejected the Nixon administration's attempt to prevent the publication of the Pentagon Papers and affirmed, in the *Richmond Newspapers* case, that the press does have some constitutionally protected position under the First Amendment, strong enough so that a trial judge must show some special reason for excluding reporters from a criminal trial. But the press nevertheless believes that it is losing ground overall.

NAT HENTOFF, in his comprehensive book on the history of the First Amendment, describes the rise of the idea of free speech and a free press in America from Peter Zenger on, and notices, in apparent sadness, the symptoms of what he plainly takes to be its present slump.[6] The book is remarkably readable and broad. It has the great merit of showing how the idea of free speech takes on different content as the underlying substantive issues change from educational policy to obscenity to reporting of criminal trials. The tone of the book seems dispassionate. Hentoff argues mostly by quoting

others. But there is no doubt where he stands. He is a partisan of free speech, and in this book there are victories and defeats for freedom, heroes and cowards of the press, friends and enemies of liberty.

But there is not much attempt at analysis of the philosophical grounds of free speech or freedom of the press, or much effort to find the limits of the freedoms and powers Hentoff wants to defend. In this respect he is typical of journalists who complain about the fate of the First Amendment in the courts, though he writes better and with more enthusiasm and knowledge than most. The press takes the Amendment as a kind of private charter, and attacks more or less automatically every refusal of the courts to find some further protection in that charter. The newspapers and networks denounced the decisions in the *Farber* and *Herbert* cases as fiercely—indeed even more fiercely—than those in the cases of *The Progressive* and *Snepp*.

But this strategy of automatic appeal to the First Amendment is, I think, a poor strategy, even if the press is concerned only to expand its legal powers as far as possible. For if the idea becomes popular that the Amendment is an all-purpose shield for journalists, warding off libel suits, depositions, and searches as well as censorship, then it must become a weaker shield, because it will seem obvious that so broad a power in the press must be balanced against other private and social interests in the community. What will then suffer is the historically central function of the First Amendment, which is simply to ensure that those who wish to speak on matters of political and social controversy are free to do so. Perhaps the surprising weakness of the First Amendment in protecting the defendants in *The Progressive* and *Snepp* cases, for example, is partly a consequence of the very effectiveness of the press in persuading the courts, in an earlier day, that the power of the First Amendment extends well beyond straight censorship cases.

In order to test this suspicion, we must consider an issue that Hentoff and other friends of the First Amendment neglect. What is the First Amendment for? Whom is it meant to protect? A variety of views is possible. The dominant theory among American constitutional lawyers assumes that the constitutional rights of free speech—including free press, which, in the constitutional language, means published speech in general rather than journalists in particular—are directed at protecting the audience. They protect, that is, not the speaker or writer himself but the audience he wishes to address. On this view, journalists and other writers are protected from censorship in order that the public at large may have access to the information it needs to vote and conduct its affairs intelligently.

In his famous essay *On Liberty*, John Stuart Mill offered a similar but more fundamental justification for the right of free speech. He said that if everyone is free to advance any theory of private or public morality, no matter how absurd or unpopular, truth is more likely to emerge from the

resulting marketplace of ideas, and the community as a whole will be better off than it would be if unpopular ideas were censored. Once again, on this account, particular individuals are allowed to speak in order that the community they address may benefit in the long run.

But other theories of free speech—in the broad sense including free press—hold that the right is directed at the protection of the speaker, that is, that individuals have the right to speak, not in order that others benefit, but because they would themselves suffer some unacceptable injury or insult if censored. Anyone who holds this theory must, of course, show why censorship is a more serious injury than other forms of regulation. He must show why someone who is forbidden to speak his mind on politics suffers harm that is graver than when he is forbidden, for example, to drive at high speeds or trespass on others' property or combine to restrain trade.

Different theories might be proposed: that censorship is degrading because it suggests that the speaker or writer is not worthy of equal concern as a citizen, or that his ideas are not worthy of equal respect; that censorship is insulting because it denies the speaker an equal voice in politics and therefore denies his standing as a free and equal citizen; or that censorship is grave because it inhibits an individual's development of his own personality and integrity. Mill makes something like this last claim in *On Liberty*, in addition to his marketplace-of-ideas argument, and so his theory can be said to be concerned to protect the speaker as well as the audience.

Theories concerned to protect the audience generally make what I have called an argument of policy for free speech and a free press.[7] They argue, that is, that a reporter must have certain powers, not because he or anyone else is entitled to any special protection, but in order to secure some general benefit to the community as a whole, just as farmers must sometimes have certain subsidies, not for their own sakes, but also to secure some benefit for the community. Theories concerned to protect the speaker, on the other hand, make arguments of principle for free speech. They argue that the speaker's special position, as someone wanting to express his convictions on matters of political or social importance, entitles him, in fairness, to special consideration, even though the community as a whole may *suffer* from allowing him to speak. So the contrast is great: in the former case the community's welfare provides the ground for the protection, but in the latter the community's welfare is disregarded in order to provide it.

The distinction is relevant to the present discussion in many ways. If free speech is justified on grounds of policy, then it is plausible that journalists should be given special privileges and powers not available to ordinary citizens, because they have a special and indeed indispensable function in providing information to the public at large. But if free speech is justified on principle, then it would be outrageous to suppose that journalists should have special protection not available to others, because that would claim

that they are, as individuals, more important or worthier of more concern than others.

Since the powers the press claims, like the power to attend criminal trials, must be special to it, it is natural that the press favors a view of free speech based on the policy argument concerned to protect the audience: that the press is essential to an informed public. But there is a corresponding danger in this account. If free speech is justified as a matter of policy, then whenever a decision is to be made about whether free speech requires some further exception or privilege, competing dimensions of the public's interest must be balanced against its interest in information.

Suppose the question arises, for example, whether the Freedom of Information Act should be amended so that the Disease Control Center is not required to make its reports available to reporters, or whether the Atomic Energy Commission should be allowed to enjoin a magazine from publishing an article that might make atomic information more readily available to foreign powers. The public's general interest in being well informed argues against confidentiality and for publication in both cases. But the public also has an interest in infection-free hospitals and in atomic security, and these two kinds of interests must be balanced, as in a cost-benefit analysis, in order to determine where the public's overall interest lies. Suppose that in the long term (and taking side effects into account) the public would lose more overall if the information in question were published. Then it would be self-contradictory to argue that it must be published in the public's interest, and the argument for free speech, on grounds of policy, would be defeated.

The problem is quite different if we take free speech to be a matter of principle instead. For now any conflict between free speech and the public's welfare is not a pseudo conflict between two aspects of the public's interest that may be dissolved in some judgment of its overall interest. It is a genuine conflict between the rights of a particular speaker as an individual and the competing interests of the community as a whole. Unless that competing interest is very great—unless publication threatens some emergency or other grave risk—the individual's right must outweigh the social interest, because that is what it means to suppose that he has this sort of right.

So it is important to decide, when the press claims some special privilege or protection, whether that claim is based on policy or principle. The importance of the distinction is sometimes obscured, however, by a newly fashionable idea, which is that the public has what is called a "right to know" the information that reporters might collect. If that means simply that the public has an interest in knowledge—that the community is better off, all things being equal, if it knows more rather than less about, say, criminal trials or grant applications or atomic secrets—then the phrase is just another way of stating the familiar argument of policy in favor of a free and

powerful press: a better informed public will result in a better society generally. But the suggestion that the public has a *right* to know suggests something stronger than that, which is that there is an audience-protective argument of *principle* in favor of any privilege that improves the press's ability to gather news.

But that stronger suggestion is, in fact, deeply misleading. It is wrong to suppose that individual members of the community have, in any strong sense, a right to learn what reporters might wish to discover. No citizen's equality or independence or integrity would have been denied had Farber, for example, chosen not to write any of his *New York Times* stories about Dr. Jascalevich, and no citizen could have sued Farber requiring him to do so, or seeking damages for his failure to write. It may be that the average citizen would have been worse off if the stories had not been written, but that is a matter of the general welfare, not of any individual right.

In any case, the alleged right to know is supposed to be a right, not of any individual citizen, but of the public as a whole. That is almost incoherent, because "the public" in this context is only another name for the community as a whole. And it is bizarre to say that even if the community, acting through its legislators, wishes to amend the Freedom of Information Act to exempt preliminary reports of medical research, because it believes that the integrity of such research is more important than the information it gives up, it must not do so because of its own right to have that information. Analysis of First Amendment issues would be much improved if the public's interest in information, which might well be outbalanced by its interest in secrecy, were not mislabeled a "right" to know.

It is now perhaps clearer why I believe that the press's strategy of expanding the scope of the First Amendment is a bad strategy. There is always a great risk that the courts—and the legal profession generally—will settle on one theory of a particular constitutional provision. If First Amendment protection is limited to the principle that no one who wishes to speak out on matters or in ways he deems important may be censored, then the single theory of the First Amendment will be a theory of individual rights. And this means that the commands of free speech cannot be outbalanced by some argument that the public interest is better served by censorship or regulation on some particular occasion.

But if the Amendment's protection is claimed when the claim must be based on some argument concerned to protect the audience—if it is said that reporters must not be examined about their editorial judgment in libel actions because they will then be less effective in gathering news for the public to read—the single theory that might justify so broad an Amendment must be a theory of policy. It is not surprising that the dissenting opinions in the cases about which the press complains—the opinions that argue that the press should have had what it asked—contain many arguments of policy

but few arguments of principle. In the *Herbert* case, for example, Mr. Justice Brennan based his dissenting opinion on a theory of the First Amendment strikingly like Mill's theory concerned to protect the audience. Brennan cited the following well-known remark of Zechariah Chafee: "The First Amendment protects . . . a social interest in the attainment of truth, so that the country may not only adopt the wisest course of action, but carry it out in the wisest way."

But of course these appeals to the general welfare of the public invite the reply that in some cases the public's real interest would be better served, on balance, by censorship than by publication. By contrast, if the Amendment is limited to its core protection of the speaker, it can provide, in its appeal to individual rights rather than the general welfare, a principle of law strong enough to provide important protection in a true First Amendment case, like that of *The Progressive*. But if the Amendment becomes too broad, it can be defended only on grounds of policy like those Brennan provided. It can be defended, that is, only on grounds that leave it most vulnerable just when it is most necessary.

IF WE ATTEND only to the core of the First Amendment, which protects the speaker as a matter of principle, then the recent record of the Court and Congress looks better, though far from perfect. Before the *Snepp* case that core of principle was threatened, even arguably, only by the obscenity decisions, about which most of the press cares very little, and in the case of *The Progressive*, which was only a district court decision, and which ended in victory for the press anyway. The other decisions that so angered journalists—like the *Farber* and *Herbert* cases—were all decisions that simply refused to recognize reporters' arguments of policy that the public would generally be better off if reporters had special privileges. The chilling effect the press predicted for these decisions has not materialized—indeed Mike Wallace, one of the reporters who resisted examination in the *Herbert* case, recently said that the press might have deserved to lose that case.

In any event, if democracy works with even rough efficiency, and if the reporters' arguments of policy are sound, then they will gain the powers they seek through the political process in the long run anyway, and so they have lost nothing of lasting importance by being denied these powers in the courts. For if the public really is generally better off when the press is powerful, the public might be expected to realize where its self-interest lies sooner or later—perhaps aided by the press's own advice. Except in cases like the *Farber* case, when the rights of individuals—in that case the right to a fair trial—would be infringed by expanding the power of the press, the public can then give the press what it wants by legislation.

The question arises, however, whether the *Richmond Newspapers* deci-

sion (in which, as I said, the Supreme Court held that in the absence of strong countervailing interests reporters have a right to attend criminal trials) shows that the Court is now committed to a theory of the First Amendment that goes beyond the core of principle and extends to the protection of the general welfare of the audience. It is certainly true that the result in that case might be justified by an argument of policy like the argument Brennan made in the *Herbert* case. Burger's opinion in the *Richmond Newspapers* case points out, for example, that the public is better off if its deep interest in the criminal process, and even its inevitable desire for retribution, is served by newspaper accounts of trials. But a careful reading of the several opinions in the case shows that though the seven Justices who voted for the press (Mr. Justice Rehnquist dissented and Mr. Justice Powell took no part in the case) proceeded on somewhat different theories, two arguments were dominant, neither of which was a straightforward argument of policy of the type advanced by Mill.

The first, emphasized especially by Burger and, apparently, by Blackmun, ties the protection of the First Amendment to history. It argues that if any important process of government has been open to the public by long-standing traditions of Anglo-American jurisprudence, then citizens have a right, secured by the First Amendment, to information about that process, and the press therefore has a derivative right to secure and provide that information. The citizens' right is not absolute, because it must yield before competing rights of the defendant, for example. But it stands in a case, like the *Richmond Newspapers* case, in which either no important interests of the defendant are in play, or the court can protect these interests by means other than barring reporters.

This argument from history seems to me a weak argument, for there is no reason why custom should ripen into a right unless there is some independent argument of principle why people have a right to what custom gives them. But it is in any case not an argument that requires the courts to decide whether the general welfare is, on balance, served by denying the press access to information or otherwise chilling speech on any particular occasion. It holds that the press must be admitted unless some special reason, and not just the balance of general welfare, argues against it.

The second argument, stressed particularly in Brennan's opinion, is both more important and more complex. It urges that some special protection for the press is necessary in order not only to advance the general good but to preserve the very structure of democracy. Madison's classic statement of this argument is often cited in the briefs the press submits in constitutional cases. He said that "a popular government, without popular information or the means of acquiring it, is but a prologue to a farce or a tragedy; or perhaps both . . . a people who mean to be their own governors, must arm themselves with the power knowledge gives."

This is not Mill's argument, that the more information people have the more likely they are to secure, overall, what they most want. It is rather the argument that the people need some information in order even to be able to form conceptions of what they want, and in order to participate as equals in the process of governing themselves. Mill's policy argument is open-ended: the more information the better. But the Madisonian argument from the structure of democracy cannot be open-ended, for then it will end in paradox and self-contradiction.

That is so because every extension of the First Amendment is, from the standpoint of democracy, a double-edged sword. It enhances democracy because public information increases the general power of the public. But it also contracts democracy because any constitutional right disables the popularly elected legislature from enacting some legislation it might otherwise wish to enact, and this decreases the general power of the public. Democracy implies that the majority has the power to govern effectively in what it takes to be the general interest. If so, then any extension of constitutional protection of speech and the press will both increase and decrease that power, in these two different ways. Any particular person may be more effective politically because he will know more about, for example, atomic energy installations. But he may also be less effective politically, because he will lose the power to elect congressmen who will vote for censorship of atomic information. He may well count this trade-off, on balance, a loss in political power overall, particularly if he himself would prefer to sacrifice knowledge of atomic information in order to have the increased security that comes from no one else having that information either.

Every decision about censorship confronts each citizen with that sort of cost-benefit issue, and it cannot be said that he inevitably gains in political power when the matter is taken out of politics and decided by the Supreme Court instead. Indeed it is tempting to argue, on the contrary, that genuine, full-blooded democracy would require no First Amendment at all, for then every single issue of censorship would be decided by majority will through Congress and the state legislatures. But that goes too far, because, as Madison warned, people need some general and protected structure of public information even intelligently to decide whether they want more of it. There is no democracy among slaves who could seize power if they only knew how.

The opposite mistake is just as serious, however, because it is absurd to suppose that the American electorate, which already has access to a great deal more, and more sophisticated, public information than it shows any disposition to use, would gain in democratic power if the Supreme Court decided, for example, that Congress could not amend the Freedom of Information Act so as to exempt Disease Control Center reports, no matter how many people thought that such an exemption was a good idea. So the

argument from the structure of democracy requires, by its own internal logic, some threshold line to be drawn between interpretations of the First Amendment that would protect and those that would invade democracy.

There is one evident, if difficult, way to draw that threshold line. It requires the Supreme Court to describe, in at least general terms, what manner of invasion of the powers of the press would so constrict the flow of information to the public as to leave the public unable intelligently to decide whether to overturn that limitation of the press by further legislation. The Court might decide, for example, that a general and arbitrary refusal of some agency of government to provide any information or opportunity for investigation to the press at all, so as to leave the public wholly uninformed whether the practices of that agency required further investigation, fell on the wrong side of that threshold.[8] But it is extremely implausible to suppose that the public would be disabled in this dramatic way if the press were excluded from those few criminal trials in which the defendant requested such exclusion, the prosecution agreed to it, and the judge thought the interests of justice would on balance be served by it. The public of a state that adopted that practice would remain competent to decide whether it disapproved that arrangement and, if so, to outlaw it through the political process. So if Madison's argument from the structure of democracy is applied to particular cases through the idea of a threshold of public competence, the *Richmond Newspapers* case should have been decided the other way.

There is another way to apply the argument from structure however, and this is suggested in Brennan's opinion in that case. He said that though the press should have full access to information in principle, some line needed to be drawn in practice, and he proposed to draw the line, not through a threshold of the sort just discussed, but through balancing the facts of each individual case. He would assume, that is, that any constraint on the press's access to information is unconstitutional, unless there are competing interests justifying that constraint, in which case the question would be which set of interests—the public's interest in information or the competing interests—were of greater weight. In the *Richmond Newspapers* case he found no such competing interests at all, and therefore found it unnecessary to discuss how much the structure of democracy would be damaged by the exclusion in question.

All this brings Brennan's argument from structure dangerously close to an argument of policy of the kind made by Mill. Though Brennan has himself been one of the most passionate advocates of free speech, his argument invites censorship in those cases in which the general welfare, on balance, would benefit from it or, rather, when the public thinks that it would. For the balance Brennan describes could fall against rather than for *The Progressive*, for example. It is not absurd to suppose that publication of atomic data increases public risk to some degree. But it is absurd to think

that a constraint on such publication, considered in itself as Brennan recommends, would impair the structure of American democracy to any noticeable degree, or leave the public, which has considerable general knowledge of atomic dangers, unable to decide whether to change its mind and remove the constraint through ordinary political action. Brennan would himself distinguish between cases concerning access to information, like the *Richmond Newspapers* case, and cases of straight censorship, like the *Progressive* case. But the theory he described to cover the former cases might all too easily develop into a general structural theory of the First Amendment, and freedom would then suffer.

THE SUPREME COURT's procedures in Frank Snepp's case were extraordinary and indefensible. But the decision was also, I think, wrong on the merits, and not simply as a matter of procedure and remedy. We may, for purposes of isolating the precise constitutional issue in question, suppose the following facts, some of which I stated earlier. When Snepp joined the CIA he signed a contract calling upon him to submit for clearance any materials he might later wish to publish about the agency. He would not have been offered the position had he refused to sign that agreement. *Decent Interval*, the book he ultimately published without submitting it, contained no classified information. If he had never worked for the CIA and had never signed such an agreement, he would have been free to publish a book containing the same information without prior clearance, and he would have been subject to no legal penalty whatsoever. Indeed, if Congress passed a law requiring authors of books about the CIA to submit manuscripts to that agency for advance clearance, that law would be unconstitutional because it would violate authors' First Amendment rights.[9]

So the question is this: When Snepp joined the CIA, and signed the agreement, did he waive his constitutional rights to publish unclassified information about the agency, a right that anyone else, not in his position, would plainly have? I put the question that way to show that one of the arguments the CIA pressed against Snepp is not in point. The agency argued that the requirement of prior clearance it imposed on him by contract did him no harm. If the review disclosed that he wished to publish classified information, then the agency would act to prevent that. But Snepp, as the CIA rightly claimed, has no constitutional rights to publish classified information. He remained free to publish any nonclassified information, once the review was completed, just as anyone else would be free to do. The contractual requirement of clearance (the CIA argues) merely gave the agency a legitimate opportunity to assess for itself whether the material proposed to be published was classified, and to take any steps to deter publication of any that was. So the contract was not a waiver of any constitutional right.

But if, as I assume, even Congress could not require those who had no connection with the CIA to submit manuscripts about it for prior review, then it is not open to the agency to argue that prior review has nothing to do with censorship. Victor Marchetti's experience with the CIA after he submitted his manuscript shows (if any demonstration were needed) how a requirement of prior review makes what an author may say a matter of compromise, negotiation, and delay, all under the shadow of the threat of litigation, rather than a matter of what the author *wants* to say, which the First Amendment insists it should be.[10]

So the question is simply whether Snepp waived whatever First Amendment rights he would otherwise have had. Once again everything depends on what view one takes of the point and force of the right of free speech. Snepp's lawyers argued, in his petition for rehearing in the Supreme Court, that "the unreviewed memoirs of former government officials who held positions of trust with access to the most sensitive national security information have made invaluable contributions to public debate and understanding. The publication of scores of such works without any demonstrated harm to the nation's welfare belies the need for prior restraint of CIA officials." That argument is unpersuasive if it is meant to suggest that allowing Snepp to waive the First Amendment would be wrong because it would work against the general welfare.

It is true that if the CIA and other security agencies are allowed to impose requirements of prior clearance of publication as a condition of employment, then the public will undoubtedly, over the years, lose some information it would otherwise gain. But the CIA's arguments of policy against this point—that the efficiency of its intelligence gathering operations would be compromised if it did not have opportunity to review publications by ex-agents in advance—are not frivolous. No doubt the agency has exaggerated the importance of this review. It says, for example, that foreign agencies would stop giving intelligence to the United States if Snepp had won his case. These foreign agencies are not so stupid as to think that books by ex-agents are the principal sources of leaks from the CIA. Nevertheless, even if we discount the exaggeration, it is still plausible to suppose that the CIA will be more efficient if it has a chance to argue about this or that passage in advance, and alert its friends, including foreign intelligence agencies, about what will soon be in the bookstores.

But that means that there is a genuine cost-benefit issue of policy to decide: does the public welfare gain or lose more, in the long run, if books like Snepp's are delayed and harassed? The question whether Snepp waived his rights is a fresh question of constitutional law. It is not settled by any earlier decision of the Supreme Court, or by any embedded constitutional policy favoring speech. If we assume that it is to be settled by some cost-benefit calculation about what will make the community better off as a whole in

the long run, as the argument of Snepp's lawyers may suggest, then the argument that it must be settled by the courts in favor of Snepp, rather than left to Congress and the people, is not very strong.

But the argument of his lawyers is much stronger, and seems to me right, if it means to call attention not to the general welfare but to the rights of those who want to listen to what Snepp wants to say. For these citizens believe that they will be in a better position to exercise their influence on political decisions affecting the CIA if they know more about the agency's behavior, and their constitutional right to listen should not be cut off by Snepp's private decision to waive his right to speak to them.

I must now say something about this constitutional right to listen. The Constitution, as a whole, defines as well as commands the conditions under which citizens live in a just society, and it makes central to these conditions that each citizen be able to vote and participate in politics as the equal of any other. Free speech is essential to equal participation, but so is the right of each citizen that others, whose access to information may be superior to his, not be prevented from speaking to him. That is distinctly not a matter of policy: it is not a matter of protecting the majority will or of securing the general welfare over the long run. Just as the majority violates the right of the speaker when it censors him, even when the community would be better off were he censored, so it violates the right of every potential listener who believes that his own participation in politics would gain, either in effectiveness or in its meaning for him, were he to listen to that speaker.

The right to listen is generally parasitic upon the right to speak that forms the core of the First Amendment, and it is normally adequately protected by an uncompromising enforcement of that core right to speak. For the right to listen is not the right to learn what no one wants to tell.[11] But the right to listen would be seriously compromised if all government agencies were free to make it a condition of employment that officials waive their rights later to reveal nonclassified information without checking with the agency first.

The law does allow private citizens or firms to extract promises of confidentiality, of course, about revealing commercial secrets or the contents of personal diaries or the like. But Snepp's case is different. The right to listen is part of the right to participate in politics as an equal, and information about the conduct of the CIA in Vietnam is plainly more germane to political activity than information about business secrets or the personal affairs of private citizens.[12]

So the issue of whether to enforce contractual waivers of the right to speak, given the constitutionally protected right of others to listen, is one that, like so many other legal issues, requires lines to be drawn. Two different lines were available to the Supreme Court in *Snepp*. It might have said that government agencies, as distinct from private persons or firms, may

never make any waiver of First Amendment rights a condition of employment. That distinction would be justified on the ground that information about government agencies is presumptively information highly relevant to participation in politics, while information about private firms, while it may be, is not presumptively so.

Or the Court might have said that a government agency may never make such a waiver a condition of employment unless that condition is expressly imposed by Congress rather than by the agency itself. That weaker requirement would be justified on the ground that this decision—the decision whether the gravity of the threat to national security posed by former agents publishing material without prior review is sufficiently great to justify overriding the right to listen—is a decision that should be taken by the national legislature itself, rather than by an agency whose own interests in confidentiality might affect its judgment. It may well be doubted whether this second, weaker requirement is sufficient to meet the standards of the First Amendment. But it is not necessary to speculate further on that question here, because either the weaker or the stronger requirement would have argued for a decision in favor of Snepp.

It is worth asking, however, whether a different argument, not relying on the rights of others to listen, but instead relying directly on Snepp's own First Amendment right to speak, would also have justified a decision refusing to enforce his contractual waiver. It might seem that such an argument, relying directly on Snepp's own rights, must fail, because his choice to accept a job at the price of the waiver was a free and informed choice. If Snepp (who knew, as the lawyer for the CIA succinctly put it, that he was not joining the Boy Scouts) freely bargained away his full First Amendment rights by agreeing to a prior review, why should the courts now release him from his bargain when it proves inconvenient? Why should the courts now disable others from making the same bargain in the future, as they would by finding for Snepp now?

That was the CIA's argument, and it prevailed. But it is not so strong as it looks, because it rests on a mistaken analogy between a constitutional right and a piece of property. The First Amendment does not deal out rights like trading stamps whose point is to increase the total wealth of each citizen. The Constitution as a whole states, as I said, the conditions under which citizens shall be deemed to form a community of equals. An individual citizen is no more able to redefine these conditions than the majority is. The Constitution does not permit him to sell himself into slavery or to bargain away his rights to choose his own religion. This is not because it is never in his interests to make such a bargain, but because it is intolerable that any citizen be a slave or have his conscience mortgaged.

The question that must be asked, when we consider whether any particular constitutional right may be waived, is this: will the waiver leave any person in a condition deemed a denial of equality by the Constitution?

Since the First Amendment defines equal standing to include the right to report what one believes important to one's fellow-citizens, as well as the right to be faithful to conscience in matters of religion, the right of free speech should no more be freely available to trade than the right to religious belief. That is why the analogy to rights in property is such a poor one. If I make a financial bargain I later regret, I have lost money. But my standing as someone who participates in politics as an equal has not been impaired, at least according to the constitutional definition of what is essential to that standing. I have not sold myself into slavery or into a condition that the Constitution deems a part of slavery.

Once again, the argument does not justify the conclusion that a person should never have the power to agree not to publish certain information or to submit it for prior review. For not every such agreement leaves that person in a position that compromises his status as a political equal. The Supreme Court must therefore find a line to distinguish permissible from impermissible waivers of the constitutional right to speak, and either of the lines we defined when we considered, just now, the audience's right to listen might be appropriate to protect the speaker's right to speak.

The Court might say, that is, either that no waiver is permissible as a condition of employment in a government agency, or that no such waiver is permissible unless specifically authorized by Congress. But the Court, in its brief and unsatisfactory *per curiam* opinion, did not consider these possible distinctions, either of which would have supported Snepp's claim. The Court assumed that anyone who is employed by a government agency might waive his First Amendment rights even without specific congressional authorization. That assumption makes the mistake of supposing that a constitutional right is simply a piece of personal property.

So Snepp should have been held not to have waived his First Amendment rights. That result is necessary to protect the rights of others to listen and also necessary to protect Snepp's own independence. But this argument for Snepp depends on the conception of free speech and of the First Amendment that I defended earlier. It depends on supposing that free speech is a matter of principle, and therefore that it is a matter of great injustice, not just an abstract threat to the community's general well-being, when someone who wishes to speak his mind is muzzled or checked or delayed. Only if free speech is seen in that light does it become clear why it is so important to protect even an ex-CIA agent who signed a contract and knew he wasn't joining the Boy Scouts. The *Farber* and *Herbert* cases show why the First Amendment so conceived will not give the press all the powers and privileges it wants. The *Richmond Newspapers* case shows why it might even take away some of what the press has gained. But the *Progressive* and *Snepp* cases show why that conception is nevertheless essential to American constitutional democracy. The First Amendment must be protected from its enemies, but it must be saved from its best friends as well.

Notes

INTRODUCTION

1. Marshall Cohen, ed., *Ronald Dworkin and Contemporary Jurisprudence* (Totowa, N.J.: Rowman and Allanheld, 1984). On the distinction between principle and policy, see particularly the essay by Kent Greenawalt and my reply to that essay.

1. POLITICAL JUDGES AND THE RULE OF LAW
Note. Originally published in the *Proceedings of the British Academy*, 64 (1978). © 1980 British Academy.

1. J. A. G. Griffiths, *The Politics of the Judiciary* (Manchester: Manchester University Press, 1977; paperback ed., New York: Fontana Books, 1977).
2. Charter v. Race Relations Board (1973), A.C. 868.
3. Dockers' Labour Club v. Race Relations Board (1975), A.C. 259.
4. Secretary of State for Education and Science v. Tameside Metropolitan Borough Council (1976), 3 W.L.R. 641.
5. Shaw v. D.P.P. (1961), 2 W.L.R. 897.
6. Liversidge v. Anderson (1942), A.C. 206.
7. *Taking Rights Seriously* (Cambridge, Mass.: Harvard University Press, 1977; London: Duckworth, 1978).
8. I explain why at greater length in ibid., ch. 4.
9. Learned Hand, *The Bill of Rights* (Cambridge, Mass.: Harvard University Press, 1962).
10. Some of the issues discussed in this essay—in particular the group-psychological theory of statutory construction—are developed below in Chapter 16, "How to Read the Civil Rights Act."

2. THE FORUM OF PRINCIPLE
Note. Originally published in the *New York University Law Review*, 56, nos. 2–3 (May–June 1981). © Ronald Dworkin.

1. Marbury v. Madison, 5 U.S. (1 Cranch) 137, 173–179 (1803).
2. See West Coast Hotel Co. v. Parrish, 300 U.S. 379 (1937) (upholding Wash-

ington's minimum wage law for women), overruling Adkins v. Children's Hospital, 261 U.S. 525 (1923). See Roe v. Wade, 410 U.S. 113 (1973) (Texas criminal abortion statute held unconstitutional).

3. United States v. Carolene Prods. Co., 304 U.S. 144, 152 n. 4 (1938). John Ely, *Democracy and Distrust* (Cambridge, Mass.: Harvard University Press, 1981).

4. See, e.g., ibid., at p. 1; Thomas Grey, "Do We Have An Unwritten Constitution?," 27 *Stanford Law Review* 703 (1975); Michael J. Perry, "Interpretivism, Freedom of Expression, and Equal Protection," *Ohio State Law Journal*, 42: 261, 263–265 (1981). Though these particular phrases are common, others are used. Paul Brest, for example, speaks of "originalism" and "nonoriginalism," meaning to distinguish "originalist" theories from theories that are interpretivist in some sense not involving interpretation of the original text. See Brest, "The Misconceived Quest For The Original Understanding," *Boston University Law Review*, 60: 204–205 (1980). The discussion in the text applies to this distinction as well.

5. See Ely, note 3 above, at pp. 43–72 (providing a critical compendium of these nontextual standards).

6. See, e.g., Raoul Berger, "Ely's 'Theory of Judicial Review,' " *Ohio State Library Journal*, 42: 87, 120–121 (1981); Robert J. Bork, "Neutral Principles and Some First Amendment Problems," *Indiana Law Journal*, 47: 1, 6 (1971).

7. See Raoul Berger, *Government by Judiciary* (Cambridge, Mass.: Harvard University Press, 1977), pp. 249–258, 387–396. (Framers did not intend for natural law to empower judges to rise above positive limitations of Constitution); Perry, "Interpretivism," note 4 above, pp. 267–270. (Framers did not constitutionalize natural law.)

8. See, e.g., Grey, note 4 above, at pp. 707–710, 718; Perry, "Interpretivism," note 4 above, at pp. 265, 296–297, 300; Terrence Sandalow, "Judicial Protection of Minorities," *Michigan Law Review*, 75: 1162, 1179–1181, 1193 (1977). Brown v. Board of Education, 347 U.S. 483 (1954); Bolling v. Sharpe, 347 U.S. 497 (1954).

9. See Jeremy Bentham, *Of Laws in General*, ed. H. L. A. Hart (Atlantic Highlands, N.J.: Humanities Press, 1970); J. L. Austin, *The Province of Jurisprudence Determined* (London, 1832), pp. 9–33; Hans Kelsen, *Pure Theory of Law* (Berkeley: University of California Press, 1978), pp. 193–195.

10. See H. L. A. Hart, *The Concept of Law* (Berkeley: University of California Press, 1976).

11. Brest, note 4 above.

12. See H. P. Grice, "Utterer's Meaning and Intentions," *Philosophical Review*, 78: 147 (1969); H. P. Grice, "Utterer's Meaning, Sentence-Meaning and Word Meaning," *Foundations of Language*, 4: 225 (1968); H. P. Grice, "Meaning," *Philosophical Review*, 66: 377 (1957).

13. It may be a mistake to suppose that a vote, in a large legislative body, is even a speech act at all. I cannot pursue that suggestion here.

14. It is interesting that the practice of constitutional textualists here seems to differ from congressional textualists. In the ordinary process of a statutory interpretation we would not be interested, I think, in letters written by a senator to his son at college. But suppose a letter were found from Madison to his niece? Compare Ely, note 3 above, at pp. 35–36 (comparing Madison's explanation of the Ninth Amendment on the floor of Congress—unfavorably—with his earlier dis-

cussion in a letter to Jefferson). No doubt the difference reflects the point noticed earlier: that convention has succeeded in making the idea of a group intention more a term of art in contexts of ordinary legislative interpretation than in constitutional interpretation.

15. Perry, "Interpretivism," note 4 above, at p. 299.

16. Perry clearly assumes his three-valued scheme is exhaustive, because his argument requires that assumption, and because he claims "to set forth the various possible relationships between the original understanding of any power-limiting constitutional provision and any present-day political practice claimed to violate the provision." Perry, "Interpretivism," note 4 above, at p. 299.

17. The distinction between abstract and concrete intention is related to, but different from, the distinction, in the philosophy of language, between "transparent" and "opaque" propositional attitudes. See, e.g., W. V. Quine, *Word and Object* (Cambridge, Mass.: MIT Press, 1960), pp. 141–146; W. V. Quine, "Quantifiers and Propositional Attitudes," *Journal of Philosophy*, 53: 177 (1956).

18. See Ronald Dworkin, *Taking Rights Seriously* (Cambridge, Mass.: Harvard University Press, 1977; London: Duckworth, 1978), pp. 131–149.

19. See, e.g., Henry P. Monaghan, "Our Perfect Constitution," *New York University Law Review*, 56: 379–380, and n. 155; Stephen R. Munzer and James W. Nickel, "Does the Constitution Mean What It Always Meant?," *Columbia Law Review*, 77: 1029, 1037–1041 (1977); Perry, "Interpretivism," note 4 above, at p. 298.

20. I said that someone who tells his children not to treat others unfairly "means" them not to do what is in fact unfair rather than what he, the parent, thinks unfair. Dworkin, *Taking Rights Seriously*, p. 134. This does not deny that if the parent thinks it unfair to cheat on exams, he intends his children not to cheat on exams. It rather touches on an issue I discuss later in this essay, the question of the parent's "dominant" intention. I mean that the parent would not have intended his children not to cheat on exams if he had not thought that cheating was unfair.

21. Perry's formulation captures the point: "Evidence supporting the proposition that the Framers of the constitutional provisions such as the free speech, free press, and equal protection clauses intended to constitutionalize broad 'concepts' rather than particular 'conceptions' is wholly lacking." Perry, "Interpretivism," note 4 above, at p. 298.

22. I follow Brest in this phrase; Brest, note 7 above, at pp. 212, 215–216, though with some reservations about calling these opinions intentions at all.

23. Dworkin, *Taking Rights Seriously*, pp. 133–136.

24. See, e.g., Munzer and Nickel, note 19 above, at pp. 1039–1041; note 21 above.

25. Brest, note 4 above, at p. 215.

26. I discuss this point at greater length, and apply it to the political theory of utilitarianism, in Chapter 17 below, "Do We Have a Right to Pornography?"

27. Griswold v. Connecticut, 381 U.S. 479 (1965) (striking down Connecticut's ban on the use of contraceptives). 410 U.S. 113 (1973) (striking down Texas' antiabortion statute). Lochner v. New York, 198 U.S. 45 (1905) (striking down New York's maximum hours law for bakers).

28. United States v. Carolene Prods. Co., 304 U.S. 144, 152 n. 4 (1938).

29. J. Ely, note 3 above.

30. I argue for it in *Taking Rights Seriously,* pp. 234–239, and in "Social Sciences and Constitutional Rights—The Consequences of Uncertainty," *Journal of Law and Education,* 6: 3, 10–12 (1977), and I shall sketch the main outline of my argument in the next section.

31. This is the burden of Ely's argument that neither tradition nor consensus provides a sound basis for discovering fundamental values. See J. Ely, note 3 above, at pp. 60–69.

32. See Hugh Thomas, *A History of the World* (New York: Harper & Row, 1979), p. 388 (quoting Churchill).

33. See Commentary, *New York University Law Review,* 56: 525, 528 (1981) (remarks of J. Ely) ("At some point . . . [my] judge will be left substantially on his or her own" in elaborating a procedural model of democracy); cf. J. Ely, note 3 above, at 75n. (participation itself can be regarded as a value; Court should pursue "participational values").

34. In praising the "theory" the Court has adopted in the First Amendment area as "the right one," Ely simply asserts that "rights like these [free association], whether or not they are explicitly mentioned, must nonetheless be protected, strenuously so, because they are critical to the functioning of an open and effective democratic process"; ibid., p. 105.

See John Stuart Mill, *On Liberty,* ed. C. V. Shields (Indianapolis, Ind.: Bobbs-Merrill, 1956), pp. 19–67. "Wrong opinions and practices gradually yield to fact and argument; but facts and arguments, to produce any effect on the mind, must be brought before it"; ibid., p. 25. Hence, the "peculiar evil of silencing the expression of an opinion" is that it robs the human race of the "opportunity of exchanging error for truth," and of gaining "the clearer perception and livelier impression of truth produced by its collision with error"; ibid., p. 21.

35. "A popular Government, without popular information, or the means of acquiring it, is but a Prologue to a Farce or a Tragedy; or, perhaps both. Knowledge will forever govern ignorance: And a people who mean to be their own Governors, must arm themselves with the power which knowledge gives." Letter from James Madison to W. T. Barry (Aug. 4, 1822), reprinted in *The Writings of James Madison,* ed. G. Hunt (1910), 9: 103.

36. Richmond Newspapers, Inc. v. Virginia, 448 U.S. 555, 587 (1980) (Brennan, J., concurring in the judgment). Justice Brennan argued that "the First Amendment . . . has a *structural* role to play in securing and fostering our republican system of self-government"; ibid. This role involves linking "the First Amendment to that process of communication necessary for a democracy to survive, and this entails solicitude not only for communication itself, but for the indispensable conditions of meaningful communication"; ibid., p. 588.

37. I adopt this distinction from John Rawls, *A Theory of Justice* (Cambridge, Mass.: Harvard University Press, 1971), pp. 204–205.

38. A. France, *The Red Lily,* trans. W. Stephens (1908), p. 95.

39. Cohen v. California, 403 U.S. 15 (1971).

40. The Court reasoned: "[M]uch linguistic expression serves a dual communicative function: it conveys not only ideas . . . but otherwise inexpressible emotions

as well . . . We cannot sanction the view that the Constitution, while solicitous of the cognitive content of individual speech, has little or no regard for that emotive function which, practically speaking, may often be the more important element of the overall message sought to be communicated"; ibid., p. 26.

41. In *Cohen,* where the ostensible harm "flowed entirely from the communicative content" of the message, the Court properly refused to designate "offensive language" as unprotected speech, recognizing "that what seems offensive to me may not seem offensive to you." J. Ely, note 3 above, at p. 114.

42. I elaborated and defended this sort of approach to justifying *some* rights in Dworkin, *Taking Rights Seriously,* pp. 234–236, 275–277. See also Chapter 17 below, "Do We Have a Right to Pornography?" And see Dworkin, "Social Sciences," note 30 above, at pp. 10–12.

43. See J. Ely, note 3 above, at pp. 82–84. Ely offers a theory of representation that embodies the idea that elected officials must show "equal concern and respect" to all (ibid., p. 82) and implicitly rejects the pure utilitarian account of what this means in favor of something like the account described in the text. The pure utilitarian account would not support Ely's own argument that minority interests constitutionally are guaranteed "virtual representation" in the political process (ibid., pp. 82–84) and that political decisions based on prejudice (unconstitutionally) deny such representation (ibid., p. 153).

44. J. Ely, "Democracy and the Right to Be Different," *New York University Law Review,* 56: 397, 399–405 (1981).

45. See, e.g., Fullilove v. Klutznick, 448 U.S. 448, 480–492 (1980) (Burger, C.J., announcing the judgment of the Court) (upholding constitutionality of Public Works Employment Act requirement that grantees use at least 10 percent of grants to procure services from minority owned enterprises); Regents of Univ. of Cal. v. Bakke, 438 U.S. 265, 320 (1978) (Powell, J., announcing the judgment of the Court) (Constitution does not proscribe state university from ever using race-conscious admissions program); ibid., pp. 328, 336–340, 350–362 (Brennan, J., concurring in the judgment in part and dissenting in part); (neither Constitution nor Title VI bars preferential treatment of racial minorities as means of remedying past societal discrimination). See J. Ely, "The Constitutionality of Reverse Racial Discrimination," *University of Chicago Law Review,* 41: 723, 727–741 (1974).

46. J. Ely, note 3 above, p. 255 n. 92 (citation omitted).

47. For the latest version of this argument, and my response to critics of it, see my reply in *Ronald Dworkin and Contemporary Jurisprudence,* note 1 above, and "Do We Have a Right to Pornography?" Chapter 17 below.

48. These claims have been criticized. See, e.g., H. L. A. Hart, "Between Utility and Rights," *Columbia Law Review,* 79: 828, 838–846 (1979), and J. Ely, "Professor Dworkin's External/Personal Preference Distinction," *Duke Law Journal,* 5: 959 (1983).

49. 410 U.S. 113 (1973).

50. Learned Hand, *The Bill of Rights* (Cambridge, Mass.: Harvard University Press, 1958), p. 73.

51. Perry, "Noninterpretive Review," note 25 above, pp. 288–296.

3. PRINCIPLE, POLICY, PROCEDURE

Note. Originally published in *Crime, Proof and Punishment, Essays in Memory of Sir Rupert Cross* (London and Boston: Butterworths, 1981). © Ronald Dworkin.

1. [1978] AC 171, [1977] 1 All ER 589.
2. British Steel Corporation v. Granada Television Ltd. (unreported).
3. [1976] AC 171, [1977] 1 All ER 589.
4. See below, Chapter 19, "Is the Press Losing the First Amendment?"
5. (1979) 123 Sol Jo 605, CA; revised [1980] 2 All ER 608, HL.
6. Ronald Dworkin, *Taking Rights Seriously* (Cambridge, Mass.: Harvard University Press, 1977; London: Duckworth, 1978), ch. 4.
7. See, e.g., Mathews v. Eldridge 424 U.S. 319 (1976); Goldberg v. Kelly 397 U.S. 254 (1970).
8. [1978] AC at 245, quoted in Rupert Cross, *Evidence*, 5th ed. (London: Butterworths, 1979), p. 315.
9. Dworkin, *Taking Rights Seriously*, pp. 307 ff.
10. See below, Chapter 5, "Is There Really No Right Answer in Hard Cases?"
11. See, e.g., Mashaw, "The Supreme Court's Due Process Calculus for Administrative Adjudication in *Mathews v. Eldridge:* Three Factors in Search of a Theory of Value," *University of Chicago Law Review*, 44: 28 (1976).
12. Laurence Tribe, *American Constitutional Law* (Mineola, N.Y.: The Foundation Press, 1978), pp. 503–504.
13. John Mackie, *Ethics: Inventing Right and Wrong* (New York: Penguin Books, 1977), pp. 106–107.

4. CIVIL DISOBEDIENCE AND NUCLEAR PROTESTS

Note. This essay has been adapted from a talk delivered at a conference on civil disobedience arranged by Jurgen Habermas, under the auspices of the German Social Democratic Party, at Bonn, September 1983. © Ronald Dworkin.

1. I use the word "majority" in a perhaps special sense: to name those who have control for the time being of the political machinery of an adequately democratic political system. They may not be the numerical majority, but they have secured their power through elections under procedures that are, at least roughly speaking, democratic.
2. It is true that some people have made arguments of principle against deploying nuclear weapons. Certain religious groups argue, for example, that because it would be wrong actually to use atomic weapons, even defensively, it is also wrong to threaten to use them, even if that threat would in itself make nuclear war much less likely. That is a rather rigid, even counterintuitive argument of principle, and most of the people who campaign against missiles make the very different argument of policy, that more missiles will not deter nuclear war but on the contrary make it more likely.
3. In a paper delivered earlier at the conference at which this essay was presented.
4. See Dworkin, *Taking Rights Seriously* (Cambridge, Mass.: Harvard University Press, 1977; London: Duckworth, 1978), pp. 206 ff.
5. Ibid., pp. 208–209.

5. IS THERE REALLY NO RIGHT ANSWER IN HARD CASES?

Note. Originally published in the *New York University Law Review*, 53, no. 1 (April 1978). © Ronald Dworkin.

1. See Michael Dummett, "Truth," in Peter Strawson, ed., *Philosophical Logic* (Oxford: Oxford University Press, 1967), pp. 64–66.

2. See Ronald Dworkin, *Taking Rights Seriously* (Cambridge, Mass.: Harvard University Press, 1977; London: Duckworth, 1978), pp. 81, 107–110.

3. *V*'s argument assumed bivalence between "is true" and "is not true." Can *R* deny this, and claim that "is true" is itself vague? *V*'s argument that vagueness produces indeterminacy relied on a distinction between "x is not ϕ" and "it is not true that x is ϕ." That distinction is necessary to his claim that "x is ϕ," and "x is not ϕ" might neither be true without either being false. We can grasp the distinction only if we have independent criteria for asserting that something is "ϕ" and asserting that it is not. (I mean, by "independent," that the criteria for asserting the one is not just the absence of the criteria for asserting the other.) Otherwise we could make no sense of the idea that our criteria may not be satisfied for asserting either. The alleged vagueness of "ϕ" consists in this independence of criteria. But can we distinguish in this way between (1) "p is not true" and (2) "it is not true that p is true"? (1) says (on the analysis just described) that the criteria for asserting (p) are not met. It does not say that the criteria for asserting $(\sim p)$ are met. But (2) seems to say nothing more than the same thing, that is, that the criteria for asserting (p) are not met. What more or less might it be taken to claim? But if (1) and (2) do not make different claims, then "is true" cannot be shown to be vague, at least on *V*'s theory of vagueness. The reader may feel that *R* has been cheated by this argument. After all, the circumstance that *R* called attention to might well arise, for all this complex argument. Someone told that if it is not true that a contract is sacrilegious he is to treat the contract as not sacrilegious may still find himself in the difficulty of being uncertain whether it is not true that the contract before him is sacrilegious. I agree. But that is a problem for *V*, not for my answer to *R*. Someone defending the bivalence thesis I described earlier may say that every contract is either sacrilegious or not, though it may be unclear which, and reasonable men may differ. *V* must show that this claim is wrong, because the proposition that a contract is sacrilegious may be neither true nor false. *R*'s practical problem provides (I think) an embarrassment for *V*'s whole approach, at least if it is taken to be an argument for the second version of the no-right-answer thesis.

4. In this essay I am concerned only with showing that legal positivism, even if it is true, does not provide a good argument for the second version of the no-right-answer thesis. This paragraph suggests an argument against positivism itself (it is, in fact, one way of stating what I have in various lectures called the "simple-minded argument" against positivism). I do not propose to pursue that argument in this essay, but it might be useful to notice these points: (1) The argument, as presented here, fails against what I called in the text semantic positivism. It fails against, for example, a form of positivism that claims that "Tom's contract is valid" *means* that judges have a duty to enforce the contract, and the proposition that "Tom's contract is not valid" *means* that judges have a duty not to enforce it. (But semantic positivism is indefensible.) (2) The argument also fails against a

form of positivism that sustains the following claims. Propositions of law can be divided into two classes, which may be called inherently positive (or inherently mandatory or something of the kind) and inherently negative (or inherently permissive, etc.), such that, for every proposition of law and its negation, one is inherently positive and the other inherently negative. If that is so, then a form of positivism can be defended which argues that a positive proposition of law is truth-functionally equivalent to some statement about lawmaking acts, so that, for example, it is true if and only if the sovereign has so commanded; but that this is not so for negative propositions of law, which may be true just in virtue of the failure of the sovereign to command the related positive proposition. But notice that this form of positivism presupposes a kind of reductionism. It supposes, that is, that all propositions of law that do not on the surface assert or deny duties or permissions can be translated, with no change or loss in meaning, into propositions that do. It also supposes that when this reduction is carried through, each proposition so reduced will belong to an opposite class from that to which its negation is reduced, rather than, for example, each being seen to be (at bottom) claims of permission that cannot, as a matter of law, both be true. It supposes, further, that the normative proposition it expresses, which is that whatever is not prohibited is permitted, is a fair description of legal practice. This assumption may be reasonable in cases in which the law intervenes on a clean slate, as when legal rules for property are provided for a community which has no (pre-legal) scheme of ownership. It is unreasonable when some area of law develops step-by-step rather than by deploying and then refining some all-embracing principle, as in the case, for example, of the development of large parts of the law of negligence. I do not regard these brief remarks as effective arguments against a canonical positive/negative (or mandatory/permissive) distinction, but only as a reminder of the difficulties such a distinction must surmount.

5. I hope that the "new" positivist will not make a different sort of claim. He might say that a *legal* system exists only if citizens and officials follow the ground rules he has stipulated, and that if they do not (but rather follow some different ground rules of the sort I describe in succeeding paragraphs) then the arrangement does not count as a legal system. He could not claim any justification in ordinary language for that piece of linguistic tyranny, so that his theory would become simply an unprofitable stipulation, as if some student of literature claimed that the different forms of literary criticism described in the next paragraph of the text were not forms of *literary* criticism. He would fall into the same banality if he were to say that, although a political arrangement might count as a legal system even if different ground rules were followed, an answer to a question about what a court should do would count as a *legal* answer only if it would be generated by his ground rules, whether or not it is generated by theirs.

6. Dworkin, "Hard Cases," *Taking Rights Seriously.*

7. Ibid.

8. I consider the relation between these two dimensions of justification in "A Reply to Critics," *Taking Rights Seriously* (paperback ed., 1978).

6. HOW LAW IS LIKE LITERATURE

Note. Originally published in *Critical Inquiry*, September 1982. Reprinted in W. J. T. Mitchell, ed., *The Politics of Interpretation* (Chicago and London: Chicago University Press, 1983). © Ronald Dworkin.

1. See Gareth Evans, "Semantic Theory and Tacit Knowledge," in Steven H. Holtzman and Christopher M. Leich, eds., *Wittgenstein: To Follow a Rule* (London: Routledge & Kegan Paul, 1981).

2. It may be one of the many important differences between interpretation in art and law, which I do not examine in this essay, that nothing in law corresponds to the direct experience of a work of art, though some lawyers of the romantic tradition do speak of a good judge's "sixth sense" which enables him to grasp which aspects of a chain of legal decisions reveal the "immanent" principle of law even though he cannot fully explain why.

3. See E. D. Hirsch, Jr., *Validity in Interpretation* (New Haven, Conn.: Yale University Press, 1967).

4. John Fowles, *The French Lieutenant's Woman* (Boston: Little, Brown, 1969), pp. 105–106.

5. Even the first novelist has the responsibility of interpreting to the extent any writer must, which includes not only interpreting as he writes but interpreting the genre in which he sets out to write. Will novelists with higher numbers have less creative "freedom" than those with lower? In one sense, no novelist has any freedom at all, because each is constrained to choose that interpretation which (he believes) makes the continuing work of art the best it can be. But we have already seen (and the discussion of law below will elaborate) two different dimensions along which any interpretation can be tested: the "formal" dimension, which asks how far the interpretation fits and integrates the text so far completed, and the "substantive" dimension, which considers the soundness of the view about what makes a novel good on which the interpretation relies. It seems reasonable to suppose that later novelists will normally—but certainly not inevitably—believe that fewer interpretations can survive the first of these tests than would have survived had they received fewer chapters. Most interpreters would think that a certain interpretation of *A Christmas Carol*—that Scrooge was inherently evil, for example—would pass the test of integrity just after the opening pages, but not toward the end of that novel. Our sense that later novelists are less free may reflect just that fact. This does not mean, of course, that there is more likely to be consensus about the correct interpretation later rather than earlier in the chain or that a later novelist is more likely to find an argument that "proves" his interpretation right beyond rational challenge. Reasonable disagreement is available on the formal as well as the substantive side, and even when most novelists would think only a particular interpretation could fit the novel to a certain point, some novelist of imagination might find some dramatic change in plot that (in his opinion) unexpectedly unifies what had seemed unnecessary and redeems what had seemed wrong or trivial. Once again, we should be careful not to confuse the fact that consensus would rarely be reached, at any point in the process, with the claim that any particular novelist's interpretation must be "merely subjective." No novelist, at any point, will be able simply to read the correct interpretation of the text he receives in a mechanical way, but it does not follow from

that fact alone that one interpretation is not superior to others overall. In any case it will nevertheless be true, for all novelists beyond the first, that the assignment to find (what they believe to be) the correct interpretation of the text so far is a different assignment from the assignment to begin a new novel of their own. See, for a fuller discussion, my "Natural Law Revisited," *University of Florida Law Review*, 34: 165–188 (1982).

6. See above, Chapter 2, "The Forum of Principle."

7. See Stanley Fish, *Is There a Text in This Class?: The Authority of Interpretive Communities* (Cambridge, Mass.: Harvard University Press, 1980).

8. See W. J. T. Mitchell, ed., *The Politics of Interpretation* (Chicago and London: Chicago University Press, 1983).

7. ON INTERPRETATION AND OBJECTIVITY

Note. This new essay draws on material in Ronald Dworkin, "My Reply to Stanley Fish (and Walter Benn Michaels): Please Don't Talk about Objectivity Any More," in W. J. T. Mitchell, ed., *The Politics of Interpretation* (Chicago and London: University of Chicago Press, 1983). © Ronald Dworkin.

1. Stanley Fish commented on my original essay in "Working on the Chain Gang," *Texas Law Review*, 60: 551–567 (1982); reprinted in *Critical Inquiry* (September 1982), p. 201. He has since published a further criticism: "Wrong Again," *Texas Law Review*, 62: 299–316 (1983).

8. LIBERALISM

Note. Originally published in Stuart Hampshire, ed., *Public and Private Morality* (Cambridge: Cambridge University Press, 1978). © 1978 Cambridge University Press.

1. I shall provide, in this note, a more detailed description of this distinction. A comprehensive political theory is a structure in which the elements are related more or less systematically, so that very concrete political positions (like the position that income taxes should now be raised or reduced) are the consequences of more abstract positions (like the position that large degrees of economic inequality should be eliminated) that are in turn the consequences of still more abstract positions (like the position that a community should be politically stable) that may be the consequences of more abstract positions still. It would be unrealistic to suppose that ordinary citizens and politicians, or even political commentators or theoreticians, organize their political convictions in that way; yet anyone who supposes himself to take political decisions out of principle would recognize that some such organization of his full position must be possible in principle.

We may therefore distinguish, for any full political theory, between constitutive and derivative political positions. A constitutive position is a political position valued for its own sake: a political position such that any failure fully to secure that position, or any decline in the degree to which it is secured, is *pro tanto* a loss in the value of the overall political arrangement. A derivative political position is a position that is not, within the theory in question, constitutive.

A constitutive position is not necessarily absolute, within any theory, because a theory may contain different and to some degree antagonistic constitutive positions. Even though a theory holds, for example, that a loss in political equality is

pro tanto a loss in the justice of a political arrangement, it may nevertheless justify that loss in order to improve prosperity, because overall economic prosperity is also a constitutive position within the theory. In that case, the theory might recommend a particular economic arrangement (say a mixed capitalistic and socialistic economy) as the best compromise between two constitutive political positions, neither of which may properly be ignored. Neither equality nor overall well-being would be absolute, but both would be constitutive, because the theory would insist that if some means *could* be found to reach the same level of prosperity without limiting equality, then that result would be an improvement in justice over the compromise that is, unfortunately, necessary. If, on the other hand, the theory recognized that free enterprise was on the whole the best means of securing economic prosperity, but stood ready to abandon free enterprise, with no sense of any compromise, on those few occasions when free enterprise is not efficient, then free enterprise would be, within that theory, a derivative position. The theory would not argue that if some other means of reaching the same prosperity could be found, without curtailing free enterprise, that other means would be superior; if free enterprise is only a derivative position, then the theory is indifferent whether free enterprise or some other derivative position is sacrificed to improve the overall state-of-affairs. We must be careful to distinguish the question of whether a particular position is constitutive within a theory from the different question of whether the theory insulates the position by arguing that it is wrong to reexamine the value of the position on particular occasions. A theory may provide that some derivative positions should be more or less insulated from sacrifice on specified occasions, even when officials think that such a sacrifice would better serve constitutive positions, in order better to protect these constitutive goals in the long run. Rule utilitarianism is a familiar example, but the constitutive goals to be protected need not be utilitarian. A fundamentally egalitarian political theory might take political equality (one man, one vote) as an insulated though derivative position, not allowing officials to rearrange voting power to reach what they take to be a more fundamental equality in the community, because a more fundamental equality will be jeopardized rather than served by allowing tinkering with the franchise. Insulated derivative positions need not be absolute—a theory may provide that even an insulated position may be sacrificed, with no loss in overall justice even *pro tanto*, when the gain to constitutive positions is sufficiently apparent and pronounced. But insulated positions might be made absolute without losing their character as derivative.

2. See Ronald Dworkin, *Taking Rights Seriously* (Cambridge, Mass.: Harvard University Press, 1977; London: Duckworth, 1978), ch. 12.

3. Ibid., p. 227.

4. See Thomas Scanlon, "Preference and Urgency," *Journal of Philosophy*, 72: 655 (1975).

5. A very different objection calls attention to the fact that some people are afflicted with incapacities like blindness or mental disease, so that they require more resources to satisfy the same scheme of preferences. That is a more appealing objection to my principle of rough equality of treatment, but it calls, not for choosing a different basic principle of distribution, but for corrections in the application of the principle like those I consider later.

6. *Taking Rights Seriously,* pp. 234 ff., 275.
7. See Ronald Dworkin, "Social Sciences and Constitutional Rights," *The Educational Forum,* 41: 271 (March 1977).

9. WHY LIBERALS SHOULD CARE ABOUT EQUALITY

Note. Originally published in *The New York Review of Books,* February 3, 1983. © Ronald Dworkin.

1. I discuss liberty as based on the concept of neutrality in "What Liberalism Isn't," the next essay.
2. In another article I tried to develop a theoretical standard for redistribution along the following lines. Suppose we imagine that people have an equal risk of losing whatever talents they have for producing wealth for themselves, and are offered insurance, on equal terms, against this risk. Given what we know about people's aversion to risk in the United States, we can sensibly speculate about the amount of the insurance they would buy and the premium rate structure that would develop. We can justifiably model a system of tax and redistribution on this hypothetical insurance market, by taxing people up to the limit of the premiums they would have paid. This would provide more taxes and a greater fund for redistribution than we currently provide, but obviously not equality of result. See "What is Equality? Part II," in *Philosophy and Public Affairs* (Fall 1981).

10. WHAT JUSTICE ISN'T

Note. Originally published in *The New York Review of Books,* April 14, 1983. © Ronald Dworkin.

1. In Chapter 9, "Why Liberals Should Care about Equality," I describe a version of equality more complex than simple equality in that way.

11. CAN A LIBERAL STATE SUPPORT ART?

Note. This essay was presented to a conference on public support of the arts, held at The Metropolitan Museum of Art, New York, in April 1984, and sponsored by The Metropolitan Museum and Columbia University. © Ronald Dworkin.

12. IS WEALTH A VALUE?

Note. Originally published in *The Journal of Legal Studies,* 9: 191–226 (March 1980). © Ronald Dworkin.

1. Richard A. Posner, *Economic Analysis of Law* (2nd ed., Boston: Little, Brown, 1977).
2. Compare Sturges v. Bridgman, 11 Ch. D. 852 (1879), and discussion of that case in R. H. Coase, "The Problem of Social Cost," *Journal of Law and Economics,* 3: 1 (1960).
3. Ibid.
4. See, for example, Richard A. Posner, "Utilitarianism, Economics, and Legal Theory," *Journal of Legal Studies,* 8: 103 (1979). The following passages from that essay (among others) illustrate the assumption that wealth maximization is a value in itself, so that the claims for wealth maximization are to be understood as claims of the same order as, and competing with, the claims of the utilitarians that happiness is a value in itself: (*a*) "the economist, when speaking normatively, tends to

define the good, the right, or the just as the maximization of 'welfare' in a sense indistinguishable from the utilitarian's concept of utility or happiness . . . But for my normative purposes I want to define the maximand more narrowly, as 'value' in the economic sense of the term or, more clearly I think, as 'wealth' " (p. 119). (*b*) "While nowadays relatively few of the people in our society who think about these things consider wealth maximization or some other version of efficiency the paramount social value, few judge it a trivial one. And, as mentioned, sometimes it is the only value at stake in a question . . . But I am unwilling to let the matter rest there, for it seems to me that economic analysis has some claim to being re-garded as a coherent and attractive *basis* for ethical judgments. I am less clear that utilitarianism has such a claim" (p. 110; italics mine).

5. Anyone who wishes a more familiar (though in certain irrelevant ways more complex) example may substitute this one. Suppose a public body needs a piece of land in private hands but the owner will not sell. In these circumstances a court might order a compulsory transfer at some price the public body is willing to pay and the seller would in fact accept if he believed it was the best he could get. If we assume that there is such a price, then (in our substitute case) the court compels transfer with no compensation whatsoever to the seller. The transaction costs of litigating to fix the precise compensation will be saved, and we assume that these are greater than any consequential costs. (See Posner, above, note 1, at pp. 40–44.) Is the situation immediately after the forced and uncompensated transfer in any respect superior to the situation just before? (The warnings I give in the text against misunderstanding the force of the text example would hold here too.)

6. Posner, note 4 above. In Posner, note 1 above, the sense of interpersonal comparisons is challenged along familiar grounds. No effort is made in the later article to reconcile the two positions.

7. *Richard III*, Act I, scene iv, 1.6.

8. Guido Calabresi, *The Costs of Accidents* (New Haven: Yale University Press, 1970). Calabresi tells me that, though the passage I cite has often been taken to call for some trade-off between justice and cost reduction, that was not his mean-ing. But see Guido Calabresi, "About Law and Economics: A Letter to Ronald Dworkin," *Hofstra Law Review*, 8: 553 (1980), and below, Chapter 13, "Why Ef-ficiency?"

9. Posner, note 4 above.

10. Posner, note 4 above, defines "Kantian" so as to describe a political theory that rejects "any form of consequentialism" (p. 104). Kant is not, on this defini-tion, a Kantian.

11. Ibid., p. 108.

12. Ibid., pp. 125–126.

13. Robert Nozick, *Anarchy, State and Utopia* (New York: Basic Books, 1974).

14. See the essays by Paul H. Rubin and George Priest in *Journal of Legal Stud-ies*, 9 (March 1980).

15. See Ronald Dworkin, *Taking Rights Seriously*, pp. 98–100, 294–327 (paper edition, 1978). See also below, Chapter 13, "Why Efficiency?" In the article I have criticized here, Posner makes several comments about my own work. His remarks are not pellucidly consistent. He cites me as his first example of a legal philosopher who argues that legal theory should not be based on utilitarianism. So

far so good. But then he speculates about whether I am a "genuine Kantian" or only something he calls a "utilitarian of the egalitarian school." And he later remands that I am "arguably" what he calls a "left-wing utilitarian." May I help? I am not a "Kantian" as defined (see note 10 above) though I am very drawn to what I regard as the essential liberalism and egalitarianism of Kant's own theory. I am an egalitarian, though I have tried to describe a conception of equality, which requires that individuals be treated as equals rather than given equal treatment under some particular description, and some of my critics argue that this is not the correct conception of equality. I do not know whether I am left-wing, because I do not understand the sense well enough to be capable with the extension. I am mystified, however, as to why I should be considered a utilitarian, closet or crypto or otherwise. I have argued that so far as utilitarian calculations have any place in political argument (and I think that something *like* utilitarian calculations over preferences do have *some* place) then they must at least be cleansed of what I call "external" preferences. But a utilitarian is not someone who argues that such calculations have some place. He argues that they must occupy all the space there is. Those who find any interest in this autobiographical matter (if there are any) may wish to consult my *Taking Rights Seriously* (Cambridge, Mass.: Harvard University Press, 1977; London: Duckworth, 1978).

16. This article, as originally published in the *Journal of Legal Studies*, contained a postscript written in rebuttal to arguments made in Richard A. Posner, "The Value of Wealth: A Comment on Dworkin and Kronman," *Journal of Legal Studies*, 9: 243 (1980).

13. WHY EFFICIENCY?
Note. Originally published in the *Hofstra Law Review*, 8: 563–590 (1980). © Ronald Dworkin.

1. See Guido Calabresi, "About Law and Economics: A Letter to Ronald Dworkin," *Hofstra Law Review*, 8: 553 (1980), in which Calabresi responds to Dworkin, "Is Wealth a Value?" *Journal of Legal Studies*, 9: 191 (1980).

2. Guido Calabresi, *The Costs of Accidents* (New Haven: Yale University Press, 1970).

3. Richard A. Posner, "The Ethical and Political Basis of the Efficiency Norm in Common Law Adjudication," *Hofstra Law Review*, 8: 487, 492–496 (1980).

4. Ronald Dworkin, "What Is Equality," parts I and II, *Philosophy and Public Affairs*, 10.3 and 10.4 (1981).

5. J. C. Harsanyi, "Morality and the Theory of Rational Behavior," *Social Research*, 44: 623 (1977).

6. R. M. Hare, *Freedom and Reason* (Oxford: Oxford University Press, 1963), pp. 112–136.

7. See generally John Rawls, *A Theory of Justice* (Cambridge, Mass.: Harvard University Press, 1971), pp. 22–27.

8. See Ronald Dworkin, *Taking Rights Seriously* (Cambridge, Mass.: Harvard University Press, 1977; London: Duckworth, 1978), chs. 9, 12.

9. Guido Calabresi did reply to my remarks; see above, note 1, at p. 533n. I responded to his reply in a paragraph that has been omitted from this reprinted article.

10. Richard A. Posner, "Utilitarianism, Economics, and Legal Theory," *Journal of Legal Studies*, 8: 103 (1979).

11. In *Hofstra Law Review*, 8 (1980).

12. Ibid., pp. 491–497.

13. *Taking Rights Seriously*, ch. 6.

14. *Hofstra Law Review*, 8: 492.

15. Ibid., pp. 491–492.

16. Ibid., pp. 494–495.

17. Ibid., pp. 497–499.

18. Dworkin, *Taking Rights Seriously*, ch. 6.

19. Posner, *Hofstra Law Review*, 8: 497–499.

20. Ibid., p. 495.

21. See Dworkin, *Taking Rights Seriously*, p. 233.

22. See A. John Simmons, "The Principle of Fair Play," *Philosophy and Public Affairs*, 8: 307 (1979).

23. See United States v. Carroll Towing Company, 159 F.2d 169, 173 (2d Cir. 1947).

14. BAKKE'S CASE: ARE QUOTAS UNFAIR?
Note. Originally published in *The New York Review of Books*, November 10, 1977. © Ronald Dworkin.

15. WHAT DID *BAKKE* REALLY DECIDE?
Note. Originally published in *The New York Review of Books*, August 17, 1983. © Ronald Dworkin.

16. HOW TO READ THE CIVIL RIGHTS ACT
Note. Originally published in *The New York Review of Books*, December 20, 1979. © Ronald Dworkin.

1. Legislators must use theories of legislation themselves in forming beliefs or making predictions about the consequences of inexplicit statutes. But a legislator cannot use, as part of his theory of legislation, the psychological concept of legislative intent that makes his own opinion, along with the opinion of others, decisive of the content of legislation. For neither he nor they could *have* such opinions unless they had already applied a *different* theory of legislation: no group can apply the theory that the content of legislation is what that group thinks it is. Unless the concept of collective understanding is carefully limited to the hopes rather than simply the beliefs of legislators, the concept becomes incoherent. It supplies a test of the content of legislation that supposes that those whose opinions this test uses have themselves used a different test of the same thing.

2. For a discussion of this important issue, see the two preceding essays, "Bakke's Case: Are Quotas Unfair?" and "What Did *Bakke* Really Decide?"

17. DO WE HAVE A RIGHT TO PORNOGRAPHY?
Note. Originally published in the *Oxford Journal of Legal Studies*, 1: 177–212 (Summer 1981). © Ronald Dworkin.

1. Cmnd 7772, HMSO, London, 1979.

2. Report, p. 55.

3. Legal purists might object that the argument of the Report here depends not on the slippery slope but on that different weapon, the bright line (or absence of the same). But it is perfectly clear what argument is meant, and I follow the Report's language.

4. Report, p. 138.

5. Report, p. 100.

6. Report, p. 139.

7. Report, p. 138.

8. Report, pp. 96–97.

9. Report, pp. 99–100. For the point about denying substantive liberty, in the penultimate sentence, the Report cites H. L. A. Hart, *Law, Liberty, and Morality* (Stanford: Stanford University Press, 1963), pp. 45 ff.

10. The Report cites Hart to support its argument here. But Hart's argument seems to consist only in the mistake just identified. "To punish people for causing this form of distress would be tantamount to punishing them simply because others object to what they do; and the only liberty that would coexist with this extension of the utilitarian principle is liberty to do those things to which *no one* seriously objects. Such liberty is plainly quite nugatory." Hart, *Law, Liberty, and Morality*, p. 47 (italics mine). The first of these sentences is a non-sequitur, and provides no argument against the suggestion described in the text.

11. See the second part of this essay; see also Dworkin, *Taking Rights Seriously* (Cambridge, Mass.: Harvard University Press, 1978 ed.), ch. 12.

12. Report, p. 55.

13. Ibid., quoted above at note 2.

14. 357 US 449 (1958).

15. Dworkin, *Taking Rights Seriously*.

16. I leave, for another occasion perhaps, the question of what background rights we should accept as trumps if we chose, as our background justification, something closer to the best-conditions-for-human-flourishing goal of the Williams strategy. But we might notice that that theory may not be so far from the more sophisticated forms of utilitarianism than at first appears, at least on the following assumption. The goal of human flourishing admits of two interpretations, which we might call a platonic and a liberal interpretation. The platonic interpretation insists that the best conditions are those in which it is most likely that people will in fact choose and lead the lives that are the most valuable lives for them to lead. The liberal interpretation holds instead that the best conditions are those that provide people the best and most informed choice about how to lead their lives. The best conditions for choice, in this liberal sense, require not simply a wide choice of possibilities permitted by law, but also a public environment in which examples of different ways to live are in evidence, a cultural tradition in which these are imaginatively explored in various forms of art, and a system of laws that both provides the institutions and relationships that many of these ways of life require and protects them from various forms of corruption. The Williams strategy tries to bring these the platonic and liberal interpretations together in its claim that the best means for discovering which lives are in fact best lies in supplying the best conditions for choice in the liberal sense. But this is only an hypothesis: we found reasons for doubting it, and the world about us does not lend it

much support. So the choice between the two interpretations is a genuine choice. The platonic interpretation does not necessarily justify brainwashing or the other techniques of thought control that we have learned to fear. But I doubt that it appeals to many people, and I shall assume that the liberal interpretation is the theory now in question. We saw, in the first part of this essay, that the various features of a good environment for choice might conflict with one another. If the law forbids pornography even in private, then it limits choice in an important way. But if it does not then it limits choice in another way: those who wish to form sexual relationships based on culturally supported attitudes of respect and beauty, and to raise their children to that ideal, may find their plans much harder to achieve if pornography has taken too firm a hold in popular culture, which it may do even without public display. So the goal of best conditions for human flourishing, at least in the liberal interpretation, requires trade offs and compromises much as any form of utilitarianism does. In that case we might plausibly (at least for some purposes) take the goal of providing these conditions to be a particularly enlightened form of utilitarianism, which measures the value of a community, not by the opportunity it offers people overall, in the aggregate, to fulfill whatever preferences in fact they have, but rather by the opportunity it offers them, again in the aggregate, to develop and fulfill coherent and informed conceptions of the most valuable lives for them to lead. (Though we should remember that Professor Williams rejects, at least as theory of personal morality, more traditional forms of utilitarianism. See J.J.C. Smart and Bernard Williams, *Utilitarianism: For and Against,* Cambridge University Press, 1973.) But I shall not insist on that assimilation here, or consider how the argument I give might have to be modified if we did take this generous interpretation of the boundaries of utilitarianism.

17. Though there are obvious dangers of a circle here. See Dworkin, "What is Equality? Part I: Equality of Welfare," *Philosophy and Public Affairs,* 10: 3 (1981).

18. Hart, "Between Utility and Rights," *Columbia Law Review,* 79: 828, 836 ff. (1980).

19. See Dworkin, *Taking Rights Seriously,* introduction, ch. 12, and app., pp. 357–358. See also Dworkin, "Liberalism," in Stuart Hampshire, ed., *Public and Private Morality* (Cambridge, Eng.: Cambridge University Press, 1978), and Dworkin, "Social Science and Constitutional Rights: the Consequences of Uncertainty," *Journal of Law and Education,* 6: 3 (1977).

20. Hart, *Law, Liberty, and Morality,* p. 842.

21. See, e.g., ibid., p. 845, n. 43.

22. See Dworkin, *Taking Rights Seriously,* pp. 266–272.

18. THE FARBER CASE: REPORTERS AND INFORMERS
Note. Originally published in *The New York Review of Books,* October 26, 1978. © Ronald Dworkin.

1. Federal Judge Lacey, in a hearing on Farber's petition for *habeas corpus,* emphasized that Farber had undertaken to write a book about the Jascalevich case. Many newspapers and columnists have since assumed that the proposed book weakens Farber's case either legally or morally. It seems to me, on the con-

trary, almost irrelevant. Farber's contract with his publisher does not make the book's publication conditional on the conviction of Jascalevich, and there is no shred of evidence either that Farber will publish in the book material that he sought to withhold from the court or that he has any financial or personal stake in Jascalevich's conviction. There is no reason to doubt that Farber would have acted just as he did even if he had not planned to write a book.

19. IS THE PRESS LOSING THE FIRST AMENDMENT?
Note. Originally published in *The New York Review of Books*, December 4, 1980. © Ronald Dworkin.

1. The earlier case was Gannett v. DePasquale, which the press especially resented. That decision permitted a judge to exclude reporters from a pre-trial hearing, and Chief Justice Burger's opinion in the Richmond Newspapers case states that the earlier decision was intended to apply only to such hearings and not to actual trials. But Burger's own opinion in the Gannett case, as well as the opinions of other Justices, seemed to cover actual trials as well, so that the Richmond Newspapers decision was probably a change of mind, as Mr. Justice Blackmun says it was in his own separate opinion in the latter case.

2. Frank Snepp, *Decent Interval: An Insider's Account of Saigon's Indecent End Told by the CIA's Chief Strategy Analyst in Vietnam* (New York: Random House, 1977).

3. Victor Marchetti and John D. Marks, *The CIA and the Cult of Intelligence* (New York: Knopf, 1974).

4. Bob Woodward and Scott Armstrong, *The Brethren* (New York: Simon and Schuster, 1980).

5. Nor did the British House of Lords in a recent case in which British Steel Corporation sued Granada television to discover the name of an informer in the Steel Corporation's management.

6. Nat Hentoff, *The First Freedom: The Tumultuous History of Free Speech in America* (New York: Delacorte, 1979).

7. See *Taking Rights Seriously* (Cambridge, Mass.: Harvard University Press, 1977; London: Duckworth, 1978).

8. The Court faced that issue in the recent case of Houhins v. KGBX, in which prison adminstrators refused a television station all opportunities to investigate prison conditions. Perhaps because two Justices were unable to participate in the case, the Court reached no effective disposition of the issues of legal principle.

9. It is a different question, which I cannot consider now, how far Congress may constitutionally forbid citizens in general, and former agents in particular, from publishing information that may be genuinely secret and dangerous, like the names of present agents, as the bill I described earlier proposes to do.

10. The CIA initially listed 339 sections of Marchetti's book that it said disclosed classified information. These included a statement about Richard Helms's briefing of the National Security Council, in which Marchetti reported that "his otherwise flawless performance was marred by his mispronunciation of Malagasy, formerly Madagascar, when referring to the young republic." Marchetti and Knopf took the issue to litigation, during which the CIA itself conceded that 171 of these sections were not classified.

11. As a legal matter, it is necessary to recognize an independent constitutional right in order to protect those who want to listen to someone who does not himself have a constitutional right to speak. The Supreme Court has held, for example, that the First Amendment protects Americans who want to receive political material from foreign authors who are not, of course, themselves protected by the United States Constitution.

12. In particular cases differences of this character may be differences in degree only. Commercial secrets, for example, may be matters of political importance. But if so, then the argument against enforcing waivers in such cases is correspondingly stronger.

Index

CONTENTS

ОГЛАВЛЕНИЕ

Зоны растительности Европейской России: 1, тундра (приполярная область с мелкой растительностью); 2, лесная зона; 3, степная зона; 4, полупустыни и пустыни; 5, субтропическая зона.

Исторические места Европейской России

1

осо́бенность (f.) peculiarity
разнообра́зие diversity
пове́рхность (f.) surface
хребе́т ridge (also backbone)
плоского́рье plateau
равни́на plain (noun)
простра́нство space
зали́в gulf
полуо́стров peninsula
однообра́зие monotony
клин wedge
матери́к continent
кочево́й nomadic

коче́вник nomad
за́суха drought
посре́дник mediator
влечь to draw, attract
привле́чь (perf.)
вла́га moisture
поле́зный useful
вре́дный harmful
расти́тельность (f.) vegetation
стихи́я element (of nature, geography)

ГЕОГРА́ФИЯ ЕВРОПЕ́ЙСКОЙ РОССИ́И

Две географи́ческие осо́бенности отлича́ют Евро́пу от други́х часте́й све́та, и от А́зии преиму́щественно: Э́то, во пе́рвых, разнообра́зие форм пове́рхности и во вторы́х, кра́йне изви́листое очерта́ние морски́х берего́в. Нигде́ го́рные хребты́, плоского́рья и равни́ны не сменя́ют друг дру́га на таки́х сравни́тельно ма́лых простра́нствах как в Евро́пе. С друго́й стороны́, глубо́кие зали́вы и далеко́ выдаю́щиеся полуострова́ образу́ют как бы берегово́е кру́жево за́падной и ю́жной Евро́пы.

Европе́йская Росси́я не разделя́ет э́тих вы́годных приро́дных осо́бенностей Евро́пы. Мо́ре образу́ет лишь ма́лую до́лю её грани́ц. Берегова́я ли́ния её море́й незначи́тельна сравнительно с её материковым пространством. Однообразие—отличительная черта её поверхности. Одна форма господствует почти на всём её пространстве. Эта форма—равнина, плоскость пространством около двух миллионов квадратных миль, т. е. площадь равняющаяся двум третям континентальной площади Соединённых Штатов—без Аляски. На севере эта равнина покрыта лесами, на юге она переходит в маловодную, безлесную степь.

По геологическому своему строению эта степь совершенно похожа на степи внутренней Азии, а географически она составляет прямое их продолжение, соединяясь со среднеазиатскими степями широкими воротами между Уральским хребтом и Каспийским морем и простираясь из-за Урала сначала широкой, а потом всё более узкой полосой по направлению к западу, мимо морей Каспийского, Азовского и Чёрного. Это как бы азиатский клин, вдвинутый в европейский материк и тесно связанный с Азией исторически и климатически. Здесь издавна шла дорога, которой через урало-каспийские ворота приходили в Европу из глубины Азии страшные гости, все эти кочевые орды, неисчислимые, как степная трава или песок азиатской пустыни. Умеренная Западная Европа не знает таких сильных засух и таких страшных зимних бурь, какие бывают на этой степной равнине, а они заносятся сюда из Азии.

Столько Азии в Европейской России. Исторически Россия конечно не Азия. Но географически она не совсем и Европа. Это переходная страна, посредница между двумя мирами. Культура связала её с Европой. Но природа положила на неё особенности и влияния, которые всегда влекли её к Азии или в неё влекли Азию.

От однообразия формы поверхности в значительной мере зависит и климат страны, распределение тепла и влаги в воздухе и частью направление ветров. Однообразие формы поверхности делает климатические переходы с севера на юг и с запада на восток более мягкими. Ветры, беспрепятственно носясь по всей равнине и мешая воздуху застаиваться, сближают в климатическом отношении места, очень удалённые друг от друга по географическому положению, и содействуют более равномерному распределению влаги с запада на восток и тепла с севера на юг.

Летом в северной и средней России преобладают западные, дождливые и поэтому полезные, орошающие поля и леса ветры. Урал задерживает облака принесённые этими ветрами со стороны Атлантического океана и заставляет их разрешаться обильными дождями. Летом в северной и средней России выпадает обыкновенно больше дождей, чем в Западной Европе. В южной, степной России напротив преобладают сухие, и поэтому вредные, восточные ветры, которым открытая степь при её связи с пустынями средней Азии даёт сюда свободный доступ. Эта воздушная борьба Азии с Европой в пределах русской равнины напоминает историческую эпоху, когда Россия служила широкой ареной борьбы азиатских народов с европейскими.

Южная степь, при постоянных сильных и сухих ветрах, в ней господствующих, не в силах питать древесной растительности. В этом главная причина безлесья степной полосы.

Лес, степь и река—это основные стихии русской природы по своему историческому значению. Каждая из них сыграла важную роль в строении жизни, культуры и понятий русского человека.

Лес сыграл крупную роль в русской истории. В лесной России положены были основы русского государства. До второй половины 18 века жизнь наибольшей части русского народа шла в лесной полосе русской равнины. Лес оказывал русскому человеку разнообразные услуги. Он давал строительный материал, отопление, обувь (лапти из коры), посуду, пищу (лесных зверей и мёд диких пчёл) и убежище от врагов, заменяя западноевропейские горы и замки.

Степь оказывала другие услуги и клала другие впечатления. Доброе историческое значение южнорусской степи заключается в её близости к южным морям, особенно к Чёрному. Но степь заключала в себе и важные исторические неудобства. Вместе с дарами она несла бедствия. Она была вечной угрозой для древней Руси. Борьба со степным кочевником, длившаяся с 8 почти до конца 18 века—одно из самых тяжёлых исторических воспоминаний русского народа.

Так степь действовала на русского человека двусмысленно. Зато никаких недоразумений не бывало у него с русской рекой. Он любил свою реку, говорил ласковые слова о ней в своих песнях—и было за что. При переселениях река указывала ему путь, при поселении она его соседка. На её берегу он ставил свой дом, деревню или город. В продолжение значительной части года она и питала его. Для торговца она готовая летняя и даже зимняя, ледяная дорога.

В древней Руси расселение шло по рекам. Река приучила людей к общежитию и общительности. Она сближала разбросанные части населения, учила человека чувствовать себя членом общества, обращаться с чужими людьми, наблюдать их нравы и интересы, меняться товаром и опытом. Так разнообразна была историческая служба русской реки.

2

век century
also: **столе́тие**
прито́к tributary
пробра́ться to wend one's way
perf. of: **пробира́ться**
погра́бить to plunder,
perf. of: **гра́бить**
покида́ть to abandon
поки́нуть (perf.)
наёмный hired
овладева́ть to seize, take possession of
овладе́ть (perf.)
превраща́ть to transform
преврати́ть (perf.)

князь (m.) prince
кня́жество principality
средневеко́вье Middle Ages
also: **сре́дние века́**
подъём rise
правосла́вный orthodox
собо́р cathedral
могу́чий mighty
ру́копись (f.) manuscript
монасты́рь monastery
ле́топись (f.) chronicle
зо́дчество architecture
жи́вопись (f.) painting
богаты́рь (m.) valiant knight
междоусо́бие feud

КИ́ЕВСКАЯ РУСЬ—ВОСТО́ЧНАЯ ОКРА́ЙНА ЕВРО́ПЫ
(9–12 века́)

Река́ Днепр с прито́ками обхва́тывает всю за́падную полови́ну ру́сской равни́ны и соединя́ет её с се́верными, ю́жными, за́падными и восто́чными областя́ми. Верхо́вьями свои́ми Днепр бли́зко подхо́дит к За́падной Двине́ и бассе́йну И́льменя о́зера, т. е. к двум важне́йшим доро́гам в Балти́йское мо́ре. У́стьем Днепр соединя́ется с Чёрным мо́рем. Пра́вые прито́ки Днепра́ приближа́ют Поднепро́вье к бассе́йнам Днестра́ и Ви́слы, т. е. к За́падной Евро́пе, а ле́вые прито́ки соединя́ют о́бласть Днепра́ с бассе́йнами Во́лги и До́на, т. е. с восто́ком и с моря́ми Каспи́йским и Азо́вским.

Благодаря́ тому́, по Днепру́ с незапа́мятных времён шло оживлённое торго́вое движе́ние. В 8 ве́ке Днепр с прито́ками сде́лался могу́чей пита́тельной арте́рией наро́дного хозя́йства славя́нских племён, занима́вших преиму́щественно лесну́ю по́лосу Поднепро́вья. Речно́й путь втяну́л славя́н в торго́вое движе́ние, кото́рое шло тогда́ в ю́го-восто́чном углу́ Евро́пы. Свои́м низовы́м тече́нием и ле́выми прито́ками Днепр потяну́л славя́н к черномо́рским и каспи́йским ры́нкам и указа́л им доро́гу в богате́йший центр мирово́й культу́ры и торго́вли того́ вре́мени, в Византи́ю.

Леса́ Поднепро́вья свои́м пу́шным бога́тством и лесны́м пчелово́дством доставля́ли славя́нам оби́льный материа́л для вне́шней торго́вли. Меха́, мёд и воск ста́ли гла́вными предме́тами вы́воза. Сле́дствием успе́хов торго́вли славя́н бы́ло появле́ние древне́йших торго́вых городо́в по Днепру́ и его́ прито́кам: Ки́ев, Переясла́вль, Черни́гов, Смоле́нск, Лю́бец, Но́вгород, Росто́в, По́лоцк и мно́гие други́е. Большинство́ э́тих городо́в вы́тянулось дли́нной це́пью по гла́вному речно́му пути́ из Балти́йского в Чёрное мо́ре. Таки́м о́бразом, пе́рвая полити́ческая и культу́рная фо́рма, образова́вшаяся среди́ славя́н в 8 и 9 века́х, э́то городова́я о́бласть, т. е. торго́вый о́круг, в це́нтре кото́рого стоя́л укреплённый го́род.

С нача́ла 9 ве́ка по окра́инам Евро́пы начина́ют появля́ться вооружённые пира́ты из Скандина́вии. На речны́х путя́х ру́сской равни́ны э́ти пира́ты с Балти́йского мо́ря получа́ют назва́ние варя́гов. Варя́г был преиму́щественно вооружённый купе́ц, иду́щий сюда́, что́бы пробра́тся да́льше в бога́тую Византи́ю, там вы́годно поторгова́ть, а иногда́ и погра́бить бога́того гре́ка, е́сли предста́вится к тому́ слу́чай. В тех торго́вых це́нтрах ру́сской равни́ны, куда́ с осо́бенной си́лой прилива́ли вооружённые компа́нии варя́гов, они́ легко́ покида́ли значе́ние торго́вых това́рищей и́ли наёмных охрани́телей торго́вых путе́й и превраща́лись во власти́телей. Вождь варя́жской компа́нии называ́лся кня́зем. Князь овладева́л городско́й о́бластью и превраща́л её в кня́жество. Из соедине́ния варя́жских кня́жеств и сохрани́вших самостоя́тельность городовы́х областе́й вы́шло вели́кое кня́жество Ки́евское и́ли Ки́евская

Русь. Основа́теля дина́стии, кото́рая объедини́ла под свое́й вла́стью славя́нские племена́ поднепро́вской о́бласти зва́ли Рю́риком.

Едва́-ли в како́й-ли́бо друго́й стране́ средневеко́вого ми́ра мо́жно встре́тить так мно́го перекрёстных культу́рных влия́ний как на Ки́евской Руси́. Она́ постоя́нно соприкаса́лась с други́ми наро́дами. Византи́я, наро́ды восто́ка и Кавка́за, За́падная Евро́па и Скандина́вия кольцо́м окружа́ли Русь. Но в формирова́нии ру́сской культу́ры осо́бое ме́сто занима́ют Скандина́вия—кото́рая дала́ Руси́ пра́вящую дина́стию Рю́риковичей—и Византи́я, са́мая передова́я страна́ европе́йского средневеко́вья. Из Византи́и Русь приняла́ христиа́нство при кня́зе Влади́мире Пе́рвом в конце́ 10 ве́ка. При Влади́мире и его́ сы́не кня́зе Яросла́ве Ки́евское госуда́рство вступа́ет на путь бы́строго культу́рного подъёма. При них установи́лись осо́бенно те́сные культу́рные свя́зи с Византи́ей, отку́да приглаша́лись церко́вные пропове́дники правосла́вной ве́ры и худо́жники для постро́йки и отде́лки но́вых зда́ний, кото́рые сотру́дничали с ру́сскими мастера́ми. Несмотря́ на иностра́нные влия́ния, в 11 ве́ке ки́евское иску́сство уже́ облада́ет свои́м со́бственным лицо́м.

Для культу́ры Ки́евской Руси́ характе́рно сочета́ние земно́го, све́тского с боже́ственным, церко́вным. Правосла́вная це́рковь не то́лько подде́рживала полити́ческую власть кня́зя, но и благоволи́ла экономи́ческим предприя́тиям и торго́вым заня́тиям населе́ния.

Центра́льный па́мятник дре́внего Ки́ева и велича́йшее созда́ние иску́сства Ки́евской Руси́—Софи́йский собо́р. По мы́сли его́ созда́теля, кня́зя Яросла́ва, он до́лжен был просла́вить как освобожде́ние ру́сской земли́ от тьмы язы́чества, кото́рая рассе́ялась под де́йствием луче́й премудрости Бо́жьей, ина́че говоря́ Софи́и, так и могу́щество госуда́рственной вла́сти вели́кого кня́зя. Снару́жи могу́чие ма́ссы собо́ра группирова́лись пирамида́льно. Двена́дцать ма́лых куполо́в размеща́лись на угла́х масси́ва хра́ма, по четы́ре с за́пада и по два с восто́ка. В середи́не возвыша́лся оди́н огро́мный ку́пол. Основно́й масси́в хра́ма окружа́ла одноэта́жная откры́тая галлере́я. Таки́м о́бразом, ма́ссы хра́ма ступе́нями нараста́ли по направле́нию к центра́льному ку́полу. Вну́треннее простра́нство собо́ра было не ме́нее великоле́пно. Ро́спись Софи́и распада́ется на моза́ики и фре́ски и отлича́ется исключи́тельной красото́й свои́х кра́сок. Прославля́ется не то́лько власть небе́сная, но и власть земна́я. Наряду́ с религио́зными сюже́тами изображены́ све́тские—портре́ты кня́зя Яросла́ва и его́ семьи́, сце́ны кня́жеской охо́ты, музыка́нты и акроба́ты.

При Софи́йском собо́ре была́ осно́вана библиоте́ка, где храни́лись и перепи́сывались ру́кописи и где создала́сь своя́ шко́ла перево́дчиков и зароди́лось лето́писное де́ло. Ва́жную роль как расса́дники пи́сьменности и просвеще́ния игра́ли монастыри́. Крупне́йшим из них был Пече́рский монасты́рь осно́ванный в 11 ве́ке в ближа́йших окре́стностях Ки́ева, по образцу́ пеще́рного монастыря́ на Афо́не. В его́ сте́нах перепи́сывались кни́ги, расходи́вшиеся пото́м по кня́жеским и церко́вным библиоте́кам, вели́сь ле́тописи, воспи́тывались пропове́дники и писа́тели. Из среды́ мона́хов вы́шли выдаю́щиеся мастера́ зо́дчества и жи́вописи.

К важне́йшим па́мятникам ки́евской культу́ры принадлежа́т та́кже дре́вние эпи́ческие пе́сни, так называ́емые были́ны. Расцве́т были́нных пе́сен совпада́ет с эпо́хой расцве́та ки́евского госуда́рства, в 10–11 века́х. Они́ я́рко отрази́ли истори́ческие фа́кты, наро́дную идеоло́гию и бытовы́е черты́ того́ вре́мени. Они́ свя́заны со вре́менем кня́зя Влади́мира Пе́рвого, кото́рого были́ны называ́ют "Кра́сное со́лнышко". Его́ весёлые пиры́, бога́тство и высо́кая культу́ра его́ го́рода Ки́ева, всё э́то ста́ло традицио́нным во мно́гих были́нах. Вокру́г Влади́мира были́ны группирова́ли о́бразы богатыре́й—хра́брых, си́льных защи́тников ру́сской земли́ от набе́гов степны́х коче́вников. Оборо́на Руси́ от вне́шних враго́в составля́ет па́фос ру́сских были́н.

В ру́сской жи́зни оста́лось о́чень ма́ло следо́в от Ки́евской Руси́, от её бы́та. Софи́йский собо́р, наприме́р, так пострада́л от пожа́ров, разруше́ний, переде́лок и ремо́нтов, что он дошёл до нас в почти́ неузнава́емом ви́де. Тем не ме́нее, ру́сский наро́д по́мнит ста́рый Ки́ев с его́ князья́ми и богатыря́ми, с его́ собо́рами и монастыря́ми, по́мнит и лю́бит его́, как не люби́л он ни одно́й из столи́ц его́ сменивших, ни Москвы, ни Петербурга. Это происходило по двум причинам. Во первых, жизнь Киевской Руси отличалась благами, которые русский народ в последствии потерял либо навсегда, либо на очень долгое время. Надолго прекратились тесные, свободные сношения с чужими странами. Татарское нашествие нарушило городскую жизнь и торговлю, а затем крепостное право, созданное московским правительством, положило конец личной свободе русского человека. Во вторых, Киевская Русь была колыбелью русской народности. Во всём обществе пробудилась мысль о Русской Земле как о чём-то цельном, общем. В летописях и былинах повторяется выражение Русская земля, и нигде, ни в одном памятнике, не встречается выражение русский народ. Из всех элементов, входящих в состав государства, территория наиболее доступна пониманию. Она и служила определением рождавшемуся чувству народности.

Главная причина упадка киевского государства состояла в том, что члены правящей династии, потомки Рюрика, находились в постоянной вражде и междоусобии. Каждый хотел владеть Киевом. Киев был сборным пунктом русской торговли. Из Киева шёл выход на степные торговые дороги. Кто владел Киевом, тот держал в своих руках ключ от главных ворот русской торговли. Уже с конца 11 века начинается процесс разложения киевского государства. Киевская Русь постепенно распадается на ряд самостоятельных княжеств и областей. Одновременно напор степных кочевников делается всё сильнее. Особенно остро этот процесс распада сказался на южных областях. Они не смогли дать отпор нападавшим кочевникам, половцам. В поэме ''Слово о полку Игореве'' южная Русь оставила нам горький плач о своей гибели и одно из выдающихся произведений древней русской литературы. В ''Слове'' соединена историческая повесть и героическая лирика. Поэма описывает поход князя Игоря Северского в 1184 году против половцев, кончившийся неудачей из-за княжеских междоусобий. Поэма—призыв русских князей к объединению.

3

независимость (f.) independence
расцвет bloom, flowering
вече popular assembly (historical term)
сосредотачивать to concentrate
    сосредоточить (perf.)
торговля trade
промысел craft, profession
рынок market
купец merchant
товар merchandise
устный oral
творчество creative power, creation

столкновение clash
битва battle
языческий heathen
улов catch
увлекать to charm (also: to carry away)
    увлечь (perf.)
покровитель (m.) patron
сдержанность (f.) restraint
стремление aspiration
достигать to achieve
    достигнуть (perf.)
терять to lose
    потерять (perf.)
потеря loss

ДРЕВНИЙ НОВГОРОД И НОВГОРОДСКАЯ КУЛЬТУРА

Новгород объявил свою независимость от киевского княжества в 1125 году и затем обратил всё своё внимание и все силы на создание особого общественного и культурного строя. Расцвет Новгорода относится к 13, 14 и 15 векам. Верховная власть принадлежала вечу. В теории всякий новгородец, граждански свободный и имевший свой двор, мог участвовать в управлении своей страны. На деле же, властью овладела новгородская аристократия—бояре.

Вся новгородская страна простиралась от Белого моря

че́рез о́бласть озёр Ла́дожского, Оне́жского и Йльменя до водоразде́ла Йльменских рек и За́падной Двины́. Её центра́льную ли́нию с се́вера на юг составля́ли ре́ки Волхо́в и Ло́вать. На за́пад от э́той ли́нии бы́ло мно́го городо́в, т. е. укреплённых мест. Они́ защища́ли Но́вгород от вне́шних враго́в. Но все они́, за исключе́нием Пско́ва и Ста́рой Руси́, бы́ли ничто́жны в экономи́ческом отноше́нии. На восто́к от ли́нии Во́лхов—Ло́вать городо́в не́ было во́все. Новгоро́дская страна́ была́ сла́бо заселена́, и всё её населе́ние сосредота́чивалось в трёх пу́нктах—в само́м Но́вгороде, в Пско́ве и в Ста́рой Руси́. Но́вгород, по коли́честву дворо́в, ви́димо превосходи́л да́же Москву́ и был одни́м из крупне́йших городо́в не то́лько в Руси́ но и в Евро́пе. В Но́вгороде в 15 ве́ке бы́ло до 6,000 дворо́в. Таки́м о́бразом, в новгоро́дском госуда́рстве соверша́лась неравноме́рность в распределе́нии населе́ния. Столи́ца как бы вобрала́ в себя́ все си́лы свое́й земли́, оста́вив о́чень ма́ло прови́нции. Она́ сосредото́чила в себе́ всю торго́влю и все про́мыслы, став в э́том отноше́нии как бы оа́зисом в пусты́не.

Причи́ны тако́й концентра́ции наро́дно-хозя́йственных сил лежа́ли в основны́х сво́йствах новгоро́дской террито́рии. Земля́ дава́ла плохи́е, ску́дные урожа́и и земледе́лие явля́лось второстепе́нным заня́тием. Гла́вное же значе́ние в новгоро́дской хозя́йственной жи́зни принадлежа́ло торго́вле и тем про́мыслам, кото́рые её пита́ли. Про́мыслы э́ти дава́ли новгоро́дскому ры́нку дорого́й това́р: меха́, воск, соль и ры́бу. Чтобы их добыва́ть, на́до бы́ло идти́ за ни́ми на́ море и в се́верные леса́, где ещё в ска́зочном изоби́лии держа́лась драгоце́нная добы́ча. Стремя́сь к э́тому бога́тству, новгоро́дцы ра́но потяну́лись на далёкий се́вер, суро́вый но оби́льный, осво́или себе́ грома́дные простра́нства по берега́м Бе́лого мо́ря, счита́ли их свои́ми зе́млями и из них вози́ли на новгоро́дский ры́нок це́нные това́ры. Из Но́вгорода э́ти това́ры шли в Евро́пу, в обме́н на то, что привози́ли в Но́вгород ганзе́йские и шве́дские купцы́—на сукно́, вино́, пря́ности и мета́ллы. Европе́йский това́р новгоро́дцы распространя́ли на ру́сском ю́ге и восто́ке, а отту́да получа́ли в обме́н, гла́вным о́бразом, хлеб. Таки́м о́бразом, в кругооборо́те свое́й торго́вли Но́вгород ничего́ не добы-вал на собственной почве. Он был только посредником между своими северными колониями, Европой и Русью.

Новгородская торговля находилась в руках бояр. Они руководили всеми стадиями торгового оборота. Они на севере захватили в своё владение громадные пространства земель, населив их своими холопами. Они в самом Новгороде господствовали на рынке, заполняя его своими товарами и поставив купцов в зависимость от себя. На пространстве всего двух веков экономическое господство новгородской аристократии выросло до степени политической диктатуры. В 15 веке Новгород стал управляться небольшим кругом боярских семей, в руках которых сосредоточились все средства власти над массами.

Новгород был богат не только в экономическом, материальном отношении. Вместе с развитием торгово-ремесленной городской жизни шло умственное и художественное развитие. Памятниками умственной культуры Новгорода служит не только устное народное творчество, но и письменная, книжная литература. На первое место письменной литературы надо поставить летописание.

Новгородские летописи резко отличаются и по содержанию и по стилю от южнорусских, киевских. Новгородские летописцы интересуются почти исключительно своим городом и областью. Рассказы о походах и сражениях у них сравнительно редки и скупы. У новгородцев на первом плане гражданские интересы—выборы, смены и смерти гражданских и церковных властей, столкновения низших слоёв населения с боярами. Новгородские летописцы также отмечают климатические явления—грозы, бури, грады, наводнения. Затем они, видимо. не упустили отметить ни одного случая окончания или ремонта общественных построек—моста, кремля, городских стен или церквей. Из прочих событий местной жизни с такой же точностью отмечаются случаи неурожая, голода, эпидемий, пожаров и других общественных бедствий.

Южные летописи пространны и часто представляют целые литературные, поэтические рассказы, в особенности на военные темы. Новгородские летописи деловиты, точны и кратки. Сравнительно сухи в них даже страницы посвящённые са́мым герои́ческим моме́нтам ме́стной исто́рии, наприме́р би́тве Алекса́ндра Не́вского про́тив шве́дов и ливо́нских ры́царей.

В у́стно-поэти́ческом тво́рчестве новгоро́дской земли́ та́кже как и в ле́тописях отража́ется жизнь и быт большо́го торго́вого го́рода и его́ огро́мной о́бласти. Одни́м из са́мых изве́стных произведе́ний новгоро́дского фолькло́ра явля́ется были́на о Садко́. В э́той были́не ме́стные бытовы́е черты́ наро́дной жи́зни и христиа́нской ве́ры Но́вгорода соединя́ются с иде́ями дре́внего се́верного мифи́ческого э́поса и язы́ческих преда́ний. В э́той были́не расска́зывается, как музыка́нт Садко́, в награ́ду за превосхо́дную игру́ получа́ет от морско́го царя́, хозя́ина воды́, необыкнове́нный уло́в рыбы́ в о́зере Ильмене. Садко́ от э́того богате́ет и стано́вится одни́м из пе́рвых купцо́в в Но́вгороде. Занима́ясь замо́рской торго́влей, Садко́ пла́вает с това́рами по моря́м, но да́ни морско́му царю́ не пла́тит. Морско́й царь се́рдится, остана́вливает корабли́ Садко́ и тре́бует его́ к себе́. Попа́в в подво́дное ца́рство, Садко́ опя́ть стано́вится музыка́нтом и увлека́ет морско́го царя́ свое́й игро́й. Царь танцу́ет, его́ бы́стрые движе́ния поднима́ют бу́рю, от кото́рой ги́бнут корабли́ на́ море. Появля́ется покрови́тель моряко́в и купцо́в, свято́й Никола, вели́т Садко́ бро́сить игру́ и у́чит его́ что де́лать, когда́ морско́й царь предло́жит ему́ жени́ться на одно́й из свои́х дочере́й. Садко́ сле́дует указа́ниям Нико́лы и благополу́чно возвраща́ется в Но́вгород. В знак благода́рности своему́ спаси́телю Садко́ стро́ит Нико́ле це́рковь.

Це́ркви занима́ли ва́жное ме́сто в новгоро́дской культу́ре. К древне́йшим па́мятникам отно́сится ка́менный новгоро́дский Софи́йский собо́р, постро́енный в середи́не 11 ве́ка, ещё в ки́евскую эпо́ху, кня́зем Влади́миром Яросла́вичем, всего́ не́сколько лет поздне́е ки́евского собо́ра. В нача́ле 12 ве́ка после́довала постро́йка це́лого ря́да други́х собо́ров в Но́вгороде. Все они́ огро́мные ка́менные зда́ния, кото́рые вели́чественно возвыша́ются и царя́т над мо́рем ни́зких деревя́нных постро́ек го́рода. Уже́ в э́тих ра́нних новгоро́дских собо́рах мо́жно усмотре́ть черту́, характе́рную и для други́х сторо́н новгоро́дской культу́ры: простоту́ и сде́ржанность.

Архитекту́ра собо́ров проявля́ет стремле́ние просты́ми сре́дствами дости́гнуть вели́чия и торже́ственности. Со второ́й полови́ны 12 ве́ка строи́телями в Но́вгороде выступа́ют уже́ не князья́, а боя́ре и купцы́. Поэ́тому архитекту́рными произведе́ниями э́того вре́мени явля́ются уже́ не огро́мные собо́ры, а сравни́тельно небольши́е це́ркви, в кото́рых большу́ю роль игра́ли практи́ческие удо́бства строи́телей— скла́ды це́нностей и това́ров в церко́вных подва́лах. Но и э́ти це́ркви отлича́ются простото́й и монумента́льностью.

Вну́треннее украше́ние хра́мов, стенна́я церко́вная жи́вопись и и́конопись, достига́ет своего́ по́лного расцве́та в Но́вгороде в 14 ве́ке. Кру́пными фигу́рами выступа́ют худо́жники Во́лохов и Феофа́н Грек. О́ба проявля́ют в своём иску́сстве любо́вь к древнегре́ческим тради́циям, интере́с к живо́му челове́ку и приро́де. Они́ приближа́ют церко́вное иску́сство к жи́зни. Их фигу́ры, свобо́дные и вырази́тельные, полны́ движе́ния и челове́ческих чувств. Произведе́ния Во́лохова и Феофа́на не уступа́ют по си́ле и реали́зму созда́ниям вели́ких мастеро́в за́падноевропе́йского Возрожде́ния.

Незави́симость Но́вгорода продолжа́лась до второ́й полови́ны 15 ве́ка. В 1478 году́ го́роду пришло́сь подчини́ться Москве́ и новгоро́дское госуда́рство переста́ло существова́ть. За сто лет по́сле поте́ри свое́й незави́симости го́род потеря́л бо́лее 80 проце́нтов своего́ населе́ния. В 1582 году́ в нём оста́лось всего́ то́лько 1,000 дворо́в.

4

междуре́чье Mesopotamia, country between two rivers
оби́лие abundance
сеть (f.) net, network
земледе́лие agriculture
also: **се́льское хозя́йство**
творе́ц creator
насле́дственный hereditary
уде́л appanage, domain, share
уде́льный appanage (adj.)
разобще́ние disunity
служи́лый service (adj.)
уча́сток section
крепостно́й fortified (also: serf—adjective and noun)

крепостно́е пра́во serfdom
стро́йность (f.) gracefulness
наше́ствие invasion
обру́шиться to descend upon perf. of: **обру́шиваться**
завоева́ние conquest
обши́рный vast
дань (f.) tribute
опустоша́ть to lay waste **опустоши́ть** (perf.)
окра́йна border region
пе́репись (f.) census
кресто́вый похо́д Crusade
и́го yoke, oppression
духо́вный spiritual

УДЕ́ЛЬНАЯ РУСЬ—ЗА́ПАДНАЯ ОКРА́ЙНА МОНГО́ЛЬСКОЙ ИМПЕ́РИИ
(от 13 до середи́ны 15 ве́ка)

На се́веро-восто́ке, в междуре́чье, образо́ванном Око́й и Ве́рхней Во́лгой, уже́ в конце́ 12 ве́ка наблюда́ются пе́рвые уси́лия отде́льных князе́й созда́ть но́вые це́нтры правле́ния и поря́дка, вдали́ от хао́са и разложе́ния Ки́евской Руси́. Результа́ты сказа́лись: В се́веро-восто́чные города́ и леса́ потяну́лись переселе́нцы с ю́га.

Междуре́чье Оки́ и Во́лги, составля́ющее центра́льную о́бласть Европе́йской Росси́и, отлича́ется заме́тными физи́ческими осо́бенностями от Руси́ Ки́евской: оби́лием лесо́в

15

и болот и паутинной сетью рек и речек, бегущих в разные направления. Эти особенности положили глубокий отпечаток на быт населения. По речной сети население расходилось в разные стороны. В этой области, слишком отдалённой от приморских рынков, внешняя торговля не могла стать главной движущей силой народного хозяйства. Значительная часть населения занимается земледелием. Деревенские поселения получают здесь решительный перевес над городами.

Старое киевское общество было старше своих князей. Первые князья, явившись в Русскую землю, вошли в готовый уже общественный строй. Они не могли назвать себя творцами общества, которым они правили. Совсем другой взгляд на себя, и на своё отношение к обществу, развили под влиянием колонизации князья в центральной области Европейской России. Здесь князь становится руководителем политического и экономического порядка, наследственным хозяином своего земельного владения—удела. Междуречье делится не на городовые области, а на княжеские уделы. Киевская Русь сменяется удельной Русью. Значение Междуречья растёт параллельно постепенному падению значения Киева.

Садясь на удел, первый князь его обыкновенно находил в своём владении не готовое общество, а область, которая только что начинала заселяться, в которой всё надо было устроить и построить, чтобы создать в ней общество. Князь руководил колонизацией, считал её делом своих рук, своим личным созданием, и поэтому считал себя личным хозяином и владетелем своего удела.

Каждый князь привыкал действовать отдельно, во имя личных выгод, вспоминая о соседе-родственнике только тогда, когда тот угрожал ему, нападал на него или когда представлялся случай поживиться на его счёт. Это взаимное разобщение удельных князей делало их неспособными к дружным союзам между собой, гасило мысль о единстве и цельности Русской земли, об общем народном благе. Самое слово "Русская земля" довольно редко появляется на страницах летописи удельных веков.

При отсутствии общего, объединяющего интереса, князь

переставал быть правителем и оставался только простым хозяином, а население удела превращалось во временных его жителей. Население распадалось на два класса: на служилых и "чёрных," т. е. низших людей. Служилыми людьми были бояре и вольные слуги, состоявшие на личной службе у князя по договору с ним. Они признавали власть его над собой, пока ему служили. Но каждый из них мог покинуть князя и перейти на службу к другому. Такие же отношения к князю были и у чёрных людей. Чёрный человек подчинялся власти князя, платил ему дань только пока пользовался его землёй. Но и он мог перейти в другой удел.

Таким образом князь видел в уделе не общество, а хозяйство. Он не правил им, а разрабатывал его. Свободный человек, служилый или чёрный, приходил в удел, служил или работал в нём, получал участки княжеской земли во временное употребление, и уходил. Он не был политической единицей, подданным, в составе местного общества, а экономической случайностью. Не закон, а личный договор определял отношения свободных лиц к князю. Создавались отношения напоминающие феодальные порядки в средневековой Европе. Но в удельных отношениях отсутствовала одна основная черта феодализма: крепостное право, прикрепление людей к земле. И бояре и чёрные люди свободно переходили из удела одного князя в удел другого.

Уделы были разных размеров. В больших и богатых постепенно развивались города, которые князья украшали храмами, дворцами и укреплениями, созданными русскими мастерами и ремесленниками. К началу 13 века самыми важными городскими центрами Междуречья были Ростов, Суздаль и Владимир. К этому времени местная архитектура всё сильнее освобождается от киевской строительной традиции и отличается простотой, стройностью и суровой мощью, несмотря на более скромные масштабы построек. Церкви похожи скорее на крепостные сооружения чем на храмы и с большой силой выражают дух своего времени, полного военных тревог и напряжения нескончаемых походов.

В начале 13 века на Русь обрушилось татарское нашествие. Татары резко отличались от предыдущих, слабо организованных кочевников, издавна появлявшихся в русских степях. Татары представляли хорошо дисциплинированную, многочисленную армию. Её создал монгольский правитель Чингис Хан с целью обширных завоеваний. Ко времени появления татар на Руси, царство Чингис Хана уже обхватывало северный Китай, Среднюю Азию, Персию и Кавказ. Поход на Русь был предпринят внуком Чингис Хана, Бату. Это было хорошо продуманное, военное и политическое предприятие.

Подойдя к Рязанскому уделу с юга, Бату потребовал дань, но получил ответ: "Когда мы не останемся в живых, то всё будет ваше." Татары вошли в Рязанскую землю и её опустошили. Оттуда они направились на Коломну, Москву, Владимир, Суздаль и другие города и поселения. Татарское нашествие обрушилось на Русь как ураган, который сносил вместе с материальными ценностями и жизни тысяч людей. В первые годы после нашествия города и селения представляли собой пепелища, которые дымились грудами развалин. Немало городов и крепостей было стёрто с лица земли татарской лавиной. Они погибли навсегда и больше в истории не встречаются.

После завоевания Русь вошла в состав монгольской империи. Киевская Русь в своё время была восточной окрайной Европы. Теперь Русь стала западной окрайной монгольской империи. Татары рассматривали русские земли как политически автономные, имеющие свою собственную власть, но находящиеся в зависимости от ханов и обязанные платить им дань. Ни один князь не имел права на правление своим уделом без разрешения хана. Дань должны были платить все. С этой целью татары производили переписи населения. От обязанности платить дань избавлено было только духовенство. Татары считали всех русских своими рабами, а князей своими слугами.

В то самое время, когда на Русь обрушилась лавина татарской армии, в Западной Европе происходит резкий перелом исторической жизни. Под влиянием крестовых походов усиливаются более широкие связи Европы со странами востока. В это время на западе начинается бурное развитие торговли и ремесла, создаётся внутренний рынок, растут городские центры. Испания прикрывает западный фланг этой расцветающей Европы от нашествия Мавров. Подобно Испании, остановившей завоевания Мавров на западе, Русь сыграла на востоке Европы историческую роль, остановив монгольское нашествие на границах западноевропейских государств. Но татары не походили на Мавров. Завоевав Россию, они не подарили ей ни алгебры, ни архитектурного стиля. Наоборот, они уводили в плен русских мастеров, строителей и ремесленников. А дань, которую русские должны были платить татарам, ложилась тяжёлым бременем на производительные силы страны. Надолго изменился быт русского народа. Со времён татарского нашествия Русь окончательно превратилась в земледельческую страну.

Тем не менее, татарское иго, продолжавшееся два с половиной столетия, не было временем полного культурного упадка, а наоборот периодом духовного роста и творчества. От суровой действительности люди спасались и отдыхали в молитвах и в мечтаниях. Татарское иго—это эпоха углубления христианской веры и расцвета волшебной сказки и сказания.

5

стро́ительство construction
возобновля́ть to renew, resume
  возобнови́ть (perf.)
пусты́нный desert (adj.)
пусты́ня desert (noun)
основа́тель (m.) founder
огра́да enclosure
мона́х monk
крестья́нин peasant
моли́тва prayer
моли́ться to pray
  помоли́ться (perf.)
пост fast, lent
наставле́ние injunction
свято́й saint
исполня́ть to fulfil
  испо́лнить (perf.)

смире́ние humility
достиже́ние achievement
бессло́ве́сный wordless, mute
кра́ска paint, color
цвет color, hue
соприкоснове́ние contact, touch
истоща́ть to exhaust
  истощи́ть (perf.)
дух spirit
сочу́вствие compassion
же́ртва sacrifice
обрека́ть to condemn
  обре́чь (perf.)
подчине́ние subordination

РУ́ССКИЙ МОНАСТЫ́РЬ

Мона́шество появи́лось на Руси́ вме́сте с христиа́нством, т. е. в конце́ 10 ве́ка. До тата́рского наше́ствия почти́ все ру́сские монастыри́ возника́ли в города́х и́ли под его́ стена́ми. Уда́р, нанесённый тата́рами ру́сской земле́, был насто́лько силён, что со второ́й че́тверти 13 ве́ка вся́кое строи́тельство в Междуре́чье надо́лго прекрати́лось. Оно́ на́чало возобновля́ться то́лько с 14 ве́ка, когда́ вое́нные похо́ды тата́р на ру́сские поселе́ния ста́ли происходи́ть ре́же и на

Руси стала возможна более спокойная жизнь по сравнению с первым столетием татарского господства.

С этого времени происходит заметная перемена в развитии монастырей. Численный перевес получают монастыри не городские, а возникавшие вдали от городов, в лесной глуши, ждавшей топора и сохи. Эти монастыри получили название пустынных или пустыней, (с ударением на первом слоге). Пустыней в понятии древнерусского человека, жившего в лесной зоне страны, считалась северная область, покрытая густыми, вековыми лесами, а не пространство покрытое песками, лишённое всякой растительности и воды.

С середины 14 века монастырская колонизация усиленно направлялась из центральных областей за Волгу на беломорский север. В продолжение следующих двух веков это движение проникало в самые отдалённые углы и усеивало монастырями обширные лесные площади северной России. К 16 веку на севере насчитывалось, сколько известно, 150 пустынных монастырей по сравнению с 104 городскими и пригородными в центре страны.

Основатели этих монастырей обнаружили много вкуса и понимания природы в выборе мест для своих построек. Везде монастырь вырастал в самом поэтическом уголке края—на берегу озера, на одиноком острове или на крутом берегу реки, сливаясь своими суровыми стенами, строгими башнями и могучими куполами в одно гармоническое целое с окружающей северной, лесной природой.

Пустынный заволжский монастырь имел очень важное значение в древнерусской жизни. Во первых он представлял сам по себе, в своей тесной деревянной или каменной ограде, земледельческое поселение. Монахи расчищали лес, разводили огороды, пахали и косили. Но в ту же сторону, оттуда же и с того же времени направлялась и крестьянская колонизация. Монах и крестьянин были спутниками, шедшими рядом или один впереди другого. Вокруг монастыря селились крестьяне, как религиозной и хозяйственной своей опоры.

Монахи пустынного монастыря отказывали себе во всех физических наслаждениях. Они жили в молитве, в строгом посту́, одева́лись в са́мую бе́дную оде́жду, не име́ли це́нных веще́й кро́ме церко́вных книг и ико́н, и проводи́ли всю жизнь в тяжёлом физи́ческом труде́. Борьба́ с приро́дой обыкнове́нно укрепля́ла их здоро́вье и большинство́ из них достига́ло глубо́кой ста́рости. К концу́ жи́зни они́ стреми́лись подели́ться свое́й духо́вной си́лой и нако́пленной нра́вственной му́дростью с те́ми, кто иска́л их сове́та и по́мощи, и нере́дко оставля́ли пи́сьменные наставле́ния.

Ру́сская це́рковь канонизова́ла мно́гих основа́телей пусты́нных монастыре́й. Жизнеописа́ния э́тих святы́х, так называ́емые "Жития́," входи́ли в соста́в наибо́лее люби́мого чте́ния дре́вней Руси́. В наро́дной па́мяти святы́е образова́ли гру́ппу но́вых си́льных люде́й, заслони́вшую собо́й были́нных богатыре́й, в кото́рых Ки́евская Русь воплоти́ла своё представле́ние о си́льном челове́ке.

Житьё свято́го бо́льше чем биогра́фия. Оно́ обращено́ со́бственно не к слу́шателю и́ли чита́телю, а к моля́щемуся. Оно́ бо́лее чем поуча́ет. Оно́ опи́сывает жизнь индивидуа́льной ли́чности, но расска́зывает о де́ятельности э́той свято́й ли́чности, чтобы показа́ть, что всё, чего́ тре́бует от нас уче́ние Христа́, не то́лько исполни́мо, но не раз и исполня́лось, ста́ло быть достижи́мо и для други́х.

Главо́й и учи́телем пусты́нного мона́шества был Се́ргий Радо́нежский, велича́йший из святы́х дре́вней Руси́ и основа́тель, в сороковы́х года́х 14 ве́ка, Тро́ице Се́ргиева монастыря́. Этот монасты́рь нахо́дится всего́ миль со́рок на се́веро-восто́ке от Москвы́, но в те времена́ э́та о́бласть была́ ещё покры́та глухи́ми леса́ми, ма́ло заселена́ и то́же счита́лась "пусты́ней."

Свои́м смире́нием, терпели́вым внима́нием к людски́м ну́ждам и сла́бостям и трудолю́бием Се́ргий оказа́л глубо́кое духо́вное влия́ние на свои́х совреме́нников. Большинство́ святы́х 14 и нача́ла 15 ве́ка бы́ли его́ ученика́ми.

Мона́хи отдава́ли всю жизнь служе́нию духо́вным и мора́льным идеа́лам. Они́ все си́лы напряга́ли, чтобы подня́ть нра́вственный у́ровень окружа́ющего их ми́ра, чтобы осуществи́ть ца́рство Бо́жие на земле́. Догмати́ческие вопро́сы теоло́гии их не занима́ли. В монастыря́х отсу́тствовала нау́чная мысль, у́мственный труд. Ни у одного́ из святы́х э́того вре́мени не́ было любви́ к зна́нию.

Са́мыми це́нными произведе́ниями э́той исключи́тельно духо́вной культу́ры бы́ли церко́вное пе́ние и ико́ны. Правосла́вная це́рковь допуска́ла в богослуже́нии то́лько вока́льную му́зыку, пе́ние, принципиа́льно отрица́я инструмента́льную му́зыку. Древне́йшее церко́вное пе́ние бы́ло византи́йского происхожде́ния. Но во вре́мя тата́рского госпо́дства начина́ют замеча́ться на Руси́ самостоя́тельные попы́тки если не компози́торства, то по кра́йней ме́ре распе́ва на изве́стные уже́ мело́дии.

Отрица́я инструмента́льную му́зыку, правосла́вная це́рковь та́кже запреща́ла скульпту́ру. Моти́вом э́того запреще́ния служи́ло опасе́ние, что ста́тую смеша́ют с и́долом. Зато́ усе́рдно подде́рживалась религио́зная жи́вопись, т. е. моза́ики, фре́ски и ико́ны. В 14 и 15 века́х в Росси́и византи́йские моза́ики и стенны́е фре́ски уступа́ют ме́сто деревя́нной ико́не. И́конопись достига́ет блестя́щего расцве́та и стано́вится одни́м из велича́йших худо́жественных достиже́ний ру́сского монастыря́.

Ру́сский мона́х выража́л своё мировоззре́ние не сто́лько слова́ми, ско́лько посту́пками и поведе́нием, стремя́сь свои́м приме́ром осуществи́ть ца́рство Бо́жие на земле́. Ико́на была́ та́кже спо́собом бесслове́сного выраже́ния той же религио́зной мы́сли, того́ же идеа́ла. Свои́ми ли́ниями и кра́сками она́ выража́ла соприкоснове́ние двух миро́в, боже́ственного и челове́ческого, ве́чного споко́йствия и земно́го страда́ния. Золото́й цвет, кра́ска све́та, госпо́дствует в ико́не. Мир изображён как весь освещённый небе́сным све́том. Ря́дом с золоты́м употребля́ются все отте́нки си́него, цве́та во́здуха и не́ба. То э́то темноси́нее, высо́кое, звёздное не́бо, то блестя́щее голубо́е сия́ние дня, то зеленова́тый тон бле́дного се́верного ру́сского не́ба под зи́мний ве́чер. На э́том фо́не выраста́ет сюже́т ико́ны—идеа́льный, не портре́тный о́браз божества́ и́ли свято́го. Фигу́ры чрезвыча́йно то́нкие, дли́нные и худы́е, как бы истощённые посто́м и́ли страда́нием. Побе́да ду́ха над те́лом вы́ражена по́лным отсу́тствием движе́ния. Всё сосредото́чено в выраже́нии глаз, так как глаза́ явля́ются це́нтром проявле́ния вну́тренней, духо́вной жи́зни челове́ка. С гру́стью и глубо́ким сочу́вствием к страда́ющему челове́честву смо́трят глаза́ свято́го с ико́ны на окружа́ющий мир.

Крупне́йшим ру́сским иконопи́сцем был Андре́й Рублёв, мона́х Тро́ице Се́ргиева монастыря́. Рублёв жил в ближа́йшем окруже́нии Се́ргия и посвяти́л его́ па́мяти своё велича́йшее произведе́ние, ико́ну Тро́ицы. Э́та ико́на изобража́ет Бо́га Отца́, Бо́га Сы́на и Бо́га Ду́ха яви́вшихся, по библе́йской леге́нде, в о́бразе трёх а́нгелов, к Авраа́му. В по́лном молча́нии, в глубо́ком разду́мье о су́дьбах ми́ра, три а́нгела расположи́лись на невысо́ких сиде́ниях. Ико́на представля́ет акт велича́йшей же́ртвы боже́ственной любви́ к челове́честву: Бог Оте́ц обрека́ет Своего́ Сы́на на смерть; но та́кже акт велича́йшего послуша́ния: гото́вность Бо́га Сы́на на страда́ние.

К концу́ 15 ве́ка монастыри́, в осо́бенности в центра́льной о́бласти страны́, на́чали заме́тно богате́ть, получа́я ще́дрые пода́рки не то́лько деньга́ми но и земе́льными уча́стками от населе́ния. Э́то привело́ к ва́жному спо́ру о церко́вном иму́ществе.

Гла́вным защи́тником церко́вной со́бственности был Ио́сиф Во́лоцкий, игу́мен бога́того Волокола́мского монастыря́ в центра́льной о́бласти страны́. Ио́сиф защища́л церко́вное иму́щество во и́мя социа́льных зада́ч це́ркви. Он утвержда́л, что монасты́рь до́лжен быть бога́т, что́бы привлека́ть выдаю́щихся люде́й в мона́хи. Без таки́х люде́й ве́ра пострада́ла бы, це́рковь не могла́ бы ока́зывать духо́вного влия́ния на наро́д. На монасты́рь Ио́сиф смотре́л как на своего́ ро́да госуда́рственное учрежде́ние, име́ющее це́лью подготовля́ть служи́телей госуда́рственной це́ркви.

Про́тив Ио́сифа вы́ступил Нил Со́рский, основа́тель пусты́нного монастыря́ на реке́ Со́ре, в Белозёрском краю́ Заво́лжья. Нил отрица́л церко́вное иму́щество во имя духо́вных зада́ч це́ркви. Он тре́бовал стро́гого отделе́ния це́ркви от госуда́рства и от земны́х бога́тств. Мона́х до́лжен жить труда́ми рук свои́х, а не на чужо́й счёт. Церко́вное иму́щество ну́жно раздава́ть бе́дным. Ва́жно вну́треннее христиа́нство, а не вне́шнее бога́тство. Нужна́ духо́вная свобо́да, разви́тие ли́чной со́вести ка́ждого челове́ка.

Це́рковь должна́ де́йствовать убежде́нием, моли́твой и приме́ром, а не си́лой и принужде́нием.

Ио́сиф был представи́телем госуда́рственного правосла́вия, враг вся́кой свобо́ды. Нил был сторо́нник бо́лее духо́вного, свобо́дного христиа́нства. О́ба встре́тились на церко́вном собо́ре 1503 го́да. Собо́р согласи́лся со взгля́дами Ио́сифа. Э́тот пе́рвый литерату́рный спор в ру́сской исто́рии и его́ реше́ние оказа́ли глубо́кое влия́ние на после́дующее разви́тие ру́сской це́ркви и подгото́вило в бу́дущем по́лное подчине́ние це́ркви госуда́рству.

6

скáзка fairy tale
сказáние legend
действи́тельность (f.) reality
чудéсный miraculous
инóй other, different
волшéбный magical
окрáска tint, hue
Жар-пти́ца Fire Bird
воображéние imagination
неви́димый invisible
скрывáть to conceal, hide
  скрыть (perf.)
ничтóжество insignificance
слия́ние fusion, merging

довéрие trust, confidence
мýдрый wise
дурáк fool
испытáние trial, test
испы́тывать to test (also: to experience)
  испытáть (perf.)
живóтное animal
зверь (m.) beast
томи́ться to languish
лягýшка frog
невéста bride
сочетáние combination
мечтá daydream, longing

СКÁЗКА И СКАЗÁНИЕ

Скáзка стрáнствует, передаётся от нарóда к нарóду. Национáльное в скáзке почти́ всегдá вариáнт общечеловéческого. Основнáя тéма скáзки всех векóв и всех нарóдов—это ухóд от гнетýщей человéка бéдности, ухóд от сурóвой, мрáчной действи́тельности и подъём к богáтству чудéсного, подъём в инóе, волшéбное цáрство. Национáльная окрáска скáзки проявля́ется в конкрéтном изображéнии этого волшéбного цáрства, в конкрéтном вы́боре герóев, котóрые и́щут это цáрство, и в конкрéтном описáнии собы́тий, происходя́щих по дорóге в волшéбный мир.

Неизвéстное, волшéбное, вмéсте с тем и дáльнее. Для обозначéния отдалённости инóго цáрства в рýсской скáзке име́ется мно́жество ра́зных выраже́ний. По одно́й ве́рсии е́хать туда́ ну́жно "три́дцать дней и три́дцать ноче́й," по друго́й "криво́й доро́гой три го́да е́хать, а прямо́й три часа́. То́лько пря́мо то прое́зду нет." Ино́е ца́рство от нас "за три́девять земе́ль," э́то тот край све́та, где "кра́сное со́лнышко из си́него мо́ря восхо́дит" и́ли "страна́, где ночу́ет со́лнце." Всё, свя́занное с ины́м ца́рством мо́жет принима́ть золоту́ю окра́ску, наприме́р Жар-пти́ца, цель иска́ний геро́ев во мно́гих ру́сских ска́зках. Это пти́ца, пе́рья кото́рой облада́ют спосо́бностью свети́ть и свои́м бле́ском поража́ют зре́ние челове́ка.

Ино́е ца́рство иногда́ нахо́дится под землёй, на горе́ и́ли под водо́й. Центра́льное ме́сто в наро́дном ру́сском воображе́нии занима́ет неви́димый Град Ки́теж. Стои́т он на о́зере Све́тлом Я́ре за Во́лгой. Цел тот го́род со времён тата́рского наше́ствия, с белока́менными стена́ми, золоты́ми купола́ми церкве́й, с бога́тыми монастыря́ми, кня́жескими дворца́ми, с боя́рскими ка́менными дома́ми. Цел град, но неви́дим.

Скры́лся он чуде́сно, когда́ безбо́жный царь Бату́, разори́в Русь Сузда́льскую, пошёл покоря́ть Русь Ки́тежскую. Подошёл тата́рский царь к гра́ду Вели́кому Ки́тежу, хоте́л дома́ сжечь, люде́й переби́ть, жён и деви́ц в плен угна́ть. Не допусти́л Бог разоре́ния христиа́нского гра́да. Де́сять дней, де́сять ноче́й Бату́ иска́л град Ки́теж, и не мог найти́. И до сих пор тот град стои́т неви́дим. А на о́зере Све́тлом Я́ре, в ти́хий ле́тний ве́чер виднє́ются отражённые в воде́ сте́ны, це́ркви, монастыри́, дворцы́ и дома́. И слы́шится по ноча́м глухо́й, печа́льный звон колоколо́в ки́тежских.

Слия́ние ме́жду ска́зочным и христиа́нским, кото́рое лежи́т в осно́ве сказа́ния о гра́де Ки́теже, о́чень хара́ктерно и для ру́сской ска́зки. Это слия́ние проявля́ется та́кже в вы́боре геро́ев волше́бной ска́зки. Иска́тель ино́го ца́рства—богаты́рь и́ли дура́к. Но в ска́зке о́браз богатыря́ ре́зко отлича́ется от были́нного богатыря́ ки́евских времён. В были́не, богаты́рь си́льная, хра́брая фигу́ра. Его́ ли́чный по́двиг стои́т в це́нтре де́йствия. В ска́зке, богаты́рь я́сно ви́дит своё ничто́жество, сознаёт свою́ беспо́мощность.

В скáзке человéк всё врéмя стáлкивается с напоминáнием о каком-то роковóм для негó предéле, о егó завúсимости свы́ше. Богатьíрь достигáет цéли магúческим путём. Напримéр сúла вливáется в негó извнé, иногдá чéрез чудéсный напúток. Он игрáет совершéнно пассúвную роль, от негó трéбуется тóлько безгранúчное довéрие, покóрность и прéданность той вы́сшей сúле, котóрая егó ведёт.

Ум герóя тáкже не игрáет никакóй рóли. Магúческий постýпок, котóрый кáжется лю́дям бессмы́сленным, нерéдко окáзывается сáмым мýдрым. Неудивúтельно, что ря́дом с богатырём скáзки являéтся дурáк, т. е. существó совершéнно лишённое вся́кого человéческого рáзума. Дурáк ничегó не дéлает и ничегó не знáет. О чём бы егó не спросúли, дáже о том, как егó зовýт, у негó одúн отвéт: "Не знáю." Все егó постýпки кáжутся лю́дям глýпыми, а мéжду тем онú всегдá окáзываются мудрéе, чем постýпки егó "ýмных брáтьев."

В э́том вы́боре герóев рýсской скáзки тáкже чýвствуются религиóзные óтзвуки христиáнства. Человéк глубокó сознаёт своё ничтóжество, бессúлие своегó рáзума и отдаёт себя́ всецéло во власть вы́сшей, чудéсной сúле. В рýсской скáзке необыкновéнно слáбо вы́ражено дéйствие снúзу. Человéк ждёт всех благ жúзни свы́ше, надéется на чудéсную пóмощь и при э́том совершéнно забывáет о своéй лúчной отвéтственности.

Э́то не знáчит, что герóй рýсской скáзки не переживáет тяжёлых испытáний. Чтóбы достúгнуть инóго цáрства, нýжно совершúть большúе пóдвиги, преодолéть мнóго препя́тствий и прéжде всегó бесконéчное расстоя́ние, отделя́ющее нáшу действúтельность от лýчшего, волшéбного мúра. Отсю́да волшéбные спóсобы передвижéния. Одúн из любúмых образóв рýсской скáзки—магúческое живóтное úли птúца, котóрые помогáют человéку перенестúсь в инóе цáрство. То э́то сéрый волк, то орёл, то сóкол. Но все онú имéют однý и ту же цель: помóчь человéку уйтú и подня́тся над действúтельностью. И всегдá э́тот ухóд трéбует велúких жертв от человéка. Óбраз Ивáна-царéвича, котóрый отдаёт сóбственное тéло на кормлéние орлá, чтóбы добы́ть невéсту, "ненагля́дную красотý," принадлежúт к числу́ люби́мых в ру́сской ска́зке и повторя́ется в ней не раз.

Челове́к свя́зывается со зве́рем про́чной свя́зью взаи́много сострада́ния. В мину́ту кра́йней нужды́ и́ли опа́сности зве́ри помога́ют челове́ку и спаса́ют его́. Но и челове́к освобожда́ет живо́тное и помога́ет ему́. Вся́кий зверь про́сит челове́ка о по́мощи и поща́де поня́тным ему́ "го́лосом челове́ческим."

С э́тим свя́зана накло́нность ска́зки ви́деть в живо́тном челове́ка, кото́рый томи́тся в звери́ном о́бразе, пока́ не я́вится до́брый челове́к—освободи́тель, кото́рый его́ пожале́ет и спасёт. Наибо́лее я́рким выраже́нием э́той мы́сли слу́жит ска́зка о Царе́вне-лягу́шке, кото́рая говори́т Ива́ну богатырю́, что он до́лжен взять её за́муж, что́бы вы́йти из боло́та, в кото́рое он попа́л. С по́мощью лягу́шки Ива́н выхо́дит из боло́та и она́ возвраща́ется в свой челове́ческий о́браз царе́вны.

Э́то уча́стие звере́й в жи́зни и подъёме челове́ка—оди́н из наибо́лее я́рких и люби́мых моти́вов ру́сской наро́дной ска́зки. Солида́рность всего́ живо́го на земле́, челове́ка и зве́ря, то́же одно́ из христиа́нских открове́ний и в ча́стности одна́ из люби́мых тем ру́сского жития́ святы́х.

Характе́рно, что му́дрость в ска́зке представля́ется не в мужско́м, а в же́нском о́бразе. Преоблада́ют два же́нских ти́па: му́драя стару́ха и му́драя неве́ста. Стару́ха обыкнове́нно носи́тельница не то́лько му́дрости, но и вла́сти, кото́рая даётся зна́нием: "Что ни есть на бе́лом све́те, всё ей покоря́ется." В неве́сте, наприме́р в Васили́се-Прему́дрой, с му́дростью соединя́ется и красота́, облада́ющая си́лой волше́бного де́йствия. Сочета́ние в же́нском о́бразе вы́сшей му́дрости, красоты́ и вла́сти над всем ми́ром напомина́ет тот о́браз Софи́и Прему́дрости Бо́жьей, кото́рая вдохновля́ла строи́телей хра́мов и иконопи́сцев Ки́евской Руси́.

Ру́сская ска́зка—э́то преле́стная поэти́ческая грёза, мечта́ о лу́чшем ми́ре, мечта́, в кото́рой ру́сский челове́к иска́л успокое́ния и о́тдыха. Ска́зка окрыля́ет его́ воображе́ние, но в то же вре́мя усыпля́ет его́ эне́ргию. В герма́нских ска́зках челове́к то бо́рется со свои́ми бога́ми, то спаса́ет

их сами́х из тру́дного положе́ния. В ру́сской ска́зке, при
встре́че с чуде́сным, челове́к как-то сра́зу опуска́ет ру́ки.
Он испы́тывает очарова́ние, восхище́ние, весь превраща́-
ется в слух и зре́ние, но не перехо́дит к де́йствию, а
ждёт бога́тства жи́зни как дар свы́ше, от Бо́жьей во́ли, от
Жар-пти́цы и́ли от се́рого во́лка.

Иска́ние ино́го ца́рства в ру́сской ска́зке представля́ло
собо́й ступе́нь в той ле́стнице, кото́рая приво́дит наро́дное
созна́ние от язы́чества к христиа́нству.

ну́лась от дере́вни и начала́ иска́ть сою́зников среди́ го-
ро́дского и фабри́чного населе́ния. Но гла́вное бы́ло то,
что в концу́ 19 ве́ка бо́лее радика́льно настро́енные чле́ны
э́той гру́ппы от наро́дничества перешли́ к маркси́зму. Этот
перехо́д был са́мым кра́йним и са́мым траги́чным в исто́рии
ру́сской интеллиге́нции. Чу́вство сострада́ния и жа́лости,
мечта́ о свобо́де и це́нности челове́ческой ли́чности, в
ру́сском маркси́зме заменя́ются моти́вами си́лы, принуж-
де́ния, отрица́ния ли́чности и безжа́лостной жесто́кости.
Для достиже́ния мо́щи и бога́тства социа́льного коллекти́ва
отноше́ние к челове́ку де́лается беспоща́дным и жесто́ким.

7

превраще́ние transformation	**прее́мник** successor
соде́йствовать to contribute, further	**блеск** brilliance
убе́жище refuge	**уме́ренность** (f.) moderation
стека́ться to flow together, merge	**поколе́ние** generation
обогаще́ние enrichment	**почти́тельный** respectful
возвыше́ние elevation (abstract)	**вы́года** advantage
награ́да reward	**образцо́вый** model (adj.)
поруче́ние commission, task	**еди́ный** sole
пото́мство posterity	**чо́порность** (f.) affectation, stiffness
власть (f.) power	**Возрожде́ние** Renaissance
	холм hill

МОСКВА́—ЕЁ ПРЕВРАЩЕ́НИЕ ИЗ УДЕ́ЛА В ГОСУДА́РСТВО

Пе́рвое изве́стие о Москве́, сохрани́вшееся в ле́тописях, отно́сится к 1147 го́ду. В то вре́мя э́то бы́ло ма́ленькое пограни́чное поселе́ние возни́кшее на перепу́тье ме́жду днепро́вским ю́гом и верхнево́лжским се́вером. Назва́ние Москвы́ совпада́ло с назва́нием реки́, на кото́рой оно́ находи́лось. Река́ Москва́ служи́ла во́дным путём ме́жду се́вером и ю́гом Междуре́чья, ме́жду ве́рхней Во́лгой и сре́дней О́кой. По ней же мо́жно та́кже бы́ло держа́ть путь на восто́к, во Влади́мир.

Тако́е центра́льное географи́ческое положе́ние мно́го соде́йствова́ло ро́сту и разви́тию Москвы́. Со всех сторо́н она́ была́ прикры́та от вне́шних враго́в. Тата́рские уда́ры па́дали на сосе́дние уде́лы—Ряза́нский, Нижегоро́дский, Росто́вский, Яросла́вский, Смоле́нский—и о́чень ре́дко достигали до Москвы, за исключением первого татарского погрома 1238 года, захватившего и Москву. Благодаря такому прикрытию московская область стала убежищем для окружающего населения, всюду страдавшего от татарских нападений. Столь редкий покой вызвал к концу 13 века движение русского населения в Междуречье с востока на запад, из старых ростовских и суздальских поселений в пустынные углы маленького московского удела.

В первой половине 14 века произошло два важных события, которые значительно ускорили начавшийся подъём Москвы. Во первых Москва сделалась церковной русской столицей. Татарским нашествием окончательно опустошена была старинная Киевская Русь, пустевшая с половины 12 века. Вслед за населением на север ушёл в 1299 году и высший иерарх русской церкви, киевский митрополит Максим и поселился во Владимире. Преемник Максима, митрополит Пётр, странствуя по Руси, часто бывал в Москве и у него завязалась тесная дружба с князем этого удела, Иваном I. Случилось так, что здесь, в 1326 году, митрополит Пётр и умер. А преемник Петра Феогност уже не захотел жить во Владимире и поселился в Москве.

Так Москва стала церковной столицей Руси задолго прежде, чем сделалась столицей политической. Богатые материальные средства, которыми располагала тогда русская церковь, освобождённая от татарской дани, стали стекаться в Москву, содействуя её обогащению. Ещё важнее было нравственное впечатление, произведённое этим перемещением церковной столицы на население. Здесь с большим доверием стали относиться к московскому князю, полагая что все его действия совершаются с благословения главы русской церкви.

Второе важное для возвышения Москвы событие тоже связано с личностью Ивана I. Ему удалось установить выгодные сношения с татарами. Видя, что на татар гораздо легче действовать смирением и деньгами, чем сопротивлением и оружием, Иван усердно ухаживал за ханом. Никто из русских князей чаще Ивана не ездил на поклон к хану. Там он был всегда желанным гостем, потому что приезжа́л туда́ не с пусты́ми рука́ми, а с бога́тыми пода́рками. В награ́ду за тако́е поведе́ние Ива́н в 1328 году́ получи́л от ха́на зва́ние вели́кого кня́зя и поруче́ние собира́ть со всех уде́лов нало́женную тата́рами на Русь дань и доставля́ть её ха́ну.

Со вре́менем Ива́н стал доставля́ть ха́ну то́лько часть со́бранной да́ни, оставля́я значи́тельные су́ммы в со́бственном карма́не. Поэ́тому он перешёл в па́мять пото́мства с прозва́нием Кали́ты, т. е. де́нежного кошеля́. Э́ти де́ньги употребля́лись для расшире́ния моско́вских владе́ний. Ива́н Кали́та на́чал скупа́ть зе́мли у други́х ру́сских князе́й, а в слу́чае отка́за прибега́л к вооружённому захва́ту си́лой. Таки́м о́бразом моско́вский вели́кий князь пе́рвый на́чал выводи́ть Русь из состоя́ния полити́ческого разобще́ния, в како́е привёл её уде́льный поря́док, на́чал собира́ть ру́сские зе́мли и заставля́ть их признава́ть власть Москвы́.

Истори́ческие па́мятники 14 и 15 веко́в не даю́т нам возмо́жности жи́во воспроизвести́ Кали́тино пле́мя, ли́чность ка́ждого из прее́мников Ива́на Кали́ты. Они́ явля́ются в э́тих па́мятниках дово́льно бле́дными фигу́рами сменя́вшими друг дру́га под и́менем Семёна, друго́го Ива́на, Дими́трия, Васи́лия, друго́го Васи́лия. Всма́триваясь в них, легко́ заме́тить, что пе́ред на́ми прохо́дят не своеобра́зные ли́чности, а однообра́зные повторе́ния одного́ и того́ же семе́йного ти́па.

Все моско́вские вели́кие князья́ до Ива́на III как две ка́пли воды́ похо́жи друг на дру́га, так что наблюда́тель иногда́ затрудня́ется реши́ть, кто из них Ива́н и кто Васи́лий. Э́то князья́ без вся́кого бле́ска, без при́знаков как герои́ческого, так и нра́вственного вели́чия. Не блестя́ ни кру́пными тала́нтами, ни я́ркими до́блестями, они́ та́кже не отлича́лись и кру́пными поро́ками и́ли страстя́ми. Э́то де́лало их во мно́гих отноше́ниях образца́ми уме́ренности и аккура́тности. Э́то сре́дние лю́ди дре́вней Руси́. В пяти́ поколе́ниях оди́н Дими́трий Донско́й далеко́ вы́дался вперёд из ря́да свои́х предше́ственников и прее́мников. Вели́кая би́тва на Дону́ в 1380 году́, пе́рвая им дости́гнутая побе́да ру́сских над тата́рами, положи́ла на него́ герои́ческий о́тблеск выдаю́щегося челове́ка.

Лу́чшей семе́йной черто́й моско́вских князе́й бы́ло то, что все бы́ли почти́тельные сыновья́. Они́ свя́то почита́ют па́мять и заве́т свои́х роди́телей. Поэ́тому среди́ них ра́но скла́дывается насле́дственный запа́с поня́тий, привы́чек и приёмов, образу́ется отцо́вское и де́довское преда́ние, кото́рое заменя́ло им ли́чный ра́зум. Отсю́да после́довательность де́йствий, ро́вность движе́ния у моско́вских князе́й. Они́ де́йствуют бо́лее по па́мяти, по заве́ту отцо́в, чем по ли́чному реше́нию. Рабо́та у них идёт ро́вной, непреры́вной ни́тью, сын по ме́ре сил продолжа́ет де́ло отца́.

Все они́ хоро́шие хозя́ева, ко́пят по мелоча́м, понемно́гу, де́йствуют во и́мя ли́чных вы́год и интере́сов. К полови́не 15 ве́ка ру́сский наро́д привы́к смотре́ть на моско́вского кня́зя, как на образцо́вого хозя́ина, а на моско́вское вели́кое кня́жество как на са́мое благоустро́енное владе́ние на Руси́.

В 1462 году́ главо́й э́того владе́ния стано́вится Ива́н III. Он был после́дним собира́телем Руси́. При нём после́дние незави́симые уде́льные князья́ призна́ли власть Москвы́. При нём произошло́ покоре́ние Но́вгорода с его́ обши́рными зе́млями. При нём же происхо́дит оффициа́льное и оконча́тельное сверже́ние тата́рского и́га. Ра́нее, моско́вский вели́кий князь был са́мым си́льным и бога́тым среди́ уде́льных князе́й, а его́ земля́ была́ одни́м из не́скольких отде́льных владе́ний. Тепе́рь моско́вский князь стано́вится еди́ным прави́телем национа́льного госуда́рства. Грани́цы э́того госуда́рства тепе́рь совпада́ют с преде́лами се́веро-восто́чной ру́сской наро́дности. До сих пор, моско́вское кня́жество бы́ло прикры́то от вне́шних враго́в други́ми, ру́сскими же кня́жествами и́ли зе́млями незави́симых городо́в. Тепе́рь самостоя́тельное моско́вское госуда́рство стано́вится глаз на́ глаз с иностра́нными держа́вами.

Ива́н III начина́ет называ́ть себя́ царём всей Руси́, начина́ет сознава́ть произоше́дшую переме́ну в своём положе́нии. Чу́вство возвыше́ния и мо́щи ещё бо́лее уси́лилось, когда́ Ива́н III, в 1472 году́, жени́лся на Со́фье Палеоло́г, племя́ннице после́днего византи́йского импера́тора, жи́вшей в Ита́лии. Она́ привезла́ в Москву́ преда́ния и обы́чаи византи́йского двора́ и го́рдость свои́м происхожде́нием. Ива́н на́чал чу́вствовать себя́ прее́мником византи́йского импера́торского до́ма, па́вшего в 1453 году́ по́сле взя́тия Константино́поля ту́рками.

При моско́вском дворе́ стал заводи́ться сло́жный и стро́гий византи́йский церемониа́л, кото́рый сообща́л большу́ю чо́порность и натя́нутость придво́рной жи́зни. В моско́вских бума́гах с той поры́ появля́ется но́вый, бо́лее торже́ственный язы́к и пы́шная терминоло́гия. С конца́ 15 ве́ка на печа́тях Ива́на III появля́ется византи́йский герб, дву-гла́вый орёл, как нагля́дное выраже́ние династи́ческой свя́зи с византи́йскими импера́торами.

Почу́вствовав себя́ в но́вом положе́нии ря́дом с зна́тной жено́й Со́фьей, Ива́н нашёл те́сной и некраси́вой пре́жнюю обстано́вку, в како́й жи́ли его́ скро́мные пре́дки. В Москву́ была́ вы́звана из Ита́лии гру́ппа италья́нских зо́дчих для постро́йки но́вых собо́ров и дворцо́в. Во главе́ э́той гру́ппы стоя́л Аристо́тель Фиораве́нти, изве́стный не то́лько в Ита́лии, но и в други́х европе́йских стра́нах как оди́н из са́мых тала́нтливых зо́дчих. Фиораве́нти был по́слан во Влади́мир, где он подро́бно осмотре́л ме́стные це́ркви. В 1478 году́ он сопровожда́л Ива́на III в похо́де на Но́вгород и сле́довательно ви́дел па́мятники новгоро́дской архите́кту́ры. Но́вые моско́вские собо́ры и дворцы́ соединя́ют ряд характе́рных осо́бенностей влади́миро-су́здальской и нов-горо́дской архитекту́ры с черта́ми зо́дчества италья́нского Возрожде́ния.

Строи́тельство Фиораве́нти и его́ помо́щников сосредо-та́чивалось в Кремле́. В дре́вней Руси́ кремлём называ́лась кре́пость, т. е. центра́льная укреплённая часть го́рода. Кремль го́рода Москвы́ возни́к на холме́ как бы само́й приро́дой предназна́ченном для постро́йки кре́пости. Э́тот круто́й холм был защищён с двух сторо́н Москво́й реко́й и впада́ющей в неё ре́чкой Негли́нной. Но́вые великоле́пные собо́ры постро́енные при Ива́не III—Успе́нский, Бла-гове́щенский и Арха́нгельский—, Грано́вита́я пала́та для пара́дных приёмов, но́вый ка́менный дворе́ц на ме́сте ста́рого деревя́нного, но́вые высо́кие сте́ны с ба́шнями окружа́ющие Кремль, всё э́то должно́ бы́ло соотве́тствовать значе́нию Москвы́ как столи́це но́вого, могу́щественного госуда́рства.

8

самодержа́вие autocracy
противоре́чие contradiction
оте́чество fatherland
привы́чка habit
колеба́ние wavering, hesitation
обяза́тельный obligatory
зна́тный distinguished, of
   noble origin
подбо́р selection, assortment
бестолко́вый stupid
ла́герь (m.) camp
неизглади́мый indelible
уча́сток section, part
принуди́тельный compulsory

уклони́ться to shun, avoid
   perf. of: уклоня́ться
поощря́ть to encourage
   поощри́ть (perf.)
по́дать (f.) tribute, tax
о́бщина commune
дохо́д income
бре́мя burden
приобрести́ to acquire
   perf. of: приобрета́ть
укры́ться to take refuge, hide
   perf. of: укрыва́ться
отря́д division, detachment
   (military)
угрожа́ть to threaten

САМОДЕРЖА́ВНАЯ МОСКО́ВСКАЯ РУСЬ
(до конца́ 16 ве́ка)

За пы́шным фаса́дом но́вых кремлёвских зда́ний, придво́рных обря́дов и ти́тулов скрыва́лось ва́жное и опа́сное противоре́чие. Ива́н III и его́ прее́мники насто́йчиво повторя́ли, что вся ру́сская земля́—их со́бственность. В уде́льные века́, когда́ ме́жду свобо́дным населе́нием и кня́зем существова́ли вре́менные догово́рные отноше́ния, князь был со́бственником то́лько террито́рии. С объедине́нием ру́сских земе́ль под вла́стью Москвы́ положе́ние измени́лось.

Страна́ населённая це́лым наро́дом, для кото́рого она́ ста́ла оте́чеством, не могла́ остава́ться ча́стной со́бственностью прави́теля. Но ни Ива́н III, ни его́ сын Васи́лий III,

ни его́ внук Ива́н Гро́зный не смогли́ сбро́сить уде́льных
привы́чек. В их созна́нии бо́рятся два противополо́жных
нача́ла: ча́стный со́бственник и национа́льный прави́тель,
самовла́стный хозя́ин и носи́тель верхо́вной госуда́рствен-
ной вла́сти. Это колеба́ние ме́жду двумя́ поря́дками при-
вело́ госуда́рство к глубо́ким потрясе́ниям, тем бо́лее, что
не то́лько царь но и населе́ние не уме́ло отвы́кнуть от
проше́дшего, от уде́льных воспомина́ний.

Уде́льные воспомина́ния храни́лись осо́бенно жи́во среди́
боя́р, среди́ бы́вших уде́льных князе́й и их пото́мков. При-
знава́я власть Москвы́ и теря́я незави́симость, уде́льные
князья́ станови́лись слу́гами Москвы́, где они́ слива́лись
с моско́вскими боя́рами в оди́н вы́сший прави́тельствен-
ный, аристократи́ческий класс. Но́вые слу́ги—боя́ре шли
в Москву́ не за но́выми служе́бными вы́годами, как это
бы́ло в уде́льные века́, а бо́льшей ча́стью с го́рьким чу́в-
ством сожале́ния о поте́рянных вы́годах уде́льной само-
стоя́тельности. Слу́жба боя́р из во́льной ста́ла обяза́тель-
ной, нево́льной. Моско́вский царь призыва́ет зна́тных
сотру́дников для управле́ния страны́, пре́дки кото́рых
некогда́ владе́ли частя́ми э́той страны́.

Но воспомина́ния о про́шлом занима́ли боя́р гора́здо
бо́льше, чем забо́та о настоя́щем, о госуда́рственных дела́х
и о слу́жбе царю́. Эти воспомина́ния служи́ли по́водом
постоя́нных генеалоги́ческих спо́ров среди́ боя́р, чей пре́док
име́л бо́льшее значе́ние и владе́л наибо́лее бога́тым и зна-
чи́тельным уде́лом. А генеалоги́ческие спо́ры привели́ к
разрабо́тке це́лой систе́мы, иера́рхии служе́бных отноше́ний
ме́жду боя́рами при моско́вском дворе́. Эта систе́ма из-
ве́стна под назва́нием ме́стничества. Поздне́йшие поколе́ния
должны́ бы́ли размеща́ться на слу́жбе и за столо́м царя́,
как ра́ньше размеща́лись пе́рвые поколе́ния уде́льных кня-
зе́й по разме́ру и значе́нию их владе́ний. Служе́бное по-
ложе́ние ка́ждого боя́рина при дворе́ не заслу́живалось, а
насле́довалось. Служе́бная карье́ра боя́рина не была́ его́
ли́чным де́лом, его́ ча́стным интере́сом. Это ограни́чивало
власть царя́ в пра́ве подбо́ра подходя́щих сотру́дников и
исполни́телей его́ во́ли.

Отсю́да выходи́ли постоя́нные столкнове́ния ме́жду мос-

ко́вским царём и его́ боя́рами. Э́ти столкнове́ния вноси́ли
драмати́ческое оживле́ние в церемо́нную жизнь моско́вского
двора́. Царь иска́л спосо́бных и послу́шных слуг, а ме́ст-
ничество подставля́ло ему́ зна́тных, но ча́сто бестолко́вых
люде́й. Служе́бная го́дность оце́нивалась происхожде́нием
пре́дков. А э́то зна́чило подчине́ние госуда́рственной слу́ж-
бы обы́чаю, кото́рый корени́лся в нра́вах и поня́тиях
уде́льной эпо́хи. И царь и боя́ре бы́ли недово́льны друг
дру́гом и госуда́рственным поря́дком, в кото́ром они́ жи́ли
и кото́рым они́ руководи́ли. Но ни та ни друга́я сторона́
не могла́ приду́мать друго́го поря́дка, не могла́ освобо-
ди́ться от привы́чек уде́льного вре́мени.

Одна́ко положе́ние ру́сской земли́ ре́зко измени́лось со
времён уде́льной эпо́хи. Сосе́дями моско́вского госуда́рства
бы́ли тепе́рь на за́паде Шве́ция, Ливо́нский о́рден и Литва́,
на ю́ге и восто́ке оста́тки тата́рских организа́ций, почти́
ежего́дно напада́вших на окра́йны моско́вской Руси́. Со
все́ми э́тими сосе́дями Москва́ вступи́ла в напряжённую
оборони́тельно-наступа́тельную борьбу́. Моско́вское го-
суда́рство походи́ло на вооружённый ла́герь, с трёх сторо́н
окружённый врага́ми. Ве́чная опа́сность легла́ неизглади́-
мой печа́тью на весь склад моско́вского о́бщества.

Для оборо́ны страны́ нужны́ бы́ли пре́жде всего́ два
ору́дия—во́йско и де́ньги. Организа́ция вое́нного, служи́-
лого кла́сса начала́сь в после́дней че́тверти 15 ве́ка. Э́та
боева́я си́ла скла́дывалась из лиц принадлежа́вших ко
всем слоя́м населе́ния и росла́ с чрезвыча́йной быстрото́й.
Гла́вным сре́дством для содержа́ния э́тих служи́лых люде́й
явля́лась земля́, так как с объедине́нием Руси́ в распоря-
же́нии моско́вского царя́ оказа́лся огро́мный земе́льный
фонд. Из э́того фо́нда моско́вское госуда́рство и ста́ло раз-
дава́ть уча́стки земли́, так называ́емые поме́стья, служи́-
лым лю́дям во вре́менное по́льзование, как вознагражде́ние
за слу́жбу.

Поме́стья отводи́лись служи́лым лю́дям преиму́щественно
в ю́жных и за́падных частя́х госуда́рства, по бли́зости от
возмо́жного теа́тра войны́. Э́ти вре́менные владе́льцы по-
ме́стий ста́ли называ́ться поме́щиками и́ли дворя́нами. Обо-
ро́на страны́ сде́лалась принуди́тельной до́лжностью э́того

кла́сса. Поме́щик, дворяни́н, уже́ не мог уклони́ться от
э́той обя́занности зако́нным путём и бро́сить да́нное ему́
поме́стье.

Разви́тие поме́стной систе́мы привело́ к тому́, что бо́ль-
ши́е простра́нства за́нятой крестья́нами земли́ бы́ли пе́ре-
даны дворя́нам, и таки́м о́бразом на э́тих земля́х создала́сь
зави́симость крестья́н от дворя́н. Э́ту зави́симость госуда́р-
ство не то́лько одобря́ло, но и поощря́ло. Дворя́не со-
ставля́ли моско́вское во́йско, а крестья́не преврати́лись в
класс, обя́занный поставля́ть госуда́рству де́ньги в ви́де
по́датей.

Крестья́не жи́ли в о́бщинах, кото́рые называ́лись мира́ми.
Среди́ чле́нов ми́ра земля́ дели́лась соразме́рно с рабо́чими
си́лами ка́ждой крестья́нской семьи́. Э́та черта́ сближа́ла
ру́сский мир с европе́йской о́бщиной, существу́ющей на за́-
паде в 8 и 9 века́х, во вре́мя расцве́та средневеко́вого фео-
дали́зма. Но там крестья́нин рабо́тал исключи́тельно на
покры́тие ли́чных нужд свое́й семьи́ и хозя́йства своего́
господи́на. А в моско́вском госуда́рстве крестья́нин стал
гла́вным исто́чником госуда́рственного дохо́да, и пе́ред
ним ста́ла тру́дная зада́ча, как увели́чить производи́тель-
ность труда́ с тем, что́бы поставля́ть казне́ тре́буемые
по́дати.

При существу́ющих примити́вных ме́тодах земледе́лия
э́та зада́ча была́ крестья́нству не по си́ле и ́ оно́ на́чало
бе́гством уклоня́ться от непоме́рно тяжёлого бре́мени.
Начался́ ма́ссовый крестья́нский вы́ход в ''ди́кое по́ле,''
т. е. в ю́жные степны́е о́бласти, освобождённые от тата́р,
но ещё не воше́дшие в соста́в моско́вского госуда́рства. Тут
беглецы́ осно́вывали свобо́дные о́бщины и ста́ли называ́ться
казака́ми, т. е. во́льными, незави́симыми людьми́. К сере-
ди́не 16 ве́ка, при Ива́не Гро́зном, в моско́вском госуда́рстве
созда́лся о́стрый хозя́йственный кри́зис, вы́званный недо-
ста́тком рабо́чих рук.

Ива́н Гро́зный ви́дел себя́ с де́тства среди́ чужи́х люде́й.
Ему́ бы́ло четы́ре го́да, когда́ у́мер его́ оте́ц, а восьми́ лет
он потеря́л и мать. Всю жизнь у него́ сохраня́лось чу́вство
одино́чества. Он ра́но усво́ил себе́ привы́чку ходи́ть огля́-
дываясь и прислу́шиваясь, ра́но привы́к ду́мать, что он

окружён то́лько врага́ми. Всего́ трудне́е бы́ло приобрести́ его́ дове́рие. Кни́ги бы́ли люби́мым предме́том его́ заня́тий. Гла́вное, что он чита́л, бы́ло духо́вного содержа́ния, библе́йские писа́ния. Его́ люби́мые те́ксты все отвеча́ют на одну́ те́му, все говоря́т о ца́рской вла́сти, о её боже́ственном происхожде́нии, о ги́бельных сле́дствиях разновла́стья. Ива́н постепе́нно со́здал себе́ из э́тих иде́й идеа́льный мир, в кото́рый уходи́л отдыха́ть от земны́х стра́хов и огорче́ний.

Ива́н был пе́рвый из моско́вских прави́телей, кото́рый жи́во почу́вствовал в себе́ царя́ в настоя́щем библе́йском смы́сле. Он сам для себя́ стал святы́ней, со́здал тео́рию ца́рской вла́сти и самообожа́ния. Усво́ив себе́ таку́ю иде́ю верхо́вной вла́сти, он реши́л, что не мо́жет пра́вить госуда́рством, как пра́вил его́ оте́ц и дед, при соде́йствии боя́р. Э́то реше́ние привело́ к созда́нию опри́чнины, в кото́рой Ива́н наде́ялся освободи́ться от боя́р и уничто́жить их сопротивле́ние ца́рской вла́сти.

Всё госуда́рство раздели́лось на две ча́сти, на зе́мщину и опри́чнину. Во главе́ пе́рвой оста́лись боя́ре, во главе́ второ́й стал сам царь. Сло́во опри́чнина в 16 ве́ке бы́ло уже́ устаре́лым те́рмином ста́рого, уде́льного языка́, кото́рый тогда́шняя моско́вская ле́топись перевела́ выраже́нием ''осо́бый двор,'' ''осо́бо вы́деленное владе́ние.'' Опри́чнина захвати́ла чуть не полови́ну всего́ госуда́рства. Сам царь Ива́н смотре́л на опри́чнину, как на своё ча́стное владе́ние, кото́рое он вы́делил из соста́ва госуда́рства. Опри́чнина получи́ла значе́ние убе́жища, куда́ хоте́л укры́ться царь от вражде́бного боя́рства.

Ива́н брал к себе́ в опри́чнину гла́вным о́бразом те города́ и центра́льные о́бласти, в кото́рых жи́ли пото́мки уде́льных князе́й. Зе́мщина же располага́лась вдоль грани́ц госуда́рства.

Но опри́чниной называ́лся та́кже но́вый, состоя́щий из дворя́н отря́д, кото́рый до́лжен был охраня́ть царя́, вы́сшая поли́ция по дела́м госуда́рственной изме́ны. Отря́д состоя́л снача́ла из ты́сячи челове́к и пото́м был увели́чен до шести́ ты́сяч. Опри́чник был оде́т весь в чёрном, на вороно́м коне́. У него́ бы́ли привя́заны к седлу́ соба́чья голова́ и метла́. Э́то бы́ли зна́ки его́ до́лжности, состоя́вшей в том, что́бы вымета́ть изме́ну и грызть госуда́рственных изме́нников. Из взя́тых в опри́чнину областе́й все опа́сные для Ива́на лю́ди, гла́вным о́бразом пото́мки уде́льных князе́й, переселя́лись в зе́мщину, на окра́йны госуда́рства. Но мно́гих опри́чники му́чили и убива́ли.

Опри́чнина оказа́лась мо́щным ору́дием Ива́на Гро́зного про́тив боя́р, с по́мощью кото́рого царю́ удало́сь вы́рвать с ко́рнем все оста́тки уде́льных поря́дков и сломи́ть сопротивле́ние боя́р самодержа́вию. Но опри́чнина име́ла и други́е после́дствия. Зре́лище крова́вых и жесто́ких распра́в опри́чников со свои́ми же́ртвами уси́ливало среди́ крестья́н недово́льство, страх и жела́ние бежа́ть за преде́лы моско́вского госуда́рства. К концу́ ца́рствования Ива́на Гро́зного недоста́ток рабо́чих рук и коли́чество необрабо́танных поле́й продолжа́ли расти́ и экономи́ческий кри́зис страны́ дости́г угрожа́ющих разме́ров.

9

сму́тный troubled (also: confused, vague)

отлича́ться to be distinguished

отличи́ться (perf.)

погаса́ть to expire, go out

пога́снуть (perf.)

отреше́ние renunciation

вы́борный elected

недоразуме́ние misunderstanding

сле́дователь (m.) investigator

потрясённый shaken

самозва́нец pretender

за́говор conspiracy

изба́виться to get rid of

perf. of: **избавля́ться**

созда́ть to create

perf. of: **создава́ть**

све́ргнуть to dethrone

perf. of: **сверга́ть**

восста́ние uprising

обя́занность (f.) duty

вме́шиваться to interfere

вмеша́ться (perf.)

броже́ние ferment

поги́бнуть to perish

perf. of: **погиба́ть**

кровопроли́тие bloodshed

СМУ́ТНОЕ ВРЕ́МЯ
(1598–1613)

Ива́н Гро́зный у́мер в нача́ле 1584 го́да. Го́да за полтора́ до свое́й кончи́ны, поссо́рясь со свои́м ста́ршим сы́ном Ива́ном, Гро́зный так си́льно уда́рил его́, что уби́л его́ на́ смерть. Поэ́тому престо́л по́сле Гро́зного перешёл к его́ второ́му сы́ну Фёдору. Фёдору предстоя́ло стать после́дним царём из дина́стии Рю́риковичей и из пле́мени Ива́на Кали́ты. По́сле Гро́зного оста́лся ещё оди́н, мла́дший, сын Дими́трий, кото́рому оте́ц дал ма́ленький уде́л, го́род У́глич с уе́здом. Но в 1591 году́, семиле́тний Дими́трий у́мер от ра́ны, нанесённой ножо́м в го́рло во вре́мя игры́ его́ на дворе́ У́глического дворца́.

Племя Ивана Калиты, построившее московское государство, всегда отличалось удивительным практическим умением обрабатывать свои материальные дела, всегда заботилось о земном, и это самое племя, погасая, блеснуло полным отрешением от всего земного, вымерло царём Фёдором Ивановичем, который всю жизнь думал только о небесном, о духовных делах. Родившись слабосильным, он вырос малорослым, бледным, худощавым человеком, с неровной, старчески медленной походкой от преждевременной слабости в ногах. Он вечно улыбался, но безжизненной, жалкой улыбкой. На престоле он искал человека, который стал бы хозяином его воли. Таким человеком стал Борис Годунов. Царь Фёдор был женат на сестре Годунова, Ирине. Борис стал править государством именем зятя. Он правил умно и 14летнее царствование Фёдора было для государства временем отдыха. Но в январе 1598 года царь Фёдор умер бездетным. После него не осталось никого из Калитиной династии, кто бы мог занять опустевший престол. В московском государстве началось Смутное время. Окончилось оно со вступлением на престол царя Михаила Фёдоровича Романова в 1613 году. За эти 15 лет московская жизнь была полна борьбой различных общественных и политических сил.

После смерти царя Фёдора на престол вступил Борис Годунов Но московские люди не могли принять мысль о выборном царе. Думали, что выборный царь—не царь. Это недоразумение в московском политическом сознании является главной причиной начала Смуты. Люди смотрели на государство не как на союз народный, который не может принадлежать никому кроме самого народа, а как на личное владение и хозяйство царской династии, как на семейную собственность Калитина племени, которое её создало и расширяло в продолжение трёх веков.

Первые годы Смуты, от 1598 до 1606 года, были периодом династической борьбы. Предметом борьбы служит московский престол. Следователи трагичной смерти царевича Димитрия в 1591 году признали, что царевич погиб от нечаянного самоубийства. Но после избрания Бориса Годунова царём, по Москве пошли слухи и молва, что Годунов

подосла́л уби́йц к царе́вичу, чтобы проложи́ть себе́ доро́гу
к престо́лу, а в 1604 году́ разнесла́сь весть, что а́генты
Годуно́ва промахну́лись в У́гличе́, что царе́вич Дими́трий
жив и идёт из Литвы́ добыва́ть престо́л.

Царь Бори́с Годуно́в у́мер весно́й 1605 го́да, потрясённый
успе́хами самозва́нца. Самозва́нцу Дими́трию удало́сь встать
на моско́вский престо́л, но он вско́ре был уби́т. Его́ паде́ние
бы́ло подгото́влено за́говором боя́р, во главе́ кото́рого
стоя́л князь Васи́лий Шу́йский. На собра́нии загово́рщи-
ков накану́не восста́ния, он открове́нно заяви́л, что при-
зна́л самозва́нца то́лько для того́, чтобы изба́виться от
Годуно́ва. Больши́м боя́рам ну́жно бы́ло поддержа́ть само-
зва́нца, чтобы све́ргнуть Годуно́ва, а пото́м све́ргнуть и
самозва́нца, чтобы откры́ть доро́гу к престо́лу одному́ из
свое́й среды́.

По́сле самозва́нца на престо́л вступи́л Васи́лий Шу́йский.
Э́то был пожило́й, 54ле́тний боя́рин небольшо́го ро́ста,
слепова́тый, неглу́пый, но бо́лее хи́трый чем у́мный. Царём
Васи́лием ма́ло кто был дово́лен. Гла́вной причи́ной не-
дово́льства была́ его́ зави́симость от кружка́ боя́р, его́ из-
бра́вших и игра́вших им, как ребёнком. Недово́льны царём
—зна́чит на́добен самозва́нец: Самозва́нство станови́лось
стереоти́пной фо́рмой ру́сского полити́ческого мышле́ния, в
кото́рую отлива́лось вся́кое обще́ственное недово́льство.
И слу́хи о спасе́нии Лжедими́трия Пе́рвого, т. е. о второ́м
самозва́нце, пошли́ с пе́рвых мину́т ца́рствования Васи́лия.
Во и́мя э́того при́зрака начали́сь восста́ния с 1606 го́да.
Движе́нием восста́вших руково́дят уже́ не династи́ческие
моти́вы, а моти́вы кла́ссовой вражды́. На верши́ну о́б-
щества восстаю́т обще́ственные низы́ в наде́жде на поли-
ти́ческий и социа́льный переворо́т. Э́то откры́тое междо-
усо́бие продолжа́ется с 1606 до 1610 го́да и мо́жет быть
на́звано вре́менем социа́льной борьбы́.

За э́то вре́мя вскрыва́ется втора́я основна́я причи́на
Сму́ты. Моско́вские зако́ны распределя́ли госуда́рственные
обя́занности среди́ кла́ссов о́бщества, но не определя́ли
прав—ни ли́чных, ни кла́ссовых. Положе́ние лица́ и́ли
кла́сса определя́лось лишь его́ обя́занностями. Дина́стия
служи́ла венцо́м в сво́де госуда́рственного зда́ния. С её

исчезновением разрывался узел, которым сдерживались все общественные отношения. Что прежде терпеливо переносили, покоряясь воле привычного хозяина, то казалось невыносимым теперь, когда хозяина не стало. Все классы общества поднялись со своими особыми нуждами и стремлениями, чтобы облегчить своё положение в государстве.

В то время, когда царь Василий боролся против народных восстаний, в московское междоусобие начинают вмешиваться иностранцы. Новгородская и смоленская окраины государства переходят под власть шведов и поляков, а в самой Москве, после свержения царя Василия в 1610 году, водворяется польский королевич Владислав на престол. Вмешательство иностранцев возбуждает в русских национальное чувство и направляет против инородных врагов все слои московского населения. С 1611 года начинается объединение всех народных сил и попытки свержения чуждой власти. Этот период Смуты, от 1611 до 1613 года, может быть назван временем борьбы за национальность.

Осенью 1612 года эта борьба окончилась успешно. Русские войска, под руководством князя Пожарского и мясника Минина, освободили Москву от поляков. Но Смута окончательно прекратилась только в 1613 году, когда удалось найти царя, которого можно было связать родством, хотя и не прямым, с династией Рюриковичей. Царь Михаил Романов был племянником последнего царя прежней династии. Первая жена Ивана Грозного была Анастасия Романова, сестра деда Михаила.

Смута внесла в московскую жизнь социальные перемены и культурные новшества. В Смуте окончательно погибла вековая московская, боярская, аристократия. Те немногие боярские роды, которые не вымерли во время опричнины и Смуты, в 17 веке обеднели и вошли в состав дворянства. Смута не изменила общественного строя Москвы, но она переместила в нём центр тяжести с боярства на дворянство. Произошла смена господствующего класса, и новый господствующий класс сохранил на будущее время за собой и право на крестьянский труд и право на придворную карьеру.

Культу́рная переме́на,, со́зданная Сму́той состоя́ла в бо́лее бли́зком знако́мстве ру́сских с иностра́нцами. До Сму́ты то́лько ца́рский двор и случа́йно отде́льные ли́ца соприкаса́лись с иностра́нцами и ви́дели их в Москве́. В Сму́тное вре́мя соприкоснове́ние с иностра́нцами у москвиче́й ста́ло постоя́нным и о́бщим. За пе́рвым самозва́нцем в Москву́ яви́лись со́тни, да́же ты́сячи, поляко́в и шве́дов, вое́нных, торго́вых и промы́шленных. Ру́сские лю́ди убеди́лись в том, что им сле́дует усво́ить европе́йскую те́хнику. Кро́ме того́, они́ уви́дели, что европе́йцы уме́ют веселе́е жить. Европе́йский костю́м, бритьё бороды́, му́зыка, предме́ты дома́шней обстано́вки начина́ют входи́ть в моско́вскую жизнь вме́сте с лати́нской и по́льской кни́гой, религио́зным вольноду́мством и полити́ческой иде́ей. В 17 ве́ке в Москве́ идёт у́мственное броже́ние, несу́щее с собо́й нача́ло той европеиза́ции Руси́, кото́рая так широко́ шагну́ла вперёд при Петре́ Вели́ком.

Сму́та оста́вила глубо́кий след в па́мяти ру́сского наро́да. Когда́, в 19 ве́ке, расцвело́ све́тское иску́сство в Росси́и, Сму́тное вре́мя послужи́ло сюже́том для многочи́сленных худо́жественных произведе́ний. Преддве́рье Сму́ты изобрази́л худо́жник Илья́ Ре́пин в свое́й карти́не ссо́ры Ива́на Гро́зного с царе́вичем Ива́ном: Гро́зный, с обезуме́вшим от отча́яния и у́жаса выраже́нием лица́, прижима́ет те́ло умира́ющего сы́на, кото́рому он сгоряча́ нанёс смерте́льный уда́р. Коне́ц Сму́ты прибли́зился по́сле наро́дного объедине́ния про́тив иностра́нного вмеша́тельства. Вождя́м э́того объедине́ния, Ми́нину и Пожа́рскому, посвящён па́мятник рабо́ты И. П. Ма́ртоса на Кра́сной пло́щади в Москве́. Но весь па́фос э́тих бу́рных 15 лет—кровопроли́тие, восста́ния, бой, уби́йства, пожа́ры, ли́чные траге́дии и обще́ственные столкнове́ния—полне́е всего́ изображены́ в двух музыка́льных произведе́ниях—в о́перах ''Бори́с Годуно́в'' Мусо́ргского и ''Жизнь за царя́'' Гли́нки.

10

поломать to break, demolish
  perf. of: **ломать**
отсталость (f.) backward-
  ness
превосходство superiority
оборона defense
роскошь (f.) luxury
раздумье hesitation, ponder-
  ing
соблазнять to tempt
  соблазнить (perf.)
государь (m.) sovereign
грамотность literacy
сомнение doubt
быт way of life
соперник competitor, rival

отшатнуться to shy away
  perf. of: **отшатываться**
служить to serve
  послужить (perf.)
лишить to deprive
  perf. of: **лишать**
седло saddle
лавка shop
личность (f.) personality,
  individual
прикрепление attachment,
  confinement
уложение code, law
поколебать to shake, disturb
  perf. of: **колебать**
раздвоение split

СЕМНАДЦАТЫЙ ВЕК И ЕГО ПРОТИВОРЕЧИЯ

Смута так много поломала старого, что самое восстановление разрушенного неизбежно получало характер обновления. Семнадцатый век—эпоха перелома в русской жизни и культуре. Два противоположных течения волнуют русское общество. Одно отталкивает его к старине, а другое увлекает вперёд, в тёмную даль неведомой чужбины.

Русские люди начинают оглядываться по сторонам, искать указаний и уроков у чужих людей на Западе, всё более убеждаясь в его превосходстве и в своей собственной отсталости. Московское правительство и общество особенно сильно почувствовали нужду в военной и промышленной технике Западной Европы. Усиленный спрос привлёк в

Москву множество иностранных техников, офицеров и солдат, врачей, мастеровых, купцов и заводчиков. Они основали иностранное поселение на восточной окраине Москвы, которое получило название Немецкой слободы. В составе её населения были представлены почти все европейские нации—французы, англичане, шведы, голландцы, итальянцы, немцы. В социальном отношении численный перевес оказался на стороне военного элемента.

Немецкая слобода скоро разрослась в значительный городок с прямыми, широкими улицами и переулками, с красивыми домами, ветренной мельницей и тремя лютеранскими церквами. Это был уголок Западной Европы, приютившийся на окраине Москвы. Это иностранное поселение и стало проводником западноевропейской культуры на Руси. Офицеры, купцы и мастера, которых правительство выписывало для внешней обороны и для внутренних экономических надобностей, вместе со своей военной и промышленной техникой приносили в Москву и западноевропейские удобства, предметы роскоши и увеселения.

Подражая иностранным образцам, царь и верхи московского общества начинают выезжать в нарядных немецких каретах, обшитых бархатом, с хрустальными стёклами, украшенных живописью. Богатые люди начинают строить каменные дома на место плохих деревянных, заводят домашнюю обстановку на иностранный лад, обивают стены золотыми кожанными обоями бельгийской работы, украшают комнаты картинами, зеркалами и часами. При дворе и в высшем кругу развивается страсть к театральным зрелищам и к балету.

В высших московских кругах также пробуждается интерес к научному образованию, к книжному знанию, охота к размышлению о таких предметах, которые раньше не входили в обычный кругозор русского человека. В Москве пытаются завести школы и правительство и частные лица.

Едва московское общество отведало плодов западной культуры и науки, как им уже начинает овладевать тяжёлое раздумье, безопасны ли они, не повредят ли чистоте веры и нравов. Это раздумье—второй момент в настроении рус-

ских умóв 17 вéка, наступи́вший вслед за недовóльством
свои́м положéнием.

Ра́ньше нау́ка и иску́сство цени́лись по их свя́зи с цéрковью, как срéдства познáния слóва Бóжья и душéвного
спасéния. Знáнию и худóжественным украшéниям жи́зни,
не имéвшим такóй свя́зи и такóго значéния, не давáли
мéста в систéме воспитáния. Цéрковь молчали́во их тер-
пéла, как дéтские и́гры, а порóй порицáла, как опáсное
развлечéние. Увеселéния бы́ли подчинены́ прáвилам цер-
кóвного поря́дка. У тогó, кто хотéл быть и́ли казáться
благочести́вым, цéрковное пéние бы́ло еди́нственным раз-
влечéнием. Му́зыка преслéдовалась цéрковью положи́тель-
но, дáже нарóдные пéсни. Однáко, ру́сский нарóд постоя́нно
соблазня́лся запрещёнными плодáми.

Глáвное внимáние педагóгии в москóвском воспитáнии
бы́ло обращенó на прáвила, как слéдует жить по христи-
áнски, а не на нау́чныє знáния. Настоя́щий нарóдный учи́-
тель в москóвской Руси́—э́то был хозя́ин дóма, отéц се-
мéйства. Хозя́ин считáл в состáве своéй семьи́, своегó
дóма, не тóлько свою́ женý и детéй, но и всех жи́вших в
егó дóме рóдственников и слуг, зави́симых от негó людéй,
с семéйствами тех и други́х. Это бы́ло егó домáшнее цáрство.
Здесь он был не тóлько муж и отéц, но и пря́мо называ́лся
госудáрем.

Этот домовóй госудáрь и был домáшним учи́телем, егó
дом был егó шкóлой. Ребёнок дóлжен был воспи́тываться
не стóлько урóками, котóрые он слу́шал, скóлько той
нрáвственной атмосфéрой, котóрой он дышáл. Грáмотность
не входи́ла в состáв óбщего воспитáния. Онá причисля́лась
к техни́ческим прóмыслам и нужнá былá тóлько в нéсколь-
ких служéбных дóлжностях. Не тот считáлся му́дрым
человéком, кто имéл обши́рные знáния, а тот, кто дéлал
мнóго добрá.

При таки́х взгля́дах на воспитáние москóвское óбщество
17 вéка не моглó не почу́вствовать тревóжные сомнéния,
безопáсно ли знакóмство с зáпадной нау́кой и культу́рой
для векови́х устóев ру́сского бы́та? Европéйская нау́ка и
культу́ра приходи́ли в Росси́ю как бы сопéрницей и́ли в
лу́чшем слу́чае сотру́дницей цéркви в дéле устроéния чело-

ве́ческого сча́стья. И моско́вская мысль, опу́танная преда́-
ниями и тради́циями, могла́ то́лько испу́ганно отшатну́ться
от тако́й сотру́дницы и́ли сопе́рницы.

Таки́м о́бразом, в 17 ве́ке за́падное влия́ние проника́ло
в Ро́ссию ме́дленно и поде́йствовало лишь на верхи́ мос-
ко́вского госуда́рства. За исключе́нием э́того то́нкого со-
циа́льного сло́я, всё о́бщество све́рху до́низу продолжа́ло
находи́ться под влия́нием поня́тий и тради́ций, сложи́вшихся
в предыду́щих двух столе́тиях. На Руси́ жить зна́чило
служи́ть госуда́рству. Кла́ссы о́бщества различа́лись друг
от дру́га не по свои́м права́м и привилле́гиям, а по ро́ду
свое́й слу́жбы, по содержа́нию свои́х пови́нностей. Все
одина́ково явля́лись раба́ми госуда́рства.

Да́же зна́тные лю́ди не так бы́ли бога́ты, как э́то каза́-
лось. Во́лей царя́ они́ всегда́ могли́ лиши́ться своего́ иму́-
щества. Интере́с госуда́рства и́ли царя́ поглоща́л все
интере́сы. Крестья́нин был обя́зан рабо́тать на дворяни́на
и плати́ть по́дати, а дворяни́н был обя́зан нести́ вое́нную
слу́жбу. Э́та слу́жба продолжа́лась до са́мой сме́рти. Ни
ста́рость, ни ра́ны не освобожда́ли вполне́ служи́лого че-
лове́ка оъ возло́женных на него́ госуда́рственных обяза́-
тельств. При э́том, ни род, ни ме́сто слу́жбы не зави́сели от
свобо́дного вы́бора дворяни́на. Ка́ждый служи́л там и так,
как ему́ бы́ло предпи́сано свы́ше.

Слу́жба купцо́в заключа́лась в обяза́тельном веде́нии
торго́во-промы́шленных предприя́тий. Как дворяни́н был
пригвождён на всю жизнь к похо́дному седлу́, так купе́ц
был пригвождён к городско́й ла́вке, в кото́рой он обя́зан
был всю жизнь торгова́ть для того́, чтобы плати́ть госу-
да́рству по́дати.

Неуваже́ние к челове́ческой ли́чности станови́лось са́мым
обыкнове́нным приёмом в администрати́вной пра́ктике мос-
ко́вского госу́дарства. К середи́не 17 ве́ка оно́ привело́
прави́тельство к оконча́тельному прикрепле́нию крестья́н
к обраба́тываемой и́ми земле́. Так как не служи́ть госу-
да́рству мо́жно бы́ло то́лько незако́нно укрыва́ясь, то
крестья́не всё бо́льше прибега́ли к бе́гству в ю́жные сте́пи,
ещё не воше́дшие в территориа́льный соста́в Москвы́. Уло-
же́ние 1649 го́да да́ло дворя́нам пра́во иска́ть и си́лой воз-

вращать бежавших от них крестьян и их потомков. Крестьяне теперь окончательно теряли право передвижения с места на место и тем самым лишались последних следов личной свободы.

Крепостное право установилось в московском государстве не столько в интересах дворян, сколько в интересах государства, для того, чтобы укрепить обязанность крестьян платить в казну деньги. В этом состоит главная черта, отличающая русское крепостное право от западноевропейского. В Западной Европе прикрепление крестьян к земле развилось в средние века, на территории политически раздробленного, феодального порядка. В России оно произошло значительно позднее, но зато сложилось в пределах обширного, национального государства.

Начала западного влияния на Россию шли из Немецкой слободы. Корни старого московского порядка исходили из Кремля. Тут жил царь, который продолжал считать государство своей личной собственностью и власти которого не было границ.

В 17 веке значительную часть Кремля занимало здание дворца, громадное, причудливое строение, состоящее из бесчисленного количества палат, теремов и разного рода хозяйственных построек, крупных и мелких, каменных и деревянных, в хаотическом беспорядке примыкавших друг к другу и сплетавшихся в лабиринт, который нарастал в течение двух столетий. Кремль кишел людьми—придворными, дворцовыми служителями, ремесленниками, мастерами разного рода и многочисленными посетителями. Дворцовое хозяйство было огромной и сложной машиной, для обслуживания которой нужны были многочисленные рабочие, составляющие обширную группу населения Москвы.

Немецкая слобода указывала России дорогу на запад, Кремль стремился держать её под своей традиционной, неограниченной властью. Столкновение этих двух противоположных течений поколебало прежнее единство русской культуры и русского общества. С 17 века начинаются раздвоение и разлад в духовной, социальной и умственной жизни русского народа, наложившие свою печать на последующие столетия.

11

раскол schism
раскольник dissenter
обряд ritual
сложный complicated
смелый bold
парус sail
предприятие undertaking
восстановление restoration
исправление correction
отступление digression (also: retreat)
преследовать to persecute
преследование persecution
ссылка exile
пытка torture

казнь (f.) execution
искажать to distort
исказить (perf.)
мозг brain
трезвый sober
скоплять to accumulate, save
скопить (perf.)
сохранить to preserve, save perf. of: сохранять
лад way, fashion
хлам rubbish
подвал cellar
чердак attic

ЦЕРКОВНЫЙ РАСКОЛ

Русским церковным расколом называется отделение значительной части русского общества от правящей православной церкви. Раскольники принадлежали, главным образом, к низшим классам населения.

Это разделение началось во второй половине 17 века вследствие церковных реформ патриарха Никона и продолжало расти и крепнуть в последующие два столетия. К концу 19 века в России было, по расчётам изучающих этот вопрос людей, до двадцати миллионов раскольников. Эти диссиденты отказывались признавать авторитет церковного правления и придерживались "старой веры," старых обрядов, существовавших до реформ Никона. Поэтому раскольников также называют староверами или старообрядцами.

Патриарх Никон был человек величественной наружности, высокий, гордый, прекрасно говоривший, но с сложным, неровным характером. В ежедневной жизни он был тяжёл, капризен, вспыльчив и самолюбив. По своим умственным и нравственным силам он был большой делец, желавший и способный делать большие дела, но только большие. От покоя он скучал, не умел терпеливо выжидать. Ему постоянно нужна была тревога, увлечение смелой мыслью или широким предприятием. Это был словно парус, который только в бурю бывает самим собой, а в тихую, безветренную погоду висит на мачте как бесполезная тряпка.

Никон увлекался смелой, и для России новой мыслью, что патриарх стоит выше царя, что духовенство выше государственной власти. А широкое предприятие, которым он занялся со свойственной ему энергией, это было восстановление полного согласия между русской церковью и греческой. Он хотел восстановить сношения, которые со времён падения Киева значительно сократились. С этой целью Никон предпринял исправление русских церковных обрядов и книг. В течение веков эти книги переписывались от руки и в них вошло не мало ошибок и отступлений от греческих источников.

Но Никон плохо понимал людей, с которыми ему приходилось считаться. На Руси духовенство никогда не ставило себя выше царя или князя, не искало светской власти. Поэтому, идея о превосходстве патриаршеской власти над царской не нашла себе сочувствия среди русских и привела, в конце концов, к падению и удалению Никона.

Предпринятое Никоном согласие между русской церковью и греческой также пострадало от резкого, властного отношения патриарха к людям. Никон слишком низко оценил первых противников исправления церковных обрядов и книг. Мечтая о сближении русской и греческой церквах, он вызвал разъединение в самой русской церкви.

Несмотря на личную неудачу Никона, начатые им изменения в церковной службе и книге продолжались и после его падения. Правительство одобряло эту реформу, так как в то время оно начинало искать более близких сношений с чужими странами во всех сферах русской жизни.

Таким образом раскольники восставали не только против церковной власти, но также против государственной. А со своей стороны, правительство жестоко преследовало и наказывало староверов как опасных для государства бунтовщиков. Но ссылки, пытки и смертная казнь, которыми старообрядцы нередко платили за свои убеждения, только подливали масла к огню, только способствовали росту и расширению раскола.

Протест раскольников выходил далеко за пределы религиозных вопросов. К староверам бежали все восстающие против существующего порядка вещей. В раскол шёл тот, кто хотел укрыться от крепостной зависимости, кто искал личной свободы, кто вспоминал о старинных традициях свободной и богатой жизни Киевской Руси.

Раскол был явление новой, а пе старой жизни. Главное в расколе было не сохранение старины, старых церковных обрядов, а построение новой жизни, основанной на учении Христа. По мнению раскольников, реформы Никона и политика Москвы исказили христианское учение, построили царство Анти-Христа, от которого нужно было бежать. Со временем, раскол разбился на множество разных сект, но центральной идеей у всех оставалось убеждение, что мир во власти Анти-Христа.

Старая вера клала на своих последователей не только религиозные обязанности, но требовала согласовать всю жизнь—семейную, общественную и хозяйственную—с требованиями христианства. Раскольник считал собственную совесть судьёй своих действий. В своих строгих требованиях к человеческой личности раскол имеет много общего с европейским протестантизмом и американским пуританизмом.

Раскольники превратились в религиозную народную интеллигенцию. Раскол расшевелил спавший мозг русского человека, заставил его думать о своей вере. Священники и монахи стали рассуждать об обрядах и их значении именно потому, что правительство хотело их заставить де́лать ина́че, а не так, как они́ привы́кли пре́жде де́лать. Оди́н из ра́нних защи́тников ста́рой ве́ры, протопо́п Авваку́м, счита́ется не то́лько кру́пным духо́вным вождём раско́ла, но и велича́йшим писа́телем своего́ вре́мени.

В моско́вском госуда́рстве госпо́дствовало отсу́тствие мы́сли и стро́гое подчине́ние вла́сти; раско́льник люби́л мы́слить, спо́рить, охо́тно учи́лся гра́моте. Церко́вная сфе́ра была́ для него́ у́мственной гимна́стикой. В ней он получа́л подгото́вку к тому́, чтобы име́ть возмо́жность уда́чно обрати́ться и к други́м сфе́рам жи́зни. Старове́ры, несмотря́ на пресле́дования, не то́лько не бедне́ли, но наоборо́т постоя́нно собира́ли в свои́ ру́ки значи́тельные бога́тства.

Тре́звые, трудолюби́вые, че́стные, осторо́жные в дела́х свои́х, раско́льники постепе́нно скопля́ли бога́тства и уме́ли сохраня́ть их в свои́х се́мьях. Остава́ясь в своём те́сном кругу́, они́ помога́ли во всём друг дру́гу, вели́ торго́во-промы́шленные дела́ вме́сте и вся́чески подде́рживали друг дру́га. В свой круг, недосту́пный для посторо́ннего богача́, они́ охо́тно принима́ли вся́кого бедняка́, лишь бы он остава́лся и́ли станови́лся ве́рным ста́рой ве́ре.

До второ́й полови́ны 18 ве́ка жесто́кие пресле́дования раско́льников заставля́ли их сели́ться на окра́йнах госуда́рства и́ли да́же бежа́ть заграни́цу. В заво́лжских леса́х выраста́ли бога́тые раско́льничие о́бщины и селе́ния. К концу́ 18 ве́ка, при Екатери́не Второ́й, отноше́ния прави́тельства к раско́льникам смягчи́лось, что да́ло им возмо́жность верну́ться в центра́льные о́бласти страны́. В нача́ле 19 ве́ка раско́льники завели́ мно́жество фа́брик и торго́вых предприя́тий в само́й Москве́ и в её окре́стностях, и составля́ли богате́йший слой ру́сского купе́чества. В э́то же вре́мя ста́рая ве́ра продолжа́ла распространя́ться. Пропага́нда её происходи́ла не то́лько в раско́льничих церква́х и монастыря́х, но и на фа́бриках и в магази́нах. Про́поведь раско́ла де́йствовала не то́лько на се́рдце, но и на карма́н после́дователей.

Раско́льники сыгра́ли кру́пную роль в сохране́нии це́нных па́мятников дре́вней ру́сской культу́ры. Когда́ дворя́нство на́чало увлека́ться европе́йской культу́рой и жить на европе́йский лад—а э́то начало́сь при Петре́ Вели́ком и усили́лось к концу́ 18 ве́ка—стари́нная ру́сская обстано́вка, ру́кописи и осо́бенно дре́вние ико́ны, попада́ли в ви́де ста́рого хла́ма в подва́лы и чердаки́ дворя́нских домо́в. Отсю́да их спаса́ли и покупа́ли раско́льники. Сохране́нием э́того це́нного материа́ла старове́ры оказа́ли неоцени́мую услу́гу ру́сской исто́рии и культу́ре. Без них мно́гое бы бессле́дно пропа́ло.

12

велика́н giant
мозо́ль (f.) callus
отвлечённый abstract
подро́бность detail
принужде́ние force, compulsion
ору́дие tool
промы́шленность (f.) industry
опира́ться to lean on
  опере́ться (perf.)
почётный honorary
поворо́т turn, change

переворо́т upheaval
преобразова́ние reform
отменя́ть to abolish
  отмени́ть (perf.)
заменя́ть to replace
  замени́ть (perf.)
нало́г tax
пожи́зненный for life
поко́йник deceased
киби́тка covered wagon
щади́ть to spare
  пощади́ть (perf.)
сопротивле́ние resistance

ПЁТР ВЕЛИ́КИЙ И ЕГО́ ВРЕ́МЯ

Лю́ди всех поколе́ний и ра́зных взгля́дов в оце́нках ли́чности и де́ятельности Петра́ сходи́лись в одно́м: его́ счита́ли си́лой. Никто́ не счита́л его́ ничто́жным челове́ком, никто́ не сомнева́лся в грома́дном его́ влия́нии на ход наро́дной жи́зни.

Пётр был велика́н, почти́ семи́ фу́тов ро́стом, це́лой голово́й вы́ше любо́й толпы́, среди́ кото́рой ему́ приходи́лось когда́-ли́бо стоя́ть. Он про́жил свою́ жизнь в постоя́нной физи́ческой де́ятельности. Ру́ки его́ бы́ли всегда́ в рабо́те и с них не сходи́ли мозо́ли. Он ве́чно куда́-то е́хал, во всём спеши́л и был го́стем у себя́ до́ма.

Он хоте́л узна́ть и усво́ить вся́кое но́вое ремесло́ и де́ло, пре́жде чем успева́л сообрази́ть, на что оно́ ему́ пона́добится. Он был как до́ма в любо́й мастерско́й, на како́й угодно фабрике. Но выше всего он ставил корабельное мастерство. Современники считали его лучшим корабельным мастером в России. Из него, родившегося в континентальной Москве, вышел настоящий моряк, которому морской воздух нужен был, как вода рыбе.

Но Пётр не был охотник до отвлечённых, общих соображений. Во всяком деле ему легче давались подробности работы, чем её общий план. Он лучше соображал средства и цели, чем следствия. Во всём он был больше делец, мастер, чем мыслитель. Несчастье Петра было в том, что он остался без всякого политического сознания, с одним смутным ощущением, что у его власти нет границ, а есть только опасности. Вся его деятельность была основана на мысли о необходимости и пользе властного принуждения. Он надеялся силой навязать народу недостающие ему блага. Потому, заботясь о народе, он до крайности напрягал его труд, тратил людские средства и жизни безрасчётно, без всякой бережливости.

По направлению своей деятельности Пётр больше привык обращаться с вещами, с рабочими орудиями, чем с людьми, а потому и с людьми обращался, как с рабочими орудиями. Пётр был великий хозяин, царь мастеровой, всего лучше понимавший экономические интересы России и искавший источники государственного богатства.

Реформа, совершённая Петром Великим не имела своей прямой целью перестраивать ни политического, ни общественного, ни нравственного порядка, а ограничивалась стремлением вооружить русское государство и народ готовыми западноевропейскими средствами, умственными и материальными. Пётр заводил в России то, что он видел полезного на западе и чего не было в России.

У России не было регулярной армии—он сформировал её. Не было флота—он построил его. Не было удобного морского пути для внешней торговли—он армией и флотом отвоевал восточный берег Балтийского моря от Швеции. Была слаба промышленность—после него осталось более двух сот фабрик и заводов. Для всего этого необходимо было техническое знание—заведены были школы, училища и академия. И призывались западные европейцы, чтобы

рабо́тать и учи́ть рабо́те ру́сских в о́бласти вое́нной, эконо-
ми́ческой, фина́нсовой и администрати́вной те́хники.

При Петре́ о́бщество оде́лось в но́вые, европе́йские
пла́тья, заговори́ло други́м языко́м, получи́ло но́вые уч-
режде́ния, но по пре́жнему оста́лось све́рху до́низу закре-
пощённым. Вое́нная, боева́я жизнь ру́сского госуда́рства
не то́лько не прекрати́лась, но обостри́лась ещё бо́лее. Ведь
всё вре́мя ца́рствования Петра́, це́лых 20 лет подря́д,
кипе́ла грандио́зная борьба́ со Шве́цией. Э́та борьба́ на-
прягла́ до кра́йней сте́пени боевы́е и платёжные си́лы
наро́да. И Пётр не то́лько не осла́бил, но ещё бо́лее уве-
ли́чил тя́гости, нало́женные госуда́рством на о́бщество. Со
времён Петра́, для всех кла́ссов тя́гость госуда́рственных
пови́нностей была́ удво́ена: ка́ждый класс по пре́жнему
нёс свою́ специа́льную пови́нность, и сверх того́ на все
кла́ссы без разли́чия была́ поло́жена ещё всео́бщая пови́н-
ность, вое́нная слу́жба в регуля́рной а́рмии.

В свое́й реформа́торской рабо́те Пётр опира́лся гла́вным
о́бразом на дворя́нство. Но э́тот класс был ма́ло подгото́влен
проводи́ть како́е-ли́бо культу́рное влия́ние. В у́мственном
и нра́вственном разви́тии дворя́нство не стоя́ло вы́ше ос-
тально́й наро́дной ма́ссы. Ну́жно бы́ло распространи́ть
среди́ дворя́н зна́ния, повы́сить их культу́ру. Пётр хоте́л,
что́бы дворя́нство счита́ло госуда́рственную слу́жбу свои́м
почётным пра́вом и до́лгом. Поэ́тому, де́ятельность Петра́
вела́, с одно́й стороны́, к возвыше́нию дворя́нства. По-
ме́стья, зе́мли, кото́рыми по́льзовались дворя́не, перешли́
в их по́лную насле́дственную со́бственность. За выдаю́щую-
ся слу́жбу Пётр раздава́л ще́дрые пода́рки и аристокра-
ти́ческие ти́тулы кня́зя, гра́фа и баро́на.

Но вме́сте с тем, Пётр тре́бовал от дворя́нства напря-
жённой слу́жбы, тяжёлой, неви́данной ра́ньше в моско́в-
ской Руси́. С пятна́дцати лет дворяни́н до́лжен был идти́
на слу́жбу. Две тре́ти дворя́нства шли на слу́жбу в а́рмию
и флот, а одна́ треть поступа́ла на гражда́нскую слу́жбу.
До-петро́вское прави́тельство счита́лось с служи́лым че-
лове́ком лишь с того́ моме́нта, когда́ он станови́лся чле́ном
боево́й си́лы. Тепе́рь, при Петре́, прави́тельственный ука́з
сторожи́т молодо́го дворяни́на у са́мой колыбе́ли, втор-

га́ется в его́ уче́бную ко́мнату, укла́дывает в определённые
ра́мки не то́лько его́ служе́бный труд, но и все направле́ния
его́ у́мственной жи́зни. Уче́бная подгото́вка ста́ла обяза́-
тельной. Для обуче́ния ру́сские дворя́не ма́ссами посы-
ла́лись за грани́цу и должны́ бы́ли держа́ть стро́гие экза́мены
по возвраще́нию в Росси́ю.

Европеиза́ция, проведённая петро́вской рефо́рмой каса́-
лась, гла́вным о́бразом, дворя́нства. Но новизна́ де́ятель-
ности Петра́ состоя́ла не то́лько в за́падничестве, но и в
секуляриза́ции, в раско́ле ме́жду прави́тельством и церковью. И́менно в э́том рефо́рма Петра́ была́ не то́лько
поворо́том, но и переворо́том. Ви́дя недружелю́бное отно-
ше́ние к свои́м преобразова́ниям со стороны́ духове́нства,
Пётр отмени́л патриа́ршество и замени́л его́ Сино́дом,
т. е. госуда́рственным о́рганом управле́ния це́рковью. Пётр
тре́бовал от це́ркви по́лного повинове́ния и подчине́ния,
отрица́я незави́симость церко́вных прав. Духове́нство пре-
враща́ется в своеобра́зный служи́лый класс, стано́вится
запу́ганным сосло́вием. Отча́сти оно́ опуска́ется и́ли оттес-
ня́ется в социа́льные низы́. А на верха́х церко́вной иера́рхии
надо́лго устана́вливается двусмы́сленное молча́ние.

Несмотря́ на свою́ реформа́торскую рабо́ту, Пётр не
успе́л сбро́сить с себя́ до́чиста древнеру́сского челове́ка с
его́ нра́вами и поня́тиями, да́же тогда́, когда́ воева́л с ни́ми.
У за́пада Пётр взял иде́и для устро́йства вое́нных сил, го-
суда́рственного и наро́дного хозя́йства, прави́тельственных
и церко́вных учрежде́ний. Но из ста́рой Руси́ Пётр сохрани́л
иде́ю о свое́й неограни́ченной вла́сти и об обяза́тельной
слу́жбе ка́ждого лица́ и кла́сса госуда́рству.

Э́та после́дняя иде́я сказа́лась осо́бенно ре́зко в отно-
ше́нии Петра́ к ни́зшим кла́ссам населе́ния, кото́рые он
отяготи́л но́выми нало́гами и но́выми спо́собами принужд-
де́ния. Ряды́ регуля́рной а́рмии Петра́ пополня́лись· рек-
ру́тами, кото́рых крестья́нство и купе́чество бы́ли обя́заны
доставля́ть прави́тельству в ука́занном коли́честве. Сол-
да́тская слу́жба была́ пожи́зненной. Провожа́я рекру́та,
роди́тели, жёны и де́ти пла́кали как по поко́йнику. Соз-
да́лся да́же осо́бый вид наро́дного э́поса, ''рекру́тские
пла́чи.''

Дере́вня не то́лько поставля́ла солда́т, но и рабо́чию си́лу для промы́шленности. Пётр со́здал но́вую фо́рму нево́льного, промы́шленного труда́. Крестья́не, ра́нее прикреплённые к земле́, перевози́лись на фа́брику и́ли заво́д и не име́ли пра́ва покида́ть э́ти предприя́тия. Фа́брика и заво́д при Петре́ не́ были вполне́ ча́стными предприя́тиями, а получи́ли хара́ктер госуда́рственных опера́ций, кото́рые прави́тельство вело́ че́рез своего́ обяза́тельного аге́нта— купца́ и́ли фабрика́нта.

Пра́вя госуда́рством из похо́дной киби́тки и с почто́вой ста́нции, Пётр ду́мал то́лько о дела́х, а не о лю́дях. Ему́ приходи́лось рабо́тать спе́шно и принуди́тельно, среди́ упо́рной и опа́сной вне́шней войны́ со Шве́цией за Балти́йское побере́жье, и при э́том боро́ться с наро́дной апа́тией и отста́лостью, разви́вшихся в допетро́вской, моско́вской Руси́.

Поэ́тому рефо́рма, скро́мная и ограни́ченная по своему́ первонача́льному пла́ну, постепе́нно преврати́лась в упо́рную вну́треннюю борьбу́, взволнова́вшую все кла́ссы о́бщества. Рефо́рма Петра́ была́ револю́цией не по свои́м це́лям и результа́там, а то́лько по свои́м приёмам и по впечатле́нию, како́е произвела́ на умы́ и не́рвы совреме́нников.

В своём преобразова́тельном разбе́ге, Пётр не уме́л щади́ть людски́е си́лы, а лю́ди в своём стоя́чем отпо́ре не хоте́ли цени́ть его́ уси́лий. Пётр шёл про́тив ве́тра и со́бственным ускоренным движе́нием уси́ливал встре́чное сопротивле́ние.

Рефо́рма Петра́ была́ борьбо́й деспоти́зма с наро́дом, с его́ отста́лостью. Он хоте́л, что́бы раб, остава́ясь рабо́м, де́йствовал созна́тельно и свобо́дно. Совме́стное де́йствие деспоти́зма и свобо́ды, просвеще́ния и ра́бства, э́то полити́ческая и культу́рная квадрату́ра кру́га, зага́дка, кото́рая разреша́ется в Росси́и со вре́мени Петра́ Вели́кого и всё ещё не разрешена́.

13

сноше́ние contact
рука́в branch of river (also: sleeve)
меша́ться to mingle
боло́то swamp
возни́кнуть to arise, spring up
perf. of: **возника́ть**
зы́бкий unstable
напереко́р in defiance of
кость (f.) bone
образе́ц model
пло́тник carpenter
уско́рить to hasten
perf. of: **ускоря́ть**

о́блик features, contour
воздвига́ть to erect
воздви́гнуть (perf.)
тюрьма́ prison
неве́жество ignorance, crudeness
изя́щный refined
дворе́ц palace (noun)
дворцо́вый palace (adj.)
властели́н master, lord
взве́шивать to weigh
взве́сить (perf.)
разби́вка layout

ПЕТЕРБУ́РГ В ВОСЕМНА́ДЦАТОМ ВЕ́КЕ

Пётр Вели́кий не люби́л Москвы́. Там встреча́л он наибо́лее упо́рное сопротивле́ние свои́м рефо́рмам. Ста́рая столи́ца, объедини́тельница ру́сской земли́, была́ опо́рой и си́мволом старины́.

Петру́ нужна́ была́ но́вая столи́ца на берегу́ мо́ря, окно́, че́рез кото́рое Росси́я могла́ бы установи́ть сноше́ния с Евро́пой. Отвоева́в себе́ от Шве́ции до́ступ к Балти́йскому мо́рю, Пётр неме́дленно, в 1703 году́, приступи́л к постро́йке го́рода Петербу́рга на том ме́сте, где река́ Нева́ впада́ет в Фи́нский зали́в, т. е. и́менно там, где в эпо́ху ки́евского госуда́рства начина́лся во́дный путь из Скандина́вии в

Византию, приведший Русь к столь обширным сношениям с чужими странами.

Устье Невы распадается на пять главных рукавов, которые образуют, вместе с рядом более мелких протоков и речек, множество плоских и низменных островов. В природе здесь нет ничего пышного, гордого, всё снизилось и словно ждёт смиренно, что воды зальют этот печальный край. Тощая трава мешается с сухим мхом и болотными растениями. Здесь царствует колючая сосна, печальная ель и чахлая берёза, эти деревья севера.

Туманы и болота, из которых возник Петербург, свидетельствуют о титанической работе, которую нужно было произвести, чтобы создать здесь, на зыбкой, пустынной почве, этот город. Здесь всё говорит о великой борьбе с природой, здесь всё наперекор стихиям. Вряд ли найдётся другой город в мире, который потребовал бы больше жертв для своего рождения. Петербург—город на костях человеческих. Водная стихия скована героическими усилиями его строителей. Периодически повторяющиеся наводнения —некоторые из них катастрофических размеров, погубившие тысячи людей—проходят через всю историю города.

Низменность берегов и болотистая почва требовали укрепления грунта. Пётр, съездив в Европу, понял, что местность и климат новой столицы ближе всего подходят к голландским—те же низкие места, так же много болот и воды. Страстный любитель воды, он хотел, чтобы это был город каналов и мостов, такой как Амстердам, который он видел, или как Венеция, которую ему не удалось посетить, но о которой он столько слышал.

В 1712 году Пётр объявил только что начинающий обстраиваться Петербург новой столицей. Московская Русь перестала существовать. Её сменила Всероссийская империя—название, которое было официально введено в 1721 году, когда Пётр принял титул Императора Всероссийского.

Не только личные вкусы Петра, но и общие идеи и приёмы его реформ отразились как в зеркале в строении Петербурга. Прежде всего появились военные здания— Петропавловская крепость на центральном острове и Адмиралтейство, т. е. верфь для постройки кораблей, на ле́вом берегу́ Невы́. Для себя́ Пётр, не люби́вший ро́скоши, постро́ил ма́ленький, ни́зкий, одноэта́жный до́мик напро́тив от Петропа́вловской кре́пости.

Го́род не то́лько стро́ился, но и заселя́лся принужде́нием. Жи́тели переезжа́ли сюда́ по прика́зу царя́. Дворя́не бы́ли обя́заны стро́ить себе́ дома́ по предпи́санным царём разме́рам. Хотя́ Пётр ли́чно не люби́л ро́скоши, он поощря́л её в свои́х помо́щниках, так как Петербу́рг до́лжен был стать образцо́м но́вой, европе́йской жи́зни для всей Росси́и. Мно́гие из домо́в, постро́енных сотру́дниками царя́, бы́ли и грандио́знее и краси́вее, чем все петро́вские дворцы́.

Пе́рвые петербу́ргские постро́йки бы́ли исключи́тельно деревя́нные. Лес име́лся под руко́й, а со́бранные сюда́ со всей Росси́и пло́тники хорошо́ уме́ли стро́ить деревя́нные зда́ния. Что́бы э́ти деревя́нные постро́йки не сли́шком напомина́ли Москву́, они́ распи́сывались под ка́мень и́ли кирпи́ч. Но постепе́нно ста́ли заменя́ть де́рево ка́мнем. Для того́, что́бы ускори́ть в Петербу́рге постро́йку ка́менных домо́в, Пётр изда́л ука́з в 1714 году́ о запреще́нии ка́менных постро́ек во всём госуда́рстве и веле́л на ка́ждом су́дне и во́зе, приходя́щем в Петербу́рг привози́ть определённое коли́чество камне́й.

С 1711 го́да лихора́дочная стро́йка идёт не то́лько в Петербу́рге, но понемно́гу начина́ет переки́дываться и на его́ окре́стности. Не то́лько царь, но и его́ приближённые стро́ят себе́ за́городные дворцы́.

Архитекту́рный о́блик Петербу́рга ко дню сме́рти его́ основа́теля был со́здан исключи́тельно иностра́нными зо́дчими. В Петербу́рг прие́хали сра́зу и италья́нцы и не́мцы и францу́зы и голла́ндцы. Живя́ и рабо́тая здесь одновре́менно, ка́ждый вноси́л в постро́йки свои́ ра́совые и индивидуа́льные осо́бенности. Благодаря́ э́тому Петербу́рг получи́л свою́ со́бственную физионо́мию. Его́ нельзя́ назва́ть ни италья́нским, ни неме́цким, ни голла́ндским, ни францу́зским. Стиль его́ то́лько ''петербу́ргский.''

Са́мая замеча́тельная черта́ в о́блике го́рода э́то то, что здесь воздвига́лись не отде́льные зда́ния, а стро́ились це́лые архитекту́рные пейза́жи далёких перспекти́в и широ́ких простра́нств. Го́род создава́лся как антите́за окружа́ющей приро́де, как вы́зов ей. Он весь из споко́йных, прямы́х ли́ний и твёрдого ка́мня, че́ткий, стро́гий, стро́йный и ца́рственный, с золоты́ми шпи́лями Адмиралте́йства и колоко́льни собо́ра Петропа́вловской кре́пости, кото́рые споко́йно возно́сятся к бледнозелёным небеса́м.

К концу́ ца́рствования Петра́ Вели́кого Петропа́вловская кре́пость возвыша́лась как си́мвол самодержа́вия. Собо́р кре́пости предназнача́лся для погребе́ния ру́сских царе́й, а вокру́г вы́росла са́мая больша́я госуда́рственная тюрьма́. Пе́рвым полити́ческим престу́пником, кото́рый сюда́ попа́л, был еди́нственный сын Петра́ Вели́кого, Алексе́й. Царе́вич относи́лся враждéбно к рефо́рмам отца́ и бежа́л за грани́цу, что́бы укры́ться от гне́ва гро́зного царя́. Но его́ верну́ли и Пётр, подозрева́я за́говор и изме́ну, пре́дал сы́на суду́. Сла́бый здоро́вьем царе́вич Алексе́й не вы́держал заключе́ния и пы́ток и у́мер в 1718 году́.

Пётр Вели́кий сконча́лся в 1725 году́ не назна́чив прее́мника. В тече́ние сле́дующих 37 лет, верхо́вная власть переходи́ла путём дворцо́вых переворо́тов от одного́ чле́на ца́рской семьи́ к друго́му. Де́сять лет на престо́ле продержа́лась племя́нница Петра́ А́нна Ива́новна Курля́ндская (1730–1740), два́дцать лет продолжа́лось ца́рствование до́чери Петра́ Елизаве́ты (1741–1761), а в 1762 году́ на престо́л вступи́ла бы́вшая неме́цкая принце́сса и жена́ вну́ка Петра́, Екатери́на II (1762–1796).

Влия́ние э́тих трёх же́нщин си́льно отрази́лось на разви́тии Петербу́рга. А́нна Ива́новна была́ же́нщина ро́слая и ту́чная, с лицо́м бо́лее мужски́м чем же́нским, гру́бая и жесто́кая. Несмотря́ на своё неве́жество, она́ явля́ется созда́тельницей ца́рского двора́ и придво́рной жи́зни в Петербу́рге, для кото́рых в своё вре́мя у Петра́ Вели́кого не́ было ни вре́мени ни накло́нности. Императри́ца А́нна устра́ивает роско́шные приёмы, одева́ется в бога́тые наря́ды и тре́бует тако́го же пра́здного и све́тского о́браза жи́зни от свои́х придво́рных. Всё э́то ещё но́во и гру́бо, сквозь вне́шний блеск и лоск ещё я́рко просве́чивают неве́жество и культу́рная отста́лость. Но при весёлой, жизнера́достной, лени́вой и беспоря́дочной Елизаве́те придво́рная жизнь становится изящнее и великолепнее. Молва о сказочно блестящих придворных балах и увеселениях в Петербурге начинает расходиться по европейским столицам.

Центром придворной жизни становится Летний дворец, построенный знаменитым архитектором Растрелли младшим. При Петре Великом, в Петербург попали лишь обломки итальянского барокко, значительно сильнее отразились формы немецкого, но не было художника великана, который мог бы властной рукой наложить свою личную печать на город. Таким властелином форм был Растрелли.

Барокко—живописная архитектура, создающая впечатление движения, непрерывного бега линий. Любимый приём барокко—центральность композиции, единство пространства, архитектура больших масс. Петербург давал богатый материал для таких приёмов. Самый блестящий период творчества Растрелли относится к сороковым и пятидесятым годам 18 века, когда не только в столице, но и в пригородах вырастают дворцы этого великого зодчего. Последней постройкой Растрелли в Петербурге был Зимний дворец, оконченный в 1762 году. Каждая отдельная часть этого огромного здания обдумана и взвешана так, что длиннейший главный фасад получил оживлённую, но всё же строгую разбивку.

При величественной и талантливой Екатерине II, Петербург достиг полного расцвета. Иностранцы стали называть его "городом дворцов." Любя все художества, Екатерина питала особенную страсть к архитектуре. Раскопки Помпеи в середине 18 века произвели полный переворот в европейском искусстве и открыли эру нового классицизма— крушение барокко и возрождение классицизма.

Екатерина, которая любила благородную простоту, всецело сочувствовала этому перевороту и пригласила ряд талантливых европейских зодчих новой школы в Петербург. Главными среди них были шотландец Чарлс Камерон, долго живший в Риме и влюблённый в классический мир, и итальянец Джакомо Кваренги. Кваренги стал для Петербурга тем, что раньше был Растрелли. Со времён Екатерины Петербург хранит на себе печать строгих форм классической, римской эпохи.

14

придавля́ть to crush
охвати́ть to encompass
  perf. of: **охва́тывать**
стя́гивать to draw together
  стяну́ть (perf.)
мятёжный mutinous
штык bayonet
раб slave
чертёжик
  diminutive of: **чертёж**
  sketch, draft
знать (f.) gentry
украше́ние decoration
увлече́ние enthusiasm, passion

просвети́тельный enlightening
недоста́ток shortcoming
размышля́ть to meditate, ponder
ску́дный scanty, sparse
избавля́ть to rid of
  изба́вить (perf.)
бичева́ть to scourge
нача́ла (pl.) principles, elements
произво́л free will, discretion
брак marriage
про́пасть (f.) precipice

НО́ВЫЙ КУЛЬТУ́РНЫЙ ЦЕНТР—ДВОРЯ́НСКАЯ УСА́ДЬБА

С оконча́нием Се́верной войны́ со Шве́цией в 1721 году́ для Росси́и ко́нчилась многовеко́вая борьба́ за свою́ самостоя́тельность. Росси́я могла́ тепе́рь обрати́ться к разви́тию свои́х духо́вных и материа́льных сил, так надо́лго прида́вленных вое́нными бу́рями. Для э́того пре́жде всего́ ну́жно бы́ло освободи́ть обще́ственные кла́ссы от бре́мени тех госуда́рственных обя́занностей, кото́рое на них лежа́ло.

Освобожде́ние ру́сского о́бщества начало́сь све́рху и к концу́ 18 ве́ка охвати́ло лишь ве́рхний обще́ственный класс—дворя́нство. По двум причи́нам дворя́нство бы́ло тепе́рь наибóлее сильным клáссом óбщества и моглó рáньше всех сбрóсить с себя госудáрственные обязанности.

Во пéрвых, в рукáх дворянства сосредотáчивалась вáжная материáльная сила: владéние землёй. Ещё со врéмени москóвского госудáрства класс дворян получил исключительное прáво на землевладéние. Дворянство 18 вéка унаслéдовало это прáво. По услóвиям тогдáшнего нарóдного хозяйства Россúи, владéние землёй стягивало в рукáх дворянства все нúти нарóдного трудá. В то врéмя Россúя ещё тóлько готóвилась вступить на путь промышленного развития. Земледéльческий труд составлял истинную оснóву всегó нарóдного хозяйства, а распоряжéние землёй и крепостнúми принадлежáло дворянству.

Во вторúх, в рукáх дворянства оказáлось, пóсле смéрти Петрá Велúкого, вáжное политúческое орýдие. Дворцóвые переворóты, повторяющиеся до сáмого начáла 19 вéка, происходúли с пóмощью гвардéйских полкóв, состоявших исключúтельно из дворян. Кáждый член цáрской семú, пóднятый на престóл мятéжными гвардéйскими штыкáми, спешúл вознаградúть дворянский класс, оказáвший емý поддéржку в лицé гвáрдии, нóвыми правáми, выгодами и привилéгиями.

При Áнне Ивáновне пожúзненная обязáтельная слýжба дворян былá огранúчена на 25 лет, а в 1762 годý совсéм отменéна. При Елизавéте, дворянство получúло прáво продавáть крепостнúх отдéльно от землú, т. е. как рабóв. Крóме тогó, онó приобрелó судéбно-полицéйскую власть над своúми крестьянами. При Екатерúне II, дворянство было обращенó в привилегирóванный класс с ширóкими правáми самоуправлéния.

Освобождáясь от слýжбы и приобретáя всё нóвые правá, дворянство мáссами хлынуло к себé в дерéвню, чтóбы наслаждáться своéй свобóдой пóсле вековóй, тяжёлой слýжбы. Здесь, в дворянских усáдьбах и имéниях, с середúны 18 вéка исполнилось желáние Петрá Велúкого, чтóбы Петербýрг стал образцóм для всéй Россúи. Развúтию городóв препятствовало крепостнóе прáво. Но распространéнию зáпадноевропéйской культýры в дерéвне способствовало прáздное и состоятельное дворянство.

Все стараются обзавестись "Растрелливским" домом. Но получить его оказывалось не легко, так как знаменитый архитектор был завален дворцовыми делами в Петербурге. Многие были счастливы, если им удавалось упросить Растрелли сделать хоть чертёжик для дома и церкви где нибудь в дальнем имении. То было первое имя зодчего, которое узнала вся Россия, и искусство его было первое, которому суждено было перешагнуть за пределы придворной знати и войти в жизнь широких масс провинциального дворянства.

Таким же успехом пользовались, во второй половине 18 века, любимые архитекторы Екатерины II. Вся знать хотела себе строить дома в дальних усадьбах по проектам Джакомо Кваренги. Огромное влияние на русское зодчество второй половины 18 века оказал также Таврический дворец, построенный архитектором Иваном Егоровичем Старовым по поручению Екатерины II для её фаворита Потёмкина. Идеал пышности и богатства, этот "пантеон" служил предметом нескончаемых подражаний. Каждый состоятельный дворянин старался завести у себя хоть некоторое подобие "пантеона"—пусть даже небольшой деревянный дом, но непременно с флигелями и во что бы то ни стало с колоннами и с куполом. В короткое время вся деревенская Россия покрылась маленькими Таврическими дворцами.

При Елизавете, главной заботой дворянства было украшение жизни плодами чужой культуры. Не только архитектура домов, но и обстановка и одежда были западноевропейскими по стилю. При Екатерине II, новой заботой общества стало украшение ума, усвоение чужих идей. Началось увлечение французской просветительной литературой. Французских философов читали, перечитывали, переводили и собирали, составляя целые библиотеки. В особенности увлекались Вольтером, благодаря его способности говорить обо всём и легко и остроумно. Но о практических результатах просвещения думали мало.

Французская просветительная литература была восстанием против феодального порядка и католического миросознания. Как практическое движение она имела чисто

местный, французский или западноевропейский, антифео-
дальный интерес. В России не было того, против чего на-
правлены были на Западе эти идеи. Все недостатки русской
жизни тогдашнего времени происходили именно из того,
что ничего не было устарелого, привычного, а всё ещё соз-
давалось на ходу. Русский образованный человек жил в
русской действительности, а ум его был наполнен содержанием совсем другого происхождения, взятым из совсем
другого мира.

В голове образованного человека екатерининской эпохи
необыкновенная масса общих идей, но он совсем не раз-
мышляет и не понимает того, что его окружает.

Этот недостаток размышления и понимания действительности даже тяготел над литературой. Никогда русская
литература не говорила о таких возвышенных и отвлечённых предметах и никогда не отличалась более скудным
содержанием.

Чужие слова и идеи избавляли русское общество от необходимости размышлять, как даровой крепостной труд
избавлял его от необходимости работать. Литература раз-
делилась на два течения: идиллию и сатиру. Она или
восхищалась современными идеями или бичевала уродли-
вые проявления современных порядков. Сатира обличала,
идиллия восторгалась, обе декламировали, ни та ни
другая не размышляла.

Самым даровитым писателем екатерининского времени
надо считать Дениса Ивановича Фонвизина, но и он понёс
на себе всю тяжесть неестественных отношений русского
человека к действительности. Его лучшие комедии "Бри-
гадир" и "Недоросль"—отвлечённые трактаты о добро-
детели и пороках.

Идеи просветительной философии о началах разума и
свободы не оказывали никакого действия на поступки
людей. Между этими идеями и русской действительностью
было безмерное расстояние. После того, как с дворян сни-
мается обязательная служба и они превращаются в приви-
легированную корпорацию, вставал логический вывод,
что и с крестьян нужно снять обязательный крепостной
труд. Но этого второго шага 18 век не сделал. Закон не

ставил власти дворян над крепостным никаких пределов
и границ. Помещик по своему произволу определял количество крестьянского труда. Помещичья власть вторгалась
во все уголки крестьянской жизни. Прежде всего помещик
старался обеспечить наиболее выгодное размножение крепостной массы. Для этой цели пускалась в ход самая гру-
бая регламентация крестьянских браков. Но семья крепостного могла распасться столь же неожиданно и быстро,
как и возникала. Помещик мог продать крестьянина на
сторону, вырвав его из родной семьи. Торговля крестьянами принимала в течение 18 века всё большие размеры.
Состояние, капитал помещика, считались не деньгами, а
"душами," т. е. числом принадлежащих ему крепостных.

В своей деревне дворянин был полновластным хозяином,
самодержцем в небольшом царстве. Он окружал себя много-
численным штатом дворни, которая производила всё нуж-
ное для хозяйства и даже работала для увеселения своего
хозяина. Многие дворяне устраивали у себя крепостной
театр, пересаживая на местную почву всё то, с чем знако-
мились в Петербурге. Крепостные артисты обучались всем
видам сценического искусства—драме, опере, балету, пению
и инструментальной музыке.

К концу 18 века, единство русской культуры, которое
было уже поколеблено в 17 веке и ещё сильнее при Петре
Великом, окончательно разбивается. Общественный строй
России отличается большой простотой, но вместе с тем и
польным, внутренним разобщением. Общество распадается на две главных части, на свободных дворян и пора-
бощённых крестьян.

Их разделяет глубокая пропасть. Крестьянские массы
продолжают хранить связь с церковным сознанием, с ре-
лигиозными началами. Монастырь является для них всё
ещё главным, если не единственным культурным центром.
А среди дворян возникает светская культура, основанная
на западноевропейских идеях вольнодумства. У русского
дворянина не стало почвы. Он говорит по французски,
читает Вольтера, Монтескье, Дидро, Руссо, одевается по
последней парижской моде, а его детей обучает францу́з-
ский гувернёр. Но французская почва, с которой он сры-

вал культурные цветки, была ему чужда, а русская почва, на которой он стоял, совсем не давала таких цветков. Ни идеи, ни практические интересы не привязывали его к родной почве. Он был русским, которому страстно хотелось стать французом. Вечно стараясь стать своим среди чужих, он только становился чужим среди своих.

Это раздвоение русского общества наложило глубокую тень на весь последующий, 19 век.

15

мысль (f.) thought	**кольцо́** ring
иску́сство art	**купе́чество** merchant class
разры́в break, rift	**обременя́ть** to burden
десятиле́тие decade	**обремени́ть** (perf.)
простота́ simplicity	**уча́сток** share, portion
поколе́ние generation	**включа́ть** to include, inclose
сра́внивать to compare	**включи́ть** (perf.)
сравни́ть (perf.)	**разложе́ние** disintegration
оби́лие abundance	**обма́н** deceit
чино́вничество officialdom	**босо́й** barefoot
чино́вник civil servant	**бося́к** tramp, pauper
прави́тельство government	

ОБЗО́Р ДЕВЯТНА́ДЦАТОГО ВЕ́КА

19 век—одна́ из са́мых замеча́тельных эпо́х в ру́сской исто́рии, мо́жет быть да́же са́мая замеча́тельная. Это век мы́сли, сло́ва, тво́рчества, и иску́сства, золото́й век литерату́ры, му́зыки и жи́вописи. Вме́сте с тем это та́кже век нараста́ющего вну́треннего разры́ва и раско́ла в о́бществе. Ка́ждое десятиле́тие прохо́дит под зна́ком но́вого значи́тельного собы́тия и́ли но́вых иде́й, меня́ющих соста́в о́бщества, его́ о́браз жи́зни, настрое́ние, интере́сы, мне́ния и мы́сли.

Простота́ обще́ственного стро́я конца́ 18 ве́ка, разде́л о́бщества на две гла́вных ча́сти, на дворя́н и крестья́н, исчеза́ет. Бы́стро и бу́рно выраста́ет ряд но́вых социа́льных групп и кла́ссов. Всех их занима́ют унасле́дованные от 18 ве́ка и неразрешённые вопро́сы: Как освободить крестьян, как снять с них обязательный крепостной труд, как уничтожить пропасть, разделяющую высшие классы от низших, как восстановить единство общества и культуры? Вопрос "Что делать?" повторяется всеми и не раз в течение века появляется в заглавии литературного произведения.

После смерти Екатерины II в 1796 году на престол вступил её сын Павел I, человек изломанный, раздражённый и озлобленный враждой, которую мать всю жизнь питала к нему. Вся деятельность Павла была направлена к тому, чтобы отменить всё, что было сделано и задумано Екатериной. При ней расцвет и возвышение дворянства достигли небывалых раньше размеров. Это то развитие Павел и старался остановить и изменить. Павел был первым настроенным против дворян царём. Своё отношение к этому классу он метко и ярко выразил словами: "В России велик только тот, с кем я говорю, и только пока я с ним говорю."

Павел уничтожил установленное Екатериной самоуправление дворянства и многие другие аристократические привилегии. Чтобы отстранить возможность дворцовых переворотов, столь способствовавших в течение 18 века к возвышению дворянства, Павел установил законом 1797 года порядок наследования престола—от отца к старшему сыну. Но эта предосторожность не спасла царя от дворянского заговора и, в 1801 году, от убийства.

Несмотря на кратковременность царствования Павла I, начавшийся при нём разлад между дворянством и правительством не прекратился при его наследнике, Александре I, а наоборот усилился и продолжал расти. Причиной этому послужили наполеоновские войны, решающим этапом которых явилось нашествие Наполеона в Россию в 1812 году, окончившееся полным разгромом французской армии.

Победа над Наполеоном увлекла русское правительство и дворянство в противоположные стороны. Александр I всецело занялся переустройством Европы, "Священным союзом," и отложил вопрос о внутреннем преобразова́нии Росси́и, столь интересова́вшем его́ до 1812 го́да. А на передовы́х люде́й ру́сского двора́нства Оте́чественная война́ 1812 го́да име́ла обра́тное влия́ние. Она́ породи́ла в них жела́ние преобразова́ть ру́сскую жизнь, преодоле́ть ту про́пасть, кото́рая отделя́ла их от наро́да.

На рубеже́ 18 и 19 столе́тий ру́сские двора́не переста́ли стреми́ться в вое́нную слу́жбу, снача́ла по́льзуясь привиле́гиями, ока́занными им Екатери́ной II, а пото́м спаса́ясь от стро́гостей и вражды́ Па́вла I. Наполео́новские во́йны сно́ва привлекли́ двора́н в ряды́ а́рмии. Заграни́чные похо́ды и пребыва́ние ру́сских войск в европе́йских столи́цах познако́мили двора́н-офице́ров с за́падноевропе́йской жи́знью и разви́ли в э́тих молоды́х лю́дях настрое́ние, ре́зко отлича́ющееся от о́браза мышле́ния их отцо́в, поколе́ния време́н Екатери́ны II.

В двора́нах конца́ 18 ве́ка просвети́тельная францу́зская литерату́ра воспита́ла холо́дный рационали́зм и суху́ю мысль, отчуждённую от действи́тельности и презира́ющую ру́сскую жизнь. Наоборо́т, двора́не времён Алекса́ндра Пе́рвого жи́во интересова́лись действи́тельностью не то́лько европе́йской, но и ру́сской. Всё, что они́ ви́дели заграни́цей, они́ сра́внивали с Росси́ей. Они́ переста́ли увлека́ться францу́зской культу́рой и закрыва́ть глаза́ пе́ред ру́сской действи́тельностью. Отцы́ бы́ли ру́сские, кото́рым стра́стно хоте́лось стать францу́зами, сыновья́ бы́ли по воспита́нию францу́зы, кото́рым стра́стно хоте́лось стать ру́сскими. В них, в отли́чие от отцо́в, удиви́тельное оби́лие чу́вства, переве́с чу́вства над мы́слью, оби́лие доброжела́тельных поры́вов, стремле́ние к о́бщему добру́, в осо́бенности к добру́ ру́сского наро́да, гото́вность же́ртвовать ли́чными интере́сами, сча́стьем и да́же жи́знью.

Из э́того поколе́ния, из э́той офице́рской, двора́нской среды́, сложи́лось та́йное о́бщество, воше́дшее в исто́рию под назва́нием Декабри́стов. Чле́ны э́того о́бщества хоте́ли сде́лать в Росси́и полити́ческий переворо́т, отмени́ть самодержа́вие, замени́в его́ конституцио́нным поря́дком, и освободи́ть крестья́н от крепостно́го пра́ва. Иде́и Декабри́стов не́ были я́сно офо́рмлены, бы́ло мно́го разногла́сий, и за́говор был пло́хо подгото́влен. Поэ́тому они́ изве́стны под названием того месяца, в котором они попытались устроить переворот—в декабре 1825 года—а не под названием идей, которым они хотели служить.

Восстание Декабристов кончилось полной неудачей. Пятерых из них казнили и более ста были сосланы в Сибирь. Но всё же это движение имело громадное значение. Во первых, Декабристы являются основателями новой общественной группы в России. Они отцы интеллигенции. Они были первыми русскими, которые действовали в России во имя идей, а не во имя лица. Ни один из дворцовых переворотов 18 века не имел целью нового государственного порядка.

Во вторых, восстанием Декабристов кончается политическая роль русского дворянства. Оно перестаёт быть правящим классом, всё более теряет своё правительственное значение. Руководство государственными делами переходит к специальным органам правительства— к чиновничеству. Чиновничество пополняется, в особенности в высших своих слоях, из дворянства. Но это уже не группа самостоятельных деятелей, а послушное орудие правительства.

Развитие чиновничества ярко отразилось на облике Петербурга первой половины 19 века. Это уже не город дворцов, а город по преимуществу административный, бюрократический и официальный. Чиновник становится главным его гражданином.

Страстью строительства, которая отличала Петра Великого и Екатерину II, горел и Александр I. Ему хотелось сделать Петербург красивее всех посещённых им столиц Европы, придать Петербургу ещё более единообразный и строгий вид. Строительство привлечённых Александром I великих зодчих сосредотачивается на правительственных зданиях, а не на частных дворцах. Классицизм продолжает расцветать, но идеал уже не Рим, как это было в 18 веке, а древне-греческие руины Пестумских храмов, с их дорическими коллонадами. Перестраиваются Адмиралтейство, Биржа, Большой Театр, Главный Штаб, строятся Александринский Театр и соединённые колоссальной аркой здания Сената и

Сино́да. Всё э́то ды́шит простото́й, суро́вым му́жеством и си́лой мо́щных форм до́рики.

В то вре́мя, как Петербу́рг станови́лся го́родом чино́вничества, у новоро́жденной ру́сской интеллиге́нции то́же создава́лся свой центр—Москва́. В Петербу́рг е́здили служи́ть, в Москву́ е́здили учи́ться. Тут находи́лся лу́чший и старе́йший ру́сский университе́т, привлека́ющий молодёжь изо все́х концо́в Росси́и. В Москве́ 19 ве́ка почти́ не́ бы́ло заме́тно ничего́ официа́льного. ''Петербу́рг стро́ился рубля́ми, а Москва́ века́ми,'' говори́т ста́рая ру́сская посло́вица. Москва́ росла́ вокру́г Кремля́ во все сто́роны ко́льцами, окружёнными сте́нами, расположе́ние кото́рых напомина́ло как бы разре́з ствола́ де́рева, по кото́рому мо́жно определи́ть его́ во́зраст. Распределе́ние коле́ц сохрани́лось да́же тогда́, когда́ сте́ны ста́ли заменя́ть бульва́рами. Свои́м смеше́нием зе́лени—па́рков, садо́в и огоро́дов—с дома́ми, Москва́ напомина́ла большу́ю дере́вню. У́лицы кри́вы и ко́сы, нет гла́вной у́лицы, кото́рую мо́жно бы́ло бы сравни́ть с Не́вским проспе́ктом в Петербу́рге.

О́блик Петербу́рга как чино́вничий го́род вполне́ сложи́лся в пе́рвой полови́не 19 ве́ка. В э́то же вре́мя Москва́ находи́лась ещё в перехо́дном состоя́нии, то́лько постепе́нно теря́я свой ста́рый, дворя́нский о́блик. Ядро́ но́вого моско́вского населе́ния оконча́тельно сформирова́лось то́лько во второ́й полови́не 19 ве́ка. Оно́ состоя́ло не то́лько из интеллиге́нции, но и из купе́чества, и отрази́ло, таки́м о́бразом, переме́ны произоше́дшие в соста́ве ру́сского о́бщества в связи́ с двумя́ собы́тиями. Разви́тию интеллиге́нции спосо́бствовало восста́ние Декабри́стов в 1825 году́. Бы́стрый рост купе́чества и промы́шленности был вы́зван освобожде́нием крестья́н в 1861 году́.

Зако́н 1861 го́да яви́лся отве́том прави́тельства на важне́йший, занима́ющий все́х вопро́с: ''Что де́лать?'' Но основны́х пробле́м ру́сской действи́тельности э́тот зако́н не разреши́л. Он не́ дал крестья́нам свобо́ды, а наоборо́т обремени́л их но́выми долга́ми и обя́занностями. Земе́льные уча́стки, кото́рые прави́тельство покупа́ло у дворя́н для переда́чи освобождённым крестья́нам не переходи́ли в ру́ки ча́стных лиц, а остава́лись во владе́нии се́льской общи́ны, ми́ра.

В тече́ние 49 лет ка́ждый член общи́ны до́лжен был плати́ть так называ́емый "вы́куп" за обраба́тываемую им зе́млю. Общи́на отвеча́ла прави́тельству за упла́ту э́того до́лга. То́лько отплати́в э́тот долг крестья́нин мог стать ча́стным со́бственником свое́й земли́. Таки́м о́бразом, бы́вшая зави́симость крестья́нина от поме́щика заменя́лась но́вой зави́симостью от общи́ны. Общи́на преврати́лась в ме́стный о́рган госуда́рственной, фина́нсовой администра́ции. Она́ включа́лась в разви́тие де́нежного хозя́йства, несмотря́ на то, что по существу́ она́ принадлежа́ла к эпо́хе средневеко́вого натура́льного хозя́йства.

Э́то противоре́чие привело́ к разложе́нию дереве́нской общи́ны во второ́й полови́не 19 ве́ка. Наибо́лее энерги́чному меньшинству́ среди́ чле́нов ми́ра, так называ́емым "кулака́м," удава́лось—нере́дко путём обма́на и наси́лия над бо́лее сла́быми крестья́нами—освобожда́ться от тя́жких долго́в, пробива́ть себе́ доро́гу и поднима́ться в ряды́ купцо́в и промы́шленников. Но большинство́ крестья́нской ма́ссы опуска́лось всё ни́же, бедне́ло и сходи́ло в ряды́ "босяко́в" и́ли дереве́нского пролета́риата.

И кулаки́ и босяки́ спеши́ли из дере́вни в города́, в осо́бенности в Москву́, пе́рвые, что́бы развива́ть там свои́ предприя́тия, вторы́е в наде́жде найти́ за́работок и, по возмо́жности, поступи́ть в ряды́ бы́стро расту́щей фабри́чной рабо́чей си́лы.

Интеллиге́нция, чино́вничество, буржуа́зия, дереве́нский пролетариа́т и промы́шленные рабо́чие бы́ли те́ми но́выми социа́льными гру́ппами, кото́рые появи́лись в Росси́и в тече́ние 19 ве́ка. Из них, интеллиге́нция оказа́ла са́мое реша́ющее влия́ние на дальне́йшую судьбу́ Росси́и.

16

у́мственный intellectual
насле́дие inheritance, legacy
ве́ра faith
ра́зум reason, intelligence
мышле́ние thinking
вы́вод conclusion
стра́стный passionate
спаси́тель (m.) savior
сжига́ть to burn, destroy by
  fire
  сжечь (perf.)
поклоня́ться to worship,
  bow
  поклони́ться (perf.)

кра́йность (f.) extreme
справедли́вый just
плод fruit
досто́инство dignity
разночи́нец commoner
отрица́ние negation
презира́ть to despise
положи́тельный positive
ка́яться to repent, confess
вина́ guilt
искупле́ние expiation
искупля́ть to expiate
  искупи́ть (perf.)

РУ́ССКАЯ ИНТЕЛЛИГЕ́НЦИЯ

В соста́в интеллиге́нции любо́й страны́ вхо́дят все, кто принима́ет уча́стие в у́мственной жи́зни населе́ния. У́мственная де́ятельность, иска́ние иде́й, э́то основна́я черта́ интеллиге́нции.

В Росси́и появле́ние э́той обще́ственной гру́ппы бы́ло подгото́влено рефо́рмами Петра́ Вели́кого и распростране́нием образова́ния во второ́й полови́не 18 ве́ка. Но как осо́бый, отде́льный класс, она́ появи́лась то́лько в 19 ве́ке.

По́сле раско́льников, э́то была́ втора́я социа́льная гру́ппа, кото́рая развила́сь незави́симо от прави́тельства, вопреки́ прави́тельству. "Не челове́к для госуда́рства, а госуда́рство для человéка''[1]—вот однá из основны́х идéй ру́сской интеллигéнции 19 вéка.

Однáко, отстáивая свобóду мы́сли, идéйную независи́мость от прави́тельства, ру́сские интеллигéнты не смогли́ освободи́ться от векового́ наслéдия христиáнской рели́гии. Ру́сская культу́ра былá, до 18 вéка, преиму́щественно духóвной, церкóвной культу́рой. Вéра, а не рáзум, былá оснóвой э́той культу́ры. И дáже тепéрь, когдá появи́лась интеллигéнция, т. е. класс, котóрый стреми́лся разви́ть свой у́мственные спосóбности, свой рáзум, котóрый хотéл начáть свобóдную рабóту мы́сли, психолóгия правослáвия остáвила глубóкий след в мышлéнии э́того клáсса.

Вéра, религиóзность, оснóвана на безграни́чной прéданности однóй идéе и на безуслóвном отрицáнии всегó несоглáсного с э́той идéей. И́менно такóй, религиóзный по своему́ существу́ подхóд, руководи́л ру́сской интеллигéнцией в её у́мственной рабóте. Онá всегдá искáла идéю, котóрую онá моглá бы приня́ть целикóм, без оговóрок. Крити́ческий, скепти́ческий óбраз мышлéния, осторóжный осмóтр возмóжных оши́бок и́ли непрáвильных вы́водов, остáлся чужд ру́сской мы́сли. Характéрно, что слóво ''прáвда'' имéет, на ру́сском языкé, два разли́чных значéния. Прáвда не тóлько то, что соответсвует действи́тельности, но тáкже морáльный идеáл, поря́док жи́зни оснóванный на справедли́вости.

И́менно в э́том, вторóм смы́сле ру́сская интеллигéнция искáла прáвды. Ею руководи́ло чу́вство, а не рáзум; чу́вство глубóкого сострадáния к ру́сскому нарóду, стрáстное желáние стать спаси́телем э́того нарóда—и́ли дáже всегó человéчества—, создáть нóвую, справедли́вую жизнь. В э́той мечтé о лу́чшей жи́зни, в сравнéнии с котóрой бледнéет реáльность, интеллигéнция сохрани́ла черты́ религиóзности. Éсли окáзывалось, что идéи, на котóрых стрóилась её мечтá, не соотвéтствовали действи́тельности, то интеллигéнт от них откáзывался и искáл нóвых, как бы говоря́: ''Я сжёг всё, чему́ поклоня́лся—поклони́лся всему́, что сжигáл.'' Поэ́тому, разви́тие ру́сской

---

[1] М. Карпóвич, ''Тради́ции ру́сской обществ́енной мы́сли,'' стр. 18.

мы́сли в тече́ние 19 ве́ка шло не равноме́рно и после́довательно, а представля́ет собо́й ряд ре́зких перехо́дов от одно́й кра́йности к друго́й.

Интеллиге́нция жила́ в разры́ве с настоя́щим, не то́лько потому́ что взаи́мное чу́вство вражде́бности отстраня́ло её от прави́тельства, но и потому́, что це́лая про́пасть отделя́ла её от наро́дных масс и от разви́тия наро́дной жи́зни. От гру́сти земны́х страда́ний она́ пыта́лась уйти́ в идеа́льную действи́тельность. Вся́кая хозя́йственная де́ятельность, все стремле́ния к разви́тию производи́тельных сил страны́, рассма́тривались интеллиге́нцией как по́шлое, ни́зкое стремле́ние к ли́чной нажи́ве. Интеллиге́нция не люби́ла бога́тства, а то́лько справедли́вое распределе́ние бога́тства. Её вражде́бность к купе́честву была́ столь же сильна́ как и к прави́тельству.

Ру́сская интеллиге́нция жила́ исключи́тельно иде́ями и для иде́й. Во и́мя свои́х иде́й она́ была́ гото́ва на тюрьму́, ка́торгу, пы́тки и смерть. Она́ не была́ социа́льным кла́ссом. В её соста́в вошли́ представи́тели ра́зных слоёв о́бщества.

По нача́лу, интеллиге́нция была́ почти́ исключи́тельно дворя́нской. Пе́рвые иде́йные тече́ния э́той гру́ппы офо́рмились в 40 года́х 19 столе́тия. Э́то бы́ло за́падничество и славянофи́льство. За́падники—наприме́р литерату́рный кри́тик В. Бели́нский и профе́ссор моско́вского университе́та Т. Грано́вский—учи́ли: По осно́вам свое́й культу́ры, ру́сские—европе́йцы, то́лько мла́дшие по своему́ истори́ческому во́зрасту, и потому́ должны́ идти́ путём про́йденным За́падом, усвоя́я плоды́ их культу́ры. Таки́ми плода́ми за́падники рассма́тривали пре́жде всего́ поня́тие о це́нности и досто́инстве челове́ческой ли́чности и о её пра́ве на свобо́дное разви́тие своего́ ра́зума.

Да, возража́ли славянофи́лы—А. С. Хомяко́в, И. В. Кире́евский и други́е—ру́сские европе́йцы, но восто́чные. У них свои́ осо́бые нача́ла жи́зни, кото́рые они́ и должны́ разраба́тывать со́бственными уси́лиями. Таки́ми нача́лами славянофи́лы счита́ли правосла́вную рели́гию и крестья́нскую общи́ну. Европе́йские рефо́рмы Петра́ Вели́кого они́ осужда́ли как национа́льную катастро́фу. Росси́я не уче-ни́ца и не спу́тница, да́же не сопе́рница Евро́пы, она́ её преёмница. Росси́я и Евро́па—это две ста́дии культу́рного разви́тия челове́чества. За́падная Евро́па—обши́рное кла́дбище, где под бога́тыми, мра́морными па́мятниками спят вели́кие поко́йники про́шлого. Лесна́я и степна́я Росси́я— э́то колыбе́ль, в кото́рой беспоко́йно во́зится и кричи́т мирово́е бу́дущее. Евро́па отжива́ет, Росси́я то́лько начина́ет жить, и так как ей придётся жить по́сле Евро́пы, то ей на́до уме́ть жить без неё.

Славянофи́лы бы́ли обращены́ к допетро́вскому про́шлому, за́падники к Западу. Но и допетро́вская Русь и за́падная Евро́па бы́ли для них не реа́льностью, а идеа́льной мечто́й. Отвлечённые филосо́фские спо́ры ме́жду представи́телями обо́их тече́ний вели́сь с необыча́йной стра́стностью и нере́дко конча́лись разры́вом ли́чных отноше́ний.

В 60 го́ды в интеллиге́нцию всё бо́льше влива́ются но́вые лю́ди—разночи́нцы. Э́то лю́ди, вы́званные к рабо́те из ни́зших слоёв о́бщества эпо́хой рефо́рм Алекса́ндра II. Большу́ю роль игра́ют в э́той гру́ппе интеллиге́нты, вы́шедшие из духо́вного сосло́вия, наприме́р Н. Черныше́вский и Н. А. Добролю́бов. Иде́йное тече́ние э́того десятиле́тия получи́ло назва́ние нигили́зма. Бы́вшие семинари́сты де́лаются нигили́стами. 60 го́ды пре́жде всего́ вре́мя крити́ческое, вре́мя отрица́ния дорефо́рменной, дворя́нской культу́ры. Слова́ми тре́тьего изве́стного представи́теля нигили́зма, Д. И. Пи́сарева: "Что мо́жно разби́ть, то и ну́жно разбива́ть. Что вы́держит уда́р, то годи́тся, а потому́ бей напра́во и нале́во, от э́того вреда́ не бу́дет."

Нигили́сты презира́ли пра́здную, изя́щную жизнь дворя́н 40 годо́в, их идеали́зм, их бесконе́чные разгово́ры и спо́ры на филосо́фские те́мы, их неспосо́бность к практи́ческой рабо́те. Но нигили́зм не весь в отрица́нии. В нём была́ и положи́тельная сторона́: увлече́ние материали́змом. На материали́зме осно́вано стремле́ние нигили́стов созда́ть но́вый тип челове́ка: си́льного, практи́чного, мы́слящего реали́ста, челове́ка незави́симого, освобождённого от вся́ких тради́ций и авторите́тов, челове́ка уве́ренного во власть ра́зума над жи́знью. Но и тут интеллиге́нция не освободи́лась от религио́зного моти́ва. Но́вый челове́к, о

кото́ром мечта́ли нигили́сты, и кото́рого Чернышéвский
описа́л в своём рома́не "Что дéлать?" это аскéт, кото́рый
отка́зывает себé во всех удóбствах жи́зни, развива́ет свой
ум, си́лы и вóлю не для себя́, а для служéния други́м,
чтобы посвяти́ть всю свою́ жизнь и ли́чность подготовлéнию
револю́ции.

Идéя о вла́сти ра́зума над жи́знью, интерéс к человéческой ли́чности сближа́ет нигили́стов с за́падниками 40
годóв, несмотря́ на глубóкие разногла́сия э́тих двух покo-
лéний. Вопрóс о нарóде, об отношéнии "мы́слящего реа-
ли́ста" к нарóду отодвига́ется нигили́стами на за́дний
план. Зато́ в 70 гóды мысль о нарóде опя́ть стано́вится
центра́льной для интеллигéнции. Поэ́тому, члéны э́той
гру́ппы получа́ют тепéрь назва́ние нарóдников. В нарóд-
ничестве ска́зывается извéстная связь с идéями славяно-
фи́лов 40 годóв. Идéйными вождя́ми нарóдников бы́ли
П. Л. Лавро́в и Н. К. Михайлóвский.

В соста́в интеллигéнции, наряду́ с разночи́нцами, опя́ть
начина́ют входи́ть дворя́не под назва́нием "ка́ющихся
дворя́н." Чу́вство вины́ и жела́ние искуплéния руководи́т
нарóдниками: дворя́нская культу́ра в прóшлом ста́ла воз-
мóжной благодаря́ труду́, пóту и крóви нарóда. Тепéрь
пришлó врéмя э́тот долг заплати́ть. Интеллигéнция шла
в нарóд, в дерéвню, чтобы искупи́ть свою́ вину́, чтобы
помóчь крестья́нству, учи́ть егó, улу́чшить егó экономи́-
ческое положéние. С э́той цéлью ты́сячи нарóдников шли
в дерéвню в ка́честве докторóв, учителéй и́ли прóсто
рабóчих.

Но и тут, дви́жущая идéя интеллигéнции не была́
реа́льностью, а мечтóй. Нарóд, с котóрым ка́ющиеся дво-
ря́не встреча́лись в дерéвне, был совсéм не такóй, каки́м
они́ себé егó представля́ли. Крестья́не не доверя́ли нарóд-
никам, не хотéли их пóмощи, ча́сто не понима́ли их речéй
и нерéдко са́ми выдава́ли их поли́ции. Судьба́ нарóдников
была́ траги́чна, потому́ что они́, готóвые отда́ть свою́
жизнь нарóду, бы́ли отвéргнуты э́тим са́мым нарóдом.

Разочарова́ние в крестья́нстве привелó интеллигéнцию
в концé 70 годóв к тому́, что она́ перешла́ от ми́рной, про-
свети́тельной рабóты к революциóнной, а затéм отвер-

нýлась от дерéвни и нáчала искáть союзников среди́ городского и фабри́чного населéния. Но глáвное бы́ло то, что в концý 19 вéка бóлее радикáльно настрóенные члéны э́той грýппы от нарóдничества перешли́ к марксúзму. Э́тот перехóд был сáмым крáйним и сáмым траги́чным в истóрии рýсской интеллигéнции. Чýвство сострадáния и жáлости, мечтá о свобóде и цéнности человéческой ли́чности, в рýсском марксúзме заменя́ются моти́вами си́лы, принуждéния, отрицáния ли́чности и безжáлостной жестóкости. Для достижéния мóщи и богáтства социáльного коллекти́ва отношéние к человéку дéлается беспощáдным и жестóким.

стих verse
воплоти́ть to embody
  perf. of: **воплоща́ть**
произведе́ние work (of an
  artist)
ли́шний superfluous
чутьё flair
по́шлый vulgar, base
поро́к vice
скита́ние wandering, roam-
  ing
ве́ха landmark
накану́не on the eve

просто́р spaciousness, scope
ги́бель (f.) ruin, destruction
ста́до herd
ста́дность (f.) herdlike
  existence
проро́ческий prophetic
подо́бие resemblance, image
собла́зн temptation
мураве́йник ant heap
расстила́ться to spread
настрое́ние mood
неле́пый absurd
при́зрак phantom

РУ́ССКАЯ ЛИТЕРАТУ́РА В ДЕВЯТНА́ДЦАТОМ
ВЕ́КЕ

В це́нтре внима́ния ру́сских писа́телей 19 ве́ка стоя́ла та
же иде́я, кото́рая занима́ла ру́сскую интеллиге́нцию вообще́:
отрица́ние совреме́нного обще́ственного стро́я. Это была́
не то́лько иде́я, но и це́лое чу́вство, си́льное и о́строе.
Моти́в сострада́ния к го́рю челове́ка и ми́ра, иска́ние
пра́вды, челове́ческого сча́стья, соверше́нной жи́зни, есть
основно́й моти́в ру́сской литерату́ры 19 ве́ка.

Её основа́телем явля́ется Алекса́ндр Серге́евич Пу́шкин.
Он роди́лся в после́дний год 18 ве́ка и преждевре́менно
сконча́лся от смерте́льной ра́ны полу́ченной на дуэ́ли в
1837 году́. Мо́лодость Пу́шкина совпа́ла с двумя́ ва́жными
собы́тиями в исто́рии Росси́и—с наше́ствием Наполео́на и с

восста́нием Декабри́стов.[1] В э́той полити́ческой и духо́вной атмосфе́ре и формирова́лся Пу́шкин. Он стоя́л о́чень бли́зко к кружку́ Декабри́стов. Из-за свои́х свободолюби́вых и напра́вленных про́тив прави́тельства стихо́в Пу́шкин провёл 6 лет в ссы́лке и всю жизнь остава́лся под надзо́ром прави́тельства.

Пу́шкин заста́л ру́сскую литерату́ру, когда́ она́ ещё жила́ чужи́ми· о́бразами и ещё не име́ла со́бственного, вполне́ сложи́вшегося языка́.[2] Ему́ одному́ пришло́сь испо́лнить две рабо́ты, в други́х стра́нах обыкнове́нно разделённые це́лыми столе́тиями, а и́менно: установи́ть язы́к и созда́ть литерату́ру. В его́ тво́рчестве как бы просыпа́лся ум и литерату́рный тала́нт ру́сского наро́да. В нём лежа́т нача́ла, семена́ всей ру́сской литерату́ры 19 ве́ка. Нет писа́теля в тече́ние всего́ э́того столе́тия, кото́рый не находи́лся бы под влия́нием Пу́шкина.

Пу́шкин довёл до вы́сшего соверше́нства своё основно́е ору́жие—сло́во; сло́во, как сре́дство изображе́ния и сло́во, как элеме́нт музыка́льный, причём изобрази́тельность и музыка́льность, смысл и звук слов, приводи́лись Пу́шкиным к еди́нству, како́го ре́дко достига́ло иску́сство. Поэ́тому поэ́т оказа́л глубо́кое влия́ние на разви́тие не то́лько литерату́ры, но и ру́сской му́зыки. Нет компози́тора в 19 ве́ке, кото́рый не воплоти́л бы в зву́ках тем и слов Пу́шкина.

Слове́сным мастерство́м далеко́ не исче́рпывается значе́ние Пу́шкина. Не ме́нее замеча́тельна разнообра́зность геро́ев и ти́пов, ру́сских и иностра́нных, со́зданных поэ́том, и порази́тельны бога́тство и глубина́ иде́й им вы́сказанных с велича́йшей кра́ткостью, вырази́тельностью и я́сностью. Отноше́ние ли́чности к о́бществу и госуда́рству, столкнове́ние ме́жду челове́ческим ра́зумом и чу́вством, европе́йским рационали́змом и ру́сской религио́зностью, страсть к деньга́м и вла́сти как основна́я пробле́ма совреме́нного челове́ка—вот основны́е иде́и, разви́тые ру́сскими писа́телями 19 ве́ка. И все они́ бы́ли вы́сказаны и наме́чены Пу́шкиным.

---

[1] См. гл. 15, стр. 75–76.
[2] См. гл. 24, стр. 130–31.

Таким же образом пушкинские герои сделались предками целого ряда родственных им фигур в произведениях последующих русских классиков 19 века. Евгений Онегин Пушкина, холодный, скучающий, неспособный применить свой ум и европейское образование в современной русской обстановке, явился родоначальником нескольких поколений "лишних людей" в русской литературе—людей оторванных от родной земли. А скромный, несчастный Евгений из пушкинского "Медного всадника"—основатель длинной портретной галлереи маленьких, жалких, забитых, беззащитных людей.

Николай Васильевич Гоголь на десять лет моложе Пушкина. Он начал своё творчество в 1830 годах, под знаком романтизма, с изучения народных былин, сказок и песен Малороссии, где писатель родился. Его первые произведения—ряд поэтических, фантастических сказок о своей родине, в которых смешное переплетается со страшным и жутким. У Гоголя было особое чутьё для наблюдения зла, для описания тёмных сил и отрицательных сторон жизни. Он видел метафизическую глубину зла, не только его социальные проявления.

Мир Гоголя не изображение действительности, а только всего пошлого, низкого в русской жизни, даже когда он от фантастических малороссийских сказок переходит к реалистическим рассказам о жизни мелких чиновников в Петербурге, а затем, в комедии "Ревизор" и повести "Мёртвые души" к описанию русского провинциального города и деревни.

Гоголь не психолог, он великий художник внешних форм, а не внутреннего развития человека. В "Мёртвых душах" каждый герой является символом одной дурной стороны русской жизни во время крепостного права. Тут и плутовство и сентиментальная мечтательность, глупость и жадность, нахальное невежество, хитрость и грубость и наконец скупость. Все эти пороки, одетые в человеческие образы, Гоголь описывает так живо и ярко, с таким реализмом и горькой усмешкой, что он заставляет читателя забывать, что это фантастические маски, а не действительные люди.

Иван Сергеевич Тургенев провёл почти всю жизнь в скитаниях по странам Запада, с более или менее продолжительными возвращениями в Россию. Близкое знакомство с западноевропейской жизнью и культурой развило в нём способность с большой объективностью, издалека следить за развитием русской жизни. Тургенев—художественный летописец своего времени, изобразивший в своих романах, на фоне замечательных описаний русской природы, те общественные перемены, которые происходили на его глазах в России от 40 до 70 годов.

Названия главных романов Тургенева—"Рудин," "Дворянское гнездо," "Отцы и дети," и "Новь"—имеют особый смысл. Это вехи того пути, который Тургенев прошёл в своих думах о судьбах русского общества. Рудин—человек 30–40 годов, преемник пушкинского Онегина. Он блестящий оратор, не знающий России мечтатель, неспособный на сильные чувства и энергичные действия. "Дворянское гнездо" уже не роман о герое, а о целой среде, о путях слабеющего и беднеющего дворянства перед освобождением крестьян. Роман поэтически овеян осенней печалью и освещён вечерней зарёй.

"Накануне" весь обращён к будущему. Герой романа иностранец, болгарин, предсказывающий, что Россия стоит накануне появления и в ней людей дела, идущих на смену мечтательным людям слова 40 годов. В романе "Отцы и дети" Тургенев описывает появление этих людей дела в 60 годах—нигилистов разночинцев—и их столкновение с "отцами," со старшим поколением 40 годов. В 1876 году Тургеневым написан последний роман "Новь." В лице героя народника, который кончает самоубийством, Тургенев простился со своим любимым героем—лишним человеком. Писатель осуждает народническое хождение в народ без знания народа, без умения подойти в нему, без реально обоснованной программы.

Современниками Тургенева были величайшие русские писатели 19 века—Лев Николаевич Толстой и Фёдор Михайлович Достоевский. Главные произведения обоих написаны в 60 и 70 годах.

Толстой художник жизни; он проникает до самых её

корней и видит все её проявления и этапы, от рождения до смерти. В его художественных, эпических произведениях царит полная гармония искусства и действительности. Голоса писателя как будто не слышно, а говорят и движутся сами герои, живёт вся обстановка, в которой они находятся, природа и животные.

Огромный художественный материал использован Толстым в его главном произведении ''Война и мир,'' описывающем период наполеоновских войн России. Тут целые народы, армии, сражения, толпы, тут жизнь целых родов русского дворянства, столичного и провинциального, но и простое крестьянство, тут исторические лица, но и развитие и судьба отдельных частных лиц. Все эти толпы людей проходят мимо читателя в полной гармонии, как живые, каждый имеет своё место, каждое лицо часть широкой, жизненной волны.

Историей движут не отдельные личности, а массы, народ. Вот главный мотив романа и основная идея Толстого, которую он за последние три десятилетия своей жизни (он умер в 1910 году) развил в многочисленных произведениях философского и морального содержания. Человек должен жить для других, не отделяя своей жизни от жизни общей. Смерть уничтожает личную жизнь, бессмертия души не существует, но жизнь общая, жизнь человеческой группы, общества, народа, продолжается и только в ней человек может найти счастье.

В произведениях Толстого чувствуется простор, необъятная ширина русской равнины. В творчестве Достоевского, с другой стороны, преобладает глубина и высота. Он художник духовного. Его герои не отдельные личности, а представители разных сторон души современного человека вообще. Достоевского занимает только одна тема— трагедия современного человека, которая в полной силе раскрывается в России, стране величайших крайностей и противоречий. Эта трагедия состоит в том, что современный человек перестал верить в Бога, объявил свою гордую независимость, силу и право действия по личному, властному усмотрению.

Достоевский не интересуется всей жизнью выпавшего из

ста́рого христиа́нского миропоря́дка челове́ка, а то́лько гла́вными мину́тами его́ вну́тренней, духо́вной траге́дии. Поэ́тому иде́и игра́ют огро́мную роль в тво́рчестве э́того худо́жника-мысли́теля. Иде́и прино́сят челове́ку ги́бель, но и спасе́ние. Лю́ди Достое́вского живу́т иде́ями, чу́вствуют мы́сли и выража́ют весь свой хара́ктер в разгово́ре. У ка́ждого своя́ осо́бенная речь и интона́ция, свой слова́рь и ритм фраз.

В судьбе́ богооста́вленного челове́ка Достое́вский ви́дит два направле́ния—человекобо́жество и ста́дность. Он проро́чески намеча́ет пути́ ру́сской коммунисти́ческой револю́ции, произоше́дшей 36 лет по́сле его́ сме́рти. Человекобо́г, т. е. си́льная ли́чность, кото́рая счита́ет, что Бо́га нет, что всё позво́лено, что ей мо́жно преступа́ть все зако́ны, теря́ет свой челове́ческий о́блик и неизме́нно погиба́ет. Челове́к то́лько и есть, е́сли он о́браз и подо́бие Бо́жье. Приро́да челове́ка соотноси́тельна приро́де Бо́га.

Христиа́нство Достое́вский понима́ет, как рели́гию духо́вной свобо́ды, свобо́ды вы́бора ме́жду добро́м и злом. Зло, преступле́ние, явля́ется испыта́нием свобо́ды. Вы́брав зло, соверши́в преступле́ние, челове́к мо́жет восстанови́ть свою́ свобо́ду то́лько страда́нием и искупле́нием. Путь свобо́ды есть путь страда́ния. Поэ́тому всегда́ существу́ет собла́зн изба́вить челове́чество от страда́ний лиши́в его́ свобо́ды, поработи́в его́, преврати́в его́ в поко́рное ста́до. Но си́лой, вла́стью, невозмо́жно созда́ть духо́вную общину, а то́лько создаётся материа́льный, живо́тный коллекти́в, коммунисти́ческий муравей́ник. О́ба пути́, человекобо́жество и ста́дность, приво́дят к одному́ и тому́ же результа́ту, к уничтоже́нию челове́ческой ли́чности.

Свобо́да и страда́ние и́ли ра́бство с живо́тным сча́стьем— вот пути́ совреме́нного челове́чества, кото́рые расстила́лись пе́ред Достое́вским с го́рных верши́н его́ тво́рчества и кото́рые он оконча́тельно указа́л в своём после́днем и велича́йшем произведе́нии ''Бра́тья Карама́зовы.''

Анто́н Па́влович Че́хов на́чал свой тво́рческий путь в 80 года́х коро́ткими расска́зами. Они́ сперва́ принесли́ ему́ сла́ву. Геро́й э́тих расска́зов—ма́ленький, сре́дний, ру́сский челове́к из всех слоёв о́бщества. Кра́ткость—гла́вная характерная черта формы и стиля Чехова. Он умеет передать на нескольких страницах целую жизнь человека, описать выбором нескольких коротких подробностей целую обстановку и вложить глубокие, сложные мысли в короткие, простые слова.

Второе достижение Чехова относится к области драматургии. Его пьесы—новая глава в истории театра. Чехов изменил понятие о действии. События на сцене представляют тончайшие, почти незаметные переходы. Вместо открытого движения, Чехов создаёт настроение на сцене, которое передаётся зрителям и показывает скрытое действие. На сцене как будто ничего не происходит, но одним словом, звуком, жестом, выбором обстановки, всё меняется и движется вперёд.

В своей лучшей пьесе "Вишнёвый сад," написанной в 1903 году, Чехов с грустной улыбкой прощается с жизнью старой, дворянской России. Конец настолько близок, что эта жизнь представляется уже нелепой и нереальной. Главные герои призраки, всё в их жизни смешно и бессмысленно. Комическое и трагическое сливаются и выступают как разные стороны одного целого.

18

подражáние imitation
объём volume
перезвóн chimes
кóлокол bell
проникновéнный expressive
жéртвовать to sacrifice
наблюдáтельность (f.) talent of observation
презрительный contemptuous
кýчка heap, group

кружóк circle
грань (f.) boundary line
разумéть to conceive
порыв impulse
преступный guilty, criminal
мýчить to torture
предáние tradition, legend
мрáчный somber
великолéпный magnificent
исповедь (f.) confession
вопль (m.) scream

РУ́ССКАЯ МУ́ЗЫКА В ДЕВЯТНА́ДЦАТОМ ВЕ́КЕ

В течéние векóв в Россúи церкóвное пéние и нарóдная пéсня существовáли рáдом, не окáзывая друг на дрýга влияния. Цéрковь преслéдовала нарóдную пéсню. В рýсском óбществе интерéс к свéтской мýзыке зародúлся в 18 вéке, одноврéменно с нарастáющим сближéнием с зáпадноевропéйской культýрой вообщé. Но до пéрвой трéти 19 вéка включúтельно царúт слепóе подражáние Зáпаду, глáвным óбразом увлечéние итальáнской óперой.

Родоначáльником рýсской мýзыки являéтся Михаúл Ивáнович Глúнка. Во мнóгих отношéниях Глúнка имéет в рýсской мýзыке такóе же значéние, как Пýшкин в рýсской литератýре. Óба положúли начáло нóвому рýсскому твóрчеству, óба покóнчили с подражáнием, óба сóздали нóвый рýсский язык—одúн в поэзии и прóзе, другóй в мýзыке. Худóжественная дéятельность Глúнки продолжáлась всегó тóлько 20 лет, и за э́то врéмя он создал очень немного по объёму, но громадное по содержанию, по новизне, силе и влиянию на дальнейшие судьбы русской музыки.

Родившись в 1804 году в помещичьей семье в деревне, Глинка прожил все детские и юношеские годы среди характернейших проявлений русского музыкального творчества—древнего церковного пения и народной песни. Ещё ребёнком он страстно полюбил гармонический перезвон церковных колоколов. В своей опере "Жизнь за царя," написанной в 1836 году, Глинка соединил эти народные ценности—старинную, то протяжно грустную, то буйно весёлую, крестьянскую песню со строгим, сдержанным и проникновенным, древнерусским церковным пением, обогащая их приёмами европейской гармонизации и оркестровки.

"Жизнь за царя" основана на историческом предании о крестьянине Иване Сусанине, который жертвует собой во время Смуты для спасения отечества. Личная трагедия народного героя вырастает в народный эпос. Образ народа как единое, могучее целое проявляется в мужских и женских хорах и наконец в мощном и величественном хоре с колоколами "Славься."

Во всю жизнь Глинки—он умер в 1857 году—его личным товарищем и художественным спутником был Александр Сергеевич Даргомыжский. Он не был рождён музыкальным колористом, был почти вовсе лишён дара инструментального творчества. Но где он превосходит Глинку, это в драматичности выражения, в психологической наблюдательности, в анализе душевных состояний и внутренних переживаний.

В своей опере "Русалка," написанной на пушкинский текст, Даргомыжский создаёт образы скромных, незаметных людей, лишённых ореола героизма и величия, но способных к сильным и глубоким переживаниям. Его самое великое произведение, это опера "Каменный гость," тоже написанная на пушкинские слова. Даргомыжский стремится звуками прямо и точно выразить слово, создаёт своей музыкой полные и верные человеческие характеры, рисует индивидуальные черты человеческие, условленные не только временем и местом, но и настроением, чувством и страстями.

Ещё при жизни Глинки и Даргомыжского, около середины 19 века, в России началось новое музыкальное движение. В Петербурге образовался музыкальный союз нескольких юношей, товарищество Балакирева, одушевлённое мыслью о необходимости нового направления в музыке. Их окрестили презрительным прозвищем "могучей кучки." Но сверх того, их постоянно прозывали "невеждами" и "дилетантами." И всё таки балакиревское товарищество завоевало себе прочное почётное положение. Прежде всего оно признало своим главой и основателем русской музыки Глинку, в то время ещё не понятого, и повело энергичную войну с русской итальяноманией и музыкальным "космополитизмом."

Милий Алексеевич Балакирев был первым из русских композиторов, самостоятельно продолживших и развивших симфонические принципы Глинки. Но он же первый привёз на русскую почву драматические и живописные элементы западноевропейского музыкального неоромантизма. Самый знающий среди членов кучки, он скоро стал признанным главой кружка и сыграл крупную педагогическую роль среди своих товарищей, ознакомляя их с проблемами музыкальной техники.

Модест Петрович Мусоргский одним из первых присоединился к балакиревскому кружку. Мусоргский хотел уничтожить грань, отделяющую музыку от других сфер человеческого мышления, и найти широко понятный и доступный язык для общения с людьми разного положения и социального состояния. Он считал призванием художника живую беседу с людьми, передачу живых мыслей, тончайших черт природы человека и человеческих масс.

Преследуя эту цель, несмотря на много недостатков в технике, Мусоргский заставляет музыку говорить и рисовать, негодовать, страдать и смеяться. Он не останавливается ни перед изображением мужиков и баб в деревне, ни перед скорбной мольбой нищей сироты. Он живописует звуками одинаково ярко и психологию ребёнка, и чувства молодой женщины, испуганной козлом, но не испугавшейся старого мужа, и мысли семинариста, учащего латинскую грамматику среди воспоминаний о поповской дочери. То шутливая, то насмешливая, музыкальная сатира Мусоргского возвышается до злого, бичующего сарказма в его музыкальных памфлетах, направленных против современных ему представителей музыкального консерватизма.

Полного расцвета талант композитора достигает в операх "Борис Годунов" и "Хованщина." Мусоргский назвал их "народными драмами." Он разумел народ как "великую личность, одушевлённую единой идеей" и изобразил в обеих операх коллективную психологию, могучие порывы народных масс.

Сюжетом оперы "Борис Годунов"[1] послужила драма Пушкина того же названия. Но не все линии трагедии писателя одинаково развиты композитором. Боярская интрига отбрасывается и образ Самозванца слабеет. В опере два главных лица: преступный царь Борис и народ. Исторически вина Годунова в смерти царевича Дмитрия никогда не была доказана, но Пушкин сделал её основой своего творческого произведения. В опере Мусоргского психологическая драма царя преступника, которого мучает совесть, и социальная драма восстающих народных масс, составляют две переплетающиеся линии действия.

Опера "Хованщина" также построена на сопоставлении личности и народа. В центре действия стоит трагедия стрелецкого офицера и старовера князя Ивана Хованского, обвинённого в заговоре против правительства и погибшего в конце 17 века. Второй главный герой—народ. Целый ряд народных групп переживают столкновение двух культур—древнерусской и западноевропейской.

Самым долговечным и плодовитым из членов балакиревского кружка оказался Николай Андреевич Римский-Корсаков (1844–1909). Он проявил великий и оригинальный талант во всех музыкальных областях, куда

---

[1] Исторический обзор Смутного времени и царствования Бориса Годунова в гл. 9, стр. 42–46.

ни обращалось его творчество. Помимо своих собственных произведений, он окончил оперу Александра Порфирьевича Бородина "Князь Игорь," оставшейся незаконченной при смерти её создателя в 1887 году. В основе оперы лежит поэма киевских времён "Слово о полку Игореве."[2]

Римский-Корсаков начал с романса и затем, вдохновлённый стариной новгородской губернии, в которой он родился, написал в 60 годах, музыкальную картину "Садко"[3] и оперу "Псковитянка." После этого он решил поближе ознакомиться с техническими приёмами композиции и занялся тщательным изучением гармонии, контрапункта и фуги. С 1873 года, Римский-Корсаков с обновлёнными силами принялся за новое творчество, возвращаясь к темам народного предания. Окончив сказочные оперы "Снегурочка," "Царь Салтан" и "Золотой петушок," он обращается к народной психике с другой, духовно-религиозной стороны и пишет оперу "Сказание о невидимом граде Китеже и деве Февронии."[4] Симфонические, инструментальные создания Римского-Корсакого также принадлежат к высшим торжествам композитора.

Пётр Ильич Чайковский любил всё русское не менее чем члены балакиревского кружка, но в музыкальной своей натуре он вовсе не носил элемента "национального," а был от головы до ног космополитом. Он не вносил никаких особенных новшеств в свои произведения и считал все новые стремления "кучки" невежеством.

Внимание Чайковского было прежде всего направлено на раскрытие внутренних душевных переживаний человеческой личности. Он пишет очень много, берёт темы из русского народного быта и великих образцов мировой литературы и драматургии. Вследствие физических и моральных причин личной жизни, Чайковский был почти постоянно мрачно, печально настроен, несмотря на чувствительный, добрый, мягкий характер. Чаще всего его сочинения имели характер меланхолический, задум-

---

[2] См. гл. 2, стр. 9.
[3] Содержание этой былины: гл. 3, стр. 13.
[4] Содержание этого сказания: гл. 6, стр. 27.

чивый и гру́стный, выража́я глубо́кую, но ти́хую любо́вь и поэти́ческие настрое́ния в соедине́нии с великоле́пно пе́реданными карти́нами приро́ды, то ми́рно споко́йной, то возбуждённо бунту́ющей. Реалисти́ческая по́весть в стиха́х Пу́шкина "Евге́ний Оне́гин," э́та "энциклопе́дия ру́сской жи́зни," преврати́лась под перо́м Чайко́вского в лири́ческую о́перу.

Са́мой лири́ческой из всех музыка́льных форм Чайко́вский счита́л симфо́нию. Она́ с наибо́льшей полното́й спосо́бна вы́разить всё то, для чего́ нет слов, но что стреми́тся быть вы́сказано. Э́та "музыка́льная и́споведь души́" име́ет несравне́нно бо́лее могу́щественные сре́дства для выраже́ния пережива́ний и бо́лее то́нкий язы́к чем слова́. Вы́сшее созда́ние Чайко́вского—6ая симфо́ния, напи́санная незадо́лго до его́ сме́рти, наступи́вшей в 1893 году́. К концу́ свое́й жи́зни мра́чное настрое́ние Чайко́вского всё уси́ливалось и воплощено́ в велича́йшем произведе́нии компози́тора, в э́том стра́шном во́пле отча́яния и мучи́тельной безнадёжности челове́ка, стра́стно люби́вшего жизнь.

19

худо́жник artist
преклоне́ние admiration, adoration
че́рпать to draw upon
  почерпну́ть (perf.)
исполне́ние execution, performance
предчу́вствие foreboding
изображе́ние representation, picture
передвижно́й transient
вы́ставка exhibit
притесня́ть to oppress
заключённый prisoner
полотно́ canvas, also: linen fabric

бурла́к workman on the Volga barges
песо́к sand
ля́мка strap
кандалы́ shackles
призы́в call, appeal
уны́лый melancholy
запро́с quest
чу́до miracle
  чудеса́ (pl.)
утра́чивать to lose
  утра́тить (perf.)
пове́рженный prostrated

РУ́ССКАЯ ЖИ́ВОПИСЬ В ДЕВЯТНА́ДЦАТОМ ВЕ́КЕ

Све́тская жи́вопись начала́ развива́ться в Росси́и в 18 ве́ке. Для украше́ния дворцо́в, кото́рые стро́ились в Петербу́рге и в дворя́нских уса́дьбах, пона́добились и карти́ны. Из-за грани́цы бы́ло вы́звано большо́е коли́чество худо́жников—не́мец Гео́рг Гроот, италья́нец Пье́тро Рота́ри, францу́з Луи Токэ́, и мно́гие други́е. Создаётся среди́ ру́сских вкус к карти́нам, на сме́ну стари́нной религио́зной жи́вописи прихо́дит све́тское иску́сство. Пре́жде всего́ развива́ется портре́тная жи́вопись.

Из Импера́торской акаде́мии худо́жеств, осно́ванной в середи́не 18 ве́ка для воспита́ния ру́сских худо́жников,

выхо́дит ряд выдаю́щихся портрети́стов. В 1773 году́
Д. Г. Леви́цкий пи́шет портре́т францу́зского мысли́теля
Дидро́, проводи́вшего в то вре́мя, по приглаше́нию Ека-
тери́ны II, не́сколько ме́сяцев в Петербу́рге. Э́тот портре́т
Дидро́ счита́л са́мым правди́вым и уда́чным из всех с
него́ когда́-ли́бо пи́санных. В 10 и 20 года́х 19 ве́ка выде-
ля́ется О. А. Кипре́нский, ма́стер романти́ческого пор-
тре́та. Осо́бенно уда́чны его́ же́нские портре́ты, но столь
же знамени́т его́ портре́т Пу́шкина, напи́санный в 1827
году́.

Акаде́мия худо́жеств с са́мого нача́ла своего́ возник-
нове́ния приде́рживалась консервати́вных тради́ций. В
пе́рвой полови́не 19 ве́ка в ней цари́ло преклоне́ние пе́ред
за́падноевропе́йским классици́змом. Основны́е сюже́ты
карти́н че́рпались из мифоло́гии, би́блии и Ева́нгелия;
преоблада́л ю́жный, преиму́щественно италья́нский, пей-
за́ж, а портре́ты должны́ бы́ли быть пара́дно-декора-
ти́вными. Тща́тельно выпи́сывалась бога́тая оде́жда, на
фо́не дорого́й ме́бели и́ли роско́шной архитекту́ры. Во
второ́й че́тверти 19 ве́ка из э́той шко́лы вы́шли два
выдаю́щихся худо́жника—Карл Па́влович Брюлло́в и
Алекса́ндр Андре́евич Ива́нов. Сюже́ты их гла́вных
карти́н соотве́тствовали тради́циям Акаде́мии, но в испол-
не́нии о́ба начина́ют освобожда́ться от холо́дной усло́в-
ности по́зднего классици́зма.

В 1830–33 года́х Брюлло́в пи́шет "После́дный день
Помпе́и." Карти́на изобража́ет ги́бель Помпе́и в моме́нт
изверже́ния Везу́вия. На фо́не ру́шащихся зда́ний и ста́туй
ме́чется толпа́, зали́тая злове́щим бле́ском мо́лнии и
пла́менем вулка́на. Карти́на производи́ла огро́мное впе-
чатле́ние на зри́телей. Изображе́ние ги́бели дре́внего
го́рода выраста́ла в о́бщее представле́ние о ма́ссовых
челове́ческих катастро́фах и коренны́х истори́ческих
переворо́тах.

Брюлло́в изобрази́л у́жас разруше́ния, Ива́нов—свет
и зарю́ но́вой истори́ческой эпо́хи. Сюже́т его́ велича́йшей
карти́ны, над кото́рой он рабо́тал бо́лее двадцати́ лет,
библе́йский: явле́ние Христа́ наро́ду. Иоа́нн Крести́тель
собра́л наро́д у реки́ Иорда́на. И́здали приближа́ется

Христо́с, по́сле до́лгого поста́ возвраща́ющийся из пусты́ни. Иоа́нн ука́зывает на Него́, как на спаси́теля челове́чества. Одни́ слу́шают его́ с наде́ждой и ра́достью, други́е с любопы́тством и недове́рием. Но все охва́чены предчу́вствием истори́ческого поворо́та.

К середи́не 19 ве́ка Акаде́мия ста́ла всё ча́ще подверга́ться кри́тике со стороны́ молоды́х худо́жников. Всё гро́мче тре́бовали, что́бы иску́сство перешло́ от идеали-зи́рованной, нереа́льной, подража́ющей За́паду жи́вописи к правди́вому изображе́нию ру́сской действи́тельности. Несмотря́ на э́то, о́сенью 1863 го́да Акаде́мия объяви́ла сюже́том для ко́нкурса на золоту́ю меда́ль те́му из сканди-на́вских саг: Пир в Валга́лле. Все 14 конкурре́нтов на золоту́ю меда́ль отказа́лись уча́ствовать в ко́нкурсе, отдели́лись от Акаде́мии и основа́ли своё со́бственное худо́жественное объедине́ние. Це́лью объедине́ния бы́ло вы́вести ру́сскую жи́вопись на свобо́дную, самостоя́тельную доро́гу и созда́ть реалисти́ческое иску́сство.

К нова́торам нача́ло примыка́ть всё бо́льше худо́жников. В 1870 году́ образова́лось ''Това́рищество пере-движны́х вы́ставок.'' Одни́м из иде́йных вожде́й э́того движе́ния был худо́жник Васи́лий Григо́рьевич Перо́в. Он воспринима́л иску́сство как обще́ственное служе́ние. Зада́ча худо́жника—дать наро́ду обще́ственно-эсте-ти́ческое воспита́ние. Ну́жно внести́ иску́сство в широ́кие ма́ссы путём устро́йства передвижны́х вы́ставок во всех города́х Росси́и. Пе́рвая вы́ставка Передви́жников состоя́-лась с больши́м успе́хом в Петербу́рге в 1871 году́. С тех пор, передово́е ру́сское иску́сство развива́ется под зна́ком э́того движе́ния.

Карти́ны Перо́ва, в кото́рых преоблада́ет серова́то-кори́чневая кра́сочная га́мма, напо́лнены печа́лью и гне́-вом. Они́ выража́ют глубо́кое сочу́вствие к го́рю, нищете́ и беспра́вию наро́да и осужда́ют и обвиня́ют тех, кто притесня́ет наро́д. Сюже́ты Перо́ва: неве́жество провин-циа́льного духове́нства, гру́бость купе́чества, самодово́ль-ство ме́лких чино́вников. В карти́не ''По́хороны крестья́-нина'' изображено́ го́ре осироте́вшей, ни́щей дереве́нской семьи́.

Са́мыми кру́пными из Передви́жников бы́ли Илья́ Ефи́мович Ре́пин и Васи́лий Ива́нович Су́риков. Иску́сство Ре́пина кра́йне разнообра́зно и бога́то. Он со́здал и замеча́тельные портре́ты и карти́ны на истори́ческие те́мы, взя́тые из про́шлого ру́сского наро́да. Но, как и Перо́в, он уделя́ет большо́е внима́ние бытово́му жа́нру. Аре́ст революцио́нного пропаганди́ста в дере́вне, полити́ческий заключённый пе́ред ка́знью, отка́зывающийся от и́споведи, революционе́р, неожи́данно возвраща́ющийся домо́й из ссы́лки—вот его́ те́мы. Изве́стнейшей из его́ бытовы́х карти́н явля́ется полотно́ "Бурлаки́."

В жа́ркий по́лдень, по раскалённому песку́ пло́ского, лишённого те́ни бе́рега Во́лги, ме́дленно иду́т оди́ннадцать бурлако́в, с широ́кой ля́мкой, охва́тывающей их грудь и пле́чи, ступа́я го́лыми нога́ми по горя́чему песку́. Их употребля́ют вме́сто живо́тных. Они́ тя́нут про́тив тече́ния ба́рку, нагружённую хле́бом. Ка́жется, бу́дто они́ уже́ це́лые столе́тия иду́т так и бу́дут идти́ ещё столе́тия— одни́ равноду́шные, други́е мра́чные, все угнетённые, но си́льные и му́жественные.

Су́риков—худо́жник истори́ческих траге́дий. На пе́рвом ме́сте в его́ карти́нах—наро́д, как истори́ческая си́ла. "У́тро стреле́цкой ка́зни" пока́зывает коне́ц ста́рого, моско́вского во́йска. За бунт про́тив европе́йских рефо́рм Петра́ Вели́кого стрельцы́ царём обречены́ на смерть. Сейча́с начнётся казнь. В стороне́, си́дя на коне́, Пётр хо́лодно и гне́вно смо́трит на свои́х побеждённых враго́в. Но стрельцы́ в э́ту после́днюю мину́ту жи́зни духо́вно не сдаю́тся. Ни оди́н из них не выража́ет стра́ха или малоду́шия, несмотря́ на слёзы и сто́ны окружа́ющих их жён и дете́й.

В "Боя́рине Моро́зовой" Су́риков изобрази́л эпизо́д из исто́рии церко́вного раско́ла.[1] В зи́мний, сне́жный день везу́т Моро́зову в кандала́х по моско́вской у́лице. Её уво́зят в ссы́лку за её старове́рческие убежде́ния. На синева́том, сне́жном фо́не выделя́ются ли́ца и пёстрые, я́ркие оде́жды провожа́ющей боя́рыню толпы́. Все взо́ры

---

[1] См. гл. 11, стр. 52–56.

обращены́ к ней. Бле́дная, вся в чёрном, высоко́ подня́в го́лову и пра́вую ру́ку в проща́льном призы́ве отста́ивать ста́рую ве́ру, е́дет раско́льница, ско́ванная но не побеждённая.

Бы́ли среди́ Передви́жников и пейзажи́сты. Ива́н Ива́нович Ши́шкин и Алексе́й Кондра́тьевич Савра́сов одни́ из пе́рвых, кото́рые обрати́лись к скро́мному, уны́лому ландша́фту се́верной Росси́и. Ши́шкин на всю жизнь вдохнови́лся берёзами и со́снами лесно́й глуши́, сде́лался худо́жником ру́сского ле́са. Савра́сов стал изобрази́телем весе́ннего пейза́жа, та́ющего сне́га и мя́гкого, ды́мчатого во́здуха.

Передви́жничество дости́гло своего́ по́лного расцве́та в 70 и 80 года́х. Основны́е стремле́ния э́того худо́жественного тече́ния соотве́тствовали о́бщему настрое́нию интеллиге́нтских слоёв ру́сского о́бщества. Жела́ние не то́лько пасси́вно созерца́ть жизнь, но её и суди́ть и измени́ть, явля́лось гла́вным интере́сом, кото́рый руководи́л и нигили́стами 60 годо́в и наро́дниками 70 годо́в.[2] Одна́ко, к концу́ 80 годо́в в ми́ре иску́сства начина́ют развива́ться но́вые настрое́ния и но́вые запро́сы. Иде́и Передви́жников начина́ют подверга́ться пересмо́тру и кри́тике, кото́рая к середи́не 90 годо́в приво́дит к по́лному разры́ву ме́жду "отца́ми" и "детьми́," ме́жду Передви́жниками и но́вым, молоды́м поколе́нием худо́жников.

Молодо́е поколе́ние обвиня́ет Передви́жников в том, что они́ бо́льше расска́зывают, чем творя́т, что они́ приглаша́ют "чита́ть" карти́ны, вме́сто того́, что́бы и́ми любова́ться, что они́ свя́зывают себе́ ру́ки стремле́нием передава́ть лишь объекти́вную реа́льность. Реали́зм вы́родился в фотографи́чность. Заговори́ли о "нигили́зме глаз" Передви́жников, кото́рый разви́л в худо́жниках э́того поколе́ния привы́чку иска́ть в приро́де то́лько то, что ви́дят все, и выража́ть на́йденное то́же так, как все ви́дят. Та́кже осужда́ли Передви́жников за изли́шнюю отчуждённость от за́падноевропе́йского иску́сства и в недооце́нке ра́нних портрети́стов конца́ 18 ве́ка и ху

---

[2] См. гл. 16, стр. 82–83.

дожников начала 19 столетия, воспитанных Академией художеств.

На смену Передвижникам, проповедникам "полезной живописи," объективной правильности, пришло поколение, лозунгом которого стала творческая, индивидуальная "бесполезность" и свобода. Идея крайнего индивидуализма проникала в то же время, под названием символизма, и в литературу. Группа художников, писателей и поэтов объединилась вокруг нового журнала "Мир Искусства." Под тем же именем начались выставки. Новое течение не было определённой школой живописи. Нужным признавалось всё яркое и самостоятельное, поощрялась способность художника "видеть чудеса," прозревать за предметом его дух и сущность.

Немало художников, начавших своё творчество под знаком Передвижников, перешло в новый лагерь. Исаак Ильич Левитан первый перенял у французских импрессионистов их живописные приёмы, их подход к задачам света и цвета, и стал поэтом русского пейзажа. Валентин Александрович Серов в своих замечательных портретах достиг слияния человека и свето-воздушной среды, не утрачивая при этом реализма в изображении. Виктор Михайлович Васнецов широко использовал для своего творчества народные былины и нашёл в своих картинах—сказках новый подход к природе сквозь сказочную грёзу. Стремление к индивидуализму нашло наиболее яркое выражение в творчестве Михаила Александровича Врубеля. Образ Демона почти два десятилетия занимал воображение художника. Последняя картина Врубеля, скончавшегося в 1910 году, "Демон поверженный"— фантастически красочное изображение трагического одиночества и гибели "духа гордости и красоты." Вся фигура и лицо демона с мрачными, горящими глазами, выражают поверженную, но не смирившуюся силу.

20

уничтожа́ть to destroy
уничто́жить (perf.)
соотве́тствующий corresponding
у́ровень (m.) level
желе́зная доро́га railroad
у́зел knot, junction
кати́ть to roll
пополня́ть to fill up, supplement
доброво́льный voluntary
пове́рхностный superficial
производи́тельный productive
произво́дство production
ча́стный private

признава́ть to acknowledge, recognize
призна́ть (perf.)
вклад contribution
тамо́женный customs (adj.)
очути́ться to find one's self (in a place)
пренебреже́ние neglect, scorn
убеди́ть to convince
  perf. of: убежда́ть
снаря́ды ammunition
отре́чься to abdicate
  perf. of: отрека́ться
смета́ть to sweep away
смести́ (perf.)

РУ́ССКАЯ БУРЖУА́ЗИЯ

Ру́сский наро́д всегда́ люби́л торго́влю и занима́лся ею, когда́ и где то́лько мог. В са́мую ра́ннюю эпо́ху ру́сской исто́рии, во времена́ ки́евского госуда́рства, торго́вля и городски́е це́нтры име́ли важне́йшее значе́ние для наро́дной жи́зни. Тем не ме́нее, буржуа́зный класс, кото́рый сыгра́л таку́ю кру́пную векову́ю роль в исто́рии За́падной Евро́пы и Аме́рики, появля́ется в Росси́и о́чень по́здно—то́лько в 19 ве́ке—и о́чень ско́ро схо́дит со сце́ны: он уничтожа́ется, вме́сте с дворя́нством, в осе́нней револю́ции 1917 го́да.

Сло́жный и ме́дленный проце́сс разви́тия за́падноевропейской буржуазии с 12 века связан с ростом городов. Купцы, ремесленники и промышленники стекались в городах. Бежавшие от феодальной тесноты и обиды люди находили в городе свободу, порядок и работу. Городской воздух делал человека свободным. В России, в продолжение веков, город не мог играть соответствующей роли. Со времён удельного порядка, русский город возникал и развивался по приказу сперва княжеской, а позднее царской, власти. Бежавшие от крепостного права люди уходили на юг, в "дикое поле" степных областей к казакам, или на север, в леса к раскольникам. Города не были независимыми и не могли сделать русского человека свободным.

В московском государстве купцы представляли собой, по подобию крестьянских миров, торговые общины, организованные ради государственных целей. Обязанность платить подати ложилась одинаково на купцов и на крестьян. Купцы находились на том же социальном уровне как и крестьяне. Они не составляли среднего класса, стоявшего между крестьянством и аристократией, по подобию западноевропейского общества.

В 19 веке произошло несколько событий, содействовавших выделению русских купцов и промышленников в особый, буржуазный класс. Во первых, со времён Екатерины II прекратились жестокие преследования раскольников правительством.[1] Многие с окраин вернулись в центральные области страны и основали свои торговые и промышленные предприятия в Москве и в её окрестностях. Со времён московского государства Москва была одним из важнейших торговых центров России.

Росту буржуазии также сильно содействовало развитие железных дорог во второй половине 19 века. И тут Москва оказалась главным узлом. К концу века, десять разных железнодорожных линий расходились от Москвы во все стороны, соединяя её с Петербургом и Балтийским морем, с Западной Европой через Варшаву,

---

[1] См. гл. 11, стр. 55.

с Сиби́рью и А́зией че́рез Ни́жний Но́вгород, и с ю́жными плодоро́дными степя́ми и с черномо́рскими порта́ми. Ста́рая ру́сская посло́вица: "Москва́ у всей Руси́ под горо́й, в неё всё ка́тится," получи́ла но́вое значе́ние. Всё Междуре́чье от ве́рхней Во́лги до Оки́ покры́лось фа́бриками и заво́дами всех видо́в и разме́ров, кото́рые располага́лись, нере́дко на расстоя́нии всего́ двух и́ли трёх миль друг от дру́га, вдоль желе́зных доро́г.

Но са́мое си́льное влия́ние на подъём буржуа́зии оказа́ла отме́на крепостно́го пра́ва в 1861 году́. После́довавшее разложе́ние крестья́нской общи́ны,[2] бы́стрый рост дереве́нского пролетариа́та, дава́л промы́шленникам и купца́м оби́льную и дешёвую рабо́чую си́лу для их предприя́тий. А подня́вшиеся с низо́в "кулаки́" пополня́ли ряды́ само́й буржуа́зии и способ́ствовали её коли́чественному ро́сту. Почти́ все выдаю́щиеся моско́вские купе́ческие се́мьи вы́шли из рядо́в крестья́нства.

Бли́зкая генеалоги́ческая связь буржуа́зии с крестья́нством не препя́тствовала бы́строму подъёму культу́рного у́ровня ру́сских купцо́в и промы́шленников. За после́дние два десятиле́тия 19 ве́ка европе́йская архитекту́ра, обстано́вка, оде́жда и предме́ты ро́скоши всё сильне́е влия́ли на вку́сы и о́браз жи́зни состоя́тельных представи́телей торго́вли и промы́шленности. Каза́лось, что буржуа́зия доброво́льно проходи́ла тот путь европеиза́ции, на кото́рый дворя́нство наси́льно вступи́ло при Петре́ Вели́ком.

Но европеиза́ция ру́сской буржуа́зии была́ пове́рхностной и каса́лась то́лько вне́шних форм обихо́да. В основны́х проявле́ниях своего́ культу́рного разви́тия, буржуа́зия пошла́ свое́й, самостоя́тельной доро́гой. Гла́вное, она́ не после́довала у́мственному пути́ дворя́нства, она́ не увлекла́сь ни плода́ми францу́зского просвеще́ния, ни после́дующими произведе́ниями европе́йской мы́сли. Порождённая дворя́нством и вы́делившаяся из него́ интеллиге́нция оста́лась глубоко́ чужда́ и вражде́бна ру́сскому купе́честву. В раско́ле ме́жду э́тими двумя́ гру́ппами корени́тся основна́я ра́зница ме́жду ру́сской буржуа́-

---

[2] См. гл. 15, стр. 77–78.

зией и западноевропейским средним классом. Русская
дореволюционная интеллигенция не смотрела на развитие
производительных, промышленных сил России как на
положительное благо. Средний класс, соединяющий
представителей умственного, идейного и торгово-про-
мышленного труда, в России не успел сложиться.

Русских купцов и промышленников не привлекали
ни философские размышления, ни политические вопросы.
В этом несомненно сказалась тесная родственная связь
купечества с крестьянством. Старинная русская культура выражалась не столько словами и мыслями, сколько
красками и звуками: иконы и церковное пение были её
важнейшими достижениями. В 19 веке русская живопись
и музыка далеко вышли за пределы церковного мира,
сделались всецело светскими, но именно эти две области
искусства больше всего привлекали русскую буржуазию.
Тесная дружба связывала русских композиторов и художников с представителями торговли и промышленнности.
Писатели, в общем, в этом союзе не участвовали.

Буржуазия сделала очень много для расцвета искусства. Железнодорожный строитель Савва Иванович
Мамонтов основал частную оперу. Тут русское общество
впервые оценило русских композиторов. Здесь создался
успех оперы Римского-Корсакова "Садко," здесь испол-
нялся "Борис Годунов" Мусоргского. Текстильный
промышленник Павел Михайлович Третьяков создал
знаменитую галлерею, в которой были собраны картины
всех выдающихся русских художников 19 века. Купец
Сергей Иванович Щукин собрал редкую коллекцию новой
французской живописи—Гогена, Матисса, Пикассо и
многих других—покупая картины того или иного мастера
в то время, когда он ещё не был признан в Европе. Кроме
этих крупнейших примеров культурной деятельности буржуазии, было ещё большое количество других ценных
купеческих вкладов в искусство—коллекции картин,
икон, фарфора, и музеи, уже не говоря о денежной под-
держке многочисленных культурных учреждений.

В художественных и культурных вопросах буржуазия
проявляла большую самостоятельность. Но в своей по-

литической психологии, в своём отношении к государству, она не могла освободиться от традиционного, сложившегося в течение веков смирения русского человека перед верховной властью правительства.

Со времён образования московского государства правительство непосредственно участвовало в процессе образования частных состояний. Оно давало богатство как награду за хорошее политическое поведение, но оно всегда его могло и отнять. Это своеобразие оставило яркий след в политических взглядах русской буржуазии. Она продолжала смотреть на правительство, как на источник милостей и благ, как на силу, которая всё может, не только в области политики, но и в области экономики, тем более, что правительство давало промышленникам огромные казённые заказы и таможенное покровительство от иностранной конкуренции. Эта психология буржуазии препятствовала развитию её самостоятельного классового сознания и ясного понятия о её роли в русском обществе, о её общественных правах и обязанностях.

Отсутствие понятия социальных обязанностей особенно сильно сказалось в отношении буржуазии к рабочим. Россия вступила на путь индустриализации позднее западноевропейских стран, и поэтому могла сразу воспользоваться последними техническими открытиями, сделанными на Западе, и оборудовать свои фабрики новейшими заграничными машинами. Для обслуживания этих машин в распоряжении промышленников находился огромный, и поэтому дешёвый, фонд рабочих рук: деревенский, бросивший землю, пролетариат. Русская фабрика жадно и безжалостно поглощала этот человеческий материал, мало заботясь об условиях работы, о жилище, гигиене и пище рабочих.

Сложные, мощные технические орудия производства очутились в руках русских промышленников раньше, чем они успели задуматься о том, что технические перемены влекут за собой перемены социальных и политических сил и вносят новые проблемы в область человеческих отношений.

Смиренное отношение буржуазии к правительству, её пренебрежение к нуждам и настроениям рабочих и её отчуждённость от интеллигенции—вот три момента, которые решили её судьбу. В русской революции, начавшейся в 1905 году и свершившейся в 1917 году, русская буржуазия не смогла сыграть той решающей роли, которую французская буржуазия столь успешно сыграла в 1789 году.

Восстание 1905 года было вызвано не только успешной пропагандой революционной интеллигенции среди рабочих, но также неудачным исходом войны с Японией и всеобщим недовольством в стране. В октябре этого года, многовековое русское самодержавие перестало существовать. Николай II обещал народу основы гражданской свободы и созыв законодательного, выбранного всеми классами населения, учреждения—Государственной Думы.

В Думе буржуазия не сумела создать своей собственной партии. Лишённая дара политической мысли и речи, не развив самостоятельного политического языка, она разъединялась и входила в разные партии, то соединяясь с дворянством, то сближаясь с более умеренной интеллигенцией.

Русской буржуазии не удалось убедить ни правительство ни общество в том, что развитие промышленных сил страны приобретало всё большее значение, в особенности ввиду надвигающейся Первой мировой войны. Уже в 1915 году русская промышленность оказалась не в силах снабжать армию нужным количеством снарядов и оборудования. Это вызвало осенью этого года необходимость общего отступления, кровавые потери и нарастающее недовольство в самой армии. Тем временем, ещё задолго до начала войны, организованное революционное движение под руководством Ленина от рабочих перешло и на крестьян. Под давлением всех этих сил и общественного недовольства, Николай II весной 1917 года отрёкся от престола. Но Временное правительство, назначенное Думой, осенью этого же года было сметено большевитской революцией.

21

отверну́ться to turn away	**преиму́щество** advantage
perf. of: **отвора́чиваться**	**меньшинство́** minority
отверга́ть to repudiate	**большинство́** majority
отве́ргнуть (perf.)	**разма́х** sweep
необходи́мость (f.) necessity	**переде́л** redistribution
преоблада́ние predominance	**подчиня́ть** to subordinate
минова́ть to avoid	**подчини́ть** (perf.)
захва́т seizure	**пленя́ть** to captivate, charm
стяжа́ние acquisition	**наси́лие** force, violence
жесто́кий cruel	**отмере́ть** to atrophy
грубова́тость (f.) coarseness	perf. of: **отмира́ть**
спор dispute	**угнете́ние** oppression
вопреки́ contrary to	

ЛЕ́НИН И РЕВОЛЮ́ЦИЯ 1917 ГО́ДА

И́мя Ма́ркса с са́мого нача́ла 70 годо́в ста́ло по́льзоваться значи́тельным уваже́нием среди́ ру́сской чита́ющей пу́блики. Уже́ в 1872 году́ был переведён на ру́сский язы́к "Капита́л" и его́ крити́ческий ана́лиз противоре́чий капиталисти́ческого стро́я был хорошо́ изве́стен ру́сской интеллиге́нции. Под влия́нием э́того ана́лиза пе́рвые ру́сские маркси́сты отверну́лись от крестья́нства, кото́рое отве́ргло и столь разочарова́ло наро́дников, и обрати́лись к фабри́чным рабо́чим как к дви́жущей си́ле в объекти́вном социа́льно-экономи́ческом проце́ссе.

Сле́дуя предсказа́ниям "Капита́ла," ру́сские маркси́сты счита́ли, что социали́зм бу́дет результа́том экономи́ческой необходи́мости, что он насту́пит благодаря́ вну́треннему, неизбе́жному разложе́нию капитали́зма. Тем не ме́нее,

110

вопрос о применении исторических теорий Маркса к судьбам русского народа решался в отрицательном смысле. Россия была всё ещё страной земледельческой, с подавляющим преобладанием крестьянства, с отсталой промышленностью и с очень немногочисленным пролетариатом. Не трудно было сделать вывод, что эти условия препятствовали, по крайней мере в ближайшем будущем, эволюции капитализма предсказанной Марксом и его переходу в социализм.

Приспособление марксизма к русским условиям, признание возможности для России миновать зрелую стадию капиталистического развития и прямо перейти к социализму, до образования многочисленного рабочего класса, были сделаны Владимиром Ильичём Лениным. Ленин создатель русского коммунистического движения и революции 1917 года.

Отец Ленина был провинциальным чиновником, дослужившимся до генеральского чина и дворянства. Первым толчком, который определил революционное отношение Ленина к миру и жизни, была казнь его брата, замешанного в 1887 году в террористическом деле.

Ленин не теоретик марксизма, а теоретик революции. Он интересовался лишь одной темой—вопросом о захвате власти, о стяжании для этого всех сил. С этим связана прямолинейность, узость его миросозерцания, элементарность его лозунгов, обращённых к массам. Он один, задолго до революции, думал о том, что будет и что делать, когда власть будет завоёвана, и как организовать власть. Он допускал все средства для борьбы, для достижения целей революции. Добро было для него всё, что служит революции, зло—всё, что ей мешает. Он проповедывал жестокую политику, хотя лично не был жестоким человеком.

Ленин потому мог стать вождём революции и реализовать свой давно выработанный план, что он был типично русским человеком, а не типично русским интеллигентом. В его характере были черты типичные для простого русского народа: простота, цельность, грубоватость, практичность мысли. В своей личной жизни Ленин любил порядок и дисциплину, любил сидеть дома и работать, не любил бесконечных споров в кафе, к которым имела такую склонность русская радикальная интеллигенция. В философии, в искусстве, в духовной культуре Ленин был очень отсталый и элементарный человек. Многое было ему недоступно и неизвестно.

Для Ленина марксизм прежде всего был учением о диктатуре пролетариата. Поэтому, вопреки теориям Маркса, он видел в политической и экономической отсталости России преимущество для осуществления социальной революции. В стране, не привыкшей к правам и свободе граждан, легче осуществить диктатуру, чем в странах с развитым демократическим строем. В стране с мало развитым капитализмом легче организовать экономическую жизнь согласно коммунистическому плану.

В марксизме Ленина пролетариат, столь ещё немногочисленный в России, перестал быть эмпирической реальностью и стал идеей пролетариата. Носителем идеи может быть незначительное меньшинство. С 1905 года Ленин организует в главных промышленных центрах России сеть зачаточных органов диктатуры пролетариата, так называемых "Советов рабочих депутатов." Депутаты были выбраны из всех фабрик и заводов данного города. Отсюда впоследствии произошло название Советской России. А Петербург переименовали в Ленинград.[1]

Миф о народе, ранее вдохновляющий народников 70 годов, был заменён мифом о пролетариате. Различие между "буржуем" и "пролетарием" стало различием между злом и добром, несправедливостью и справедливостью, между заслуживающим порицания и одобрения. И в этом мифе по новому восстановился миф о русском народе: крестьянство, от которого отвернулись первые русские марксисты, в марксизме Ленина опять стало важнейшей силой. Оно было объявлено революционным классом и ближайшим союзником пролетариата.

Тем самым подготовленная Лениным революция приобретала стихийный размах. В начале 20 века две трети

---

[1] Во время Первой мировой войны Петербург назывался Петроградом.

крестьянства состояли из "бедняков," т. е. жили очень бедно и несомненно желали радикальных перемен. Кроме того, русские крестьяне вообще всегда считали присвоение земли дворянами такой же несправедливостью, как и крепостное право. Коллективное владение землёй было более свойственно русскому народу, благодаря существованию крестьянской общины. Крестьяне мечтали о переделе земли. Русская коммунистическая революция и совершила этот передел, отобрав всю землю у дворян и у частных владельцев, и передав её крестьянам.

Орудием для осуществления диктатуры пролетариата Ленин сделал коммунистическую партию. Целью Ленина было создание сильной организации, представляющей хорошо дисциплинированное меньшинство. Самая организация партии была уже диктатурой, каждый член партии был подчинён центральной и верховной власти вождя. Отрицание Лениным свободы внутри партии не обошлось без сопротивления его сотрудников.

На состоявшемся в Лондоне в 1903 году съезде партии— тогда известной под названием Социал-демократов—произошёл раскол на Большевиков, поддерживающих Ленина, и Меньшевиков, восстающих против него. Первоначально, слово большевики было совершенно бесцветно и означало только сторонников большинства. Но постепенно оно приобрело символический смысл. Со словом большевики связывается понятие силы, со словом меньшевики—уже не просто меньшинство, а понятие сравнительной слабости. В бурной стихии революции 1917 года, восставшие народные массы пленялись большевизмом как силой, которая больше даст, в то время как меньшевизм представлялся слабым, намеренным дать народу меньше.

Русская коммунистическая революция в значительной степени была определена Первой мировой войной и её неудачным для России исходом. Это был самый благоприятный момент для производства опыта коммунистической революции. Война способствовала победе Ленина. Именно война с её навыками, методами и переживаниями породила новый тип русского интеллигента. Появился новый тип милитаризованного человека. В отличие от старого типа

интеллигента он был гладко выбрит, подтянут, сдержан,
с твёрдой походкой. Он имел вид завоевателя, который не
стесняется в средствах и всегда готов к насилию, одержим
волей к власти и хочет быть не только разрушителем и
критиком, но и строителем и организатором. Именно такие
люди из рабочих и крестьян нужны были Ленину, чтобы
сделать революцию. Её нельзя было бы сделать с мечтательным, сострадательным, мягким и добрым типом старой
интеллигенции 19 века.

Большевизм вошёл в русскую жизнь, как в высшей
степени милитаризованная сила. Проблема власти была
основной и центральной у Ленина. Но такой же она бывала
и раньше в русской истории, во времена московского
государства и Петра Великого. Ленин соединил в себе две
исторические традиции: традицию русской интеллигенции,
состоящей в искании справедливого порядка жизни, и традицию русской государственной власти, склонной к не-
ограниченному самодержавию и деспотизму. В 19 веке
эти две традиции и их носители—интеллигенция и правительство—находились в смертельной вражде и борьбе.
В 20 веке Ленин их соединил.

Насилие над людьми, диктатуру, Ленин считал вре-
менным явлением. Он думал, что государство отомрёт,
когда под влиянием принуждения, люди привыкнут соблю-
дать элементарные условия общественности, приспособятся
к новым условиям. Ленин не признавал в человеке никакого внутреннего начала, не верил в дух и свободу духа.
Но он бесконечно верил в общественную муштровку человека, верил, что принудительная общественная организация может создать какого угодно нового человека. Одного
он не предвидел—что диктатура пролетариата, усилив
государственную власть, может принять совершенно новые
формы классового угнетения. Это процесс, который раз-
вился в Советской России при преемнике Ленина, Иосифе
Виссарионовиче Сталине.

осуществле́ние realization, conversion into reality
разоре́ние devastation
восстановля́ть to restore
восстанови́ть (perf.)
изли́шек surplus
усту́пка concession
уси́ливаться to gather strength
хи́трость (f.) cunning
ту́ловище torso
о́спина pock mark
связь (f.) connection

жа́жда thirst
мощь (f.) might
кирпи́ч brick
усоверше́нствовать to perfect
ра́мка frame, framework
о́трасль (f.) branch
держа́ва power (nation)
располага́ть to dispose
зажи́точный well-to-do
го́лод famine
спрос demand
схо́дство resemblance

СОЦИА́ЛЬНЫЙ СТРОЙ СО́ЗДАННЫЙ СТА́ЛИНЫМ

Большеви́стская па́ртия, кото́рую в тече́ние мно́гих лет создава́л Ле́нин, должна́ была́ дать образе́ц но́вой организа́ции всей страны́. Ле́нин не до́жил до осуществле́ния э́того пла́на. Наоборо́т, в после́дние го́ды жи́зни ему́ пришло́сь отступи́ть от социалисти́ческого переустро́йства Росси́и. Разоре́ние и упа́док произво́дственных сил, вы́званные поте́рями во вре́мя Пе́рвой мирово́й войны́, а зате́м гражда́нской войно́й и иностра́нной вое́нной интерве́нцией 1918–20 годо́в, заста́вили Ле́нина провозгласи́ть, в 1921 году́, "Но́вую экономи́ческую поли́тику," изве́стную под сокраще́нием Нэп.

При Нэ́пе в изве́стных преде́лах была́ восстано́влена свобо́да ча́стной торго́вли. Крестья́нам разреша́лась свобо́дная прода́жа изли́шков их произво́дства на ры́нке. А ча́стным предпринима́телям бы́ло разрешено́ открыва́ть ме́лкие промы́шленные предприя́тия. Э́ти ме́ры спосо́бствовали восстановле́нию наро́дного хозя́йства.

Несмотря́ на части́чные усту́пки капитали́зму и иде́е ча́стной со́бственности, сде́ланные при Нэ́пе, госуда́рственная власть, осно́ванная на диктату́ре пролетариа́та, продолжа́ла уси́ливаться. Неизбе́жным после́дствием э́того явле́ния бы́ло разви́тие бы́стро расту́щей бюрокра́тии, находя́щейся в зави́симости и под руково́дством коммуни́стической па́ртии. И́менно при э́той нараста́ющей бюрократиза́ции Сове́тской Росси́и сложи́лся и осуществи́лся план Ста́лина захвати́ть власть.

До револю́ции 1917 го́да Ста́лин игра́л в па́ртии ничто́жную роль, послу́шно исполня́я во́лю и поруче́ния Ле́нина. Но уже́ тогда́ он отлича́лся исключи́тельной практи́ческой хи́тростью и беспринци́пностью, никогда́ не остана́вливаясь ни пе́ред каки́ми сре́дствами.

Ста́лин был челове́к ро́ста ни́же сре́днего, с дли́нным ту́ловищем и коро́ткими нога́ми, с кре́пким сложе́нием, с лицо́м покры́тым о́спинами, с ма́ленькими, тёмно-ка́рими глаза́ми и ни́зким лбом. По у́мственным спосо́бностям он стоя́л ни́же сре́днего у́ровня парти́йного рабо́тника, был ма́ло культу́рным и ма́ло образо́ванным челове́ком.

По́сле револю́ции 1917 го́да, Ста́лин терпели́во завя́зывает ли́чные свя́зи в парти́йной верху́шке. В 1922 году́ он ока́зывается подходя́щим кандида́том на ме́сто секретаря́ па́ртии. Под коне́ц жи́зни Ле́нин переста́л доверя́ть Ста́лину, неоднокра́тно осужда́л его́ и намерева́лся его́ смени́ть, но у́мер в 1924 году́ не осуществи́в э́того реше́ния.

По́сле сме́рти Ле́нина Ста́лин продолжа́ет поднима́ться в парти́йной иера́рхии. Он бьёт проти́вников не рассужде́нием, а голоса́ми, заране́е подо́бранными в ряда́х парти́йной бюрокра́тии. Отстрани́в своего́ гла́вного врага́, Тро́цкого, от вла́сти сра́зу по́сле сме́рти Ле́нина, он зате́м принима́ется за свои́х вре́менных сою́зников, Зино́вьева и Ка́менева. Его́ ме́тод—удаля́ть си́льных сопе́рников и собира́ть вокру́г себя́ послу́шных, зави́симых люде́й. Всё подчиня́ется его́ жа́жде вла́сти. С 1927 го́да Ста́лин стано́вится самовла́стным прави́телем и принима́ется за строи́тельство социалисти́ческого о́бщества, за организа́цию всей страны́ по образцу́ стро́я большеви́стской па́ртии.

Ле́нин отрица́л свобо́ду внутри́ па́ртии и э́то отрица́ние свобо́ды бы́ло перенесено́ Ста́линым на всю страну́. Весь ру́сский наро́д оказа́лся подчинённым не то́лько диктату́ре коммунисти́ческой па́ртии и её центра́льному о́ргану, но и доктри́не самого́ дикта́тора. Отрица́ется свобо́да мы́сли и со́вести. Вы́сшей це́нностью признаётся не челове́к и его́ ли́чное благополу́чие, а экономи́ческая мощь госуда́рства. Ли́чность рассма́тривается лишь как сре́дство и ору́дие для э́той це́ли, как кирпи́ч, ну́жный для строи́тельства социалисти́ческого о́бщества.

При Ста́лине бы́ли устро́ены многочи́сленные концентрацио́нные лагеря́, гла́вным о́бразом на се́вере, вдоль Беломо́рского побере́жья, и в отдалённых частя́х Сиби́ри. Заключённые стро́или кана́лы, рабо́тали в каменно-у́гольных ша́хтах и обслу́живали ра́зные промы́шленные предприя́тия. К середи́не 30 годо́в число́ ла́герников, по всей вероя́тности, дошло́ до пяти́ миллио́нов челове́к и возросло́, накану́не Второ́й мирово́й войны́, до десяти́ миллио́нов.

Вла́стное принужде́ние как гла́вное ору́дие социа́льной револю́ции бы́ло офо́рмлено Ле́ниным. Ста́лин разви́л, усоверше́нствовал и примени́л э́то ору́дие уже́ не в ра́мках одно́й коммунисти́ческой па́ртии, а в преде́лах всего́ сове́тского госуда́рства. Но он та́кже воспо́льзовался вторы́м насле́дием Ле́нина: традицио́нной мечто́й, руководя́щей ру́сской интеллиге́нцией с са́мого нача́ла её возникнове́ния, об устро́ении лу́чшей, справедли́вой жи́зни. Сознава́я, что организова́ть власть, подчини́ть себе́ ма́ссы нельзя́ одно́й си́лой и чи́стым наси́лием, Ста́лин создаёт си́мвол и иде́ю для обще́ственного еди́нства. Он провозглаша́ет иде́ю о построе́нии социали́зма в одно́й стра́не: т. е. в Сове́тском Сою́зе, и объявля́ет, для руково́дства э́тим строи́тельством с 1929 го́да, пятиле́тние пла́ны разви́тия всех о́траслей наро́дного хозя́йства.

Э́ти пла́ны игра́ют роль принуди́тельных зако́нов. Выполне́ние предпи́санных объёмов произво́дства явля́ется для всех и ка́ждого обяза́тельной до́лжностью. Но э́тим принужде́нием далеко́ не исче́рпывается значе́ние пятиле́ток. Пятиле́тний план был не то́лько тре́звой, сухо́й, прозаи́ческой, статисти́ческой реа́льностью. В созна́нии наро́да он превраща́ется, в осо́бенности по нача́лу, в вдохновля́ющую, поэти́ческую, тво́рческую мечту́, в ору́дие и сре́дство для акти́вного измене́ния жи́зни, для созда́ния мо́щной, бога́той, промы́шленной страны́.

Гла́вное внима́ние пятиле́ток обращено́ на уско́ренное, гига́нтское разви́тие промы́шленности, пре́жде всего́ тяжё-лой инду́стрии. Ну́жды наро́да, лёгкая промы́шленность, производя́щая предме́ты широ́кого потребле́ния, далеко́ отступа́ют на за́дний план по сравне́нию с постро́йкой каменно-у́гольных шахт, нефтяны́х про́мыслов, желе́зных и ме́дных руднико́в, электри́ческих ста́нций и машино-строи́тельных заво́дов. Из земледе́льческой страны́ Сове́тская Росси́я превраща́ется в промы́шленную держа́ву.

Одновре́менно с бы́строй индустриализа́цией Ста́лин про-вёл радика́льную реорганиза́цию крестья́нства созда́нием коллекти́вных хозя́йств и́ли колхо́зов. Ча́стные и ме́лкие о́б-щинные крестья́нские хозя́йства бы́ли переведены́ и соединены́ в кру́пные земледе́льческие предприя́тия, осно́ванные на механиза́ции произво́дства, т. е. располага́ющие тра́кторами, комба́йнами и други́ми сельско-хозя́йственными маши́нами.

Коллективиза́ция дере́вни представля́ла собо́й глубо-ча́йший обще́ственный переворо́т, це́лую но́вую револю́цию. Она́ проводи́лась не то́лько для того́, чтобы осуществи́ть механиза́цию се́льского хозя́йства и тем са́мым повы́сить земледе́льческое произво́дство, но та́кже для того́, чтобы уничто́жить ча́стную со́бственность на сре́дства произ-во́дства и тем са́мым укрепи́ть госуда́рственный контро́ль над земледе́лием. Накану́не Пе́рвой мирово́й войны́ за-жи́точные крестья́не—кулаки́ составля́ли 15% всего́ се́ль-ского населе́ния, а крестья́не сре́днего доста́тка—20%. При Нэ́пе ча́стные элеме́нты в дере́вне опя́ть получи́ли возмо́жность расти́ и развива́ться. Когда́ прави́тельство на́чало их наси́льно загоня́ть в колхо́зы, они́ оказа́ли упо́рное сопротивле́ние, обрати́вшееся в жесто́кую, кро-ва́вую борьбу́ и разоре́ние дере́вни. То́чных да́нных о числе́ поги́бших в э́той но́вой, агра́рной револю́ции нет, но встреча́ются ци́фры от пяти́ до двена́дцати миллио́нов крестья́н.

После́довавший зате́м в 1932–33 году́ го́лод та́кже унёс в моги́лу не́сколько миллио́нов челове́к.

Но́вое, колхо́зное крестья́нство сближа́ется, по своему́ положе́нию, и о́бразу жи́зни, с кла́ссом промы́шленных рабо́чих. Крестья́не, как и рабо́чие, тру́дятся на госуда́рственных предприя́тиях (колхо́з лишь форма́льно чи́слится обще́ственным предприя́тием), находя́щихся в по́лном распоряже́нии коммунисти́ческой па́ртии. Крестья́не, как и рабо́чие, явля́ются исполни́телями еди́ного наро́дно-хозя́йственного пла́на и веду́т свою́ рабо́ту в соотве́тствии с э́тим обяза́тельным для них пла́ном. Крестья́не, как и рабо́чие, явля́ются принуди́тельно организо́ванной рабо́чей си́лой. Они́ прикреплены́ к ме́сту свое́й рабо́ты, подчинены́ парти́йным надсмо́трщикам и не име́ют пра́ва отка́зываться от рабо́ты и меня́ть ме́сто рабо́ты.

Тре́тьим основны́м кла́ссом, по́сле крестья́н и рабо́чих, явля́ется сове́тская интеллиге́нция. По объёму э́тот класс превосхо́дит во мно́го раз ста́рую дореволюцио́нную интеллиге́нцию. Бы́стрый рост индустриализа́ции со́здал грома́дный спрос на люде́й с вы́сшим техни́ческим и академи́ческим образова́нием. Но по своему́ положе́нию э́тот класс стои́т, как крестья́не и рабо́чие, в по́лной материа́льной зави́симости от прави́тельства и под его́ иде́йным контро́лем. Интеллиге́нция преврати́лась в служи́лый класс специали́стов по культу́рным дела́м. Гла́вная их зада́ча состои́т в том, что они́ должны́ помога́ть прави́тельству в перевоспита́нии масс, в возде́йствии на мышле́ние наро́да, в созда́нии но́вого ти́па челове́ка, гото́вого бесприкосло́вно слива́ться с коллекти́вом и ста́вить служе́ние госуда́рству вы́ше свои́х ли́чных интере́сов. Сове́тские писа́тели пря́мо называ́лись Ста́линым "инжене́рами челове́ческой души́."

По своему́ стро́ю, со́зданное Ста́линым госуда́рство име́ло большо́е схо́дство с моско́вским крепостны́м ца́рством 17 ве́ка. Все кла́ссы населе́ния поста́влены в крепостну́ю зави́симость от госуда́рства. На Руси́ жить тогда́ зна́чило служи́ть. Э́то ве́рно и сейча́с, с той ра́зницей, что совреме́нные ме́тоды и приёмы принужде́ния неизмери́мо возросли́ по сравне́нию с про́шлым.

23

итог sum total
уровень (m.) level
давление pressure
обучение instruction
усилие effort
примкнуть to join
  perf. of: примыкать
рабство slavery
порабощение enslavement
проявление display, mani-
  festation
ослаблять to weaken
  ослабить (perf.)

барсук badger
страдание suffering
разгром havoc, devastation
размер meter (of verse), also:
  dimension, size
самоубийство suicide
упадок decline
взыскание penalty
оттепель (f.) thaw
изгнание expulsion
наблюдать to observe
ложь (f.) lie
сомневаться to doubt

СОВЕТСКАЯ КУЛЬТУРА

Рассматривая итоги советской культуры, необходимо раз-
личать два вопроса. Во первых, насколько поднялся
культурный уровень народных масс, насколько выросли
и распространились грамотность, образование, знания,
усвоение культурных памятников и художественных цен-
ностей? Во вторых, что происходит в области нового
творчества? Создаются ли новые культурные достижения и, если они имеются, то в каких отраслях культуры?
Как действует давление правительства, отрицание свободы мысли и слова, на творческие силы народа?

Ответ на первый вопрос является положительным. В
области культурного просвещения широких масс достиг-
нуты серьёзные успехи. Советское правительство уделило
большое внимание ликвидации неграмотности и введению

всеобщего, бесплатного, первоначального обучения. Наряду с организацией начальных школ правительство употребляет большие усилия для развития средних школ и высших учебных заведений, вузов. Очень значительные средства выделяются на научную работу и научные учреждения, но также на расширение сети театров, кино и музеев.

Все эти усилия исходят из соображения, что от воспитания будущих поколений зависит закрепление всего того, что было создано и перестроено революцией. Народное образование поэтому является прежде всего политическим. Во всех своих отраслях оно основано на обязательном обучении диалектического материализма, теорий Маркса и Ленина и истории коммунистической партии. Произведения, посвящённые этим вопросам, издаются и расходятся массовыми тиражами в несколько миллионов экземпляров. Но и художественная литература имеет свою многомиллионную читающую публику. Не только советские писатели, но и русские классики 19 века и многие переведённые произведения мировой литературы изданы миллионными тиражами. В особенности Пушкин и Толстой пользуются огромной популярностью.

Ответ на второй вопрос, встающий при обзоре советской культуры, вопрос о состоянии нового советского творчества, гораздо сложнее. Большие творческие достижения сделаны советскими учёными в области науки и техники. Поскольку работа единичного человека не противоречит генеральной линии коммунистической партии, поскольку она, наоборот, способствует развитию промышленной, технической, и в особенности военной мощи государства, она получает щедрую поддержку от правительства. В этом направлении и в указанных пределах, личности предоставляется свобода творчества.

Это крупное, но не единственное проявление культурных достижений. Рядом с многочисленными фигурами научных и технических творцов в советской культуре также выделяются одинокие фигуры лиц, создавших себе имя ещё до революции и продолжавших своё творчество в России при советской власти. Главными являются писа́тель Макси́м Го́рький и компози́тор Серге́й Серге́евич Проко́фьев.

Макси́м Го́рький счита́ется родонача́льником сове́тской литерату́ры. Он был пе́рвым среди́ кру́пных писа́телей 19 ве́ка, кото́рый вы́шел из низо́в о́бщества. С пе́рвых свои́х расска́зов, появи́вшихся в 1890 года́х, он воспе́л си́лу, тала́нт и мора́льные ка́чества боояко́в и бродя́г, находя́щихся "на дне" жи́зни, но сохрани́вших ве́ру в досто́инство и тво́рческие си́лы Челове́ка. Го́рький примкну́л к революцио́нному движе́нию, призыва́я наро́д в свои́х произведе́ниях восста́ть про́тив "ра́бства де́нег," кото́рое пришло́ в Росси́ю на сме́ну "ра́бства земли́." На рост ча́стной промы́шленности и капитали́зма Го́рький смотре́л, как на но́вое порабоще́ние наро́да, кото́рое смени́ло бы́вшее, дереве́нское крепостно́е пра́во.

В социалисти́ческом о́бществе Го́рький наде́ялся и мечта́л уви́деть небыва́лый расцве́т свобо́ды челове́ческой ли́чности. Необходи́мо отме́тить, что по́сле револю́ции Го́рький не посвяти́л ни одного́ худо́жественного произведе́ния изображе́нию Сове́тской Росси́и (в кото́рой его́ мечта́ о свобо́де ли́чности не осуществля́лась), а продолжа́л, до са́мой свое́й сме́рти в 1936 году́, писа́ть о "тёмном ца́рстве" дореволюцио́нных купцо́в, промы́шленников и консервати́вных интеллиге́нтов.

Проко́фьев с 1908 го́да на́чал выступа́ть как пиани́ст с исполне́нием свои́х произведе́ний, пленя́я свое́й све́жестью, мо́лодостью и жизнера́достностью. Во вре́мя револю́ции он поки́нул Росси́ю и верну́лся туда́ то́лько в 1932 году́. Он за́нял ва́жное ме́сто в сове́тской музыка́льной культу́ре, в осо́бенности в о́бласти о́перного и бале́тного тво́рчества и му́зыки к ря́ду выдаю́щихся кинофи́льмов, наприме́р к фи́льмам "Алекса́ндр Не́вский" и "Ива́н Гро́зный." В нача́ле Второ́й мирово́й войны́ рома́н Толсто́го "Война́ и мир" вдохнови́л Проко́фьева написа́ть о́перу того́ же назва́ния.

Тре́тье проявле́ние тво́рческих сил в сове́тской культу́ре свя́зано с переме́ной в полити́ческой обстано́вке. Появле́ние худо́жественных произведе́ний бы́ло после́дствием, результа́том э́тих переме́н, а не самостоя́тель-

ной, дви́жущей си́лой культу́рного подъёма. В разви́тии
Сове́тской Росси́и бы́ло два пери́ода, когда́ давле́ние
прави́тельства на наро́д бы́ло осла́блено. Пе́рвый тако́й
моме́нт отступле́ния от при́нципа по́лного вла́стного
принужде́ния наста́л с объявле́ния Ле́ниным Нэ́па[1] в
1921 году́, второй—по́сле сме́рти Ста́лина в 1953 году́. Оба
ра́за после́довало оживле́ние тво́рческой мы́сли, вы́шли
многочи́сленные живы́е, оригина́льные худо́жественные
произведе́ния, в осо́бенности в о́бласти литерату́ры.

Для книг появи́вшихся во вре́мя Нэ́па характе́рно
правди́вое описа́ние мучи́тельных страда́ний, жертв и
потрясе́ний, кото́рых потре́бовала револю́ция. В 1924
году́ появля́ется рома́н Леони́да Макси́мовича Лео́нова
"Барсуки́," кото́рый даёт я́ркую карти́ну крестья́нского
сопротивле́ния намере́ниям сове́тской вла́сти собра́ть с
дере́вни непоси́льный для крестья́н нало́г. В 1925 году́
Алекса́ндр Алекса́ндрович Фаде́ев начина́ет писа́ть "Раз-
гро́м"—психологи́ческий ана́лиз партиза́нского отря́да во
вре́мя гражда́нской войны́. Э́та психоло́гия то́нко изобра-
жена́ не то́лько в положи́тельных, но и отрица́тельных
проявле́ниях и отте́нках. В том же, 1925 году́, изве́ст-
нейший сове́тский писа́тель Михаи́л Алекса́ндрович
Шо́лохов начина́ет рабо́тать над эпи́ческим рома́ном
"Ти́хий Дон." Центра́льная те́ма—вну́тренние колеба́ния
гла́вного геро́я, казака́ Григо́рия Ме́лихова, ме́жду но́вой
и ста́рой жи́знью, ме́жду сторо́нниками революцио́нного
движе́ния и его́ проти́вниками.

К пери́оду Нэ́па та́кже отно́сится тво́рчество сове́тского
поэ́та Влади́мира Влади́мировича Маяко́вского. Мая-
ко́вский стреми́лся сде́лать иску́сство ма́ссовым досто-
я́нием, созда́ть но́вую, агитацио́нную поэ́зию "площаде́й
и у́лиц," обращённую к ма́ссам и досту́пную им. Он
вводи́л разгово́рную речь, ора́торские призы́вы, поли-
ти́ческий и бытово́й слова́рь в свою́ поэ́зию и прида́л
стиху́ но́вые фо́рмы ритми́ческого разнообра́зия, смеши-
вая ра́зные разме́ры—ямб, хоре́й и други́е. В 1930 году́
Маяко́вский поко́нчил жизнь самоуби́йством.

---

[1] См. гл. 22, стр. 115–16.

При Сталине давление власти на направление народного творчества было прочно установлено и привело к резкому упадку художественного достоинства характерных для этого периода произведений. Темы творчества теперь оффициально задаются правительством не только писателям, но и художникам и даже композиторам. Главные сюжеты: жизнь коммунистической партии, её борьба за генеральную линию, создание промышленной базы, социалистическая переделка деревни, ликвидация кулачества как класса. Писателям предлагают перестать быть художниками и превратиться в пропагандистов правительства. Невыполнение партийного заказа нередко приводило к суровым взысканиям. Даже музыка не избежала политического давления. Крупнейший советский композитор Дмитрий Дмитриевич Шостакович в 40 годах подвергся суровой критике за "субъективизм настроений и чрезмерное усложнение музыкального языка."

Есть писатели, которые чувствуют себя настоящими художниками и перестают писать. Выдающийся поэт Борис Леонидович Пастернак прекращает творческую работу и занимается переводами—сперва грузинских поэтов, потом "Фауста" Гёте и затем Шекспировских трагедий. Характерно его замечание: "Маяковский застрелился, а я перевожу."

После смерти Сталина наступил второй период смягчения правительственного давления на народ, так называемая "оттепель." Эта оттепель имела особое значение и силу, потому что она наступила вслед за историческими впечатлениями, вынесенными русским народом из Второй мировой войны. В Советской России эта война называется Великой, или Второй, отечественной войной. Первой было нашествие Наполеона в 1812 году. Параллель в названии основана на том, что главной целью военных действий России в обоих случаях было изгнание врага с отечественной территории. Но параллель применима и для другого сравнения. Наполеоновские войны, походы русских войск в Европу, впервые дали русскому обществу возможность непосредственно ознакомиться с западноевропейскими порядками и сравнить их с русскими. Отсюда вышли Декабристы,[2] тут находятся истоки русской интеллигенции.[3]

То же самое повторилось, в более широком масштабе, во время и после окончания Второй мировой войны. Заграничные походы советской армии впервые дали широким массам советских солдат-граждан возможность непосредственно наблюдать чужие порядки. Всё, что они видели, они сравнивали не только с действительностью в Советской России, но и с тем, что советское правительство сообщало им о жизни и людях заграницей.

Выводы из этих наблюдений и сравнений стоят в центре тех умственных брожений и исканий, которые народ получил возможность хоть частично высказывать после смерти Сталина. Самое значительное произведение этого времени—роман Бориса Леонидовича Пастернака "Доктор Живаго," за который автору в 1958 году была присуждена Нобелевская премия. От этой чести писатель принуждён был отказаться ввиду суровой критики, поднявшейся против него в Советском Союзе. Главное лицо романа, доктор медицины Живаго—искусный диагност, который редко ошибается в своём определении болезни. Недуг, который Живаго рассматривает с объективностью учёного и с болью человека, страстно любящего жизнь, это порабощение мысли и слова в Советской России. Лечение от этой болезни диагност Живаго находит в христианской религии и её учении о достоинстве и духовной свободе человеческой личности.

Другое важное произведение периода "оттепели"—роман Владимира Дудинцева "Не хлебом единым" (слова взяты из Евангелия), появившейся в конце 1956 года. В этой книге стоит знаменательная фраза: "Кто научился думать, того полностью лишить свободы нельзя." Это говорит герой романа после своего возвращения из сибирского концлагеря.

Если оглянуться на исторической путь, пройденный русской мыслью, то эти слова приобретают величайшее

[2] См. гл. 15, стр. 75–76.
[3] См. гл. 16, стр. 79–84.

значе́ние. Ду́мать зна́чит иска́ть пра́вды. В нове́йших произведе́ниях сове́тской литерату́ры э́то сло́во неоднокра́тно повторя́ется. Наро́д и́щет пра́вды. Он и́щет её в тех двух значе́ниях, кото́рые э́то сло́во име́ет на ру́сском языке́.[4] Он зна́ет, что совреме́нное сове́тское о́бщество не осно́вано на справедли́вости, что челове́к порабощён, как нигде́ в ми́ре, что свобо́да явля́ется достоя́нием привиллеги́рованного меньшинства́ коммунисти́ческой аристокра́тии. И ру́сский наро́д та́кже зна́ет, что мно́гие прави́тельственные сообще́ния о жи́зни за рубежо́м и в само́й стране́ не соотве́тствуют действи́тельности, а осно́ваны на лжи.

В каки́е фо́рмы в дальне́йшем бу́дущем вы́льются э́ти мы́сли и ду́мы, никто́ не мо́жет предсказа́ть. Но что они́ существу́ют и занима́ют широ́кие слои́ населе́ния, в э́том сове́тские произведе́ния после́дних лет не позволя́ют сомнева́ться.

---

[4] См. стр. 80.

24

отразиться to be reflected perf. of: **отражаться**
проповедывать to preach
азбука alphabet
Евангелие Gospel
приобщать to acquaint, bring close to
  приобщить (perf.)
торжественность (f.) solemnity
судебник law code
достояние legacy (abstract)
совпадать to coincide
  совпасть (perf.)
заимствование borrowing, imitation

приспособление adaptation
опередить to outstrip
взаимный mutual
меткость (f.) exactness
поток stream, flow
исчезать to disappear
  исчезнуть (perf.)
сокращение abbreviation, contraction
слог syllable
плавный fluent
гибкий pliable
переимчивый imitative

РАЗВИТИЕ РУССКОГО ЛИТЕРАТУРНОГО ЯЗЫКА

В истории русского языка отразилось всё развитие русского народа, все главные эпохи его жизни.

Одним из самых знаменательных событий в истории культуры и просвещения всего славянства был приезд братьев миссионеров Кирилла и Мефодия около 863 года из Византии в Моравию. Их послал византийский император Михаил III, чтобы проповедывать христианство местному населению на его родном, болгарском языке. Братья знали болгарский язык, так как они были родом из Салоники, тогда окружённого болгарскими поселе-ниями. Ещё до въезда в Моравию Кирилл составил с большим лингвистическим чутьём славянскую азбуку и начал переводить Евангелие на болгарский язык.

Славянские языки, при всех различиях, существующих между ними в 9–10 веках, были всё же настолько ещё близки друг к другу, что письменный язык, созданный Кириллом и Мефодием на болгарской основе, оказался вполне понятным и в других славянских землях. Этот язык стал таким образом как бы международным письменным языком славянства в раннюю пору его истории. Громадное культурное значение переводов Кирилла и Мефодия заключалось в том, что они приобщали славянство к византийской культуре, сохранившей, хотя и в своеобразной форме, прочную связь с античным миром. В то время, как на западе Европы латынь оставалась единственным языком религии и культуры, непонятным для низших классов народа, на Востоке христианство распространялось на языке доступном широким массам населения.

На Руси письменный славянский язык появился вместе с принятием христианства в конце 10 века. При списывании старославянских текстов и при составлении оригинальных текстов по старославянским образцам, древнерусские литераторы иногда невольно, а иногда и сознательно, допускали отступления от источников в пользу своей родной речи. Этот старославянский язык русской редакции и был первым письменным языком Киевской Руси.

Благодаря быстрому развитию материальной культуры в городских, торговых центрах Киевской Руси, письменный язык употреблялся не только для церковных рукописей, но и для документов светского содержания. Каждый из этих разделов письменности имел свой особый стиль речи. На церковно-книжном стиле лежит печать торжественности и учёности. Полярной противоположностью этому стилю является речь в документах светского содержания, основанная на обиходных средствах языка. К числу крупнейших памятников этой бытовой письменности относится киевский судебник "Русская Правда." Она написана деловым языком, в ней отражается забота о материальных ценностях, о безопасности капитала.

К числу самых важных культурных достояний, полученных Московской Русью по наследству от Киевской, принадлежит письменный язык. За время, отделяющее эпоху возвышения Москвы от упадка Киева, в живом говоре русского народа произошло очень много изменений. В бытовую жизнь Руси вошло большое количество новых слов. Многие из них были татарского происхождения. Одни обозначали одежду или предметы домашнего хозяйства. Другие касались местной администрации и татарского правления.

Поэтому письменный язык киевской эпохи для московской Руси 15–17 веков был уже вполне книжным. Разговорная речь Москвы далеко ушла от языка киевских памятников не только церковной, но и светской письменности. А преобладание духовной, церковной культуры, отсутствие светских влияний на московский ум, препятствовали слиянию книжного и разговорного языка. Литературные памятники обиходной речи московской эпохи поэтому скудны. Самым замечательным из этих памятников были произведения протопопа Аввакума, выдающегося вождя церковного раскола в 17 веке. Его "Житиё" написано живым, ярким, идиоматическим языком, пестрящим пословицами и поговорками.

При Петре Великом понятие книжного языка перестало совпадать с представлением о языке церковно-славянском. Появился новый русский литературный язык, в котором большая роль принадлежала переводам с западноевропейских языков. В процессе этих переводов русский язык должен был приобретать средства нужные для передачи соответствующих понятий западноевропейской цивилизации. Эта цель достигалась двумя путями. Из них более простой—заимствование термина. Привычными и своими для русского языка становились французские, немецкие, голландские, английские слова, касающиеся военного и морского дела, государственной администрации, науки, техники и ежедневной жизни вообще, вроде: солдат, лагерь, марш, гавань, киль, руль, император, министр, горизонт, температура, практика, фут, сюртук, фрукты. . . . Второй путь переводов сложнее. Он состоял в приспособлении русских слов к буквальным переводам соответствующих иностранных слов, например: предрассудок, переворот, трогательный, противоречие.

В петровскую эпоху также меняется старая церковнославянская азбука. Пётр её преобразует, начертание букв упрощается, удалены лишние буквы. Новой, гражданской азбукой начали писать все светские книги, а старую азбуку продолжали употреблять в богослужебных книгах. Создание новой азбуки обозначало резкий раздел между светской литературой и церковной, между новой и старой русской культурой.

Вопрос о взаимном отношении разговорного русского языка и церковно-славянского был поднят в середине 18 века великим учёным и поэтом Михаилом Васильевичем Ломоносовым. Он видит в церковно-славянском языке как бы основание для языка русского. По его мнению, только тот может правильно писать по русски, кто тщательно изучал церковно-славянские книги. Ломоносов составляет русскую грамматику, первую научную разработку языка.

Но блестящие мысли Ломоносова опередили его век. До создания единого русского языка было ещё далеко. Увлечение русского дворянства французской культурой во второй половине 18 века коснулось и языка. Привычка читать и говорить по французски, обучение французскому языку с детства, создали двуязычную атмосферу. Повседневным явлением стали разного рода галлицизмы, т. е. обороты речи буквально переведённые с французского. Таким образом, после раздела между светским и церковным языком, окончательно совершившегося при Петре Великом, произошло новое раздвоение речи. К концу 18 века язык образованного общества отделился от языка простого русского народа.

Для того, чтобы русский литературный язык стал подлинно национальным, нужно было разрушить все эти преграды и соединить все эти элементы речи в цельное единство. Это сделал Пушкин в начале 19 века.

Народную речь Пушкин называл "живым и кипящим источником." Охотно беседуя с крестьянами и нищими, поэт не упускал случая записывать поговорки, пословицы, песни и сказки, которые он слышал, восторгался меткостью и образностью простонародных выражений и вводил их в свои произведения. Но Пушкин также понимал, что за церковно-славянским языком стоит многовековая культура слова. В тех случаях, когда поэт говорит о высоких и важных предметах или переносит читателя в дальнюю эпоху прошлого, церковно-славянские слова, дышащие торжественностью, величием и напоминающие о седой старине, оказались незаменимым изобразительным материалом. Слова иностранного происхождения, вошедшие в русский язык, Пушкин также одобрял и считал их обогащением, если они давали новые и жизненно необходимые речевые средства.

Простота, естественность, точный лаконизм, чувство меры и полная свобода в подборе языковых средств характеризуют художественную речь Пушкина. В ней нельзя ни одного слова отнять, но и прибавить нельзя. Сделав синтез трёх раньше резко отделённых друг от друга стилей, Пушкин определил основные пути дальнейшего развития русского литературного языка.

Начиная с Гоголя во второй четверти 19 века одним из главных интересов русского писателя стала передача характерных подробностей и оттенков языка различных групп русских людей. Также были сделаны громадные достижения в области психологического анализа в произведениях Льва Толстого, Достоевского и их преемников. Начиная с эпохи Гоголя, в русскую литературу широким потоком влились разнообразные словесные материалы, имеющие свой источник то в крестьянских говорах, то в языке ремесленников, купцов, чиновников и других, то в своеобразных состояниях душевной жизни мелкой, подлой или наоборот глубокой, благородной натуры.

Весь этот материал стал средством для построения диалога. Эта особенность русской литературы 19 века значительно осложняет вопрос перевода на иностранные языки. В переводе многие из этих тонкостей и оттенков русской речи неизбежно теряются или слабеют. Поэтому всю глубину и значение произведений русских классиков может всецело постичь только тот, кто читает их по русски.

Язык сложившийся во второй половине 19 века целиком вошёл в советскую жизнь, хотя он и испытал сильные изменения в связи с событиями революции и перестройки политического, общественного и экономического порядка. Из русского языка стали исчезать слова, употреблявшиеся для названия старых учреждений, чинов и должностей, вроде слов: барин, лакей, городовой, губернатор, гимназия. Характерно также для советской эпохи переосмысление значения раньше существовавших слов и выражений, например: совет, октябрь, ударник (старое значение этого слова—деталь винтовочного затвора, новое—передовой советский человек).

Но самое значительное пополнение словарного состава и фразеологии русского языка произошло созданием огромного количества новых слов путём сокращения. Эти новые слова служат главным образом для обозначения новых советских учреждений, должностей или социальных групп. Иногда новые термины состоят из соединения первых букв нескольких слов, при чём каждая буква произносится согласно своему алфавитному названию: СССР, КП (коммунистическая партия), ЦК (Центральный комитет). Или же происходит слияние первых слогов нескольких слов: колхоз (коллективное хозяйство), совхоз (советское хозяйство), комсомол (коммунистический союз молодёжи). Из последних часто развиваются новые термины с помощью суффиксов: колхозник, комсомолец.

Пушкин называл русский язык ярким и звучным, простым и точным, выразительным и плавным, гибким и мощным в своих оборотах и средствах, переимчивым в своих отношениях к чужим языкам. Это определение и сейчас не потеряло своего значения.

ИСТОЧНИКИ

Глава

Академия Наук СССР. *История культуры древней Руси.* Москва, 1951.................... 2, 4

———. *История русского искусства.* Москва, 1953..... 2

Анцыферов, Николай П. *Душа Петербурга.* Петербург: Брокгауз-Ефрон, 1922.................... 13

———. *И. С. Тургенев.* Москва: Государственный литературный музей, 1947.................... 17

Бенуа, А., и Муттер, Р. "Русская живопись в 19 веке," *Артист* (Москва), Но. 36 (1894).......... 19

Белинский, Виссарион. *Сочинения.* Москва: А. И. Мамонтов, 1882, т. 12......................... 13

Бердяев, Николай. *Русская идея.* Париж, 1946....... 16

———. *Истоки и смысл русского коммунизма.* Париж, 1955.................................... **21, 22**

Билл, Валентина Ч. *Забытый класс—русская буржуазия* (по английски). Нью Иорк: Ф. А. Прегер, 1959.. 20

Варшавский, Л. П. *Передвижники.* Москва: Государственное издательство, 1937.................... 19

Винокур, Григорий О. *Русский язык, исторический очерк.* Москва: Государственное издательство, 1945 24

Грабарь, Игорь. *История русского искусства.* т. 3: *Петербургская архитектура в 18 и 19 веках.* Москва: И. Кюбель, 1909–13............. 13, 14, 15

Греков, Борис Д. *Киевская Русь.* Москва, 1953........ 2

Дорофеев, В. и Черемин, Г., изд. *Пушкин в русской критике* (сборник статей). Москва: Государственное издательство художественной литературы, 1950..................................... 17

Глава

Ермилов, Владимир В. *Драматургия Чехова*. Москва: Советский писатель, 1948 17

Ефимов, А. И. *История русского литературного языка*. Москва: Государственное учебно-педагогическое издательство министерства просвещения РСФСР, 1955 24

Забелина, И. Е., памяти. *Москва в прошлом и настоящем*. Москва: Образование, 1908 10

Карпович, М. М. "Традиции русской общественной мысли," *Судьбы России*. Сборник статей. Нью Иорк: Братья Раузен, 1957 22

Келдыш, Ю. *История русской музыки*. 2 тома. Москва-Ленинград: Государственное музыкальное издательство, 1948 18

Кизеветтер, А. А. *Русское общество в 18 столетии*. Ростов на Дону: Донская речь, 1903 14

———. *19 век в истории России*. Ростов на Дону: Донская речь, 1903 15

Кириллов, И. А. *Правда старой веры*. Москва: Товарищество Рябушинских, 1916 11

Ключевский, Василий О. *Курс русской истории*. Москва: Синодальная типография, 1904.

том I 1, 2, 4

том II 5, 7, 8

том III 9, 10, 11, 16

том IV 12, 14

том V 14, 15

Маковский, Сергей. *Силуэты русских художников*. Прага: Наша речь, 1922 19

Мельников Печерский, П. Н. *Сочинения*. Москва, 1898 . . . . 6, 11

Мережковский, Дмитрий С. *Л. Толстой и Достоевский*. Петербург: Мир искусства, 1901–3 17

Мочульский, К. *Достоевский, Жизнь и творчество*. Париж, 1947 17

Овсянико-Куликовский. *История русской литературы 19 века*. Москва, 1910 16

Глава

Платонов, Сергей Ф. *Смутное время*. Прага: Пламя, 1924...................................... 3, 9
———. *Пётр Великий, его личность и деятельность*. Париж: Н. П. Карбасников, 1927................. 12
Порфиридов, Н. Т. *Древний Новгород*. Москва, 1947.... 3
Стасов, В. В. *Избранные сочинения*. Москва: Государственное издательство "Искусство," 1952.......... 18
Трубецкой, Евгений. "Иное царство и его искание в русской сказке," *Русская мысль* (Прага), т. 1–2 (1923)...................................... 6
Флоровский, Г. *Пути русского Богословия*. Париж, 1937.. 12

SOURCES

Chapter

ERMILOV, VLADIMIR V. *Chekhov's Playwriting*. Moscow: The
Soviet Writer, 1948.   17
EFIMOV, A. I. *History of the Russian Literary Language*. Moscow:
State Publishing House, 1955.   24
ZABELIN, I. E., in memoriam. *Moscow in Past and Present*.
Moscow: Education, 1908.   10
KARPOVICH, M. M. "Traditions of Russian Social Thought,"
in *The Fate of Russia*. New York: Rausen Brothers,
1957.   16
KELDYSH, IU. *History of Russian Music*. 2 vols. Moscow-
Leningrad: State Musical Publishing House, 1948.   18
KIZEVETTER, A. A. *Russian Society in the 18th Century*. Rostov
on the Don: Donskaia riech, 1904.   14
———. *The 19th Century in the History of Russia*. Rostov on
the Don: Donskaia riech, 1903.   15
KIRILLOV, I. A. *The Righteousness of the Old Faith*. Moscow:
Riabushinsky & Co., 1916.   11
KLIUCHEVSKY, VASSILY O. *A History of Russia*. Moscow:
Synod Typography, 1904.
  Vol. I. 1, 2, 4
  Vol. II. 5, 7, 8
  Vol. III. 9, 10, 11, 16
  Vol. IV. 12, 14
  Vol. V. 14, 15
MAKOVSKY, SERGE. *Profiles of Russian Artists*. Prague: Nasha
riech, 1922.   19
MELNIKOV PECHERSKY, P. N. *Collected Works*. Moscow,
1898. . . . . 6, 11
MEREZHKOVSKY, DMITRI S. *Tolstoy and Dostoyevsky*. Peters-
burg: The World of Art, 1901–3.   17
MOCHULSKY, K. *Dostoyevsky, His Life and Works*. Paris:
YMCA Press, 1947.   17
OVSIANIKO-KULIKOVSKY. *History of Russian Literature in the
19th Century*. Moscow, 1910.   16
PLATONOV, SERGE F. *The Time of Trouble*. Prague: Plamia,
1924. . . . . 3, 9
———. *Peter the Great, His Personality and His Work*. Paris:
N. P. Karbasnikov, 1927.   12

Chapter

PORFIRIDOV, N. T. *Ancient Novgorod*. MOSCOW, 1947........ 3

STASSOV, V. V. *Selected Works*. MOSCOW: State Publishing
House, 1952..................................... 18

TRUBETSKOY, EUGENE. "The Magic World and Those Who
Seek It in the Russian Fairy Tale," *Russian Thought*
(Prague), Vols. I and II (1923)................... 6

FLOROVSKY, G. *Development of Russian Theology*. Paris: YMCA
Press, 1937..................................... 12

РОДОСЛОВНЫЕ ТАБЛИЦЫ

Род Ивана Калиты
(см. гл. 7–9)

Иван I Калита	1325–41
Семён Гордый	1341–53
Иван II Красный	1353–59
Димитрий Донской	1359–89
Василий I	1389–1425
Василий II Тёмный	1425–62
Иван III	1462–1505
Василий III	1505–33
Иван Грозный	1533–84
Фёдор I	1584–98

Род Романовых
(см. гл. 9–20)

Михаил	1613–45
Алексей	1645–76
Фёдор II	1676–82
Пётр I Великий	1682–1725
Екатерина I (жена Петра Великого)	1725–27
Пётр II (внук Петра Великого)	1727–30
Анна Курляндская (племянница Петра Великого)	1730–40
Анна Брауншвейгская (внучка брата Петра Великого)	1740–41
Елизавета (дочь Петра Великого)	1741–61
Пётр III (внук Петра Великого)	1761–62
Екатерина II (жена Петра III)	1762–96
Павел I	1796–1801
Александр I	1801–25
Николай I	1825–55
Александр II	1855–81
Александр III	1881–94
Николай II	1894–1917

Владимир Ильич Ленин; родился 1870, умер 1924
(см. гл. 21).

Иосиф Виссарионович Сталин; родился 1879, умер 1953
(см. гл. 22 и 23).